FROM THE WAGNER ACT
TO TAFT-HARTLEY

FROM THE WAGNER ACT
TO TAFT-HARTLEY

*A Study of National Labor Policy
and Labor Relations*

By

HARRY A. MILLIS

and

EMILY CLARK BROWN

THE UNIVERSITY OF CHICAGO PRESS

THE UNIVERSITY OF CHICAGO PRESS, CHICAGO 37
Cambridge University Press, London, N.W. 1, England
W. J. Gage & Co., Limited, Toronto 2 B, Canada

PREFACE

THIS study is an analysis of the development of national labor policies and an appraisal of them in the light of our experience. It is hoped that such a study will contribute to the process of public discussion by citizens and in the legislatures by which a democratic society seeks to find the better solutions for its difficult and pressing problems. Neither the Wagner Act nor the Taft-Hartley Act gave final answers as to governmental policy in relation to labor organization and collective bargaining. The authors of this volume hoped that this analysis and appraisal of our experience would contribute to the understanding needed in order to achieve democratic and workable solutions in this area of our national life. At the same time the study had in mind the needs of specialists in the field for detailed analyses of some of the more important policies. The more technical parts of the volume will, it is hoped, prove useful to government administrators, to lawyers, and to the union and management representatives upon whom rests the major responsibility for developing efficient, democratic, and responsible solutions for the problems of labor relations in our society.

The collaboration which this volume represents resulted from the force of events in the area under investigation, which brought together two separately planned and begun research projects. Dr. Millis, following his retirement as Chairman of the National Labor Relations Board in 1945, began a study of the developing movement for change in the national labor policy and an analysis of the important issues involved. The undersigned began a study of Wagner Act experience during her two years as operating analyst for the NLRB in Washington in 1942–44 and planned in a year's leave of absence in 1947–48 to complete a book on the Wagner Act. The adoption of the Labor Management Relations Act, in June, 1947, made it clear to both authors that each study needed the other to complement it, and the plan of collaboration followed.

From the start of the partnership a division of responsibility was clearly laid down. The full responsibility for the study of the experience under the Wagner Act was to be that of the undersigned. While she had the great pleasure and profit of opportunity for long talks with the senior author on the experience and on matters of fact and

v

policy, the conclusions and judgments are in every case her own. Dr. Millis, in fact, did not necessarily agree in every instance with her appraisal and conclusions and took no responsibility for them. Part I was written by the undersigned, and she alone is responsible for it.

The analysis of the Taft-Hartley Act was planned to be the responsibility of Dr. Millis. Unfortunately his death on June 25, 1948, made necessary certain changes in the original plans. Chapter 8, on the background in union, employer, and government actions, was planned and in large part written by Dr. Millis. The account of developments in state legislation was largely based upon his work in collaboration with Harold A. Katz. The remainder of chapter 9 and chapter 10 were the work of Seymour Z. Mann. Dr. Millis wrote the basic chapters 11–13 analyzing the 1947 Act as well as substantial parts of chapters 14 and 15. The rest of Part III was written by the undersigned. Chapter 16 on the experience under the Act was from the start planned to be her responsibility. Unfortunately she also had to write the final appraisal of the 1947 Act. The Epilogue is the brief statement which Dr. Millis wrote and intended to expand for his last chapter, with the addition of two other brief notes which seem appropriate for his final word.

This work is based on study of the documents, on the long and rich experience of the former NLRB Chairman both in administration of the Wagner Act and as arbitrator in many industries, and on two years' study by the undersigned of the administration of the Wagner Act from within the agency and extensive interviews in 1947 and 1948 with employers, union representatives, counsel for employers and unions, and present and former members of the NLRB and its staff in many different parts of the country. Grateful acknowledgment is made to the many people, too numerous to name, who gave generously of their time to help in the project. But several must be mentioned for their special help: Judge J. Warren Madden, who read several early chapters; Dr. William M. Leiserson for his extensive comments on many chapters; Ivar Peterson and Harold A. Katz, who read all the manuscript; and, among others, Louis G. Silverberg and Professors Frederick H. Harbison, Charles O. Gregory, Charles A. Myers, and Helen D. Lockwood. Their suggestions have at many points helped to eliminate errors and to strengthen the analysis and the writing; but only the authors, and in the end the undersigned, are responsible for any errors of fact or omission or of judgment which others may find in our discussion of these controversial matters.

Thanks are due to the Rockefeller Foundation and to the Social

Science Research Committee of the University of Chicago for making funds available for this study; to Vassar College for a Faculty Fellowship, which freed a year for this work; and to the Department of Economics of Vassar College, whose forebearance made the completion of the book possible. The Industrial Relations Center of the University of Chicago gave generous assistance at all stages. Seymour Z. Mann contributed much more to the study than only the chapter and a half for which he carried the major responsibility; and the expert and tireless work of Raulston G. Zundel and Elizabeth Warrick in the library and in final preparation of the manuscript also played a large part in the good partnership which began under the leadership of "The Boss" and continued to completion of the work. Elizabeth Murr and Aiko Hirada also helped in the typing at different times.

Acknowledgment is made to the Bureau of National Affairs, Columbia University Press, Funk and Wagnalls Company, Harper and Brothers, McGraw-Hill Book Company, Macmillan Company, Oxford University Press, American Academy of Political and Social Science, American Management Association, *Business Week,* the *Quarterly Journal of Economics,* and the *Columbia, Iowa, Harvard,* and *University of Chicago Law Reviews* for permission to quote copyrighted material. A portion of the analysis of union security was presented first to the New York University Second Annual Conference on Labor and appears in the *Proceedings* (Albany: Mathew Bender & Co., 1949).

EMILY CLARK BROWN

VASSAR COLLEGE
March 1949

TABLE OF CONTENTS

PART I. THE WAGNER ACT

1. WHENCE THE WAGNER ACT? 3
2. THE NATIONAL LABOR RELATIONS ACT AND ITS ADMINISTRATION 30
3. NLRB CASES AND THE LABOR MOVEMENT 76
4. FREEDOM FROM INTERFERENCE AND THE RIGHT TO BARGAIN . 95
5. UNIONS OF THEIR OWN CHOOSING 129
6. FREEDOM OF SPEECH, FREEDOM TO STRIKE, FREEDOM FROM COERCION IN RIVAL UNION DISPUTES 174
7. A TWELVE-YEAR BALANCE SHEET 234

PART II. HOW THE TAFT-HARTLEY ACT CAME ABOUT

8. THE BACKGROUND OF THE TAFT-HARTLEY ACT. I. LABOR, EMPLOYERS, AND GOVERNMENT 271
9. THE BACKGROUND OF THE TAFT-HARTLEY ACT. II. STATE LEGISLATION AND ATTEMPTED LEGISLATION IN CONGRESS . . . 316
10. TAFT-HARTLEY AND THE EIGHTIETH CONGRESS 363

PART III. THE TAFT-HARTLEY ACT

11. THE TAFT-HARTLEY ACT: IN GENERAL AND ADMINISTRATIVE PROCEDURES 395
12. UNFAIR LABOR PRACTICES UNDER TAFT-HARTLEY 420
13. REMEDIES UNDER TAFT-HARTLEY 482
14. REPRESENTATION AND ELECTIONS UNDER TAFT-HARTLEY . . 514
15. OTHER PROVISIONS OF TAFT-HARTLEY 561
16. EXPERIENCE UNDER TAFT-HARTLEY 610
17. CONCLUSIONS: THE NATURE OF THE TAFT-HARTLEY ACT . . 655

Table of Contents

EPILOGUE

WHAT INDUSTRIAL RELATIONS ROAD FOR THE UNITED STATES? .   669

SELECTED BIBLIOGRAPHY

SELECTED BIBLIOGRAPHY 681

INDEXES

INDEX TO MAJOR CASES CITED 691

GENERAL INDEX 699

x

PART I

The Wagner Act

CHAPTER 1

WHENCE THE WAGNER ACT?

A terrible thing.

T HE National Labor Relations Act of 1935, commonly known as the Wagner Act, was an act of faith in the democratic process for industry as an essential for a democratic society and "the indispensable complement of political democracy." As Senator Wagner said in 1937, "The right to bargain collectively is at the bottom of social justice for the worker, as well as the sensible conduct of business affairs. The denial or observance of this right means the difference between despotism and democracy."[1] And again: "Let men know the dignity of freedom and self-expression in their daily lives, and they will never bow to tyranny in any quarter of their national life."[2]

The policy adopted in the Wagner Act was one of positive protection of labor's right to organize and of encouragement of collective bargaining. Along with the increased freedom to act which resulted from the Norris–La Guardia Act of 1932, this meant a drastic change from the preceding decades and even more from the eighteenth and early nineteenth centuries. In May, 1937, shortly after the Supreme Court held the Wagner Act constitutional, a distinguished student of law, writing in a great law journal, said:

Surveying the American scene for the past fifty years, it appears that for the greater part of that period the influence of the law has tended to prolong, and perhaps encourage, the needless fight over recognition. Of course, the courts had discarded the earlier notion that labor organizations per se were criminal conspiracies. But . . . the courts have allowed employers a pretty free hand to defeat such organization if they could. . . .

We seem to be moving slowly toward a more rational relationship between capital and labor. For the greater part of the past half century, the law tended, on the whole, to retard this consummation. In the latter years its influence, decisively, has been in the right direction. Such progress as

1. Senator Robert F. Wagner in address, May 8, 1937, quoted in Louis G. Silverberg, *The Wagner Act: After Ten Years* (Washington: Bureau of National Affairs, 1945), p. 13.

2. Senator Wagner in *New York Times Magazine*, May 9, 1937, p. 23.

we have made has been at needless cost of blood and tears, and economic wastage. . . . The old ways will not work, could not work, really. It is time for an act of faith.[3]

In 1806, in the famous case of the Philadelphia Cordwainers, a court had said: "A combination of workmen to raise their wages may be considered in a two fold point of view: one is to benefit themselves . . . the other is to injure those who do not join their society. The rule of law condemns both."[4] In America, as in other countries, by a long, slow process labor moved from the early master-servant relationship —for many even bond servitude or slavery—toward that equality of status and bargaining power between free employees and their employers, resulting in joint determination of the conditions under which people worked, that was envisioned by the Wagner Act. It was a process by which workers gained, although never universally, freedom to act in concert for their common benefit and power to act effectively. Governmental policy moved from one of suppression to more or less toleration and finally to acceptance and encouragement of labor organization and collective bargaining. The meaning and influence of the Wagner Act, the culmination of this development, can be understood only against this long history.

REGULATED LABOR AND THE CRIMINAL CONSPIRACY DOCTRINE

In Colonial America, as a recent study shows, "overt acts by employees, individually or collectively, to better their working conditions"[5] were frequently recorded. But workers, whether indentured servants, or apprentices, artisans, or other free labor under contract, were enjoined to obedience and strict observance of their contracts; and the courts were available to insure specific performance of labor contracts or for suits for damages—or criminal action in some colonies —for breach of contract by workers.[6] Combinations of workers to better their conditions were ephemeral, although there were some "strikes, slow-downs and conspiracies to desert." These were generally disapproved by the authorities, but no such sweeping prosecu-

3. Calvert Magruder, "A Half Century of Legal Influence upon the Development of Collective Bargaining," *Harvard Law Review*, 50 (1937), 1071–1117, at 1078, 1117.

4. Philadelphia Cordwainers (1806), in John R. Commons (ed.), *Documentary History of American Industrial Society* (Cleveland: A. H. Clark Co., 1910), Vol. 3, p. 233.

5. Richard B. Morris, *Government and Labor in Early America* (New York: Columbia University Press, 1946), p. 522. This is a very valuable and interesting study of the sources. See especially ch. 3, "Concerted Action among Workers."

6. *Ibid.*, pp. 522–23.

tions occurred as those in eighteenth-century England. In general, court enforcement of contracts and statutes permitting compulsory labor and penalizing absenteeism and desertion were effective hindrances to the development of any real movement for collective activity by workers. After the Revolution changing economic conditions turned the skilled workers, who found their standard of living threatened, toward strikes and permanent labor organization. As the movement became more extensive and effective and more of a threat to their interests, American employers turned to the English common-law doctrine of criminal conspiracy in an effort to stamp out the danger through the criminal courts.[7]

In England the common-law restrictions on labor activity came out of a long history. From the time of the Black Death in the fourteenth century any efforts of workers to combine and use their economic power to improve their conditions of employment had been punishable.[8] Industrial expansion during the Elizabethan period improved the conditions of artisans but brought no recognition of any right to use their bargaining power to promote their interests. By the eighteenth century, greatly increased activity of labor combinations resulted finally in the general Combination Acts of 1799 and 1800, which outlawed any concerted action by workers or employers and made violators criminally liable. Meantime, the common law, built up by decisions of the courts, had developed the doctrine of conspiracy under which actions done in combination might be illegal, although lawful when done by one, if either the purpose or the means were unlawful. When all collective activities of employees were brought under this doctrine and considered criminal conspiracies, a powerful weapon was available against the rising labor organizations. During the first quarter of the nineteenth century, although trade-union activities increased and collective bargaining took place when employers were willing, many union leaders were prosecuted and harshly punished for concerted activities under the Combination Acts or the common law.[9] Later, when statutes limited the common-law conspiracy

7. *Ibid.*, pp. 206–7; John R. Commons and Associates, *History of Labour in the United States* (New York: Macmillan Co., 1926), Vol. 1, Pt. 1, chs. 1–5, esp. pp. 138–39.

8. This brief treatment relies heavily on James M. Landis and Marcus Manoff, *Cases on Labor Law* (Chicago: Foundation Press, 1942), ch. 1; and Harry A. Millis and Royal E. Montgomery, *Organized Labor* (New York: McGraw-Hill Book Co., 1945).

9. Landis and Manoff, *op. cit.*, pp. 11–16. The Combination Acts and the common-law conspiracy doctrine supposedly applied to employers as well as employees, but concerted action by employers was not interfered with. They were

doctrine in some respects, courts developed the notion that any combination of workers to improve their conditions was illegal at common law as a combination in restraint of trade, and prosecutions on this basis became frequent and hampering, especially in the 1850's. In England on the whole, however, from 1825 on, the development was toward replacing the uncertain and restrictive common law by statute law and freeing trade-unions from the old restrictions.[10]

The heritage of the English common-law doctrines of criminal and civil conspiracy was to plague the American labor movement for a long time, while English labor was gradually being freed from them. That the common law was applicable in this country was made clear in a series of dramatic prosecutions of journeymen shoemakers and tailors for criminal conspiracy from 1806 on into the 1830's. It was not surprising that the federalist judiciary followed the thinking of the English courts rather than the democratic pleas of the journeymen. So a Philadelphia court in 1806 found quite simply that a combination to raise wages was a criminal conspiracy. In 1810 a New York court based its findings of conspiracy upon illegality of the *means* of the strike rather than upon unlawfulness of the aim to increase wages. Since prosecutions for attempts to raise wages were politically unpopular, some courts made their decisions turn on coercion or other illegal means. As late as 1835 and 1836 in New York State, however, journeymen shoemakers and tailors were convicted and fined under a state law for conspiracy to raise wages.[11] Mass protests against these

---

used against labor by employers and by the courts, which, as Dean Landis indicates, "perceived concretely enough the dangers to their traditional economy involved by any recognition of the legality of collective action. . . . By making the legality of combination depend upon the test of 'illegal purposes' or 'unlawful means' they were enabled to mould a legal doctrine that would serve the end of keeping their civilization true to what they conceived to be its objectives." *Ibid.*, p. 14. Cf. also Charles O. Gregory, *Labor and the Law* (New York: W. W. Norton & Co., 1946), ch. 2.

10. The Act of 1824–25 permitted workers to combine and enter agreements as to wages and hours, though limiting them in other respects as to both objects and means. The Acts of 1871 and 1875 eliminated completely the doctrine of criminal conspiracy as applied to labor organizations and legalized peaceful picketing. The Act of 1906 finally eliminated also the doctrine of civil conspiracy under which unions had been found subject to injunction and suit for damages. This gave to English labor "the least restrictive labor code till then known." The Act of 1927, following the General Strike of 1926, imposed a number of limitations, but no significant cases arose under it, and it apparently had little or no effect upon collective labor activity before its repeal by the Labor government in 1946. Millis and Montgomery, *op. cit.*, pp. 491–98; Landis and Manoff, *op. cit.*, pp. 22–30.

11. Landis and Manoff, *op. cit.*, pp. 30–34; Commons, *History of Labour*, Vol. 1, pp. 138–52, 405–11.

convictions may have had some relationship to the acquittals in several later cases. Finally in the important *Commonwealth* v. *Hunt*[12] decision the conspiracy doctrine was clarified and somewhat limited. This case involved efforts of the journeymen bootmakers of Boston to enforce a closed shop. The Chief Justice of the state refused to find an illegal conspiracy in the mere fact of a combination not to work with nonmembers. While the earlier precedents were not expressly rejected, he held that combinations to raise wages were not per se illegal; rather their legality depended upon the *ends* and the *means* used. In effect, therefore, unions had a right to exist, but their actions could still be found illegal. Prosecutions on the earlier bases came to an end. But the door was still open for other attacks, and in numerous cases courts were to attempt to draw the line between the permissible and the forbidden in union activities.

After the Civil War as industry expanded there was renewed growth of labor unions. In the extensive unrest and strikes, some of them involving violence, in the seventies and eighties, prosecutions for criminal conspiracy occurred again. Several states in the sixties, seventies, and eighties passed laws aimed at strikes or their conduct or limiting other union activity. But there was also wide sympathy for the strikers, and a number of states, including New York, New Jersey, Pennsylvania, and Illinois, attempted by statute to legalize collective labor action which had been under attack in the conspiracy cases. As Landis says, the criminal conspiracy doctrine had in the main spent itself.

A broader consciousness of the need for collective action to combat the swift rise of corporate power was afoot. Juries might incline too sympathetically towards workers seeking to use the only effective means available to them to improve their conditions. But, principally, the new remedy of the injunction ma[de] resort to the more ponderous means of indictment for criminal conspiracy unnecessary and less efficacious.[13]

And courts were still to use the common-law approach, judging whether union activity was justifiable in its purposes and its means, as they decided suits for injunctions or for damages against unions.

LABOR INJUNCTIONS, ANTITRUST ACTS, AND THE BASIC LAW OF LABOR

An injunction was first used in a labor dispute in England in 1868, but this way of handling labor disputes was short-lived there.[14] In the

12. 4 Metcalf 111 (Mass., 1842); Landis and Manoff, *op. cit.*, pp. 34–36.
13. Landis and Manoff, *op. cit.*, p. 38.
14. Millis and Montgomery, *op. cit.*, pp. 629–30. Even under the somewhat restrictive Act of 1927, only the government could seek an injunction, and so far as is known this power was never used.

From the Wagner Act to Taft-Hartley

United States a court order to restrain strikers came first in the railway strike of 1877. In the next decade of rapid upswing of labor organization—the Knights of Labor and others—and of extensive and bitter strikes, injunctions were widely used: in Maryland and Ohio in 1883 against glassworkers; in Iowa in 1884 against coal-miners; in the 1888 railway strike in upward of fifteen cases in both state and federal courts. Their use was thoroughly established after the Massachusetts Supreme Judicial Court in 1888 expressly approved an injunction to restrain picketing and after the United States Supreme Court approved a lower court's action in finding Eugene V. Debs in contempt of court for violation of a court order in the great Pullman strike of 1894.[15]

From then on injunctions were very frequent until in the thirties a real effort was made to limit their use in labor disputes. Their great significance was that labor controversies were brought increasingly into the courts, and court-made law came to dominate the field. Moreover, the doctrine of conspiracy found a new lease on life, for judges frequently used it as a basis for their restraining orders when they considered either the object or the means used by labor in its concerted activities unlawful. Injunctions in labor cases increased steadily in number. Dr. Witte found 508 cases in federal courts and 1,364 in state courts in which injunctions were issued on application of employers prior to May 1, 1931. A total of 28 were issued in the eighties, 122 in the nineties, 328 from 1900 to 1909, 446 in the next decade, and 921 between January 1, 1920, and May 1, 1930.[16] Thus to quote:

> For almost a generation and a half, from the 1890's to the early 1930's . . . the power of the courts was invoked to assist in defeating most of the more important strikes—among them, the Pullman strike of 1894, the coal strike of 1919, the shopmen's strike of 1922—and only a smaller proportion of the relatively less important ones . . . to prevent the successful spreading of labor boycotts . . . and . . . to prevent organizing activities where the workers were engaged under individual nonunion or "yellow-dog" contracts.[17]

The injunction, a restraining order issued by a court, in theory is used only in extraordinary cases where there is no adequate remedy at law for a threatened injury to property rights, the injury would be irreparable, and the party seeking relief comes into court "with clean hands." Violation is punishable as contempt of court. Labor disputes

15. Landis and Manoff, *op. cit.*, pp. 38–39; *in re* Debs, 158 U.S. 564 (1895).
16. Edwin E. Witte, *The Government in Labor Disputes* (New York: McGraw-Hill Book Co., 1932), p. 84.
17. From H. A. Millis and R. E. Montgomery, *Organized Labor* (1945), p. 631. Courtesy of McGraw-Hill Book Co.

were brought within the scope of the injunction when the right to do business was recognized as a property right. This was clearly established in early cases when not only physical damage to property was enjoined but also interference by the union with access to the labor and other markets, that is, the right to do business.[18] From then on the courts, in deciding whether particular union activities were illegal, weighed the injury to business or the restraint of trade which was inevitable from any effective strike, picketing, or boycott and considered whether it was justified by self-interest of the labor group.

The antitrust laws also were important in the development of the use of courts in labor disputes. The Sherman Act of 1890 prohibited combinations or conspiracies in restraint of interstate or foreign commerce and provided for criminal prosecution, injunctions, and suits for triple damages for violations. Whether Congress intended it to apply to labor organizations as well as to the industrial combinations which were the main object has been debated at length.[19] But, in any event, the injunctions in the railroad strikes of the 1890's relied on the Act, holding the strikes to be in illegal restraint of interstate commerce. In 1908 in the famous Danbury Hatters case, where there had been a strike in an attempt to organize and finally a nationwide boycott aided by the American Federation of Labor, the boycott was held illegal under the Sherman Act, and heavy damages were assessed against the individual union members. The Supreme Court after long litigation upheld the judgment.[20]

Fears on the part of the unions that their existence was in danger under this ruling led to a campaign in the national elections of 1908–12 for amendment of the Sherman Act. In the Clayton Act of 1914 labor believed that it had achieved its object of being freed from attack under the antitrust laws. Again the intent of Congress has been debated, a recent detailed study of legislative history concluding that clearly Congress meant to exempt labor from these restrictions.[21] But the Supreme Court in the Duplex[22] case decided that the exemption of labor organizations applied only to the *lawful* carrying-out of *legitimate* objects. In other words, the law had not been changed, and still

18. Commons, *History of Labour*, Vol. 2, pp. 505–7.
19. For opposite conclusions see Edward Berman, *Labor and the Sherman Act* (New York: Harper & Bros., 1930), Pt. 1; and Alpheus T. Mason, *Organized Labor and the Law* (Durham: Duke University, 1925), chs. 7–9.
20. Loewe v. Lawlor, 208 U.S. 274 (1908), 235 U.S. 522 (1915).
21. Joseph Kovner, "The Legislative History of Section 6 of the Clayton Act," *Columbia Law Review*, 47 (1947), 749–65. But cf. Witte, *op. cit.*, pp. 66–69.
22. Duplex Printing Press Co. v. Deering, 254 U.S. 443 (1921).

9

in the individual case courts would decide whether the particular activity was lawful in its objects and its means. In fact, the Clayton Act, by permitting suits for injunctions to be brought by private parties, increased the use of labor injunctions in the federal courts. State anti-injunction laws, most of them modeled on the Clayton Act during this period, also proved disappointing to labor. When Arizona construed its law broadly so as to prevent an injunction against picketing, the Supreme Court held the act, so construed, to be unconstitutional.[23]

From the 1890's through World War I, the postwar period, and the 1920's, accordingly, organized labor was faced with the danger that its activities might be attacked in the courts, not only if they violated the laws against violence and destruction of property, but also for violating the less clearly defined antitrust laws, federal and state. In addition, there were state statutes against conspiracy and a variety of other state laws against coercion, boycotts, picketing, and other activities. Some of these merely declared the common law; some were broader. When states, on the other hand, attempted to prohibit discrimination by discharge of union members or by requiring the signing of individual nonunion contracts—"yellow-dog" contracts—these statutes were held unconstitutional.[24] In general, common-law concepts ruled, and the details of what labor organizations might and might not lawfully do were determined by decisions of many courts in the various jurisdictions. The law was, therefore, different in different states and uncertain. It varied from state to state in the extent to which it restricted labor's activities. It was largely affected by the "bias or economic and social predilections of the court,"[25] which more often than not was more favorably disposed toward the employer and toward the common law's anticombination slant than toward efforts of employees to organize and act collectively for their own benefit.

Key decisions of the Supreme Court, most of them coming under the federal antitrust acts, indicate the state of the law before 1930 and how the law was weighted against labor activities.[26] In the first place, efforts of the federal government or the states to protect the right to organize were generally unsuccessful. In 1908 the Supreme

23. Truax v. Corrigan, 257 U.S. 312 (1921).

24. Witte, *op. cit.*, pp. 77–81; John R. Commons and John B. Andrews, *Principles of Labor Legislation* (New York: Harper & Bros., 1936), pp. 385–88, 405–8.

25. Millis and Montgomery, *op. cit.*, p. 638.

26. A number of these cases and the problems involved will be analyzed further in Part III, *infra*, chs. 12 and 13, in connection with issues under Taft-Hartley.

Court declared unconstitutional a provision in the Erdman Act which prohibited discharge for union membership by the railroads,[27] holding it beyond the power of Congress to regulate interstate commerce and an interference with the constitutional right of free contract. In 1915 a Kansas law which prohibited an employer from requiring employees to sign individual nonunion contracts was similarly voided as an interference with the rights of property and contract.[28] The capstone was added to this structure in the Hitchman[29] case, fought through the courts for ten years. The Supreme Court finally supported injunctions restraining the Mine Workers from organizing activity in West Virginia, the great nonunion stronghold in the industry, after employers required "yellow-dog" contracts as a condition of employment. Any attempt to organize these men then was held an illegal attempt to induce breach of contract.[30] Accordingly, under this decision, and those in most states, such contracts were protected by the courts. They were widely used, especially in the coal industry, and seriously interfered with the efforts of unions to organize. State laws against the employers' black list, also, which were on the books in more than half the states by 1932, proved generally ineffective. The black list operated secretly and was very hard to prove, although its existence was often well known, and it was effective.[31]

Efforts of workers to organize and to promote their interests by using strikes, boycotts, and picketing were limited in a series of significant decisions under the antitrust laws during the 1920's. In the Duplex Printing Press Company[32] case the Supreme Court held that labor was not exempt from these laws. An injunction was approved against the Machinists in New York, when, by boycotting Duplex presses, they attempted to aid their fellow union members in an effort to organize a plant in Michigan and eliminate substandard wages and working conditions there. The Supreme Court held that these New York workers had no such interest in the controversy as to justify their interference with interstate commerce. This policy was carried

27. Adair v. United States, 208 U.S. 161 (1908).
28. Coppage v. Kansas, 236 U.S. 1 (1915).
29. Hitchman Coal and Coke Co. v. Mitchell, 245 U.S. 229 (1917).
30. One is reminded of the Colonial statutes and the prosecutions and damage suits for "enticement of servants." "In addition to enticement, the mere counseling of servants to seek their freedom by legal means might be considered by the courts as an unwarranted interference with the property interests of others." Morris, *op. cit.*, p. 430.
31. Witte, *op. cit.*, pp. 213–18.
32. Duplex Printing Press Co. v. Deering, 254 U.S. 443 (1921). Cf. *infra*, ch. 12, pp. 462–63.

11

further in the Bedford Stone Cutters[33] case in 1927. A local union at the Indiana limestone quarries had been broken following a strike, and the company was operating on a nonunion basis. Fellow union members, in an effort to promote renewed recognition at the quarries, refused to set stone cut by their opponents and thus interrupted building operations in different sections of the country. The Supreme Court upheld the resulting injunctions on the ground that this was an illegal combination in restraint of trade.

Whatever may be said as to the motives of the respondents or their general right to combine for the purpose of. . . protecting themselves or their organizations, the present combination deliberately adopted a course of conduct which directly and substantially curtailed, or threatened thus to curtail, the natural flow in interstate commerce of a very large proportion of the building limestone production of the entire country. . . .[34]

Justice Brandeis, however, in a dissent, in which Justice Holmes joined, said:

If, on the undisputed facts of this case, refusal to work can be enjoined, Congress created by the Sherman Law and the Clayton Act an instrument for imposing restraints upon labor which reminds of involuntary servitude. . . . It would, indeed, be strange if Congress . . . willed to deny to members of a small craft of workingmen the right to cooperate in simply refraining from work, when that course was the only means of self-protection against a combination of militant and powerful employers. I cannot believe that Congress did so.[35]

If a union violated the antitrust acts, it could be sued for triple damages, as was established in the Coronado Coal cases. A bitter struggle resulted at a mine in Arkansas from an effort to operate on a nonunion basis after having been under a regional union agreement. There was violence on both sides, several nonunion miners were killed, and property was destroyed. When the company sued for damages, the Supreme Court held that a union though unincorporated could be sued under the Antitrust Act. The Court finally concluded that the purpose of the union had been to stop the production and shipment of nonunion coal which "would by competition tend to reduce the price of the commodity and affect injuriously the maintenance of wages for union labor in competing mines." This was held a violation of the federal Antitrust Act, and the local union was there-

33. Bedford Cut Stone Co. v. Journeymen Stone Cutters' Association, 274 U.S. 37 (1927), *infra*, ch. 12, pp. 463–65.
34. 274 U.S. 37, 54 (1927).
35. *Ibid.*, p. 65.

fore liable for triple damages.[36] This decision was relied on in another attack upon the Mine Workers' efforts to organize West Virginia. Sweeping restraining orders were sustained by the circuit court of appeals,[37] and the Supreme Court refused to review the case. The Court considered that the union had engaged in "an actual combination and conspiracy in restraint of trade in a manner quite foreign to the normal and legitimate objects of the union." Apparently any union in an interstate industry was in danger of the antitrust laws if in its attempt to organize and act effectively for its own protection it interrupted to a substantial degree the interstate flow of commodities.

Picketing also was restricted under the antitrust acts, although the Clayton Act in Section 20 had expressly provided that peaceful picketing was not to be enjoined by the federal courts. In the American Steel Foundries case in 1921 the Supreme Court held that the right to combine, to strike, and to persuade peacefully was protected. But picketing in numbers was inevitably intimidating. Accordingly, the number of pickets permitted should be declared by a court in the light of the particular circumstances. Here one picket at each entrance was considered proper, "but with special admonition that their communication, argument, and appeals shall not be abusive, libelous or threatening, and that they shall not approach individuals together but singly."[38] In the Truax[39] case the same year, when a state court attempted to interpret a state law so as to permit picketing more freely than this, the Supreme Court held the Act thus interpreted to be unconstitutional. These decisions had wide influence on lower state courts as well as federal and resulted in extensive restriction of picketing.

Labor organizations, therefore, before the significant changes in governmental policy in the thirties, were substantially restricted in their activities under the common law, the antitrust laws, and various state statutes. For the most part, the law was declared by court decisions, especially in the injunction cases. Frequently because of the uncertainty of the law, inadequate procedures, and, it must be said also, biases of some courts, things which were entirely lawful, such as

36. United Mine Workers v. Coronado Coal Co., 259 U.S. 344 (1922); Coronado Coal Co. v. United Mine Workers, 268 U.S. 295 (1925). Cf. also United Leather Workers v. Herkert & Meisel Trunk Co., 265 U.S. 457 (1924).

37. United Mine Workers *et al.* v. Red Jacket Consolidated Coal & Coke Co., 18 F. 2d 839 (C.C.A. 4, 1927).

38. American Steel Foundries v. Tri-City Central Trades Council, 257 U.S. 184, 207 (1921).

39. Truax v. Corrigan, 257 U.S. 312 (1921).

peaceful persuasion, were enjoined. When these injunctions were modified on appeal to higher courts, it was small comfort to workers whose strikes had been broken in the meantime. In addition, injunctions were used against acts which were crimes under common or statutory law. Violations were then punishable at the will of the court, under common law, without the protection of jury trial. Possibly the effect of injunctions has been exaggerated by both employers and labor. They were frequently ignored, and sometimes they strengthened the solidarity of workers determined to win. But they were frightening to less experienced workers, hampered the effectiveness of picketing, encouraged active and severe restrictions by the police, and cost the unions time, effort, and money to fight court cases. They were especially hampering in the face of "yellow-dog" contracts.[40] And they did not prevent the violence which continued to be an accompaniment of industrial disputes. Rather, by encouraging employers in fighting unionization rather than settling disputes through collective bargaining, they increased the bitterness of the struggle. At the same time, the uncertainty of the law and sometimes its patent unfairness made the problem of policing more difficult.

The result was that the labor injunction "weakened and undermined the courts"[41] and so respect for law and government, since unions considered the law so unfair and unduly restrictive of their right to act in self-protection. In addition, the courts emphasized the right to do business and protected it as a property right against efforts of workers to improve their conditions. Labor's "right to organize" often was a hollow one. Effective exercise of this right frequently ran into collision with the employer's right to do business, which received the protection of the courts.

The inequality of the law is seen further when we remember that lockouts were unrestricted by the common law, except in case of violation of a contract; that black lists, though illegal in many states, were used with little or no danger; that employers used antiunion discrimination, espionage, and strikebreaking services with impunity; and that "yellow-dog" contracts and company unions were often effective accompaniments of antiunion programs which were successful against efforts of workers to organize. The record fully supports the statement quoted early in this chapter that the influence of the law had tended

40. Cf. Witte, *op. cit.*, ch. 6.
41. Millis and Montgomery, *op. cit.*, pp. 638–40.

"to prolong and perhaps encourage the needless fight over recognition."[42]

American trade-union membership, after its peak of possibly one million members in 1886, declined to less than half a million during the difficult years of the nineties and did not pass the million mark again until 1901. During a brief "honeymoon period" it rose to over two million by 1904 and remained fairly stable for the rest of that decade, then rose rapidly to nearly 2.7 million by 1914. The great mass of unskilled and semiskilled workers, however, remained unorganized.[43] This was in spite of the fact of increased industrialization and urbanization and the growth of large-scale industry under the corporate form of organization as market areas expanded. While national wealth and income increased, moreover, there was little increase in the real earnings of workers.

During a brief period over the turn of the century, collective agreements were established in a number of important industries as the natural outcome of successful collective bargaining. But by 1901 many employers were becoming alarmed at the increasing strength of the labor movement. An organized open-shop drive resulted which was participated in by many employers' associations. The National Association of Manufacturers, the National Metal Trades Association, the National Founders Association, the American Anti-Boycott Association, and the Citizens' Industrial Association, were leaders in the drive. They urged members to maintain open shops, sometimes maintained black lists, gave assistance to employers engaged in industrial disputes, and opposed legislation sponsored by the unions. And they carried on extensive efforts to mold public opinion against unions and in favor of what was called "the right to work."[44] Success of their

42. Cf. also *Final Report of the Commission on Industrial Relations* (Washington: Government Printing Office, 1916), pp. 90–97.

43. Leo Wolman, *Ebb and Flow in Trade Unionism* (New York: National Bureau of Economic Research, 1936), pp. 15–20.

44. The attitudes were not usually quite so frankly expressed as they were in 1902 in the classic statement of President Baer of the Philadelphia and Reading Railroad Company: "The rights and interests of the laboring man will be protected and cared for, not by the labor agitators, but by the Christian men to whom God in his infinite wisdom, has given control of the property interests of the country." *Cleveland Citizen*, August 26, 1902, quoted in Selig Perlman and Philip Taft, *History of Labor in the United States, 1896–1932, Labor Movements* (New York: Macmillan Co., 1935), p. 43.

efforts is suggested by the fact that the growth of union membership was stopped for the most part during the later years of that decade.[45] For a few years before the war, perhaps because employers became less vigilant, perhaps mainly because of efforts to organize on an industrial basis in such industries as the garment trades, there was again an increase in organization and experiment with joint agreements in new areas. Fears on the part of the unions, resulting from the antiunion tactics of employers during this period, however, were influential in bringing the Clayton Act, which the unions had hoped, vainly, would free them from some of the restrictions felt so sharply.

During the first World War all conditions were favorable for a growth of unionism, and union membership nearly doubled, rising to over five million by 1920. Prosperity, with rising prices and profits, increased demand for labor, unwillingness of employers to risk strikes, and co-operation in the war effort combined with a new governmental labor policy to advance unionism and collective bargaining. The growth of unions was to a large extent concentrated, however, in the industries most essential to the war—fields in which the unions already had at least some organization. Because of the importance of avoiding strikes, the government, with the agreement of employers and the American Federation of Labor, established a number of tripartite bodies to work for the settlement of labor disputes. The most important was the War Labor Board, set up in April, 1918. Its agreed-upon statement of principles and policies provided that there should be no strikes or lockouts and that the right of workers to organize and bargain collectively was not to be denied or interfered with. Employers were not to engage in discrimination, nor were unions to engage in coercion of workers or employers in efforts to increase their membership. The status quo was to prevail: where unions had been recognized, this was to continue; where there had been open shops, unions were not to demand closed shops or to consider it a grievance that nonunion workers were employed. This public policy gave unions a protection which they never had previously experienced. Yet their expansion was limited by the status quo provision. In addition, when in open-shop industries the need for joint machinery to settle disputes became evident, the War Labor Board and other similar boards encouraged and sometimes ordered the establishment of employee rep-

45. Millis and Montgomery, *op. cit.*, pp. 95–98. See also U. S. Senate, Committee on Education and Labor, *Violations of Free Speech and Rights of Labor*, cited as *La Follette Committee Reports: National Association of Manufacturers*, Report No. 6, Pt. 6; *National Metal Trades Association*, Report No. 6, Pt. 4, 76th Cong., 1st Sess., 1939.

resentation plans. Thus "company unionism" was given an impetus which was to persist until the Wagner Act made any "company-dominated" organizations illegal.[46]

In the immediate postwar years American labor organizations rose to a new peak of membership and power. Rising cost of living and lagging wage rates, along with a tendency of some employers to withdraw their recognition of unions, led to great unrest and an unprecedented number of strikes. Railroad strikes, the coal strike, and the great steel strike of 1919 all failed. A drastic injunction obtained by the Attorney-General in the coal case was a warning to labor of things ahead. Warning was seen also in the refusal of Judge Gary, chairman of the board of directors of United States Steel, to meet leaders of the twenty-four craft unions which had largely closed down the industry. In 1919 a National Industrial Conference of representatives of labor, employers, and the public was called by President Wilson. But the conference failed, and the labor group left when industry representatives refused to agree that employers must be obligated to meet with representatives of national unions chosen by their employees for collective bargaining purposes. It was clear that the wartime truce was over and that employers were prepared to challenge the position of the unions. A changed "public temper" toward the unions was apparent, too, related in part to the fear of revolutionary influences in the "red hysteria" of 1919–20.[47]

When postwar prosperity was interrupted, union membership dropped sharply. By 1923 it had declined to about 3.6 million from its 1920 peak of 5 million, and through the rest of the decade it drifted downward. The percentage of nonagricultural employees who were in unions declined from 19.4 in 1920 to 10.2 in 1930.[48] The largest part of the losses in the first drastic years of deflation was in war industries, but other unions suffered from shifts in the location of industry from old organized to new nonunion areas and from economic difficulties such as in the coal and textile industries. Many factors ran against efforts to organize or to hold existing labor organization during the 1920's. Among them were technological developments and the growth of giant corporations and mass production; a tendency toward displacement of craftsmen and some technological unemployment; and an increase in real earnings. Moreover, the larger employers

46. Cf. Lewis L. Lorwin and Arthur Wubnig, *Labor Relations Boards* (Washington: Brookings Institution, 1935), pp. 8–13.
47. Millis and Montgomery, *op. cit.*, pp. 140–49.
48. Wolman, *op. cit.*, pp. 26, 34, 116.

17

adopted positive programs of "welfare capitalism" and "an economy of high wages," designed to increase the security and well-being of employees and their sense of attachment to the companies for which they worked. Especially important was the development of company unionism, which in mass-production industries gave at least a means of handling some disputes and developing some feeling of common interest between employer and employee. In addition, many employers joined again in an open-shop offensive which took the name of "the American Plan." Comparable in some respects to the antiunion drive of the early 1900's, this campaign emphasized more positive aspects such as employee representation plans and welfare programs. But it used also the "yellow-dog" contract, sanctioned by the courts since 1917; and the open-shop associations often assisted their members by supplying strikebreakers and by other services designed to help them maintain a nonunion position. The campaigns were in part directed against racketeering and corruption, of which there was evidence in the building trades and others. But they did not stop there. And, aided by the labor injunction, which reached its peak of use during this period, and other restrictive court decisions, these methods were effective and discouraging to unions which tried to develop or use economic power.

On the whole, therefore, except for the brief period of the war, and with some variations among the states, the influence of government and the courts had for decades given support to employers in labor disputes and allowed them a large degree of freedom to fight unions, while unions, on the other hand, were liable to attack in the courts if they used methods which were effective, even peaceful ones. The American Federation of Labor with its traditional structure and methods, trying to adapt itself to the temper of the twenties by emphasizing co-operation and promising increased productive efficiency as a basis for increased wages, was unable to make progress or to do more than hold its existing membership in a few better-organized fields.

In one industry, nevertheless, there was a straw in the wind which foreshadowed a change in governmental policies. This was in the railroad industry, long subject to governmental intervention for the settlement of disputes because of the essential character of its service. In 1926 the Railway Labor Act[49] was enacted by Congress, in the form agreed upon by a conference of railway executives and union officials

49. 44 U.S. Stat. 577.

who wished to emphasize collective bargaining instead of the settlement of disputes by a national board, as under the previous law. The Act made it the duty of both sides to exert every effort to make agreements and to settle disputes. It provided a Board of Mediation to assist in the settlement of disputes and for voluntary arbitration, emergency fact-finding boards to be appointed by the President in case of need, and adjustment boards to be set up by the parties to settle disputes arising over the application of agreements. For present purposes the most significant feature was that representatives were to be chosen by both groups "without interference, influence or coercion" by the other party. Interpreting this clause in a highly important decision[50] in 1930, the Supreme Court held that the Texas and New Orleans Railway could be enjoined from establishing an employee representation plan and coercing its employees by threats of discharge to give up their union membership and join the new organization. In effect, this decision overruled the Adair case of 1908, which had permitted the railroads to discharge employees for union membership.[51] It encouraged the effort to obtain a broad protection of the right to organize which was to materialize in a few years in Section 7(a) of the National Industrial Recovery Act and finally in the National Labor Relations Act.

DEPRESSION AND A NEW NATIONAL LABOR POLICY

Then came the Great Depression and the decade of the 1930's which was to see a new governmental policy, restriction of the use of labor injunctions, positive protection of the right to organize, new vitality in the labor movement as it changed its structure and methods, and great extension of union membership and collective bargaining under two competing union federations.

As unemployment grew from 1929 to 1933, reaching an estimated sixteen million, union membership fell to its lowest point since before the war, under three million.[52] Unemployment, insecurity, and declining standards of living faced not only manual wage-earners but white-collar workers and others in all walks of life. There was as a result a widespread loss of confidence in the ability of unregulated free enterprise to maintain full employment and the rising standards which had been foreseen during the twenties. It came to be rather commonly

50. Texas & New Orleans Railway Co. v. Brotherhood of Railway and Steamship Clerks, 281 U.S. 548 (1930); Millis and Montgomery, *op. cit.*, pp. 520–21, 737–40.
51. *Supra*, p. 11.
52. Wolman, *op. cit.*, pp. 33–34.

believed, also, that an increase in mass purchasing power was necessary to sustain full production and employment under conditions of modern mass production; and, if this was so, then support for unionism and collective bargaining was desirable, to balance the unrestrained power of the great corporations. Measures to promote greater equality of bargaining power, therefore, began to appear proper public policy, in order to increase wages. Among workers themselves, moreover, the experience of depression and mass insecurity turned them toward the unions. Many of them had lost confidence in the promises of "welfare capitalism" after years of depression. In addition, the long-run trends which had been seen in the 1920's, but which were overbalanced then by other factors, in the thirties began to show their effects. The labor force was more homogeneous, increasingly American-born and the product of American schools. Many more workers were employed by great corporations under conditions of mass production. Resentment at "being pushed around" was widespread and ready to become articulate and to add its force to a rush into the unions once conditions were propitious.

This experience of widespread insecurity, and the piling-up of evidence as to the inequity of the use of injunctions in labor disputes,[53] led a Republican-controlled Congress to pass the Norris–La Guardia Anti-injunction Act[54] on March 23, 1932. It had been drafted by a subcommittee of the Senate Judiciary Committee with the aid of a group of eminent legal scholars. For the first time it spelled out a federal labor policy favoring full freedom of association of workers and freedom from interference by employers with this right. The statement of policy will be quoted in full.

SECTION 2. . . . The public policy of the United States is hereby declared as follows:

Whereas under prevailing economic conditions, developed with the aid of governmental authority for owners of property to organize in the corporate and other forms of ownership association, the individual unorganized worker is commonly helpless to exercise actual liberty of contract and to protect his freedom of labor, and thereby to obtain acceptable terms and conditions of employment, wherefore, though he should be free to decline to associate with his fellows, it is necessary that he have full freedom of association, self-organization, and designation of representatives of his own choosing, to negotiate the terms and conditions of his employment, and that he shall be free from the interference, restraint, or coercion of employers of labor, or their agents, in the designation of such representatives or in self-

53. Cf. Felix Frankfurter and Nathan Greene, *The Labor Injunction* (New York: Macmillan Co., 1930); Witte, *op. cit.*
54. 47 U.S. Stat. 70.

20

organization or in other concerted activities for the purpose of collective bargaining or other mutual aid or protection; therefore, the following definitions of, and limitations upon, the jurisdiction and authority of the courts of the United States are hereby enacted.

This Act drastically limited the power of federal courts to issue injunctions in labor disputes, unless fraud or violence were involved. "Labor dispute" was broadly defined to give wide latitude to the right to strike, picket, or boycott. Individual nonunion contracts, "yellow-dog" contracts, were made unenforceable. Substantial procedural safeguards were provided, such as limiting the issuance of temporary restraining orders, requiring adequate notice and hearings, and providing the right of jury trial in case of violations. Liability of union officers or members for damages for unlawful acts was limited by requiring clear proof of actual participation in, or authorization of, the unlawful acts. Many states also passed similar legislation in succeeding years.[55] When Supreme Court decisions finally interpreted these acts, it was clear that they effectively freed labor from many of the restrictions of the old decisions under the antitrust laws, other statutes, and the common law.[56]

After the national election of 1932, a new administration and Congress went to work to carry out their mandate to "do something" about the depression. A major recovery measure, the National Industrial Recovery Act,[57] became law on June 16, 1933. Since the antitrust acts were being relaxed to permit agreements within industries, in the interest of increasing employment, production, and purchasing power, and organization by employers was encouraged, protection of organization by workers was a necessary corollary. Accordingly, in spite of the anxiety of some employers, the famous clause 7(a) was included,[58] reminiscent of the protection of the right to organize under the War Labor Board, and borrowing much of its crucial language from the statement of policy of the Norris–La Guardia Act:

Sec. 7(a) Every code of fair competition, agreement, and license ap-

55. Millis and Montgomery, *op. cit.*, pp. 647–48. By 1941 there were twenty-four states with anti-injunction laws, seventeen of them modeled after the Norris–La Guardia Act, and nineteen had anti-"yellow-dog" contract laws.

56. Senn v. Tile Layers' Protective Union, 301 U.S. 468 (1937); Lauf v. E. G. Shinner & Co., 303 U.S. 323 (1938); Milk Wagon Drivers' Union v. Lake Valley Farm Products, 311 U.S. 91 (1940). This Act and some of the decisions under it are discussed further in Part III, ch. 13, pp. 458–59; ch. 13, pp. 485–89.

57. 48 U.S. Stat. 195.

58. Similar policy had been declared in the Railway Labor Act of 1926 (44 U.S. Stat. 577) and in amendments to the Bankruptcy Act, March 3, 1933 (47 U.S. Stat. 1467).

proved, prescribed, or issued under this title shall contain the following conditions: (1) that employees shall have the right to organize and bargain collectively through representatives of their own choosing, and shall be free from the interference, restraint, or coercion of employers of labor, or their agents, in the designation of such representatives or in self-organization or in other concerted activities for the purpose of collective bargaining or other mutual aid or protection; (2) that no employee and no one seeking employment shall be required as a condition of employment to join any company union or to refrain from joining, organizing, or assisting a labor organization of his own choosing; and (3) that employers shall comply with the maximum hours of labor, minimum rates of pay, and other conditions of employment, approved or prescribed by the President.

Unions naturally took this as a green light for an organizing drive and began an extensive campaign, especially in the coal, clothing, textile, and iron and steel industries, with considerable success. Many employers, on the other hand, quickly turned to the organization of company unions which they believed permissible under 7(a). This occurred notably in the steel, rubber, chemical, and automobile industries. Company-union coverage increased from 1933 to 1934 even more than that of trade-unions, although union membership had increased by the summer of 1934 more than half a million.[59] Conflicts arose early over the meaning of the right to organize and the freedom from interference by employers with this right which 7(a) purported to guarantee. Furthermore, under the influence of rising employment, prices, cost of living, and wages, and the opposition of many employers to organization of their employees, an increase in strikes threatened the recovery program. Accordingly, on August 5, 1933, on the recommendation of the Labor and Industrial Advisory Boards of the National Recovery Administration, the President established a National Labor Board, consisting of Senator Robert F. Wagner as chairman, the chairmen of the Labor and Industrial Advisory Boards, and two representatives each of labor and industry. Not until December 16, 1933, was there an Executive Order which formalized the power of the Board and approved and ratified actions already taken. The Board's functions were then, broadly, to settle by mediation, conciliation, or arbitration any controversies between employers and employees which tended to impede the purposes of the NIRA. In February, 1934, further Executive Orders authorized the holding of elections for choice by employees of representatives for collective bargaining pur-

59. Wolman, *op. cit.*, p. 34. By 1935 it was estimated that company-union coverage was nearly 60 per cent of union membership, compared with 40 per cent in 1932. Millis and Montgomery, *op. cit.*, p. 841.

poses and authorized the Board, if it found that an employer had refused to recognize such a chosen representative of the employees or in any other way was in violation of 7(a), to report this to the Compliance Division of the NRA or to the Attorney-General for appropriate action.[60]

The National Labor Board inevitably combined the function of trying to settle strikes, including disputes over recognition, and the quasi-judicial function of interpreting 7(a) and trying to prevent its violation. The work was on an emergency basis, with much overlapping of functions and authority among the Code agencies, local compliance boards, and the National Labor Board with its regional boards. During the first months, nevertheless, the Board with its great prestige had considerable success in settling strikes by obtaining agreements for elections. In November, 1933, however, the National Association of Manufacturers made a public attack upon the Board, claiming that its policies were interfering with sound employment relationships. Shortly thereafter the Board was defied by the Weirton Steel Company and the Budd Manufacturing Company, both of which refused to co-operate in elections to determine whether their employees chose to be represented by employee representation plans or by outside unions.[61] From then on the Board had increasing trouble with recalcitrant employers.

The great sources of difficulty in the experience of this Board were that it combined the function of mediation of disputes with that of obtaining compliance with law and that on the latter point it had no effective means of forcing an unwilling employer to comply. The Board always tried to mediate and obtain agreement, even after a Board decision was necessary. If finally noncompliance was clear, there was difference of opinion within the Board as to whether compulsion should be attempted. But the only compulsion possible was to submit the case to the Administrator, or later to the Compliance Division or to the Attorney-General, for "appropriate action." All that the Compliance Division could do was to "remove the Blue Eagle"— "NRA Member—We Do Our Part"—the symbol of compliance with the NIRA which decorated store windows and business letterheads during the boom period. The Attorney-General could institute injunction proceedings or prosecute. In only four cases, however, were

60. For text see *Decisions of the National Labor Board, August 1933–March 1934* (Washington, 1934), pp. v–viii.

61. Lorwin and Wubnig, *op. cit.*, pp. 102–6; cf. *infra*, ch. 4, pp. 123–24.

Blue Eagles removed during the National Labor Board's life.[62] The Weirton case was still before the courts when the NIRA came to an end in 1935.

Despite its difficulties in securing compliance, the Board in its interpretations of 7(a) began to lay the groundwork for a new common law which would protect the right to organize. Its decisions on discrimination for union activity, company-union cases, majority rule, and the meaning of recognition and collective bargaining were all significant beginnings of the definition of employers' obligations under the emerging national labor policy.

By March, 1934, Senator Wagner and others concerned with the work of the National Labor Board had become convinced that if the policy of 7(a) were to be made effective, it required further elaboration and provision for enforcement. Senator Wagner, therefore, introduced a bill to create a National Labor Board, on which hearings were held during March and April.[63] The bill declared the right to organize, defined unfair labor practices of employers which interfered with this right, and gave the Board power to seek enforcement of its orders through the federal courts. The proposal was at once attacked by the National Association of Manufacturers, the United States Chamber of Commerce, other important employer associations, and individual employers, many of whom brought in representatives of their employee representation plans to speak against it. It was attacked as class legislation, imposing restraints on employers but not on unions, as tending toward compulsory unionism, and as unconstitutional. It was supported, on the other hand, by many in the NLB organization, by the AFL, and by numerous experts in the field who considered it necessary to carry out the policy of 7(a) and to protect true collective bargaining from interference by employers. When it was evident that prompt action could not be obtained on this proposal, however, and in view of a mounting strike crisis, a simple resolution was transmitted to Congress by the President and enacted and signed on June 19, 1934.[64]

Public Resolution No. 44 authorized the President to establish a board or boards to investigate any controversies arising under 7(a)

62. Lorwin and Wubnig, *op. cit.*, p. 268.

63. U.S. Senate, Committee on Education and Labor, *Hearings, To Create a National Labor Board,* 73d Cong., 2d Sess., March 14–April 9, 1934, Pts. 1–3, 1028 pp.

64. For text of Public Resolution No. 44 and the Executive Order establishing the National Labor Relations Board see *Decisions of the National Labor Relations Board, July 9, 1934–December 1934* (Washington, 1935), pp. v–vi.

which obstructed commerce. Such boards were empowered to conduct elections and in connection with them to order the production of documents or the appearance of witnesses. Except for orders in connection with elections, which could be enforced or reviewed by the courts in the same manner as orders of the Federal Trade Commission, the Board could obtain enforcement of orders, as before, only through the compliance machinery of the NRA or the Department of Justice. The resolution also did not settle such a basic issue as that of majority rule, over which there had been conflicts in the interpretation of 7(a) between the NLB and the Administrator of the NRA.[65] This compromise was accepted without great opposition, since it was to continue only until the end of the NIRA on June 16, 1935.[66]

Under the authority of this resolution the President on June 29, 1934, established a National Labor Relations Board. It consisted of three full-time public members.[67] The Board continued the system of regional boards, with panels of industry and labor members, which had been set up by the earlier Board. Unavoidably, although it sought to function only on disputes involving 7(a), it continued to emphasize mediation and the effort to obtain prompt settlement of disputes in the regional offices. When necessary, there were formal hearings and decisions by panels in the regional offices. Cases went to the national Board then on appeal or when employers refused to agree to elections or to comply with local decisions. Basic policies were set by the formal decisions of the National Labor Relations Board, and regional boards were expected to act in harmony with these decisions interpreting 7(a). Many elections were conducted on consent or order, but in some cases employers went to the courts to obtain review of the Board's election orders.[68] The great problem, as in the case of the

65. Lorwin and Wubnig, *op. cit.*, pp. 231–62, 268–72. Settlement of an automobile dispute by the President on March 25, 1934, had provided for proportional representation, contrary to the policy of the NLB. Cf. also D. O. Bowman, *Public Control of Labor Relations* (New York: Macmillan Co., 1942), pp. 33–38.

66. Perhaps typical was a letter from "the Vice-President of one of the largest corporations," in June, 1934, quoted later by Senator Wagner. This industrialist said that he viewed the passage of the resolution with equanimity, as it meant a temporary measure substituted for a permanent one, and he did not believe the Wagner bill would have again as good a chance of passage...."The trade is a mighty good compromise.... My personal opinion is that it is not going to bother us very much." *Cong. Rec.*, 79:7569.

67. The members were Chairman Lloyd K. Garrison, H. A. Millis, and Edwin S. Smith. Mr. Garrison resigned and was replaced by Francis Biddle in November, 1934. For the history of this and the special industry boards set up under Public Resolution No. 44, cf. Lorwin and Wubnig, *op. cit.*

68. *Ibid.*, ch. 11, esp. pp. 309, 329.

NLB, was that of enforcing orders against recalcitrant employers. During its first six months the Board succeeded in having Blue Eagles removed by the Compliance Division in twenty-four cases, but later this became more difficult. Moreover, the Blue Eagle itself received less public respect in the later months of the NRA. Attempts to obtain enforcement by the Department of Justice failed. The Department brought suit in only one case of thirty-three referred to it.[69] The Board with its regional boards was able to settle a large number of disputes. But it could not enforce the protection which 7(a) purported to provide against an employer who was unwilling to comply. The Board reported frankly: "The Board is powerless to enforce its decisions. In the ultimate analysis its findings and orders are nothing more than recommendations."[70]

Nevertheless, when Congress came to consider a longer-range policy, it was aided by the experience of this Board, which had attempted to administer the national policy expressed in 7(a) and to build up by its interpretations a body of common law based on recognition of the right of free choice of bargaining representatives. Much of this experience was reflected in the Wagner Act.

By spring of 1935, the unions, aided by improving business conditions, the stimulus of the new national labor policy, and whatever protection they obtained from the boards, had gained a million or more new members and had even encroached on old open-shop strongholds in mass-production industries. Company unions had expanded even more. The new militance and increased organization of the unions met acceptance of collective bargaining by many employers, especially in highly competitive industries where the stabilization of competition by the NRA codes could be strengthened by the influence of strong unions. But many other employers, especially in mass production, opposed any change from their old ways of handling labor relations. They supported company unions, and many used espionage and discrimination and preparations to fight strikes by force[71] as weapons against union organization. Important companies, also, had been able by court action to block the holding of elections by the Board to determine the choice of their employees as to repre-

69. The Houde Engineering Corp. case. This and the Weirton case, carried over from the National Labor Board, were dropped with others after the Schechter decision held the NIRA unconstitutional. *Ibid.*, pp. 302–4, 324–26, 329–30.

70. Quoted in *ibid.*, p. 324.

71. Cf. ch. 4, *infra*, pp. 100–101.

sentation, and unrest was mounting as a result.[72] Meantime, there had been some improvement in business conditions, but there were still twelve million or so unemployed, and great uncertainty prevailed as to the future.

In view of the coming expiration of the NIRA, as well as of the breakdown in enforcement of 7(a), and with the depression experience vivid in his mind, Senator Wagner in February, 1935, introduced a revised bill for a permanent National Labor Relations Board, and hearings were held during March and April.[73] The Senator emphasized the aim to establish as permanent national policy an effective protection of the right of workers to organize which would not be destroyed by court decisions. This was thought necessary as a basis for a sound economy, since concentration in industry had increased and the bargaining power of individual workers had decreased accordingly. Moreover, if employers were allowed to associate, the same privilege must be accorded to employees. It was hoped that greater equality of bargaining power, as a result, would increase wages and thus act as a corrective to undue concentration of wealth and income and promote a balanced economy. In addition, the wastes of bitter conflicts over recognition, such as had been seen even the year before, should be avoided.[74]

Committee hearings brought forth again opposition from the major employers' associations and many individual employers, as well as from a large number of officers of employee representation plans. A few employers spoke in favor of the bill. The major arguments in opposition held that the bill was unconstitutional and objected to the majority-rule provision, the outlawing of company-supported company unions, and the failure to include control over unions or to prohibit coercion from any source. The Senate Committee unanimously supported the bill, however. In two days of debate the major test was on Senator Tydings' amendment to prohibit coercion or interference by *any* person; this was defeated by a vote of 21 to 50. The bill was then adopted, 63 to 12.[75]

72. Lorwin and Wubnig, *op. cit.*, pp. 309, 329.
73. U.S. Senate, Committee on Education and Labor, *Hearings, National Labor Relations Board*, 74th Cong., 1st Sess., 1935, p. 890, cited as Senate Committee on Education and Labor, *NLRB Hearings, 1935*. The bill was called "A Bill To Promote Equality of Bargaining Power between Employers and Employees, To Diminish the Causes of Labor Disputes . . . and for Other Purposes."
74. *Ibid.*, pp. 32–38; *Cong. Rec.*, 79:7565–73.
75. *Cong. Rec.*, 79:7675, 7681.

From the Wagner Act to Taft-Hartley

Before the House Committee reported, the Supreme Court on May 27, 1935, invalidated the NRA codes as unconstitutional.[76] The House Committee reconsidered the bill in the light of this development. When it reported, strongly supporting the bill with minor amendments, on June 10, it had reformulated the declaration of policy and the title of the bill, in order "to emphasize the intent . . . to promote industrial peace," by preventing unrest arising from interference with the right to organize. Somewhat more opposition developed in the House, and there were unsuccessful attempts to add a "coercion from any source" amendment, to limit the power of the Board to decide units appropriate for collective bargaining, and to stiffen the rule as to use of evidence. On the last point there was a record vote, of 84 to 117. Fears were expressed also for "company unions" and for minority rights. Several congressmen spoke of hundreds of letters and telegrams they were receiving from employers against the bill and indicated resentment of "propaganda" and "misrepresentation" and of the activities of "the men responsible." The National Association of Manufacturers was very active in organizing the opposition. After one day's debate, nevertheless, the bill was passed without a record vote.[77] Differences between the two houses were easily adjusted, and the Conference Report was adopted by the House by a vote of 132 to 45, and by the Senate without a record vote, on June 27, 1935. The bill was signed by the President on July 5, 1935.[78] The surprisingly small opposition in Congress was undoubtedly related to the gravity of the economic situation and uncertainty of the future accentuated by the end of the NRA.

The National Labor Relations Act[79] went far beyond Section 7(a) of the NIRA in its effort to provide effective protection of the rights of

76. Schechter Poultry Corp. v. U.S., 295 U.S. 495 (1935). The Court held that there had been an unconstitutional delegation of legislative power and that the interstate commerce power had been exceeded.

77. *Cong. Rec.*, 79:9676–9711, 9715–31, esp. 9680, 9683, 9727, 9729–31. For a documented account of the management of the opposition to the bill and the stimulation of pressure against it by the National Association of Manufacturers, with co-operation of other associations, see *La Follette Committee Reports, National Association of Manufacturers*, Report No. 6, Pt. 6, 76th Cong., 1st Sess., 1939, pp. 75–122.

78. *Cong. Rec.*, 79:10259, 10300. Cf. Bowman, *op. cit.*, pp. 51–57. The *Senate Committee Report*, No. 573, 74th Cong., 1st Sess., May 1, 1935, and the *House Committee Report*, No. 1147, 74th Cong., 1st Sess., June 10, 1935, are easily available in National Labor Relations Board, *Statutes and Congressional Reports Pertaining to the National Labor Relations Board* (Washington, 1943), pp. 33–103.

79. 49 U.S. Stat. 449.

labor. It declared the right of employees to organize and to bargain collectively through representatives freely chosen by the majority and to engage in concerted activities for their mutual aid and protection. It defined and prohibited a series of interferences by employers with these rights. It provided for an independent Board of impartial members to administer the Act, with power on their own initiative to seek enforcement of their cease-and-desist orders in unfair labor practice cases in the circuit courts of appeal. Recognizing how employers had been able to hamper efforts to secure compliance with 7(a) by resorting to the courts to delay elections, also, Congress restricted the right of appeal to the stage of cease-and-desist orders.[80] Conciliation and mediation of labor disputes were entirely outside the scope of the agency. It was limited to preventing unfair labor practices and settling issues over representation.

The wheel of governmental policy toward combination of workers to promote their interests by collective action had turned far, from disapproval and repression, through sharp limitations on concerted activities, to toleration and the removal of many such limitations on actions not illegal when done singly, and finally to positive protection of the right to organize, and therefore to encouragement of organization, by prohibiting interference by employers with that right. It remained for experience to show whether Senator Wagner's Act, the culmination of the revolutionary national labor policy which developed in the thirties, and which he saw as "permeated with principles of freedom,"[81] would prove an effective instrument to further the freedom of workers and free and democratic industrial relations as an essential basis for a sound economy.

80. The Act is analyzed further in the next chapter. Special points in its terms and its legislative history will be considered later in connection with particular issues.

81. Senate Committee on Education and Labor, *NLRB Hearings, 1935*, p. 41.

CHAPTER 2

THE NATIONAL LABOR RELATIONS
ACT AND ITS ADMINISTRATION

THE National Labor Relations Act of 1935,[1] the Wagner Act, brought to fruition in a brief, carefully drawn statute a revolutionary national labor policy—that workers were to be protected in the right to organize and bargain collectively through freely chosen representatives. Through the twelve years' life of the statute, in the face of widespread hostility of the press and continuing opposition of influential groups in industry, the Board sought to solve the new and difficult problems of administering such a law and making its policies effective. Experience showed that industry increasingly accepted these policies. But the Board never obtained the public understanding of its purposes, powers, methods, and accomplishments as well as of the limits of its functions which might have protected the Act from the attack of critics many of whom wished not so much to improve it as to destroy it.

The Act itself was essentially simple, with a limited purpose. That purpose is set forth in the statement of findings and policy:

... to eliminate the causes of certain substantial obstructions to the free flow of commerce ... by encouraging the practice and procedure of collective bargaining and by protecting the exercise by workers of full freedom of association, self-organization, and designation of representatives of their own choosing, for the purpose of negotiating the terms and conditions of their employment or other mutual aid or protection.[2]

Congress found that the denial by employers of these rights and the refusal of employers to bargain collectively led to strikes and unrest which interfered with interstate commerce and that inequality of bargaining power between unorganized employees and employers "organized in the corporate or other forms of ownership association" tended to depress wages and prevent stabilization of competitive

1. 49 U.S. Stat. 449.
2. Cited in full, with additions made by the Taft-Hartley Act in 1947, *infra,* ch. 11, p. 397.

wage rates and hence to aggravate recurrent business depressions. Experience had proved, Congress stated, that protection by law of the right to organize and bargain collectively promotes the flow of commerce by removing "certain recognized sources of industrial strife and unrest," encouraging the friendly adjustment of industrial disputes, and making for equality of bargaining power.

The Act was not intended to deal with all types of labor relations questions, or the prevention of strikes in general, any more than it was with issues over wages or with possible abuse of power by unions or by employers in other areas of activity. Whether wise or not, whether or not experience would show need for additional legislation to deal with matters growing out of the experience under this Act, the Wagner Act gave to the Board which was to administer it only limited powers, to prevent practices of employers which interfered with the right of workers freely to organize and bargain collectively and to determine questions of fact as to whether groups of workers had chosen labor organizations to represent them in dealing with their employers.

The basic rights of employees were stated in Section 7.

Employees shall have the right to self-organization, to form, join, or assist labor organizations, to bargain collectively through representatives of their own choosing, and to engage in concerted activities for the purpose of collective bargaining or other mutual aid or protection.

Five unfair labor practices were defined and forbidden to employers: (1) any interference, restraint, or coercion of employees in the exercise of the rights guaranteed; (2) domination or interference with the formation or administration of a labor organization or contributing financial or other support to it; (3) discrimination to encourage or discourage union membership, except that closed-shop contracts were not illegal if made with a union representing the majority of the employees in an appropriate bargaining unit and without illegal assistance by the employer; (4) discrimination against an employee for filing charges or testifying under this Act; and (5) refusal to bargain collectively with the legal representative of employees in an appropriate bargaining unit.

A National Labor Relations Board of three members, appointed by the President with the advice and consent of the Senate, was to administer the Act. Like other independent administrative agencies, the Board was to investigate, to hold hearings, and to issue decisions and orders. Its orders were not self-enforcing, however; it could petition a circuit court of appeals for the enforcement of an order in an unfair labor practice case, and similarly any person aggrieved by such an order could petition the circuit court for review. As was the case with other similar agencies, the Board was not bound by the technical rules of evidence, and its findings of fact, if supported by evidence, were to be controlling in the courts. There were no penalties for violation of the Act, only the power to prevent unfair labor practices by cease-and-desist orders and the power to require affirmative action to effectuate the policies of the Act.

Throughout its history, operating as it was in a highly controversial field, in which old established habits were being forced to change under pressure from the government, the Board was subject to sharp criticism. A minority of a House of Representatives committee in 1940 said:

> Justly or unjustly, the consensus of public opinion is that the Board is biased, prejudiced, and has been guilty not only of grabbing and using power never delegated to it by the act, but that it has been unfair and unjust in its actions.[3]

Similarly the Hartley report in 1947 stated:

> The committee's investigations, as well as those of preceding Congresses, have shown bias and prejudice to be rampant in the Board's staff, and among some members of the Board itself.[4]

Many criticisms were badly informed, failing to understand the functions of the Board and its limitations or simply reflecting dislike of the purposes of the Act. Most of them ignored large segments of the evidence as to the work of the Board. Yet real issues were raised as to proper administrative procedures for the enforcement of such a law as this. Now that an era has ended with the substitution of the Taft-Hartley Act for the Wagner Act, it is desirable to review the experience as objectively and with as much perspective as is possible at this time. What were the problems in administration? Did the Board succeed in solving them? What was the testimony of courts and impartial investigators on these questions? Was need for changes in the law indicated by the experience? The present chapter is concerned only with these questions of administrative procedures and their

3. U.S. House of Representatives, Committee on Labor, *Minority Report, Proposed Amendments to the National Labor Relations Act*, Report No. 1928, Pt. 3, 76th Cong., 3d Sess., April 12, 1940, p. 10, cited as House Committee on Labor, *Minority Report, NLRA (1940)*.

4. U.S. House of Representatives, Committee on Education and Labor, *Labor-Management Relations Act, 1947*, Report No. 245, 80th Cong., 1st Sess., April 11, 1947, p. 26, cited as *Hartley Report*.

results. Policies as to the actual rights and duties under the law will be discussed later.

In fairness to the Board the factors which made its job tremendously difficult must be recognized. First was the novelty of the problems. For the first time the federal government was attempting to enforce widely its policy of outlawing employer interference with the right of workers to organize and to bargain collectively. The Board itself, and ultimately the courts on review of Board orders, had to define what this meant in the innumerable different situations which came before the Board. Unions had to learn what this Act could and could not do, employers to learn their duties under the new statute, courts to learn the points at which former protection of property rights had to give way to other rights. And the Board and its staff and the courts had to develop the meaning of "due process" in the enforcement of this new type of law. Moreover, personnel had to be trained for a task needing objectivity and thoroughness as well as tact and common sense in dealing with emotionally charged situations. Especially after April, 1937, when, as Chairman Madden pointed out, "no ready-made personnel, experienced in the field of labor relations, was available,"[5] the Board needed quickly to recruit and train a large staff to meet an avalanche of cases. It was not surprising if not all employees were as objective and efficient as the Board desired or as they became later through experience and training.

Another crucial factor in the difficulties of the Board was the continuing opposition in industry and in Congress. The fight on the constitutionality issue consumed much of the energy of the Board until April, 1937. When that issue was settled by the Supreme Court, the major associations of industry began a drive for amendment[6] which continued, with a partial recess during the war, until its success in 1947. The three lengthy congressional investigations in both House and Senate in 1939–40 took much time and harassed the Board at a period when it was overwhelmed with a heavy case load and inadequate staff. When this attack upon the Act failed to result in amendment, opposition took the form of hostility in the appropriations com-

5. U.S. House of Representatives, Committee on Labor, *Hearings, Proposed Amendments to the National Labor Relations Act*, 76th Cong., 1st Sess., May 23, 1939, Vol. 2, p. 317, cited as House Committee on Labor, *NLRA Hearings* (*1939*).

6. Cf. Chamber of Commerce of U.S., *Federal Regulation of Labor Relations* (Washington, D.C., May, 1937), p. 4. National Association of Manufacturers, *Why and How the Wagner Act Should Be Amended* (New York, June, 1939), pp. 19–20.

mittees and inadequate appropriations.[7] Again at the close of the war the drive for amendment or repeal was renewed, actively promoted by the National Association of Manufacturers, and the relations with Congress, as to appropriations and the necessity of supplying material for the investigating committees, once more absorbed a large share of the time and energy of the Board and its staff. Through most of its life the Board worked in a hostile atmosphere, in which opposition and misunderstanding were promoted by much of the press.

The division in the labor movement also added enormous complications which had not been foreseen when the Act was passed. The rapid growth of labor organization increased the number of cases, while the rivalries between AFL, CIO, and independent unions brought to the Board cases which sometimes posed touchy and difficult questions and exposed the Board to harsh criticisms of "bias," from whichever group lost as a result of particular policies.

Finally, the abnormal conditions of the defense, war, and postwar periods ruled for more than half of the life of the Wagner Act. They gave the Board difficult questions of policy, swamped it for a time with the irrelevant job of conducting War Labor Disputes Act strike votes, and in the two years of strife following V-J Day turned public ire against the NLRA for conditions which were outside the area of the powers of the Board.

It has been said truly that the Board never had a chance to function in a "normal" period, with adequate staff and speed and efficiency in handling of cases, and to show what it might have done for the elimination of strife. Instead it had first the bitter opposition of most of industry and the fight on constitutionality; then the deluge of cases after the establishment of the constitutionality of the Act and the increase of union membership following the organization of the CIO; then, before it could get its work onto a current basis, the hampering

7. Cf. U.S. Senate, Subcommittee of the Committee on the Judiciary, *Hearings, Investigation of the National Labor Relations Board,* 75th Cong., 3d Sess., January 28, 1938, pp. 47–48, cited as Senate Committee on the Judiciary, *NLRB Hearings,* quoting David Lawrence in the *Washington Star;* U.S. Senate, Subcommittee of the Committee on Appropriations, *Hearings, Labor–Federal Security Appropriations Bill for 1948,* 80th Cong., 1st Sess., April 7, 1947, p. 867, cited as Senate Appropriations Committee, *Hearings, 1948.*

The Board's total expenditures and obligations, by fiscal year, were as follows, from *Annual Reports.* For a comparison with the much more sharply rising work load, see *infra,* ch. 3, Table 1.

1935–36	$ 620,571	1941–42	$3,069,275
1936–37	788,528	1942–43	3,598,992
1937–38	2,456,884	1943–44	3,435,780
1938–39	2,845,771	1944–45	3,623,867
1939–40	3,184,021	1945–46	4,250,951
1940–41	2,867,212	1946–47	4,436,650

congressional investigations; next the war; and, finally, the postwar avalanche and the renewed attack upon the Act. And through most of the twelve years' history, appropriations and staff were inadequate, and the backlog of cases grew. It may be added also that the constant shift in personnel of the Board, none being reappointed after a full five-year term,[8] while giving certain advantages in fresh points of view, lost what might have been a more consistent and increasingly efficient administration by an expert and experienced Board.

The Board, facing all these problems and difficulties, worked at solutions along four main lines. First, it improved its personnel and methods by careful selection and training and by building upon the experience of the most efficient of the staff, getting their advice and making it available to others through staff committees and field conferences. Second, it improved the Washington control over work in the field and gradually developed standard procedures which did much to eliminate regional differences in handling of cases and to put the work on a high level of efficiency. Third, the Board itself over the years developed a high degree of separation of functions within the agency and clear and extensive delegation of authority to officers and committees in Washington and to Regional Directors in handling cases in the field. Finally, the policies of the Board developed through the years on the basis of experience, influenced by court decisions on Board cases, public and congressional criticism, the Board's study of its own experience, and the attitudes of the members of the Board. The problems of the NLRB were of special difficulty because of the complex relationships with which it dealt. Nevertheless, in many respects the Board's experience and the attacks upon it paralleled that of other administrative agencies during these years.

1935–37

The members of the Board, who were appointed by the President late in August, 1935, were Chairman J. Warren Madden, professor of law at the University of Pittsburgh, Edwin S. Smith, a member of the old NLRB and with other experience in labor relations, and John M. Carmody, member of the National Mediation Board. Mr. Carmody resigned a year later and was replaced by a lawyer, Donald Wakefield Smith.

The Board inherited from the old NLRB a small staff, divided be-

8. Mr. Edwin S. Smith was reappointed for five years after serving a one-year term. Mr. Houston and Mr. Herzog each served short periods before their five-year terms.

tween Washington and some twenty-one regional offices, much of which it retained as an experienced group. It appointed a Regional Director and a Regional Attorney in each regional office. In Washington the General Counsel through a Litigation Section and a Review Section was responsible for conducting hearings and for representing the Board in all judicial proceedings and for the review of records of hearings and assisting the Board in preparing formal decisions. He also supervised the work of attorneys in the field. The Secretary of the Board was responsible for the general administrative work and the supervision of the regional offices as well as for the administrative handling of cases in Washington and the field. He acted also as Chief Trial Examiner in charge of the Trial Examiners' Division, whose members presided over hearings and prepared reports for the Board. He had of course nothing to do with the decision-making process following hearing. An Economic Division prepared necessary materials for the Board on questions of fact as to the interstate commerce aspects of cases and on labor relations questions.

Even before the Board had completed its organization and published its first rules and regulations the attempt to prevent administration of the Act began. On September 5, 1935, the American Liberty League published a report of a committee of prominent lawyers which held that the Act was clearly unconstitutional, as an unreasonable interference with individual rights, and beyond the power of Congress to regulate interstate commerce.[9] This issue would have to be decided by the Supreme Court before real enforcement of the Act could begin.

Nonetheless, cases began to come in; 203 in October, 1935, and from then on through the early months of 1937 an average of some 100 or more cases were filed each month.[10] In the first year four-fifths of them charged employers with unfair labor practices. In the second year over 70 per cent were such charges, while representation cases increased to about 30 per cent of the cases filed. At the start there was only loose supervision of the field offices, and the handling of cases varied from region to region depending upon the experience and personalities of the staff. But the general outlines of Board procedures began to be set. When a charge was filed that an employer had dis-

9. National Lawyers Committee of the American Liberty League, *Report on the Constitutionality of the National Labor Relations Act*, September 5, 1935, quoted in House Committee on Labor, *NLRA Hearings* (1939), Vol. 8, pp. 2241–87. Cf. *infra*, ch. 8, p. 295.

10. For complete data on cases handled by years see *infra*, ch. 3, Table 1.

criminated against employees for union activity, maintained a company-dominated union, or otherwise interfered with the rights guaranteed by the Act, the Regional Director or a field examiner investigated, with the help of the Regional Attorney on legal points. Interviews with complaining employees and others and with employers and management—often bitterly hostile and unco-operative—and study of records were all designed to learn whether in fact the Act was being violated. If it appeared from the investigation that the employer was violating the law, an attempt was made to show him what would be necessary to bring himself into compliance with the requirements of the Act and to settle the case on that basis by agreement. If, however, the charge proved not to be well founded, unions were asked to withdraw the charge, or, failing that, the Regional Director would dismiss it, refusing to issue a formal complaint. Appeal could be made to the Board against his action.

Somewhat similarly, when a petition was filed by an employee or a labor organization asking for an investigation of a question as to the right of employees to a representative chosen by the majority of the group, it was handled in the regional office. Sometimes in the course of this preliminary investigation the case could be settled by an agreement of the employer to recognize the union, on proof of its majority, or by agreement for a secret election to be held by the Regional Director to determine the desires of the employees. If the investigation failed to support the claim that a real question of representation existed, the Regional Director could report to the Board, recommending either that the union be permitted to withdraw its petition or that the petition be dismissed.

It was surprising, in view of the organized opposition to the Act, that it proved possible to settle some cases by these informal procedures.[11] In the first year, of 865 complaint cases filed, over 60 per cent were disposed of informally. More than 30 per cent were withdrawn or dismissed when the evidence did not support the charge that violations had occurred. But 240 cases, nearly 28 per cent, were "settled" in compliance with the Act by the reinstatement of employees who had been discriminated against, by payment of back pay, by recognition of a labor organization, by abolition of a company union, or by agreement by employers to cease interfering with em-

11. Cases handled in the regional offices without the necessity of issuing a formal complaint, or a formal notice of hearing, or carrying the case up to the Board for formal order in either a representation case or an unfair labor practice case are called "informal cases." Conversely those requiring "formal" action, hearing and Board order, are called "formal cases."

ployees' rights and to post notices to this effect. Of the 203 representation cases filed in this first year, too, 90, or 44 per cent of those closed, were disposed of informally. Some were withdrawn or dismissed, but in 29 cases employers agreed to recognize the union, and in 23 there were elections by consent to determine the issue.[12] These settlements in many instances occurred where strikes were in process or threatened. They showed that industrial strife could be reduced by use of the peaceful processes of the Board.

Where cases could not be disposed of by these informal processes, however, the Board proceeded to use its full powers of formal action. In a complaint case the Regional Director requested authorization from the Board to issue a formal complaint. In the hearing held before a Trial Examiner of the Board, or sometimes before Board members themselves, an attorney for the Board was responsible for getting into the record the evidence as to the alleged violations. The employer and his counsel had every opportunity to present evidence and argument in defense. Often the hearing could be completed in a day or a few days. Occasionally, as when mass discriminatory discharges or a complex of other violations were charged, it might run for weeks.[13] After the hearing the Trial Examiner prepared an Intermediate Report giving his findings of fact on the evidence and his recommendations. This report was served on the parties and opportunity given to file exceptions. Oral argument before the Board would be granted on request of the employer or union party to the case. The Review Section analyzed the record for the Board and gave any assistance required by the Board in making its final decision and order.

In representation cases which could not be disposed of by informal methods the Regional Director similarly requested from the Board authorization to proceed to a hearing. The hearing was held before a Trial Examiner, before whom both sides had full opportunity to present the evidence on the issues. After an informal report by the Trial Examiner and review of the record by the Review Section, the Board made its decision, either dismissing the case, certifying a union as representative of the employees in an appropriate unit, or ordering an election conducted by the Regional Director to determine whether the employees had chosen a representative. After the election, if a

12. National Labor Relations Board, *First Annual Report* (Washington: Government Printing Office, 1936), pp. 35, 40.

13. The Remington Rand hearing extended from October 14 to December 11, 1936. *Second Annual Report,* p. 161.

majority of the votes were for a union, that union was certified by the Board.[14]

The Board's orders against employers in unfair labor practice cases could be enforced only by petitioning the proper circuit court of appeals to enforce the order, subject to review by the Supreme Court. The obstructionists, however, were unwilling to follow this orderly procedure and tried by injunction suits in federal district courts to prevent the Board from functioning at all. This campaign beginning in November, 1935, resulted in the filing of nearly one hundred such suits to prevent the Board from holding hearings. The Board fought these cases vigorously. Fortunately the majority of the district courts, all but one of the circuit courts, and finally the Supreme Court completely upheld the Board, denying that district courts had any power or jurisdiction in these cases. But in the meantime for much of the first two years the work of the Board was seriously hampered; in fact, "in some areas where the District Judges were particularly hostile, the Board's work was forced to a standstill."[15]

Even more important for the long run was the Board's success in establishing the constitutionality of the Act. Recognizing how essential it was to establish the work on a "firm and broad constitutional basis," the Board was on the lookout for important cases which would test squarely the major issues as to constitutionality. Meantime it encouraged the regional offices to settle informally the small and less significant cases and, if necessary, induce employees to postpone pushing their cases. The Board refused to take jurisdiction of some cases which it considered beyond its constitutional authority or where it did not yet wish to test the issue of its jurisdiction.

In a number of important early cases the Board went in person to hear the case in place of a Trial Examiner, and in many others individual members of the Board were appointed Trial Examiner. This meant that they had the experience themselves of sitting for days and hearing the evidence as to discrimination, espionage, violence against union adherents, or other interference with the rights of employees under the Act, and then analyzing for themselves the record on which they based their decision. The Board insisted in all cases going to hearing that there be the most careful investigation and preparation

14. For more discussion of Board methods in these first years see J. Warren Madden, "Birth of the Board," in Louis G. Silverberg, *The Wagner Act: After Ten Years* (Washington: Bureau of National Affairs, 1945), pp. 34–42. Also *First* and *Second Annual Reports* of the National Labor Relations Board.

15. Charles Fahy, "The NLRB and the Courts," in Silverberg, *op. cit.*, pp. 44–45; *First Annual Report*, pp. 46–50; *Second Annual Report*, pp. 31–32.

of the case and "legal craftsmanship" in order to build a sound foundation for the court tests. In the first year the Board issued only 56 decisions finding unfair labor practices and ordering employers to cease and desist and 3 decisions dismissing charges. In the second year there were only 39 cease-and-desist orders and 8 dismissals.[16] Petitions for the enforcement of orders were filed promptly in a few carefully selected cases which would test broadly the constitutionality and application of the Act.

That Congress and the Board had built soundly was demonstrated when the Supreme Court on April 12, 1937, issued its five crucial decisions holding the Act constitutional and applicable to manufacturing industries as well as those in transportation and communication. The Court held also that the procedures afforded "adequate opportunity to secure judicial protection against arbitrary action."[17]

By the end of the Board's second year, despite the action of the courts, there had been only four cases in which companies had complied with the Board's order against unfair labor practices. But as in the first year the regional offices had been able to settle a substantial number of both the complaint and the representation cases by informal methods.[18] In addition, elections had been held, 31 in the first year and 265 in the second, to determine whether employees desired representation for collective bargaining purposes. In many instances, however, the Board had been unable to prevent discrimination or other illegal tactics under which many workers were still suffering. The Board felt that it had made a sound start, nevertheless. It had established the legal basis for its work and also the informal procedures which could handle cases expeditiously with the co-operation of employers and unions, in order to achieve the purposes of the Act which was now established as the law of the land.

1937–40

The next three years, the final period of the leadership of Chairman Madden, were years of greatly increased activity and considerable strain, as the Board sought to develop the concrete meaning of the Act in practice and to obtain acceptance of its purposes by employers and unions. Any hope that after the constitutionality of the Act was

16. Madden, in Silverberg, *op. cit.*, pp. 38–42; *First Annual Report*, pp. 35–37; *Second Annual Report*, pp. 21–22.

17. NLRB v. Jones and Laughlin Steel Corp., 301 U.S. 1, 47 (1937).

18. *First Annual Report*, pp. 37, 45; *Second Annual Report*, pp. 20–22, 25–27, 29–30.

established employers would promptly accept the law proved mistaken. The Chairman early in 1938 reported to a Senate committee that widespread violations had continued. "The resistance to that law has continued and has been encouraged by very important people."[19] Moreover, the dramatic organization campaigns following the establishment of the CIO brought disputes involving union rivalry as well as those over the basic right of organization and collective bargaining. The Supreme Court decisions were followed by a flood of new cases, many of which had been held up pending the court tests, and which came from the period when employers, on what they considered good authority, had believed that the law would not stand. While earlier cases filed had averaged 130 a month, in April, 1937, they increased to 477, in May to 1,064, in June to 1,283, and in July to 1,325. Then the tide receded slightly, but for the year ending July 30, 1938, a total of 10,430 cases were filed, about two-thirds of them unfair labor practice cases. The year before had seen 4,068 cases filed. In the next two years the case load leveled off at 6,000–7,000.[20]

The Board received additional funds in August, 1937, in order to be able to expand its staff and handle its cases.[21] Its personnel increased from 272 in June, 1937, to 692 a year later, and to over 800 in 1939 and 1940. Slightly more than half of the staff were in the regions in 1938, slightly less than half in 1939 and 1940.[22] The Chairman, in retrospect, called the 1937 addition to the funds "adequate,"[23] but he always chose to operate as economically as possible, and during these years in spite of hard work and long hours the staff was never able to get its work on a current basis, the backlog of pending cases grew, and unions complained bitterly of delay in handling cases. Salaries were relatively low, and as a matter of policy the Board employed many young and inexperienced people, believing that it could thus obtain a more able staff than if it took older men who would come for such salaries.[24]

19. Senate Committee on the Judiciary, *NLRB Hearings* (*1938*), pp. 70–71.
20. *Eleventh Annual Report*, p. 75; *Third Annual Report*, p. 285.
21. See *supra*, n. 7.
22. D. O. Bowman, *Public Control of Labor Relations* (New York: Macmillan Co., 1942), p. 379, from U.S. House of Representatives, Subcommittee of the Committee on Appropriations, *Hearings, Department of Labor–Federal Security Agency Appropriations Bill for 1942*, 77th Cong., 1st Sess., 1941, Pt. 1, p. 535.
23. Silverberg, *op. cit.*, p. 41.
24. Bowman, *op. cit.*, pp. 375–83. The staff considered the Chairman a hard bargainer, and there were many inequities in salaries especially in the field offices, until Civil Service Classification was applied to the entire staff after 1941. In 1939 the most common salary for field examiner, for example, was $2,600 or $2,900,

It would have been surprising indeed if a staff collected under these circumstances had not been on the whole of a liberal disposition, believing in the purposes of the Act, and sympathetically disposed toward the employees and labor organizations that filed their charges and petitions with the Board. Some of the staff had had labor relations experience, more of them had not. There were among them some "zealots" and some "crackpots, prima donnas, and irresponsibles." The Board had to train its enlarged staff, both in techniques of the job and in the necessary objectivity, and eliminate those who could not be trained. There were warnings from Washington against improper fraternization with unions or union attorneys, or improper pressure on employers to accept settlements, or the various indiscretions which were sometimes brought to the attention of the Board, and insistence upon absolute impartiality in dealing with employers and unions.[25] Impartiality was difficult to maintain when so many prominent companies proved to be hostile to the Act and the Board, were unco-operative during the investigations, sometimes even encouraged or instigated threats of violence against Board staff as well as union representatives, and continued interfering with the rights of their employees. It was not to be wondered at that when hostile congressional investigations got under way in 1939 it was possible to find for the record instances in which employers and sometimes unions claimed that there had been bias or inefficiency or at least a lack of understanding of the realities of industrial relations.

The Board turned out an enormous volume of work during these years. In the crisis year of 1937–38 it closed 8,799 cases, about 70 per cent of all on its docket of both the complaint and the representation cases. About half of all those closed were settled informally by agreement for the adjustment of the charge or for settling a representation dispute by a consent election, check of union cards against pay rolls, or agreement for recognition. Another large group were withdrawn or dismissed before formal action. In a few cases, only 29, there was compliance with a Board cease-and-desist order. The problem of getting compliance with Board and court orders was to plague the Board for a long time. The backlog of cases pending for investigation or in the later stages before the Board cast a heavy shadow, as it rose to over 3,700 cases on June 30, 1938, and to over 4,000

and only very few were paid as much as $3,500 or $4,000. House Committee on Labor, *NLRA Hearings* (1939), Vol. 2, pp. 391–402.

25. Cf. Board memos M-629 to Regional Directors, August 23, 1938, and M-851 to Regional Attorneys, May 1, 1939.

a year later, although it was finally reduced to about 2,800 in the year 1939–40.[26] In 1938–39 the Board closed only 61.5 per cent of the cases on docket, but in 1939–40, with some improvements in administration and a level load, it closed 72 per cent of its cases.

By the summer of 1938 the Board became very much concerned about the increased proportion of cases which were going to formal hearing, with the result that the Washington staff was swamped with cases waiting decision. It was becoming more difficult to get agreement of the parties to informal settlements. The Board decided therefore to limit the number of cases heard, to select cases which were strong on jurisdiction or on the merits and key cases in the region or industry, even if small, less important, or weaker cases had to be compromised or dropped. "The Act will become more quickly and firmly established if the Board succeeds in winning a limited number of key cases rather than . . . a larger number of run-of-the-mill cases. . . . The Board desires to conserve its energies for the major effort of getting itself generally accepted."[27] The Secretary circulated also a CIO memo, indicating that the CIO planned to concentrate its Board cases on key employers and clear cases, in the hope that other companies would "give up without a fight" if the dominant employers were "brought into line."[28] But, in spite of the efforts to increase the number of settlements, the cases requiring formal action increased for 1938–39 to nearly 10 per cent for complaint cases and 27 per cent for representation cases closed. The problem of delay was extremely serious. The average number of days between the filing of an unfair labor practice charge and the issuance of the Board's decision, in cases which went to hearing, was 389 in 1937–38 and 210 in 1938–39. Even the informal cases took more than two months from filing to closing in a third of the complaint cases and a fifth of the representation cases in 1938.[29]

26. *Twelfth Annual Report*, p. 83, and others.
27. Memo M-611 from Secretary to Regional Directors, August 8, 1938.
28. Memo to Regional Directors, September 30, 1938.
29. U.S. Senate, Attorney-General's Committee on Administrative Procedure, *Monograph, National Labor Relations Board*, Sen. Doc. No. 10, Pt. 5, 77th Cong., 1st Sess., p. 37, cited as Attorney-General's Committee, *Monograph;* Report of the NLRB in U.S. Senate, Committee on Education and Labor, *Hearings, National Labor Relations Act and Proposed Amendments*, 76th Cong., 1st Sess., April 26, 1939, Pt. 3, pp. 604–5, cited as Senate Committee on Education and Labor, *NLRA Hearings* (*1939*).

In an effort to decrease the number of cases requiring decision, the Board developed also the stipulation for election and certification. "Consent elections" were considered private agreements by which the parties agreed to an election to

A major difficulty during this period was that the Board had no adequate administrative plan and organization to handle expeditiously the mass of its work. When the flood of cases struck in 1937–38, the Board and its Washington staff were swamped, and no one of the Board or staff had the time or the authority, even if the ability, to solve the administrative problem. By 1939–40, when the Board was fully aware of the problem, the pressures of work in connection with the congressional investigations delayed the solution.[30] When Dr. William M. Leiserson replaced Donald Wakefield Smith on the Board in 1939, he was extremely critical of some phases of the administration and supervision. Instructions were going to regional offices from a number of different officers in Washington—the General Counsel, the Secretary, and members of the Secretary's staff—and there was no clear line of authority or provision for prompt handling of the relations between the field and the central office.

The Board had felt that a large degree of centralization of authority was necessary, in order that policies should be very carefully developed to meet the court tests. For all formal cases, therefore, the Regional Director could proceed only after authorization from the Board. Novel questions as to how to proceed, cases to be taken to hearing, and methods of investigation needed to be decided as matters of policy by the Board.[31] The Secretary's office, through which all case supervision was channeled, proved the first bottleneck.[32] Often the regional offices had to be asked for further information. Many cases could be handled as a matter of routine, but where necessary the Secretary reported to the Board for decision. Rapid disposal was hampered by "inadequacies in interoffice com-

---

be conducted by the Regional Director, but no certification by the Board of a winning union resulted. The new system provided that the parties waive their right to hearing and agree upon an election, but the results would be certified by the Board. Stipulated elections were never very numerous, however, in comparison with either consent or ordered elections. Bowman, *op. cit.*, pp. 313–14; *Twelfth Annual Report*, p. 89.

30. Cf. statement of Chairman Madden to House Appropriations Committee, cited in Bowman, *op. cit.*, pp. 392–93.

31. Attorney-General's Committee, *Monograph*, pp. 8–10.

32. Requests for authorization to proceed to hearing in both complaint and representation cases continued to be required, as well as requests to approve withdrawal or dismissal in representation cases at any time, and of complaint cases after authorization. Settlements after authorization also had to receive the approval of the Board. The requests were reviewed by the Secretary's office, consulting with the Litigation Division or the Division of Economic Research where necessary.

munication"[33] and by the mass of cases coming through the office, although requests for authorization or for dismissal or withdrawal were seldom denied. There was difference of opinion among Board members as to the efficiency of the Secretary. Dr. Leiserson criticized the work on authorization requests and reports to the Board and believed that the Board sometimes acted on inadequate understanding of the facts.[34]

In 1939 a committee of four Regional Directors was appointed by the Board to report on the administrative organization. Their report criticized the concentration of functions in the Secretary's office which overburdened it with work and the poor co-ordination between different divisions in Washington and between Washington and regional offices. They thought that the Board itself was participating in too many administrative details and delegating too little responsibility. They urged the appointment of a director of personnel and of an administrative examiner to handle authorization requests[35] in the interest of eliminating the delays which caused so much criticism. In November, 1939, a personnel chief was appointed, and in February, 1940, a chief administrative examiner, to assist the Secretary; but there was not yet any relaxing of the central controls.

In spite of the desire of the Board at this time for centralization of responsibility and control over the work in the field, the regional offices to a considerable extent went their own way, with only loose supervision during the early years. The informal cases were the great bulk of the load, and their handling varied with the personality and attitudes of Regional Directors and others of the field staff, as well as the local pressures upon the office. Some Regional Directors took little responsibility and checked all important decisions with the Secretary. Others followed their own bent and persuaded, mediated, settled cases, or dismissed them or secured their withdrawal, according to their own patterns. Late in 1937 two special examiners had been appointed to visit regional offices in an effort to improve administration, but there was little immediate result.[36] Personnel difficulties in some of the offices, although known to the Board, were not all

33. Attorney-General's Committee, *Monograph*, p. 10.

34. See quotations from Leiserson memos in U.S. House of Representatives, Special Committee To Investigate the National Labor Relations Board, *Intermediate Report*, Report No. 1902, 76th Cong., 3d Sess., March 29, 1940, Pt. 1, pp. 26–33, cited as *Smith Committee Report*. Cf. also Bowman, *op. cit.*, pp. 388–95.

35. *Smith Committee Report*, pp. 30–31.

36. Bowman, *op. cit.*, pp. 389–90.

straightened out during this period. Handling of complaint cases varied from careful and objective investigation by many of the staff in accordance with the terms of the Act to instances at one extreme where almost all cases were found to be without merit and at the other where employers were "bulldozed" into settlements beyond the legal requirements, perhaps "shot-gun settlements."[37] In representation cases methods varied also, for example, in the arrangements for elections by consent or other informal methods of settling the question. The Secretary's office during this time tried by its correspondence on cases and by general instructions to improve methods of case handling.[38] But large variations in practice remained.

In the cases which went to hearing, the Board through the Legal Division made continuing efforts by letters and advice on particular matters to improve the quality of the work of the field attorneys, so that the record would be complete and contain all the relevant evidence on the issues. In 1939 a more extensive system of supervision of field attorneys by the Litigation Division was established.[39]

The Trial Examiners' Division by 1938 was entirely separated from the Legal Division and under the supervision of a Chief Trial Examiner. Trial Examiners had strict instructions not to fraternize with the Board attorney trying a case and to provide a fair and full hearing. They could consult with the Chief Trial Examiner on matters of policy, however. Most of the Trial Examiners were lawyers. They were instructed to play an active role, questioning witnesses when necessary in order to get all the facts into the record.[40] After the hearing in an unfair labor practice case the Trial Examiner prepared his Intermediate Report containing his findings of fact, conclusions, and recommendations. At first there was little or no supervision, and reports were written hastily in the field in some cases between hear-

37. Cf. statement of D. R. Clarke, Illinois Manufacturers Association, in House Committee on Labor, *NLRA Hearings* (1939), Vol. 8, p. 2220.

38. There were forms for the requests for authorization, for reports on closed and adjusted cases, and for notices of dismissal or withdrawal; instructions as to notices to employers and to competing unions; instructions to conform consent election procedure to Board policy for ordered elections by including a place on the ballot for a vote of "no union," the use of observers at the polls, the handling of challenged ballots, and run-off elections; instructions as to handling of settlements and that settlements should be in harmony with the Act and for efforts to secure compliance with Board and court orders. Early in 1940 a standard outline of forms was provided to be posted by employers in connection with compliance before unfair labor practice cases were closed.

39. Attorney-General's Committee, *Monograph*, p. 20; *Third Annual Report*, p. 5; *Fourth Annual Report*, p. 11.

40. *Fourth Annual Report*, pp. 149–51.

46

ings. For a time, too, per diem men were used as Trial Examiners, sometimes with poor results. By 1939, however, there was a real effort to improve the quality of Intermediate Reports by a system of review within the Trial Examiners' Division on the basis of which the Trial Examiner made any revisions he wished in his report before final issuance.[41] But in 1940 the Attorney-General's Committee on Administrative Procedure criticized the reports as not being "of great value to either the parties or the Board," although they did serve as a useful outline of the issues.

In representation cases until 1940 staff Trial Examiners were used and wrote informal reports for the use of the Board. But after that time as a measure of economy it was found possible in all but the most complex cases to appoint a member of the field staff as Trial Examiner for representation case hearings. These hearings were not generally "adversary" in nature but rather a part of the Board's investigation of the question of representation and could be much less formal than the trial of an unfair labor practice case.

In unfair labor practice cases where the Trial Examiner found violations of the law, occasionally employers agreed to comply with the recommendations, and cases were closed upon completion of compliance. But usually the record along with briefs and exceptions of the parties, and oral argument before the Board on request, then went to the Board for formal decision. At this point the Review Section within the Legal Division took charge for a thorough review of the record of the hearing. Review attorneys had strict instructions not to consult with the Trial Examiner or (after March, 1939) to use the informal files which included the preliminary investigation material. They studied the record, exhibits, and briefs, as well as the Trial Examiner's report, listened to the oral argument, and analyzed the evidence and the issues. After thorough discussion with an experienced supervisor they reported orally to the Board, sometimes with written memos, on the issues and the evidence. The Board discussed the evidence, sometimes requested further study of certain points, and finally after thorough deliberation on the case in one or more such conferences made decisions on the various issues and instructed the review attorneys as to the decision to be drafted. Occasionally the Board consulted the Trial Examiner on matters of credibility. Sometimes matters of policy were discussed with the Chief Economist, the General Counsel, or the Secretary. But the decision, after final

41. *Ibid.;* Attorney-General's Committee, *Monograph,* pp. 21–22; Cf. also Bowman, *op. cit.,* pp. 274–76.

review, revision, and redrafting if necessary, was the decision of the *Board* itself, based on the record.[42] The Board members had had no contact with the prosecuting of the case since their usually routine authorization of the issuance of complaint, and they came freshly, some time later, to the consideration of the evidence and the issues. When the Board found the allegations not supported by the evidence, it dismissed the case. More usually, because the careful investigation at earlier stages had screened out most of the weak cases, it found the employer guilty of unfair labor practices and ordered him to cease and desist and to take appropriate action to bring himself into compliance with the law. In representation cases, if the Board found that a question of representation existed, it usually ordered an election, although occasionally until a 1939 decision it certified a union on the evidence in the record that it had a majority in the unit in question.[43]

The problem of getting compliance with Intermediate Reports, Board orders, or even court decrees when they were secured, had rather haphazard attention in the stress of handling too many cases at the earlier stages. In August, 1938, the Secretary sent instructions to Regional Directors in an effort to obtain uniform procedure in reporting on compliance. It was the responsibility of the Regional Director to seek compliance with Intermediate Report or Board order and to report to the Board for approval any proposed settlement. After court orders the Regional Directors were to make no commitments without submission to the Litigation Division. Thus the regional offices did not have complete responsibility. When they could not get compliance, cases were referred to the Litigation Division to consider enforcement in the circuit court.

By fall and winter of 1938–39 the Board was swamped with cases in which there had been no compliance. Some were Board-order cases which had not been enforced; others had court decrees, but still compliance had not been achieved. It was impossible for the Board to take all cases to court, either for original enforcement or for contempt action. Some cases were too old, some not strong enough, and some were border-line cases as to details of compliance. The Board, facing a difficult situation, decided to try to clear the decks by a drive to "settle" many of these cases. It appointed a lawyer to specialize in settlement work and in January, 1939, established a special Settlement Section. Their efforts, with those of the field staff

42. Attorney-General's Committee, *Monograph*, pp. 24–25, 28; Bowman, *op. cit.*, pp. 283–87.
43. Cf. *infra*, ch. 5, p. 133.

under pressure to put more work into compliance efforts, resulted in an increase in the number of cases closed "on compliance" after Board and court orders in the next two years—from 29 in 1937–38 to 207 in 1938–39 and 324 in 1939–40.[44] The settlements were supposedly in compliance with the Act and the orders. But inevitably many were compromises, some on minor points and entirely in harmony with the purposes of the Act; others the best compromise that could be obtained. This meant frequently that some of the victims of discrimination were not reinstated or that less than the full amount of back pay necessary to compensate for the loss of earnings of workers discriminated against was paid or that no mention was made in the notice posted by the employer of the fact that the employees were free to join a union if they so desired. Regional Directors were supposed to be consulted as to the merits of proposed settlements made from Washington.[45] However, the "Chamberlain squad" appellation which grew up among the Board's staff for the Settlement Section indicated the belief that unnecessary compromises were made and that "good cases" sometimes were "sold down the river." There was considerable criticism from unions to this effect, as well as some from employers of an opposite sort.[46] This system, which continued into 1940, speeded up some of the difficult cases and cleared the docket;[47] but bad effects from poor settlements were felt for a long time.

The Board continued, by taking its orders to the courts for enforcement, to get the check on its procedures and policies which was necessary in order to establish the policies of the Act. And in this it was strikingly successful. Occasionally courts disagreed with the Board in interpretation of the facts or of the law. But by June 30, 1940, the circuits courts had set aside only 27 orders of the Board out of 133 cases decided and had enforced the others in full or with modifications in about equal numbers. The Supreme Court in 22 decisions on Board orders had set aside only 2, modified and enforced 2, and enforced in full 18 of the orders of the Board.[48]

In addition to this check by the judiciary, the Board and the Act were subjected during the months of 1939–40 to three full-dress investigations by congressional committees, by the Senate and House Committees on Labor, and by the Special Investigating Committee sponsored by Congressman Howard Smith of Virginia. The Board

44. *Annual Reports.*
45. Memo M-812 from Secretary to Regional Directors, March 2, 1939.
46. Attorney-General's Committee, *Monograph*, p. 7.
47. For further discussion cf. Bowman, *op. cit.*, pp. 320–31.
48. From *Annual Reports.* See *infra,* ch. 3, Table 2.

itself was heard at considerable length and given opportunity to present statements, and the critics of the Board and the Act were encouraged to air their grievances. The Smith Committee subpoenaed Board records and combed the files for instances where misconduct and bias or inefficiency could be charged. A few such instances were found, of which much was made. AFL officials gave substantial aid to the critics by their charges that the Board was pro-CIO. The Committee criticized the Board and its staff for bias and partiality, inefficiency and misconduct; and it claimed that the procedures did not afford fair protection of rights and that particular policies were unreasonable. It made much of isolated instances and disregarded the evidence from the large support given by the courts to the Board's procedures and policies.[49] It proposed sweeping amendments to the law, which were passed by the House but not by the Senate. Some of the issues raised then and again in 1945–47 will be discussed later. Suffice it to say here that criticism could legitimately be made, as we have indicated. But the sweeping attack upon the Board was not justified by any complete review of the available evidence.

The most thorough study of the Board's procedures to that time had been made at the Columbia Law School.[50] After an exhaustive study of the Board's handling of cases and the courts' review, it concluded: "The Board has made a largely successful effort to perform a difficult assignment by a procedure which, while minimizing the chance of mistake, fully preserves the basic values of traditional judicial processes."

In addition, the Attorney-General's Committee on Administrative Procedure made a detailed study of the NLRB during this period and reported as of January, 1940.[51] It made no sweeping criticisms. Its recommendations were chiefly designed to increase efficiency and the internal separation of functions, for example, by further delegation of authority and by increasing the importance of the hearing officers and of their reports.

Finally, the Board's own defense of its stewardship during these years deserves quotation.

49. *Smith Committee Report;* cf. also its *Minority Report,* 76th Cong., 3d Sess., Report No. 1902, Pt. 2, April 11, 1940.
50. Walter Gellhorn and S. L. Linfield, "Politics and Labor Relations—NLRB Procedure," *Columbia Law Review,* 39 (1939), 339–95.
51. Attorney-General's Committee, *Monograph;* U.S. Senate, Attorney-General's Committee on Administrative Procedure, *Final Report,* Senate Document No. 8, 77th Cong., 1st Sess., pp. 158–60, cited as Attorney-General's Committee, *Final Report.*

Our charter has been the statute itself, as enacted by the Congress. Our ambition has been to do an orderly, workmanlike, professional job within the limitations of that charter. We have seen millions of American workmen avail themselves of a freedom which they never had before. . . . We have seen thousands of employers put their relations with their employees upon a basis of equal and mutually self-respecting bargaining, who had never done so before. We have seen telling blows dealt at the despicable practice of corrupting American workingmen by hiring them to spy upon and betray their fellow workmen for exercising their natural and legal rights.

Unquestionably we have made mistakes. We regret those mistakes. We have done our best to correct them when they have been called to our attention. We shall continue to do so.

We have been severely criticized. Much of that criticism could have been avoided by compromising the principles of the act. We have chosen instead to vigorously put into effect the principles of the act. And we shall continue to do so.[52]

And the Board's General Counsel in 1939:

. . . Changes leading to improvements in methods have from time to time been found desirable and put into effect. We will continue this process as experience justifies. But I say now, without hesitation, that our procedure has not only survived as fiery a testing as history affords an example of, but that it is as full and as fair as any ever devised for the administration of any law by any agency of government.[53]

Some of the improvements in administration which came during these years have already been indicated, and others were to come shortly. Two changes were made especially in response to criticism from employers. A new rule, adopted in 1939, permitted an employer to petition for an election when he was faced by conflicting demands of two unions for recognition, and instructions were given Regional Directors to notify employers as to the disposition of charges against them, which had not always been done before.

In addition, the Economic Research Division, which had done essential service in providing economic materials needed as background for establishing the application of the law in the early cases, but which had been much criticized by Congress, was abolished in October, 1940, after a rider banning it had been attached to the appropriation bill.[54] Its place was taken by a smaller Technical Service Unit, to work on technical problems such as pay-roll analy-

52. Chairman Madden to Senate Committee on the Judiciary, *NLRB Hearings* (*1938*), p. 68.
53. Charles Fahy in Senate Committee on Education and Labor, *NLRA Hearings* (*1939*), Pt. 2, p. 338.
54. *Fifth Annual Report*, pp. 9, 124.

sis in connection with discrimination cases and other such assignments.

1940–45

By 1940 under Chairman Madden's leadership, the major outlines of the application of the law had been established by Board and court decisions, and there were signs of increasing acceptance of the purposes of the Act by industry. The old preponderance of unfair labor practice cases in the Board's work was to give way increasingly to representation cases and the holding of elections. The great need in the Board's work was to improve administration, in the interest of prompt, efficient, and economical handling of cases, and to increase the emphasis on good and workable industrial relations practices, which had to some degree been lost sight of in the tendency to legalistic emphasis in the first five years. The war made these needs all the more urgent if the Board was to perform its wartime duty of removing causes of labor strife which might interfere with production. When Chairman H. A. Millis, economist, arbitrator, and former member of the old NLRB, took office in November, 1940, the Board proceeded promptly to act on problems of administration, some of which had been under consideration before. Gerard D. Reilly's appointment in October, 1941, following the expiration of the term of Edwin S. Smith, reintroduced a legalistic emphasis which was to grow in influence during his term. Mr. Reilly had been Solicitor for the Department of Labor. When Dr. Leiserson resigned in February, 1943, and was replaced by John M. Houston, former businessman and member of Congress, the experienced industrial relations slant on Board problems was somewhat subordinated for a time; but the basic improvements which had been introduced in administrative organization, personnel, and procedures were to continue.

The case load rose sharply in the first two years of defense and war production, reaching nearly 11,000 cases in the year 1941–42, then dropping to 9,000 or more for each of the next three years. But the work shifted in character, until in 1942 representation cases were more than half of all cases filed, and by 1944 and 1945 around 7,000 representation cases were filed each year, but only 2,500 complaint cases. To handle this load the Board at no time had more than 900 employees. Congressional antagonism had cut the appropriation for 1941, but a supplementary fund was later given. Again in 1942 a cut forced a reduction of staff from 889 in July, 1942, to 736 by October,

1943.[55] Throughout the war period the loss of experienced personnel, nearly 40 per cent of the male employees during one year, made efficient operation even more difficult. By stringent economies and increased efficiency in methods, however, the Board succeeded in closing nearly 80 per cent of the cases on the docket during the war years and in steadily reducing the backlog until 1945. In 1943, as a result of improved procedures, the time required for handling cases had been greatly reduced.[56] But the delays were still too great and a constant source of criticism. These problems were accentuated in 1944 and 1945 by the necessity of conducting strike votes required under the Smith-Connally War Labor Disputes Act, a duty which finally interfered seriously with the major functions of the Board.[57] By summer of 1945 the backlog of pending cases had risen sharply.

The approach of the "Millis Board" to administrative questions was made clear when the Board sent a letter to all regional offices in January, 1941, and a few months later called conferences of regional personnel, where "the major importance" of the regional offices in the work of the Board was emphasized. The Chairman expressed appreciation of the "tough jobs" in the field and promised to work for more help and decent pay for the field staff. He asked full and frank discussion from them in the effort to improve methods of operation. For some years less than half the staff had been in the field, but now there was increased emphasis on the field work. By 1946 nearly 60 per cent of the staff were in the regional offices.[58] Moreover, the policy of occasional area or general regional conferences of the field staff gave opportunity for very useful pooling of experience and discussion of methods. Such conferences bore good fruit in improving procedures and efficiency and in the training of new members as well as in the intangibles making for high morale in a hard-working staff.

The establishment of a Field Division, early in 1941, was of major importance. Before that a chief administrative examiner in the Secretary's office had been given the work of handling Washington relations with the field on cases. But now all such matters were separated from the Secretary's office and put in the hands of the Field

55. *Eighth Annual Report*, p. 3. See n. 7, *supra*, for total expenditures.
56. *Eighth Annual Report*, pp. 13–14.
57. *Ibid.*, pp. 74–81; *Ninth Annual Report*, pp. 72–74; *Tenth*, pp. 76–77. See discussion below, p. 61, and ch. 8, p. 299.
58. Cf. Bowman, *op. cit.*, p. 379; U.S. House of Representatives, Subcommittee of the Committee on Appropriations, *Hearings, Department of Labor–Federal Security Agency Appropriation Bill for 1947*, 79th Cong., 2d Sess., Pt. 1, May 29, 1946, p. 749.

Division, with a director and three assistant directors. They had the responsibility of general supervision of the regional offices, handling all case work, and co-ordinating the work of the regions with that of the Board. All requests for advice, requests for authorization, appeals, questions as to compliance, and instructions were to be handled through the Field Division. The Legal Division continued to supervise the work of attorneys in the field. The assistant directors of the Field Division were to visit the regional offices and advise and assist the Regional Directors in improving their methods, but the Regional Directors were instructed that the Board expected them to stand on their own feet.[59]

The Attorney-General's Committee on Administrative Procedure had recommended that the Board delegate more authority and decentralize administrative functions. In line with this recommendation the Board delegated to the new Field Division complete responsibility for deciding requests for authorization to proceed in representation cases, unless advice was desired from the Legal Division, or if a new principle or matter of general policy was involved, in which case the problem would be referred directly to the Board. For complaint cases the Board set up an Authorization and Appeals Committee with power to act, except for cases which should be referred to the Board because of disagreement or a new question or policy matter.[60] The Board thus had no connection with any cases at this stage, unless on a matter of general policy. The new procedure provided for prompt and simplified handling of cases, with clear lines of responsibility.

Experienced Regional Directors had long been asking for more authority and autonomy, especially in issuing complaints and notices of hearing in representation cases. The Board had been unwilling to give them this authority as long as great differences in efficiency and

59. *Sixth Annual Report*, pp. 3–9; Field Division Letter No. 2, June 10, 1941. No discussion of the work of the Field Division can omit tribute to the work of Oscar S. Smith, first assistant director, and then director from September, 1942, until the complete reorganization of the work of the Board in August, 1947. His great administrative ability and understanding of labor relations were largely responsible for the successful building of organization, staff, and methods during these years.

60. The Field Division handled requests for authorization first, then sent them to a Case Clearance Unit in the Legal Division. If both groups agreed, the Regional Director could proceed to issue complaint and notice of hearing. If they disagreed, the matter went to the Authorization Committee, consisting of the Director of the Field Division, the General Counsel, and the head of the Case Clearance Unit, whose decision was final unless any member wanted to refer a case to the Board. *Sixth Annual Report*, p. 8.

methods continued in different regions. But this centralized control meant unnecessary paper work and delay, even after the increased efficiency of operations under the new Field Division organization. By the fall of 1942 the Board felt that the organization and personnel had been sufficiently strengthened, and policies were by then well enough established, for it to risk further decentralization. Accordingly in October, 1942, the Regional Directors were given authority to proceed without authorization from Washington in both complaint and representation cases. Only where there were issues of policy or novel questions of fact or law, or where the Regional Director and the Regional Attorney disagreed, was it necessary to request authorization from Washington. Regional Directors could then investigate cases, settle them by consent methods, permit their withdrawal, dismiss them subject to appeal to Washington, or proceed to hearing on their own authority. A year later the Board reported evidence of successful handling of the increased responsibilities by the field staff. About 70 per cent of the complaints and 86 per cent of the notices of hearing in representation cases had been issued by the Regional Directors without prior advice to Washington, and the later action by Board or Trial Examiner in these cases upheld the Regional Director in nine-tenths of the cases. The time from filing of cases to the opening of hearings also had been substantially reduced.[61] As time went on, more and more of the work was thus handled by the regional staff on their own responsibility, with much saving of time and an increase in effectiveness because of the addition to the prestige of the local staff when they could speak with authority. Separation of functions was a reality for a very large part of the work.

Before the Board could grant this degree of autonomy to regional offices it was necessary to standardize methods and policies, especially for the handling of the new great bulk of representation cases. Efforts along this line were made before 1940, as indicated above, and much more was done in the first year and a half of the Field Division. The great contribution of the Field Division continued to be the development of simplified and standardized procedures and forms. In 1941 a series of regional conferences studied various problems, among them public relations, representation procedures, compliance problems, and standardization of forms. Their reports were circulated to the regional offices for comments, and these and later studies resulted in the adoption of standard practices, which were revised on the

61. *Seventh Annual Report*, pp. 11–14; *Eighth*, pp. 12–14.

basis of experience.[62] With the growing importance of representation cases and the necessity for efficient and speedy handling of hundreds of elections, much attention was given to improving methods, in order to be sure that there was every opportunity for free choice of representatives and that procedures were beyond possibility of complaint.[63]

It was more difficult to standardize procedures for handling charges of unfair labor practices, but here also progress was made in eliminating undesirable differences in the methods of different regions. The possibility of standard forms for written settlement agreements, and for notices to be posted by employers in connection with compliance, had long been considered. The Board had adopted the policy that all such settlements should be put in writing, and in December, 1942, a set of standard agreement forms for the settlement of various kinds of charges and an accompanying set of standard notice forms were sent to the regional offices for trial. Finally, late in 1944, the Board decided to use a similar standard set of forms for notices to be posted by employers, to be attached to the Board's orders in formal cases.

The Field Division during this time was developing a field manual, which was sent out in April, 1943. It was not "designed as a straitjacket for field employees—to serve as a substitute for thinking, initiative, growing, or use of good judgment—but as a series of guide posts to a better job." This manual, with suggestions on ways of handling different problems, as well as the standard procedures, was revised during the years and kept current, especially for the use of the new staff members. There was also a complete forms manual, kept up to date as revisions were made.[64]

Significant developments were made also in the handling of formal cases between the hearings and the issuance of Board orders. Earlier weaknesses in the Intermediate Reports had led the Board to put its

62. By early 1942, forms had been accepted for consent election agreements and for reports on elections, and the best practice in election procedure had been codified, with appropriate forms. By October, 1942, forms were available for withdrawal and dismissal letters as well as notice of hearing. There was a standard form for recognition agreements, for agreements for a check of union cards against company pay roll in lieu of elections, and for stipulations for consent elections to be followed by Board certification of a winning union.

63. Cf. *Seventh Annual Report*, pp. 32–38; *Eighth*, pp. 15–16. Ch. 5, *infra*, pp. 129–31, describes an election.

64. The procedures as they had been developed by 1944 were described in some detail in the *Ninth Annual Report*, pp. 7–15. Cf. also Bowman, *op. cit.*, chs. 13–16.

chief reliance on the report of the attorney who reviewed the record. But now the Board determined to increase the importance of the Trial Examiner and of his report. After June, 1940, a cut in the budget necessitated turning most of the hearing of representation cases over to the field staff, and the Trial Examiners were allowed to concentrate on their complaint cases. A staff of attorneys was assigned to assist them in various ways in preparation of their reports, by reviewing records, checking facts, and working on legal precedents. Although the Trial Examiners were supervised by the Chief Trial Examiner, the Board's policy was that nothing was to be "dictated" to the Examiner and that his report was to be his own.

Intermediate reports had in some instances been neglected by the attorneys of the Review Section. But now the Board voted that the attorneys should study the report of the Trial Examiner, along with briefs, exceptions, and records of oral argument, before beginning examination of the record of the hearing. The Intermediate Report was to be used as the basis for the Board's decision, and review attorneys were to indicate to the Board any points at which they found that report not supported by the record and correct in law and fact. Review attorneys, under careful supervision of a more experienced attorney, prepared a written memorandum for the Board on these points. The Board then had for its own study the Intermediate Report and its accompanying documents and the memorandum of the review attorney indicating any disagreements with the Intermediate Report. Each member of the Board had a legal assistant who aided in the member's analysis of the case. Memoranda were circulated among the Board members indicating their judgment as to the proper decision, before the Board meetings at which decisions were finally made. Sometimes the Trial Examiner was consulted on issues of the credibility of witnesses, often a difficult point on which he was in position to be of great assistance. The Board sometimes discussed the evidence further with review attorneys and supervisors. The number of times that Trial Examiners were overruled on major or minor points was evidence of the independence of the Board when finally they made their decisions. Often from this time on the final decision of the Board was a fairly brief statement which incorporated the Intermediate Report, adopting its finding of facts and conclusions, except for any points of difference especially noted. By these changes in procedure more efficient use was made of the experienced Trial Examiners, and the Board felt itself in a better position to judge the evidence and decide the issues. Moreover, a substantial saving in time in the posthearing processes was achieved by eliminating some of the duplication of effort which had been present before.[65]

The handling of compliance activities had continued in an unsatisfactory state, with responsibility divided between Washington and the field, as has been indicated above. Early in 1943, however, the regional offices were given the primary responsibility of obtaining compliance with Intermediate Reports, Board orders, and court orders. They were to report periodically to the Field Division. When they reported with full details that compliance on a case was complete, if Washington approved the case was closed and the employer was so notified. When the Regional Director reported that he could not obtain compliance, the case moved on for a decision in Washington as to the next step.[66] Except when cases were taken over by the Enforcement Section for legal action, the regional offices were given credit in their case load for the cases at the stage of compliance and were expected to give adequate attention to this part of the work.

A significant development during this time was the change of terminology, from the "settlement" phraseology, which implied bargaining and compromise, to that of "adjustment" in compliance with the law and "compliance" with orders of the Board or the courts. Compliance with the law was the aim in both the informal cases and those which reached formal stages. Sometimes the purposes of the law were achieved by accepting less than technically full compliance. But experience showed that in the earlier years lack of attention to compliance in the field and division of responsibility had resulted in long delays and too frequently in a failure to obtain the essence of compliance with the law. Such failures then militated against the possibility of securing compliance with the law by informal adjustments. The plan adopted at this time assumed clear allocation of responsibility to the regional offices except when the Enforcement Section took over for legal action, and complete co-operation between the various divisions in Washington and the regions in an effort to obtain full compliance. The regional offices could obtain technical aid from the Compliance Unit when compliance involved complicated prob-

65. Cf. *Fifth Annual Report*, p. 123; *Sixth*, pp. 4–5, 9; Bowman, *op. cit.*, pp. 281–96. The first "short-form" decision was issued on November 4, 1942 (45 NLRB 355).

66. In Washington the Field Division considered cases first and referred them to the Enforcement Section. A Compliance Committee, representing both groups, considered difficult cases and made recommendations to the Board for action. A Compliance Unit in the Enforcement Section had in 1940 replaced the old Settlement Section. But it worked only on cases especially assigned, with the Regional Director fully informed.

lems, as of back pay due to large groups of employees. But the responsibility was that of the regions.

A study made for the Board in 1944 found that compliance handling had improved following the increase in regional office responsibility. Time necessary to secure compliance had been noticeably decreased, and there were fewer instances where the quality of compliance seemed doubtful. But there were still problems needing solution before prompt compliance could be obtained, especially in a small group of difficult cases. Many regional offices felt that there should be still further delegation of authority to them to determine when compliance had been achieved. They welcomed a decision of the Board late in 1944 to order the specific form of notice which must be posted by an employer as part of his compliance; that issue was no longer one to be bargained over.

In its effort to obtain compliance with its orders, the Board during these years, 1940–45, increased its litigation for the enforcement of orders and substantially improved its record of obtaining court approval. The Supreme Court in the five years enforced in full 22 Board orders, modified and enforced 6, set aside none, and remanded two for further action. The circuit courts, in deciding 461 cases, set aside only 10 per cent, in contrast to 20 per cent in the earlier period, and enforced Board orders in full in over 60 per cent, compared to 40 per cent in the first four years.[67] The procedures and policies of the Board thus had substantial support from the courts.

The ultimate sanction for obtaining compliance was through a petition to the circuit court to find an employer in contempt for failure to obey the order of the court enforcing the Board's order. The Board had been slow to use this technique, and the earlier results had not been encouraging. In 1938 and 1939 there were only four contempt cases, in three of which the petition was denied, and in only one was the employer found in contempt of court. But in 1940 ten petitions were filed, and in the next years more use was made of this device. By the end of 1945 a total of sixty-eight contempt petitions had been filed. The filing of the petition was enough to bring about compliance in twenty-two of the cases, and in thirty cases the company was found in contempt. There had been a substantial increase in the willingness of courts to stand behind their orders and require compliance.[68] No employer was punished for contempt, however, but they were permitted to purge themselves by bringing themselves into compliance,

67. From *Annual Reports*. See *infra*, ch. 3, Table 2.
68. *Annual Reports*, esp. *Eighth*, pp. 62–63; *infra*, ch. 3, Table 3.

paying the back pay required, or otherwise complying with the order.

By 1945, then, the Board had achieved much in improving and standardizing its methods in the important work in the regional offices and increasing the efficiency of the work in Washington. It had delegated substantial responsibility to Regional Directors and to other officers in Washington, thus increasing the internal separation of functions. It had established a habit of studying its experience through staff committees and special studies by an operating analyst and continuing study of methods and policies in consultation with its field offices. In spite of large turnover during wartime, the key positions were filled by experienced and competent people, and the agency was operating at a creditable level of efficiency. And its record in the courts had continued to be good.

1945–47

The NLRB came into the postwar years, its last two years under the Wagner Act, with a firm basis in law and experience which had been tested by the courts and an efficient administrative organization which had been improved through the years as a result of criticism and appraisal by the public, governmental committees, and the Board itself. Administrative developments during these two years were only to carry further the trends toward greater internal separation of functions by delegation of authority and decentralization.

Changes in the personnel of the Board itself were reflected more in certain changes in direction or emphasis in the decisions on cases, to be discussed later, than in administrative organization. Upon the retirement of Dr. Millis, on July 5, 1945, Paul M. Herzog, a lawyer who had been a member and later Chairman of the New York State Labor Relations Board from 1937 to 1944, became Chairman. When Mr. Reilly's term expired, he was replaced on August 27, 1946, by James J. Reynolds, whose experience had been in personnel work in industry and in labor relations work in the Navy.

The case load during these years rose to all-time highs. Labor shifts during reconversion, new organization drives by AFL, CIO, and independent unions, with possibly some increase of resistance by industry after the end of the war, brought representation petitions to 10,600 and unfair labor practice cases to over 4,000 new cases in 1946–47. More than 5,500 elections for the choice of bargaining representatives were conducted during the first postwar year, and 6,900 during the second. In addition, for the first six months of this period the Board was still required to hold strike votes under the War Labor Disputes Act. During the year ending June 30, 1945, there had been 573 such elections, but in the months following the Board was swamped with a deluge of strike notices. In September, 307 were filed; in October, 666; in November, 587. By that time four of the regional offices were doing nothing but handling these cases. In six months 1,214 strike votes were conducted, including the polling of the employees of Ford, General Motors, and Chrysler. Finally by a rider to the Appropriations Act the Board was relieved of the duty of holding any further such elections, effective December 28, 1945.[69] But its regular work had been seriously set back during the time.

Congress had not permitted an increase in staff, and until December, 1945, the personnel was still under 800. A deficiency appropriation then permitted an increase in staff, which reached 990 by June, 1946. Nevertheless, the backlog of pending cases had risen by that time to 4,600. In spite of this, the antagonism to the Board, shown in the rising attempt to change the law, resulted in an appropriation which required the Board to drop more than 20 per cent of its staff, reducing it by April, 1947, to 720.[70] With unprecedented numbers of representation disputes needing to be determined, and a large number of charges of violations of the law, and in spite of continuing efforts to increase efficiency of operations, the Board was able to close only about two-thirds of the cases on its docket during these years, and by the end of the period over 5,000 cases were still pending. Delays in operations were very serious, to the disadvantage of both employers and unions. Cases which had to go to formal hearing and decision by the Board took six or seven months in representation cases, and eighteen to twenty months for complaint cases, the Chairman reported in early 1947.[71]

Instructions were sent to the field to make every effort to reduce the number of cases going to hearing by settling them at informal stages whenever reasonably possible. Representation cases were to be given priority. The Board curtailed its taking of jurisdiction in marginal cases, where the company was small or shipped little out of the state, and dismissed many such cases "for budgetary reasons,"

69. *Eleventh Annual Report*, pp. 68–69, 91; *NLRB Press Release*, November 12, 1945.
70. *Eleventh Annual Report*, p. 6; Senate Appropriations Committee, *Hearings, 1948*, p. 870. See *supra*, n. 7.
71. U.S. House of Representatives, Subcommittee of the Committee on Appropriations, *Hearings, Department of Labor–Federal Security Agency Appropriation Bill for 1948*, 80th Cong., 1st Sess., 1947, Pt. 1, p. 648.

as well as a feeling that it was unwise for the federal government to step in. It created several subregional offices, close to the source of cases, in order to reduce travel time and expense.[72] The Bureau of the Budget was asked to survey the Washington office in the interest of economies. Increased delegation of authority to regional offices also cut down time and unnecessary duplication of effort. The Board had earlier begun the practice of holding public hearings for the consideration of proposed changes in policies or procedures, as in regard to a change in the system of run-off elections, a proposed extension of employers' right to petition, and the issue of supervisors' rights under the Act.[73] In 1945, also, the Board instituted a plan for an annual conference of union and management attorneys to consider problems and proposals for changes in methods.[74]

A very significant innovation during this time was the prehearing election, which Regional Directors had long wanted, and which was discussed at the attorneys' conference in October, 1945. The Board hoped to decrease the number of hearings and ordered elections, by providing that in simple cases involving only one union and with only minor issues in dispute, the Regional Director might hold an election without waiting for a hearing and Board order, but without prejudice to the right to a later hearing if desired by either party. It was of course desirable to have the co-operation of the employer to the extent of supplying a pay roll and observers for the election; but some elections were successfully conducted without his co-operation by taking affidavits from each worker as to his eligibility to vote. Either side could challenge the ballot of any person whose right to vote in the unit was in doubt, and such ballots were segregated. After the election, a hearing and decision by the Board could be asked for by either party. As was hoped, the great majority of cases were closed by agreement after the election, with recognition of unions which won, or an agreement for certification by the Board. The result was a great saving of time in resolution of disputes.[75] There were no sub-

72. *Ibid.*, p. 646.

73. *Eighth Annual Report*, p. 14; *NLRB Press Releases*, January 24, 1944, and May 20, 1944.

74. *Eleventh Annual Report*, p. 6.

75. *Ibid.*, pp. 6–8. *Twelfth Annual Report*, pp. 3, 89. In the seven months ending June 30, 1946, of 118 cases closed after prehearing elections, only 16 had required a hearing and Board order after the election. In the next fiscal year, 1946–47, of 626 prehearing election cases closed, only 172 required subsequent hearings. During 1946–47 there were 644 such elections. The increase in the use of the prehearing election device also must have been an important factor in the decrease of Board-ordered elections from nearly 1,200 in the previous year to 876 for this year.

stantial objections, and the method was being used with success even in some two-union cases.

As a result of this variety of pressures, restraints, and improvements in methods the Board succeeded during these two years in reducing the proportion of cases closed which required formal action to about 7 per cent of the complaint cases and 20 per cent of the representation cases. Of the latter in 1946–47 more than half of those closed were adjusted informally. Of the complaint cases, however, only 20 per cent were adjusted informally, and more than 70 per cent were withdrawn or dismissed, an unprecedented proportion to be found not "good cases."[76] It was impossible to measure the extent to which budgetary limitations and "tougher standards" by the Board for finding unfair labor practices may have resulted in eliminating cases where there was, in reality, interference by employers with the right to organize. The trend, whether good policy or not, was toward a less complete protection of labor's rights under the Act.[77]

In 1946 after the passage of the Administrative Procedure Act,[78] the Board carefully reconsidered its organization and procedures to see what changes were made necessary. That law had followed many years of study, by the Attorney-General's Committee on Administrative Procedure and by congressional committees. It set up "standards of fair play" to guide all the administrative agencies, including the NLRB, which had had much consideration during these investigations. Since 1941 the Board, as we have seen above, had increased the separation of functions and delegation of powers within the agency. After careful study of the new law by a committee of personnel from its major divisions, the Board concluded that it was already meeting in all substantial respects the requirements of the law.[79] The Board rewrote its *Rules and Regulations*, however, making

76. *Twelfth Annual Report*, p. 71.
77. An unpublished M.A. thesis at the University of Minnesota, by Frank Fager, former field examiner for the Board, on *Informal Procedures of the NLRB*, points out that withdrawals by the unions are often involuntary, and "if this be true, and it certainly seems to be, a large amount of worker unrest caused by real or imaginary violations of the Act is not remedied by the Board."
78. Public Law 404, 79th Cong., 2d Sess., June 11, 1946. This Act was the culmination of a long study of the administrative agencies. Earlier bills such as the Walter-Logan Bill, which failed of passage, had attempted more drastic regulation of the independent administrative agencies.
79. David Findling, "NLRB Procedures: Effects of the Administrative Procedure Act," *American Bar Association Journal*, 33 (1947), 14–17, 82; U.S. Senate, Committee on Labor and Public Welfare, *Hearings, Labor Relations Program*, 80th Cong., 1st Sess., 1947, Pt. 4, pp. 1925–31, 1896–1901. As required by the law, the Board published a detailed report on its organization and pro-

what changes were necessary, making the rules more explicit, and adding language of the new Act where pertinent. The new rules also incorporated some recommendations made at the area conferences of regional staffs during that year as well as the details of well-established practices. One major change made by the APA itself was to give the Trial Examiners independence and security of tenure, protected by the Civil Service Commission, independent of ratings by the agency itself.[80]

The autonomy of the regional offices further increased during these two years. As before, Regional Directors could issue complaints and notices of hearing in representation cases without prior authorization from Washington except in cases involving doubts as to jurisdiction, novel issues, or a few particularly difficult kinds of situations. The Appeals and Review Committee, representing the Field and Legal Divisions in Washington, handled requests for advice and could if necessary take the question to the Board, but only rarely was this necessary. Appeals from the dismissal of petitions or charges were considered by this committee, which then gave their recommendation to the Board. Committee members might not after that advise the Board in regard to the decision of those or related cases. Cases which were closed by adjustment did not require approval from Washington, except where there was a stipulation for a Board order or court order, or if there was disagreement between the Regional Director and the Regional Attorney.

On the perennial problem of getting compliance with the formal orders, a regional conference committee in June, 1946, urged that more responsibility be given to the regional offices, even to the extent of initiating and handling contempt action. As a result, new instructions put complete responsibility for compliance upon them, and

cedures in the *Federal Register,* Vol. 11 (September 11, 1946), No. 177, Pt. 2, Sec. 3, pp. 177A-602-23.

80. The Board changed its terminology to call the field personnel who conducted hearings in representation cases hearing officers as distinct from the trial examiners. Their brief memoranda indicating the issues and their recommendations after hearings were to go directly to the Review Section with the record. For both representation cases and complaint cases rules were changed to permit intervention of interested parties at hearings with less formality. In complaint cases the Board made clear that, in addition to using the assistance of review attorneys, it consulted sometimes with Trial Examiners but not with any agents who participated in the prosecuting or investigation of the case. A new rule, required by the APA, provided that, when Regional Directors dismissed charges or petitions, the reasons were to be stated in writing. Previously there had usually been informal notification of the reason for such action, but now a more formal notice was to be given.

cases were closed on compliance when the Regional Director sent in his closing compliance report. He could ask for technical assistance or advice and could recommend further legal action, but those later steps would be taken only when the Enforcement Section agreed and began action. Often, however, attorneys in the field argued cases in the circuit courts. After a decree or contempt adjudication, it was again the full responsibility of the regional office to obtain compliance. Some sources of delay were thus eliminated.

As to representation cases, also, the Regional Director had a large degree of authority, initiating formal action in most instances without prior advice from Washington, holding prehearing elections, or dismissing cases subject to appeal to Washington as in complaint cases. Where he was able to obtain agreement for determination of representatives by consent election or consent cross-check of cards against pay roll, his rulings were held to be final, unless arbitrary or capricious.

Thus the Board, by delegating such authority to the Regional Directors, had largely decentralized the handling of the great bulk of its case work, informal and formal, in the investigating and prosecuting stages and the handling of representation elections. By delegating authority to the Committee on Appeals and Review, it kept clear of consideration of cases in the early administrative stages except for the rare case where a policy question was involved or where it had to consider an appeal from the Regional Directors' action. It was increasingly careful to segregate itself in its decisional activities from the Field Division or regional officers who had handled cases at the earlier stages. The Review Section functioned as a general pool of law clerks for the Board, with no connection in their handling of cases with the personnel who earlier investigated or prosecuted these cases. The Trial Examiners were assured independence in their conduct of hearings and in preparing their Intermediate Reports, and the Board consulted them in connection with the decision process only when their special experience with the case would help in the weighing of the evidence. But with all this degree of separation of functions and decentralization, a unified policy could be attained, since the Board was responsible in general for the determination of policy and for the administrative organization which carried out the policies.

In spite of the growing criticism of the Act and the Board in Congress and the public press during these two years, the Board continued successfully to perform the important functions for which it was established, especially through the elections to determine representatives in nearly 7,000 cases. Through *informal* processes also it continued to dispose of the great bulk of the cases which came before it, in the spirit of the administrative process. It achieved compliance with the law in a substantial number of cases, either by informal adjustment or by compliance after formal orders. The courts, moreover, continued to uphold the Board's decisions in the great majority of cases.[81]

CONCLUSION—THE CRITICISM AND THE EVIDENCE

Criticisms of the NLRB that stemmed from dislike of the Act itself and its purposes, or opposition to certain practices over which the Board had no control under the Act, or criticisms of particular policies of the Board in its case decisions are not the issue at this point. But a number of criticisms of the *administration* of the Act continued to be repeated in various forms throughout the life of the Wagner Act. The chief of these charged: (1) that the Board, being its own "prosecutor, judge, and jury," had prejudged cases before they came up for decision and could not therefore make a fair decision; related was the charge that the actual decisions were often, in effect, made by subordinates; (2) that due process was denied also because bias and partiality prevented fair investigation, fair hearing, and impartial decision; (3) that the Board did not adequately weigh all the evidence and based decisions upon evidence which would not stand up in court, while the courts were prevented by the law from going behind the Board's findings of fact to make their own appraisal of the evidence. Such charges were made so frequently for so long a period that by sheer weight of repetition they received large credence. It is important to look at the record, however, to see whether they were justified.

The "prosecutor, judge, and jury" charge is a general attack upon the administrative agency system, not only on the NLRB. It is very significant that Congress itself in passing the Administrative Procedure Act in 1946 continued the inclusion of all the functions of administration of certain laws within the agencies set up for the purpose, but with provisions to insure the internal separation of functions. The NLRB, as we have seen above, through the years increased its delegation of authority and its own separation, as the decision-making group, from the earlier functions of investigating and prosecuting cases, in the interest of meeting the public criticism on this score. There is no real evidence of abuse under the earlier system.

81. *Twelfth Annual Report,* p. 41. See *infra,* ch. 3, Table 2.

Moreover, in the early stages of administering a new law it was essential that the Board keep a close check on the handling of cases while policy was being established. In the later years the separation had gone so far that many of the critical statements about the Board's administration bore little if any resemblance to what actually was being done. The Board had largely solved the problem of maintaining separation between the different parts of the agency: those which investigated, handled the great bulk of cases informally, administered the determination of representation questions in the field, and prosecuted the complaint cases requiring formal action; the Trial Examiners who heard such cases; and the Board itself which with the assistance of the review attorneys decided the formal cases. Yet it was able to maintain the unity of policy which resulted in its very successful record for informal settlements, what the Attorney-General's Committee called "numerically and otherwise, the life-blood of the administrative process—negotiations and informal settlements."[82] If there had been any basis in the early history for the charge that review attorneys exerted undue influence on decisions, this also was reduced as time went on. The Board improved its posthearing procedures by increasing the value and importance of the Trial Examiners' report and requiring that review attorneys use these documents and prepare written reports for the Board on their analysis of the record and the Intermediate Report. The machinery itself seemed to provide adequate safeguards for the integrity of the quasi-judicial process, subject only to the possibility of human error.[83]

The sweeping charges of bias and prejudice made against the Board and its staff must be viewed in the light of the fact that, as the Attorney-General's Committee pointed out, sincere belief in the policies and principles of the Act "cannot be called bias or prejudice, however distasteful such an attitude may be to parties or counsel who believe these policies and principles to be unwise or unfair."[84] In the early days of the Act, with an inexperienced and enthusiastic staff, operating in an atmosphere of great hostility, some of the criticism had a basis in fact. The Board did not entirely solve

---

82. Attorney-General's Committee, *Final Report*, pp. 58–59.

83. Cf. U.S. House of Representatives, Committee on Education and Labor, *Labor-Management Relations Act, 1947, Minority Report*, Report No. 245, 80th Cong., 1st Sess., April 11, 1947, pp. 74–75. "No claim has been made that the NLRB has not fully complied with its provisions [in the Administrative Procedure Act]. . . . The hearings before the committee did not, in our opinion, disclose any abuses arising out of the present procedures of the . . . Board."

84. Attorney-General's Committee, *Monograph*, p. 17.

its problem of developing a competent staff, and especially in the first years the work in the field was very uneven. To some extent the unevenness continued. But, with experience and training, the development of methods of supervision and standards of procedure, and the elimination from the staff of people not suited to the job of thorough, impartial investigation, the Board had to a large degree solved this personnel problem, and this despite the tremendous turnover in staff incidental to the war. Moreover, the fact that in the first ten years about half of all charges of unfair labor practices were withdrawn or dismissed at the informal stages, and a still larger proportion in the last two years, gives no support to the claims of prolabor bias in case handling.[85] Mistakes there could still be, and undoubtedly were, but the question is whether the procedures were such as to protect all parties from the effects of individual shortcomings, if they existed.

It must be admitted that there were widespread complaints by employers of bias and prejudice. By 1947 these charges seemed to be made more frequently in the areas where the purposes of the Act were less generally accepted and where "old-fashioned" unfair labor practices still were frequently found. The correlation appears more than accidental. Many employers who felt that there had been bias earlier had no complaints to make of recent years or complaints based on their own experience. Some of them acknowledged candidly that it was difficult to separate their feeling toward the Act, which at least at first was very "hard to take," and their appraisal of the Act's administration. The fear and insecurity aroused by the drastic changes in industrial policy which were forced by the Wagner Act were not conducive to approval of the actions of the administrative agency, however honest and objective it might be. The staff, moreover, did not achieve the superhuman feat of administering the Act so tactfully that those who came in conflict with it enjoyed the experience. To some extent it was a question of manners, of field examiners and

85. Cf. statement of Chairman Madden in a 1938 broadcast: "Here then are many hundreds of cases where the employer is exonerated on the merits. . . . Yet our critics go on parroting the statement that we always find that the employer is wrong. . . . Would they have us spend our time and that of the employer and his employees and the public's money going through the motions of a formal hearing in order to prove to ourselves what we already have learned from our investigation? . . . I ask our critics what they have to suggest as an improvement over our method of eliminating cases which are not well founded, and I ask them, in all decency, not again to mouth or write the falsehood, hundreds of times false, that we proceed against employers whenever unions request us to do so." Quoted in Joseph Rosenfarb, *The National Labor Policy and How It Works* (New York: Harper & Bros., 1940), pp. 486–87.

trial attorneys who were young and lacking the polish of professional courtesy. Some of them let their enthusiasm for the purposes of the Act show when cold objectivity in the investigation of a particular set of facts was called for. But the facts were very human, emotionally charged facts in many cases, and complete objectivity was difficult to achieve. To some extent this resulted in overwriting in early decisions, when the facts would have spoken for themselves adequately in colder, less colorful language.[86] All these problems were much on the minds of the Board members, and, as administration improved, there can be no doubt that there was less basis for criticism than there may have been earlier. And always there were safeguards if abuses occurred, by appeal to Regional Directors against any improper action of the staff, and to the Board from actions of Regional Directors, and finally to the courts. No doubt some cases were adjusted simply because employers could not afford to fight cases through the courts. But study of the available evidence makes it seem very doubtful that much if any actual injustice was done to employers—and weighed against that is a considerable volume of violations of the Act which were never remedied by the Board.

It was charged also that the Board and staff were pro-CIO. This will be considered further in connection with discussion of the craft-unit issue.[87] The AFL with the rise of the CIO felt its interests endangered at a number of points, and it reacted with fear and anger when Board decisions failed to protect the claimed "vested rights" of older unions against the new rivals. Especially important were the issues as to craft units, as to setting aside of contracts made by minority unions or with illegal assistance by employers, the holding of elections in spite of contracts claimed to be a bar to the petition, and protection of individuals from discharge for advocating a shift to the CIO. All these will be discussed below. Study of the record shows that the Board in general impartially applied its carefully thought-out policies, however they fell. But on each of these issues it was most often older unions that were hurt, and newer groups who were aided, by these policies. The AFL Executive Council protested bitterly against "pro-CIO bias" and "abuse of power" by the Board.[88] In a time of the rapid rise for the first time of a rival to the AFL, it

86. Cf. the comment by the Second Circuit Court in enforcing the Remington Rand order, *infra*, ch. 4, n. 9.

87. *Infra*, ch. 5, pp. 143–44.

88. Cf. American Federation of Labor, *Report of Executive Council to Annual Convention, 1938*, pp. 69–71, 75; *1939*, pp. 116–20; *1943*, pp. 36–37; *1944*, pp. 54–60; and others.

would have taken more than a Solomon to protect the interests of a large group of new unionists without arousing the ire of the old-line craft union group. Undoubtedly the staff as a whole was sympathetic to the new expanding labor movement on an industrial basis and sometimes glad to see a challenge to particular old unions which had been intrenched without much democratic control or genuine concern for the interests of their members. This is not to say, however, that the staff was prejudiced in its handling of cases. Its job was to administer the Act, not to protect an old union against a new one if the employees desired a change. The charge of biased administration is not upheld by the record of handling AFL and CIO cases.

The issue of whether fair hearings were provided and requirements of due process met is crucial. Company counsel have often held that a hearing was unfair, and in a few cases the Board itself set a record aside and ordered a new hearing. The critics, however, always cited a small group of cases[89] in which courts criticized the conduct of hearings or the attitudes of Trial Examiners[90] and the four cases in which orders were set aside on the ground that there had not been a full and fair hearing.[91] They omitted to mention that these are only a handful of instances out of the more than seven hundred court decisions on enforcement of Board orders by 1947. And they suppressed the much longer list of court opinions in which there were comments on the fairness, courtesy, and impartiality with which hearings were conducted. The Supreme Court, in early cases, upheld the basic procedures as affording due process.[92] We have found also some twenty-four decisions by ten different courts, in which courts denied the

89. Cf. T. R. Iserman, *Industrial Peace and the Wagner Act* (New York: McGraw-Hill Book Co., 1947), p. 62. See also *infra*, ch. 4, n. 1.

90. Consolidated Edison Co. v. NLRB, 305 U.S. 197, 226 (1938); Cupples Co. Manufacturers v. NLRB, 106 F. 2d 100, 113 (C.C.A.8, 1939); NLRB v. Ford Motor Co., 114 F. 2d 905, 909 (C.C.A.6, 1940); NLRB v. Air Associates, Inc., 121 F. 2d 586, 589 (C.C.A.2, 1941).

Others which could be added are: NLRB v. Cleveland Cliffs Iron Co., 133 F. 2d 295, 302 (C.C.A.6, 1943); NLRB v. Western Cartridge Co., 138 F. 2d 551, 553 (C.C.A.2, 1943); NLRB v. McGough Bakeries Corp., 153 F. 2d 420, 421–22 (C.C.A.5, 1946); also in Donnelly Garment Co. v. NLRB, 151 F. 2d 854 (C.C.A.8, 1945), the case was remanded for the taking of evidence which had been excluded by the Trial Examiner, but the Supreme Court on review found no want of due process in the Board's proceedings. 330 U.S. 219 (1947).

91. Montgomery Ward and Co. v. NLRB, 103 F. 2d 147, 156 (C.C.A.8, 1939); Inland Steel Co. v. NLRB, 109 F. 2d 9, 14–17 (C.C.A.7, 1940); NLRB v. Washington Dehydrated Food Co., 118 F. 2d 980, 986 (C.C.A.9, 1941); NLRB v. Henry K. Phelps Jr., 136 F. 2d 562, 566 (C.C.A.5, 1943).

92. NLRB v. Jones and Laughlin Steel Corp., 301 U.S. 1, 47 (1937); Myers v. Bethlehem Shipbuilding Corp., 303 U.S. 41 (1938).

charge that the hearing had been unfair or made specifically favorable comments on the conduct of hearings.[93] The final proof of the fact that due process cannot have been denied extensively is seen in the fact that the Supreme Court set aside only two out of fifty-nine of the Board's orders which it reviewed through June, 1947, and the

93. A few of the more recent might be quoted: "The record does not justify a finding that the Board's decision was reached as a result of bias and prejudice or that the manner in which the hearings were conducted denied the company due process of law. On the contrary we are left with strong impression that much of the conduct complained of was deliberately provoked by counsel for the Company, possibly to lay a basis for a defense to charges which otherwise could not be met." NLRB v. Weirton Steel Co., 135 F. 2d 494, 497 (C.C.A.3, 1943).

". . . without indicating an agreement with the Trial Examiner in all the rulings, we think his attitude was fair and impartial to both sides under conditions which it is understatement to describe as difficult." Berkshire Knitting Mills v. NLRB, 139 F. 2d 134, 138 (C.C.A.3, 1943).

"We have carefully read the entire record for the atmosphere and course of the proceedings. . . . The Trial Examiner properly manifested and exercised the courtesy, consideration, patience and restraint necessary on the part of a hearing officer. He accorded the parties liberal and equal scope in introducing evidence and cross-examining witnesses." NLRB v. May Department Stores, 154 F. 2d 533, 539 (C.C.A.8, 1946).

The entire list of such decisions found is as follows:

NLRB v. Mackay Radio and Telegraph Co., 304 U.S. 333, 350–51 (1938)

NLRB v. Remington Rand, Inc., 94 F. 2d 862, 873 (C.C.A.2, 1938)

Jefferson Electric Co. v. NLRB, 102 F. 2d 949, 954 (C.C.A.7, 1939)

Wilson and Co. v. NLRB, 103 F. 2d 243, 245 (C.C.A.8, 1939)

NLRB v. Stackpole Carbon Co., 105 F. 2d 167, 177 (C.C.A.3, 1939) (cert. den. 308 U.S. 605)

Kansas City Power and Light Co. v. NLRB, 111 F. 2d 340, 357 (C.C.A.8, 1940)

Subin, et al., v. NLRB, 112 F. 2d 326, 332 (C.C.A.3, 1940)

Continental Box Co. v. NLRB, 113 F. 2d 93, 96 (C.C.A.5, 1940)

Eagle-Picher Mining and Smelting Co. v. NLRB, 119 F. 2d 903, 906 (C.C.A.8, 1941)

Bethlehem Steel Co. v. NLRB, 120 F. 2d 641, 652 (C.A.D.C., 1941)

NLRB v. Luxuray, Inc., 123 F. 2d 106, 109 (C.C.A.2, 1941)

NLRB v. Newberry Lumber and Chemical Co., 123 F. 2d 831, 833 (C.C.A.6, 1941)

NLRB v. Baldwin Locomotive Works, 128 F. 2d 39, 47 (C.C.A.3, 1942)

NLRB v. Condenser Corp., 128 F. 2d 67, 79–80 (C.C.A.3, 1942)

NLRB v. Goodyear Tire and Rubber Co., 129 F. 2d 661, 663 (C.C.A.5, 1942)

NLRB v. Acme Evans Co., 130 F. 2d 477, 482–83 (C.C.A.7, 1942)

NLRB v. Gallup American Coal Co., 131 F. 2d 665, 668 (C.C.A.10, 1942)

NLRB v. Weirton Steel Co., 135 F. 2d 494, 497 (C.C.A.3, 1943)

Jacksonville Paper Co. v. NLRB, 137 F. 2d 148 (C.C.A.5, 1943)

Berkshire Knitting Mills v. NLRB, 139 F. 2d 134 (C.C.A.3, 1943)

NLRB v. Thompson Products, Inc., 141 F. 2d 794, 799 (C.C.A.9, 1944)

NLRB v. Grieder Machine Tool and Die Co., 142 F. 2d 163, 166 (C.C.A.6, 1944)

NLRB v. May Department Stores, 154 F. 2d 533, 539 (C.C.A.8, 1946)

J and H Garfinkel v. NLRB, 162 F. 2d 256–57 (C.C.A.2, 1947)

circuit courts set aside only 12.6 per cent in their 705 decisions on Board orders.[94]

Critics complained also that the Board based its decisions upon inadequate evidence and that the courts' power of review was too limited to insure proper protection of the rights of employers. The Act required the Board to base its decisions upon findings of fact from "all the testimony taken," and the rules of evidence prevailing in courts were not to be controlling. The power of the courts to review Board orders was limited by making the findings of the Board conclusive, if "supported by evidence." This arrangement was based on the usual theory of administrative law, that in a complex field "decisions based upon evidential facts under the particular statute [should be] made by experienced officials with an adequate appreciation of the complexities of the subject."[95] The Supreme Court early made clear, however, that "supported by evidence" means by "substantial evidence," and "substantial evidence is more than a mere scintilla. It means such relevant evidence as a reasonable mind might accept as adequate to support a conclusion."[96] In two cases where the Supreme Court found the Board's decisions not supported by substantial evidence, it set them aside, although in both instances some of the Justices agreed with the Board.[97] Circuit courts, applying the same test, did not hesitate to set Board orders aside when they did not find them supported by substantial evidence, but, as we have seen, the denials of enforcement were relatively few among the cases which reached the courts.

Some of the sharply critical comments by courts which are often cited came in the early years when the Board, guided by the courts, was working out its standards as to evidence.[98] Occasionally courts accepted reluctantly their limited power to review the Board's findings, although they recognized that there was substantial evidence to support the Board's conclusions.[99] In other decisions, on the con-

---

94. *Eleventh Annual Report,* p. 52; *Twelfth,* p. 41. Cf. *infra,* ch. 3, Table 2.

95. Republic Aviation Corp. v. NLRB, 324 U.S. 793, 800 (1945).

96. Consolidated Edison Co. v. NLRB, 305 U.S. 197, 229 (1938).

97. NLRB v. Columbian Enameling and Stamping Corp., 306 U.S. 292 (1939); NLRB v. Sands Manufacturing Co., 306 U.S. 332 (1939).

98. Cf. NLRB v. Union Pacific Stages, 99 F. 2d 153 (C.C.A.9, 1938); NLRB v. Thompson Products, 97 F. 2d 13 (C.C.A.6, 1938); Ballston-Stillwater Knitting Co. v. NLRB, 98 F. 2d 758 (C.C.A.2, 1938); NLRB v. Empire Furniture Corporation, 107 F. 2d 92 (C.C.A.6, 1939); NLRB v. Reynolds International Pen Co., 162 F. 2d 680 (C.C.A.7, 1947).

99. Cf. Wilson and Co., Inc., v. NLRB, 126 F. 2d 114 (C.C.A.7, 1942); NLRB v. Columbia Products Corp., 141 F. 2d 687 (C.C.A.2, 1944).

trary, courts indicated that they recognized the case for giving to specialized expert agencies the original right to determine questions of fact and draw conclusions from them.[100] Several court decisions specifically denied charges that the Board had ignored evidence favorable to the employer.[101]

The Attorney-General's Committee in its report on the NLRB found that the Board had in the main followed the traditional rules of evidence with no major departure from established principles, although hearsay was admitted "if the evidence appears likely to open up a new line of inquiry previously undeveloped or if the parties are able, by virtue of their own knowledge, to explain or contradict the statement if it is inaccurate."[102] The Administrative Procedure Act, moreover, did not change the requirements as to substantial evidence or the limitation of the power of review by the courts of the agency's findings of fact.

The record therefore does not support the charges that there was inadequate protection of the rights of the accused through Board procedures and the right of appeal to the courts. Occasional mistakes, if they were made, or if the majority of the court believed that they had been made, were rectified by the setting-aside of the Board's orders. Only by a rejection of the basic theory of administrative law can a case be made against the Board's record as a whole on these issues. The criticisms stemmed in the main from dislike of the legislation itself. As one student of the subject has said: "Business men subject to these unpopular types of regulation would in general be glad indeed to have the broadest possible judicial review in the hope of watering down and delaying the effectiveness of the regulation."[103] The propagandist technique of repeating falsehoods so often and with such assurance that they are believed almost had a parallel here. Certainly some employers in 1947 had no criticism to make from their own experience of the Board's hearings or use of evidence, although they reported hearing criticisms by others. Apparently actual criticism based on personal experience was much less widespread than

100. Cf. NLRB v. Standard Oil Co., 138 F. 2d 885 (C.C.A.2, 1943); International Association of Machinists v. NLRB, 110 F. 2d 29 (C.A.D.C., 1939); Republic Aviation Corp. v. NLRB, 324 U.S. 793, 800 (1945).

101. Cf. NLRB v. Sartorius and Co., 140 F. 2d 203 (C.C.A.2, 1944); NLRB v. Laister-Kauffman Aircraft Corp., 144 F. 2d 9 (C.C.A.8, 1944).

102. Attorney-General's Committee, *Monograph*, pp. 19–20; cf. also its *Final Report*, pp. 70–71; and Gellhorn, *op. cit.*, pp. 363–77.

103. Robert E. Cushman, *The Independent Regulatory Commissions* (New York: Oxford University Press, 1941), p. 692.

was implied by the most vocal objectors. One employer, perhaps typical of some others, said: "Of course we have been well taught by Senator ———."

A different set of issues, not considered by the critics who won their case in 1947, was whether the Board at any time failed to enforce the law with the vigor needed for full effectuation of the purposes of the Act. Unions tended to this point of view in the later years. In so far as the issue refers to particular policies in decisions, it is outside the scope of this chapter. But the "ubiquitous Congressman" asking favors for his constituent,[104] fears of Appropriations Committee reprisals for vigorous prosecution of cases against politically important companies, and organized group pressures on behalf of particular unions or employers in certain cases were all difficult to withstand and might conceivably result in dropping or delaying cases or in "watering-down" decisions. Somewhat similar were the pressures, when any member of the Board showed signs of being "politically minded," which could and probably did occasionally result in a staff appointment less than the best available. There was a question, too, whether the Board, or Board members, should be available to confer with parties to a case or their supporters. The Board never thought it necessary to shut itself off from conferences which might help to achieve understanding and compliance with the Act. Yet there were dangers, especially if an individual member had private conferences —a practice definitely not approved by most of the Board members. And there was danger of the charge of yielding to pressure, if not the fact, when there were such conferences. Proof of whether this actually happened in any cases is difficult, but, as former Chairman Millis once said, "There have been embarrassing attempts to see a Board member, rather than the Board itself, and assertions have been made that to do this was a matter of legal right. It might be that a member of the Board would badly wish to be free from such things and to protect himself against rumors, which, all will agree, are superabundant in Washington." The protection against such dangers lies of course in the integrity and courage of the members of the Board. Certainly most, if not all, of the members of the NLRB through the years were beyond the possibility of suspicion of yielding to such

104. Cf. discussion of inaction by administrative agencies as a result of such improper influence in Joseph P. Chamberlain, Noel T. Dowling, and Paul R. Hayes, *The Judicial Function in Federal Administrative Agencies* (New York: Commonwealth Fund, 1942), p. 90.

improper influence.[105] If at any point this Board, or any other administrative agency, failed to live up to the responsibility to decide cases honestly and courageously, this would be a matter of human error and of the men appointed to the Board. It should not be held the fault of the administrative procedures or of the law itself.

A study of the record of the Board's administration leads inevitably to the conclusion that the Board on the whole had solved the major problems of efficient and fair administrative processes, except as limited by inadequate funds and staff. It had listened to the criticisms and had steadily improved its organization, staff, and methods of operation in order to insure equitable and impartial handling of cases in the informal stages and a judicial consideration of the merits of cases which required formal decision. While the Board might, and we think did sometimes, make mistakes or fail to act when action was needed, and there was room for difference of opinion among experts on matters of policy, the commonly accepted criticisms of its administrative processes largely disregarded the available evidence on its operations. It is significant that, during these years while administrative problems were being solved, the virulence of the attacks upon the Board increased, especially after V-J Day. And finally, in 1947, this structure was largely destroyed by the extensive revision of administration under the Labor Management Relations Act of 1947.

105. Cf. another statement of former Chairman Millis: "Qualifications for membership on the Board consist of integrity, a sense of responsibility, impartiality and freedom from influence by any special group or organization, general sympathy with the Act to be administered, knowledge of men and relationships, and great industry. These present, other special qualifications may be important. One of these is an intimate knowledge of law, particularly industrial relations law. Another is an extensive knowledge of industrial relations, the variations in customs in industry, etc., and along with these, there must be a balanced mind and an ability to team with others who may have different views with regard to some matters."

CHAPTER 3

NLRB CASES AND THE LABOR MOVEMENT

THE living process of how the government, through the National Labor Relations Board, protected the right of workers to organize and achieve collective bargaining and thereby encouraged the growth of the labor movement and the extension of collective bargaining as an industrial way of life cannot be told by the cold statistics of the Board's case load any more than by a description of administrative procedures. Yet a rather brief look at some of the crucial statistics of cases filed and handled, elections held and their results, remedies obtained, along with those of the growth of union membership and collective bargaining, will give a framework against which can be seen and understood some of the problems met and handled by the Board, and their impact on the habits, practices, and feelings of employers, employees, and unions.

The outlines of the story are shown in Table 1. During the twelve years of the Wagner Act, American workers and their representatives filed with the NLRB more than 45,000 charges of unfair labor practices against employers and nearly 60,000 representation petitions. The Board conducted almost 37,000 elections or checks of union cards against pay rolls to determine whether a union had been chosen as bargaining representative and counted the votes of more than seven and a half million workers for or against union representation. During these years, and at least partly as a result of the protection given by the Act, membership in unions in the United States grew from less than four million in 1935 to about fifteen million by 1947. Meanwhile the extent to which workers were covered by collective bargaining agreements between unions and employers increased from an estimated 19.5 per cent in manufacturing industries and 26.1 per cent in all industries included in a 1935 study[1] to 69 per cent of the workers in manufacturing and 48 per cent of all workers in occupations where

1. U.S. Bureau of Labor Statistics, *Characteristics of Company Unions, 1935,* Bulletin No. 634, p. 37.

unions were organizing and seeking collective bargaining agreements in 1946.[2]

The first great flood of cases[3] came after the Supreme Court upheld

TABLE 1

NATIONAL LABOR RELATIONS BOARD CASES FILED AND ELECTIONS HELD, UNION MEMBERSHIP, AND THE EXTENT OF COLLECTIVE BARGAINING, 1935–47

YEAR*	CASES FILED†		REPRESENTATION ELECTIONS AND CROSS-CHECKS HELD†		UNION MEMBERSHIP‡	COVERAGE OF COLLECTIVE BARGAINING AGREEMENTS§	
	Unfair Labor Practice Cases	Representation Cases	Number	Votes Cast		Number of Employees Covered	Per Cent of Total Eligible for Coverage
Total.....	45,649	59,692	36,969	7,677,135	....	....	......
1936......	865	203	31	7,572	4,164,000	....	26‖
1937......	2,895	1,173	265	164,135	7,218,000		......
1938......	6,807	3,623	1,152	343,587	8,265,000		......
1939......	4,618	2,286	746	177,215	8,980,000		......
1940......	3,934	2,243	1,192	532,355	8,944,000	....	30
1941......	4,817	4,334	2,568	729,933	10,489,000	10,300,000	30
1942......	4,967	6,010	4,212	1,067,037	10,762,000	12,500,000	40
1943......	3,403	6,141	4,153	1,126,501	13,642,000	13,800,000	45
1944......	2,573	6,603	4,712	1,072,594	14,621,000	14,300,000	47
1945......	2,427	7,311	4,919	893,758	14,796,000	13,800,000	48
1946......	3,815	8,445	5,589	698,812	14,974,000	14,800,000	48
1947......	4,232	10,677	6,920	805,474	15,414,000	#	#
July 1– Aug. 21, 1947....	296	643	510	58,162	....	....	......

* Data for NLRB cases are for fiscal years ending June 30.

† National Labor Relations Board, *Twelfth Annual Report*, pp. 83, 89, 90.

‡ United States Bureau of Labor Statistics, *Handbook of Labor Statistics*, Bulletin 916 (1948), p. 130.

§ *Monthly Labor Review*, 64 (1947), 765–69. The number "eligible for coverage" is the number "engaged in occupations in which the unions have been organizing and endeavoring to obtain written agreements."

‖ This is not entirely comparable with the later series but is based on the Bureau of Labor Statistics survey of 14,725 establishments with nearly 2,000,000 employees in April, 1935. United States Bureau of Labor Statistics, *Characteristics of Company Unions*, Bulletin No. 634, pp. 35–38.

Not available.

the constitutionality of the Act in 1937, with more than 10,000 cases filed from July 1, 1937, to June 30, 1938, two-thirds of them involving charges of unfair labor practices. The complaint cases never dropped

2. *Monthly Labor Review*, 64 (1947), 765.

3. Unless otherwise indicated, all figures in this chapter are from the Board's *Annual Reports* or from other data supplied by the Board.

much below 4,000 in a year until 1942–43. Before that, however, an increased acceptance of the policies of the Act had brought about a growing use of the machinery of the Board to determine questions as to representation. Representation petitions numbered more than 6,000 by 1942 and in that year for the first time accounted for more than half of the cases filed with the Board. From then on during the war, and in the postwar years, the major activity[4] of the Board was the handling of representation elections of enormous importance for avoiding strikes over the issue of representation during conversion to war production, the war itself, and postwar conversion. During the last four years these representation cases were more than 70 per cent of the Board's work load—in terms of cases, not time and work involved. During the war unfair labor practice charges decreased, partly no doubt because of the state of the labor market, partly because the National War Labor Board's handling of dispute cases removed issues which might otherwise have come to the NLRB as complaint cases, and partly because to organize workers and win elections was proving to be the best way to eliminate unfair labor practices in many situations. But with the close of the war and the end of the WLB, and the renewed organization drives, especially in the South, both types of cases increased. In the final year of the Wagner Act cases filed were at an all-time high, nearly 15,000, more than 4,000 charges of unfair labor practices, and over 10,000 representation petitions. Nearly 7,000 elections were conducted in that year.

Part of the story is told also by the character of the complaints filed, with their changes over the years. Always "the heart of the Act" was Section 8(3), which forbade discrimination against employees for union activity. About 30,000, or two-thirds of all the charges filed during the twelve years, included charges of discrimination, and this proportion continued steady after starting slightly higher in the first two years.[5] Of great importance for the development of free collective bargaining was the elimination of company-dominated unionism. Charges under Section 8(2), prohibiting domination or other interference with or support to a labor organization, were involved in about one in five of the complaint cases filed in the first three years, but after that they decreased and were less than one in ten cases filed

4. For some months, in addition, the Board was swamped by the necessity of conducting strike-vote elections under the War Labor Disputes Act. In the fiscal year 1945 it held 573 elections and from July to December, 1945, a total of 1,214, many of them very large. Cf. ch. 2, *supra*, p. 61.

5. Section 8(4), prohibiting discrimination for testifying or filing charges under the Act, brought relatively few charges—only 495 during the period.

in the last five years. Numerically more important were the charges of refusal to bargain, under Section 8(5), almost 15,000 of them over the years. They were included in nearly half of the cases in the first year. But with the growth of the representation procedures to settle issues as to the right to recognition, and some increase in acceptance of the Act as the law of the land, and finally the War Labor Board's period of activity, these cases decreased until they were around 20 per cent of all cases filed in the later war years. After the war, with the end of the WLB and with organization drives that encountered the old type of employer opposition in unorganized areas, the number of such cases rose sharply to over 30 per cent of all complaint cases in the last two years of the Wagner Act. In 1947 a total of 1,347 cases charging refusal to bargain were filed. A final type of case was that which charged only general interference, under Section 8(1) of the Act, without other specific charges. These were very few in the early years, but, as employers learned to avoid specific violations of the other sections of the Act, this type of charge increased in numbers and amounted to more than 10 per cent of all filed in the later years.[6]

All areas and all industries contributed to the charges and petitions. If the figures were available, they would undoubtedly show concentration in the metropolitan industrial areas at first, followed by growth in the number of cases coming from small towns and rural areas, as union activity spread to the periphery. The regional offices serving the southern areas—Baltimore, Atlanta, New Orleans, Fort Worth, and Los Angeles—handled less than one-fifth of the complaint cases and about one-fourth of the representation cases in 1937, but by 1947 their share had increased to over 30 per cent.[7] The great bulk of the cases in 1947, well over 70 per cent, came from manufacturing industries. During the war years more than half of the Board's work was concentrated in industries essential to the war: iron and steel, ordnance, aircraft, shipbuilding, machinery, electrical equipment, chemicals, textiles, foods. By 1947 over 10 per cent of the cases came from wholesale and retail trade and finance, nearly 10 per cent from transportation, communication, and other public utilities, and over 3 per cent from services.[8] Labor organization and the resulting call for the services of the Board to settle representation disputes and prevent illegal interference with organization were evident in every sector of the American economy included under the Act.

6. From *Annual Reports, Twelfth*, p. 68; and others.
7. *Second Annual Report*, pp. 24, 28; *Twelfth*, p. 70.
8. *Annual Reports*, esp. 1941 ff.

From the Wagner Act to Taft-Hartley

During the great upsweep of organization in the mass-production industries by the Committee for Industrial Organization, the CIO unions were the greatest users of the Board, but even in 1937–38, the first year for which separate figures are available, AFL unions filed 3,692 cases as against CIO's 5,542. In the following years sometimes one group, sometimes the other, had more cases, depending partly upon shifts of affiliation of such active unions as the International Ladies' Garment Workers Union, the United Mine Workers, and the International Association of Machinists. CIO unions in most years filed somewhat more charges than did AFL unions, partly because of a greater tendency of employers to oppose CIO unions when both AFL and CIO unions were present. The AFL affiliates just before the war, and again after the war, filed more representation petitions than did the CIO. Over a ten-year period, 1938–47, AFL unions filed 16,774 charges and 24,784 representation petitions; CIO unions, 18,508 charges and 24,026 representation petitions; unaffiliated unions, 2,545 charges and 7,218 representation petitions; individuals, 3,774 charges; and employers, 648 representation petitions.

HOW CASES WERE HANDLED

The Board's decisions in the minority of cases which required formal action were crucial, since it was there that the policies under the Act were worked out. Nevertheless, the great bulk of the work of the Board was not that of quasi-judicial decision-making but rather the informal investigation, negotiation, and settlement of cases (including in this agency the conducting of elections) which has been called "the life-blood of the administrative process."[9] During the twelve years of the Wagner Act more than nine-tenths of the unfair labor practice cases closed were handled informally and nearly three-fourths of the representation petitions. Only 3,154 decisions in complaint cases and 11,419 decisions in representation cases, including decisions based upon stipulations of the parties, were issued in the more than 100,000 cases closed. To consider the work of the Board primarily that of a court, therefore, was a grave misconception of its functions.

The Board was always concerned about any tendency toward an increase in the proportion of formal cases. Informal handling of cases

9. Cf. *supra*, ch. 2, p. 67. "Formal cases" are those which required issuance of complaint or notice of hearings and usually thereafter a formal decision by the Board; "informal cases" are those handled administratively in the regional offices to a conclusion without the necessity of hearing and decision, or other "formal action."

meant speedier disposition of the issues, less expense to the parties and to the government, and adjustment near at home rather than the intervention of a distant government agency. Moreover, as the Board developed its methods and controls, it was able to achieve a considerable measure of administrative decentralization without sacrificing the unity of basic policies and methods which was essential for equitable and uniform handling of cases. Yet the trend was strong toward more formal action in representation cases and during the war in complaint cases also. The trend resulted partly from the fact that, as labor organization extended, new and more difficult problems arose on which employers wanted the decision of the Board, such as on claims to recognition of new groups like foremen, guards, and clerical employees. There were also border-line cases involving charges of more subtle violations, as in some of the free-speech cases, in which Board decision was necessary. Perhaps there was an increased resistance by employers who thought that the changed composition of the Board and certain trends in court decisions gave them a greater chance of success in formal proceedings. During the war also when organization reached into areas and industries hitherto untouched, many companies, coming into contact for the first time with the requirements of the Act, were unready to accept the interpretation of the regional offices as to their obligations. Delaying tactics also, by employers or their lawyers, who found a financial advantage in postponing acceptance of the unions, were responsible for part of the trend toward an increased proportion of cases requiring formal action.[10] In the two years after the war, nevertheless, under pressure of the mounting case load and inadequate funds, but with an increase in the level of experience and competence of the staff as old employees returned to the Board, it was possible to reverse the trend. The device of the prehearing election was instrumental in increasing the proportion of representation cases which could be handled by informal methods, including consent elections.[11]

Further analysis of the informal cases is needed. They were reported as either adjusted, withdrawn, or dismissed. Of the complaint cases in the first years of the Act, half or even more were reported as adjusted. But it is clear that frequently in some regions these were compromises without a real meeting of minds, or settlements made by the union and the employer without the intervention or approval of

10. Cf. discussion in the writer's "Free Collective Bargaining or Government Intervention?" *Harvard Business Review,* 25 (1947), 190–95.

11. Cf. *supra,* ch. 2, p. 62.

the regional office. As the different offices began to develop their own standards, however, and particularly after 1942 when the Field Division established standards for reporting and for written settlement agreements, the proportion of cases reported as informally adjusted dropped sharply. In the last three years it was only about 20 per cent of all complaint cases closed. The cases reported as dismissed remained fairly steady, averaging about 15 per cent. The cases withdrawn, meanwhile, rose, until in the last two years they were about 57 per cent of all cases closed. Cases withdrawn included those where the union and employer had made a private settlement, without action by the regional office; where the union withdrew for its own reasons, sometimes to push a representation case instead; or where the union withdrew on the recommendation of the Regional Director, who would otherwise have dismissed the case.

During the entire period of the Wagner Act, accordingly, of all the charges against employers, more than half of those closed were withdrawn or dismissed without any formal action. In the final two years this proportion had gone up to over 70 per cent. What did this mean from the standpoint of the law and its enforcement? A variety of factors are involved to which it is impossible to assign a definite weight. Changes in the law itself, through the more "liberal" interpretations by the Board of later years, undoubtedly resulted in throwing out as without merit some of the charges of discrimination and of interference with elections, for instance, which in earlier years would probably have been considered clear violations of the Act.[12] More careful investigation, also, as standards of administration developed, must have resulted in screening out more of the weaker cases. Perhaps the increase in charges filed after the end of the war also brought more weak cases, some of them really grievances or other disputes calling for settlement by collective bargaining, which inevitably led to more withdrawals. Moreover, as it became clearer that the more obvious kinds of antiunion activities were proscribed, violations or alleged violations became more subtle and harder to prove. Always some of the charges filed were without merit, some of them being filed merely for propaganda as an organizing device. The question remains, nevertheless, whether inadequate funds and staff may not have resulted in a failure to enforce the law in some instances, which was reflected in

12. There was a rather general feeling that the Board applied somewhat different standards of decision after the November, 1946, election. Cf. comments on "administrative legislation" by the *Labor Relations Reporter*, 19 (March 3, 1947), Analysis 75; *Business Week*, March 8, 1947, pp. 5–6; *CIO News*, March 10, 1947, p. 13.

the large proportion of withdrawals. It was during 1945, when the staff was swamped with Smith-Connally strike votes, that the withdrawals rose most sharply,[13] and they continued high during the final two years when the staff was small relative to the new level of cases. The heavy case load, with a necessary priority for representation cases, resulted in long delay for complaint cases. Sometimes the evidence could no longer be obtained when investigation finally got under way, although there may have been a good case originally, and sometimes unions withdrew cases, thinking that it would be impossible to get any relief. All these factors undoubtedly resulted in failure to file at all many cases where unions were sure that the law was being violated, and probably resulted in a failure of the Board effectively to enforce the Act in some of the cases actually filed. The fact that more than 2,000 complaint cases were still pending when the Wagner Act came to an end, in spite of the very large numbers withdrawn and dismissed, also suggests that the Board had not been able fully to perform its duty of protecting labor's rights under the Act.

As to the right of employers to a fair administration, many discussions of the experience under the Act neglect to emphasize that the original investigation and, where necessary, the formal hearing and Board order resulted in a screening process by which the majority of employers were cleared of the charge of violation of the Act. Over the twelve-year period, in the more than 43,000 complaint cases closed, only about 45 per cent found employers guilty of violations. These were in the cases adjusted, or closed on compliance with Intermediate Report or Board or court order. During the last year the proportion found to have violated the Act dropped to 25.5 per cent. Unions of course felt that the actual violations were much greater. There is considerable support for the inference that for many years the Board had leaned over backward in its efforts to avoid unfairness to employers. It is significant that even after the careful preliminary screening through all the earlier phases of investigation and prosecution, in its final decisions on contested unfair labor practice cases the Board completely dismissed the complaint in 268[14] instances, more than 12 per cent of all during the twelve years. Very frequently, in addition, it dismissed some of the charges and found employers guilty of only a part of the violations alleged in the formal complaint.

When employers refused to comply with its orders, the only re-

13. Withdrawals before formal action were 43.1 per cent of complaint cases closed in 1943–44; 51.5 in 1944–45; 57.1 in 1945–46; 56.5 in 1946–47.

14. Computed from *Annual Reports.* This is an average of over twenty cases for each of the twelve years.

course for the Board was to ask the circuit court of appeals for an enforcement order. In the early years the Board took a few carefully selected cases to the courts, in order to establish the basic principles of the Act, and other cases reached the courts on appeal of employers for review. Later, court orders in litigated cases ran in some years as high as one-fourth or even one-third of the number of Board orders of

TABLE 2*

RESULTS OF LITIGATION FOR ENFORCEMENT OR REVIEW
OF BOARD ORDERS JULY 5, 1935, TO JUNE 30, 1947,
BY FISCAL YEARS

RESULTS	1935–40		1941–45		1946–47		1935–47	
	No.	Per Cent	No.	Per Cent	No.	Per Cent	No.	Per Cent
Cases decided by U.S. Circuit Court of Appeals.	133	100.0	461	100.0	111	100.0	705	100.0
Board orders enforced in full.................	53	39.8	293	63.6	74	66.7	420	59.6
Board orders enforced with modification.....	50	37.6	117	25.4	18	16.2	185	26.2
Board orders set aside...	27	20.3	46	10.0	16	14.4	89	12.6
Remanded to Board....	3	2.3	5	1.0	3	2.7	11	1.6
Cases decided by U.S. Supreme Court.........	22	100.0	30	100.0	7	100.0	59	100.0
Board orders enforced in full.................	18	81.8	22	73.4	5	71.4	45	76.3
Board orders enforced with modification.....	2	9.1	6	20.0	1	14.3	9	15.2
Board orders set aside...	2	9.1	0	......	......	......	2	3.4
Remanded................	......	......	1	3.3	1	14.3	2	3.4
Board's request for remand or modification of enforced order denied................	......	......	1	3.3	......	......	1	1.7

* Compiled from *Twelfth Annual Report*, p. 41, and earlier *Annual Reports*.

the previous year. The Board had an increasing degree of success in its cases, as is shown in Table 2. In the crucial Supreme Court decisions on appeal from the circuit courts, of 59 cases, only 2 Board decisions were set aside, and 9 others modified, while the Board's orders were enforced in full in 45 cases. The circuit courts early were skeptical of the Act and the Board and set aside about 2 in 10 orders coming before them, and modified another 4, enforcing only 4 in full. After 1940, however, the number of orders set aside decreased to about 10 per cent in the subsequent five-year period and about 14 per cent in the last two years. Moreover, the orders enforced in full jumped to nearly two-thirds of the total. By the end of the twelve-year period, of 705 circuit court orders, 420, or 59.6 per cent, had enforced Board orders in full, another 26.2 per cent enforced with modifications, and only 12.6 per cent set orders aside. In the last year 70 per cent of the orders enforced Board orders in full. The record is an outstandingly good one in comparison with records of other administrative agencies in their first decades or later.[15]

In a final small number of cases it was necessary for the Board to bring employers back into court on contempt charges, in order to

15. Comparisons of the Board's record in the Supreme Court in the ten years 1937–47 with those of the first ten years' litigation of some of the other agencies are all to the credit of the NLRB. The Interstate Commerce Commission in its first ten years in the Supreme Court, 1892–1901, had no order enforced in full, one enforced in part, ten set aside. The Federal Trade Commission, 1920–29, had three orders enforced in full, one enforced with modifications, and eleven set aside. In the period 1926–38, also, the record of four agencies in the Supreme Court can be summarized as follows, from D. O. Bowman, *Public Control of Labor Relations* (New York: Macmillan Co., 1942), pp. 453–54.

DECISIONS OF SUPREME COURT, 1926–38 TERMS	BOARD OF TAX APPEALS		FEDERAL TRADE COMMISSION		INTERSTATE COMMERCE COMMISSION		NATIONAL LABOR RELATIONS BOARD	
	No.	Per Cent	No.	Per Cent	No.	Per Cent	No.	Per Cent
Total orders reviewed.....	157	100	8	100	57	100	14	100
Affirmed...............	94	60	4	50	41	72	10	27
Modified...............	3	2					2	14
Reversed..............	60	38	4	50	16	28	2	14

A more recent analysis of decisions of the Supreme Court in administrative agency cases in the 1941–46 terms shows the following. It notes that the NLRB was "the most effective agency" in securing Court approval of its actions. C. Herman Pritchett, *The Roosevelt Court: A Study in Judicial Politics and Values, 1937–47* (New York: Macmillan Co., 1948), pp. 189–90.

AGENCY	TOTAL DECISIONS OF SUPREME COURT, 1941–46 TERMS	DECISIONS UPHOLDING AGENCY	
		Number	Per Cent of Total
All agencies.........................	146	104½	72
National Labor Relations Board.......	28	24	86
Securities and Exchange Commission..	9	7	78
Federal Power Commission..........	10	7½	75
Interstate Commerce Commission.....	46	34	74
Wage and Hour Administration.......	21	14	67
Office of Price Administration........	19	12	63
Federal Trade Commission..........	5	3	60
Federal Communications Commission..	8	3	38

obtain compliance with the order of the court. Sometimes, especially in the early years, the employer was in flagrant disregard of the court's order. More often later there was a difference of opinion between the employer and the Board as to whether he was complying in full with the requirements of the order. Since a finding of contempt is an extreme measure, laying the one guilty open to punishment at the will of the court, courts apply very stringent rules of proof, requiring "clear and convincing evidence"[16] before they make a finding of con-

TABLE 3*

PETITIONS FOR CONTEMPT ADJUDICATION FILED BY THE
NATIONAL LABOR RELATIONS BOARD, 1937–47

YEAR PETITION FILED	NUMBER FILED	RESULTS		
		Compliance before Court Action	Employer Held in Contempt	Petition Denied
1937–38........	2	....	....	2
1938–39........	2	....	1	1
1939–40........	10	2	4	4
1940–41........	14	6	7	1
1941–42........	19	4	10	5
1942–43........	10	7	3	....
1943–44........	7	3	3	1
1944–45........	4	....	2	1
1945–46........	2	....	....	2
1946–47........	4	....	3	1
Total.......	74†	22	33‡	18‡

* Compiled from *Compliance Problems*, study made for the NLRB, July, 1944, *Annual Reports*, and other data supplied by the Board.
† One case was still pending in 1949.
‡ In several, part of the issues were settled by agreement before adjudication.

tempt. Hence the Board was hesitant to attempt use of this final weapon, and indeed its first attempts were discouraging. Nevertheless, as appears in Table 3, when petitions for contempt were filed, it succeeded increasingly in convincing the courts that their orders had been violated. Of a total of 74 such petitions filed, to the end of the fiscal year 1946–47, 22 resulted in compliance before it was necessary for the court to act. In 33 cases employers were found in contempt and obeyed the order of the court in order to purge themselves of the contempt. It is significant that no employer suffered any penalty as a result of his defiance of the court in these cases. In 18 instances the

16. Cf. Kansas City Power & Light Co. v. NLRB, 137 F. 2d 77 (C.C.A.8, 1943).

petitions were dismissed. In later years the Board followed the practice of asking courts to remand certain cases to the Board after enforcement, in order that the Board might determine such technical matters as the amount of back pay due. This practice, initiated by the Second Circuit Court of Appeals, seemed more appropriate than contempt action for the settlement of some of the more technical aspects of compliance.[17] The possibility of contempt action continued to be a necessary weapon for an occasional flagrant case.

Of the representation cases filed over the years, nearly half were reported as adjusted without formal action. Agreements for consent elections or cross-check of cards against pay rolls accounted for 24,520 of these, or 42 per cent of all cases closed. Unions were recognized by agreement in another 5.5 per cent of the cases. And 445 cases were adjusted, following a prehearing election, in the last two years. The proportion of cases that could be adjusted informally decreased during the war years but rose to nearly 53 per cent in the last year under the influence of the efficient and equitable device of the prehearing election. In the final year consent elections reached their peak of 4,825, or 46 per cent of all cases closed. About 25 per cent of all petitions also were withdrawn or dismissed informally during the years.

When representation cases required formal action, a few more were adjusted or otherwise disposed of before hearing, but the larger group, about 15 per cent of all in the twelve years, had formal hearings and Board-ordered elections, and another 4 per cent had stipulated elections providing for Board certification of a winning union. In the last year, again the beneficial effect of the prehearing election device was shown in a marked drop in the proportion of cases requiring Board-ordered elections, to only 8 per cent of all cases closed, while in only 1.6 per cent was it necessary for the Board to hold a hearing and make a decision in situations where prehearing elections had already been held. In that final year there were 876 ordered elections, 571 stipulated elections, 644 prehearing elections, 4,183 consent elections, and 646 consent "cross-checks" of union cards against pay rolls.

In the final year of the Wagner Act the Board succeeded in closing only 62 per cent of the complaint cases and 80 per cent of the representation cases on its docket. It ended the Wagner period, on August 21, 1947, with 2,093 unfair labor practice cases and 1,840 representation cases still pending.

17. *Eleventh Annual Report*, p. 65; *Twelfth*, pp. 60–61.

From the Wagner Act to Taft-Hartley

Full appraisal of the work of the Board and its results needs the study of major types of cases which is to follow in the next chapters. Some objective evidence of results, however, may well be considered here. First is the matter of the remedies obtained as a result of adjustments or of compliance with Board orders in unfair labor practice cases. In the twelve years of the Wagner Act some 19,500 cases ended in compliance after informal or formal action by the Board. What was involved, objectively, in this compliance? Unfortunately the records for the first three years are incomplete. But in the remaining nine years, 8,156 employers posted notices in conspicuous places in their plants, mines, offices, or other places of employment, indicating to their employees that in accordance with a law of the United States they would refrain from interfering with the right of self-organization, or specified violations of the law, and that they would do certain specified things, such as reinstate employees who had been discriminated against, often with back pay, cease recognition of company unions or of other unions with whom they had made contracts in violation of the majority preference of employees, or bargain collectively with a specified union which was the majority choice of the employees. Concrete evidence of the effect, if any, of these notices, is not available, but there are indications that to at least some of the workers this first evidence of the interest of the federal government in their affairs was dramatic and effective.

More concrete and direct in its effects was the disestablishment of company unions as bargaining representatives. While the largest number of company-union charges was filed in 1937–38, from 1939 on a total of 1,709 such plans were ended directly as a result of Board cases. Many more must have come to an end without direct disestablishment orders or adjustments, as employers learned that they were illegal and as legitimate labor organizations moved in and took over by organizing and winning elections. Related to this was the beginning of collective bargaining, after unions had filed charges of refusal to bargain, in some 5,000 cases from 1939 to 1947. A relatively small number this seems, but the possibility of such orders, and the knowledge of what the Act meant by bargaining in good faith, must have had a much broader effect than indicated merely by these numbers.

The most directly effective remedy was that of the order of reinstatement and back pay. Workers reinstated to remedy discriminatory discharge numbered 76,268 from 1938 to 1947, in addition to 226,488

88

strikers reinstated, and 727 workers placed on preferential hiring lists, since no opening was available for them at the time. Back pay amounting to $12,418,000 was paid to 40,691 workers in the last nine years. The payment of back pay, to compensate workers for losses due to discrimination by employers, was the one remedy under the Act which involved in effect a penalty for violations. Experience indicates that back pay, along with the reinstatements, provided probably the most effective deterrent to the antiunion employer from open violation of the Act as well as the best evidence that the law did actually provide some protection to workers who wished to exercise their right to engage in union activity.

The results of the representation cases are highly significant, also, for their indication both of the freely expressed desires of American workers as to union representation and of the extent to which the merits of claims for recognition were determined by the peaceful processes provided by the Act. Unfortunately, no complete information is available as to the extent to which stable collective bargaining followed the winning of elections by unions. But of the total of 36,969 elections and cross-checks conducted by the Board in its twelve years, 30,110, or more than four of every five, were won by unions. More than 80 per cent of the votes, or 6,145,834 against 1,531,-301, were cast in favor of representation by a union. This is especially significant, since three-fourths or more of the elections involved only one union rather than a contest between unions. Union success in elections was greatest in 1937, when unions won over 94 per cent of the elections and nearly 87 per cent of the votes, and in 1942 and 1943, when they won 86 per cent of the elections and more than 82 per cent of the votes. After the war the record dropped somewhat, as they attempted to win elections in new territory, geographically and industrially; but even in 1947, in the midst of a vigorous propaganda drive against the Act and unions, labor organizations were able to win 75 per cent of the elections and 77 per cent of the votes cast. Here is one electorate, moreover, which takes its democratic power and responsibility seriously and turns out to vote. In the early years valid votes cast sometimes ran as high as 90 per cent of those eligible to vote and from 1942 to 1946 ranged from 80 to 83 per cent. Interestingly, 86.2 per cent voted in 1947, an unusually high proportion which was perhaps related to the fact of a higher than usual nonunion vote in that last year.

The AFL affiliates won 12,353 elections during the twelve years, the CIO 13,837, and unaffiliated unions 3,920, while 6,859 elections were won by none. The relative success of the various union groups was not greatly different over the whole period. From July 1, 1937, to December 31, 1946, a period for which information is available, the AFL unions won 65.4 per cent of the elections in which they participated, the CIO unions 69.9 per cent of theirs, and unaffiliated unions 58.9 per cent of theirs. The CIO unions were markedly more successful at first. The AFL unions gained rapidly and toward the end of the war were a close second, while in the last two years their rate of winnings declined less than did that of CIO affiliates. Unaffiliated unions started with a lower rate of success but increased markedly, due in part to the shift to unaffiliated status of the Machinists and for a time the Mine Workers. For the year 1946–47 the unaffiliated unions were more successful than either AFL or CIO, winning 65.3 per cent of their elections, compared to 61.3 for the AFL and 62.7 for the CIO. In view of the frequently made allegations of disparity in treatment by the Board of independent unions and others, it is significant also that, for the 1937–46 period used above, independent unions participated in 89 elections for every 100 petitions which they filed, compared to 78 for the CIO and 75 for the AFL.[18]

There was variation between different industries and areas over the years in the success of unions in winning elections, as is shown in the *Annual Reports.* Certain industries, such as textiles and clothing, furniture manufacture, and retail and wholesale trade, stand out year after year with unusually large percentages of elections lost by the unions. Some of the reasons will be suggested in later discussion of cases. In the last year of the Wagner Act, however, in face of the hostility of the press and influential forces in the community, unions won nearly 59 per cent of their elections in textiles, 69 per cent in the clothing industries, 72 per cent in furniture and lumber and in food products, 75 per cent in wholesale trade, and 64 per cent in retail trade, to name only some of the important industries where there were many elections and a smaller than average success in winning elections.

One type of election of special interest, though it is only a minority of all, is that where one union held a contract and under appropriate circumstances the Board nevertheless directed an election. Rival unions won a substantial proportion of such elections. In all cases where the Board ordered an election although there was a closed-shop contract, between July 1, 1940, and November 30, 1942, the petition-

18. Statement of Chairman Herzog, U.S. Senate, Committee on Labor and Public Welfare, *Hearings, Labor Relations Program,* 80th Cong., 1st Sess., 1947, Pt. 4, p. 1912.

ing unions won 46 per cent of the 95 elections. In 140 elections during the same period ordered in the face of nonclosed-shop contracts, the petitioners won 72 per cent.[19] In the year 1946–47 also there were 47 Board-ordered elections in which a contract was held by a union which did not participate in the election, and 40, or 85 per cent, of the elections were won by the petitioning union. At the same time 237 elections were ordered in which a union holding a contract intervened. Of these elections, 139, or 59 per cent, were won by the petitioning union. The inference seems justified that such elections tend to promote democratic and responsible collective bargaining by permitting a bargaining agent which is not the choice of the majority of the employees to be replaced by another, through an election at a proper time.

It was sometimes argued that the readiness of the Board to hold elections, although a bargaining agent had been established, encouraged instability in bargaining relations—or, on the contrary, that "certifications tended to be permanent," that employees could never "free themselves" from a union once intrenched. While there is no conclusive evidence, neither presumption seems to be justified by the facts available. It has been seen that the Board's processes did make it possible for dissatisfied workers to change their bargaining agent. Moreover, there were many other cases where the union lost the support of employees and became inactive, and recognition lapsed. But evidence from a number of studies made for the Board indicates that a representation question settled by election tended to remain settled, for at least some years, as was indicated by the absence of later petitions to the Board within the period studied. In only a very small minority of the cases were numerous successive elections held for choice of bargaining representatives.[20] In only 82 cases in a four-year period ending July 1, 1946, was there a second election within a year.

Strikes for recognition were not eliminated by the work of the NLRB, in spite of its provision of a peaceable means of settling issues over claims to recognition. The United States Department of Labor reports almost 10,000 strikes involving the issue of recognition from 1935 through 1946,[21] 2,200 of which occurred during the great organization drive of 1937. Included, however, are intrastate disputes not

19. National Labor Relations Board, *Studies of the Results of National Labor Relations Board Activities* (Washington: Government Printing Office, 1946), pp. 76–81.

20. *Ibid.*, pp. 84–85.

21. Compiled from annual reports on strikes, *Monthly Labor Review*, 64 (1947), 780–800, and earlier numbers.

under the Act. Moreover, strikes over this issue, which were 30 per cent or more of all strikes in 1934 and the first years of the Act, greatly decreased during the war to less than 500 annually, under 10 per cent of all strikes, and even in 1946 were back only to 16 per cent. Meantime the 37,000 elections conducted by the Board during the twelve years prevented many potential strikes and developed habits of peaceable procedures. The increase in recognition strikes in the two postwar years can probably be attributed in large measure to the fact that inadequate appropriations for the Board made it impossible for the staff to handle cases promptly and led many unions to resort to use of their economic power in order to avoid delays.

It was frequently charged during the debate on the amendment of the Wagner Act after the war that the Act had increased strikes rather than reduced them, as had been the stated purpose of the Act.[22] The Act did not deal with the matter of preventing strikes, however, except as it was intended to remove "the causes of certain substantial obstructions to the free flow of commerce." This was done, as shown above, in so far as use of the orderly processes provided by the Board reduced the use of the strike for recognition. It is desirable, however, to look somewhat more carefully than was often done at the facts as to strikes during the twelve years of the Act in comparison with earlier times of stress. Although the working force increased to unprecedented levels, and union membership more than trebled during the life of the Act, the percentage of all employees who were engaged in strikes during the year never reached the 1919 level of 20.8. From 1935 to 1941 it fluctuated between 2.3 and 8.4 in different years, with no clear trend. In 1945 and 1946, years of postwar adjustment and strife, it reached only 12.2 and 14.5 per cent. The estimated percentage of all working time lost by strikes, also, which had been 0.37 per cent in 1927, the first year for which the figure is available, from 1935 through 1941 fluctuated between .10 and .32, except for the one year (1937) when during the great upswing in organization it reached .43 per cent. From 1942 to 1944 it sank to the very low levels of .05, .15, and .09, respectively, and in 1945 and 1946 rose to only .47 and 1.43 per cent of available working time.[23] It is well known that wage disputes were the major cause of the strikes in the postwar period. The National Labor Relations Act could be blamed for that strife only on

22. Cf. U.S. House of Representatives, Committee on Education and Labor, *Labor-Management Relations Act, 1947*, Report No. 245, 80th Cong., 1st Sess., April 11, 1947, pp. 10–11; Theodore R. Iserman, *Industrial Peace and the Wagner Act* (New York: McGraw-Hill Book Co., 1947), pp. 14–15.

23. *Monthly Labor Review,* 64 (1947), 782. Cf. *infra,* ch. 8, pp. 300–302.

an assumption that a strong labor movement which the Act had made possible was undesirable from the standpoint of public welfare. In any case, public action to encourage peaceful settlement of labor disputes, other than those in regard to claims to recognition, had purposely not been put within the sphere of action of the NLRB.

Finally the question must be considered whether the Act and its administration were actually responsible for the trebling of union membership and the extension of collective bargaining until it covered nearly half of all workers in those large segments of the economy where unions were attempting to organize. The question as put cannot be answered, except to say that the protection given by the Act undoubtedly was one of the major factors that made possible so rapid a development during little more than a decade. Without the Act it is hardly conceivable that by 1946 even with the active business and full employment of the war and postwar periods, so many of the basic industries could have had from 80 to almost 100 per cent of their wage-earners covered by union agreements, with many other industries having a coverage of 40 per cent or more of the workers.[24]

More specific evidence is available from some sample studies of the results of Board cases to indicate that collective bargaining resulted in a large majority of establishments where NLRB unfair labor practice cases had been adjusted or had resulted in compliance after Board orders. One such study of all cases adjusted or closed on compliance in the two years 1941 and 1942, in six of the Board's regional offices, found collective bargaining in effect in about two-thirds of the cases by 1943. The proportion was a little more in the cases adjusted, and in those at the other extreme where there had been court orders, and a little less where there had been only Board orders or consent decrees. It was a little less in cases where there had been only charges of discrimination or charges of general interference only, types of cases which arose often in early stages of organization campaigns. It was larger where company unions had been disestablished and more than 80 per cent after charges of refusal to bargain. The union which filed the original charge was the bargaining representative in more than 60 per cent of the informal cases and in half of the formal ones, with some other union established in 10 per cent of the latter, and in about 7 per cent of the adjusted cases. In about a third of the cases, however, no union had won recognition by the time the study was made.[25] It was estimated that nearly three-fourths of the em-

24. *Monthly Labor Review*, 64 (1947), 766.
25. NLRB, *Studies of Results*, pp. 4–10.

ployees involved in these cases were covered by collective bargaining at the time the study was made, although the United States Bureau of Labor Statistics estimated about that time that the coverage of union agreements in general was 45 per cent of all workers in private industry and 60 per cent of wage-earners in manufacturing. It seems a fair conclusion, therefore, that the Board's success in obtaining compliance with the law in these cases resulted in a larger degree of coverage by union agreement than was true generally at the time. While later charges of violation of the law were filed in 17 per cent of the formal cases and 19 per cent of those adjusted, these were sustained, or were still pending when the study was made, in only 4 per cent of the formal cases and less than 10 per cent of the adjusted ones.[26] A high degree of success in obtaining compliance with the law and a subsequent more than average coverage by collective bargaining agreements seem to have resulted from this representative sample of the Board's work during the period.

Comparable results were found in a study of cases where company-dominated unions had been disestablished during the two years 1940–42. By 1943 collective bargaining was found under way in 70 per cent of the cases where there had been informal adjustments and in 68 per cent where they had been closed on compliance after formal orders. Collective bargaining was less extensive, however, following cases where there had also been discrimination and more extensive where unions already had a majority of the employees and had obtained orders upon the companies that they must bargain with the union. Even when cases had been fought through the courts and were not closed on compliance until more than three years after the charge was filed, 33 of 48, or more than two-thirds, reported collective bargaining in effect by 1943.[27] It is clear that after violations of the Act were eliminated, however long it might take, in a large majority of cases unions finally succeeded in establishing collective bargaining relationships.

26. *Ibid.*, pp. 10–12.　　　27. *Ibid.*, pp. 22–29.

CHAPTER 4

FREEDOM FROM INTERFERENCE
AND THE RIGHT TO BARGAIN

T HE National Labor Relations Board had as its first duty to
protect employees from interference by employers with their
rights under the Act. Many employers of course continued as
before to accept unions and to bargain collectively with them. But in
the early years of the Act the Board's case records were full of instances where other employers violated the Act blatantly, violently,
using spies to report on activities of union adherents and to undermine union organizations, discriminating against employees for union
activities, instigating violence, establishing and maintaining company-dominated unions, refusing the right of collective bargaining to
legitimate organizations representing the majority of the employees
concerned, and in other ways coercing employees and interfering with
the rights guaranteed by the Act. As time went on and the policies of
the Act gained more acceptance, the lurid cases became fewer in
number, and the complaint cases coming to the Board more often involved issues of subtle violations and more technical questions of fact
and law as to the rights of employees and employers under the Act.
A decreasing proportion of complaint cases and an increase in representation cases further indicated that to some extent the Board had
accomplished its first major job of eliminating from American industrial life the bitter opposition to the right of labor to organize which
had characterized large sections of it before.

The work of the Board can be described in rather broad terms by
using a series of key cases which illustrate some of the most important
basic policies. No attempt will be made here to discuss all points
which were important in the decisions that filled seventy-four volumes
by the end of the Wagner Act period.[1] Leaving technicalities for

1. A note on method. This and the following chapters attempt to give a balanced discussion of the major trends of policy and the relationship of particular
parts of that policy to the whole. It is hoped to avoid any basis for criticisms such
as have been made of certain earlier studies of Board policy which emphasized
single cases or details of cases, sometimes out of context. The sweeping criticisms

other places and discussions, we are concerned here only with the most basic policies and their impact on industrial relations, how they worked in practice, and what problems remained to be solved.[2] The present chapter deals with crucial unfair labor practice cases and principles and their effects, the next with representation cases, and chapter 6 with a series of difficult and more controversial issues with which the Board struggled during its life.

Much of the typical experience under the Act is summed up by the important case in which the Supreme Court decided the constitutional question, that of Jones and Laughlin Steel Corporation.[3] This company, like most of the basic steel industry, had fought unionization for many years. The company dominated the life of Aliquippa, the site of its main plant. In June, 1933, during the NRA, the company established an employee representation plan and invited employees to elect representatives. A year later when the Amalgamated Association of Iron, Steel and Tin Workers tried to organize, its efforts were met by a systematic campaign of terror. Officers were shadowed by the "J and L Police"; the house of one at which an organization meeting had been held was surrounded continuously, and persons entering were noted and questioned; some were beaten as they walked on the streets. It was impossible in the fall of 1934 to obtain a place for a public meeting in Aliquippa, and the union had to cross the river to Ambridge to meet in an open lot. The first open meeting in Ambridge was addressed by Mrs. Pinchot, wife of the governor of the state. After the NIRA was declared unconstitutional, in May, 1935, foremen put pressure on employees to vote in the elec-

---

of Board policies made by these studies we think are not justified by the facts. Cf. Harold W. Metz and Meyer Jacobstein, *A National Labor Policy* (Washington: Brookings Institution, 1947); Theodore R. Iserman, *Industrial Peace and the Wagner Act* (New York: McGraw-Hill Book Co., 1947). On the Brookings study, cf. Senator Wayne L. Morse, *Labor and Nation*, 3 (May–June, 1947), 14–16, and further correspondence by Harold G. Moulton, president of Brookings Institution, Senator Morse, and Dr. William M. Leiserson, in *ibid.*, 3 (July–August, 1947), 36–40. On the Iserman book, cf. E. E. Witte, *Journal of Political Economy*, 55 (1947), 479; *Harvard Law Review*, 60 (1947), 682; cf. also footnote comment on both books in "The Taft-Hartley Act: An Administrative Chimera," *University of Pennsylvania Law Review*, 96 (1947), 67.

2. The *Annual Reports* of the Board give useful summaries of policies, and there are numerous professional journal articles on particular points. A brief summary of principles to 1947 is available in Charles O. Gregory and Harold A. Katz, *Policy Development under the National Labor Relations Act* (Chicago: Industrial Relations Center, University of Chicago, 1947). (Processed.)

3. 1 NLRB 503 (1936), enforced April 12, 1937, in NLRB v. Jones and Laughlin Steel Corp., 301 U.S. 1 (1937).

tions under the employee representation plan; moreover, an apparently systematic campaign was begun, which continued over a period of months, to break the union by discharging active members and officers. Under the NLRA, however, after July 5, 1935, such discrimination was unlawful. After charges were filed, the Board itself heard the evidence in open hearing, taking evidence on the background for whatever light it threw on the motives of the company, and found that ten men had been discriminatorily discharged. They included the president, vice-president, and financial secretary of the local union and others "active and vigorous in pursuit of the union's aim." As the Board described it:

> In nearly every case the pattern is the same. The victim is an old employee—the least length of service seems to have been six years, the longest 26 years. During his entire employment he has served to the apparent satisfaction of the respondent. Then suddenly with seeming caprice he is discharged for a routine fault or omission, to which, normally, slight penalty or no penalty attaches. . . . The cases taken together reinforce each other, reveal the plan.

The Board ordered the company, therefore, to cease any interference or discrimination, to offer reinstatement to the discharged men, and to "make them whole" for any losses suffered as a result of their discharge, by paying them what they would have earned less any amounts earned during the period. The company was required also to post notices in conspicuous places in the works to the effect that it would not discriminate for union activity.

The company's defense was primarily that the Act was unconstitutional, although it pointed out that each discharge involved an admitted fault on the part of the employee. It refused to comply with the order, and, on petition of the Board to the courts for enforcement, the order was ultimately upheld by the Supreme Court. The Court upheld the power of the federal government to regulate labor relations in manufacturing industries; moreover, the procedures under the Act were found to afford proper protection of the rights of the employer. In approving the particular order, the Court pointed out that the Act did not interfere with the employer's normal right to hire and fire but that "the employer may not, under cover of that right, intimidate or coerce its employees."

The outcome was that the company complied with the order, and the union, by then the Steel Workers Organizing Committee, CIO, continued its organizing campaign. In May, 1937, after the Carnegie-Illinois contract had been signed, there was a short strike, followed

97

by an agreement for an NLRB election, which the union won with some 17,000 votes against 7,000 nonunion, and an agreement was signed.[4] The adjustment to the new bargaining relationship was made with surprisingly little friction, and a year or so later both sides were inclined to be proud of their success.[5] Rank-and-file workers in the union offices here and in other steel towns spoke of being treated with more respect, of not being afraid, of union meetings held openly, of grievances settled. One man said: "Things are different now because the union has power. Before the management gave only what it wanted. Now the union helps decide." For the entire steel industry, which had followed much of the pattern of this company, by 1946 more than 80 per cent of the employees were working under union agreements,[6] in contrast to 1935, when nearly three-fourths were covered by company unions.[7] Labor relations in this industry, except for a few remaining spots, had shifted from the level of a fight over the right of collective bargaining through freely chosen labor organizations to that of making collective bargaining work.

Another early case illustrates the use of professional spies and strikebreakers, instigation of violence, and the promotion of back-to-work movements, along with mass discrimination, in an effort to break a strike and destroy effective labor organization. The Remington Rand Company[8] in 1934 signed an agreement with a joint council representing AFL unions in four of its plants, which was later extended to cover several others. Rumors of a pending shift of production to a new plant, about which the union was unable to obtain satisfactory conference with top officials, led to a strike in May, 1936, closing all plants. The union filed charges with the Board of refusal to bargain, discrimination, and other interferences with the rights under the Act. The Board's decision, issued on March 13, 1937, described a planned effort to break the union. Before the strike the employer secured the services of Pearl L. Bergoff, who operated a strikebreaking service, the Burns

4. *Steel Labor*, May 25, 1937, June 5, 1937; Frederick H. Harbison, "Steel" in Twentieth Century Fund, *How Collective Bargaining Works* (New York: Twentieth Century Fund, 1942), p. 525.

5. This was one of the situations studied in the writer's "The New Collective Bargaining in Mass Production: Methods, Results, Problems," *Journal of Political Economy*, 47 (1939), 38–45.

6. *Monthly Labor Review*, 64 (1947), 766.

7. U.S. Bureau of Labor Statistics, *Characteristics of Company Unions, 1935*, Bulletin No. 634, p. 42.

8. Remington Rand, 2 NLRB 626, decided March 13, 1937; cf. also U.S. Senate, Committee on Education and Labor, *Violations of Free Speech and Rights of Labor, Strikebreaking Services*, Report No. 6, Pt. 1, 76th Cong., 1st Sess., 1939, pp. 117–26, cited as *La Follette Committee Reports*.

Detective Agency, and other similar agencies. They supplied spies, strikebreakers, "missionaries" to conduct whispering campaigns and spread propaganda, and "guards" who provoked violence. Thirty union leaders were discharged. Fears of businessmen and of local authorities that the plants would move were stimulated by agents of the company. Rumors of threatened violence were planted, until in Ilion, New York, a "state of emergency" was declared by the town authorities. Then it was easy for foremen to visit employees and induce them to return to work. When all this was successful and the plant opened, the head of the company himself came to a celebration, and congratulated the local businessmen and authorities upon their successful program, which he named "the Mohawk Valley Formula." In other towns also the company succeeded in getting public support, stirring up violence and fear of violence, and promoting back-to-work movements, until the strike was lost.

The Board held that the company by its illegal refusal to bargain collectively had caused and perpetuated the strike and that its efforts to end the strike "by defeating it, in contrast to settling it by the method of collective bargaining," were therefore violations of the Act. It ordered the company to cease all interference with the rights of the employees under the Act and on request to bargain collectively with the union. In addition, to restore the status quo as far as possible, the company was ordered to reinstate with back pay those who had been discriminatorily discharged and to offer reinstatement to all the strikers who had not yet received "regular and substantially similar employment elsewhere." Since one plant had been closed, a new one opened and a substantial amount of equipment shifted, and since large numbers of new employees had been hired after the strike, there were nearly 4,000 employees to be reinstated, displacing the new employees if necessary.

The company announced that it would not obey this order. Before compliance was finally achieved the Board had to obtain a circuit court enforcement order, on February 18, 1938, another order to comply on June 1, 1938, and finally an order holding the company in contempt, on September 29, 1942,[9] and ordering specific reinstatement and back pay in some of the disputed instances. At long last the

9. NLRB v. Remington Rand, 94 F. 2d 862 (C.C.A.2, 1938), cert. den., 304 U.S. 576, 585 (1938); 97 F. 2d 195 (C.C.A.2, 1938); 130 F. 2d 919 (C.C.A.2, 1942). In enforcing the order, the court denied the company's claim that the trial had been unfair, although it said: "The underlying tone and style of the decision may not indeed have evinced that judicial detachment which is the surest guarantee of even justice" (p. 873).

99

highly complex details of compliance were completed and the case closed. Meantime collective bargaining had gone on.[10]

Stories similar in many respects could be repeated from many industries and many parts of the country. In Harlan County, Kentucky, in coal-mining, the Board found management-instigated sluggings and shootings, as well as antiunion propaganda, espionage, threats, and discharges for union activity.[11] In the Tri-State lead-mining area[12] there was use of violence against strikers, intimidation, organization of a company-dominated labor organization, and extensive discrimination for union activity. The Ford Motor Company[13] was found guilty in a number of cases of a relentless campaign of intimidation and coercion against the UAW-CIO, assaulting union organizers, intimidating and coercing employees by using strong-arm squads, distributing antiunion propaganda which was coercive in its effects, spying on its employees, and discriminating for union activity. When the United Rubber Workers began their organization at the Goodyear plant in Gadsden, Alabama,[14] they were met by a campaign of terror in the plant and in the town. There were beatings of union organizers and failure by the company to provide reasonable protection for employees in the plant or to discourage antiunion violence; in addition, a company-dominated union and discrimination against union men were involved. In these and many other such situations it was necessary for the government, through the Board and the courts, to enforce its policy of protecting labor's right to self-organization, before it was possible for the unions to achieve collective bargaining.

These and other cases found in the Board's early records may seem exaggerated. But it is necessary only to turn to the hearings and reports of the La Follette Committee, the Senate committee appointed to investigate violations of free speech and the rights of labor, for further evidence. Its report on industrial espionage[15] listed 1,475 companies which during the years 1933–36 were clients of detective agencies, for "espionage, strikebreaking, guards in connection with

10. In a number of plants union affiliation shifted to the United Electrical, Radio and Machine Workers, CIO, while the Machinists won an election in the Elmira plant in 1942. 41 NLRB 789 (1942). After the passage of the Taft-Hartley Act in 1947, and the refusal of the UE-CIO to qualify for use of the Board's facilities, the company announced that it would not bargain further with the union, claiming that it doubted its majority. Cf. *infra*, ch. 14, pp. 537–39, 555.

11. Clover Fork Coal Co., 4 NLRB 202 (1937).

12. Eagle-Picher Mining and Smelting Co., 16 NLRB 727 (1939).

13. Ford Motor Co., 4 NLRB 621 (1937), 14 NLRB 346 (1939), 26 NLRB 322 (1940), and others.

14. Goodyear Tire and Rubber Co. of Alabama, 21 NLRB 306 (1940).

15. *La Follette Committee Reports, Industrial Espionage*, Report No. 46, Pt. 3, 75th Cong., 2d Sess., Nov. 16, 1937, pp. 26, 28, 74, 79, 89.

labor disputes, or similar service." Expenditures on espionage, munitioning, and strikebreaking in 1933–37, by about 300 companies on which it had evidence, amounted to nearly $9.5 million. Pinkerton spies were operating in practically every union in the country, one hundred of them holding union offices. Demoralization of unions by the fear and suspicion engendered by this system was found again and again. The Committee concluded: "It is safe to say that the right of genuine collective bargaining will never be realized in American industry until the industrial spy is abolished." Further evidence of the extent to which many industries relied on force and intimidation rather than collective bargaining to settle disputes with their workers was given in other reports.[16]

Wherever the Board found evidence of the use of spies to defeat the right of self-organization, it ordered the practice eliminated. An example is again found in one of the first group of cases the Supreme Court decided, that of the Fruehauf Trailer Company.[17] A spy hired by the company had joined the union, became its treasurer, and furnished the company lists of members, some of whom were then discharged.

Another type of weapon against unionization, formerly widely used, was the "yellow-dog contract" by which as a condition of employment men agreed not to join a union. The illegality of such contracts was made clear in an early lumber case.[18] Among other types of intimidation frequently used in the early period under the Act were open interrogation of employees as to their union membership, as in another lumber case,[19] and circulation[20] at company instigation of "loyalty" petitions, renouncing desire for representation by a union. The manifold methods of interference with employees' rights under the Act were met by the Board on a case-to-case basis. Many of them involved the spoken or written word in a context where the Board found it to be coercive and therefore illegal, but this issue of free speech in Board cases will be taken up in a later chapter.

DISCRIMINATION

Discriminating against employees for union activity continued to be the most frequently met violation of the Act. Charges of discrimi-

16. *La Follette Committee Reports, Strikebreaking Services,* Report No. 6, Pt. 1; *Industrial Munitions,* Report No. 6, Pt. 3, 76th Cong., 1st Sess., 1939.
17. Fruehauf Trailer Co., 1 NLRB 68 (1935), enforced in 301 U.S. 49 (1937).
18. Carlisle Lumber Co., 2 NLRB 248 (1936), enforced in NLRB v. Carlisle Lumber Co., 94 F. 2d 138 (C.C.A.9, 1937), cert. den., 304 U.S. 575 (1938).
19. Greensboro Lumber Co., 1 NLRB 629 (1936).
20. American Manufacturing Co., 5 NLRB 443 (1938).

nation were involved in almost two-thirds of all the complaint cases filed through the years. While the Act was concerned with the public interest in protecting the right to organize rather than private rights, the best preventive against illegal discrimination was to require employers who had been guilty of discrimination to restore the status quo as far as possible. Therefore, as in the cases which we have discussed above, the Board ordered employers to put back the victims of discrimination to their old jobs or substantially similar ones and to make good their loss of earnings.[21]

The Board did not interfere with the employer's right to select his employees, or to discharge for cause, provided the action was not motivated by antiunionism. This was a question of fact in each case, which the Board determined by considering all the evidence, including statements and other actions of supervisors and employers themselves.[22] The care with which these issues were weighed is seen in the decisions themselves where very frequently some of the charges of discrimination were upheld, and others dismissed for want of proof.

Charges of discrimination were made frequently following strikes. The Board held that in strikes caused by unfair labor practices, as in the Remington Rand case, strikers were entitled to reinstatement to their old or similar jobs upon application, even though others hired during or after the strike had to be displaced. No back pay was awarded, however, unless they were discriminated against after their application for reinstatement. The situation was quite different where the strike was only an "economic strike," over issues as to wages and other conditions of employment. There the strikers "took their chances," and if the strike failed, and their jobs had been filled, they had no recourse. Nevertheless, if jobs became available later, the employer might not discriminate among applicants because of their union activity. Thus in the Mackay Radio case, the Supreme Court declared that the employer had the right to fill places of the strikers, but in filling certain jobs which were still available he had arbitrarily discriminated against the union leaders. Accordingly it upheld the Board's order to reinstate these men with back pay from the date of their application.[23] Such protection of strikers from later discrimination did not, however, prevent discharges of strikers who were guilty

21. Cf. *supra*, ch. 3, pp. 78, 88–89.
22. See the Board's discussion of proof of discrimination, in *Third Annual Report*, pp. 81–88.
23. Mackay Radio & Telegraph Co., 1 NLRB 201 (1936), enforced in 304 U.S. 333 (1938).

of such violent and unlawful acts as engaging in sitdown strikes.[24]

In a relatively small proportion of all the discrimination cases the issue arose because of a closed-shop contract, sometimes valid, sometimes illegal because made collusively or as a result of coercion or with a company-dominated union. These special cases are left for later discussion. Here we have been concerned only with the basic protection from antiunion discrimination.

The effects of this protection against discrimination cannot be measured, but they permeated all the work of the Board. As workers who had been discriminated against were put back to work, and given back pay, encouragement was given to others to engage in efforts to organize. A successful discrimination case was widely recognized by unions as a most useful morale-builder and organizing device, and such cases, valid or not, were frequently filed during organization drives. Even when the efforts to organize failed, or strikes were lost, greater confidence in the possibility of ultimate success came from the knowledge that individuals could be protected from reprisals. Conversely, when through poor settlements or unsatisfactory decisions workers failed to receive the protection supposedly guaranteed by the Act, a handicap was imposed which sometimes took years to overcome by successful organization. The sanction of a financial remedy for violation of this section of the Act was a powerful weapon available for use by the Board to prevent infringement of the basic policies of the Act.

COMPANY-DOMINATED UNIONS

To prevent employers' interference in or domination of labor organizations was one of the major duties of the Board under the Wagner Act. In 1935 "company unions," or organizations confined to workers of a particular plant or company,[25] were widespread. A Bureau of Labor Statistics study[26] found them covering one-fifth of all workers in the large sample studied, and one-fourth of those in manufacturing. According to this study

a large number of company unions—more than half— . . . performed none of those functions which are usually embraced under the term "collective bar-

24. NLRB v. Fansteel Metallurgical Corp., 306 U.S. 240 (1939). Cf. Board discussion in U.S. Senate, Committee on Labor and Public Welfare, *Hearings, Labor Relations Program,* 80th Cong., 1st Sess., 1947, Pt. 4, pp. 1921–23, cited as Senate Committee on Labor and Public Welfare, *Hearings, 1947.* For discussion of a trend in later decisions to restrict further the protection of strikers, cf. *infra,* ch. 6, pp. 194–202.

25. *Characteristics of Company Unions,* 1935, p. 3.

26. *Ibid.,* p. 37.

gaining." ... Another group, ... about one-third, were undertaking only a few of the activities in which trade-unions normally engage. ... With careful cooperation by management about half of the company unions in this group had become effective avenues for the adjustment of individual grievances. The third group ... —about 15 per cent of the total studied— were seriously attempting to function in those fields commonly ascribed to collective bargaining. They represented the interests of the workers with a vigor not entirely attributable to management encouragement.[27]

It was to be expected that after "company domination" was made illegal, a large number of charges of such activity would come to the Board, and this was the fact. In the first three years about one of each five charges filed involved this issue, and smaller numbers in later years. Some of them concerned new temporary organizations created to break a strike or fight the effort of a bona fide union to get established. Such organizations appeared in the Remington Rand case[28] and were part of the pattern of illegal conduct by that company. Another early case was that of the Clinton Cotton Mills,[29] of Clinton, South Carolina, where after the 1934 strike of the United Textile Workers, AFL, officers of the union were refused reinstatement, and a so-called Friendship Association was organized with the leadership and active support of overseers and "second hands," who were also supervisors. Many union members joined the association because of fear of losing their jobs. These activities continued after the Wagner Act was in force. Union meetings were spied upon and a number of union members discharged. Finally a closed-shop contract was signed with the association. The Board found unquestionable evidence that the association had been established and dominated by the company through its supervisors and was therefore illegal. The remedy ordered was to cease all such interference, withdraw all recognition from the association as a representative of the employees and "completely disestablish" it as such representative, to offer employment without discrimination, and to "make whole" the employees who had been discriminated against. In addition, the company was to post notices in the mill and the mill village to the effect that the association was disestablished, that membership in the association was not needed for employment, that the contract was null and void, and that the company would not discriminate against members of the union. This case, with endless variations but increasing subtlety, was typical of many that came to the Board through the years.

Company unionism in a purer form, unadulterated by the cruder

27. *Ibid.*, pp. 204–5.   28. 2 NLRB 626 (1937).   29. 1 NLRB 97 (1935).

antiunion tactics of discrimination, espionage, and intimidation, was brought before the Board in some of the cases filed against older employee representation plans or works councils extending back to World War I or NRA company unions. The International Harvester[30] case is one of the former. This decision is interesting for its very detailed description of the organization and functioning of one of the "good company unions." There were annual elections of representatives to the joint council but no membership meetings, no dues, no independent activity of the employees through the organization, and no formal agreements resulting from the meetings of the joint council. Any changes in conditions were announced by the company, not jointly. Inevitably, the Board found that the plan was "the creature of management," completely controlled by management, and therefore illegal under the Act. The employees under it possessed "only the shadow, not the substance, of collective bargaining." The company was ordered therefore to withdraw all recognition from the plan and completely disestablish it as representative, "since disestablishment is the only effective remedy in the case." The company at first appealed to the circuit court for review. After the Act was held constitutional, however, the company accepted the order and announced to its employees that the plan was being dropped and that it was for the employees themselves to decide how they wished to deal with the company.[31] An independent union won a consent election the following year at Fort Wayne, the locale of this case, but eventually the UAW-CIO won bargaining rights there, as well as in some other plants of the company.

"Disestablishment," or the requirement of "refraining from bargaining with an organization corrupted by unfair labor practices," had been used, and approved by the Supreme Court, as a remedy in cases under the Railway Labor Act and was noted in reports of congressional committees when the Wagner Act was under consideration. In the first Wagner Act case which raised the issue the Supreme Court upheld the Board, saying: "There was ample basis for its conclusion that withdrawal of recognition of the Association by the respondents, accompanied by suitable publicity, was an appropriate way to give effect to the policy of the Act."[32] Even where there was evidence that employees favored the old plan, the Court held that the Board could disestablish, when it concluded that "the purpose

30. 2 NLRB 310 (1936).
31. *New York Times*, April 22, 1937, p. 10.
32. NLRB v. Pennsylvania Greyhound Lines, 303 U.S. 261, 271 (1938).

of the law could not be attained without complete disestablishment of the existing organization which had been dominated or controlled to a greater or less extent" by the employer.[33]

Once these policies were established, many of the old company unions went out of existence, and their place was taken by new so-called "independent unions." The issue then arose whether these were truly independent organizations or whether they were merely successors which still carried the influence of the earlier employer domination. For example, the Westinghouse Electric and Manufacturing Company had a representation plan dating back to 1919. A case came to the Board involving one of the plants, where in 1933 the plan had been somewhat changed and in 1937, after the CIO began organization, had been replaced with an "independent" under the leadership of representatives under the old plan. The Board found that the plan had never been formally "disestablished" by the company, that there was no "line of fracture" between it and the independent, and that the employees had never been advised by the company of the separation or that the company was indifferent whether they joined the new union. Under the circumstances the Board found the independent company-dominated and ordered its disestablishment, and the courts agreed.[34]

Later history in the International Harvester Company illustrates developments in many companies and industries after the old company unions were found to be illegal. After the company ceased recognition of the old works council plans, independent unions were organized in many plants by leaders among the old employee representatives. In 1938 the company reported that it had fourteen con-

33. NLRB v. Newport News Shipbuilding and Dry Dock Co., 308 U.S. 241, 251 (1939).

34. 18 NLRB 300 (1939), enforced in Westinghouse Electric and Manufacturing Co. v. NLRB, 112 F. 2d 657 (C.C.A.2, 1940), 312 U.S. 660 (1941).

Somewhat similar issues were involved in the Western Union case decided about the same time and in the Southern Bell Telephone and Telegraph Co. case. In the former the circuit court, in enforcing the Board's order except for the reimbursement of checked-off dues which had been ordered, said: ". . . Some . . . absolute and public cleavage between the old and the new was a condition upon further recognition of the Association. . . . An unaffiliated union, known for long to be favored by the employer, carries over an advantage which necessarily vitiates its standing as exclusive bargaining agent. It cannot remain such until measures are taken to disabuse the employees of any belief that they will win the employer's approval if they remain in it, or incur his displeasure if they leave." Western Union Telegraph Co. v. NLRB, 113 F. 2d 992, 996 (C.C.A.2, 1940), enforcing 17 NLRB 34 (1939). Cf. also NLRB v. Southern Bell Telephone and Telegraph Co., 319 U.S. 50 (1943), enforcing 35 NLRB 621 (1940).

tracts, three of them with CIO unions, others with local independents.[35] The Farm Equipment Workers Organizing Committee, CIO, however, had filed a series of charges in different plants claiming that the independents were company-dominated. After some time, in 1939 the Board held a hearing on the charges in six plants, but the decision was not issued until February 8, 1941. The company claimed that it had had no part in the organization of the independents—that they were instead the result of the initiative of employees who, after having dealt with the company through the old plan, wanted their independent organizations. The Board, however, found extensive evidence in different plants that management had encouraged the independents in the interest of retaining representation in the hands of "old and trusted councilmen," had disparaged the CIO, and had given preferential treatment to the independents in their campaigns for membership. The Board held, therefore, that company interference had prevented real freedom of choice, and the independents were therefore incapable of functioning as bargaining representatives and must be disestablished.[36] As a result, a series of elections took place in different plants, and by 1947 the company was bargaining in some with the Farm Equipment Workers, CIO, in some with the UAW-CIO, and in still others with independents which had not been successfully challenged and which had won elections.

In later cases the Board continued to apply this test of "cleavage" or what came to be known as the "fracture doctrine." Where it found identity of officers between the old company-dominated union and the new independent, similarity of structure, transfer of assets between the organizations, or evidence of favoritism by the employer, among other factors which indicated that there had not been a sharp break with the past, it continued to order disestablishment. But where there was a distinct "fracture," the employer had announced his disinterestedness to the employees at large, and the facts showed that the current organization was substantially different from the earlier company-dominated union, the Board accepted the independent as bona fide.[37] As time went on and there had been some years of collective bargaining between the successor independents and the companies, the issue developed whether the "fracture" requirement should be rigidly applied or whether rather by the process of growth

35. International Harvester Co., *Employee Relations* (Chicago, 1938).
36. International Harvester Co., 29 NLRB 456 (1941).
37. E.g., in Wisconsin Telephone Co., 12 NLRB 375 (1939). Cf. Board statement in Senate Committee on Labor and Public Welfare, *Hearings, 1947*, Pt. 4, pp. 1912–13.

the once-dominated organization might have become truly independent. In 1944 the Board instructed its Regional Directors to ask advice from Washington before issuing complaints where the charge of company domination was based principally on lack of cleavage of the new organization from an old company union and where two years or more had elapsed since the failure of "fracture." It is probable that as a result many cases were dismissed or otherwise handled informally in the field. In clear cases of company assistance to the independent the Board continued to disestablish.[38] But doubt as to the universal applicability of the "fracture" requirement was shown in a late case, Detroit Edison Company,[39] where a majority of the Board found the independent to be a successor organization which had received the illegal support of the company. Nevertheless, the Board ordered only that the company cease recognition of the association unless and until it should be certified by the Board as bargaining representative. Chairman Herzog believed the effects of the unfair labor practices had

to a large extent been dissipated, and that, on this record, the requisite freedom of self-organization of the employees may be fully restored by posting an appropriate notice for 60 days, without complete disestablishment of the Association. . . . [The] employees should themselves be permitted, after the facts have come to their attention through our order and notices posted for a reasonable period, to decide whether the Association is fit to be their representative.

Outside unions frequently wanted to proceed with elections even when a charge of company domination was pending against an independent union, especially when long delays were to be expected in handling cases. A union which had been found to be company-dominated was of course not permitted on a ballot in an election. Occasionally, in order not to delay unnecessarily the determination of a representation dispute, the Board heard evidence in the representation hearing as to whether an independent was in fact a successor, dominated organization. Sometimes consent elections were held, including

38. As in Tappan Stove Co., 66 NLRB 759 (1946).
39. 74 NLRB 267 (1947). Cf. *infra*, n. 42. Cf. also Western Electric Co., 72 NLRB 738 (1947), where after a long company-union history an independent union was charged with being company-dominated. A Trial Examiner recommended disestablishment in 1945. But before the Board decided the case, which was admittedly a close one, the CIO union asked to withdraw its charge, on the ground that the independent by its 1946 strike had demonstrated its sincerity and good faith. The Board in the end ordered the company to end any discrimination or other interference with the rights of employees but did not require it to cease recognizing the independent.

on the ballot organizations against which charges had been filed and later withdrawn, or waived as a basis for objection to the elections. In rare cases the Board permitted the challenged independent to appear on the ballot in an ordered election, subject to the outcome of the pending complaint case. But, as in two Standard Oil of California cases, if the independents were later found to be company-dominated, elections in which they had won were then set aside.[40]

It was frequently said that the Board's policy toward "company-dominated unions" resulted in unfairness to independent unions and to disregard of the wishes of employees when they preferred such unaffiliated unions rather than the AFL or CIO.[41] But, as we have seen, the Board disestablished "independents" only when there was clear evidence that there had been such interference by the management with the right of employees to an unimpeded free choice, that in its judgment the organization was "company-dominated" and incapable of acting as the independent representative of employees; and the courts upheld the theory of the Board on this point. Every case was decided on its own facts. The record shows that many independents were accepted as bona fide and given the use of the Board's machinery of elections. Chairman Madden testified in 1939 that many unaffiliated unions had been certified by the Board.[42] In the twelve years of the Wagner Act independent unions won 3,920 elections. From July 1, 1937, through December 31, 1946, they were on the ballot in 89 per cent of the cases in which they petitioned, more than

40. 58 NLRB 560 (1944), 61 NLRB 1251 (1945), 63 NLRB 1174 (1945); 58 NLRB 554 (1944), 62 NLRB 449 (1945), 62 NLRB 1068 (1945). See also *Eleventh Annual Report*, p. 11, n. 9; p. 20, n. 55; p. 60.

41. Cf. U.S. Senate, Committee on Labor and Public Welfare, *Federal Labor Relations Act of 1947*, Report No. 105, 80th Cong., 1st Sess., April 17, 1947, p. 12; U.S. House of Representatives, Committee on Education and Labor, *Labor-Management Relations Act, 1947*, Report No. 245, 80th Cong., 1st Sess., April 11, 1947, pp. 7, 29, 38, 42; T. R. Iserman, in U.S. House of Representatives, Committee on Education and Labor, Hearings, *Amendments to the National Labor Relations Act*, 80th Cong., 1st Sess., 1947, Pt. 4, p. 2724, cited as House Committee on Education and Labor, *Hearings, 1947*; T. R. Iserman in Senate Committee on Labor and Public Welfare, *Hearings, 1947*, Pt. 1, pp. 168–72; Earl F. Reed, *ibid.*, Pt. 2, pp. 731–37.

42. U.S. Senate, Committee on Education and Labor, *Hearings, National Labor Relations Act and Proposed Amendments*, 76th Cong., 1st Sess., April, 1939, Pt. 2, pp. 308–11. The Board from 1942 on distinguished cases of assistance to independent unions which it found to fall short of domination, and in such cases ordered only withdrawal and withholding of recognition unless and until the organization was certified by the Board, exactly as it did in such cases of assisted affiliated unions. Heather Handkerchief Works, 47 NLRB 800 (1943) and other cases cited in *Eighth Annual Report*, p. 30.

was true for either AFL or CIO unions. In the last year of the Wagner Act independent unions were involved in about one-sixth of the elections held, and won 860, or 65 per cent of those in which they participated.[43]

Significantly also, though in each of the last two years under the Wagner Act more than three hundred charges of company domination were filed, only 51 company unions were disestablished as a result of Board action in 1946 and only 36 in 1947, in cases closed in those years.[44] Evidently the extreme remedy of disestablishment was rarely used, although allegations of company domination were still filed. Frequently unions found that the only real remedy was to organize and win elections, and they preferred to take their chances with the ballot rather than push for Board action on the charge. Evidence is not available as to whether the increased success of independents in winning elections in the last years of the period may have resulted to some degree from failure of the Board to eliminate remaining instances of illegal company interference in labor organization. Many independents were of course unquestionably bona fide. In any event the record clearly refutes the charge that the Board was unfair to bona fide independents.

The Wagner Act was largely responsible for the elimination of the company union from major sections of the economy where it had been predominant. Such industries as basic steel, agricultural implements, petroleum refining, rubber products, electrical machinery, and meat-packing, where from 50 up to 80 per cent or more of the employees were covered by company unions in 1935, by 1947 had equal or even larger proportions under union agreements.[45] Some independents continued, and there were still charges of company domination. But it was clear from Board cases and the broader experience that when interference by companies in labor organization was made illegal, and eliminated, collective bargaining through legitimate organizations was not long in flowing in to fill the vacuum.[46] Not infrequently where the old plan had been one of the minority which functioned actively to represent employees, not just to keep unions out, that experience served as a training school for management and em-

43. *Twelfth Annual Report*, pp. 73, 89; Senate Committee on Labor and Public Welfare, *Hearings, 1947*, Pt. 4, p. 1912.

44. *Eleventh Annual Report*, pp. 76, 81; *Twelfth*, pp. 68, 72.

45. *Characteristics of Company Unions, 1935*, pp. 42–45; *Monthly Labor Review*, 64 (1947), 766.

46. National Labor Relations Board, *Studies of the Results of NLRB Activities* (Washington: Government Printing Office, 1946), esp. pp. 22–24.

ployees for the more mature system of industrial relations that developed under the Wagner Act. And some at least of the employers, after their adjustment to the new relationship, found even certain advantages to them in the vitality and increased discipline of the new collective bargaining system.

A related and very difficult situation was presented when an employer interfered with his employees' right of self-organization not by supporting a company union but by assistance to a union affiliated with the AFL or the CIO. When the Board found this to be the fact, it ordered the company to cease bargaining with that union, or any favoritism in its behalf, unless and until the union had been certified. These cases will be discussed later,[47] along with other problems arising out of union rivalry.

REFUSAL TO BARGAIN

Successful labor organization normally results in collective bargaining between the representatives of the workers and of the employer or employers to determine basic conditions of wages and hours and many other matters affecting the interests of the two groups. The Wagner Act, accordingly, forbade employers to refuse to bargain with the representatives of their employees chosen by a majority in an appropriate unit as their exclusive representative.[48] This was the crux of the Act, if the congressional purpose of encouraging the practice and procedure of collective bargaining was to be achieved. But these terms needed definition in practice. The Board had no power to engage in conciliation or mediation or to decide the terms of agreements. It could only work out in individual cases the meaning of bargaining in *good faith*, try to induce employers to accept their obligations under the law, and, when necessary, go to court for enforcement of its orders to bargain. It might appear to be difficult for the Board to decide that an employer was failing to bargain in good faith, without indicating what he ought to have agreed upon. In the early days when many of the staff in the field came from experience under the NRA where mediation was part of the function of the old boards, there was undoubtedly some mingling of mediation of disputes with the attempt to secure bargaining in good faith. But as the Board developed its standards, and especially as Board and court decisions clarified the

47. Ch. 6, *infra*, pp. 204–7.
48. Cf. U.S. Senate, Committee on Education and Labor, *National Labor Relations Board*, Report No. 573, 74th Cong., 1st Sess., May 1, 1935, in National Labor Relations Board, *Statutes and Congressional Reports Pertaining to the National Labor Relations Board*, June, 1943, pp. 46–49.

meaning of the obligation under the law, progress was made in separating the narrow function of the Board from that of other agencies concerned with settling industrial disputes.

The first Supreme Court decision[49] on the Act outlined in rather general terms the duty of the employer. He must "treat with" the representatives chosen by the employees and refrain from making an agreement with any other representative, but he was not compelled to *agree*. "The theory of the Act is that free opportunity for negotiation with accredited representatives of employees is likely to promote industrial peace and may bring about the adjustments and agreements which the Act in itself does not attempt to compel." As the individual cases began to come to the Board for decision, some of them, especially in the early days of the Act, were fairly simple and obvious, where there was no real doubt that the union represented a majority of the employees claimed, and where the employer refused to recognize the union, or to meet the representatives, or to discuss terms of a contract with them. Objection to the union, preference for some other union, objection to meeting nonemployee representatives, for instance, or a union's demand for a closed shop, or a strike, were no defense against the duty to bargain. Thus in the Remington Rand case there could be little doubt that the company had refused to bargain with the union that represented its employees, both before and during the strike. Moreover, it was illegal for a company to deny exclusive recognition to the majority union, and, when agreement was reached, it was not enough for the company unilaterally to post a notice of terms, without giving the union credit by a jointly signed document. The principle that the union had a right to insist upon a written agreement, once agreement was reached, was approved by the Supreme Court in the important Heinz case.[50]

After such obvious and objective tests of refusal to bargain had been made clear, the main work of the Board in enforcing this provision of the Act became that of analyzing the myriad individual situations which came before it, to decide in the light of all the circumstances whether or not the employer was bargaining in *good faith*. The requirement never meant that an agreement must in any event be reached. Management had to confer and bargain in good faith—which could be tested by number of conferences held, atti-

49. NLRB v. Jones and Laughlin Steel Corp., 301 U.S. 1, 45 (1937).
50. 10 NLRB 963 (1939), enforced in H. J. Heinz Co. v. NLRB, 311 U.S. 514 (1941). For a good summary of the early cases see *Third Annual Report*, pp. 90–108.

tudes expressed, offers and counteroffers made—but it did not have to agree to anything to which a reasonable man might object under the circumstances. For example, an employer did not have to accede to a demand for the closed shop or similar things. The chief question was the question of fact, in each case, whether the employer entered into discussion "with an open and fair mind, and a sincere purpose to find a basis of agreement . . . and if found to embody it in a contract . . . which shall stand as a mutual guarantee of conduct, and as a guide for the adjustment of grievances."[51] The Board made its decisions on all the facts of the particular case.

For example, there was the case in Knoxville, Tennessee, which according to at least one observer "taught the hosiery industry to bargain."[52] The union had been active from 1934. In a 1939 order the Board had found illegal the company's refusal to sign a written agreement after agreement was reached. In the negotiations that followed that order the company refused full recognition. A resulting strike was settled, but the agreement provided for recognition of the union only until the company should have reason to believe that the union no longer had a majority and petitioned the Board for an election. From 1940 to 1942 some grievances were handled by the union committee—but only by speaking to the superintendent through a window from a passageway into his office or later standing in the passageway —never in the office. No wage increase was ever put into effect, although a Department of Labor survey showed that wages were less than in comparable mills. When a second charge of refusal to bargain was filed and went to hearing, the Trial Examiner found that the union had received such qualified recognition as to be no recognition at all and to make it impossible for it to treat on a basis of equality or as an effective instrument for representation of the employees. He held that the union was entitled to full recognition for a reasonable period of time. Moreover, the negotiations showed opposition to the union, not just to its demands, and gave no indication of good faith in an attempt to reach agreement. The strike had been caused by the refusal to bargain, and there had been discrimination in the refusal to reinstate strikers. Accordingly he recommended that the company bargain and reinstate strikers with back pay. The fact that the back-pay obligation was mounting after the Trial Examiner's Intermediate Report was probably one reason why the company chose to settle the case with a stipulation for a Board order and con-

51. Globe Cotton Mills v. NLRB, 103 F. 2d 91, 94 (C.C.A.5, 1939).
52. Holston Manufacturing Co., 13 NLRB 783 (1939); 46 NLRB 55 (1942).

113

sent decree, without fighting it further through the Board and the courts. Back pay of over $4,000 resulted, and collective bargaining proceeded. But it had been a long time from 1934 before the union finally achieved full recognition.

One of the cases in which the Board and the courts worked out most thoroughly the meaning of lack of good faith in bargaining was that of the Singer Manufacturing Company of South Bend. The case illustrates also the long delays which many unions met as they attempted to secure their rights through using the Board's procedures.[53] When union organization began late in 1936, several conferences took place with the company, but without reaching agreement. From then on there followed occasional fruitless conferences, a charge of refusal to bargain, renewed conferences, a representation election won by the union, more negotiations—until in April, 1939, the union called a strike and filed a second charge of refusal to bargain. The Board issued its decision in June, 1940, finding that the company had failed to bargain in good faith. The Board analyzed in detail the course of negotiations on some of the principal subjects, such as duration of the agreement, wages, hours, seniority, paid holidays and vacations, and discrimination, strikes, and lockouts. It found throughout that the union receded from its original demands and offered many compromise proposals in an effort to reach agreement, but the company continued to insist rigidly upon certain of its demands. A quotation will summarize the Board's findings:

Thus, the United was required to accept the respondent's proposals as to wages, hours, seniority, paid holidays, and vacations—among the most important elements of a collective agreement—without any evidence that such proposals were, as asserted by the respondent, necessary for business reasons or, in the case of the seniority clause, a statement of . . . existing practice. The respondent made no real effort to persuade the United to accept its proposals by communicating to it facts peculiarly within the respondent's knowledge. On the contrary, the United was required to accept the respondent's bare statements with regard to such matters as fact, even though the United was plainly entitled . . . to doubt, as it obviously did, the respondent's motives in insisting upon its proposals. The United was also required to accept a clause as to strikes and discrimination which denied it status and dignity as an equal in the bargaining process. Moreover, although acceptance by the United of the respondent's proposals, under the circumstances disclosed by this record, would manifestly have seriously

53. 24 NLRB 444 (1940), enforced as modified in Singer Manufacturing Co. v. NLRB, 119 F. 2d 131 (C.C.A.7, 1941), cert. den., 313 U.S. 595, rehearing denied, 314 U.S. 708 (1941). See statement of James J. Matles, United Electrical, Radio and Machine Workers, in Senate Committee on Labor and Public Welfare, *Hearings, 1947*, Pt. 3, pp. 1478–79.

discredited the United and threatened its continued existence as the collective bargaining agency of the respondent's employees, the respondent made no genuine effort to seek to enable the United to point out to its members the justice of the respondent's proposals or the propriety of the United's acceding to them . . . we think the conclusion is inescapable that the respondent entertained no desire to reach an agreement . . . and made no effort in good faith to do so; and we so find. . . .[54]

Thus the Board found that the company was not justified in insisting on treating holidays and vacations as matters for unilateral determination by the company and that throughout, since 1938, it had failed to bargain in good faith. The company refused to comply with the Board's order and petitioned the circuit court for review, claiming that it had negotiated for over a year and that the Board was ordering "a state of mind," not actions. But the court upheld the Board, holding that "collective bargaining is an act; pretended collective bargaining is an omission to perform the act. . . . Existence or non-existence of good faith, just as existence or non-existence of intent, involves only inquiry as to fact."[55] While the Board might not dictate the terms of the bargain, it was entitled, when the evidence supported the finding that there had been no bona fide attempt to bargain, to direct the company to do that which the Act required, "to conduct negotiations with an honest attempt to arrive at an agreement in conformity with the spirit and intent of the Act." The court agreed with the Board that the record disclosed no attempt so to modify demands as to meet any of the proposals of the union upon any of the matters in dispute; that to insist on the right to act unilaterally on matters involving legitimate collective bargaining was a refusal to bargain; that the company could not refuse to include in the contract a proper bargaining clause on wages; that on seniority its failure to produce the facts as to present practice did not carry the implication of good faith. It found the Board justified, therefore, and enforced an order that the company cease refusing to bargain or any other interference with the union's effort to negotiate. The company carried the case to the Supreme Court, which denied certiorari. Even then no collective bargaining agreement was reached until after the company had been threatened with contempt action.[56]

54. 24 NLRB 444, 467–68 (1940).
55. 119 F. 2d 131, 134 (C.C.A.7, 1941); cert. den., 313 U.S. 595.
56. Two cases involving one company, in only one of which did the Board sustain the charge of refusal to bargain, illustrate how the Board weighed the facts in deciding whether or not there was such a refusal. The Montgomery Ward Company in the first of these was found not to have bargained in good faith when it refused to take any initiative in negotiations, engaged in delay, and failed

Failure of companies to make counterproposals in the course of negotiations was frequently one of the evidences of bad faith, but counterproposals were not an absolute requirement. Good faith could not be tested without consideration of what the union did in negotiations also, and sometimes in view of the union's actions the failure to make counterproposals was not conclusive.[57] In one case where the Mine Workers presented their standard contract with a "take-it-or-leave-it" ultimatum, the Board held that this in itself would have relieved the employer of the duty to make specific counterproposals, although this employer was guilty of refusal to bargain, since he failed to recognize the union and was guilty of other antiunion acts.[58] In a 1947 case the Board was even more explicit as to the effect if a union refused to bargain.[59] Here the Typographical Union, faced with the Florida anti-closed-shop amendment, induced the employer to post a union statement of "conditions of employment" which provided in effect a closed shop and that the laws of the international union should govern. Later when the employer was charged with refusal to bargain, in connection with a strike, he raised the question whether an employer was "under a legal duty to bargain with a union that contemporaneously declines to negotiate on certain subjects." While the Board dismissed the charges on other grounds, not pertinent here, it stated: "A union's refusal to bargain in good faith may remove the possibility of negotiation and thus preclude the existence of a situation in which the employer's own good faith can be tested. If it cannot be tested, its absence can hardly be found."

The duty to bargain was naturally a continuing one and included the duty to negotiate over grievances and the interpretation of an agreement during its life.[60] But here also union actions were to be considered in judging whether the employer had fulfilled his obligation. An important case involving the charge of failure of a large

---

to discuss issues fully and openly. The circuit court enforced the order, finding in the cumulative effect of the evidence "a studied design of aloofness, of disinterestedness, of unwillingness to go forward . . . which found its answer in the Board's conclusion of refusal to bargain." 37 NLRB 100 (1941), enforced in 133 F. 2d 676, 687 (C.C.A.9, 1943). In the second case the Board dismissed the charge, holding that but for "honestly taken but irreconcilable positions" on basic issues in regard to seniority, arbitration, and the closed shop, the negotiations would have resulted in agreement. 39 NLRB 229 (1942).

57. Cf. Easton Publishing Co., 19 NLRB 389 (1940); and statement of Chairman Herzog in House Committee on Education and Labor, *Hearings, 1947*, Pt. 5, pp. 3095, 3173–75.

58. Central Minerals Co., 59 NLRB 757 (1944).

59. Times Publishing Co., 72 NLRB 676 (1947).

60. Cf. Carroll's Transfer Co., 56 NLRB 935 (1944).

aircraft company[61] to bargain with the union may be cited as an example. The evidence showed that on the points at issue the union had not really sought to use the grievance procedure contained in the agreement. Without disavowing any authority vested in it, the Board declined to assume the role of "policing collective contracts . . . by attempting to decide whether disputes as to the meaning and administration of such contracts constitute unfair labor practices under the Act," and left such matters to take their course as grievances under the grievance machinery.

Another controversial issue as to good faith in bargaining involved the claim of "management prerogatives," which was raised in an increasing number of cases in the last years of the Wagner Act. The Board held that merit increases, for instance, were subject to collective bargaining and that unilateral wage increases or changes in working conditions, denying the union the right to negotiate, were unfair labor practices.[62] A number of other important cases in which it was urged that it was not necessary to bargain over insurance or pension plans and other matters claimed as management prerogatives were pending when the Wagner Act came to an end.[63] Significantly in the Labor-Management Conference of 1945 a strong committee of representatives of management and labor held long, forthright, and candid discussions over the problem of "management's right to manage" but was unable to agree on any classification of matters properly subject to collective bargaining and those properly excluded.[64] The Board held that these issues could be decided only case by case. "The appropriate scope of collective bargaining cannot be defined in a phrase; it depends upon the industry's custom and history, the previously existing employer-employee relationship, technological problems and demands, and other factors. It may vary with changes in industrial structure and practice." This was an appropriate matter therefore for determination at the administrative discretion of a skilled Board.[65]

Occasionally an employer refused to bargain after a certification

---

61. Consolidated Aircraft Corp., 47 NLRB 694 (1943).

62. J. H. Allison and Co., 70 NLRB 377 (1946), enforced in 165 F. 2d 766 (C.C.A.6, 1947), cert. den., 335 U.S. 814 (1948); Crompton-Highland Mills, 70 NLRB 206 (1946).

63. For later action, see *infra*, ch. 15, p. 568.

64. U.S. Department of Labor, Division of Labor Standards, *The President's National Labor-Management Conference, November 5–30, 1945*, Bulletin No. 77, pp. 56–62.

65. Senate Committee on Labor and Public Welfare, *Hearings, 1947*, Pt. 4, p. 1914.

of a union by the Board or after an order to bargain, on a claim that the union no longer represented a majority of the employees. The courts supported the Board in holding that "a bargaining relationship once rightfully established must be permitted to exist and function for a reasonable period in which it can be given a fair chance to succeed."[66] Whether the claimed loss of majority was the result of influence by the employer, of uninfluenced defection of the employees, or of turnover after the majority was established, the union had a right to require the employer to bargain. This paralleled the Board's policy of refusing, in the interest of stability of bargaining relationships, to hold a new election within a year after a certification except in very exceptional circumstances. The reasonableness of this policy was supported by an investigation made for the Board of the results of cases where courts had enforced orders to bargain despite claims that the union had lost its majority. Information was available in 46 situations, nearly all of those where this issue had been raised in the courts by 1944. Contracts had resulted in 39 of them, and, of the 26 beyond their first term, 20 had been renewed, from one up to four times. Apparently stable bargaining relationships had resulted in a great majority of these situations when the court's order to bargain gave opportunity for the union to revive.[67]

Before there could be a refusal to bargain under the Act, a union

66. Franks Brothers v. NLRB, 321 U.S. 702, 705 (1944). In a small number of cases also issues rose as to the application of the majority rule established by the law, where employers claimed the right under some circumstances to bargain with individuals. The Supreme Court upheld the Board in giving full application to the majority rule to the exclusion of individual bargaining, once employees had chosen their majority representative. J. I. Case Co. v. NLRB, 321 U.S. 332 (1944); Medo Photo Supply Corp. v. NLRB, 321 U.S. 678 (1944). For an excellent analysis of these issues see Ruth Weyand, "Majority Rule in Collective Bargaining," *Columbia Law Review*, 45 (1945), 556–97.

The Board held also that under the proviso to the majority-rule clause, Section 9(a), permitting individuals "to present grievances to their employer," they were free to appear at every stage of the grievance procedure set up by the contract, but the majority representative was entitled to be present and negotiate concerning the disposition of the grievance, in accordance with the practice and philosophy of collective bargaining. U.S. Automatic Corp., 57 NLRB 124 (1944); Hughes Tool Co., 56 NLRB 981 (1944), enforced with modifications in Hughes Tool Co. v. NLRB, 147 F. 2d 69 (C.C.A.5, 1945). Cf. also North American Aviation, 44 NLRB 604 (1942), set aside in 136 F. 2d 898 (C.C.A.9, 1943); Weyand, *op. cit.*, pp. 584–90. The Supreme Court had not yet determined finally the issues in certain conflicting decisions of circuit courts. For discussion of related decisions under the Railway Labor Act, see Richard F. Watt, "The New Deal Court, Organized Labor and the Taft-Hartley Act," *Lawyers Guild Review*, 7 (1947), 206–8. Cf. *infra*, ch. 12, pp. 453–54.

67. NLRB, *Studies of Results*, pp. 37–42.

must have made a clear request for recognition and must have been able to present evidence that it did in fact represent a majority of the employees in a unit appropriate for collective bargaining. The employer was entitled to refuse recognition where in good faith he doubted the union's majority status, and in that event the appropriate procedure was for the union to file a petition for a representation election. Certification by the Board, or a report of the union's majority status by a Regional Director after consent election or card check, was ordinarily adequate evidence of majority for a reasonable period. Moreover, without such evidence from Board procedures, if the Board found that an employer's expressed doubt of the majority was not in good faith, he could be ordered to bargain. Toward the end of the Wagner Act, however, there was some indication of reluctance by the Board to find a violation of the duty to bargain unless there had been Board certification. Recognizing that the signing of cards was not so sure a guaranty of the freely expressed desires of employees as a secret election, the Board decided in 1946 that in a refusal-to-bargain case it would give the same weight to a majority status established by a cross-check of cards against the employer's pay roll only where the results had been posted in the plant and an opportunity given to any interested party to object.[68] In two other late cases charges were dismissed, where one member of the Board thought the proof of majority entirely adequate and the employer's doubts not bona fide.[69] These and other cases were much criticized as unnecessarily encouraging employers to require resort to the Board's machinery, unduly burdening the agency and causing delays in settling issues as to the right to recognition. Moreover, such delays were an invitation to unions to resort to strikes for recognition rather than to use the peaceful procedures provided by the Act.

How effective the Act was in its requirement that employers bargain collectively with representatives of the majority of their employees cannot be said with much assurance. There is little specific evidence, although a number of studies of the outcome of Board cases found collective bargaining proceeding in a very large proportion of companies where charges of refusal to bargain had been adjusted or closed on compliance.[70] This section of the Act was a very difficult one to enforce effectively. If an employer was in fact illegally refus-

68. Joe Hearin, Lumber, 68 NLRB 150 (1946). Cf. discussion of evidence of majority, *infra*, ch. 5, pp. 133–34.

69. I. Spiewak & Sons, 71 NLRB 770 (1946); Roanoke Public Warehouse, 72 NLRB 128 (1947).

70. NLRB, *Studies of Results*, pp. 9, 26, 37–42, 48.

ing to bargain, and chose to exercise his right to full hearing and to appeal to the courts for review of a Board order, the final order that he must bargain might come down from the circuit court or Supreme Court two or three years from the time of the first violation and the filing of the charge. Only rarely would a local union have survived as a functioning organization through this long period. If it had not, would the international union find it worth while to use its limited manpower to go back in and try to reorganize in order to utilize the order? Some cases died at this point, without any attempt of the union to bargain. There was no penalty upon the employer, only the order to bargain upon request. Only when discrimination also had been involved, with substantial liability for back pay to discharged employees, was there the financial or other pressure which made a recalcitrant employer eager to bring himself into compliance with the law. In addition, the matter of good faith in bargaining was not one that could be defined with simple objective tests, although experience showed that border-line cases where it was difficult for experienced people to decide the fact as to good faith or its lack were relatively few.

Critical employers and their lawyers had much to say about this provision of the Wagner Act.[71] They complained that the tests of bargaining in good faith were uncertain; but the court's statement in the Singer case is in point: "We have no doubt that if petitioner so acts as to indicate its bona fides, it will experience no difficulty."[72] They sometimes said it amounted to compulsory arbitration. Badly administered, this could have been true, but there is little if any such evidence. It was claimed too, critically, that certifications or Board orders to bargain were "permanent"—a statement indicative of failure to accept collective bargaining fully as well as contrary to the fact. Actually, if the union lost its majority or became inactive, after a reasonable time from the certification or Board or court order, the employer was entitled to refuse to bargain and naturally did, frequently without challenge.[73] Some employers objected to the obligation to bargain when there was no specific parallel obligation upon the union. While this was in general adequately handled in the Board's treatment of cases, there may in rare cases have been some real justification for employers' feeling of inequality on this point.

71. Cf. C. E. Wilson of General Motors, Senate Committee on Labor and Public Welfare, *Hearings, 1947*, Pt. 1, pp. 476–81; T. R. Iserman, *ibid.*, pp. 156–59; House Committee on Education and Labor, *Hearings, 1947*, Pt. 4, p. 2725.
72. 119 F. 2d 131, 134 (C.C.A.7, 1941).
73. Cf. discussion of the problem of employer petitions and "decertification," ch. 5, *infra*, pp. 160–63.

And finally some employers who wanted the scope of collective bargaining narrowly limited objected to the Board's case-by-case handling of these issues.

Attorneys exerted great influence in the Board's refusal-to-bargain cases. Some who were vocal in criticism of the Board's policies on these matters encouraged their clients to refuse to bargain, and their influence could be clearly seen, notably in the South, where it resulted in a large number of such cases. Especially after the war, with the end of the War Labor Board, was this a problem which the Board had not solved. One lawyer in a southern city, whose clients throughout the state were at that time the subjects of a considerable number of refusal-to-bargain charges, said frankly, "We never give a contract if we can avoid it." The problem was particularly acute in textiles and in the small clothing plants scattered through the South.

When the Board persisted in its effort to achieve compliance with the law, carrying a case if necessary through to Board order and to court and even through contempt action, and when the union continued to maintain its organization, or revived it and functioned actively, then the law could be said to have been effective. But when unions were weak, even after full Board action there was little long-run effect. Collective bargaining in a true sense, typically, resulted only if unions were strong enough to make it necessary for employers to bargain with them. Nevertheless, conversations with many union representatives and many employers over the country and in many industries lead to the conclusion that this provision in the law did serve a useful purpose. Although actual enforcement was relatively ineffective, there was still a code of ethics to the effect that, when workers had organized and chosen their representatives, it was the duty of the employer to bargain with them. Over the years, as the Board interpreted the meaning of the code in practice, and as Board staff and union representatives and employers' representatives who wished to comply with the law worked on problems as they arose, habits in industry were unquestionably affected. Increasingly employers were willing to conform to the law, once they knew what their duty was. The existence still in 1947 of recalcitrance, in some areas, industries, and companies, did not obscure the fact that over all the industrial climate had changed since 1935. The presence in the Act of the specific duty to bargain with the representatives chosen by employees in accordance with the law was one of the factors that prevented violations of the right to organize. Perhaps the greatest effect of this section of the law was where no charges were filed rather than in the actual cases handled by the Board, though these were of course essential for the defining of policy.[74]

THE RESULTS

Many of the cases described here were big and dramatic. Others were those in which crucial matters of policy were decided. But for every one of these there were hundreds of run-of-the-mill cases, in which some of the same types of violations were found. The great majority, more than 90 per cent, were handled informally in the regional offices. During the twelve years of the Wagner Act there were only 3,154 decisions in unfair labor practice cases, but more than 16,000 such cases were adjusted by agreement of the parties for compliance with the Act. In addition, some of those withdrawn, one may assume, were settlements in accord with the law, accomplished without the intervention of the Board. Like the widening circles from a stone dropped in the water, the decisions in formal cases by the Board and the courts set standards which affected the informal settlements, and all built up a body of common law as to what was required by the Act. As a result the behavior of management over the years tended to adopt the new standards set by the Act, recognizing the right of employees to self-organization and collective bargaining on the basis of free choice. In thousands of instances the fight against collective bargaining ended, and employers and unions began working out the problem of how to live together. If they had not solved all those problems, this was not to be blamed on the Board, which had been given a limited function to perform, or on the Act.

The assumption of the National Labor Relations Act that if the right of workers to organize was protected, union organization and collective bargaining would increase, was clearly correct. Collective bargaining was established in a relatively short time in a substantial majority of the Board's cases where compliance with the Act was achieved, if the group of studies made for the Board in 1943–44 were representative, as they probably were.[75] But the purposes of the Act failed of achievement when there was long delay, bargaining rights

74. Cf. Dr. Taylor's discussion of the "duty to bargain" provisions. He suggests a disadvantage in such a clause, directed against either management or unions, in that it tends to lead to government regulation of the collective bargaining process itself, and argues that the usefulness of the section should have decreased as unions became more widely organized and more firmly established. George W. Taylor, *Government Regulation of Industrial Relations* (New York: Prentice-Hall, Inc., 1948), pp. 279–84.

75. NLRB, *Studies of Results*, Pt. 1. Cf. discussion *supra*, ch. 3, pp. 93–94.

were blocked, and the right of individual workers to be free of interference in their right to engage in concerted activity was not protected. Poor settlements were sometimes made which were not in accord with the spirit and intent of the Act. Unions frequently died while the struggle to eliminate unfair labor practices was carried through the Board and the courts. Some cases were dropped without enforcement and without compliance for budgetary or other reasons. Occasionally even there was suspicion that the Board, or one of its members, or staff members, had yielded to improper direct pressure, from a member of Congress, or an influential employer, or an influential rival union—or, less directly, had been too timid to proceed energetically in action which would be unpopular with influential members of the public or members of congressional appropriations committees. Moreover, the Board was inadequately staffed for much of its life, and as a result there was such delay in investigating cases, or carrying them forward, that the public policy was never fully enforced. Nevertheless, the record shows that much had been accomplished.

Some of the outstanding failures under the Act must be mentioned, also. These are such cases as those of Thompson Products, Inc., and Weirton Steel, whose representatives were among the bitter critics of the Board and the Act.[76] From no standpoint could there be much satisfaction with the record. The companies claimed that they had been harassed by the Board for ten years and satisfactory labor relations interfered with. Unions claimed that company-dominated unions had been permitted to survive and other unfair labor practices to continue. Board records showed a succession of unfair labor practice cases and failure to achieve full compliance with the law and Board orders. Cases were still pending before the courts in 1947. In Weirton the company had organized an employee representation plan in 1933 after the Amalgamated Association of Iron, Steel and Tin Workers began organizing. In 1936, after the Steel Workers Organizing Committee came in, according to the Board decision issued in 1941,[77] there followed a company-inspired campaign of anti-CIO

76. Statement of Raymond S. Livingstone, vice-president, Thompson Products, Inc., in House Committee on Education and Labor, *Hearings, 1947*, Pt. 3, pp. 1489–1534; cf. also statement of Hugh Sperry, *ibid.*, Pt. 5, pp. 3281–3478; *infra*, ch. 5, p. 170; ch. 6, p. 200.

Statement of Earl F. Reed, attorney for Weirton Steel Co., Senate Committee on Labor and Public Welfare, *Hearings, 1947*, Pt. 2, pp. 731–47; and statement of the Board, *ibid.*, pp. 747–52.

77. 32 NLRB 1145 (1941), enforced with a minor modification in 135 F. 2d 494 (C.C.A.3, 1943).

propaganda, demonstrations, and violence, along with discrimination against seventeen workers, although charges of discrimination against another long list were dismissed as not proved. The independent formed in 1936 was held to be company-dominated. The resulting order, except for the one point on espionage, was held to be fully supported by the evidence and was enforced by the circuit court in 1943. Long efforts to settle the case followed. But meantime new charges of violations were brought in, alleging continued company domination of an independent, and new discriminations and violence against union adherents. After long consideration by the Board as to whether to charge the company with contempt or to try a new case itself, finally in August, 1944, the Board filed a petition for adjudication in contempt. The court ordered the case to be heard by a Master who would find the facts and report to the court.[78] Very lengthy hearings followed, extending from March, 1945, through April, 1947, and in 1949 a report by the Master was still awaited. Whatever the result, the Board's judgment was that, after ten years, compliance with the law had still not been obtained. Its own mistakes in handling the case and lack of effective insistence upon prompt compliance at various stages had been at least partly responsible.

In 1947 there was still need for effective enforcement of the Wagner Act's prohibition of unfair labor practices by employers, if employees were to be free to enjoy the right to organize and bargain through representatives of their own choosing. For instance, consider the case of Salant & Salant, Inc.,[79] New York manufacturers of work clothing with a series of plants in Tennessee. In March, 1946, after extensive investigation and hearing the Board issued its decision. It found that the company had engaged in an "intensive and extensive" campaign to defeat the union's efforts to organize. The company had stimulated members of the local communities to form "citizens' committees" which in some cases took up grievances with the company and operated openly as antiunion groups. It provided antiunion propaganda, enlisted the aid of local editors, engaged in espionage against union activities, failed to provide reasonable protection against assaults by nonunion employees, and discriminated against union members. After the appropriate order, there were long negotiations with the company for a possible settlement rather than prompt enforcement; and at the end of 1947 the case was still not closed. Meantime other charges had been filed in some of the plants, and in one where the Amalgamated Clothing Workers had won an election the Board had

78. 146 F. 2d 144 (C.C.A.3, 1944). 79. 66 NLRB 24 (1946).

124

found a refusal to bargain and issued a bargaining order.[80] There was need for effective action to prevent such organized interference with employees' rights, both by companies and by community groups who acted in the interest of the employer.

The southern organizing drives after the war brought forth a renewal of violent opposition to the unions, even though in many instances elections won by unions were followed by peaceable collective bargaining. Organized community antiunion drives appeared in a considerable number of cases in 1946, as they had earlier. For instance, in the Blue Ridge Shirt Manufacturing Company case in Fayetteville, Tennessee,[81] the Board found that the Chamber of Commerce had engaged in an active campaign against the CIO and in support of a local independent by mass meetings, newspaper ads, distribution of the antiunion *Militant Truth*,[82] and warning that the plant would close if organized by the CIO. The Board ordered this interference stopped. In the Mylan Manufacturing Company case,[83] of Sparta, Tennessee, the Board did not find substantial evidence to confirm its "suspicion" that the Chamber of Commerce joined with the employer in fostering the local antiunion campaign and dismissed that charge. A local businessman, however, had been permitted to make an antiunion speech in the plant, in which he recited how other companies had closed down after being organized, and warned against the same outcome for this plant. Since the company did not repudiate his actions, it was held responsible, and both the company and the businessman, with "his agents," were ordered to cease all illegal interference with the rights of the employees under the Act. In an important earlier case in southern California the Board's authority to act when the evidence showed interference by community organizations had been upheld by the circuit court in an order against the Merchants and Manufacturers Association of Los Angeles and other "institutional respondents" for their active and long-continued "open-shop" campaign among employers. The court held that the Board was entitled to issue an order against this "broad and long continuing conspiracy to frustrate and thus violate the NLRA."[84] The

80. 74 NLRB 1405 (1947).
81. 70 NLRB 741 (1946).
82. For use of another similar publication cf. *infra*, pp. 126–27.
83. 70 NLRB 574 (1946).
84. NLRB v. Sun Tent-Luebbert Co., 151 F. 2d 483, 488 (C.C.A.9, 1945), enforcing 37 NLRB 50 (1941). For representation cases where the Board considered such organized antiunion campaigns in elections, cf. *infra*, ch. 5, pp. 168–69.

ability to move against those responsible for such campaigns to frustrate the rights of employees was an important weapon for the Board.

Many cases on the books of the southern offices of the Board in 1947 were more like the most violent of the Board's early cases than what one might have expected twelve years after the Wagner Act became law. We will name just a few of such extreme cases from the Atlanta and New Orleans offices. An Intermediate Report issued May 15, 1947, found Macon Textiles, Inc.,[85] guilty of vigorous anti-union activity through management and supervisors, by surveillance of union meetings, warnings against the union, and discriminatory discharges; when union representatives were distributing handbills before an election, the manager drove up on the sidewalk, apparently in an effort to run them down, then took copies of the sample ballots, marked them nonunion and distributed them to employees, and tried to provoke a fight. In the case of Dorsey Trailers, Inc.,[86] the hearing had had to be moved from Elba, Alabama, to another town because of the fear of certain witnesses. The Trial Examiner found the superintendent and therefore the company at least partly responsible for the planned beating of a union organizer to run him out of town. In the case of Russell Manufacturing Company, of Alexandria City, Georgia,[87] the Trial Examiner found a company-dominated mill town, where the mayor was vice-president of the company and worked closely with the police in antiunion activities in behalf of the company; one organizer left town after being threatened by the police; another, who was beaten on the street by two employees who left their work after making the plan in the presence of supervisors, was himself then arrested and jailed. In another case, that of Bibb Manufacturing Company,[88] with plants in four counties in Georgia, the Trial Examiner found that police had kept a twenty-four-hour surveillance of the activities of union organizers, trailing them openly by foot or car, so that employees were afraid to talk to them, especially as there were a number of discharges of people who had been seen with the organizer. The company also had distributed, among a considerable number of other publications, some 1,000 and later 2,000

85. 80 NLRB 1525 (1948). The Board's decision, issued December 30, 1948, agreed for the most part with the Trial Examiner.

86. Intermediate Report, September, 1947. The Board in its decision late in 1948 commented on this aspect of the case: "A more flagrant violation of the Act would be difficult to find." 80 NLRB 478 (1948).

87. Intermediate Report, October, 1947, decided April, 1949, 82 NLRB No. 136 (1949).

88. Intermediate Report, August, 1947. The Board's decision, in March, 1949, found these actions violations of the Act. 82 NLRB No. 38 (1949).

annual subscriptions to the *Trumpet*, a "hate sheet" which devoted 90 per cent of its space between June, 1946, and March, 1947, to attacks upon the CIO. It was, the Trial Examiner found, illiterate, ill-informed, dishonest. As he said:

> The *Trumpet* utilized every conceivable propaganda device from fear, hatred, race discrimination, bias and prejudice to loyalty to country and to employer, to promises and inducements of better wages and better conditions purporting to come from the manufacturers, in order to prevent the textile employees from joining the Union. . . . All this propaganda purported to be solidly based on religion. . . .

These are extreme cases, but all the offices handling southern cases found many such violent instances in the later years as well as other run-of-the-mill discrimination and refusal-to-bargain cases. And no regional office in 1947 was without cases where their investigations showed that violations of the law were still to be found, even though to a greater or less extent in different areas most employers were living within the law. The time had not yet come when there was no need for the basic protection of workers' rights under the Act.

Many employers, probably a large majority, had accepted the policy of the Act and were seeking to work out their relations with their employees within the law. There were many companies whose firm instructions to their management representatives were to make every effort to avoid even the filing of a charge—or, if a charge were filed, to settle it informally. This attitude was by no means universal, however. There were still many to whom a violation of this law involved no "sense of sin." Highly significant was the incident in an important southern city in the later years of the Act, when a prominent attorney addressed the local Bar Association on handling labor cases. A mimeographed outline, at the point where he discussed pre-election company activities, said: "Risk violation of Section 8(1) if efforts have reasonable chance of success—same as to Sections 8(2) and 8(5). . . . Do not ever . . . violate or even threaten to violate Sections 8(3) or 8(4)." In other words, he recommended the use of "free speech" and other actions to keep the union out if possible—but the danger of financial penalty for discrimination was apparently too great to risk. Thus a respected member of the Bar told his colleagues to risk violating a federal labor law if they thought they could do it successfully. This lawyer, however, different from some of his colleagues, recommended that if the union won: "Better learn to live with it. . . . Chances of getting rid of union do not warrant trouble incident to getting rid of it."

From the Wagner Act to Taft-Hartley

A quite different set of problems from those discussed here came to the Board in some of the unfair labor practice cases arising out of rival union disputes. Some of them involved unjustifiable types of action by unions over which the Board had only limited control if any. These, with some other controversial problems of special difficulty, will be discussed in a later chapter, after the basic questions in representation cases have been considered.

CHAPTER 5

UNIONS OF THEIR OWN CHOOSING

FULL freedom of association" and "representatives of their own choosing," under the protection of the Wagner Act, were essential for the free and democratic collective bargaining which Congress believed would promote a healthy economy. Accordingly, one of the major functions given to the NLRB was to provide a sure and democratic means by which, when question arose, the facts could be determined as to whether employees wanted union representation. Before an employer could be required to bargain, any doubt had to be removed as to whether a union was in fact the representative chosen by a group of workers, and disputes between competing unions needed to be decided by a method which had the full confidence of all concerned. Especially after 1940, when from four thousand up to over ten thousand petitions were filed each year, the Board made a contribution to peaceful and democratic labor relations by providing a way to settle such disputes without the older method of strikes for recognition. About four out of five of these cases involved only one union. The minority where there were competing unions were often more difficult, but even there the disputes were usually settled by the orderly procedures provided under the Act.

Rules had to be developed in these representation cases so that everyone would know what to expect and have confidence in the Board's machinery. The decisions in formal cases set these standards, developing them over the years on the basis of experience and changing needs. The great majority of cases, however, were handled informally, by consent elections and other means.

For the benefit of any readers who have had no experience with such matters, it may be well to describe an actual election. Assume a small machine plant in one of the smaller towns in the Middle West. There is little organization in the town, and none in this plant. A group of active men in the plant are dissatisfied and get in touch with a representative of a union in a neighboring city. Or possibly

129

the union makes the first move, finding a center of dissatisfaction in the plant which made it appear ripe for organization. In any event a union representative comes in and works with the local nucleus for some weeks, getting cards signed which authorize the union to act as bargaining representative. Then, believing that it represents a majority, the union asks for recognition. The employer knew of the organizing move, but, being unaware of any trouble in the plant, he is shocked at the idea and doubts that the union has a majority. When he therefore refuses recognition, the union files a petition with the Regional Director of the Board. The petition names the unit claimed and states that no other union is claiming to represent the employees and that the employer has refused recognition. The cards which the union relies on to prove its majority are given the Board at the same time. The case is assigned for investigation to a field examiner, who arranges a joint conference. Since it appears from the evidence—the cards and a current pay roll which the employer brings in—that the union does have a substantial representation and a real question of representation has arisen, and since the employer as well as the union sees an advantage in settling the issue as promptly as possible, they agree on a "consent election," which does not require an order from the Board itself. The written agreement provides for the appropriate unit, "all production and maintenance employees, excluding supervisors and office employees," and the time and place of the election. The employer agrees to recognize the union if it gets a majority of the votes. The most recent pay roll is agreed on for the list of voters. The field examiner arranges the details of the election, usually holding a pre-election conference at which both parties check the list of voters and work out any issues as to eligibility to vote or other details. Notices of the election in official form, with a sample ballot, are posted in appropriate places in the plant. The ballot asks: "Do you wish to be represented for purposes of collective bargaining by the —— Union? Yes—— No——." Arrangements are made for official observers for the union and the employer. The election may be conducted in a convenient place in the plant, or outside, with hours arranged so as to avoid unnecessary interference with production. A voting booth has been rented from the election officials of the town.

The union of course electioneers, with greater or less vigor depending in part on the character of the opposition. If this election takes place in one of the later years, the employer probably, with the advice of his lawyer, circulates to the employees one or more very carefully phrased letters in which he urges all employees to vote but indicates his opinion that no union is necessary or could obtain for the employees more than they otherwise would get, in this situation where company and workers "have gotten on so well in the past." Perhaps he skirts closely the limits of privileged, noncoercive "free speech."[1] When election day comes, a ballot is handed to each eligible voter by the Board agent, as the eligibility list is checked by the agent and the observers. Ballots are marked in the voting booth, folded and put into the ballot box which is guarded by the observers. Anyone whose right to vote is in doubt may be challenged, and in that case the challenged ballot is segregated for later consideration if necessary. Ballots are carefully counted by the Board agent with the help of the authorized observers, and a tally is immediately announced. If this election is typical of those in the later years, more than 80 per cent of those eligible vote, probably much more in a small plant, and nearly 80 per cent vote for the union. The one or two challenges are so few that they are disregarded. Were they enough to determine the outcome of the election, the Regional Director would investigate, rule upon eligibility, and count any ballots which were entitled to be counted. If objections are filed to the election, the Regional Director investigates and rules upon their validity and could void the election and conduct a new one. In a consent election the ruling of the Regional Director is final. But in the typical case we are assuming there are no such complications, the results are accepted, with due rejoicing by the union and understandable regret by the employer—and recognition follows. Negotiations between the representatives of the local union, probably assisted by an international union representative, and the employer with any assistance he chooses result in a contract.

This was a simple case, but similar informal procedures were often possible in larger plants, or in cases involving more than one union, when all parties were able to agree on the unit or units appropriate and on eligibility and other details. When this was impossible, or the employer or one union refused to co-operate, or wanted Board decision on certain matters, the issues might go to the Board for determination.[2] Then after investigation a public hearing was held in order to make a record for the Board of the pertinent facts and the issues and arguments of all parties. After a final decision by the Board, the

1. Cf. *infra*, ch. 6, pp. 174–89.
2. The prehearing election, used extensively in the years 1945–47, is discussed *supra*, ch. 2, pp. 62–63.

131

election was held by the Board agents, again with as much co-operation of all interested parties as possible, and with all the safeguards of secrecy of the ballot and suitable conditions so that a free choice could be obtained from the carefully prepared list of eligible voters. After the ballots were counted, a tally was at once reported. If there were challenged ballots in sufficient number to affect the result, or objections to the election, the Regional Director investigated and reported to the Board with his recommendations. The Board finally made its decision, as to ballots to be counted, or whether in a rare case the election should be set aside, or more generally certifying the union which won, or dismissing the petition if no union had a majority.

Many elections through the years were conducted in large units, as in a textile plant of 12,000 employees in a southern mill town, for many of whom this must have been their first experience of casting a vote in a publicly conducted election; or in a steel corporation's mills where more than 116,000 voters were eligible in plants throughout the country, voting for a national union after a long company-union history; or in steamship companies where it took months before all the ships returning from the far seas could be counted when they touched American ports; or in telegraph offices all over the country; or in canneries scattered over the state of California; or in a war-time airplane plant with 30,000 employees. Many smaller elections involved their special difficulties and their own elements of drama, as when lumberjacks voted in the woods, or Negro workers in a cotton-seed-oil mill dared community opposition to come out and vote for a union, or in a southern meat-packing town where Negroes were intimidated by threats of fiery crosses and voted "No." As will be seen, there were cases where the evidence indicates that the Board was not able to achieve a full and fair test of the desires of the employees. Nevertheless, over all, the elections conducted by the Board were an experience with the democratic process, meeting some of its difficulties as well as giving the lift of spirit that often comes to the participant in such undertakings. It is hard to believe, though proof is difficult, that this experience among some millions of Americans in twelve years has not left an imprint upon ways of thinking and acting both in labor organizations and in community life generally.

Some of the special problems in representation cases need consideration next. Since the Board in its decisions was laying down the rules for the handling of some thousands of cases each year, inevitably they involved many technicalities, not all of which can be avoided here.

132

The next sections, on majority questions, appropriate units, and existing contracts as a bar to new elections, are therefore necessarily somewhat technical.

MAJORITY CHOICE

Majority rule was provided in the Act. The representative chosen by the majority was to be the exclusive representative for collective bargaining purposes. The congressional committees had accepted the conclusions of the old National Labor Relations Board functioning under Public Resolution No. 44 that majority rule was necessary for collective bargaining to be effective, as well as in accord with the basic traditions of American democracy, "which empower representatives elected by the majority of the voters to speak for all the people."[3] Proof of majority was accordingly one of the chief questions to be settled when a petition was filed asking the Board to determine a question of representation. In many early cases evidence introduced at the hearing was thought to be adequate proof, and unions were certified as representatives on this record, on testimony of employees or admission of the employer that the union represented the majority of the employees, or the introduction of signed petitions, signed membership cards, or authorizations to the union to act as representative. If the Board had any doubt as to the validity of this evidence, as when an employer contended that many of the signatures were the result of coercion,[4] it directed a secret election. By 1939, however, the Board decided that generally elections would be the best basis for certification. Thus any possible doubt would be removed as to whether the union really was the free choice of the employees.[5] From then on elections were normally used to determine a question of representation in the formal Board-ordered cases, although occasionally a union

3. The decision of the old National Labor Relations Board which first analyzed and adopted this principle was that in Houde Engineering Corp., Case No. 12, August 30, 1934, *Decisions of the National Labor Relations Board, July 9, 1934–December 1934* (Washington, 1935), Vol. 1, p. 35; U.S. House of Representatives, Committee on Labor, *National Labor Relations Board*, Report No. 1147, 74th Cong., 1st Sess., June 10, 1935, pp. 20–22, cited as House Committee on Labor, *NLRB Report, 1935*.

4. Cf. Belmont Stamping and Enameling Co., 1 NLRB 378 (1936). Evidence as to whether there had been union coercion to sign cards sometimes had to be considered in complaint cases charging refusal to bargain, also. Cf. Dahlstrom Metallic Door Co., 11 NLRB 408 (1939), enforced in 112 F. 2d 756 (C.C.A.2, 1940); Dadourian Export Corp., 46 NLRB 498 (1942), set aside in 138 F. 2d 891 (C.C.A.2, 1943).

5. Cudahy Packing Co., 13 NLRB 526 (1939); Armour and Co., 13 NLRB 567 (1939). Mr. Smith dissented, however.

was certified on the record when there had been agreement for a cross-check of union cards against the company pay roll, as in Carnegie-Illinois Steel in 1942.[6] Cross-checks continued to be used by agreement in some informal cases, but there was enough doubt as to whether signed cards were a trustworthy indication of the wishes of the employees, especially in the case of certain unions, to argue strongly for the more usual practice of holding elections. In the later years it became standard practice in "consent cross-checks" for the Regional Director to post the result in the plant for five days, giving any interested party a right to raise objection, before the determination was made final.

A majority of those voting would decide an election, the Board ruled in an early case. In an R.C.A. Manufacturing Company conflict it appeared that a minority group could otherwise have prevented the resolution of the question which was causing unrest. A bitter strike had been settled with an agreement for an NLRB election, but shortly before the vote an Employees' Committee, which was party to the election, decided to boycott it, and put on a strenuous campaign of propaganda predicting violence should the union win. The CIO won 3,016 of the 3,163 votes cast, but 9,752 had been eligible. The Board certified the union, nevertheless, saying that to fail to do so would perpetuate the conditions which caused the strike.[7] This policy was uniformly followed in the later years, unless the Board found the number of votes cast so small as not to be "substantial" or "representative."[8]

In order to insure that election results represented a free expression of the desires of the majority of the employees, the Board decided by late 1937, after some experimentation, that the ballots should include a space for voting against any organization, in multiple-union elections as well as when only one union was involved. Two members of the Board considered this necessary, since the Act "does not require an unwilling majority of employees to bargain through representatives."[9] In view of the fact that a majority of the voters might desire representation, but disagree on a representative, the Board

6. 40 NLRB 532 (1942).

7. 2 NLRB 159 (1936).

8. Cf. Northwest Packing Co., 65 NLRB 890 (1946). The Board's policy was upheld in NLRB v. Central Dispensary and Emergency Hospital, 145 F. 2d 852 (App. D.C., 1944), cert. denied 324 U.S. 847 (1945).

9. American France Line *et al.*, 3 NLRB 64 (1937); Interlake Iron Corp., 4 NLRB 55 (1937). For an argument against ever including a "No-Union" choice, see Louis B. Boudin, "Representatives of Their Own Choosing," *Illinois Law Review*, 37 (1943), 400–402.

therefore decided, in the Interlake Iron case, that in inconclusive elections it would order a run-off. But the form of the run-off ballot was a difficult point, on which debate continued, within the Board and between unions and employers, through the whole Wagner Act period. Mr. Edwin S. Smith argued in a dissent to the Interlake Iron decision and later that, unless the vote for "Neither" was a majority, a run-off should be held including only the names of the contending unions. Others argued that unless an opportunity were always given to vote for no representation, a union might be certified when it had only minority support. The question was whether a majority of the employees by their votes had shown that they wanted representation even if they could not have the union of their first choice; or whether union rivalry was so intense that many preferred none rather than a second-choice representative. Since no one could be sure of the answer, and there was no entirely satisfactory solution, the Board tried to evolve a workable policy and changed the rule a number of times as its membership changed and experience was studied.[10]

Eligibility to vote was determined partly by the definition of the unit, partly by the pay-roll date used. The pay roll immediately pre-

10. The first run-offs followed the Interlake Iron rule (4 NLRB 55 [1937]), giving opportunity to vote for or against the union with the largest vote in the first election. After Dr. Leiserson became a member, although he thought run-offs were not provided for at all by the Act, he agreed with Mr. Smith on the form of ballot, and the policy of dropping "Neither" and running the two unions was adopted, on the theory that a majority had already voted in favor of some representation. (R. K. LeBlond Machine Tool Co., 22 NLRB 465 [1940].) This also did not prove entirely satisfactory, since sometimes the choice of representative was then in fact made by a minority of the eligible voters. After study of this experience the Board considered a new, more flexible policy, which would carry on the ballot the two interests receiving the largest votes, whether two unions or a union and the "Neither" option. A public hearing was held in 1943, at which unions strenuously objected to a "no union" place on the run-off ballot. The Board finally adopted a compromise, complexly worded and detailed, that with some qualifications provided for a "no union" option if that interest ran first, but otherwise a contest between the two top unions. (*Eighth Annual Report,* pp. 14–16. Cf. discussion in D. O. Bowman, *Public Control of Labor Relations* [New York: Macmillan Co., 1942], pp. 142–55.) Chairman Herzog in a 1947 concurring opinion questioned the then current rule and thought that when "Neither" was second, that option should appear on the run-off ballot. (B. F. Goodrich Co., 73 NLRB 1250 [1947].) That the 1943 compromise had not satisfied the critics was seen when in the 1947 Taft-Hartley Act, Congress provided that run-offs should always carry the two top interests, the policy that had been seriously considered and argued for within the staff in 1943. Perhaps the conclusion to be drawn is that such a complex problem can best be decided administratively on the basis of experience but that a Board should not hesitate to make the choice that seems most sound from the over-all view, regardless of special interests that may protest at the time.

ceding the election was generally used, though a great variety of special circumstances, such as in seasonal industries, and in expanding or contracting plants, required some other date which would best insure that employees were able fully to express their desires as to representation. Probably the most difficult question as to eligibility to vote was in strike cases. Under the Act, "employee" included anyone whose work had ceased as a consequence of a "current labor dispute." Accordingly a pay roll preceding the strike was used, even where a strike had run for several months.[11] When the issue arose as to whether people hired during the strike as replacements had a right to vote, the Board at first excluded them, on the theory that to give them a voice in selecting the bargaining agent might foreclose the possibility of settling the strike, since the dispute was still current.[12] Otherwise it might be possible for twice as many to vote as there were jobs. However, after watching the experience, the Board later decided upon a modification, although Mr. E. S. Smith dissented. In a strike caused by unfair labor practices only the strikers could vote. In an "economic strike," not caused by unfair labor practices, however, and where most strikers had returned to work, but a few replacements had been hired, the replacements as well as those still on strike were permitted to vote.[13] While this rule was applied with some variations in special circumstances, the basic distinction between unfair labor practice strikes and economic strikes seemed to lead to a reasonable result, on this problem of eligibility to vote as well as others. Later in a complex situation involving a jurisdictional dispute in a Columbia Pictures case, the Board adhered to its usual policy that both strikers and replacements should vote, saying, "It is impossible during the currency of an economic strike to determine, despite what an employer may predict, whether or not the strikers will return to their jobs."[14]

The development of another set of policies, as to when a "question of representation" exists, illustrates again the flexible administrative process through which the Board watched experience and tried to establish the most workable and reasonable rules. Especially after the great bulk of the work came to be that of handling representation

11. Saxon Mills, 1 NLRB 153 (1936).

12. A. Sartorius and Co., 10 NLRB 493 (1938).

13. Rudolph Wurlitzer Co., 32 NLRB 163 (1941). The employer had of course the right to fill the places of strikers in a strike not caused by unfair labor practices. Cf. further discussion of issues as to strikes in ch. 6, *infra*, pp. 189–203.

14. Columbia Pictures Corp., 64 NLRB 490, 520 (1945); *infra*, ch. 6, pp. 199–200.

cases, delays were a serious problem. It was essential to avoid waste of time and money for both the Board and the parties, as well as disturbance of existing relationships by holding elections on frivolous claims or where there was little or no chance that a union could demonstrate that it was the choice of a majority. In a number of early cases petitions were dismissed where the Board found that the evidence of interest in a union was too small, or too old, to be sufficient,[15] but smaller showings of interest were accepted where there was a closed-shop contract or a history of unfair labor practices, either of which might make supporters of the petitioning union fear to sign cards. In general, the requirement came to be a 30 per cent showing in the form of authorization cards or other documentary evidence, although smaller showings continued to be accepted in special circumstances. By 1946, also, a larger than usual showing was required for a new election on petition of a union less than a year after it had lost an election. An "intervening union" was permitted on the ballot, on the other hand, when an election was to be held following petition of another union, if it made "some showing," either by reason of an existing or expired contract, or by some showing of cards.[16]

In the spring of 1947 the entire question of "showing requirements" was under study by the Board. Was intervention by other unions permitted too freely, especially when an intervening union could block agreement for a consent election? Was there still need to accept petitions on small showing in union-security cases, since this seemed to be an encouragement to raiding, and since, with the development of Board policies protecting the right of employees under closed-shop contracts to change their bargaining agent, there was less need for special rules for these cases?[17] Several studies of the results of elections showed some correlation between showing and success in

15. General Electric Co., 15 NLRB 1018 (1939).

16. *Tenth Annual Report*, p. 16; *Eleventh*, pp. 10–11. In NLRB parlance an intervening union is one which claims an interest in a representation case after another union files a petition for an election. The "intervenor" therefore might be an old-established union which had held a contract for years in the unit claimed by the new union or, on the contrary, another union whose only interest was a claimed jurisdiction, without support of any showing of employee interest.

It should be noted also that the practice of accepting a 30 per cent showing meant that where a union had been certified after an election in which there was a 40 or 45 per cent nonunion vote, a year later a new election might be ordered on a showing of only 30 per cent. Was this enough to indicate a question of representation? The question indicates the difficulty of deciding between the interests of stability and of assuring free choice to employees.

17. Cf. Rutland Court Owners, 44 NLRB 587 (1942), discussed *infra*, ch. 6, pp. 212–13.

elections, even when there was long delay in holding the election. Nevertheless, occasionally unions with only small showings were successful. Moreover, elections were won in spite of the presence of closed-shop or other contracts in a large enough proportion of cases to indicate that the purposes of the Act were served by enabling such dissenting groups of employees to express their preference in an election.[18] Here, on the problem of "showing requirements," as on others, the Board tried to balance, in its administrative wisdom based on experience, the sometimes opposed interests of assuring free choice for employees by their majority vote and of protecting stable collective bargaining which should not be upset by policies that might encourage raiding.

THE APPROPRIATE UNIT

Determination of "the unit appropriate for collective bargaining," a necessary step before it could be known whether a majority of the employees had chosen a representative to bargain for them, turned out unexpectedly to be one of the thorniest of the problems with which the Board was faced. The Act, and the preceding discussion in Congress, gave the Board little guidance. The Act provided[19] only that the Board should decide in each case whether, "in order to insure to employees the full benefit of their right to self-organization and to collective bargaining, and otherwise to effectuate the policies of this Act," the unit appropriate for the purposes of collective bargaining should be "the employer unit, craft unit, plant unit, or subdivision thereof."

For a number of reasons these decisions were difficult. It had been expected that disagreements would occur between employers and unions as to units, which the Board would decide in order to effectuate the broad purposes of the Act. But there were also disputes involving the desire of small groups of employees, or unions claiming to represent them, for small units such as a craft, or a department, or one plant, against the interest of a larger group who wanted a unit covering an entire plant or a group of plants. These disputes involved the issue of the right of free choice for the larger as against the small groups and issues as to what units for collective bargaining would "insure to employees the full benefit" of their rights. Moreover, members of the Board were of different opinions as to the congressional intent. Were they expected to take the initiative in deciding *the most*

18. National Labor Relations Board, *Studies of the Results of National Labor Relations Board Activities* (Washington, 1946), pp. 76–85.
19. Section 9 (b).

effective unit for collective bargaining when the issue was presented to them? Or were they merely to decide in accordance with the wishes of the employees? And, if the latter, which should rule—the interest of the larger majority of employees or the right to self-organization by minority groups?[20]

The greatest difficulty arose from the split in the labor movement, which had not been foreseen when the Wagner Act was passed in 1935. The rise of the CIO not only brought the organization of the mass-production industries on an industrial basis, which clashed with "vested rights" of craft unions; it brought also the challenge of young, militant unions to old organizations in many industries, and rivalry between AFL, CIO, and nonaffiliated unions in extending organization into many new fields. This competition led often to conflicting claims as to the units for collective bargaining, depending more upon the chance of the current strength of particular unions than upon differences in theory as to union structure. In a dynamic and highly unstable time of rapidly increasing organization, furthermore, changes in the form of organization and in affiliation occurred with unprecedented rapidity. Competing organizations sought the support of the Board for the units they claimed to be appropriate in particular cases, even when at other times they inconsistently claimed different types of units. Altogether it was an almost impossible situation for the agency forced to make the decisions.

Attempting to weigh the facts and circumstances of each case in which a unit decision was necessary, the Board developed certain standards, although it was wary of rigid rules, and insisted upon the need to decide on the facts of the particular case. Inevitably, as the volume of cases increased, there was more tendency to apply rather rigidly the rule which seemed to fit. While in some special circumstances this may have worked injustice or created unworkable situations, certainty and consistency as to the application of rules were generally approved by the Board's clients. The Board listed the major factors which were important in determining whether a group of employees had such a community of interest that they could appropriately be grouped for the purpose of collective bargaining.[21] Among

20. For a discussion of the different points of view in the Board to 1940 see Bowman, *op. cit.*, ch. 10.

21. *Third Annual Report*, pp. 156–97; *Eleventh*, pp. 23–32. There were many unit problems involving special groups, such as guards, professional employees, and foremen, but since the issues are somewhat apart from the central problems under the Act, their consideration is omitted; cf. also the group of cases where the Board refused to find units appropriate when based on distinctions of race

these factors were the duties, skill, wages, hours, and working conditions of the employees; the extent[22] and type of self-organization; the history of collective bargaining in this or other plants in the industry; the desires of the employees; the eligibility of employees for membership in the union; and the relationship between the proposed unit or units and the administration and organization of the employer's business. When there was no disagreement on the unit, ordinarily the Board found appropriate the unit requested by the petitioning union, unless it was clearly contrary to well-established principles such as the exclusion of supervisory employees from units of rank-and-file workers.[23]

By the summer of 1937 conflicts between the CIO and the AFL over the craft versus industrial unit issue and between competing unions in other situations posed for the Board a crucial problem. In the precedent-setting Globe[24] case, where rival unions claimed craft and industrial units, and where there had been both a history of separate craft negotiations and more recently a plant-wide agreement, the Board decided that either a craft or an industrial unit was feasible and that the considerations were so evenly balanced that the deciding factor should be the desires of the employees themselves. It therefore ordered an election in which the two craft groups would vote separately. If they voted for the industrial union, they would be included in a plant-wide unit; if they voted for the craft unions, they would be given separate craft units. In this case the industrial union won, although the device protected the craftsmen by giving the deciding voice to them rather than to the larger group.

This device, which came to be known as the "Globe election," from then on was used in a great many cases involving the issue of separate plants or of crafts or departments against possible larger units, where the Board felt that "evenly balanced factors" could make either unit

---

and color, *Tenth Annual Report,* pp. 17–18; *Eleventh,* p. 11; on the latter point cf. Joseph Rosenfarb in Louis G. Silverberg, *The Wagner Act: After Ten Years* (Washington: Bureau of National Affairs, Inc., 1945), pp. 95–97.

22. For discussion of the Board's consideration of the extent of organization as one among other factors in determining the appropriateness of a unit, in order not to deprive a group of organized employees of the right of collective bargaining pending more extensive organization, see *Twelfth Annual Report,* pp. 20–21. The Supreme Court upheld the Board on this in NLRB v. Hearst Publications, 322 U.S. 111 (1944).

23. The Board, however, permitted supervisors to be included in units in the maritime and printing trades and occasionally others where supervisors had traditionally been included.

24. Globe Machine and Stamping Co., 3 NLRB 294 (1937).

appropriate. Since in a large majority of the cases the union desiring the small unit won the election, as it would hardly have opposed the large unit unless it believed that it had the support of the employees in the smaller group, this policy in general ran counter to the desires of those wanting larger units. The case against such policy was argued in a number of dissenting opinions[25] by Mr. Edwin S. Smith, although he had agreed in the original case and continued to approve where there had been a history of separate bargaining by the small group. He argued, however, that the Board should not abandon its judicial function of determining the unit which would insure the full benefit of collective bargaining and promote industrial stability and peace. He thought that to permit a small minority to set themselves off, contrary to the desires of the great majority, would weaken the bargaining power of the employees and was plainly contrary to the purposes of the Act. Although the "Globe election" continued to be used extensively, there were always differences of opinion within the Board as to when it should be applied.

CRAFT VERSUS INDUSTRIAL UNITS

The most frequent controversies on units were over the craft-industrial unit issue. A bit of history is needed for the setting. Contrary to a rather general impression, the American Federation of Labor had never been entirely craft in form. The organizations of mine, clothing, brewery, and textile workers, among others, had for longer or shorter periods been predominantly industrial. One analysis[26] found, by subtracting the membership of industrial unions from the total for all American trade-unions, that "craft unions" included from 75 to 83 per cent of the total from 1914 to 1929, and only 67 per cent in 1934. When under the New Deal a strong interest developed in organizing mass-production workers, the AFL in 1934 adopted a resolution designed to provide a needed revision of its policies, since it was realized that "in many of the industries in which thousands of workers are employed a new condition exists requiring organization

25. Allis-Chalmers Manufacturing Co., 4 NLRB 159 (1937).
26. Leo Wolman, *Ebb and Flow in Trade Unionism* (New York: National Bureau of Economic Research, 1936), p. 92. Another more detailed analysis of AFL structure in 1939 found 16 per cent of AFL membership in craft and multiple-craft unions, 27 per cent in "trade-unions," which included craftsmen and related semiskilled or unskilled workers, 47 per cent in industrial and semi-industrial unions, with a remaining 10 per cent miscellaneous. David J. Saposs and Sol Davison, "Structure of AFL Unions," 4 *Labor Relations Reference Manual* 1042 (1939), summarized in Bowman, *op. cit.*, p. 204.

141

upon a different basis to be most effective."[27] Accordingly the Executive Council was directed to issue charters for national unions in the automotive, cement, aluminum, and "such other mass-production... industries" as the Council judged necessary and to inaugurate a campaign of organization in iron and steel. Unfortunately this attempted reconciliation of interests failed, and ultimately the CIO became a rival federation. The resulting extensive organization on an industrial basis as well as on a great variety of less broad lines, on the part of both AFL and CIO, led to the conflicts which caused so many headaches for the NLRB.

"Globe elections" were the solution chosen for many of the disputed unit cases before the Board. But as time went on frequently an industrial unit had been established either by collective bargaining or by a Board decision, and later a craft group claimed the right to carve out for itself a separate unit. Chairman Madden would have "Globed" these cases generally. When Dr. Leiserson came to the Board, however, Mr. E. S. Smith joined him in establishing an important limitation upon application of the "Globe" device in the American Can case.[28] A collective bargaining history on an industrial basis was held to preclude a later determination of a smaller unit by which small groups could "break up an appropriate unit established and maintained by a bona fide collective bargaining contract" against the will of the majority of the employees. Dr. Leiserson thought that the Board should look primarily to "established custom and practice as embodied in collective bargaining agreements" for the appropriate units. Mr. Smith emphasized rather the greater bargaining strength of the large unit and thought that, in the absence of a collective bargaining history by crafts, they should not be permitted to split off. Chairman Madden thought the result unfair to the crafts, since it would freeze the industrial unit, although it was a fortuitous circumstance that organization in that form had happened to get established first in a plant. For the next five years at least, however, the American Can doctrine continued to be important in the thinking of the Board, although it was never applied rigidly, and many exceptions were made in favor of craft unions.[29] The desire to promote stability in

27. American Federation of Labor, *Report of Proceedings of the Fifty-fourth Annual Convention*, 1934, pp. 586–98.

28. 13 NLRB 1252 (1939). Cf. Dr. Leiserson's discussion in U.S. House of Representatives, Special Committee To Investigate the NLRB, *Hearings, National Labor Relations Act*, 76th Cong., 2d Sess., 1939, Vol. 1, pp. 139–40.

29. Cf. Bendix Products Division of Bendix Aviation Corp., 39 NLRB 81 (1942).

collective bargaining and to avoid encouraging "raiding" gave support to the dismissal of craft petitions in clear cases.

The reaction from the AFL Executive Council to the American Can policy was loud and angry. As early as 1937 the AFL had been worried by the Board's handling of AFL-CIO cases, although it admitted the difficulty of the problems. In 1938 the Executive Council protested that the Board was undertaking "to shape the form and structure of our labor movement." By 1939 it was in full-fledged attack upon the Board, proposing amendments to limit the discretion of the Board in finding appropriate units and especially to compel it to find craft units whenever requested.[30] Although AFL unions were by no means unanimous in their interest on these issues, the Executive Council, dominated as it was by the old craft unions, ignored the fact that the convention in 1934 had approved the industrial form of organization for at least a limited number of industries.

In view of this AFL attack it is important to look at the record. The most extensive information is available for the calendar years 1943–44 from a study made for the Board.[31] Some of the results were rather surprising. Plant-wide units were most frequently requested by all union groups: by AFL unions and local independent unions each in about 57 per cent of their cases, by national independents in 62 per cent, and by CIO unions in 75 per cent of theirs. Craft units were asked for in only 22 per cent of all petitions filed—even for the AFL in only 29 per cent of their petitions. Employers tended to favor larger units, approving industrial units in over 70 per cent of the cases where they expressed a preference. There was widespread agreement between unions, too, on the industrial form of unit—in 75 per cent of the Board's formal cases where there was agreement on the unit. Great variety was found in the units requested by individual AFL unions. The Carpenters, Machinists, and Boilermakers asked for industrial units in over half of their cases but for craft units in a significant portion. Operating Engineers, Electricians, and Teamsters were among the most inconsistent, seeking craft and industrial units in about

---

30. American Federation of Labor, *Report of Executive Council to the Annual Convention,* 1937, p. 66; 1938, p. 70; 1939, pp. 116–24.

31. Unpublished study made for the Board by Bernard W. Stern, industrial analyst, dated June, 1945. Excluding cases in public utilities, communications, and pipe-line systems, where the unit problems were of a specialized nature, the study covered all other petitions filed, a total of 12,634 in the two years; all cases with Board orders involving two or more unions where all agreed on the scope of the unit, 566 cases; and the 711 contested cases where two unions or a union and the employer disagreed on the unit.

equal numbers. CIO unions, also, while mainly industrial, occasionally requested craft or departmental units.

In the contested cases where the Board had to determine the unit, requests for craft units were granted in the great majority, outright in nearly 30 per cent of the cases, and provisionally with "Globe elections" in another 42 per cent. Moreover, the AFL fared far the best before the Board in terms of its requests granted in these contested cases. It received the unit wanted, outright or provisionally, in 64.5 per cent of its cases, compared to only 50 per cent for the CIO in their cases. In only 54 cases in these two years did the Board deny an AFL request for a craft unit as against an industrial or semi-industrial unit. In 40 of those, collective bargaining history was the primary factor in the decision. But at the same time in 38 other cases the Board granted craft units despite a previous history of bargaining on a wider basis. In the 260 cases where craft "Globe elections" took place, the craft union won in 80 per cent.

The record clearly shows the extreme complexity of the problems faced by the Board in these contested cases and that it tried to weigh all the facts in each case and arrive at a reasonable conclusion. There was room for honest difference of opinion as to what would best effectuate the policy of the Act. Cases were differentiated in terms of their own special circumstances, at the same time that certain standards such as that of collective bargaining history were applied where it seemed reasonable. There is no support in this record for the charge of anti-AFL bias[32]—unless on an assumption that the interest of a craft or other small group was *always* superior to that of an industrial union, regardless of circumstances. The Board, of course, could not under the Act proceed on any such assumption.

From 1944 to 1947, nevertheless, there was substantial reconsideration and modification of policy in regard to the severance of craft groups when they requested it. Chairman Millis, while concerned for the interest of stability, had long thought the American Can doctrine unduly static, freezing the industrial unit and sometimes resulting in inequity to true craft groups.[33] Accordingly, the question was opened in a case involving pattern-makers in the General Electric Lynn plant.[34] A "Globe election" was granted, although there had been an

32. Cf. the conclusion in "The G—— D—— Labor Board," *Fortune,* 18 (October, 1938), 120, that the record does not bear out the general impression of pro-CIO prejudice.

33. Mr. Reilly tended to support the craft unit requests. He was generally believed to be very sensitive to AFL criticism and to think it wise policy to try to satisfy the AFL.

34. 58 NLRB 57 (1944).

industrial contract since 1936, on the ground that the pattern-makers were a true craft, highly skilled, with nearly 100 per cent organization in the plant and a commanding position in the trade, and that they had consistently adhered to their union through the period of industrial bargaining. For a time the Board applied this new theory cautiously. In the spring of 1945 the Chairman dissented sharply when in a Phelps Dodge case[35] the majority of the Board permitted "Globe elections" on AFL petitions in a series of craft and semi-departmental units on the theory that the crafts had retained their separate identity. The Chairman objected to the disregard of a long and successful history of bargaining on a plant-wide basis, first by an independent, then from 1941 to 1943 with the AFL Metal Trades Council, and from 1943 with the CIO Mine, Mill and Smelter Workers after they won an election in the plant-wide unit. As late as August, 1946, Mr. Reilly dissenting, the Board applied the American Can doctrine in a Philip Morris case,[36] where it found a persuasive history of industrial bargaining and no persistent, aggressive refusal of the crafts to merge with the production unit.

From November, 1946, on through 1947, however, the final three-man Board moved far toward readiness to permit "craft" groups to sever themselves from established broader units. A unit of electricians was permitted in the potash industry,[37] although there had been four years of industrial bargaining, when the Board found an "apprentice-able and well-defined craft," which had not previously had "an opportunity to vote on this issue," and that craft bargaining was common in the industry. Succeeding decisions relaxed the tests still further, especially where the issue was before the Board for the first time. Experience in other parts of the industry or the area, or even in a comparable industry, as copper-mining when the issue arose in open-pit iron-mining,[38] was used to support the case for "Globe elections" in the smaller units. The new policy was not strictly limited to true craft groups, as was seen in a miscellaneous unit of powerhouse and refrigeration plant and allied groups which the Board spoke of as "having craft characteristics," although there had been four years of plant-wide bargaining following a Board election.[39] The issue was

35. Phelps Dodge Corp. (Morenci), 60 NLRB 1431 (1945). The description of the units required seven pages!
36. Philip Morris & Co., 70 NLRB 274 (1946). Cf. also Proctor and Gamble Manufacturing Co., 70 NLRB 1121 (1946); Consolidated Vultee Aircraft Corp., 70 NLRB 1357 (1946).
37. International Minerals and Chemical Corp., 71 NLRB 878 (1946).
38. Kaiser Co. (Vulcan Mine), 73 NLRB 931 (1947).
39. E. I. DuPont de Nemours and Co., 73 NLRB 1167 (1947).

permitted to be opened even in basic steel,[40] where the Board had consistently dismissed petitions from crafts.

Many employers with experience with plant-wide bargaining were concerned over the prospect of having to deal with several unions instead of one and opposed craft severance. The AFL, of course, approved the trend, but it continued to argue for an amendment to make craft units mandatory when the craftsmen wanted it.[41] The CIO was sharply critical, arguing that the policy promoted jurisdictional strife and raiding and needlessly upset established bargaining systems.[42]

What can be said in conclusion with regard to the Board's handling of this difficult issue? Chiefly that it was unfortunate that a divided and competing labor movement forced a government agency to make choices for which there was no completely satisfactory basis. Despite Mr. Smith's persuasive argument for choice of the *most effective unit,* Congress had not given the Board any mandate to establish a national policy as to the structure of collective bargaining. Rather the question of appropriate units was to be decided case by case.[43] Reliance upon experience and evidence as to the desires of employees was a natural consequence. Faced with the dilemma of conflicting desires of different groups of employees, however, the "Globe" device was a useful way out for many cases. Administrative decision in the light of all the facts of the particular case, also, was far better in its results than would have been any rigid rule. Mistakes were undoubtedly made, earlier in too rigid application of the "collective bargaining history" test, when circumstances had changed, and later when sensitiveness to AFL criticism led to permitting severance to more than very carefully defined true craft groups. The argument for workable and effective collective bargaining on a broad basis, which employers also approve, should be overcome by the separatist desires of small groups only when the case is extremely clear. Otherwise incentive is given to

40. The Board ordered a hearing on the question of a bricklayers' request for a craft unit, in American Rolling Mill Co., 73 NLRB 617 (1947). Cf. Tennessee Coal, Iron and Railroad Co., 39 NLRB 617 (1942). For the outcome, cf. *infra*, ch. 14, pp. 523–24.

41. Statement of President William Green, U.S. Senate, Committee on Labor and Public Welfare, *Hearings, Labor Relations Program*, 80th Cong., 1st Sess., 1947, Pt. 2, pp. 1008–9, cited as Senate Committee on Labor and Public Welfare, *Hearings, 1947.*

42. Frank Donner, in *CIO News*, March 24, 1947, May 26, 1947; President Philip Murray, *Report to the Eighth Constitutional Convention of the Congress of Industrial Organizations*, November, 1946, p. 34.

43. House Committee on Labor, *NLRB Report, 1935*, p. 22.

raiding and instability. There was danger in 1947, even before the amendments to the Act, that the breaking-up of effective plant-wide units would be encouraged by Board policy.[44]

MULTI-PLANT UNITS

The question whether a single plant or a group of plants constituted the appropriate unit came to the Board in a relatively small number of cases,[45] of which a minority involved bitter controversy between rival unions. Most involved issues as to company-wide units and a few of them multiple-employer units or association- or industry-wide units.[46] Often there was no disagreement between bona fide unions as to the scope of the unit. The Board ordinarily recognized a unit as broad as was clearly in accordance with the desires of employees and their community of interest if it was justified by the form of organization of the business or businesses and permitted by the terms of the Act.

In communication and transportation systems and other public utilities the Board early held that the integrated nature of operations made system-wide units appropriate when organization had proceeded far enough, but it established local units when otherwise employees who had only organized locally would have been denied the benefits of collective bargaining pending more extensive organization.[47] In manufacturing, also, multiple-plant units were established when there was both sufficient community of interest among employees of the different plants of a company and centralization of management to make the broader unit feasible for collective bargaining and desirable in order to prevent interplant competition to the detriment of employees in different areas.[48] Employers sometimes agreed with the union on the scope of unit; but they sometimes argued for a company-wide unit when the union was able only to assert a claim to separate plants, or for separate units when a union asserted

44. But see the Board's statement of its position, in Senate Committee on Labor and Public Welfare, *Hearings, 1947,* Pt. 4, pp. 1915–16; *Twelfth Annual Report,* pp. 19–20.

45. Only 499 multi-plant petitions were filed in the two calendar years 1943–44, and the Board decided only 173 such cases in those years, for example. Stern study, *supra,* pp. 143–44.

46. The development of Board policy to 1941 was analyzed in detail by the writer in "The Employer Unit for Collective Bargaining in NLRB Decisions," *Journal of Political Economy,* 50 (1942), 321–56.

47. Cf. Postal Telegraph-Cable Co., 7 NLRB 444 (1938); Western Union Telegraph Co., 17 NLRB 683 (1939).

48. Cf. Alpena Garment Co., 13 NLRB 720 (1939); Pittsburgh Plate Glass Co., 10 NLRB 1111 (1939).

that it had a majority in the broad unit. Opposition to the union itself was evident in many such arguments over units.

For a time the Board was divided as to proper policy where one union had a majority in a company unit covering several plants but where in one plant that union was rejected by the local employees. In two important glass-company cases early in 1939 the Board refused to establish separate plant units, on the ground that to permit small groups, representing small minorities of all the employees, to separate themselves would "seriously impede and obstruct the efforts of the far larger number of employees at the other plants effectively to organize and bargain collectively."[49] Dr. Leiserson's appointment, however, brought a reconsideration. A newly adopted policy of ordinarily holding elections rather than checking union cards, in order to remove all doubt as to the real choice of employees, directed attention to the question whether a union had in fact a majority at all the plants claimed in an employer-wide unit. Normally from then on a broad unit was limited to those plants where the union had a majority. In an important group of decisions beginning with a Chrysler case,[50] the majority reversed the policy of the earlier glass cases and consistently refused to establish a multi-plant unit when on the evidence it appeared that the broad unit might impose a bargaining agency upon the employees of a plant against their choice, in the absence of a clear history of collective bargaining on the broader basis. In 1941 after Dr. Millis became Chairman, the Board granted a separate plant election to the employees in the Libbey-Owens-Ford plant[51] which had been in controversy in the original case, and the local union won the election by a large majority. Mr. E. S. Smith dissented in all these cases, consistent with his policy on craft units. He believed, as stated most fully in the Libbey-Owens-Ford dissent, that the Board should determine the unit "on the basis of the broadest industrial unit in which self-organization has been effective"; otherwise the Board was permitting the scope of unit to be determined by the desires of employees in the smallest unit claimed, thus weakening bargaining power, multiplying the problems of management in dealing with employees, and aggravating existing divisions in the labor movement.

In practice the Board's policy which continued to rule, though exceptions were made in particular circumstances, meant that company-

49. Libbey-Owens-Ford Glass Co., 10 NLRB 1470 (1939); Pittsburgh Plate Glass Co., 10 NLRB 1111 (1939).
50. Chrysler Corp., 13 NLRB 1303 (1939).
51. 31 NLRB 243 (1941).

wide units were postponed only until the union in the broad unit had demonstrated its majority in the plants in question.[52] A soundly based evolution took place as a result, and when majorities were demonstrated in individual plants, these plants were incorporated into the structure of "company-wide" bargaining. This pattern could be watched in many industries: automobile, rubber, steel, electrical manufacturing, and shipbuilding, for example.[53] It reflected a Board policy adapted to a period in which bargaining on a broad basis was developing.

After broad units had been established, either by agreement or by Board decision, sometimes controversy broke out later over an attempt of part of the unit to break away. Bitter jurisdictional disputes and raids by rival unions were sometimes involved, sometimes real dissatisfaction of local groups of employees with the results of bargaining by their existing representative. The Board, concerned for stability of labor relations, was very loath to permit the breakup of such established units. This was made clear in an important case involving the Bethlehem shipyards. An eight-yard agreement had resulted in 1942 after elections had been won in a series of shipyards by the CIO Marine and Shipbuilding Workers Union. The Baltimore Metal Trades Council, AFL, later petitioned for a separate unit in the Bethlehem Fairfield Shipyard,[54] where one of the elections had been held. The Board unanimously held that a separate unit was inappropriate after the broad unit had been established by agreement and effectively consolidated through joint action. Similarly it dismissed a CIO petition in a tobacco case,[55] where a four-plant unit had been built up after certification of AFL unions at various times and a master-agreement had been operating since 1940. The Board held this unquestionably a multi-plant unit, "there being actual bargaining on a multi-plant basis, stabilized by agreement." This doctrine was applied even in a much less clear case[56] where a two-plant unit had been established four years earlier after an independent union won separate elections in the two plants, but where the independent had for more than a year been completely inactive in one plant, and an AFL

52. Cf. Briggs Manufacturing Co., 17 NLRB 749 (1939); Chrysler Corp., 28 NLRB 328 (1940); 31 NLRB 400 (1941).

53. The UAW-CIO, for instance, reported 60 General Motors plants under contract in 1940 and 81 in 1941. *United Automobile Worker*, August 1, 1941, p. 4.

54. Bethlehem-Fairfield Shipyard, 58 NLRB 579 (1944).

55. P. Lorillard Co., 58 NLRB 1112 (1944).

56. Allied Laboratories, 60 NLRB 1196 (1945). Mr. Reilly took occasion to state the conditions, however, under which he approved of permitting *craft* severance, in spite of the American Can doctrine.

union filed a petition. The petition was dismissed, the Chairman considering the four years' history conclusive, and Mr. Reilly concurring on the basis of the precedents against permitting "a dissident faction to secede from the organic structure which it helped to establish." Mr. Houston's dissent made clear the dilemma facing the Board in such cases where the bargaining agent had really ceased to function in the part of the unit which wished to secede, so that collective bargaining was at a standstill. He did not think that stability could be served by attempting to maintain the status quo here; the problem could be solved only by an election.

ASSOCIATION UNITS

By 1947 more than four million workers were covered by association-wide bargaining agreements.[57] While relatively few of the Board's cases involved the issue of whether multiple-employer units were appropriate,[58] decisions on this issue were sometimes influential in the development of area- and industry-wide bargaining.

Board policy on multi-employer units paralleled in important respects that as to company-wide units. Before a multi-employer unit could be found appropriate under the Act, however, the Board required clear evidence that the association was authorized to act and was acting for the employers in collective bargaining,[59] as well as that bargaining in such a broad unit was feasible. Collective bargaining history was an important element to be considered for proof of these points. In early cases association units were found appropriate in a number of longshoremen's cases and in clothing, fisheries, fish-packing, stone-working, and motion-picture cases, among others; but

57. U.S. Bureau of Labor Statistics, *Collective Bargaining with Associations and Groups of Employers,* Bulletin No. 897, 1947.

58. The Board decided only 19 cases involving question as to multi-employer units in the calendar years 1943–44. Stern study, *op. cit.* The Board reported also that in fiscal year 1946 "cursory examination" of the records found only 10 decisions finding multi-employer units appropriate. U.S. House of Representatives, Committee on Education and Labor, *Hearings, Amendments to the National Labor Relations Act,* 80th Cong., 1st Sess., 1947, Pt. 5, p. 3178, cited as House Committee on Education and Labor, *Hearings, 1947.*

59. Shipowners' Association of the Pacific Coast, 7 NLRB 1002 (1938). Cf. also statement of the Board: "Thus the Board will never establish a multiple-employer bargaining unit in any case unless it appears that the employers themselves, either as members of an employer association or otherwise, have already established a practice of joint action in regard to their labor relations and have demonstrated, by negotiations through an effective employer organization and the customary adherence to uniform labor agreements resulting therefrom, that they desire to be bound by group rather than individual action." House Committee on Education and Labor, *Hearings, 1947,* Pt. 5, p. 3157.

they were refused in the absence of evidence that employers had given the association "antecedent legal authority" to bargain for them.

As in the company-wide unit cases, the greatest difficulty arose where a rival union wished to break up an established unit. Following its theory on "stability" and the interest of effective collective bargaining as shown by bargaining history, the Board refused in early cases to permit units of single companies to be withdrawn on petition of rival unions, where association bargaining had improved labor conditions and stabilized highly competitive industries. Cases in the doll and toy industry in New York City, the scrap-iron industry of San Francisco, and coal-mining[60] are examples.

While these cases posed the issue as between effectiveness of a broad unit for collective bargaining and the claim of smaller groups to a right of self-determination, serious division among Board members on the weight to be given to the factors in association cases was later in appearing than on the craft issue. In 1941, however, the majority of the Board, Chairman Millis and Dr. Leiserson, permitted reopening of an issue as to the association unit in the first Pacific longshoremen's case. In 1938[61] the Board had established a coast-wide unit, in spite of the protest of the AFL longshoremen. Four locals in northern ports with about nine hundred members had remained AFL, while the rest of the locals with over ten thousand members had transferred to the CIO International Longshoremen's and Warehousemen's Union. The Board originally held that the contrary desires of the men of the four ports were outweighed by the need for an effective coast-wide unit, in view of the coast-wide organization of the employers. The majority of the Board in 1941, on the contrary, permitted "Globe elections" in the three ports, including Tacoma, which were still claimed by the AFL. It found that the AFL longshoremen had refused to accept coast-wide decisions in some matters, had continued their organization, and had bargained locally with their employers on all local matters, and that, since they had never had an opportunity to vote as to whether they should be included in the broad unit, they should now be permitted to do so.[62] These elections were won overwhelmingly by the AFL.

Mr. E. S. Smith dissented strongly, arguing that the decision placed in jeopardy the gains of the longshoremen resulting from years of

60. Admiar Rubber Co., 9 NLRB 407 (1938); Hyman-Michaels Co., 11 NLRB 796 (1939); Alston Coal Co., 13 NLRB 683 (1939); Stevens Coal Co., 19 NLRB 98 (1940).
61. Shipowners' Association of the Pacific Coast, 7 NLRB 1002 (1938).
62. 32 NLRB 668 (1941); 33 NLRB 845 (1941).

effort to build up the coast-wide unit and that it would "tend to disrupt a workable and stabilized bargaining relationship established by certification and contract and thus frustrate the bargaining process." This decision was as sharply criticized by the CIO as the earlier one had been by the AFL. In 1947 it was still an issue, as Tacoma had continued to remain out of the coast-wide unit. The separateness in fact which the Board had recognized continued, with its accompanying danger to union strength should serious conflict break out between unions and employers.

The majority of the Board had made clear in the longshore decision, however, that it was not changing its established policy. Appropriately established and practically functioning bargaining units would not be split and smaller units set up on the desire of employees in smaller groups. The policy of maintaining broad units which had been established by collective bargaining history continued. In New Bedford cotton textiles accordingly the Board ordered an association-wide election instead of the separate company elections which the CIO requested—and the CIO won in the broad unit.[63] In the southern soil-pipe industry it dismissed a CIO petition for a separate company election, on the ground that an industry-wide contract with the Moulders Union, AFL, was a bar—although there was doubt whether the contract had in fact been administered in the plant in question.[64] In an important case in the pulp and paper industry of the Pacific Northwest,[65] where collective bargaining had been conducted by AFL unions on a multiple-employer basis since 1934, it dismissed the petition of a dissatisfied local which had joined the CIO. The decision emphasized the fact that employees as well as employers in this industry had long considered bargaining on an association basis desirable and that this system of dealing had been conducive to orderly functioning of collective bargaining and to stability and uniformity in labor conditions.

From then on the Board continued to apply these principles as well established, where it found collective bargaining histories on a multiple-employer basis and "actual bargaining on a multi-plant basis, stabilized by agreement." The same principles were used also in cases where a small group of companies had negotiated jointly, although without a formal association.[66] It was possible to distinguish cases,

63. 47 NLRB 1345 (1943).
64. Central Foundry Co., 42 NLRB 265 (1942); 46 NLRB 676 (1943); 48 NLRB 5 (1943).
65. Rayonier, Inc., 52 NLRB 1269 (1943).
66. Dolese and Shepard Co., 56 NLRB 532 (1944); Standard Slag Co., 63 NLRB 313 (1945).

however, and one-plant units were sometimes found proper, in the face of claims for an association unit. In a glass case, a new plant was not assimilated to the association unit until after a one-plant election.[67] In a Pepsi-Cola Bottling Company case, where there was an association contract of long standing, but no indication that the Brewery Workers had ever bothered to organize the employees or provide for any participation by them in bargaining, even on grievances, the Board found the Teamsters' claim for a separate company unit justifiable and ordered an election.[68] In a hotly contested case in the clothing industry[69] where the AFL claimed that the Union Label Agreement to which the employer was a party made a separate company unit inappropriate, the Board held that the national agreement was of such limited scope that it did not pre-empt the field of collective bargaining. A local unit was therefore appropriate, and the Amalgamated Clothing Workers was certified after having won an election. This case was distinguished from other association cases where the Board found that individual company bargaining on some details was only within the limits left after basic conditions were determined by the association-wide contract.[70]

Although it was extremely difficult for a union to make a case before the Board for breaking off a small unit from a larger one established by collective bargaining history, paradoxically an employer could pull out, if he indicated his intention "to pursue an individualistic course of action with regard to his labor relations." If he resigned from the association, and was permitted by its constitution to do so, the association was no longer his legal bargaining representative, and the Board could no longer include his employees in the association unit. The Board therefore found the employer's intent controlling and separate company units appropriate.[71]

67. Demuth Glass Works, 53 NLRB 451 (1943).
68. Pepsi-Cola Bottling Co. of Kansas City, 55 NLRB 1183 (1944).
69. Cohn-Goldwater Manufacturing Co., 53 NLRB 645 (1943), 55 NLRB 1164 (1944), 56 NLRB 749 (1944). For AFL criticism see American Federation of Labor, *Report of the Executive Council to the Annual Convention, 1944,* pp. 57–58.
70. New Bedford Cotton Manufacturers Association, 47 NLRB 1345 (1943).
71. Cf. Great Bear Logging Co., 59 NLRB 701 (1944); Marcellus W. Murdock, 67 NLRB 1426 (1946). In a Haverhill shoe case a multi-employer unit covered association members and those nonmembers who approved the broad unit and expected to continue to follow the lead of the association. George F. Carleton and Co., 54 NLRB 222 (1943). In two leather cases a little later association units were limited to the members of the association, although the independents had been in the habit of signing identical contracts; this was not considered true area-wide bargaining, since the independents were not obligated to follow the lead of the association. Advance Tanning Co., 60 NLRB 923 (1945); R. E. Rappaport & Sons, 62 NLRB 1118 (1945).

The issue of area-wide bargaining was presented to the Board in 1946 in complex form in the San Francisco metal trades. There had been a long history of collective bargaining between the Machinists and the California Metal Trades Association, which set the standards then followed by the entire local industry. A schism occurred in the union and part shifted to the CIO. In the resulting representation case the association contended for an area-wide unit, in order to restore stability and uniformity in labor conditions. But the Board[72] held that true association-wide bargaining existed only when employers had specifically given the association authority to bargain for them; it ruled that the association unit would include only such employers, all others to constitute separate units. As a result one union won some of the independents, the other the association unit. Area-wide unity had been shattered by the union split, and the Board decision was unable to contribute toward a solution. In view of the collective bargaining history it appeared to the association unrealistic to require such specific evidence of authorization by the individual employer, before his employees were included in the broad unit which had been in fact established by long history.[73]

To summarize late policy on association units, by 1947 the Board set up such broad units only when employers indicated by their actions or explicitly that they were bound by the joint action of the group. If inclusion of any part of the unit was questioned by a union, the employees of that group were permitted to vote as to their desires.[74] If an old established collective bargaining system on a broad basis was challenged by a union wishing to withdraw a small unit, this was denied, except when employers indicated that they did not choose to be bound by association action or failed to indicate that they did. "Stability of collective bargaining" ran, therefore, against the desires of a seceding group, unless supported by independence on the part of individual employers. The latter qualification, however, opened the way to disruption of established area-wide bargaining in such situations as in the California metal trades.

72. California Metal Trades Association, 72 NLRB 624 (1947); cf. also California State Brewers Institute, 72 NLRB 665 (1947).

73. For an interesting later case, in which the majority of the Board reaffirmed this line of doctrine and specifically the Advance Tanning decision (*supra*, n. 71), see Associated Shoe Industries of Southeastern Massachusetts, 81 NLRB No. 38 (January 19, 1949).

74. Cf. Waterfront Employers Association of the Pacific Coast, 71 NLRB 80, 71 NLRB 121 (1946). In these cases the multi-employer unit was established, despite objections by the associations and some of the individual companies, when the association activities indicated that the broad unit was appropriate. *Twelfth Annual Report*, p. 21.

Such multiple-employer and multiple-plant cases were often difficult, especially when bitter jurisdictional disputes between rival unions were involved. Faced with the necessity of making decisions, the Board developed a policy which worked reasonably well on the whole. Possibly in some cases it would have been better to permit the dissenting local group to vote. Yet sometimes the dispute died down, and the incumbent union later was able to achieve greater acceptance. It was questioned, also, whether the terms of the Act required the Board to go as far as it did in the last two years in permitting employers to determine the scope of units which had been stabilized previously by their joint action in dealing with the unions. The rather widespread adverse comment on industry-wide bargaining in the later years may have had some influence on these decisions. But employers could not under the law be deprived of their right to make their own decisions as to their own bargaining agent, and this, as well as the complex factors as to stability and collective bargaining history and the interest in free choice of employees so that the union acting for them could be their responsibly chosen agent, had to be weighed in making these decisions in the individual cases.

CONTRACTS AS A BAR TO REPRESENTATION ELECTIONS

Issues as to the relative importance of stability and free choice of representatives arose also in an important group of cases involving contracts. The question whether an existing contract should prevent the holding of an election during its life was an increasingly important one as more and more of industry came to be covered by collective agreements. Was the right of employees to be represented by a union of their own choice, in accordance with the terms of the Act, paramount, or the interest of the incumbent union and perhaps of the employer in a contract? The Act was of course designed to encourage collective bargaining, and therefore collective agreements, as well as freely chosen representation. The Board built up a body of precedent in deciding case by case on these issues, but its evolving theory was seldom explicitly stated.[75]

In the early period, when a "prevailing disregard of collective contracts" by the Board was commented on,[76] matters were relatively simple, since most frequently the contracts which were urged as a bar to proceeding were clearly not valid under the Act. The Board had no trouble ordering elections in the face of contracts that had

75. Some of these cases involved also jurisdictional disputes, policy as to which is discussed *infra*, ch. 6, pp. 220 ff.

76. W. G. Rice, Jr., "The Legal Significance of Labor Contracts under the NLRB," *Michigan Law Review*, 37 (1939), 693–724, at 716.

been signed with company-dominated unions or with unions not representing the free choice of a majority of the workers when signed, or during a dispute over representation, or contracts of unreasonably long duration or of indefinite term.[77] In the first year one decision assumed "the freedom of employees to change their representatives, while at the same time continuing the existing agreements under which the representatives must function."[78] But this theory did not appear later in any such sweeping form, and petitions were frequently dismissed during the term of a contract without prejudice to renewal at any appropriate time. By 1939 the issues were clearly drawn, and differences of approach within the Board shown, in the National Sugar Refining Company case.[79] There the majority refused to order an election, "in the interest of stabilization of industrial relations," since the contract was not to last for more than a year, the contracting union had represented a majority when the contract was signed, and no opposing union had given prior notice of its claim to the employer. Mr. E. S. Smith dissented, however, since there was evidence that the contracting union no longer represented a majority, and it was two years since a consent election. He would have expected recognition of the contract to continue until its expiration or change by agreement.

From 1940 to 1945, although there were still disagreements among the Board members, the basic rules were laid down as to the effects of contracts in representation cases. Dr. Leiserson thought that if "a real dispute" over representation existed, it was best to order an election. Chairman Millis, however, put more emphasis on the desirability of stability for satisfactory industrial relations. And Mr. Reilly tended to think in terms of commercial contract law. The basic theory as to whether unions in making contracts were simply acting as agents for the employees,[80] or whether they were principals, with enforceable rights in the contracts, was never completely worked out or stated. A workable compromise was sought which would give due weight to

77. *Third Annual Report,* pp. 134–38. Issues as to collusive contracts are considered *infra,* ch. 6, pp. 204–10.
78. New England Transportation Co., 1 NLRB 130 (1936).
79. 10 NLRB 1410 (1939); *Fourth Annual Report,* p. 75.
80. This was said in one decision, Mill B, Inc., 40 NLRB 346 (1942). Cf. also Columbia Pictures Corp., 64 NLRB 490 (1945). For discussions of the effect of the Wagner Act upon rights under collective contracts, see B. F. Willcox, "The Tri-Boro Case, Mountain or Molehill?" *Harvard Law Review,* 56 (1943), 576–609; "Change of Bargaining Representative during the Life of a Collective Agreement under the Wagner Act," *Yale Law Journal,* 51 (1942), 465–81; T. R. Witmer, "Collective Labor Agreements in the Courts," *Yale Law Journal,* 48 (1938), 195–239.

the need both for stability and for protecting free choice. As time went on, and the industrial relations scene changed to one where contracts were very common and appeared frequently in the cases before the Board, it was inevitable that more weight was given to them and that rules were developed as to the appropriate time to permit a new determination of representation. By 1945–47 this trend had gone so far that the Board was thinking in terms of the "status" of contracting unions, and protection of this status for reasonable periods was given more weight than the freedom of employees to choose their representative. A better-established labor movement possibly made proper this increased institutionalism.

The basic rules as to what contracts would bar elections during their term can easily be summarized. Valid contracts, made with the representatives of the majority of the employees in an appropriate unit, fixing some important terms and conditions of employment, and extending for a reasonable period, normally acted as a bar, in the absence of a prior claim by a rival union.[81] Agreements had to be written and signed, however, before they received such weight.[82] The important "one-year rule" held that normally a contract, or a certification after an election, would bar a new election for a period of one year. The reasonableness of contracts of longer duration was determined by consideration of the custom of the industry. A contract which had been extended under an automatic renewal clause, in the absence of desire of either party to open its terms at the renewal date, usually thirty days or sixty days before the end of the contract period, had equal weight with a new contract, but only, after the Mill B case, if there had not been notice of the claim of the rival union before the automatic renewal date.[83] If the contract was opened for negotiation, however, a petition for an election would be entertained, as was true during negotiation of a new contract, until its effective date. However, when an AFL union opened negotiations and secured a modification of its contract, extending its term, after a CIO organization drive began, such a "premature extension" or renewal was not permitted to foreclose the right of employees to seek a change of representatives.[84]

Petitions sometimes were filed where there had been shifts of substantially the entire group of employees, or a change of affiliation of a

81. *Tenth Annual Report*, p. 19.
82. Eicor, Inc., 46 NLRB 1035 (1943).
83. Mill B, Inc., 40 NLRB 346 (1942). Dr. Leiserson dissented, thinking that it put a premium on inaction to permit an automatically renewed contract to act as a bar unless the rival gave notice before the renewal date.
84. Wichita Union Stockyards Co., 40 NLRB 369 (1942).

local union, or a schism such that there was doubt what union represented the employees, or where the contracting union was defunct and the contract not being administered. Sometimes it was claimed even in the last-named situation that a contract had been automatically renewed in the absence of a prior claim of a rival before the renewal date and was hence a bar; and some petitions were dismissed on such grounds. The Board finally made clear that a union which no longer represented a group of employees was incapable of renewing a contract in their behalf; hence, such a contract could not bar an election.[85] On the basis of the complex facts in the various cases of these sorts, the Board frequently ordered elections,[86] but in others, in close cases, it dismissed the petitions "in the interest of stability" during the life of the contract.[87] The issues were discussed in 1945 in the Container Corporation case.[88] The Pressmen's Union, AFL, had won a consent election and signed a contract and the next year a new contract. A few months later a CIO union claimed recognition and petitioned for an election. The AFL local was no longer functioning, no dues being collected or grievances negotiated. The company and the international union, however, claimed that the contract was a bar. The majority of the Board held that under these circumstances the contract failed to fulfil its statutory function, since it was not being administered, and that it could not therefore serve to stabilize labor relations. While carefully avoiding *ipso facto* setting aside the contract, or necessarily affecting "whatever legal rights may have survived the destruction of the union which negotiated and signed it," the Board ordered an election.[89] Mr. Reilly, dissenting, held the contract a valid one and could find "no legal theory" for setting it aside. He held that the employees' right to revoke the authority of their agent could apply only prospectively and was concerned that certifications might be frustrated "if they are repugnant to enforceable contracts."

The issue in such cases was of course whether, realistically, stable industrial relations could be achieved without an election to settle the representation dispute. A bit of pertinent evidence came from reports of Regional Directors on the results of such cases in 1940–42. In thir-

85. Cf. Aladdin Industries, 63 NLRB 76 (1945); Perfection Spring and Equipment Co., 72 NLRB 590 (1947); Sunshine Mining Co., 48 NLRB 301 (1943).
86. Cf. Harbison Walker Refractories Co., 44 NLRB 1280 (1942); Gelatin Products Co., 49 NLRB 173 (1943).
87. Great Lakes Carbon Corp., 44 NLRB 70 (1942).
88. 61 NLRB 823 (1945). Cf. also Trailer Co. of America, 51 NLRB 1106 (1943).
89. Cf. News Syndicate Co., 67 NLRB 1178 (1946).

teen instances where petitioning unions won the elections, nine of the old contracts were taken over and administered to their expiration, and another was kept until new terms were agreed upon. In only two cases were new contracts made at once.

During the two postwar years increased competition between rival unions made the Board more than ever concerned with the interest of stability and inclined its thinking toward protecting the "status" of incumbent unions for at least reasonable periods. For newly certified unions the Board extended the one-year rule, to hold that contracts renewed or newly written at any time during the year after certification would bar an election for the term of the contract.[90] Only in a few exceptional circumstances did the Board order an election in spite of this rule.[91]

Already in early 1945 contracts of more than one year, also, were coming to be accepted as reasonable. Two-year contracts were held presumptively valid, in the worsted industry, when a rival union could not prove that they were contrary to custom in the industry. Even a three-year contract was found valid and a bar when the incumbent union proved that such contracts were common in the industry and area.[92] Finally, in 1947, the Board went further and held that, in the light of the experience in administering the Act, a two-year contract could not be said to be unreasonable. The Reed Roller Bit Company[93] had signed a two-year agreement with the Steelworkers, and after a year the Machinists petitioned for an election. The company and the Steelworkers both held that the contract should be considered a bar. The Board in its unanimous decision made a strong case for the position that collective bargaining had passed through an "experimental and transitional period," in which it was important to emphasize "the right of workers to select and change their representatives," but that the time had come when "stability of industrial relations can be better served, without unreasonably restricting employees in their right to change representatives, by refusing to interfere with bargaining relations secured by collective agreements of two years' duration." Accordingly the petition was dismissed.

In addition, the Board developed a series of other rather technical

90. Swift and Co., 66 NLRB 1288 (1946); Con. P. Curran Printing Co., 67 NLRB 1419 (1946); *Eleventh Annual Report*, pp. 19–23.
91. Electric Sprayit Co., 67 NLRB 780 (1946); Carson Pirie Scott and Co., 69 NLRB 935 (1946).
92. Uxbridge Worsted Co., 60 NLRB 1395 (1945); United States Finishing Co., 63 NLRB 575 (1945).
93. 72 NLRB 927 (1947). Cf. also Puritan Ice Co., 74 NLRB 1311 (1947).

rules as to when a petition would be accepted, all in the interest of stability. A claim to recognition alone was not enough to prevent a new contract from becoming a bar to an election, unless the claim was followed up within ten days by a petition filed with the Board.[94] This was to prevent frivolous claims—a "dog-in-the-manger" attitude— when a union was not ready seriously to press its claim, especially since under Board policies an unsettled question of representation prevented further negotiation.[95] Moreover, the petition of a rival union, to be accepted, had to be filed before the automatic renewal date of an old contract, even if the contract was opened for negotiations.[96] Board Member Houston was concerned lest the new rules unduly restrict the right of workers to change representatives at reasonable periods. The rules were complicated and technical, but union officers and business agents who watched Board decisions carefully seemed to have adjusted easily to them.

The question in all this development was whether for good industrial relations there was too much support to union "status" and stability when democratic and responsible industrial relations might better be promoted by more assurance that the union recognized had the support of the employees concerned. On the other hand, the discouragement of raiding and useless instability was salutary.[97] Appraisal of all the factors involved in each case continued to be needed. Mistakes were sometimes made when rules were applied rigidly without adequate attention to all the factors in particular cases. But, as the Board studied its experience, it tended to find and eliminate the major difficulties in its policies. From a long-run view the basic policies which had been developed appeared on the whole to strike a reasonable and workable balance between the needs of "stability" and free choice. There was still need for careful administration, based on thorough and objective investigation of the facts of each case.

EMPLOYER PETITIONS AND THE DECERTIFICATION ISSUE

Whether and to what extent employers should have the right to initiate representation proceedings by filing petitions with the Board was controversial throughout the twelve years of the Wagner Act.

94. General Electric X-Ray Corp., 67 NLRB 997 (1946).
95. Midwest Piping and Supply Co., 63 NLRB 1060 (1945).
96. Northwestern Publishing Co., 71 NLRB 167 (1946); Mississippi Lime Co., 71 NLRB 472 (1946); Greenville Finishing Co., 71 NLRB 436 (1946).
97. Cf. the interesting discussion by Gerhard P. Van Arkel, former General Counsel for the Board, 19 *Labor Relations Reference Manual*, 130–35 (1946).

There were real problems from the standpoint of employers who were caught between the fire of two unions claiming recognition or faced with one union which tried by threat of strike or boycott to force recognition though it had not proved and sometimes could not prove that it had the adherence of a majority of the employees. The Board decided at the start that it would not accept petitions from employers, since they might otherwise take advantage of the Board's processes, "under conditions which would frustrate rather than effectuate true collective bargaining."[98] In 1939, however, after congressional hearings showed extensive criticism, the Board adopted a rule permitting employers to petition when they were faced by rival claims of two unions.[99] The Smith Committee in its report in 1940 urged amendent of the Act on this point but limited its recommendation to these two-union situations.[100]

In view of the extensive discussion of this problem, it was surprising how few employers took advantage of the right to petition. Only 74 petitions were filed by employers in the first year, 1939–40, and for the entire eight years under the 1939 rule only about 650 employer petitions were filed, out of a total of nearly 60,000 representation petitions. An analysis of the 507 cases which had been closed by October, 1946, showed that more than half were withdrawn or dismissed before decision by the Board. One-fourth were settled by agreement, by consent elections, stipulated elections, or agreements for recognition or for cross-checks of union cards. Only 18 per cent needed a decision by the Board, most of these resulting in a Board-ordered election. Apparently the employers' right of petition was helpful in settling representation disputes in some of these situations, though these cases were a very minor part of the Board's work.

Controversy continued as to whether employers should have the right to petition when only one union was involved. The Board was concerned lest giving the right to petition in such circumstances would let an employer force a premature test when a union was only beginning to organize, and thus frustrate the right to organize. Moreover, there was danger of encouraging employers to question the union's majority at the end of every contract term and so delay col-

98. *First Annual Report*, p. 26.
99. *Fifth Annual Report*, p. 12; cf. also Board statement in U.S. Senate, Committee on Education and Labor, *Hearings, National Labor Relations Act and Proposed Amendments*, 76th Cong., 1st Sess., 1939, Pt. 3, pp. 540–43.
100. U.S. House of Representatives Special Committee To Investigate the NLRB, *Intermediate Report*, Report No. 1902, 76th Cong., 3d Sess., March, 1940, pp. 77–78.

lective bargaining and interfere with the rights of the employees, especially where there was a history of unfair labor practices.[101] Yet it was recognized that occasionally a petition filed by an employer might help to solve a problem.

During the war the War Labor Board sometimes ordered an employer to make a contract with a union, although he claimed that the union no longer represented his employees. The NLRB therefore in 1944 considered adopting a rule which would have permitted an employer who was involved in a dispute before another government agency to file a petition with the Board in order to have a speedy settlement of any representation issue. A public hearing was held on the proposal; but the unions protested strongly, fearing a flood of petitions which would lead to disruption of relationships and encouragement of antiunion minorities at a time when the unions were trying to maintain the no-strike pledge, and the matter was dropped.

A closely related question was whether the Board should accept a petition to decertify a union as bargaining agent. The Board decided against it in the Tabardrey case in 1943.[102] A petition was filed by a group of southern textile employees alleging that the CIO no longer represented the majority in the plant, after the union had been certified more than two years earlier, but had never been able to obtain a contract. A petition had been presented to the company, signed by an apparent majority, asking it not to enter into any contract for the employees. All this was while a dispute was before the War Labor Board. The NLRB dismissed the petition after hearing the case, on the ground that the petitioners were not seeking representation but rather an election to test the claim of the CIO, and the CIO was not asking an election. The dismissal did not act as a recertification of the CIO, however, or any decision as to duties or rights of the company; those questions were not "properly" before the Board in this case. The Board's refusal to hold elections on such petitions was criticized by employers who argued that the Board disregarded the rights of individual employees and made it more and more difficult for them to get rid of a union—the claim that certifications were "perma-

101. Board statement, Senate Committee on Labor and Public Welfare, *Hearings, 1947*, Pt. 4, pp. 1887, 1916–17; cf. also statements from regional offices, House Committee on Education and Labor, *Hearings, 1947*, Pt. 5, p. 3119.

102. Tabardrey Manufacturing Co., 51 NLRB 246 (1943). Cf. also the Board's dismissal late in 1945 of a group of petitions for decertification filed by employers who were before the WLB. The NLRB held that any dispute over representation could be resolved by the established procedures under the Act. Toledo Steel Products Co., Colonial Life Insurance Co., Landis Machine Co., 65 NLRB 56, 58, 60 (1945).

nent."[103] The Board, however, felt that elections under these circumstances would be counter to the purposes of the Act, by opening the way for encouragement of dissident minorities or of antiunion interference by employers.

There was in fact already ample protection of the legitimate interests of individual employees and employers. At appropriate times, at the end of contract periods, employees were free to shift their union affiliation or to repudiate the union, and employers were free to refuse further recognition if in good faith they doubted the continuing majority status of the union. The Board then would accept a petition from the union claiming to represent the employees, or would investigate any charge of refusal to bargain. Charges that the employer had encouraged an antiunion minority, and that his "doubts" were not in good faith, had to be considered sometimes in such "refusal-to-bargain" cases. The Board had the problem also of how to handle such cases without encouraging employers to challenge the union's majority at the end of every contract. Sometimes there was very long delay as the Board was unable to reach a decision on a close case.

Nevertheless, in view of the widespread criticism on this point, it is not impossible that the Board might have modified its rules further, as to employer petitions at least, to meet the criticism as it did in 1939. The strongest case for a relaxation of the rule was for the benefit of an employer faced by a union which preferred to use its economic power rather than the orderly processes of the Act to secure recognition. In some other cases where the union in fact no longer was desired by the employees, possibly an election on an employer petition or a decertification petition would sometimes have been the most simple and direct way to clarify the facts. But in the natural course of events, if the union really had lost its hold, employers could and did stop bargaining. There was no real hardship in these cases under the existing rule, unless from the standpoint of some who were excessively concerned for the rights of dissident minorities,[104] and those who in close cases would prefer all the benefit of any doubts to be given to those who opposed collective bargaining. This was not of course the basic premise of the Wagner Act or of its administration.

103. For criticisms, and statements by the Board and by union representatives, see Senate Committee on Labor and Public Welfare, *Hearings, 1947*, Pt. 1, p. 154; Pt. 2, pp. 889–90; Pt. 3, p. 1534; Pt. 4, pp. 1917–18; House Committee on Education and Labor, *Hearings, 1947*, Pt. 2, pp. 243–56; Pt. 5, pp. 3153–54.

104. Cf. statements of Leo Wolman and T. R. Iserman, Senate Committee on Labor and Public Welfare, *Hearings, 1947*, Pt. 1, pp. 118, 151–56.

THE INTEGRITY OF ELECTIONS

For the purposes of the Act to be achieved it was essential that elections for the choice of representatives make possible a free and uncoerced choice by the employees. The Board developed its standards of election procedure, to insure proper control of eligibility lists, suitable arrangements for voting, secrecy of the ballot, and safeguards for counting and reporting on the results. The integrity of the Board's conduct of elections was universally recognized. In a rare case where the Board found defects in its own handling of an election, it set the election aside.[105] It was crucial also that the surrounding circumstances permit a free election. The Board considered carefully any objections filed, and elections were set aside when investigation convinced the Board that any interference had impeded full freedom of choice.

Occasionally charges were sustained that violence or other coercive conduct by a union had interfered with the employees' freedom to choose their representative, and, as a result, the Board set aside or postponed elections.[106] In a number of cases employers filed objections on the ground that unions had circulated false and misleading statements and thus interfered with a free election. The Board held, however, that it could not and should not attempt to censor or police union electioneering, unless the conduct was coercive in character and so related to the election as to have had a probable effect upon the votes. It spoke of a strong presumption that secret ballots reflect the true desires of employees, and so certified the unions which had won these elections.[107] Employers were of course free to answer any misstatements. In two 1947 cases, also, elections were set aside on objections of employers that supervisors who were members of the union had participated in organizing employees and thus had interfered with the employees' freedom of choice. Mr. Houston dissented from what appeared to him a refusal to certify the union that was the choice of the employees, on objection of the employer, when the employer had violated the Act through permitting interference by supervisors.[108]

105. *Twelfth Annual Report,* pp. 16–17. Cf. Bercut-Richards Packing Co., 65 NLRB 1052 (1946), *infra,* ch. 6, pp. 224 ff.

106. Cf. National Tea Co., 41 NLRB 774 (1942); La Follette Shirt Co., 65 NLRB 952 (1946).

107. Maywood Hosiery Mills, 64 NLRB 146 (1945); Kroder-Reubel Co., 72 NLRB 240 (1947).

108. Robbins Tire and Rubber Co., 72 NLRB 157 (1947); Parkchester Machine Corp., 72 NLRB 1410 (1947).

More frequently the objections to elections were filed against employers. Over the years a considerable number of elections were set aside when the Board found that freedom of choice had been interfered with by activities of employers or supervisors, such as by threatening economic reprisals should the union win, or warning that the plant might close, or conversely campaigning with pre-election wage increases, or with promises of benefit once the union was defeated.[109]

When competing unions were involved, the employer had no right to give preferential treatment to one of them. Accordingly the Board set aside an election in the Joshua Hendy Iron Works[110] case where an independent union held a contract, and an election was conducted on an AFL petition. In addition to other indications of the employer's preference for the independent, its members were permitted to circulate in the plant on company time for campaign purposes, while AFL adherents had no such freedom; the independent used its bulletin board in the plant for campaign purposes, while the AFL had no comparable opportunity; and the company permitted the independent to use the company's conference room for an election meeting of the shop stewards. While the Board did not here decide whether the employer had been entitled to continue to apply the terms of the independent's contract, including the handling of grievances, it found the special privileges outside the contract sufficient evidence of unequal treatment to sustain the union's objection to the election.

This issue of the status of a contract during an election period was a very difficult one, since it was necessary for normal production to continue, with as little interruption as possible, and also that employees be free to choose their representative without undue influence or coercion from any source. In a Phelps Dodge[111] case in 1945 the Board dismissed CIO objections to the election and certified the AFL, which held a contract under which grievances had continued to be handled during the pre-election period. The Trial Examiner found that the AFL had the advantage of a superior position inseparable from the fact that it held the contract, but that to have abolished the grievance procedure for the period of the election would seriously have threatened production. A month later in an unfair labor practice case[112] the Board held that when an employer signed a contract with

109. Cf. S. Frieder & Sons Co., 62 NLRB 880 (1945); Hudson Hosiery Co., 72 NLRB 1434 (1947).
110. 53 NLRB 1411 (1943).
111. Phelps Dodge Copper Products Corp., 63 NLRB 686 (1945).
112. Midwest Piping and Supply Co., 63 NLRB 1060 (1945); *Twelfth Annual Report*, p. 26.

one of two competing unions, while awaiting determination of a representation question by the Board, this constituted violation of his obligation to neutrality. This doctrine was applied later in a group of cases involving a long-drawn-out rival-union dispute in the California canning industry, when the Board declared that after the expiration of an existing contract the companies were under obligation to refrain from exclusive recognition of either union until the question of representation was settled.[113] But the problems had not been solved, especially when during long delays before representation disputes were settled, closed-shop contracts were enforced to the benefit of one of the contending unions. The Board toward the end of the Wagner Act period was seeing the danger of applying this doctrine in such a way as to interrupt continuous collective bargaining and held that it was to be applied with caution and only in situations where it was necessary in order to protect freedom of choice.[114]

The most frequent basis for objections to elections was the charge that coercion by employers by written or spoken word had prevented a free election. The issue of free speech was of course involved—an issue which in its various aspects in Board cases will be discussed later.[115] Here it need only be said that after the courts had spoken on this subject, in the Virginia Electric and Power case and the American Tube Bending case and others, the Board followed the courts in their judgment that employers had a right to discuss the issues in a representation election campaign, so long as they refrained from speech which in its context was coercive. The limits of privileged free speech were not always clear, and unions felt that in the later years many employers did in fact succeed with impunity in coercing employees, in situations where speech itself could be coercive. The increase in the proportion of elections which were lost may have been related to this development.

When unfair labor practices were still unremedied, or charges against employers still pending as they sometimes were for long periods before the Board or the courts, it was always a question whether an election was possible which would reflect the free choice of employees. The Board preferred not to hold elections while such cases were pending. However, this policy would sometimes long delay the attainment of collective bargaining by a union which was ready to prove its right to recognition. Accordingly the Board sometimes

113. *Infra,* ch. 6, pp. 224 ff.
114. Ensher, Alexander & Barsoom, Inc., 74 NLRB 1443 (1947).
115. *Infra,* ch. 6, pp. 174–89.

held consent or ordered elections in spite of the risks involved from unremedied unfair labor practices. Ordinarily it did so only if the union filed a "waiver," agreeing not to rely on the unfair labor practices as a basis for a subsequent objection to the election, or in the alternative withdrew the charges. A study of the cases during one year, 1942, in which charges were withdrawn in favor of proceeding with an election, found that elections were won in about 80 per cent of the cases, though the proportion of losses was larger than usual. Later charges filed and upheld, or still pending two years later, in about 10 per cent of these cases, indicated that in some of them unfair labor practices had continued.[116] No similar over-all study is available as to the effects of the waivers. But problems sometimes reached the Board where objections to the elections were filed in spite of the waiver. In the May Department Stores[117] case, the Board set an election aside because of extensive and varied interferences by the company before the election. The majority of the Board held that a waiver did not "obliterate the past unfair labor practices," and the effects upon employees of the company's pre-election conduct could be determined realistically only by reference to events in the past. Mr. Reilly, concurring specially, would in general have given much broader effect to the waiver, on the theory that the union had knowingly incurred the risk that the unfair labor practices would still exert a coercive effect. In an earlier case[118] a two-man Board had followed Mr. Reilly's theory and refused to set aside an election, holding that a pre-election speech of the employer was not coercive in itself and that the union's waiver precluded the Board from considering the earlier unfair labor practices as relevant to the question of the possible coerciveness of the speech. By 1947, somewhat similarly, the Board had developed a theory of "separability" between speech and acts. This further protected the employer's freedom to speak during elections; and it resulted in weakening the earlier doctrine that a context of unfair labor practices might make words coercive when they would not be otherwise.[119]

116. NLRB, *Studies of Results*, pp. 43–54.
117. 61 NLRB 258 (1945). Cf. also unfair labor practice cases against this company, 53 NLRB 1366 (1943), 59 NLRB 976 (1944), both enforced, in May Department Stores Co. v. NLRB, 326 U.S. 376 (1945) and 154 F. 2d 533 (C.C.A. 8, 1946).
118. Charles H. Bacon Co., 55 NLRB 1180 (1944). Cf. also Mr. Reilly's dissent in Monumental Life Insurance Co., 69 NLRB 247 (1946), enforced in 162 F. 2d 340 (C.C.A.6, 1947). *Eleventh Annual Report*, p. 20; *Tenth*, pp. 26–27; *Eighth*, pp. 49–50.
119. Discussed *infra*, ch. 6, pp. 182–83.

Community activities in support of employers against unions have been mentioned earlier. In a number of cases through the years, especially in the South and in rural areas, organized antiunion activities of community groups went so far as to be unquestionably coercive in their effects upon employees, preventing fair and free elections. In one Iowa case[120] the Board found that this had been true. In addition to the employer's and supervisors' pre-election statements, which included warnings against economic loss should the union win, the Chamber of Commerce engaged in an active antiunion campaign which the Board found to have been coercive. Both the company and the Chamber were ordered to cease interference, but the circuit court enforced the order only against the company, finding no connection of the Chamber of Commerce with the company. In another case[121] the Board found no conclusive evidence connecting the company with the community campaign against the union. But it found that under all the circumstances the election was not conducted "in an atmosphere conducive to the sort of free, unintimidated choice of representatives which the Act contemplate[d]." Therefore the election was set aside. This election occurred in 1946 in a small town, Smithfield, Virginia, which depended largely upon the meat-packing plants of the company concerned. About 80 per cent of the employees were Negro. The anti-CIO campaign organized by the newspaper publisher and an insurance salesman used personal contacts with influential Negroes in the town, newspaper publicity, a mass meeting shortly before the election, at which "flaming crosses" and the return of the Klan were strongly implied, and threats of violence against CIO organizers. All this created a "hostile and threatening atmosphere," in which 112 valid votes were cast of 114 eligibles—85 of them against the union. The Board investigated the union's objections to the election, held a four-day public hearing, and issued its decision setting the election aside a little over a year after the election had been held. Shortly thereafter the union withdrew its petition.

In another case an almost equally strong community campaign against the union failed in its purpose to dissuade employees from voting for the union. A prehearing election was held in the fall of 1946 in a unit of five small jointly owned shirt plants, in New Albany, Ecru, Hickory Flat, and Pontotoc, Mississippi.[122] A Citizens' Committee, active in the antiunion campaign, represented according to

120. American Pearl Button Co., 52 NLRB 1113 (1943), modified and enforced in 149 F. 2d 311 (C.C.A.8, 1945). Cf. also *supra*, ch. 4, pp. 124–26.
121. P. D. Gwaltney, Jr., and Co., 74 NLRB 371 (1947).
122. Irwin Manufacturing Co., Case 15-R-1878.

their own statement "the substantial, sound business men, preachers, farmers and others. . . . They are people who have some money invested here. Who have a stake in these communities. Who should and do have the best interests of everyone in these communities at heart." The local newspaper[123] the day before the election devoted more than half of its six pages to the campaign, with a full-page ad by the company, page-and-a-half ads by the Citizens' Committee, statements from a senator and three congressmen, a column headed "What Comes Down Our Alley?" an editorial headed "A Local Union, Yes; CIO, No," and a news story carrying a statement by a local minister. All rang the changes on the themes of "outside organizers" interested only in dues, "foreign-born, communistic Yankees," attack on the southern way of life and white supremacy, doubts that the company could pay higher wages, fears that the plants would move. The company denied CIO statements that wages were only 40 cents. It showed an average of $.649 an hour, with 345 of the 655 employees getting between 50 and 60 cents, only 10 temporarily below 50 cents, and 52 making 90 cents or over. The minister's front-page statement indicated his outrage at a CIO "scurrilous attack" which had attributed to him "more enthusiasm than brains." His statement began, "It takes no brains to see the CIO won't do in the South," and ended after an extreme use of all the going slogans, with "No Christian citizen who prays about this will vote for CIO." The Citizens' Committee urged all to vote and to give the matter "serious and prayerful thought." Surprisingly, when the votes were counted they stood 333 for the CIO, 285 against. As the last vote was counted a shout rose in the street outside, and union supporters piled into their cars and went parading through the streets, singing the union adaptation of an old Gospel hymn, "Just like a tree standing by the water, we shall not be moved." The company then agreed to recognize the union without going to hearing.

Such extreme examples should not obscure the fact that in a much larger proportion of cases the elections were quiet, orderly, democratic proceedings in which it was clear that the result could and did reflect the true desires of the employees. Where the Board found that interference prevented a fair test of employee desires, however, it set elections aside, or postponed holding them. Charges of unfair labor practices were not infrequently filed in such cases, and Board orders resulted requiring companies to refrain from such interferences in

123. *New Albany Gazette*, New Albany, Mississippi, Vol. 57, No. 8, October 3, 1946.

the future. In one case in 1944 where enforcement of a previous order was still pending in circuit court, the Board used its power to apply for and get a temporary injunction restraining a company from interfering with an election.[124] The Board had noted an increased tendency to exert pressure on employees in elections and asserted its intention to preserve the integrity of its election processes. Such pressures increased rather than decreased, however, in the remaining years under the Wagner Act.

THE RESULTS

The direct results of the Board's representation cases have already been shown in chapter 3, in elections won, unions recognized, and collective bargaining contracts made, but a number of other points need discussion. To many unions, probably most, by 1947, the representation procedures were the most important of the Board's functions, although the basic protection of rights under the Act was still an essential foundation. The great majority of the petitions continued to be handled informally. The formal decisions, however, like those in the unfair labor practice cases, set the standards and built up over the years, flexibly, a body of common law for the handling of representation disputes and for behavior in industry. Just as the unfair labor practice cases affected the behavior of employers primarily, so the representation cases affected union habits in a number of crucial ways. Both sets of precedent also, inevitably, affected the habits of the other party.

In several ways union habits were modified by the representation processes under the Wagner Act. First was as to organizing methods. Too often in the past employers were "signed up" by unions without much regard for whether the employees had been organized. The statement by an old union organizer, "I don't have a majority but I have jurisdiction," was a throwback to the time when organizing the people was not always prerequisite to signing closed-shop contracts covering them. Such habits still persisted, especially when long

124. NLRB v. Servel, temporary injunction issued by Seventh Circuit Court of Appeals, September 29, 1944. The Board order was enforced later in 149 F. 2d 542 (C.C.A.7, 1945). Cf. *Tenth Annual Report*, pp. 69–70; *Ninth*, p. 3. The Sixth Circuit Court, on the contrary, denied without opinion the Board's request for a temporary injunction against Thompson Products, on October 19, 1945, when the Board claimed that the employer's antiunion campaign was preventing a free election. Twice earlier the Board had set aside elections at this company's plants on the ground of interference by the company. *Eleventh Annual Report*, pp. 64–65. Cf. *supra*, ch. 4, p. 123. Cf. also the Board's attempt to obtain a contempt adjudication in the California canneries case, *infra*, ch. 6, p. 229.

delays made it more difficult to use effectively the orderly processes provided by the Board, and in areas where picket lines or boycotts were very effective. Nevertheless, it was widely recognized that the union was under obligation to prove support by the majority of employees before it was entitled to recognition.[125] Employers who required Board certification before they would recognize a union sometimes found this a useful delaying device, but on the whole use of the Board's democratic processes contributed toward a sound base for collective bargaining resting on the free choice of the employees. When employers were ready to accept the result of Board elections, also, strikes for recognition were made unnecessary, and to a large extent Board elections replaced such strikes.[126] Sometimes a short strike was a preliminary to getting the employer's agreement for a consent election.

The Board's rules protecting the choice of the majority of the employees, and providing that existing contracts were a bar to new elections only for reasonable periods and under proper safeguards, all weakened unions which tried to maintain their position without adequately serving the needs of the employees and keeping their support. Orderly means were provided by which workers could assert a preference for different representation, and many shifts of affiliation took place.[127] Old and responsible union officers sometimes complained that they were forced as a result to give excessive attention to keeping members satisfied, even at the expense of discipline and sound economics. But the net effect must have been to promote democracy and rank-and-file participation in their unions. The major loss was to the weak or inefficient union, or the "racketeering union," since, given a free choice, in general the votes go to the organizations that serve their members best. The decline in union racketeering, and its relative absence in the industries under Board jurisdiction, may well be related to the wide use of the orderly representation procedures under the Act.

As the Board increased its emphasis on "stability" over the years, to some degree it limited freedom of choice and freedom to change representatives. In part this was inevitable, when labor organization and collective bargaining got beyond its period of rapid expansion.

125. For an old-line union defense of the earlier system of obtaining recognition see Paul R. Hutchings, "Effect on the Trade Union," in Silverberg, *op. cit.*, pp. 73–74.

126. *Supra*, ch. 3, pp. 91–92.

127. *Supra*, ch. 3, pp. 90–91. Extreme instability with numerous successive elections as employees shifted back and forth between unions was, however, rare.

171

From the Wagner Act to Taft-Hartley

The policies laid down in Washington, however, were general policies applicable to the entire nation, even though parts of the country and of certain industries were still in some respects in a "pre–Wagner Act stage." The "freezing" of contracts for two- or even three-year periods, which was possible under the later rules, along with a tendency to think in terms of union "status," sometimes hampered democratic self-organization where there had not yet been time for organization to settle down on a stable, freely chosen basis.

The problem of organizing by "raids" on already organized groups, however, rather than by organizing new employees, increased as organization extended. Some of the "raids" were the more or less spontaneous, more or less assisted efforts of workers to change their affiliation to unions which they believed would serve them better. The rules as to contracts, timeliness of petitions, and "showing requirements" all tried to control these shifts and regularize them by limiting them to appropriate times. Generally these rules were accepted as reasonable, and unions adapted their practices to them without much dissent. That the rules were clear and definite, and impartially applied, was more important than what the particular rule was, in the opinion of many of the Board's clients. But when a change was made, as in the trend toward craft severance, there was an encouragement to raiding and instability.

Board policies also affected the structure of the labor movement and of collective bargaining. The extension of the industrial form of organization, essential if mass production was to be effectively organized, received protection at a crucial period. Later, greater liberality in permitting craft severance was a potential danger to the broad units that employers as well as industrial unions approved in many industries, and encouraged continued agitation by craft organizations which might otherwise have accepted a more limited field where the craft form was still needed. Multi-plant and multi-employer units, found appropriate by the Board under proper safeguards, permitted collective bargaining on a broad basis, with the accompanying advantage of stabilization of competition, though some limitation on local self-determination. Government controls inevitably, therefore, influenced the character as well as the extent of collective bargaining.

The greatest difficulty in the representation cases was delay. Inadequate appropriations made it impossible for the Board to keep up with its case load, even with every effort to increase efficiency.[128]

128. Cf. *supra*, ch. 2, pp. 61–62. In 1945 great delay in holding elections was caused by the necessity for holding War Labor Disputes Act strike votes on the thirtieth day after the notice was filed.

Sometimes exceptionally long delay was caused by serious disagreement within the Board on a close case or matter of policy. Occasionally there was suspicion that political or other pressures were responsible for the Board's failure to issue a decision.[129] Whatever the reasons, such delays made unions far more ready to resort to economic pressure to settle their disputes over recognition.

The most severe criticisms of the Board's handling of representation questions came from the unions in connection with disputes over units and from employers in regard to the right of employers to petition. Over the years changes were made in policy as a result of criticisms when they appeared reasonable. There is room for difference of opinion as to details of some of the policies. Yet a study of the Board's handling of representation cases leads to the conclusion that on the whole the Board built soundly in developing a common law which would protect the right of employees freely to choose their bargaining representatives. Handicapped by inadequate staff and by the enormous difficulties presented by the divided and competing labor movements, and faced by a tremendous volume of cases which made it difficult to apply the rules as flexibly as was most desirable, the Board nevertheless achieved a very large degree of respect and acceptance of its work in this field. It made an outstanding contribution toward the establishment of collective bargaining on a freely chosen and democratic basis. Its record is convincing proof of the fact that such a law should provide for flexible administration by an expert Board under suitable general safeguards laid down by Congress. Policy could then be developed in view of the changing needs shown by experience rather than being based on rigid detailed rules laid down in the law itself.

129. Cf. United Steelworkers of America, *Report of Officers to the Third International Convention,* May, 1946, p. 34.

CHAPTER 6

FREEDOM OF SPEECH, FREEDOM TO STRIKE, FREEDOM FROM COERCION IN RIVAL UNION DISPUTES

FREEDOM of workers to organize and to bargain through unions of their own choice, the basic freedoms which the Wagner Act meant to protect, and how the Board implemented them, have already been considered. Several of the most difficult and controversial problems with which the Board struggled are still to be discussed. All bear directly on the issue as to whether the Wagner Act was adequate, or whether amendments were needed fully to carry out the original purposes of the Act or related and newly recognized public purposes. Among these problems are employers' freedom of speech, freedom of workers and unions to strike, and the right of employees, individually and collectively, to be free of coercion, by either unions or employers in rival union or jurisdictional controversies. Each of these is complicated by the presence of rival and conflicting claims of different groups. They raise crucial questions as to sound public policy.

THE EMPLOYER'S FREEDOM OF SPEECH

Was the constitutional right of free speech actually limited as the Board enforced the Wagner Act's prohibition of interference with the rights of workers? This was often said by the critics. A real clash of rights was of course possible, if employers claimed an unlimited right to speak about union matters to their employees. In fact, such speech in concrete cases did sometimes result in intimidation or coercion of employees. The issue was sharpened as the years went by and the more overt forms of interference were clearly outlawed and to a considerable extent dropped out of use. The greater attention to this issue in the discussion of the Act in the postwar years than in 1939 is significant. Policy of the Board and the courts evolved gradually. The Supreme Court laid down basic criteria for decision in 1941,

174

and later cases further defined the standards. But remaining issues shown in divergent interpretations in some of the circuit courts and in Board cases had not yet been settled by the Supreme Court when the Act was amended in 1947.

The function of the Board, it must always be remembered, was to protect the right of workers to be free of interference or coercion in connection with their right to organize and bargain collectively. Protection of the basic constitutional right of free speech, on the other hand, was in the hands of the courts. They would and should check the Board if it should unintentionally go so far in performing its own function as to encroach on the right of employers as well as of all others to free speech. What did the Board actually do? And how did the courts reconcile these rights?

In many early cases the Board cited as unlawful statements by employers which were plainly intimidatory or coercive, such as threatening or implying that the plant would close down or move or employees would be in danger of discharge if they supported the union. Other types of statements found unlawful, such as describing union organizers as "racketeers" or interested only in the money to be collected, or the union as corrupt, or union members as "thugs" and "reds," or explaining the Wagner Act without mentioning its guaranties of rights to the employees, might at first glance seem to indicate that the Board had interfered with the employer's right to express his opinion. But the Board made clear that such statements were found coercive only when the name-calling was associated with and an integral part of extensive acts of interference and coercion.[1] "The time and the place and the circumstance, these are the controlling factors at all times," explained Chairman Madden.[2] Employers' utterances were often strong supporting evidence where employees had been discriminatorily discharged and other unfair labor practices engaged in, and they were included among the interferences by such employers which the Board ordered stopped. It was not until the Ford case in 1939, however, that the Board specifically ordered an employer to cease distributing antiunion propaganda to his employees. In that case, in addition to the antiunion pamphlets there had

1. Cf. *Third Annual Report,* 1938, pp. 59–60.
2. U.S. Senate, Committee on Education and Labor, *Hearings, Proposed Amendments to the National Labor Relations Act,* 76th Cong., 1st Sess., 1939, Pt. 2, pp. 170–72; Pt. 3, pp. 496–97, 507, cited as Senate Committee on Education and Labor, *NLRA Hearings, 1939.*

been a reign of terror, and union organizers had been beaten by the company's "service men."[3]

During this early period the Board's theory was that the Act required the employer to maintain strict neutrality, keep his hands off, during any efforts of the employees to organize.[4] It was thought that in the employer's position of economic power any indication of his preference might prevent the employees from exercising free choice. Board orders where statements were among the unfair labor practices ordered ended were upheld by a number of circuit courts; and the Supreme Court itself, in a case involving primarily the question of an employer's support of one union as against another, said, "Slight suggestions as to the employer's choice between unions may have telling effect among men who know the consequences of incurring that employer's strong displeasure."[5]

By 1939, nevertheless, there was extensive criticism that employers were being deprived of their constitutional rights, and various proposals for amendment of the Act included free-speech guaranties. The Smith Committee, while disavowing any intent to impair the rights of labor or permit coercion, recommended specific protection of expressions of opinion, provided they were "not accompanied by acts of coercion, intimidation, discrimination, or threats thereof."[6] The Board[7] considered any such amendments dangerous; they might tend to encourage interference with employees' rights, and they were unnecessary, since the courts would protect the constitutional rights of employers should the Board overstep the bounds.

The issue was not directly considered by the Supreme Court until

3. Ford Motor Co., 14 NLRB 346 (1939), enforced with the omission of the order on distribution of propaganda, in 114 F. 2d 905 (C.C.A.6, 1940), cert. den., 312 U.S. 689 (1941). Cf. also 23 NLRB 342 (1940); 23 NLRB 548 (1940).

4. Statement of Board in U.S. House of Representatives, Committee on Labor, Hearings, *Proposed Amendments to the National Labor Relations Act,* 76th Cong., 1st Sess., 1939, Supplement, p. 23.

5. International Association of Machinists v. NLRB, 311 U.S. 72, 78 (1940); cf. also NLRB v. Link-Belt Co., 311 U.S. 584 (1941); also *Fourth Annual Report,* pp. 135–36, *Sixth,* p. 89. The Board's policy against permitting such utterances by employers as might interfere with the freedom of employees found support also in two earlier decisions under the Railway Labor Act, Texas & New Orleans Railroad Co. v. Brotherhood of Railway Clerks, 281 U.S. 548 (1930); Virginian Railway Co. v. System Federation No. 40, 300 U.S. 515 (1937).

6. U.S. House of Representatives, Special Committtee To Investigate the National Labor Relations Board, *Intermediate Report,* Report No. 1902, 76th Cong., 3d Sess., 1940, Pt. 1, pp. 83, 90–91, cited as *Smith Committee Report.* 533 (1943).

7. For statements of its position see citations, *supra,* nn. 2, 4.

1941, in the important Virginia Electric and Power Company case.[8] The Board had found a long background of antiunion activity by the company. Then in 1937, when the AFL attempted to organize, the company by a bulletin and by speeches of high company officials announced to employees that it recognized their rights under the Wagner Act and would not discriminate for any reasons of union affiliation; but it encouraged them to set up an "inside" organization. The independent was quickly organized with company assistance. A closed-shop contract was signed, and employees were discharged for refusal to join the independent. The Board found that the bulletin and speeches, as well as the other activities, were illegal interferences with the rights of employees under the Act. The company protested strongly that the order was an invasion of its right of free speech. The Supreme Court, holding that the statements standing by themselves were not coercive, remanded the case to the Board for further determination as to whether these were found coercive by reliance on surrounding circumstances. The Board rewrote its decision, making its findings more detailed. The Court then upheld the Board, enforcing the order in full. It held that these utterances were not privileged, though noncoercive in themselves, when they were part of an entire pattern of conduct which was violative of the Act.

In its first decision on this case the Supreme Court laid down a general rule to guide the Board and the courts on the free-speech issue.

The employer . . . is as free now as ever to take any side it may choose on this controversial issue. But, certainly, conduct, though evidenced in part by speech, may amount, in connection with other circumstances, to coercion within the meaning of the Act. If the total activities of an employer restrain or coerce his employees in their free choice, then those employees are entitled to the protection of the Act. And in determining whether a course of conduct amounts to restraint or coercion, pressure exerted vocally by the employer may no more be disregarded than pressure exerted in other ways.

Moreover, in determining whether a company actually interfered, "the Board has a right to look at what the Company has said as well as what it has done."[9]

In other words, employers had a right to express their views on labor matters to their employees, but they were not free to coerce by words any more than by acts. And the fact of whether words were coercive was to be reasonably determined in the light of the entire

8. 20 NLRB 911 (1940), 44 NLRB 404 (1942), 314 U.S. 469 (1941), 319 U.S. 533 (1943).
9. 314 U.S. 469, 477, 478 (1941).

context. This seems to have been what the Board had been trying to do, though the underlying theory of a duty to "neutrality" which the Board had sometimes stated was apparently rejected. The Board still had to decide in particular cases whether speech was privileged, or whether, because of the particular circumstances, it interfered with the employees' rights.

Development of the law continued with two important circuit court cases, one upholding the Board and one setting its order aside, both of which the Supreme Court on the same day declined to review.[10] The American Tube Bending case, in which the Board was reversed, understandably received much more attention in the press. The Board, two members participating, had found that the president of the company had entered into an election campaign and had stated his position in a letter and a speech to the employees, after which a large majority voted against the union. He had emphasized the right of the employees to choose and the secrecy of the ballot. But he argued that the issue in the election was whether a union could get more for the employees, or an outsider do more for them; could their status be improved by choosing someone else for leader? The Board, emphasizing the company's lack of neutrality, found it guilty of an unfair labor practice and set the election aside. The circuit court considered itself bound by the Virginia and Electric Power decision, since it found nothing in the record but the speech, "an argument, temperate in form, that a union would be against the employees' interests as well as the employer's, and that the continued prosperity of the company depended on going on as they had been," and reversed the Board.

In the Trojan Powder case, on the contrary, which also involved a series of letters, carefully phrased and without explicit threats, the Board was upheld. There had been an earlier attempt to organize, which failed after a series of letters to the employees. In 1941 a CIO attempt to organize brought forth another series which implied that unless a no-strike pledge were signed the amount of work might be adversely affected. There were also some anti-CIO statements by supervisors. The Board found that under all the circumstances the conduct had amounted to interference and coercion, and the Court upheld this conclusion, enforcing the order. The result then seemed

10. American Tube Bending Co., 44 NLRB 121 (1942), set aside in 134 F. 2d 993 (C.C.A.2, 1943), cert. den., 320 U.S. 768 (1943); Trojan Powder Co., 41 NLRB 1308 (1942), enforced in 135 F. 2d 337 (C.C.A.3, 1943), cert. den. 320 U.S. 768 (1943).

to stand, as before, that the context of surrounding circumstances was conclusive as to whether any particular set of statements on behalf of a company could be enjoined as an unlawful interference but that in the absence of a background of unfair labor practices employers were free to speak if their words were not coercive in themselves.

By 1947 the Supreme Court had not in any Board case given further guidance as to the conditions under which the Board could restrain employers' statements. In the 1945 *Thomas* v. *Collins* case,[11] however, involving another issue, important statements were made which affected later development of Board and court policies. There the issue was whether Texas might require registration of union organizers. The Court held the requirement invalid when its application limited the right to make a public speech to enlist support for the union movement. Any regulation of labor unions must not infringe the rights of free speech and assembly, which may only be limited in face of a showing of "clear and present danger." The right "to discuss and inform people concerning the advantages and disadvantages of unions" is protected. Similarly,

. . . employers' attempts to persuade to action with respect to joining or not joining unions are within the First Amendment's guaranty. . . . When to this persuasion other things are added which bring about coercion, or give it that character, the limit of the right has been passed. . . . But short of that limit the employer's freedom cannot be impaired.[12]

The American Tube Bending and Trojan Powder decisions were cited with approval. Justice Douglas, however, concurring, commented that one who "uses the economic power which he has over other men and their jobs to influence their actions . . . is doing more than exercising the freedom of speech protected by the first amendment," whether employer or employee. And Justice Jackson, concurring, suggested that if either violence on the part of labor or discrimination or intimidation by the employer were associated with the speech, "the constitutional remedy would be to stop the evil, but permit the speech, if the two are separable; and only rarely and when they are inseparable to stop or punish speech or publication."[13] But still the question remained for the Board and the courts as to what was permissible in the particular situation; and circuit courts differed

11. 323 U.S. 516 (1945). Cf. also the cases in which picketing was held protected under the First and Fourteenth Amendments. Thornhill v. Alabama, 310 U.S. 88 (1940), and others.
12. 323 U.S. 516, 537–38 (1945).
13. *Ibid.*, p. 548.

in the extent to which they accepted the Board's findings of coercion.

Several circuit court decisions encouraged employers who thought the American Tube Bending decision meant greater freedom than earlier to discuss issues with their employees. In the Budd Manufacturing Company case,[14] the court refused to find the company in contempt, although on the same day that it posted the notice required for compliance with a Board and court order it sent a lengthy letter to its employees in which it spoke favorably of the long history of relationships under the representation plan, now being disestablished. The letter assured employees of their freedom to choose but suggested the organization of an independent union. The court held that the background of unfair labor practices prior to compliance could not then be used to determine the coerciveness of later speech; otherwise the employer would never again be free to speak on these matters to his employees. Another circuit court, the Eighth, also, set aside two Board orders, with comments that further extended the employer's freedom to enter into campaigns against unions. In the Brandeis[15] case the Board had set aside an election in a department store and found the company guilty of unfair labor practices. There had been a campaign, vigorous on the part of both union and company, with antiunion articles and statements by the company, its manager, and supervisors, the circulation of an antiunion petition in the store with the knowledge of the company, and surveillance of union representatives. The court nevertheless held that as a matter of law the employer could disseminate facts, express his opinion, indicate a preference for individual dealing, and express hostility to a labor organization, "so long as the reasoning power of the employee and not his fear is appealed to. . . . Certainly, effectiveness of statement is not a test of its constitutionality; neither is accuracy." In a Montgomery Ward[16] case the Board found a pre-election speech not privileged when it was made against a background of discriminatory discharges and antiunion remarks by supervisors and when employees were required to attend and listen. The court set the order aside, holding that the discharges were for adequate cause and that isolated remarks of minor supervisors were not to be taken as reflecting company policy. The speech itself was considered privileged, since the employer had a right to answer attacks by the union, employees were not inconvenienced by being required to attend, the employer had as much right to speak at one time as another, and

14. 142 F. 2d 922 (C.C.A.3, 1944).
15. J. L. Brandeis & Sons, 145 F. 2d 556, 566 (C.C.A.8, 1944).
16. 157 F. 2d 486, 500 (C.C.A.8, 1946).

freedom of speech was not to be limited by "subtleties . . . invoked as the basis for inference" of coerciveness.

On the other hand, the Seventh Circuit Court held the Reliance Manufacturing Company[17] in contempt for its newspaper ads and other pre-election activities after a court order enforcing the Board's order. The court held that the right under some circumstances to express an opinion as to a union "certainly does not extend to the point where it becomes a participant in a contest to which it is not a party." The Third Circuit Court, also, in spite of its earlier decision in the Budd case, upheld the Board in the M. E. Blatt Company[18] case, in finding coercive the company's notices to employees that it "was not necessary" for them to join any organization, when this was a part of the pattern of an offensive against the union. And the Sixth Circuit Court in the Hal Peterson[19] case, referring to earlier cases where it had held that employers had the right to express their views and to distribute pamphlets to their employees, distinguished cases where the disparaging statements were "couched in such phrases, or attended by such circumstances, that they tend to exercise undue influence and coercion upon employees." When there had been discriminatory discharges, and the manager had stated to his men that if they joined the union they were "sticking their necks out," the reasonable inference was that discharge and discrimination were being threatened. Accordingly the order was enforced.

It is apparent that there were no simple and clear rules as to what was permissible. In the later years many employers and their lawyers tested out in action the question of how far they could go in exercising their right to discuss organization matters with their employees. The Board dismissed an unprecedented number of cases which came before it, when it found other charges of interference not supported by the evidence, and the speeches or statements, usually made in connection with elections, not coercive in themselves.[20] Some were close cases where the Trial Examiner had believed the statements in their context to be coercive. In two Mr. Houston dissented.[21] In

17. 143 F. 2d 761, 763 (C.C.A.7, 1944).

18. 143 F. 2d 268 (C.C.A.3, 1944), cert. den., 323 U.S. 774 (1944).

19. 157 F. 2d 514 (C.C.A.6, 1946), cert. den., 330 U.S. 838 (1947), enforcing 63 NLRB 1426 (1945).

20. Cf. Strathmore Packing House Co., 68 NLRB 214 (1946); Ebco Manufacturing Co., 67 NLRB 210 (1946); Philadelphia Gear Works, 69 NLRB 11 (1946); Oval Wood Dish Corp., 62 NLRB 1129 (1945); General Motors Corp., 73 NLRB 74 (1947).

21. Merrimack Woolen Mills, 68 NLRB 229 (1946); Arkansas-Missouri Power Corp., 68 NLRB 805 (1946).

June, 1947, the Board unanimously dismissed[22] a charge where the employer had predicted a decline in jobs should the union win. The Board said: "These are matters upon which the employees were able, equally with the respondent, to exercise reason and judgment, and the [employer's] formulation of the consequences it prophesied from unionization carried no connotation that its own economic power would be used, if necessary, to make its prophecy come true." This was a policy far removed from the earlier decisions which found coercion in such statements. In some cases, also, speeches were held to be privileged even though there were other unfair labor practices.[23]

Late in 1946 the Board began to develop a theory of "separability" between speech and earlier unfair labor practices, under which speech was privileged, following the suggestion of Justice Jackson in *Thomas* v. *Collins*. Mr. Reynolds first stated this theory in the Fisher Governor Company[24] case, where he thought that a speech was "separable" although it was only ten days after discriminatory discharges of two union leaders, and it announced a wage increase and showed clearly the company's opposition to the efforts to organize. He held that discrimination could be prevented, and then the employees would be free "to listen to their employer and weigh for themselves the merits of his opinions in an atmosphere free from fear of discriminatory action." Both the other members of the Board considered ten days too short an interval for a realistic "separability" doctrine; but since the Chairman did not agree that the discharges were discriminatory, the charge that the speech was an unfair labor practice was dismissed.

Two weeks later the Board dismissed a complaint against the Bausch and Lomb Optical Company.[25] A vigorously antiunion pamphlet distributed to employees was held to be privileged, although statements by supervisors seven months before had been found coercive and in violation of the Act, in an earlier case. Again, in the La Salle Steel Company[26] case, the Board found illegal assistance to an independent union, coercive and intimidatory remarks by management representatives, and interference with the free choice of employees by announcing a wage increase on the day of an election, and

22. Electric Steel Foundry, 74 NLRB 129 (1947).
23. Ross Gear and Tool Co., 63 NLRB 1012 (1945), set aside in 158 F. 2d 677 (C.C.A.7, 1947); Libby-Owens-Ford Glass Co., 63 NLRB 1 (1945).
24. 71 NLRB 1291, 1295 (1946). Mr. Reilly in April, 1945, had suggested that a letter was separable from other unfair labor practices, in his dissent in Republic Aviation Corp., 61 NLRB 397 (1945).
25. 72 NLRB 132 (1947).
26. 72 NLRB 411 (1947).

so set an election aside. Nevertheless, the majority held that an anti-union letter was privileged. It had been distributed to employees the day before the election by attaching copies to their time cards; but the Board found that it was not in itself coercive or inseparably connected with the unfair labor practices which had occurred six months earlier. Mr. Houston dissented strongly, believing the letter an integral part of a totality of unlawful and coercive tactics. Finally in the United Welding Company[27] case the Board found it not an illegal interference when the company went over the head of the union during a strike by sending letters to individual employees. Altogether the Board was far less ready, by the spring of 1947, to find that speech itself was unlawful when "the total activities of an employer restrain or coerce his employees" than it had been earlier, or than the Supreme Court decisions seemed to permit. Skeptical commentators pointed to a probable relationship of this trend to impending amendments then being discussed in Congress.[28]

A line was drawn, nevertheless, beyond which speech was held to be coercive. In the last two years the line was perhaps clearest when employers campaigned before an election with wage increases, "for the presentation of economic benefits to employees in order to have them forego collective bargaining is a form of pressure and compulsion no less telling in its effect on employees because benign."[29] Clear threats of detriment also continued to be held coercive. There were, however, serious differences of opinion within the Board as to how far they should go in considering speech illegal because of its circumstances and background. Mr. Reilly in the last year or so of his term put increased emphasis on freedom to speak. Where the unions had waived prior unfair labor practices as a basis for objection to elections, he was unwilling to consider the earlier conduct even as context for later speeches which were challenged.[30] He suggested the separability doctrine as early as April, 1945, and always opposed the theory, then being considered, that when employees were compelled to assemble and listen to a speech, this element of compulsion made words otherwise privileged, coercive.[31]

27. 72 NLRB 954 (1947). Cf. also Fafnir Bearing Co., 73 NLRB 1008 (1947); *infra*, pp. 201–2.

28. *Labor Relations Reporter,* 19, Analysis 93–95 (April 17, 1947).

29. Hudson Hosiery Co., 72 NLRB 1434 (1947); Roots-Connersville Blower Corp., 64 NLRB 855 (1945). Cf. Medo Photo Supply Corp. v. NLRB, 321 U.S. 678 (1944).

30. Cf. discussion *supra*, ch. 5, pp. 166–67.

31. *Supra*, n. 24. Continental Oil Co., 65 NLRB 1400 (February, 1946); Van Raalte, Inc., 69 NLRB 1326 (August, 1946). Cf. also dissent in Goodall Co., 68 NLRB 252 (May, 1946).

The "compulsory audience" doctrine, adopted by the Board in the Clark[32] case in August, 1946, was the one clear extension, during the last years, of restriction upon the employer's freedom to speak. This case involved the only large plant in a small city, and the Trial Examiner had emphasized this setting as intensifying the coercive effect of the acts found. The company had staged a full-fledged anti-CIO campaign before a run-off election, after a close vote in the first election. This included leaflets, newspaper ads, and a speech in the plant broadcast one hour before the polls opened, as well as preferential treatment of the independent union. The Board found the campaign statements an integral and inseparable part of a coercive course of conduct. It considered that the compulsory audience, which gave the company exclusive access to the employees, made freedom of speech meaningless. The Board commented on its function of "protecting employees against that use of the employer's economic power which is inherent in his ability to control their actions during working hours." Mr. Reilly, on his last day on the Board, dissented strongly, arguing that the case was covered by the American Tube Bending decision, and opposing any theory that a national industrial union needed protection from the greater economic power of the company. The Board, in asking for enforcement of its order, argued that the employees had a right, under the Act and the First Amendment, to determine for themselves whether or not to receive advice and information concerning their self-organization, and that this right was violated when the employer used his economic power to compel them to assemble and listen to speeches. The circuit court declined in that case to lay down so broad a rule, although it found the order justified under all the circumstances. In enforcing the order against requiring employees to assemble during working time to listen to speeches against self-organization, it added a proviso—unless the employer accorded a similar opportunity to the union to address the employees. The Board meantime had been hesitant to use the doctrine in later cases, pending court decision.[33] The Board's decisions in the last year only rarely and in the clearest cases held that employers' statements

32. Clark Brothers Co., 70 NLRB 802 (August 26, 1946), enforced as modified in 163 F. 2d 373 (C.C.A.2, 1947). For an interesting note defending this doctrine, cf. *University of Chicago Law Review*, 14 (1946), 104.

33. Chairman Herzog's statement in his opinion in Fisher Governor Co., 71 NLRB 1291 (December, 1946). But cf. Bergman's, Inc., 71 NLRB 1020 (December, 1946). Another circuit court, in the Montgomery Ward case, had held that an employer had as much right to speak at one time as another. 157 F. 2d 486 (C.C.A.8, 1946).

went beyond mere persuasion and under the circumstances were coercive and therefore violations of the Act.[34]

Through the twelve years of the Wagner Act the Board's policies, as stated in its formal decisions and checked and modified by the courts and by its own developing experience, established the standards as to what kinds of statements by employers, under what conditions, were illegal interferences with the rights of employees under the Act. The larger body of cases handled informally followed these standards and so affected in far-reaching manner habits of action in the still greater number of companies and plants which had no direct contact with the administrators of the law. In the early years, when violations were very widespread, the employer who wished to live within the law generally was careful to avoid discussing any issue as to unionization with his employees. After the Supreme Court in 1941 laid down the rule that the employer was as free as ever to take any side he chose, barring a context of total activities which were coercive, and especially after the American Tube Bending decision supplied a pattern which was considered noncoercive, many employers, urged by their associations and lawyers, hastened to use their "new freedom." Few were as candid as the representative of the prominent printer who admitted that the company desired "to do everything legally permissible to prevent the employees from joining the union,"[35] but the attitude was widespread. Some miscalculated, as did the printer, and the Board and the courts found that they had overstepped the bounds of legitimate free speech, in a totality of coercive conduct. But "American Tube Bending letters" were very widely used in elections and in organizing campaigns, especially in the postwar years. Objections to elections and charges of unfair labor practices were still filed in some of these cases, but the latitude permitted to employers was broad. The increased proportion of Board cases which were withdrawn or dismissed, and the noticeable increase in the proportion of elections lost in these years may be assumed to have been related to this trend.

In view of all this, the violence of the attack upon the Act on the free-speech issue may appear surprising. This was one of the points most often and strongly argued in the congressional hearings in

34. Cf. statement of the Chairman in U.S. House of Representatives, Committee on Education and Labor, *Hearings, Amendments to the National Labor Relations Act*, 80th Cong., 1st Sess., 1947, Pt. 5, pp. 3117, 3110, cited as House Committee on Education and Labor, *Hearings, 1947.*

35. R. R. Donnelley and Sons Co., 60 NLRB 635, 715 (1945), enforced in 156 F. 2d 416 (C.C.A.7, 1946).

1947.[36] Some of it can be discounted as simply use of a stereotype for propaganda purposes. But the issues are important and merit serious consideration. The major points made on behalf of employers in public utterances and private conversation can be summarized. Some thought that the Board was unduly restrictive earlier but that this was no longer true. Others held that even in 1947 the Board was too restrictive—an argument hard to take seriously in view of the care with which the Board sorted out the few cases where it was willing, because of the whole context, to find statements to have been coercive. There was, however, widespread feeling that employers were not free to answer union attacks and misstatements, even by honest factual statements. Moreover, many employers were afraid to speak or write to their employees on issues of mutual concern, lest they be charged with unfair labor practices. The complaint that the law was uncertain, and that employers could not tell what was permissible and what beyond the law, was basic to the two prior complaints. On the other hand, many employers in different parts of the country admitted frankly that there had been no serious difficulty over the right to speak and that they themselves had never felt restricted in anything which they wished to say to their employees. The proponents of a free-speech amendment argued thus: an amendment is necessary so that the employer may be free, without using coercion, to discuss any issues with his employees, to express his opinion about union matters, and to answer union propaganda.

Union representatives[37] also varied in their comments on the issue. Many of them pointed out that since the American Tube Bending decision, and especially with the later trend in Board decisions, there had been "a lot of trouble." Pre-election statements and letters were very common and were often effective and difficult to combat. Their effectiveness, however, depended upon the area and the conditions. They were much more effective in rural areas and in the South and other newly organized situations. Many organizers, especially in the well-established unions, were finding that they "could meet it," by preparing workers in advance and being ready to meet the particular statements when they came. Some found that employers' statements

36. Cf. U.S. Senate, Committee on Labor and Public Welfare, *Hearings, Labor Relations Program*, 80th Cong., 1st Sess., 1947, Pt. 1, pp. 105–9, 551, 554–55, 588–89; Pt. 2, p. 966; Pt. 4, p. 1799, cited as Senate Committee on Labor and Public Welfare, *Hearings, 1947;* House Committee on Education and Labor, *Hearings, 1947*, Pt. 4, pp. 2722–23; Pt. 2, pp. 490, 536–37.

37. Cf. Senate Committee on Labor and Public Welfare, *Hearings, 1947*, Pt. 1, p. 434; Pt. 2, pp. 1011, 1115; Pt. 3, pp. 1339, 1473, 1478.

were occasionally helpful to the union cause, by stirring up interest, giving the union more talking points, and even arousing antagonism among employees so that they came out to vote "against the boss." A considerable number saw their own interest in free speech so great, and so closely related to free speech for the employer, that they thought he also must be free to talk, so long as he avoided coercion. Union representatives generally insisted, however, that the employer should not be allowed to coerce employees by subtle threats or inducements or to use the unequal advantage of his economic position to reach employees, either in the plant or by use of his mailing list.

These arguments do not meet all the issues, however. Some employers who had failed by 1947 fully to accept the right of employees to organize wanted to be free to use at least the antiunion weapon of speech, now that other weapons were denied them, and to know how far they could legitimately go. Some unions preferred not to have to meet the stronger test presented by the employers' freedom to talk, which forced them to do a better job in order to win elections and hold their membership.

The Board's regional offices were in good position to observe the effects of pre-election statements by employers. They reported great variation early in 1947 in the extent to which such statements were used, depending on industry and area and the influence of particular attorneys. They were widely used in the South. Many of the regions noted some elections lost when there were such pre-election campaigns by employers, although some thought the importance of these letters overestimated. In general, the statements had little effect in the better-organized cities or long-organized areas, but in the "hinterlands" the story was quite different. They were especially effective in isolated, rural areas where employees were unsophisticated, sometimes illiterate, and newly organized, and the unions were weak. They were sometimes effective also where there had been a history of good labor relations. Sometimes, however, the effect was opposite to that which had been intended. It was clear that greater freedom of employers to enter into the campaign as employees tried to organize was a real handicap to unions in some of the industries and areas where organization was still in an early stage and where freedom to organize was not yet thoroughly established.

This experience gave some indications as to the needs of sound policy. If the purposes of the Act were still to be accomplished, it was important for the Board to be willing and able to make a realistic appraisal of all the factors in particular situations and not hesitate to

187

enjoin statements when they were clearly coercive in the entire context, including consideration of the social milieu. The fact of employers' dominance in one-industry towns and backwoods areas could not be ignored in deciding whether statements were coercive. Nor could the fact that 1947 was different from 1937—at least in many parts of the country. Even in 1947, however, the doctrine of separability of words and acts could easily lead to permitting actual coercion in some circumstances. The meaning of "coercion" needed careful analysis. Moreover, the experience in 1947 showed how important it was to continue to use statements as evidence of motive in connection with other evidence of discrimination or other unfair labor practices, if employees were still to be protected from interference by some employers with their rights under the Act.

On the other hand, it was an unhealthy atmosphere for labor relations if employers who were dealing honestly with the union representing their employees did not feel free to talk. A study of Board decisions gives little if any support for these fears where employers were not motivated by desire to break the unions; and the anti-Board propaganda must be held partly responsible for these anxieties. Moreover, the extent to which employers did in fact talk makes one question the extent of their fears. Perhaps the Board could have made more clear than it did, however, that, in the absence of acts indicating a motive to interfere with the rights of employees, the employer had every right to speak freely with his employees, and to answer union statements, and that the Board would lean over backward to avoid any interference with that right. There was no real occasion for the decent employer to feel restricted, any more than was dictated to him by his own estimate of the probable effects upon his relations with his employees.

By 1947 the Board was giving the benefit of the doubt to free speech, except where it found clear coercion, and this was as it should be. There were cases, however, where unions and others thought that the Board had failed to give sufficient weight to factors which made the totality of the employer's action coercive. Still it was reasonable to make the decisions in the light of the fact that by 1947 the labor movement was in many sections and industries well established and strong and able to stand on its own feet, and even in areas where it was still weak it had, nevertheless, the prestige of a strong national movement. Except when coercion was very clear, therefore, it was proper to give the benefit of the doubt to free speech, since, as Woodrow Wilson said, "in this free air of free speech men get into that sort of communication with one another which constitutes the basis of all common achievement."[38] If unions found this free discussion a delaying factor in their growth, still those that won out would have a sounder basis in the clearer understanding of issues by their rank and file.[39] Employers, on the other hand, needed to weigh the question of whether, if they succeeded in delaying organization by entering into election campaigns, they might not suffer as a result of the emotions aroused in a period of sharp conflict.[40] The delicate problems involved in government control in this area called for sound analysis of actual situations, self-restraint by the Board to avoid undue interference in labor relations, and courage and authority to stop the use of words when they were integral parts of campaigns of coercion.

In sum, there was in the experience little evidence of unreasonable restraint of employers by Board decisions and considerable evidence of abuse of "free speech" by a minority of employers even in the later years. Yet if a carefully drawn free-speech amendment could have made clearer to employers that they had every right to discuss any matters of common interest, barring interference with the rights of their employees, it might have served a useful purpose in removing one of the grievances of employers under the Act. This does not mean that speech could be removed from a context of other unfair labor practices, when it was an integral part of such conduct or gave crucial evidence of the nature of such conduct, if real protection was still to be given to the right to organize.

FREEDOM TO STRIKE

Protection of "the right to strike" was explicit in the Wagner Act. Did the Act and its administration therefore increase strikes "by taking most of the risk out of striking"? Did it encourage unlawful and violent strikes by removing the penalties for misconduct? These charges were frequently made.[41] An incomplete description was often given of what the Board actually did, with little or no regard for the carefully thought-out bases in public interest for the policy of the Act and the decisions of the Board on these matters. What did the Act

38. Noted by Justice Jackson in Thomas v. Collins, 323 U.S. 516, 546 (1944).
39. Cf. the election discussed *supra*, ch. 5, pp. 168–69.
40. Cf. B. M. Selekman, *Labor Relations and Human Relations* (New York: McGraw-Hill Book Co., 1947), pp. 14–25.
41. Cf. Theodore R. Iserman, *Industrial Peace and the Wagner Act* (New York: McGraw-Hill Book Co., 1947), pp. 16–23; Harold W. Metz and Meyer Jacobstein, *A National Labor Policy* (Washington: Brookings Institution, 1947), ch. 7; see also *supra*, ch. 4, n. 1.

itself provide? Most important was the general statement, "Nothing in this Act shall be construed so as to interfere with or impede or diminish in any way the right to strike."[42] Strikes were protected also by Section 7, which included among the rights of employees "and to engage in concerted activities, for the purpose of collective bargaining or other mutual aid or protection." The definition of *employee*[43] included "any individual whose work has ceased as a consequence of, or in connection with, any current labor dispute or because of any unfair labor practice, and who has not obtained any other regular and substantially equivalent employment." Finally, power was given the Board to devise remedies for unfair labor practices—"and to take such affirmative action, including reinstatement of employees with or without back pay, as will effectuate the policies of this Act."[44]

Policies were worked out in early cases and approved by the courts in the Remington Rand and Mackay Radio and other cases.[45] The duty of an employer to bargain with a representative chosen by the majority of his employees continued during a strike and required him to bargain for the settlement of the strike. After an ordinary strike over economic matters, the employer could not lawfully discriminate later against the strikers. Their reinstatement could be ordered when jobs were available, with back pay from the time of any discriminatory refusal to reinstate, although employees hired during the strike did not need to be replaced. When a strike had been caused or prolonged by unfair labor practices, on the other hand, in order to reestablish the status quo as far as possible the employer could be ordered to displace strikebreakers and to rehire the strikers without discrimination. Back pay ordered from the time of a discriminatory refusal to reinstate did not mean pay during the strike, but only after application for reinstatement. Moreover, strikers in a current labor dispute were entitled to vote in an election for choice of representatives.[46] These policies were clearly in accord with the intent of Congress, "of encouraging the practice of collective bargaining and protecting the rights upon which it is based."[47]

There were difficult problems, however, on which differences of opinion arose within the Board, and sometimes between the Board

42. Sec. 13.   43. Sec. 2 (3).   44. Sec. 10 (c).

45. *Supra*, ch. 4, pp. 98–99, 102; *Third Annual Report*, pp. 76–80, 92, 209–12, 229–33.

46. *Supra*, ch. 5, pp. 135–36.

47. U.S. Senate, Committee on Education and Labor, *National Labor Relations Board*, Report No. 573, 74th Cong., 1st Sess., May 1, 1935, pp. 6–7, cited as Senate Committee on Education and Labor, *NLRB Report, 1935*.

and the courts. Did violence or other misconduct by strikers remove them from the protection of the Act so that employers could legally refuse to reinstate them? And were some strikes removed from the category of concerted activities which were protected by the Act, because they were for an unlawful purpose? These questions appeared in a relatively small proportion of the Board's cases but were important, perhaps chiefly as giving a target for criticism whether or not well founded.

Congress had explicitly rejected proposals that the Act should include prohibitions of coercion or violence by employees or unions. Committee reports indicated that the Act was not to be "a mere police court measure" and that the Board should not be diverted from its main task by the addition of such functions. Remedies for fraud and violence or threats of violence were considered available and adequate, through local police authorities and the state and federal courts.[48] Violence on both sides had, in fact, been a long-standing accompaniment of industrial strife in America.[49] The first years of the Wagner Act were no exception, especially as long as many employers refused to accept the policies of the Act.[50] When employers argued that they should not be required to reinstate strikers who had been guilty of violence, the Board decided, and was generally upheld by the courts, that such minor violence as often accompanied bitter strikes, while not to be condoned by the Board, yet should not prevent a return to work.[51] Persons guilty of more serious offenses, on the contrary, were ordinarily not ordered reinstated. The Board considered all the circumstances in deciding whether the purposes of the Act would be effectuated by ordering reinstatement, and, when the employer had himself been guilty of serious infractions of the Act and violence, this gave support to a liberal policy. The Republic Steel[52]

48. *Ibid.*, pp. 16–17.
49. Harry A. Millis and Royal E. Montgomery, *Organized Labor* (New York: McGraw-Hill Book Co., 1945), pp. 667–89; E. E. Witte, *The Government in Labor Disputes* (New York: McGraw-Hill Book Co., 1932), ch. 9.
50. The evidence is available in numerous decisions of the Board as well as in the La Follette Committee hearings and reports. Cf. *supra*, ch. 4.
51. Cf. Stackpole Carbon Co., 6 NLRB 171 (1938), enforced in 105 F. 2d 167 (C.C.A.3, 1939), cert. den., 308 U.S. 605 (1939). For a contrary decision, NLRB v. Indiana Desk Co., 149 F. 2d 987 (C.C.A.7, 1945), modifying 56 NLRB 76 (1944).
52. 9 NLRB 219 (1938); 107 F. 2d 472 (C.C.A.3, 1939), cert. den. except as to another issue, 310 U.S. 655 (1940). Cf. also U.S. Senate, Committee on Education and Labor, *Violations of Free Speech and Rights of Labor* (cited as *La Follette Committee Reports*), *The "Little Steel" Strike and Citizens' Committees*, Report No. 151, Pt. IV, 77th Cong., 1st Sess., 1941.

case presented the issues on a large scale. The company, before and during the "Little Steel" strike of 1937, had engaged in an extensive campaign against the union, including the incitement of violence. In Massilon, Ohio, an unprovoked attack by police had killed three strikers and wounded others. There were numerous arrests and convictions of strikers for offenses ranging from felonies involving use of explosives down to assaults and minor disorders on the picket line. The Board decided that it must rely on the local authorities and would not retry any evidence as to misconduct, although it took notice of any convictions and pleas of guilty and of the fact that penalties under state and local law had already been paid in such cases. In view of all the circumstances the Board held that to remedy the employer's unfair labor practices required reinstatement of the strikers, even those who had violated other laws, except those whose crimes were exceptionally grave. In the exercise of its discretion, therefore, it excluded any guilty of felonies or of more serious misdemeanors, including destruction of property to a value of $300, while any with less serious violations were included among those entitled to be reinstated. The circuit court upheld the Board generally, although, following the Supreme Court's Fansteel decision, it excluded a somewhat larger list of offenders.[53] The Supreme Court refused to consider an appeal from the company on this issue.

Four months after the Board had worked out its solution for such problems in the Republic case, the Supreme Court in the much-publicized Fansteel[54] case reversed the Board and set a limit to reinstatement of strikers after violence. This again was a conflict which followed refusal of the employer to recognize the right of collective bargaining and other antiunion activities. A sit-down strike took place, in the course of which public authorities ejected the strikers from the plant after violent resistance. Substantial damage occurred to the company's property, 93 strikers were arrested for contempt following an injunction, and 37 of them were sentenced to fines and jail terms. The company had announced the discharge of all the sit-downers during the strike but later invited applications for reinstatement and took back 35 who applied, abandoning the strike. The Board held that the company had not effectively discharged the men, since it took back those who could be induced to come during the

53. *Fourth Annual Report*, pp. 105–7; *Fifth*, pp. 101–2, 105.
54. NLRB v. Fansteel Metallurgical Corp., 306 U.S. 240 (1939), reversing on this issue, enforcing others, 5 NLRB 930 (1938). Cf. discussion in H. M. Hart, Jr., and E. F. Prichard, Jr., "The Fansteel Case; Employee Misconduct and the Remedial Powers of the NLRB," *Harvard Law Review*, 52 (1939), 1275–1329.

strike, and that union activity rather than misconduct was the basis of the objection to the others. It therefore ordered reinstatement. The circuit court, disregarding the employer's unfair labor practices, set aside the entire order. The Supreme Court enforced the order against unfair labor practices but disapproved the order to reinstate the strikers, holding that the Board had exceeded the limits of its discretion. It held that since the sit-down strike was clearly illegal, the employer had a right to discharge those engaging in such unlawful conduct; to require reinstatement, therefore, would not effectuate the purposes of the Act to encourage peaceable settlements. Two members of the Court, however, Justices Reed and Black, agreed with the Board and would have required reinstatements. They thought that punishment for illegal acts should be left to the peace officers and that the Board should have discretion, depending on the circumstances, to order reinstatement when "both labor and management had erred," in order to restore both to their former status.

The law was then established that employers could discharge or refuse to reinstate strikers for serious violence or destruction of property or for an illegal sit-down strike. The Board still had to decide, in the exercise of its discretion in the particular case, whether the line had been passed, or whether the purposes of the Act would be effectuated by requiring offers of reinstatement to all the strikers. The Supreme Court disagreed with the Board again in 1942. It held that maritime workers who struck aboard ship, although their vessel was moored in a safe domestic port and the strike was provoked by an illegal refusal to bargain, were in violation of the federal mutiny statute; and as a result their concerted activities were not of a sort protected by the Act. The Court admonished the Board not to be so "single-minded" in effectuating the policies of the Act as to ignore "other and equally important Congressional objectives."[55]

A related question was whether a strike in violation of a contract was protected under the Act, or whether an employer was entitled to discharge such strikers and refuse to reinstate them. The Board at first considered that the Act made no distinction based on the issues in a dispute. Therefore in the important Sands[56] case, where it found a real difference of opinion over the interpretation of a contract, it held that even if there had been a violation of the contract the strikers

55. Southern Steamship Co. v. NLRB, 316 U.S. 31, 47 (1942), modifying 23 NLRB 26 (1940). Four justices dissented, thinking the Board's decision reasonably within its discretion.
56. Sands Manufacturing Co., 1 NLRB 546 (1936), set aside in 306 U.S. 332, 344 (1939).

were still employees and entitled to reinstatement without discrimination. The Supreme Court, however, reversed the Board; this was one of only two Board decisions which it reversed completely. It held that there had been a violation of the agreement by the men, and "the Act does not prohibit an effective discharge for repudiation by the employee of his agreement, any more than it prohibits such discharge for a tort committed against the employer." Justices Reed and Black, however, dissented, without opinion.

When this issue arose in later cases, it often involved close questions as to whether in fact there was a violation of contract, or, if there was, whether under the circumstances the employer could still be enjoined from later discrimination. In one case, Hazel-Atlas,[57] the Board was upheld in its principle that the employer must not discriminate later among strikers, when he had condoned their violation of contract by reinstating them. The court, however, upheld the discharge of a foreman who had aided the unlawful strike. In another, the United Biscuit[58] case, the Board found that a strike in violation of a no-strike agreement had been induced by unfair labor practices which the employees believed threatened the existence of their union. Under the circumstances the Board, without condoning breaches of contract, held that the strikers should be reinstated. The circuit court disagreed, holding such a strike without legal justification and the employer entitled to discharge as a result.

After the war there was much public discussion of the issue of strikes in violation of contracts. The Board then took a firm position that strikers who had violated contracts were not protected from effective discharge. Early in 1946 in the Scullin Steel[59] case the Board held that discharges were not discriminatory when a group of men had struck for wage increases in 1943, in the face of a contract with an independent union. The strike was not caused by unfair labor practices, although the Board found that later there was illegal assistance to the independent. Since the contract was considered valid at the time of the strike, the discharge of the strikers was held permissible. A year later the same principle was firmly reasserted, in the Dyson case,[60] although again there could be considerable doubt as to the nature of the contract. The claim that discharges of a group of

57. Hazel-Atlas Glass Co., 34 NLRB 346 (1941), modified and enforced in 127 F. 2d 109 (C.C.A.4, 1942).

58. United Biscuit Co., 38 NLRB 778 (1942), modified and enforced in 128 F. 2d 771 (C.C.A.7, 1942).

59. 65 NLRB 1294 (1946).

60. Joseph Dyson & Sons, 72 NLRB 445 (1947).

striking employees were justified by a violation of a no-strike contract
had not been made before the Board in the original hearing. The
Board, nevertheless, found that the contract was a valid one made
with an exclusive representative and that the strike in violation of the
no-strike clause rendered the strikers vulnerable to loss of their jobs.
The principle was applied once more, in May, 1947, in the Fafnir
Bearing case,[61] where eight union leaders had been discharged for
alleged violation of a no-strike agreement. The Trial Examiner found
such doubt as to the proper construction of the clauses in question
that he considered it in derogation of the basic rights under the Act
to deprive an employee of the protection of the Act, under the circumstances. The Board, however, construed the contract to mean an
obligation not to strike before a certain date and held the discharges
permissible.

The cases so far discussed all involved the issue of whether certain
acts by strikers deprived them of the protection of the Act, so that
they could lawfully be discharged or refused reinstatement. The
Board followed the directions given by the courts, and strikers guilty
of serious violence or destruction of property, or violent sit-down
strikes, or violation of such a federal statute as that against mutiny,
or violation of contracts, were not protected. There is no need to
quarrel with the policy, but it called for application in the light of
the whole circumstances and consideration of its effects in industrial
relations. This in general seems to have been done, without falling,
on the one hand, into the mistake of trying to take on the job of
policing strikes, not the function of the Board, or, on the other hand,
seriously limiting the protection of "concerted activities."[62] Any context of unfair labor practices by the employer needed realistic consideration in deciding these cases. It was reasonable, also, that the Act
should not be applied to limit the employer's right to discipline in
regard to violation of agreements as well as in other areas. Such problems are normally a matter for collective bargaining, however, where
mature bargaining relationships have been established, and are best
handled in that way. The "company security clauses" in the Ford
Motor company agreement of 1946 are an illustration. There was
danger in the spring of 1947 that the Board's decisions would make

61. Fafnir Bearing Co., 73 NLRB 1008 (1947).
62. For an excellent discussion of the development of policy and the issues in
the earlier period, see Joseph Rosenfarb, *The National Labor Policy and How It
Works* (New York: Harper & Bros., 1940), pp. 145–47, 549–75.

unions reluctant to sign no-strike agreements.[63] Under all the circumstances, including the uncertainty as to the contractual obligations, the three much-publicized applications of the policy in 1946–47 discussed above are subject to question.

A quite different issue was presented in a series of cases beginning in 1944, when it was claimed that illegality of the object of the strike removed strikers from the protection of the Act. State courts under the common law and federal courts in interpreting the Sherman Antitrust Act and the Clayton Act in labor cases had long seriously limited the right to strike, by applying the test of legality of purpose. It was largely as a result of inequities arising from these decisions that the Norris–La Guardia Act (and similar acts in a number of the states) limited the use of injunctions in labor disputes and declared that employees were not to be enjoined from the exercise of full freedom to engage in concerted activities, barring fraud or violence. The Wagner Act incorporated the same unrestricted language in protecting "concerted activities" in Section 7.

In the American News Company case,[64] nevertheless, the majority of the Board held that strikers were not protected from discharge and refusal of reinstatement when they struck for the illegal purpose of compelling the employer to grant wage increases without prior approval of the National War Labor Board. The national wage stabilization policy, under the Price Control Act of October 2, 1942, and the Executive Order of October 3, 1942, prohibited any wage increases until approved by the WLB, and provided fine or imprisonment for violators. In this case when for more than two months there had been no action by the WLB on a joint application for approval of a wage increase, the union demanded immediate increases, which the employer refused on the ground that they could not lawfully be granted. The following day the men struck. Ten days later, on the advice of the Regional War Labor Board, the men decided to abandon the strike and requested reinstatement. This was refused, although the jobs had not been permanently filled, and the union filed an unfair labor practice charge.

The NLRB in its decision pointed out that for the employer to have granted the increases would have been illegal and subject to

63. Cf. discussion in *Labor Relations Reporter*, 19, Analysis 61–63 (February 17, 1947); 20, Analysis 5 (May 12, 1947). This was an issue also under Taft-Hartley. For an important later case involving an alleged violation of a no-strike clause cf. United Elastic Corp., 84 NLRB No. 87, decided in June, 1949.

64. 55 NLRB 1302 (April 14, 1944). On the timing of this decision see *infra*, ch. 7, n. 17.

penalty. Moreover, the Price Control Act expressly enjoined this Board, with other agencies, "to work toward a stabilization of prices, fair and equitable wages, and cost of production"; this was a kind of statute to which the National Labor Relations Act, therefore, should be accommodated if it could reasonably be done. The majority went on to hold that they were not required by the terms of the Act to give protection to such a strike for an illegal purpose. They granted that Congress had rejected proposals to broaden the Act to include regulations of employee misconduct; nevertheless, misconduct had been held to remove employees from protection against discharge. They agreed that neither the Norris–La Guardia Act nor the NLRA had given the Board or the courts any broad discretion to determine proper objectives of concerted activity. Nevertheless, they held that Congress could not have meant the Board to ignore the character of a strike to compel violation of another federal law. Accordingly the Board dismissed the complaint.

Chairman Millis dissented in a vigorous, thoroughly documented opinion. Under these circumstances he would have ordered reinstatement of the employees upon application, but because of the nature of the strike he would have denied them the usual remedy of back pay. After studying the congressional reports and debates he concluded that Congress could not have intended any limitation of the rights of the employees under the Act. The language was explicit that the right to strike was not to be impeded or diminished in any way. Congress had specifically rejected numerous proposals to deny its protection to employees who strike for an unlawful purpose, since it did not consider the Act "a fitting instrument for the regulation of coercive conduct by employees or labor organizations . . . [and] on broad considerations of policy did not intend to vest the Board with authority to inquire into the objectives of employee concerted activity in determining substantive rights under the Act." Congress, in adopting in the NLRA the unrestricted language of the Norris–La Guardia Act, clearly meant to "guard against a revival of the discredited legality-of-object test." The Fansteel and other cases were not controlling in the Chairman's view, since they involved actions which were in themselves unlawful, apart from purpose. The Chairman warned also that this decision might be used to resurrect "as a measure of permissible union conduct the vague and uncertain test of legality of objective," by applying it to a wide variety of conduct deemed to be in violation of some federal, state, or local law or court decision. Finally, he held that the decision of the majority was not

197

in accord with the wartime federal labor policy. Congress had not made strikes illegal or denied strikers the protection of federal laws, and the Board should not do what Congress had been unwilling to do. By ordering reinstatement but without back pay, when the jobs had not been filled, the Board would discourage such ill-advised strikes but would promote prompt settlement of disputes and the best use of manpower. It would avoid the possibility that the employer might refuse reinstatement for the purpose of breaking a union. Such a policy, he believed, would support the entire governmental scheme for wartime labor policy without excessive emphasis to any one aspect.

As the Chairman had expected, employers then tried to extend the American News doctrine to other situations. In a series of cases the Board, unanimously or by majority, distinguished the facts in the case and ordered reinstatement of strikers where a strike was found to have followed an impasse in negotiations over wages, or to have been an effort to compel negotiations over wages, rather than a demand for wage increases without WLB approval.[65] In one of these the circuit court disagreed, holding the strike an illegal attempt to force a present increase. A similar question arose when employees struck without the prior notice required by the War Labor Disputes Act, and employers claimed the right to discharge them under the American News doctrine. In the Republic Steel[66] decision in June, 1945, where foremen had struck without filing the required notice, Mr. Reilly, the strongest advocate of the American News doctrine, would have denied them reinstatement on the ground of their breach of a federal law. The majority, however, including Chairman Millis, held that the War Labor Disputes Act had not intended to affect the rights of employees under the NLRA and that the wartime labor policies of the government were best effectuated by giving the strikers the protection of the Act.

Altogether the criticisms of the American News doctrine seem well justified. It limited the right to strike, when Congress had not given any authority to the Board to inquire into the objective of strikes, and when the governmental policy was to rely on the no-strike pledge rather than compulsion to prevent strikes. It was not forced by the Supreme Court decisions which had held certain *acts* in strikes outside the protection of the law. It ignored the long history of restric-

65. Indiana Desk Co., 56 NLRB 76, 58 NLRB 48 (1944), set aside as to reinstatement of strikers in 149 F. 2d 987 (C.C.A.7, 1945); Union-Buffalo Mills Co., 58 NLRB 384 (1944); Rockwood Stove Works, 63 NLRB 1297 (1945).

66. 62 NLRB 1008 (1945). Cf. also Union City Body Co., 69 NLRB 172 (1946); Kalamazoo Stationery Co., 66 NLRB 930 (1946).

tions on labor's right to act, through application of the objectives test. And, if widely applied, it would have encouraged employers to continue fights rather than promoting prompt settlement of disputes and return to work, which was needed especially in wartime and is a sound objective of governmental labor policy at any time. The Board in the exercise of its discretion could adjust the remedy to the facts, without removing in such situations all the protection of concerted activity which the Act provided by its terms.[67]

Strikes for recognition while representation cases were pending before the Board were sometimes challenged as illegal attempts to force violation of the Act and therefore outside the protection of the Act, under the American News doctrine. The question was considered first in the Columbia Pictures Corporation[68] case, involving a bitter jurisdictional dispute of long duration. After a change of affiliation of set decorators the employers had refused to recognize the new union, although a War Labor Board arbitration award made that recommendation. The union finally struck, while its petition with the NLRB was still pending, and notices of discharge were sent to all the strikers when they failed to return to work as the WLB ordered. Most of the jobs were filled. The specific issue before the NLRB was whether strikers could vote in the election. Mr. Reilly, dissenting, thought that their discharges were valid and that they should not vote. He held that they had flouted the law by attempting to compel recognition at a time when the producers were prohibited from recognizing any union because of an unsettled representation case before the Board.[69] The purpose of the strike, therefore, was to compel a violation of the Act, and as such it was not within the concerted activities protected by the Act, under the American News doctrine. He argued also that the Board should encourage use of its administrative processes rather than industrial strife. The majority, on the other hand, held that both strikers and replacements should have the right to vote.[70] They refused to apply the American News doctrine to a case where employees had struck for an objective to which they believed themselves entitled under the Act, even though their action in striking while the issue was before the Board was ill considered.

---

67. For discussion of this and related points see "Availability of NLRA Remedies to 'Unlawful' Strikers," *Harvard Law Review*, 59 (1946), 747–68. The minority position in the American News Case was indorsed, pp. 766–67.

68. Columbia Pictures Corp. *et al.*, 64 NLRB 490 (October 26, 1945).

69. He cited Mid-West Piping and Supply Co., 63 NLRB 1060, decided September 21, 1945; *supra*, ch. 5, pp. 165–66.

70. *Ibid.*, p. 136.

Such a strike was within the concerted activities protected by the Act, and strikers could not be discharged and deprived of their status as "employees" as a result. They were therefore entitled to vote. In a number of later representation cases, somewhat similarly, the majority of the Board ordered elections despite recognition strikes, on the theory that an election was the best method to terminate the dispute, although Mr. Reynolds objected to making the election machinery available until work was resumed.[71]

In the Thompson Products[72] case, however, the American News doctrine was applied more broadly than a majority of the Board had been willing to do in Columbia Pictures. Here the Board found that a strike for recognition by the UAW-CIO, in the face of an existing certification of another union, was an illegal attempt to induce the employer to violate the Act. As such it was not a protected "concerted activity" under the Act. Mr. Houston by 1946, when three separate opinions were issued on the complex case, had become convinced that the American News decision was not based on valid principles and would have overruled it. He found this strike protected by the Act and would have ordered reinstatement and back pay for the discharged strikers. Mr. Reilly argued strongly that the strike was an illegal attempt to coerce violation of the Act and wished to dismiss the complaint against the employer. Chairman Herzog, on reconsideration of the facts in 1947, agreed with Mr. Reynolds, who by then had replaced Mr. Reilly on the Board, that the American News doctrine was applicable. A new decision was issued, therefore, and the discharges were accepted as valid, since the strike had been for an illegal purpose, to coerce recognition in the face of an outstanding certification of another union.

The argument that the Board should protect its own certifications by not giving the protection of the Act to employees who struck to compel their disregard by employers has considerable appeal. There were problems also in a number of other types of cases where minority unions used their economic power to compel violations of the Act. Nevertheless, the Wagner Act did not provide any limits upon the concerted activities which were to be protected. It was a dangerous precedent when the Board began to consider the object of strikes as giving justification to employers in some instances for later dis-

71. National Silver Co., 71 NLRB 594 (November 5, 1946); Seneca Falls Machine Co., 71 NLRB 1106 (December 16, 1946); Whiting & Davis Co., 71 NLRB 1200 (December 17, 1946); Horton's Laundry, 72 NLRB 1129 (1947).
72. 70 NLRB 13 (August 15, 1946), 72 NLRB 886 (February 21, 1947).

crimination for concerted activities; and it is very doubtful whether the facts in these cases justified the extreme measure of refusing any protection to the striking employees. But these and related problems involving union coercion will be considered further below.[73]

Another question which was sometimes difficult to answer was that of permissible action by an employer during a strike. The duty of the employer to bargain with the representative of the majority of the employees for the settlement of the strike was well-established doctrine. It was held coercive, furthermore, for the employer to "go over the head of the union" and attempt to bargain with individuals.[74] But in a strike not caused by unfair labor practices the employer had a right to replace strikers if he could. If a real impasse was reached in negotiations, and the strike broken and strikers replaced, eventually the duty to bargain could be dissipated, though the employer must not have used any unfair labor practices for that purpose. The later tendency to permit a larger degree of freedom to employers to speak to their employees in such situations sometimes made it difficult to draw a line between permissible and really coercive conduct. Three cases decided in 1947 were much criticized by unions as a retreat from the protection provided by older decisions. In the Times Publishing Company[75] case the Board dismissed a charge of refusal to bargain when the publisher hired replacements and posted unilateral conditions of employment, after he had been unable to reach agreement with the union during a strike. He had announced to the union and in the public press that he would give preference in employment to union members. The case was complicated by the Florida anti-closed-shop amendment and the Typographical Union's insistence that the employer accept conditions in accordance with the union's international laws. The Board held that under all circumstances this had not been an illegal rejection of the bargaining agent and attempt to deal with individuals.

In the Fafnir Bearing[76] case where the Board found the strike one in violation of a contract, the Trial Examiner held that a series of newspaper ads and a letter to individual strikers, suggesting a secret ballot on the question of return to work and offering them the inducement of an advance against future pay checks, constituted unlawful

73. *Infra,* pp. 216 ff.
74. Cf. Remington Rand, *supra,* ch. 4, pp. 000–00; Biles-Coleman Lumber Co., 4 NLRB 679, enforced in 98 F. 2d 18 (C.C.A.9, 1938); Acme Air Appliance Co., 10 NLRB 1385, enforced in 117 F. 2d 417 (C.C.A.2, 1941).
75. 72 NLRB 676 (1947), discussed *supra,* ch. 4, p. 116.
76. *Supra,* p. 195.

interference and attempts to induce repudiation of the strike and the union. The Board, however, held that in the entire context these attempts to terminate the strike were not unlawful. In the United Welding Company[77] case the company had been involved in the nation-wide steel strike of January, 1946, and had failed after long efforts to reach a settlement with the union. It had sent a series of letters to employees during the negotiations explaining its position and describing the course of negotiations. Late in March a petition was signed by a bare majority of the employees offering to return to work and renouncing the union. The company opened the plant, and finally in May the union called off the strike, and the remaining strikers returned to work. The Trial Examiner considered the employer's actions an illegal attempt to undercut the union's authority and induce abandonment of the strike. But the Board under all the circumstances found the actions not illegal and dismissed the complaint. These three cases illustrate the complexity and difficulty of some of the cases in which it was necessary to decide realistically whether action had been coercive or privileged. There was some justification for the unions' fears that under these precedents employers might be permitted a dangerous leeway to deal with individuals rather than the bargaining agent chosen by the majority.

Criticism of the work of the Board in strike cases seemed often to be based on an assumption that the government should outlaw a number of types of strikes. But the Wagner Act had no such provisions. Sometimes actions by the Board were taken out of context and criticized when, under all the circumstances, they were easily justifiable as reasonable and in accordance with the purposes of the Act.[78] While many cases were difficult to decide, and reasonable men might differ on particular decisions, except for the American News doctrine there is little real foundation for criticism of the basic policies. Study of the cases does not indicate unreasonable protection of strikers. The Board did not take all the risk out of striking. Employers who refrained from the prohibited unfair labor practices could still use their economic power to defeat a strike, and strikers ran the risk of being replaced. Strikers continued to be subject to local law-enforcement authorities for their acts, and in case of serious violations of law they could be discharged. But the Board, although its processes

77. 72 NLRB 954 (February, 1947).
78. Cf. statements by T. R. Iserman, Senate Committee on Labor and Public Welfare, *Hearings, 1947*, Pt. 1, pp. 147–51; Pt. 4, pp. 2216–18; Raymond S. Smethurst, *ibid.*, Pt. 4, pp. 1798–1800; Earl F. Reed, *ibid.*, Pt. 2, pp. 737–43; Board statement, *ibid.*, Pt. 2, p. 752; Pt. 4, 1920–23.

were long and frequently slow, and there was sometimes failure effectively to push for compliance, yet did give some protection to strikers by preventing later discrimination, even where strikes were lost. The Act and the Board did, in fact, remove some of the risk of striking and strengthen the hands of the unions. It was the intent of the Seventy-fourth Congress to protect the full freedom of employees to engage in concerted activities, in the interest of the purposes of the Act. Only in the case of concerted activity to thwart rights of other employees under the Act does there appear to be a sound case for any limitation of freedom to strike, in the context of problems within the scope of the Wagner Act. This is not to say that there might not be a case for additions to the Act to deal with other problems, such as "national emergency strikes," and perhaps others.[79]

CLOSED-SHOP PROBLEMS

Competition of rival unions brought the Board some of its most difficult problems. This was especially true when closed-shop contracts were involved. Under some of them there was coercion by unions or by collusive action of unions and employers, contrary to the right of the majority of the employees to be represented by the union of their own choosing and the right of minorities to reasonable protection.

The closed-shop proviso to Section 8 (3), the anti-discrimination section, provided only that nothing in the Act should

preclude an employer from making an agreement with a labor organization (not established, maintained, or assisted by any action defined in this Act as an unfair labor practice) to require, as a condition of employment, membership therein, if such labor organization is the representative of the employees as provided in section 9 (a), in the appropriate collective bargaining unit covered by such agreement when made.

The committee reports made clear that the intent was only to leave the status quo, not illegalizing closed shops in states where they were legal, except for two limitations. A requirement for union membership was permissible *only* if the union was the choice of a majority of the employees concerned and if the union had not been illegally assisted by the employer.[80]

Three types of related problems came to the Board: where a rival union claimed that it had replaced the contracting union as majority

79. Problems of this sort are discussed in Part III, *infra*, esp. ch. 12, pp. 455–76; ch. 15, pp. 574–86.
80. Senate Committee on Education and Labor, *NLRB Report, 1935*, pp. 11–12.

representative; where the contracting union had not represented an uncoerced majority of the employees when the contract was made; and where the contract was valid but discharges under its terms interfered with rights guaranteed by the Act.

In the first group of cases, where local unions had shifted their affiliation or a rival claimed that the contracting union had lost its majority, the Board, balancing the interests of stability and of free choice, permitted the change of representative to be made at proper times on the evidence of election results. Such elections where there were closed-shop contracts frequently were won by the rival petitioning unions.[81] Closed-shop contracts were not always in accord with the desires of the employees covered, and the Board's elections, which permitted orderly indication of that fact and the establishment of the bargaining agent which the employees wanted, gave important protection to the rights of employees under the Act. Protection of the rights of the majority from collusive closed-shop contracts was a more difficult problem.

COLLUSIVE CONTRACTS—THE ASSISTED UNION

Under the Act a closed-shop contract made with a minority union, or with a union which received the assistance of the employer, was unquestionably illegal. The mandate of Congress was clear, and the Board recognized the validity of a contract only if there had been an uncoerced majority when it was signed. But sharp controversy resulted over the setting-aside of illegal contracts. Older unions felt that they had vested rights in contracts and in jurisdiction over certain industries, and old habits were upset of sometimes signing contracts without seeing first that the employees had agreed. As the habit grew of using elections to establish the right to recognition, however, this type of problem was less frequently met.

One of the most bitter attacks upon the Board came from the American Federation of Labor,[82] when the Board found certain AFL contracts illegal and ordered employers to cease recognizing the union. Competitive organizing by the AFL and the CIO, especially in the electrical manufacturing field, brought the issue to the Board in several important cases in 1937. Employers faced by the prospect that their employees were going to organize often preferred, understandably, to take their chances with the older, supposedly more conserva-

---

81. The development of policy is discussed *supra,* ch. 5, pp. 137–38, 155–60; election results, ch. 3, pp. 90–91.

82. American Federation of Labor, *Report of the Executive Council to the 58th Annual Convention,* 1938, pp. 69–76; *59th,* 1939, pp. 116–24.

tive organization as the "lesser evil." They frequently let their wishes be known to employees by words and acts. The storm broke when the first such case was decided by the Board, that of the National Electric Products Corporation,[83] in Ambridge, Pennsylvania. The UE-CIO began organizing in 1936. Then in March, 1937, the AFL electrical workers began a campaign, with the consent and aid of the company and its supervisors. In May, without any evidence of an AFL majority, and when the CIO claimed a substantial majority, an AFL closed-shop contract was signed. A bitter and violent strike followed, which was settled by agreement that the Board would determine the issues. The Board found the contract illegal, since it had been made with an organization assisted by unfair labor practices. It ordered the contract set aside, an appropriate notice posted by the employer renouncing the unfair labor practices and ending discrimination, and an election held to determine the choice of employees. In this instance, as in many others, the assisted union finally won the election.

By March, 1939, the Board had set aside sixteen contracts made with affiliated unions, fifteen of them AFL and one CIO, where it found that the union had not represented a majority at the time the contract was entered into or that the contract was the result of illegal assistance or interference by the employer with the efforts of employees to organize freely. All but one of these were closed-shop contracts. By this time also the Board had set aside sixty-two contracts with company-dominated independent organizations.[84]

The AFL, deeply concerned over the rise of a competing organization, frankly justified its willingness to have the assistance of employers in organizing and bitterly protested that the Board was violating the sanctity of contracts and building up a straw man by use of the term "favoritism."[85] By 1939 the AFL was supporting amendments to the Act which would have legalized contracts made, other than with "company unions," even if the employer had favored and assisted the union.[86] The Board, on the other hand, as Chairman

83. 3 NLRB 475 (1937).

84. Report of Board in Senate Committee on Education and Labor, *NLRA Hearings, 1939*, Pt. 3, pp. 512–14.

85. AFL, *Executive Council Report*, 1938, p. 72. The AFL General Counsel, Mr. Padway, argued before the Supreme Court in the Consolidated Edison case that employers must have the right to "engage in and indulge in" certain preferences, and "to make certain statements respecting preferences for labor organizations." Quoted in Rosenfarb, *op. cit.*, p. 294.

86. AFL, *Executive Council Report*, 1939, pp. 117, 121–24; Board report in Senate Committee on Education and Labor, *NLRA Hearings, 1939*, pp. 488–89, 510–16. Cf. discussion in Rosenfarb, *op. cit.*, pp. 283–94. See also *infra*, ch. 9, pp. 347–49.

Madden told the AFL in an address to their convention in 1937,[87] held that coercion by an employer to force his employees to join a union was illegal, whether the union was AFL, CIO, or independent, and it argued before congressional committees that any relaxation on this point would open the way to serious hazard to the right of employees to self-organization.

Ultimately the power of the Board under the Act to invalidate such contracts was upheld by the courts, although there was an adverse decision by the Supreme Court in the first important case on this issue, that involving the Consolidated Edison Company of New York.[88] The Court enforced the Board's order against a variety of interferences by that company with the employees' efforts at self-organization. It held, however, that there was no sufficient basis for finding that the contracts were the result of unfair labor practices and setting them aside pending choice by the employees of a bargaining agent. The Board had found that, while the CIO was attempting to organize, the company assisted the AFL electrical workers in taking over the members after an employee representation plan was given up. The AFL agreement, while nominally for members only, had been interpreted as giving exclusive recognition. The Supreme Court, holding that the AFL should have been made a party to the case and given official notice that its contracts were under attack, set aside this portion of the order. The Board, as a result, was careful in succeeding cases to see that the contracting union was always made party to any case in which its contract was at stake.

In later cases the Supreme Court upheld the Board in invalidating contracts where there was substantial evidence of assistance to the union by unfair labor practices. In the Serrick[89] case a Machinists' contract was set aside, when the Board found that there had been active support of this union by the employer. The Supreme Court approved, holding it within the Board's discretion to determine the appropriate remedy where "as a result of unfair labor practices a union cannot be said to represent an uncoerced majority." In the long-contested Electric Vacuum Cleaner Company[90] case also the Board was upheld. The AFL commented[91] that this gave further proof of the need for amendments to limit the powers of the Board.

87. Quoted in Rosenfarb, *op. cit.*, p. 253.
88. 305 U.S. 197 (1938), modifying 4 NLRB 71 (1937).
89. Serrick Corp., 8 NLRB 621 (1938), enforced in International Association of Machinists v. NLRB, 311 U.S. 72, 82 (1940).
90. 18 NLRB 591 (1939), enforced in 315 U.S. 685 (1942).
91. AFL, *Executive Council Report*, 1942, pp. 70–71.

It continued to be settled policy that employers were not entitled to give preferential treatment to one of two competing unions and that contracts resulting from illegal assistance to one of them should be set aside, unless and until the union was certified as representative. This was the policy applied both when affiliated AFL or CIO unions received illegal assistance and in cases involving independent unions. When independent unions were found to be "company dominated," however, and therefore incapable of acting as the free representative of the employees, not only were contracts set aside, but the company-dominated union itself was given a "death sentence" by being ordered disestablished. This difference in treatment was much criticized in the later period of attack on the Board but had a sound basis in the differences in the situations.[92] There is, however, some doubt as to the effectiveness of the Board's remedy in the "assisted union" cases where contracts were set aside, only to be followed later by the winning of elections in many instances by the union which had been illegally assisted. But a more severe remedy in the collusive contract cases, by "disestablishing" the local union even if AFL or CIO, would hardly have been practicable at this time, politically at least.[93] And in the long run the Board's election procedures gave opportunity for employees themselves to assert their independence and shift their bargaining representative, if the once assisted union did not prove one which served them well. These procedures gave incentive to the assisted union to win the allegiance of its members by doing its job of representation properly.

Closed-shop contracts under certain wartime conditions presented the Board with another problem which led to the "Frey rider" to the Appropriation Act. In a considerable number of instances an employer about to start a new business enterprise found that a certain union was the only source of labor supply available from the beginning. Accordingly he made a contract to hire labor only from the union. When charges were filed with the Board under these circumstances, in the absence of evidence of discrimination when the contract was entered into, such charges were dismissed in the regional offices. Cases of a different sort were those where it was charged that, although management itself had to secure its help from far and near, these employees were required to join a union with which a closed-shop contract had been entered into when only a few employees had

92. Cf. *supra,* ch. 4, pp. 109–10.
93. For the policy of equal treatment of affiliated and independent unions adopted in 1948 under the amended Act, see *infra,* ch. 12, pp. 425–28.

been hired. The most famous of such cases was that of the Kaiser Shipyards, in Portland, Oregon, where the CIO claimed that closed-shop contracts had been entered into with the AFL Metal Trades Council when there were only 67 men employed in one yard and about 190 in another, while two years or so later there were 90,000 employees in three yards. Discriminatory discharges of about 700 men were alleged. The CIO wanted the contracts set aside, and ultimately an election to be held by the Board to determine the bargaining agent. The AFL, on the other hand, argued that since most of the Pacific Coast shipyards were under contract with AFL unions and covered by a coast-wide stabilization agreement, it was entirely proper for these new yards to come under the agreement. It protested against a CIO "raid" and argued that contracts should be stabilized for the war period. The Board made every effort to obtain a satisfactory adjustment not in conflict with the law but, this failing, finally issued a complaint and began a formal hearing, in December, 1942. Even after that it offered to dismiss the case if the AFL would agree to strike out the closed-shop clause of the contracts, but the AFL refused. A campaign directed to Congress, holding that war production would be adversely affected by any upset to the contracts, resulted finally in the "Frey rider" to the Appropriation Act for 1944. This prohibited the Board from using any of its funds in connection with a complaint case arising over an agreement that had been in effect for three months without complaint having been filed. For the future it was provided that, for any such agreement to be protected,[94] notice of it must have been posted in the plant.

The Board immediately dropped the Kaiser and other important cases, and the CIO withdrew from any further activity at the Kaiser plants. The evil of such legislation through riders was clear when it was discovered that this rider went much further than had been intended. The Board announced in October, 1943, that the Comptroller-General, on consultation as to the meaning of the rider, had ruled that it applied to company-union cases where an agreement of more than three months' standing was involved. At the end of the fiscal year the Board reported that it had been precluded from proceeding on 95

94. U.S. Senate, Subcommittee of the Committee on Appropriations, *Hearings, Labor–Federal Security Appropriation Bill for 1944*, 78th Cong., 1st Sess., pp. 296–348, 389–444. AFL, *Executive Council Report*, 1943, pp. 36–37; 1944, pp. 60–61. The rider took its name from John Frey, president of the AFL Metal Trades Department, at whose instance this limitation on the Board's expenditures was made.

cases, 46 of them involving allegedly company-dominated unions, and 49 illegal assistance to other unions; 52 of them alleged also discriminatory discharges, and 13 refusal to bargain with the majority union. The rider had acted as an amendment to the Act, protecting illegal contracts and in many instances making it impossible for the Board to protect employees from discrimination or from refusal of employers to bargain with their majority representative. Charges filed by AFL unions as well as by CIO and independents were included.[95] The Board and a number of CIO representatives testified a year later that in some cases unrest had continued and that a number of strikes had occurred in plants involved, partly as a result of the Board's inability to continue processing cases.[96] The AFL continued to support the limitation, although it was willing to have it modified in some respects. A rider was again attached to the appropriation for 1945, but excluding company-dominated union cases from its coverage.[97] While this permitted the Board to go ahead with these cases, it still restricted the Board's ability to act against some types of conduct which were illegal under the Act itself. The rider was continued in the same form for the year 1946 and again for 1947 with a minor amendment.[98]

Some of the protection of contracts for which the AFL had argued was won in this way. In the Kaiser and other cases it prevented a test of whether the employees wished to be represented by the AFL or by some other union. Thousands of workers therefore had their first taste of union membership during the war under conditions of "compulsory unionism" where there had never been an opportunity to vote as to representation. It is at least questionable whether more contribution was made to stability and war production by freezing these contracts than would have been made by prompt holding of elections. In 1942–43, for instance, the Board held 127 elections in shipyards, where 115,000 votes were cast, resulting in choice of the AFL in 38 per cent of the cases, of the CIO in 30 per cent, and of independent unions

95. *Eighth Annual Report*, pp. 6–10; *Ninth*, pp. 4–6.

96. U.S. House of Representatives, Subcommittee of the Committee on Appropriations, *Hearings, Department of Labor–Federal Security Agency Appropriation Bill for 1945*, 78th Cong., 2d Sess., pp. 614–31, 657–750.

97. It also made clear that a renewed contract was to be considered as a new contract, subject to attack within three months. However, a charge filed in cases involving these contracts had to be filed by an employee, not by a labor organization.

98. *Ninth Annual Report*, pp. 4–6; *Tenth*, pp. 54–55; *Eleventh*, p. 51; AFL, *Executive Council Report*, 1946, pp. 161–62; 1947, p. 103.

in 14 per cent.[99] The limitation on the appropriation was disastrous in the first year in its effects upon protection of the rights under the Act in an important group of cases. Later, as modified, and after adequate notice of the requirement that charges be filed within three months, it gave slight difficulty. In so far as it promoted the healthy habit of full publicity to contracts, it was salutary. But the basic principles of giving protection to illegal contracts and of legislation by appropriation were both unjustifiable.

All this experience, despite occasional AFL and independent union criticisms, made clear the need for prompt and decisive action by the Board to protect rights under the Act—"calling them as they see them" —however they fell. When the Board and the courts, and employers, stood firm, generally the right of free choice was maintained in spite of occasional coercive efforts by minority unions. The administrative agency was in best position, also, to judge whether in a particular case the organization with which an illegal contract had been made was so completely under company domination that it should be "disestablished" rather than simply having its contract set aside. If there was any case for amendment of the Act at this point, it was not to limit the discretionary powers of the Board but rather to give it additional power against the occasional union which attempted coercion to maintain its illegal contract.

UNION COERCION: DISCHARGES UNDER THE CLOSED SHOP

The third problem came to the Board rather early, but no settled policy for its solution was worked out until 1942. As the numbers of workers covered by closed-shop and other types of union-security contracts increased, from about four million in 1941 to eleven million in 1946,[100] there were more possibilities of abuse. To the extent that the Board had authority it dealt with the problem and established reasonable standards for protection of individuals against discrimination instigated by unions because of the exercise of rights under the Act.

Discharges for nonmembership were permissible under the Act, as the Board decided in early cases, only when the contract clearly required union membership, involved an unassisted labor organization representing the majority of the employees in an appropriate unit when entered into, and was known to the employees.[101] Otherwise

99. *Eighth Annual Report*, p. 97.
100. *Monthly Labor Review*, 64 (1947), 766–67.
101. *Third Annual Report*, pp. 88–90; *Fifth*, pp. 40–43. Cf. Clinton Cotton Mills case, discussed *supra*, ch. 4, p. 104.

any such discharges were violations of the Act, and employees could be ordered reinstated with back pay. The difficult questions of policy arose when there had been shifts of union affiliation, or employees were advocating such shifts, and discharges were used to prevent their exercise of free choice. Such discharges were shown in the Board's records, in a group of cases studied in 1942, in a substantial minority of the closed-shop contract cases where the Board ordered elections. The danger of loss of job by advocates of the rival union was a reason for the Board's policy of ordering elections in these closed-shop cases on a smaller showing of interest in the form of signed cards than was usually required. In representation cases the Board could only order the election, without giving specific protection to individual employees; but sometimes charges of discrimination were filed. In an important early case, M. & M. Woodworking Company,[102] after a local carpenters' union had voted to transfer its affiliation to the CIO and returned its AFL charter the carpenters' international union chartered a new local and insisted that the employer continue to apply the closed-shop clause of the contract. The employer, thereupon, faced with a boycott by the AFL, discharged those refusing to join the new local. The Board decided that the discharges were illegal, since the contract was with the local union and the withdrawal from the international had been in accordance with the union's constitution. The Ninth Circuit Court disagreed, holding that the contract was enforceable to the benefit of the AFL carpenters' union.

Again when a series of bitter jurisdictional disputes broke out in New York City radio manufacturing plants between AFL and CIO electrical workers' unions, the Board was divided as to what it could and should do. In the Ansley Radio Corporation[103] case late in 1939 the Board found that early in the life of a closed-shop contract a majority of the employees had shifted to the CIO, although the employer gave illegal assistance to the AFL, the contracting union. The majority of the Board held that discharges of CIO adherents were permitted, on request of the AFL, for failing to maintain their AFL membership but not for mere "talk and advocacy of a change in affiliation." Mr. E. S. Smith would have held that the shift of majority precluded the employer from any discharges on demand of the contracting union, in spite of the closed-shop contract. The Chairman empha-

102. 6 NLRB 372 (1938), set aside in 101 F. 2d 938 (C.C.A.9, 1939).
103. 18 NLRB 1028 (1939). Cf. discussion of contracts as a bar to representation proceedings, *supra*, ch. 5.

sized the interest of stability for reasonable periods. Dr. Leiserson thought that full effect must be given to a valid closed-shop contract during its term and would have dismissed the entire complaint.

The question remained whether under the Act a valid closed-shop contract could be used to enforce discharges in order to protect indefinitely the status of the contracting union, even when the desires of the employees had changed. The Board's answer in the negative became fixed policy after the Rutland Court Owners'[104] case in 1942. This case involved a Washington apartment house where a closed-shop contract had been signed for the year 1939 after the seven employees had joined an AFL local union. The employees became dissatisfied, however, and in December six of them signed cards designating a CIO local to represent them. One was discharged at once on the claim of the AFL that he had not paid his dues and was creating dissension. An AFL representative questioned the others in the presence of the employer as to their intentions for the following year, and the next day the four who did not redesignate the AFL were discharged and their places taken by other members of the AFL local. A closed-shop contract was then signed for 1940, and the CIO filed a charge of discrimination. The Board found the discharges and the new contract illegal and ordered the company to offer reinstatement and back pay to the discharged employees and to cease recognizing the AFL unless and until it was certified by the Board. AFL representatives had argued in briefs and oral argument that the Board should not put so much emphasis on the right to choose representatives and to change bargaining agents. The primary purpose of the Act, they held, was "to attain contracts and maintain them." Employees who became dissatisfied should improve their own unions, not shift to another; and the closed-shop union had a right to expel members for advocating another union. "People are fired right and left now, under all closed-shop contracts, for advocating dual unionism." The Board held, on the contrary, that while discharges for nonunion membership were permissible for a reasonable period, any effort of

104. 44 NLRB 587 (1942), 46 NLRB 1040 (1943). The case was long delayed partly because of the changes in Board membership and the controversial and difficult issues of policy. The case was heard before Chairman Madden's retirement; a Proposed Findings of Fact and Order was issued in August, 1941, Mr. Smith dissenting to a proposal to dismiss on the ground that the case involved local industry not covered by the Act; he would have held the employer "in commerce" in the District of Columbia, and guilty of unfair labor practices. In September, 1942, the Board decision was issued, signed by Chairman Millis and Mr. Reilly, Dr. Leiserson dissenting.

212

the union to establish itself in perpetuity, regardless of the desires of the employees, was contrary to the purposes of the Act and not protected. "Effectuation of the basic policies of the Act requires, as the life of the collective contract draws to a close, that the employees be able to advocate a change in their affiliation without fear of discharge by an employer for so doing." Dr. Leiserson, however, dissented on the ground that the 1939 contract was valid and that Congress had not given the Board authority to suspend enforcement of a valid closed-shop contract, even if there were undesirable effects.

A second major bulwark for employees against abuse under closed-shop contracts was provided in the Wallace decision in 1943 which was approved by the Supreme Court.[105] In a West Virginia wood products plant the efforts of the United Construction Workers, CIO, to obtain recognition led to a strike during which an independent union was organized with the aid of the company. The strike was settled by an agreement for a consent election, with the understanding that, if either union won, it would obtain a closed-shop contract. The independent won by a small majority. Thereupon the employer signed a closed-shop contract, after receiving a letter in which the union made clear that it intended to eliminate from the plant those who were opposed to its interests. The applications of some forty employees were then rejected by the independent, and they were discharged. The Board found the company guilty of illegal assistance to the independent and discrimination. It made clear that an employer might not under the Act enter into a closed-shop contract when he knew it was designed "as an instrument for effecting discrimination against his employees solely because of their prior union activities." The Supreme Court upheld the Board, laying down the important principle that a bargaining agent is under a duty to represent the interests of all in the unit, impartially and without discrimination. To a similar effect was the Monsieur Henri Wines case[106] where a closed-shop contract was signed after the employees had designated the union as their representative, but they were then denied union membership and discharged.

These two doctrines continued to be applied. Activity on behalf of a rival union was protected during a certain period against discharge for dual unionism; and a closed-shop contract could not be entered into for the purpose of discrimination for prior union activity. Union-

105. Wallace Corp., 50 NLRB 138 (1943), enforced in 323 U.S. 248 (1944), four Justices dissenting.
106. 44 NLRB 1310 (1942).

shop and maintenance-of-membership clauses were held to be included under the closed-shop proviso and subject to the same conditions. The Board in 1945 added the condition that a discharge was discriminatory under the Act only if the employer knew that the reason for the requested discharge was expulsion or refusal of membership because of dual union activity.[107] But given such knowledge, as when a man was discharged after being expelled for having acted as observer for the rival union in an election, the employer was guilty of discrimination even though he had acted in good faith.[108] The democratic freedom of employees to reconsider their bargaining agent without fear of reprisal was thus supported by the Board and the courts even though it was the union rather than the employer which caused the violation of the Act. A union-security contract, also, could not act retroactively, making union membership before the date when the contract became effective a condition of employment.[109] But discharges for dual union activity were held permissible, even if the individual tendered his dues to the contracting union, when the activity in behalf of the rival union began so early in the life of the contract that, if successful, "it might well have undermined the status of the existing bargaining representative in the middle of the contract term."[110]

In the last months of the Wagner Act, in a series of cases[111] where discharges for dual unionism were clearly discriminatory under the established precedents, Mr. Reynolds dissented. He argued that the contracting union should be made a co-respondent with the employer, on the theory that a closed-shop contract, giving a union effective control of the tenure of employees, made it an "employer" within the meaning of the Act. He thought also that the Board's reliance upon the employer's knowledge of the reason for a discharge gave employees inadequate protection in the free exercise of their right to choose representation. He thought that the Board could and should, therefore, impose "effective restrictions on a union's power to utilize a

---

107. Diamond T Motor Car Co., 64 NLRB 1225 (1945); American White Cross Laboratories, 66 NLRB 866 (1946), enforced in 160 F. 2d 75 (C.C.A.2, 1947); Spicer Manufacturing Corp., 70 NLRB 41 (1946).

108. Portland Lumber Mills, 64 NLRB 159 (1945), enforced in 158 F. 2d 365 (C.C.A.9, 1946), cert. granted, 331 U.S. 798 (1947); cert. dismissed, 332 U.S. 845 (1948).

109. Colonie Fibre Co., 69 NLRB 589, 71 NLRB 354 (1946), enforced as modified in 163 F. 2d 65 (C.C.A.2, 1948).

110. Southwestern Portland Cement Co., 65 NLRB 1, 8 (1945).

111. Lewis Meier & Co., 73 NLRB 520 (April 24, 1947); Durasteel Co., 73 NLRB 941 (May 13, 1947), and others.

closed-shop contract as a weapon of industrial tyranny." If this was not possible, then the Act should be amended. The majority of the Board held that they had no such power under the Act and were unwilling to take such a step of "administrative legislation."

Dual unionism was traditionally a major crime in the calendar of American unions. But the unions' efforts to protect themselves and their security sometimes conflicted sharply with the freedom of individuals to exercise their right of free choice under the Act and were susceptible of other abuses. Evidence is not available as to the extent to which these abuses existed, though that they did exist is clear from Board records and elsewhere.[112] The Board's policies gave a major safeguard against such abuses, both by the elections to determine the choice of the majority of the employees and by limiting discharges for dual unionism. Board records showed that often the employees ordered reinstated after dual union discharges did not accept the offers, but there were cases where they did and where they were accepted into the union and the plant without trouble. Unions came to accept as proper the prohibition of expulsions and discharges during the protected period toward the end of a contract. The Board was considering, in 1947, whether this protected period should be specifically defined, perhaps to correspond exactly with the period during which a petition would be accepted for a new election. There was a question also whether it should not be made the duty of the employer to inquire into the reason when he was asked to discharge a nonmember. Mr. Reynolds' proposal that the union itself be joined with the employer and held financially responsible was clearly outside the authority of the Board under the Wagner Act, but it did raise a real question as to whether amendment of the Act on this point might not be desirable. The Board itself was inclined to favor such an amendment.

Closed-shop discharges which came before the Board were of several different sorts, calling for different remedies. Some were clearly the result of union-employer collusion that smelled of racketeering. Some were simply a form of illegal assistance to a preferred union. And some were the result of a union's attempt to prevent its own overthrow by a change of choice by the employees. Sometimes it was not easy to tell the difference, and careful analysis of the actual situation was called for with a fitting of the remedy to the facts through

112. Cf. a group of letters received by Senator Ball, sixteen of them from individual workers, Senate Committee on Labor and Public Welfare, *Hearings, 1947*, Pt. 4, pp. 2063–71.

the administrative process. Added power to the Board to act against the union itself in some of these cases would have helped to protect employees against abuses under union-security agreements.[113] It was still a question whether any discharges should be permitted for dual unionism or other discharges resulting from nonvoluntary lack of union membership. This was a problem on which more evidence was needed before any drastic change should be made in public policy.

UNION COERCION NO DEFENSE

The Board was troubled for some years by the problem of what to do when an employer claimed that his admitted violation of the Act was coerced by union action, strike or boycott, or threats of economic reprisal. Employers were sometimes in an extremely difficult position, in the middle between two contending unions, as the Board recognized. The rule adopted in 1939 to permit employers to petition for an election when faced by rival claims of two unions helped in some cases, but there was still a problem if a union used its economic power regardless of the choice of the majority of the employees. In 1937 the issue arose in a jurisdictional dispute between the American Newspaper Guild and the Teamsters over the circulation department employees of the *Seattle Star*.[114] After the men involved had joined the Guild, the Teamsters claimed that they had jurisdiction over all circulation department employees and refused to haul papers unless the men joined the Teamsters. This the employees refused to do, but they were unable to guarantee delivery themselves in view of "goon squads." The employer then hired Teamsters, displacing the original employees. When the Guild filed charges of discrimination, the Board found unmistakable violation of the law and ordered reinstatement and back pay, although commenting that the employer "was placed in an unenviable position by the Teamsters' ultimatum." The circuit court enforced the order, saying that the Act permitted no immunity on the ground that the employer thought the exigencies of the moment required infraction.

In later cases the Board continued to hold that threats of boycott

---

113. *Business Week*, March 1, 1947, p. 70, reported a case where an AFL union agreed to the reinstatement of seven employees whom it had required to be discharged for pro-CIO activity, and to pay them back pay itself, in order to settle a case and proceed to a Board election. For Board discussion of the problem, cf. House Committee on Education and Labor, *Hearings, 1947*, Pt. 5, pp. 3155–56, 3162; Senate Committee on Labor and Public Welfare, *Hearings, 1947*, Pt. 4, pp. 1860, 1905, 1934–35.

114. Star Publishing Co., 4 NLRB 498 (1937), enforced in 97 F. 2d 465 (C.C.A.9, 1938). Cf. also Pittsburgh Plate Glass Co., 4 NLRB 193 (1937) and Zellerbach Paper Co., 4 NLRB 348 (1937).

or strike, or of economic disadvantage resulting from union reprisals, could not be held to relieve the employer from his responsibility for any violation of the Act.[115] Temporarily in 1941 a highly questionable theory of a "technical violation" only was used in the New York and Porto Rico Steamship Company[116] case, and the usual remedies were not ordered. The case involved a jurisdictional dispute over radio operators. The employer maintained a neutral position and sought a settlement of the dispute; but finally he replaced the AFL operators, who were in a majority, by CIO men, after he was convinced by CIO strikes and threatened strikes that he could not man the ships unless he gave in to the CIO. The Board held that it could properly consider the coercion in determining the proper remedy and ordered the discrimination ended but without reinstatement or back pay. Mr. E. S. Smith dissented, pointing to the danger of collusion to undermine the purposes of the Act under this doctrine. A little later, in the Greer Steel case[117] where a CIO man had been kept out of the plant because of a threat of a strike by the AFL union, the Board distinguished this from the earlier case by the fact that there had been no actual showing of the use of economic power by the union to coerce. And later in the same month, in another case involving discrimination induced by a local CIO union, the Board held clearly that pressure by a local union gave no immunity from the duty to avoid discrimination.[118] This remained settled policy, as two 1946 cases show. In one of them the company had urged the employees to vote for the AFL crafts rather than the United Steel Workers because of fear of an AFL boycott; but, as the Trial Examiner had said, "It is now well settled that an employer's fear of economic reprisal, or loss of business, resulting from the unionization of his employees, does not justify a commission of unfair labor practices."[119] In the other,[120] involving a long-standing jurisdictional dispute, the employer signed a contract with the AFL printing trades unions although his employees had long had a Lithographers' contract. He justified it by an old award of jurisdiction by the AFL to the printing trades and by fear of economic

115. Cf. M. & M. Woodworking Co., *supra*, p. 211; McQuay-Norris Manufacturing Co., 21 NLRB 709 (1940), enforced in 116 F. 2d 748 (C.C.A.7, 1940); Wilson & Co., 26 NLRB 297 (1940), enforced with modifications in 123 F. 2d 411 (C.C.A.8, 1941); Hudson Motor Car Co., 34 NLRB 815 (1941), enforced in 128 F. 2d 528 (C.C.A.6, 1942).

116. 34 NLRB 1028 (1941).

117. 38 NLRB 65 (1942).

118. Borg-Warner Corp., 38 NLRB 866 (1942).

119. O'Keefe and Merritt Manufacturing Co., 70 NLRB 771, 788 (1946).

120. Albert Love Enterprises, 66 NLRB 416 (1946).

reprisal. The Board, nevertheless, required him to bargain with the union which represented the majority of the employees in question, and it specifically denied the defense of "technical violation." It held that any attempt to distinguish cases on the ground of compulsion would open the door to collusion and encourage the use of force and succumbing to force.

This policy was sound. Any relaxation would have increased the number of cases where the defense of union coercion was urged. Besides, it would have been a practical impossibility to decide always whether coercion was the fact, or whether there was collusion between employer and union. Experience showed that in many instances when the employer took a firm stand the coercive union withdrew, and the dispute was settled in accord with the law. Nevertheless, there were also cases where the employer was in fact the victim of a jurisdictional dispute, and where an aggressor union was ready to force its will by the use of economic power, regardless of the rights of employees to a union of their own choosing. Teamster locals were the most notorious for such actions, but they were not the only unions known to use them on occasion. The Board had no power to act specifically against the union which was trying to force a violation of the law. In two cases, however, the issue came before a court, and a possible remedy was suggested.

The first involved the long-standing dispute between Brewery Workers and Teamsters,[121] as a result of which the Brewery Workers finally left the AFL and affiliated with the CIO. The "beer war" went on in many sections of the country, accompanied by boycotts and violence, as the Teamsters tried to establish jurisdiction over the brewery drivers and in some areas over the brewery workers themselves. In the Gluek Brewing Company in Minneapolis only the drivers were involved. When the Teamsters threatened a boycott, the company discharged its drivers and contracted for delivery through another company, as it feared harm to personnel and trucks and to its local business if it tried to oppose the Teamsters. The Board, however, pointed out that the company had made no effort to settle the dispute in some other way and had not sought any legal action against the Teamsters; accordingly the company was ordered to reinstate the men with back pay. The case went to circuit court where the order was enforced, although the Teamsters had filed a brief in which they threatened to disregard any decision upholding the Board's order. The court commented sharply on a union's thinking that it had "un-

121. AFL, *Executive Council Report*, 1939, pp. 23–25.

controllable power to disregard and to nullify a determination of the Labor Board and an order of a court sustaining the Board." If the threat ripened into action, the court implied that something could be done in a contempt action; but the court thought that it would be desirable for the statute law to be clear on such matters as to the power of the Board and the courts to protect freedom of association.[122] The company complied with the order, and the men were offered reinstatement and given back pay. The Teamsters were for the time quiet, though one participant commented, "They never give up." The following spring a St. Paul city-wide brewery strike was settled in the governor's office by agreement of all the unions involved, with the acceptance of a "general principle" for Minnesota that drivers and helpers were to go to the Teamsters, and inside men in breweries and soft-drink plants to the Brewers. The Minneapolis Gluek drivers were included in this settlement. So the Teamsters achieved their purpose by agreement. The court's threat of contempt action had at least induced compliance with the law at that time.

Another case where the court warned a union against possible contempt action involved the Musicians, in the National Broadcasting Company case.[123] The Board had certified the National Association of Broadcast Engineers and Technicians as the representative of the "platter-turners" in a system-wide radio station unit, excluding Chicago, where by reason of collective bargaining history the platter-turners were in the Musicians' Union. The Musicians, however, threatened strikes should the company recognize NABET in the broad unit and held that, irrespective of the Board's holding, the Musicians were entitled to that work. The Board ordered the company to bargain with the certified union, since economic pressure was no defense. The order was taken to court and promptly enforced by the Second Circuit. The court considered whether its order should run against the American Federation of Musicians as well as against the company, but it assumed that the Musicians would respect the order. The court said: "If an attempt to prevent the companies from complying with our order should be made it would seem that the ordinary contempt procedures available against a person with knowledge of the decree although not named in it would enable the court to protect its order." Apparently no contempt action was necessary.

By 1947 no attempt had yet been made to use the weapon of contempt against a union which tried to coerce an employer to violate a

122. 47 NLRB 1079 (1943), enforced in 144 F. 2d 847, 858 (C.C.A.8, 1944).
123. 61 NLRB 161 (1945), enforced in 150 F. 2d 895, 900 (C.C.A.2, 1945).

219

court order in NLRB cases. It had not yet been demonstrated whether such action was prevented by the Norris–La Guardia Act.[124] In any event it was clear that occasionally there was need for some effective sanction against a union which tried to force violation of the rights of other employees under the Act.

JURISDICTIONAL DISPUTES, UNION COERCION, AND THE BOARD'S REMEDIES

"Juridictional disputes" were involved in many of the troublesome cases discussed above. Traditionally jurisdictional disputes involved conflicts between different unions over their claimed right to organize certain workers or to control certain work, in the trade or industrial territory over which their "jurisdiction" extended. Under the theory of trade autonomy and exclusion of any "dualism," the American Federation of Labor aimed in granting charters to affiliated unions to define and delimit their exclusive jurisdiction, and when necessary later to iron out disputes between them. Even before the advent of the CIO, however, there were jurisdictional disputes, some of which defied solution by the accepted union methods, between craft unions, between craft and industrial unions, and between industrial unions with overlapping jurisdictions, or with different long-run objectives, or resulting from secession movements. Changing products, materials and methods and expanding organization made conflicts inevitable. When a rival federation, largely organized on an industrial basis, brought greatly expanded organization, rival union disputes of many sorts inevitably increased.

"Jurisdictional disputes" most narrowly defined, involving claims of different unions to certain work, the kind most familiar in the building trades, were outside the scope of the NLRB's authority and were left to settlement with only more or less success to the unions themselves or by collective bargaining. Jurisdictional disputes over which union was to organize and represent certain workers also could be settled in accordance with the American trade-union tradition, by award or agreement as to jurisdiction within the labor movement itself without necessarily consulting the workers involved. As soon as the larger part of these disputes cut across federation lines, however, they were not easily susceptible of resolution by that means. They then became

124. Some states with "Little Norris–La Guardia Acts" interpreted them to permit enjoining a union from strikes to force violation of a certification of a union by the state board. Statement of G. D. Reilly in Senate Committee on Labor and Public Welfare, *Hearings, 1947*, Pt. 4, pp. 2054–55.

"representation disputes," to be settled according to the Wagner Act by the choice of the workers themselves as to which union, if any, they wanted to represent them. The election processes of the Board were successful in determining these disputes peacefully in most of the rival union cases which came to the Board.[125]

The Board attempted, wisely, to avoid interfering in the internal affairs of labor organizations and held that the federations should themselves work out the solution to their jurisdictional disputes. Accordingly, representation petitions involving disputes between two AFL unions were dismissed as a matter of policy in the early years.[126] But it proved impossible to hold strictly to this policy. When cases were filed involving the suspended CIO unions, where the authority of the AFL was no longer accepted, the Board ordered elections.[127] When the conflict was a three-way one, including two AFL unions and an outside one, the Board finally decided that it must hold an election to settle the representation dispute, though its election did not settle the internal issue of juridictional claims.[128] By 1942, also, while the Board still stated that it ordinarily dismissed "jurisdictional dispute" petitions where only unions belonging to one federation were involved, it found that some such disputes could not be solved without its intervention. So in the Harbison-Walker case,[129] where the CIO had been unable to settle a dispute between a local industrial union and District 50 of the United Mine Workers, and one union refused to recognize the authority of the parent-organization, an election was ordered as the only way to resolve the dispute. Increasingly it was found necessary in an occasional case to settle such disputes by holding an election, where there was little or no chance of the dispute

125. Board statement, Senate Committee on Labor and Public Welfare, *Hearings, 1947*, Pt. 4, pp. 1858–59, 1887–91, 1918. For other definitions of jurisdictional and rival union disputes cf. Walter Galenson, *Rival Unionism in the United States* (New York: American Council on Public Affairs, 1940), pp. 1–2; Florence Peterson, *American Labor Unions* (New York: Harper & Bros., 1945), pp. 225, 266.

126. Aluminum Co. of America, 1 NLRB 530 (1936); Axton-Fisher Tobacco Co., 1 NLRB 604 (1936); *Second Annual Report*, pp. 119–22.

127. Interlake Iron Corp., 2 NLRB 1036 (1937).

128. Showers Brothers Furniture Co., 4 NLRB 585 (1937); Long-Bell Lumber Co., 16 NLRB 892 (1939); Campbell, Wyant & Cannon Foundry Co., 32 NLRB 416 (1941).

129. 43 NLRB 936 (1942). For an AFL case where President Green told the Board that it was impossible for the AFL to settle a long-standing dispute, see Iowa Electric Light and Power Co., 38 NLRB 1124, 46 NLRB 230 (1942). For the 1939 discussion as to whether the Board should act in these disputes, cf. Galenson, *op. cit.*, pp. 146–47.

being resolved without use of the Board's machinery.[130] The disputes between the Lithographers and the other printing trades, and the Teamsters and Brewery Workers, were only the best known of such controversies. From 1944 on the Board permitted its Regional Directors to proceed with many such cases without consulting Washington, as when a petition was filed by an employer in a long-standing jurisdictional dispute which the parent-organization had been unable to resolve, or where consent elections could be arranged. Regional Directors continued to notify the federations and give them opportunity to settle the dispute if they could. It might be said that the unions to some extent had abdicated, by leaving the Board to settle these conflicts. On the other hand, in many instances the best way to resolve the issue was by the method contemplated in the Act, that workers should freely choose the union which they wished to represent them.[131]

Jurisdictional disputes thus merged into the larger problem of union rivalry in extending organization. Some could still be settled by agreement of the unions, directly or through decisions of the parent-organizations, to delimit their fields or to avoid "raiding" each others' plants or territories. Practically that was often the most desirable solution, although it had possibilities of abuse and of undercutting the right of employees to unions of their own choice. The democratic election process, on the other hand, was usually the most feasible means to settle these disputes when they involved unions of different affiliation, and sometimes those within one of the federations. Many of the long-standing disputes which began as intra-federation jurisdictional disputes, moreover, became ordinary rival union disputes subject to resolution by elections, as a result of shifts of affiliation in the very fluid labor movement of the ten years after the birth of the CIO.

Success in settling these disputes by the Board's election process depended upon freedom from coercion by either employers or unions. Fortunately this was the fact in the great majority of instances. But

130. *Eighth Annual Report*, p. 44; *Ninth*, p. 24; *Eleventh*, p. 12. Occasionally elections were ordered without special mention in cases involving two affiliates of a parent organization.

131. The Board was not bound by the terms as to jurisdiction or eligibility to membership in union constitutions, and, when it was claimed that a union could not be certified for a certain unit because its constitution did not provide jurisdiction or eligibility to membership covering the group in question, the Board held this immaterial, in the absence of showing that the union would not provide adequate representation for these employees. Cf. Texas Co., 61 NLRB 885 (1945); Virginia Ferry Corp., 67 NLRB 698 (1946).

defiance of the Board's processes and standards in a minority of cases, some of which have been mentioned above, was difficult to meet and occasionally thwarted a free choice by employees. The Board developed methods to meet such challenges. When a union had been certified, or was unquestionably the choice of the majority of the employees in an appropriate unit, the employer could not justify a refusal to bargain or discriminatory discharges by the fact of threats of strikes or boycotts or other economic pressure by a rival union. Union coercion was no defense.[132] Twice circuit courts in enforcing Board orders warned unions that they might be subject to contempt action if they failed to respect the order.[133] In a 1947 case where a union struck to induce the employer to recognize it in a violation of his obligation under the law to bargain with a certified union, the strike was held to have been for an illegal purpose, and the strikers were not protected against discharge.[134] Discharges for dual unionism at the instance of unions holding closed-shop contracts were strictly limited, and the rules permitting them defined, in an effort to protect the right of employees at proper times to choose freely between competing unions.[135] Finally, an employer did not have a right to give assistance to a preferred union in rival union disputes or to sign a contract with it when a representation dispute was still unresolved. Collusive contracts were set aside, and employers were ordered not to interfere with the right of their employees to choose freely between the competing unions.[136] But the question of whether an employer could give exclusive recognition to a union with which he had an old contract, and continue to handle grievances, or whether there had to be a "hiatus" in collective bargaining during the pre-election period, had come up in the later years and had not been satisfactorily solved. There was a real possibility of collusive assistance to a preferred union under such circumstances, although when there was long delay in handling cases it was impossible to stop all relations with a union pending the election.

Public opinion was justly aroused against the much-publicized cases where unions used economic power to thwart the rights of other employees under the Act by strikes or boycotts. This was one of the points on which there was a strong demand for legislation in the congressional hearings of 1946 and 1947. In the President's Labor-Management Conference of 1945 the management representatives

132. *Supra*, pp. 216–20.
133. *Ibid.*, pp. 218–19.
134. *Ibid.*, p. 200.
135. *Ibid.*, pp. 210–16.
136. *Ibid.*, pp. 204–6; ch. 5, pp. 165–66.

recommended that, after a determination by the Board of a bargaining representative, any interference by another union should be made an unfair labor practice. Union representatives recommended only that no union should engage in a strike or boycott in protest against the results of noncollusive agreements or determinations by the Board, but, mistakenly, we think, they opposed amendment of the Act on this point.[137]

The extent of such coercive action by unions was probably over-estimated, although in some areas and industries it was a real problem. Early in 1947, on inquiry from the Board, the regional offices reported on their experience in the previous year. Only eight reported cases filed in which unions had attempted by strikes or boycotts or threats to coerce employers into recognizing them, contrary to the results of a Board certification of another union; another four knew of other cases in the area of such coercion by unions not representing a majority. About half of the cases reported involved Teamsters, the rest other AFL or independent unions. In some the result was still inconclusive; in some the aggressor union had won out, by agreement of all parties; in some where the employer and employees stood firm for their rights under the law, the aggressor had withdrawn. It was clear that the Board was not able in all cases to protect the right of employees to have union representation *only* when the majority had made that choice.

Problems involved in interunion rivalry, when powerful unions were prepared to force their will regardless of the orderly processes provided under the Act, and especially when employers, whether by free choice or under coercion, "went along" with such unions, can perhaps be made most clear by describing in some detail an extreme example. The long conflict in the California cannery industry will illustrate these problems.

The 1945–48 struggle over representation of the fruit and vegetable cannery workers of northern and central California had as background conflicts over jurisdiction within the AFL and between AFL and CIO going back to the middle thirties. This highly seasonal industry, scattered up and down the agricultural valleys and in the Bay cities, employed at the summer peak over 50,000 workers—a polyglot group including Mexicans, colored, "Oakies and Arkies," students—in more than sixty canneries. AFL contracts had been in effect since

137. U.S. Department of Labor, Division of Labor Standards, *The President's National Labor-Management Conference, November 5–30, 1945,* Bulletin No. 77, pp. 63–64, 69.

1937, when the State Federation of Labor made an industry-wide master-contract with the California Processors and Growers, covering a group of federal labor unions of cannery workers. The AFL had given the State Federation control over the local unions, many of which had been organized earlier with left-wing support. The powerful Teamsters union supported the AFL, while the Longshoremen and Warehousemen supported the CIO cannery workers. The methods of the AFL in extending control and excluding the CIO were criticized even within AFL groups. According to one careful study of this period, also, "cannery employers, as represented by the California Processors and Growers and other organizations, had indicated a decided preference for dealing with the conservative union bloc."[138] Charges filed by the CIO against the employers and the association, or the CP&G, that they illegally assisted the AFL unions, were settled in 1940 with a consent decree ordering the companies not to interfere in any way with the organization of their employees but specifically permitting the AFL contract to continue. A State Council of Cannery Unions had been formed from the federal locals late in 1937, and this group continued to negotiate with the CP&G contracts which were ratified by the various local unions and covered most of the industry.

In 1945 serious unrest[139] began when the cannery locals, long eager to form an international union within the AFL, were assigned by the AFL Executive Council to the Teamsters. Opposition on the ground that they were "cannery workers, not truck drivers" led a group of important locals to refuse to accept this decision. Some of them even

138. U.S. Bureau of Labor Statistics, *Labor Unionism in American Agriculture,* Bulletin No. 836, p. 154. This study by Stuart Jamieson, especially ch. 11, pp. 149–55, 174, 186–92, gives an excellent, well-documented history of this period.

139. The major sources used for the following account are: (1) Board decisions, Bercut-Richards Packing Co. *et al.,* 64 NLRB 133 (1945), 65 NLRB 1052, 68 NLRB 605, 70 NLRB 84 (1946); Flothill Products, 70 NLRB 119 (1946); G. W. Hume Co., and California Processors and Growers, 71 NLRB 533 (1946); Ensher, Alexander and Barsoom, 74 NLRB 1443 (August 21, 1947).

(2) Documents in connection with the contempt petition filed by the Board in 1946 against *CP&G; Board petition* for rule to show cause; *Return* of CP&G; *Board motion* to strike response and answer; *Brief* for Respondents (CP&G); *Brief* for Intervenors (AFL).

(3) Mathew O. Tobriner, "Labor's Suicide at Cannery Row," *Labor and Nation,* 2 (November–December, 1946), 41–42, 64; Donald Henderson, "Not Suicide, but Attempt at Resurrection," *ibid.,* 3 (March–April, 1947), 2, 47; Daniel V. Flanagan, "Out California Way," *American Federationist,* 54 (March, 1947), 24–26, 29.

(4) Interviews with representatives of employers, AFL, CIO, and of the Board, in Washington and California.

appealed to the AFL Seafarers Union for charters, and, when the AFL stopped that, they tried to set up independent unions. Some of the leaders of the California State Council of Cannery Unions were active in this movement. Petitions for representation elections were filed with the Board in the summer of 1945 by independent unions and by the Food, Tobacco, Agricultural and Allied Workers Union, CIO. The Teamsters meantime had been recognized by the employers as the legal successor to the federal locals and to the master-contract.

The Board then had to decide whether it should and could hold elections in this highly seasonal industry in which the 1945 season was already well under way. Hearings were held in July on some of the local petitions, and then, after an unexplained delay in the Washington office, the petitions were consolidated for further hearings in August and September. The AFL and the CP&G held that their contract of 1941 running to March, 1946, was a bar to an election. In addition, the AFL protested that it was too late in the season for an election to be representative. The fruit season during which around 50,000 were employed was over, the tomato season used only about 20,000, and during the off season from November to March there would be only a minimum of 4,000 to 5,000 employees. But stoppages had occurred in a number of plants, and there was anxiety to avoid interruptions of production for the coming season. A letter from the Department of Agriculture to the Board suggested the desirability of holding the election in the interest of uninterrupted food production.

Finally, on October 5, the Board ordered a prompt election,[140] sending its order to the West by wire. It held that the contract was not a bar, as it was to expire in March, and that the election would determine the representative for the following period. The CIO's showing of over 10,000 members in the CP&G plants was considered sufficient to raise a question of representation. Moreover, the tomato season had a larger proportion of full-time and regular employees and fewer casual and part-time workers than the peak of the season and so was considered a reasonable time for an election. If no election were held then, resolution of the issues would be delayed until the following summer. An association-wide unit was found appropriate, based on the history of collective bargaining, with the independent companies as separate units. The CIO was permitted on the ballot in all units where it had any showing of interest. The difficulties were recognized of holding such an election in a widely scattered

140. 64 NLRB 133 (October 12, 1945). The telegraphic order was issued on October 5.

seasonal industry, closely related to agriculture, where the number of employees fluctuated from day to day, and some employees moved from plant to plant, especially when the time for preparation for the election was short. But the Board set up certain standards, permitting those who had worked twenty-five days in the season to vote.

The elections were held during the week of October 11, 1945. Although there had not been time for all the usual procedures, eligibility lists of twenty-five-day employees were available and were used in most of the plants; in a few, people were allowed to vote on other evidence or on affidavits. Observers for all parties were present and challenged any doubtful cases, Board staff challenging even more than did the others. The Regional Director reported that in the association unit the AFL won 4,701 votes, the CIO 6,067, there were 200 votes for an independent union or none, and 1,291 ballots were challenged. The CIO needed 63 more votes for a majority. In the independent units, the CIO won seven and the AFL five, while two were inconclusive.

Then came a long period of extreme pressure upon the Board to set the elections aside. The Teamsters, backed by the powerful Pacific Coast Teamster leader, Dave Beck, and the AFL, protested both that the election should not have been held at all and that irregularities made the result unrepresentative. The Regional Director investigated the objections, reported in detail the methods used, and concluded that the vote, for instance of 12,000 in the CP&G unit out of 18,000 employed, at a date that the Board had considered representative, did represent the free choice of the employees. He recommended that the challenged votes be considered and counted. The CP&G appealed to the Secretary of Labor for help in its "dilemma," since CIO unions were trying to expand their membership while AFL unions were insisting on exclusive recognition and demanding discharge of employees who transferred to the CIO.[141] The California delegation in Congress entered the controversy, saying that strikes were already threatening production and that the food crop for the next season was at stake, as the AFL threatened state-wide picketing should the CIO be certified.[142] The Teamsters on February 1, 1946, notified the CP&G that they stood on their award of jurisdiction from the AFL, and plainly implied a boycott of any processor who should recognize the CIO.[143] A congressional subcommittee questioned the Chairman on the matter.[144]

141. CP&G Return, *op. cit.*, Exhibit G.
142. *Ibid.*, Exhibit H.
143. *Ibid.*, Exhibit I.
144. Henderson, *op. cit.*, p. 47.

The Board finally by majority decision signed by Chairman Herzog and Mr. Reilly on February 15, 1946, four months after the elections, set them all aside,[145] even those in the independent plants, many of which had been won by very large majorities by AFL or CIO. The Board held that while some of the objections were highly technical, consistent with the AFL's "unremitting attempts to block or discredit" the elections, under all the circumstances the elections had not been conducted with such procedural safeguards as to make sure that the results were truly representative of the desires of the employees; moreover, it was of vital significance that the integrity of the Board's procedures be maintained at all cost. Mr. Houston, dissenting, thought that, while irregularities must have occurred in the extreme difficulty of an election under these circumstances, there was no reason to think that they affected the chances of either participant. He would have overruled the objections in the interest of prompt settlement of the dispute for the coming season. The majority of the Board warned that pending a determination of the issue of representation by a new election during the next season the companies were not entitled to give preferential treatment to either union or give effect to the "closed-shop provisions" of the existing contract after its expiration on March 1, 1946.

If the Board expected peace as a result of its decision, it was mistaken. The CP&G immediately protested that they were in an impossible position, with the CIO demanding negotiations and the Teamsters demanding exclusive recognition. The companies protested that it was unrealistic to think they could operate without continuing regular relations with the AFL and stated that the AFL in November had given them evidence of a majority in each of their plants. Attempts were made through various groups, including the Conciliation Service, to secure agreement for a truce, but none was forthcoming. The Teamsters threatened and in March applied a blockade, when the plants ceased giving them exclusive recognition during the beginning of the new season. The CIO claimed that the boycott was "phony," that little production was affected, and that the Teamsters permitted spinach to be brought to certain plants and processed, although other plants refused to receive loads.[146] Be that as it may,

145. 65 NLRB 1052 (1946).
146. Senate Committee on Labor and Public Welfare, *Hearings, 1947*, Pt. 3, pp. 1564–65; news reports in *San Jose Mercury-Herald,* March 2, 1946, March 23, 1946. For an interesting analogy cf. a report of a 1937 strike in which the California Processors and Growers were said to have inflamed the growers against the union "by a skillful and misleading campaign of publicity. There was an entirely

on March 31 the CP&G resumed recognition of the Teamsters, claiming that the spinach crop was in jeopardy. Their position was that the old contract had not expired on March 1 but was a continuing one. The AFL insisted on treating the contract as requiring union membership, although the actual terms of the old contract provided only preferential hiring. "Clearance" by the Teamsters was required of all employees, and many CIO adherents were refused employment. The Board meantime had instructed the regional office to issue complaints on any charges that companies had granted exclusive recognition to the Teamsters in advance of certification. Such charges were shortly filed. It was obvious that there was open defiance of the Board.

More negotiations ensued, of which there are no public records. It was essential that the crops not be interfered with, but if possible that a fair election be permitted to determine the choice of the employees. Was such an election possible? Emotions ran high; the CIO picketed some plants; the AFL insisted that it was entitled to performance of its contract in spite of the Board's policy against preferential treatment of one union during an election campaign. The Board finally decided to charge the CP&G with contempt of court for violation of the old 1940 decree against interference with the rights of employees under the Act. On May 23, 1946, it filed a petition with the Ninth Circuit Court, claiming that the action of the employers threatened to make a free election impossible. The employers and the AFL as intervenor alleged primarily that the AFL was the established bargaining agent and that its status continued until a new determination of representation was made. The court dismissed the Board's petition without opinion on July 15. Then the Board had to decide whether to proceed with charges of unfair labor practices against the companies. It did so only in the case of some individual companies, not against the CP&G, for reasons not stated. Meanwhile, on June 13, 1946, it had ordered new elections, in spite of the known hindrances to a fair and free election.[147]

These second elections were to be held during a representative week in the height of the season; eligibility to vote was limited, with some qualifications, to those who worked in that week. A supple-

false emphasis on the losses faced by the growers although other processing facilities were available." *La Follette Committee Reports, Employers' Associations and Collective Bargaining in California*, Report No. 398, Pt. 1, 78th Cong., 1st Sess., 1943, p. 756.

147. 68 NLRB 605 (1946).

mental direction, on August 16,[148] said that since the CIO had not waived the charges of unfair labor practices as a basis for objection to the election, the Board itself would not permit the subject matter of the charges to constitute a valid basis for setting aside the election, should there be objections. The CIO, nevertheless, went on with the election. On August 19 the Board issued decisions against two of the independent companies,[149] in which it found them guilty of unfair labor practices through their exclusive recognition of the Teamsters while the representation case was pending. There was considerable evidence also of discrimination under the contracts, though no decision on a discrimination case was issued until later.[150]

The elections on August 29–30, 1946, resulted in the association unit in a vote of 16,262—less than a majority—for the AFL and 14,896 for the CIO, with 674 for neither, and 2,056 ballots challenged. In the independent units some went CIO, some AFL. The total vote was nearly 40,000. The CIO at once challenged the results, claiming that interference and preferential treatment by the employers, and the "shaping of the electorate" by discrimination, had made free choice impossible. The Board certified the CIO in plants where it had won and began an investigation of the rest, along with the charges of discrimination and other unfair labor practices. Since the issues were extensive and the number of cases of alleged discrimination very large, the investigation was a long process. The Board proceeded on a number of cases against independent companies, but not against the Association, and in no case before the end of 1947 was there enforcement by court of a Board order against any of these companies. On July 31, 1947, the Regional Director recommended that the Board hold a hearing on the objections; and on the same day a complaint was at last issued against the CP&G group, charging coercion and discrimination through entering into an illegal contract with the Teamsters. Most of the companies had continued through 1946 and again through the 1947 season to deal with the Teamsters as exclusive representative. Finally, on January 20, 1948, some seventeen months after the elections, the Board set aside those which had been challenged, saying that in view of the objections and challenges they

148. 70 NLRB 84 (1946).
149. Flothill Products, 70 NLRB 119 (1946); Lincoln Packing Co., 70 NLRB 135 (1946). In the former the election had been inconclusive; in the latter the ballots had been impounded pending determination of the question whether this company belonged in the CP&G unit.
150. Cf. G. W. Hume Co., 71 NLRB 533 (October 31, 1946); Califruit Canning Co., 73 NLRB 290 (April 10, 1947).

were inconclusive but that, since the CIO had not complied with the filing requirements of the new Act, the Board was precluded from further investigation of the petition. After three years of upset the Teamsters remained in control, except in a few plants where the CIO had won elections and had contracts; but AFL contracts in CP&G and other units were still under challenge before the Board and in some cases in the courts.[151] And there was still no conclusive evidence as to what union was the real choice of the majority of the employees.

This long-drawn-out case must be considered one of the Board's worst failures. It seriously hurt the Board's prestige on the Pacific Coast. For more than two years there was defiance of the Board by a powerful union and a group of employers who either by preference or by coercion went along with that union. The Board's own delays and lack of decisive action were to a large extent responsible and resulted in failure to bring about a solution within the terms of the Act of a difficult jurisdictional dispute. But several major factors in the complex story need to be considered.

First, the Board had not entirely solved the difficult technical problem of how to conduct an election in such a seasonal industry with adequate safeguards and proper timing, so that the results would be beyond question. Secondly, it had not solved the question of relation-

151. For the Board orders finding the contracts unlawful and ordering certain companies to withhold recognition of the Teamsters, see nn. 149 and 150. In one case, on the contrary, on August 21, 1947, the majority of the Board dismissed a complaint, on the ground that, while a representation question was still pending, technically, when the contract was entered into, actually the AFL was the only union then claiming to represent the employees. Mr. Houston dissented against the dismissal of the complaint, "although the Employer's conduct in executing his closed-shop contract with the AFL . . . was in direct defiance of a Board order not to do so issued only 12 days before. If there is anything more calculated to bring into ridicule the processes of this Board than this abdication in the face of such contumacy, I cannot conceive of it." Ensher, Alexander and Barsoom, 74 NLRB 1443, 1445.

On September 2, 1949, the Board announced a negotiated settlement of the case against the CP&G and certain other companies, after extensive hearings between August, 1948, and May, 1949. The companies and the Teamsters agreed to entry of a Board order and court decree providing for back pay up to $205,000 and reinstatement of 1,326 employees, and for the ending of any illegal interference with rights of employees. The Teamsters agreed to revoke fines against employees who suffered discrimination, and that there should be no black list. In addition a union-shop election, on petition of the Teamsters, was to be held in September in CP&G plants, with reinstated employees entitled to vote. *NLRB Press Release,* September 2, 1949. It is significant also that the CIO union, the Food and Tobacco Workers, had finally in August, 1949, filed non-Communist affidavits in order to be able to use the NLRB's processes.

ships between employers and a union which had long been the bargaining agent, when a question of representation was left unsettled for months or years. The Midwest Piping[152] doctrine was reasonable for short periods but was not workable for a very long interim. It was unrealistic for the Board to think that its dicta against exclusive recognition of either union in setting aside the first election by itself would solve the problem. Prompt resolution of the dispute, to clarify the rights and obligations for at least one season, would have been the only real solution. Mr. Houston's argument against setting aside the first elections was sound.[153]

A third factor was the terrific pressure upon the Board at various points in this long history—from Congress, the AFL, employers, other government offices. Board members tended by experience to develop considerable immunity to such pressures, in self-defense and recognition of their responsibility under the Act; but in the fall of 1945 a new Chairman was subjected to one of the worst barrages of pressure in the history of the Board. The general impression that the Board "yielded to pressure" has considerable support in the record. And any signs of weakness made a solution impossible to obtain. Fourth, however, the inadequacy of staff and appropriations, especially in the first crucial months of the fall of 1945, when the Board was swamped with strike-vote elections under the War Labor Disputes Act,[154] was an obstacle to the needed prompt investigation and decision which must not be overlooked.

Finally, the Board needed more power to act effectively against a union or employers who interfered with the Board's orderly processes and whose action, or threatened action, interfered with other rights under the Act. Power to find a union guilty of unfair labor practices and power to obtain temporary injunctions against both unions and employers whose actions threatened to interfere with rights under the Act would have aided the Board in its efforts to protect these rights in this case. It must be said, however, that the Board through indecision and delay failed to make the most effective use of the powers which it did have.

152. Discussed *supra*, ch. 5, pp. 165–66.
153. Bercut-Richards Packing Co., 65 NLRB 1052 (1946).
154. Cf. *supra*, ch. 2, p. 61. It was not sufficient justification, however, for a delay of four months before the decision to set aside the first election, nearly two months to the petition for contempt action and five months to the first finding of unfair labor practices in connection with the contracts of March, 1946, eleven months from the second election to the complaint against the CP&G, and seventeen months from that election to the dismissal of the representation petition.

Freedom of Speech, Freedom To Strike

This experience strengthens conclusions as to the problem of jurisdictional disputes where different unions claim to represent a group of workers. The process of elections under the Act was a satisfactory method to solve such disputes. But it needed speed, with prompt and vigorous action against any who would violate the integrity of the process or interfere with the right of employees to uncoerced free choice of representation. Added power for the Board to make cease-and-desist orders against unions, supplemented by power to get injunctions against unions or employers in rare cases, seemed to be called for, in order to demonstrate that no union however powerful was beyond the law. Specifically, strikes or boycotts against a union that had been certified as bargaining representative, or that held a valid, effective contract, or other strikes or boycotts to compel violation of this Act, needed to be made unfair labor practices, with the Board given power to obtain temporary injunctions against such action. Such powers would not often need to be used. But such additional powers would have aided the Board in its efforts to protect freedom of choice and of collective bargaining through chosen representatives in accordance with the purposes of the Act.

CHAPTER 7

A TWELVE-YEAR BALANCE SHEET

FOR twelve years the Wagner Act remained unchanged on the
statute-books. Although it was subjected to sharp attack on
numerous occasions,[1] it was not until after the war that its
critics were able to muster sufficient support to bring about the drastic amendments that they had long sought. But the charged atmosphere of a period of reconversion strife and postwar struggles over
economic and political power[2] was not conducive to an objective
appraisal of the experience under the Act. The appraisal by history
may differ substantially from that made by the Eightieth Congress.

The policy of the Wagner Act was in many respects revolutionary,
with its purpose to use federal power to prevent long-established
practices of interference with efforts of workers to organize and to
encourage instead the practice of collective bargaining. Was its faith
in the democratic process for industry justified? The Act attempted
no detailed regulation of employment relationships, rather choosing
to leave these matters to be worked out freely by collective bargaining, in conformity with broad basic standards and protections of
workers' rights laid down in the Act. It relied upon protection of the
right to organize and bargain collectively, and an expected greater
equality of bargaining power, to promote the free flow of commerce
by furthering collective bargaining and the "friendly adjustment of
industrial disputes." It did not go further, however, into the field of
collective bargaining itself. It had no provisions for conciliation or
mediation for the prevention of strikes when collective bargaining
ended in disagreement, a point often forgotten by critics who blamed
the Act or the Board when increased union organization led to increased strikes.

Appraisal of twelve years' experience under the Wagner Act with
this somewhat limited scope must consider how the Act was administered and how it directly affected American industrial life, whether

1. The efforts to amend the Act are analyzed *infra*, chs. 9, 10.
2. *Infra*, ch. 8.

it furthered sound and democratic ways in industry, whether perhaps it needed to be supplemented to achieve its basic purpose. Final appraisal, too, needs to go beyond the Act itself, to consider the effects of expanded unionism and collective bargaining upon the whole economy. But this broader problem is beyond the scope of the present study.

Answers to even the more limited questions considered here are not simple. They call for consideration of all aspects of a complex history, a need too seldom recognized in the discussion of the Act, in Congress or elsewhere. They must recognize, too, that this was a revolutionary Act, operating during years of rapid change[3] resulting both from the Act itself and from the shifts from depression to defense and war and to postwar conditions. It always operated in a hostile atmosphere promoted by those who never fully accepted the premises of the Act or co-operated in bringing about compliance with its demands. The divided labor movement enormously increased the difficulties. Altogether there had been by 1947 no complete test of the assumptions of Congress in adopting the Wagner Act in 1935 or of the long-run possibilities of that Act.

THE BOARD

Change and development were characteristic of the administration of the Act, as of the industrial scene of which it was a part. No discussion of the history under the Act, therefore, can validly ignore the changes. This was true of the National Labor Relations Board itself. Despite much continuity as the institution developed and policies became established, it is still perhaps not an undue simplification to speak of three different Boards, under the three Chairmen. As the membership of the Board changed and different men came to exert large influence, changes in emphasis appeared only gradually. But the three Boards differed enough to justify an attempt to characterize them, with their own strengths and weaknesses.

First was the Madden Board, whose job required pioneering, experiment, militance in getting the new law accepted. It did in many ways a brilliant job, especially in establishing the legal basis in court decisions supporting the Act and its administration, so that the policies of the Act could be made effective. Its weakness was in administration. While this should not be overemphasized, the first Board clearly did not solve the problems of personnel selection and training and effective control from Washington, with decentralization

3. Cf. *supra*, ch. 2, pp. 33–35.

where feasible, that were needed for the most efficient, practical, and uniformly fair administration of the Act.

Next came the Millis Board, from 1940 to 1945. It was a time for consolidation, improvements in administration, emphasis on workable, realistic industrial relations under the Act, perhaps increased attention to criticism where found justified. Under the Millis-Leiserson team administration was greatly improved, both in the regional offices and in Washington, with increased delegation of powers and decentralization. Policies were modified at some points on the basis of experience, in the interest of sound industrial relations. Unions considered the Board less militant in protection of labor's rights; some employers at least considered that the Act was being administered more fairly. Chairman Millis' influence declined for a time, temporarily, when Mr. Houston early in his term supported Mr. Reilly on a number of issues in dispute, but later a Millis-Houston majority was again established.

Finally under Mr. Herzog's chairmanship Mr. Reilly's point of view came to have more influence. Mr. Houston was sometimes in dissent against Reilly-Herzog and later Herzog-Reynolds decisions on crucial matters on which there were differences of opinion. These were years of increasing attack upon the Act and a climate of opinion apparently more critical of union actions. The trend in the Board in these years, perhaps necessarily, was toward conciliating the opposition, political-mindedness, conservatism in enforcing the Act, renewed legalism in interpretation of the Act, waiting for the courts to speak rather than seeking to lead the courts as an expert agency as the Board had done earlier by its decisions. Administratively the trend toward decentralization and separation of functions continued until the Board itself approached the position of a detached court. No longer the strong Board of earlier years, it was bitterly criticized by many unions, even more than before, and won some approval from employers for "fairer decisions." But it could not stop the attack upon the Act.

THE CRITICISMS

Most of the commonly made criticisms of the Board and the Act have appeared in the discussion of the work of the Board in earlier pages. Without repeating the evidence it will be well to take them in order and see what conclusions follow from an attempt to "look at the record." The major criticisms[4] fall into four groups, two of them

4. The criticism that the Board increased strikes by taking the risk out of striking (cf. *supra,* ch. 6, pp. 189–203) needs only brief comment here. The Act

236

concerning primarily the Board and its administration, the other two the Act itself. The Board was charged with bias and maladministration, though this in part reflected objection to the Act; the Board also was charged by others with weakness and ineffectiveness in administering the Act; the Act was sharply criticized for inequality in its treatment of employers; and the Act and its administration were held to violate the rights of individuals and minorities. These serious charges, frequently made in the press, the propaganda, and in congressional hearings, debates, and reports, call for careful consideration.

BIAS AND MALADMINISTRATION

Probably the most frequent complaint against the Board was that it was biased.[5] These charges came from all sides—employers, AFL, CIO, and independent unions—and accordingly to a considerable degree they neutralized each other. For the most part they reflected the cries of groups who were hurt by the basic policies of the Act, though with rare exceptions these were applied objectively and in forms that reasonable men, in the exercise of their discretion, could think reasonable. The distribution of power was affected by the Act and developments under it, and reactions of insecurity, fear, and anger were inevitable. The antiunion employer, the old union with a collusive contract or a dissatisfied membership, the craft or industrial union whose unit contention did not receive support, the independent union which was still tainted with the company domination of its predecessor—all were prone to claim that the Board was biased, however much it might be applying its basic policies—and the policies of the Act—consistently. These charges were in essence criticisms of the Act itself, although put in the form of complaints against a "biased Board." In fact, most if not all of the members of the Board and the staff through the years quite properly believed in the purposes of the Act which they were employed to administer, as the policeman is "against crime" and the minister "against sin." This could not properly be called bias, however. On the whole the policies were applied objectively. Only rarely does the evidence suggest that action or lack of action was influenced by concern over special interests or pressures, from AFL,

---

meant to protect the right to strike as well as the right to organize, and preventing strikes was within its province only so far as strikes arose over the recognition issue and could be prevented by holding elections and by stopping employers' interferences with the right of organization.

5. Cf. *supra*, ch. 2, pp. 67–70; ch. 5, pp. 143–44.

CIO, employers, or Congress, other than interest in carrying out the policies of the Act.

Charges against the administrative organization, claiming that fair administration was not given because the Board was "prosecutor, judge, and jury,"[6] are not supported by the evidence no matter how frequently they were repeated. They ignored the real nature of the administrative process established by Congress for this Board and others—emphasis on informal handling of the great bulk of the work and on unified administration and centralized control to avoid waste motion, at the same time that there was administrative separation between those who investigated and prosecuted and those who decided cases. There were real problems both on these matters and on the need for thoroughly objective administration, but these problems were increasingly solved during the years.

The earlier weaknesses in administration need not be repeated here.[7] With a staff necessarily inexperienced in the administration of such a law and with varied backgrounds, and with the Board members preoccupied with the necessity of gaining court acceptance of the basic principles of the Act, administration in the regional offices was very uneven. It ranged from efficient and objective though necessarily vigorous law enforcement at best, through efforts at mediation and conciliation in some offices, to some "bull-dozing" of employers in others. But there was more evidence of annoyance resulting from the failure of young and inexperienced staff members to maintain the required detachment of manner, and the dislike of the violator of the Act at having his violations investigated, than of bias in administration. It was of course unfortunate when enthusiasm for the job made some staff members appear "anti-employer" or "pro-CIO." Just cause for criticism was naturally less often present later than in the earlier years when methods of administration were being developed. Similarly, some of the early decisions might better have been more judicial in tone. The Board from the start gave very thorough consideration to every formal decision, but, as the volume of work increased, possibilities of abuse through inadequate control by the Board of the post-hearing review and decisional processes became evident.

All these problems were for the most part solved through the years, especially after 1940.[8] Improved selection and training of personnel and standardization of methods through the work of the Field Division greatly strengthened the work in the regional offices. For the

6. *Supra*, ch. 2, pp. 66–67, 70–72.
7. *Ibid.*, pp. 35–50.   8. *Ibid.*, esp. pp. 53–60.

formal cases, increased importance and independence of Trial Examiners and improved control over the review process gave greater assurance to the Board that, when cases came to them for decision, the necessary full and accurate information was at hand. Unified policy was essential and required at the start a large degree of central control of operations. Later it was possible to delegate more authority and to separate more completely the functions of handling informal cases, and the preliminary investigation and hearing of formal cases, from the review of records and final decision by the Board. There was still at the end some unevenness in the efficiency of the regional offices. But over all, despite tremendous turnover due to the war, the Board had developed a staff of which it was entitled to be proud and which set a high standard of government service. The Board had largely solved the problems of establishing and maintaining standards of efficient and objective administration, with adequate controls from Washington along with a large degree of decentralization, delegation of authority, and separation of functions. It had profited from its own study of its experience and from the criticisms in Congress and those of the Attorney-General's Committee. It was highly significant that when the Administrative Procedure Act was passed the Board was already meeting most of its requirements.

One indication of successful administration was that informal administrative processes in the field were able to handle the great majority of the Board's cases. This meant the screening-out at an early stage of many poor cases and adjustment by consent of many others, including those with obvious violations. It resulted in great saving of time and money to employers, unions, and the government, as well as the advantage of settlement near home. For the formal cases the major objective test was the record of the Board in the courts, and here also there was outstanding success.[9] The courts upheld the Act and the procedures under it as meeting the test of due process, and only in a very small minority of cases was the Board held to have failed in this respect. Court decisions made clear, also, that findings of the Board had to be accepted by the courts only if based on substantial evidence. Yet the record of the Board in having its orders enforced by the courts was a remarkable one for an agency administering a new and highly controversial law.

These facts, and the detailed study of administration and of cases in preceding chapters, give little support to the charges of widespread bias and injustice in the administration of the Act. It does not seem

9. *Ibid.*, pp. 70–73; ch. 3, Table 2.

likely that much if any actual injustice can have been done to employers even in the first years. If there were such injustices, history must weigh them against the fact that open and extensive violations of the Act continued. The Board had largely solved the problems of administration, in spite of the difficulties inherent in its job. Experience indicated no sound case for special administrative experiment with the NLRB, unless unified, efficient administration by an expert Board was no longer wanted in this controversial field.

The major policies developed by the Board in its decisions also stood remarkably well the test of court review. No substantial upsets occurred on such basic matters as the tests of company domination, disestablishment of company-dominated unions, setting-aside of collusive contracts, tests of refusal to bargain, tests of discrimination, and many others. The Supreme Court in a few cases limited the Board: setting limits to reinstatement orders as to strikers after violence or violation of contracts; holding that a contract could not be set aside when the contracting union had not been a party to the case and clearly on notice that its contract was under attack; defining further the extent to which employers' freedom of speech was a protection from charges of unfair labor practices; limiting blanket orders to refrain from unfair labor practices when only limited violations had been found; and denying that the Board could require an employer to reimburse government agencies for work-relief funds paid to employees who had been discriminatorily discharged. But these were relatively minor as against the broad support given the Board on basic policies.

Similarly, the test of experience showed that on the whole the Board developed policies that were sound and workable from the industrial relations standpoint, although it started its task in an uncharted field filled with problems of great complexity and difficulty. The division in the labor movement particularly made it an almost impossible task to administer the Act, since problems created by this split had not been foreseen by Congress. A number of policies were very sharply criticized by different groups. But it seems probable that the verdict of history will be in favor of the Board, that it met the challenge with a high degree of statesmanship. Some of the policies were changed as time went on and experience showed need. Probably mistakes were made. Undoubtedly occasional mistakes were made on particular cases, some of which were rectified by the courts. Perhaps the Board was unduly slow to recognize that a history of independent action might change a union which started as successor to a company-

240

dominated union into a bona fide independent. Sometimes it was unduly cautious in holding contracts to bar a new election, although more realistic consideration might have found that the old union had ceased functioning. Perhaps for a time it applied the test of collective bargaining history too rigidly and thus prevented true craft groups from expressing their choice as to representation; and later it let separatist groups pull out from well-functioning units without defining strictly enough the conditions under which such separations should be permitted. Possibly it could have made more clear the extent of freedom of employers to speak and the conditions which limited the use of that freedom to interfere with rights under the Act.

The major criticisms of policy which the present review of the Board's history finds, however, concern developments of the later years which limited the protection of the rights of employees under the Act. These were the temporary removal of foremen from the protection of the Act;[10] limitations on the protection of the right to strike by the American News doctrine;[11] permitting greater freedom of speech to the employer even where a background of other unfair labor practices and the community milieu made the speech inevitably coercive in its effects;[12] and an apparent trend toward requiring the evidence of a Board certification before a refusal to bargain would be found, thus encouraging unnecessarily the use of the Board's machinery.[13]

Employers and unions sometimes complained that the Board abused its powers by excessive interference in the affairs of industry or of unions. Largely this was a denial of the purposes of the Act, which required interference at certain points if its policies were to be

10. On the highly controversial issue of foremen's unions, the Board was bitterly criticized by many employers both for its inconsistency and shifts of position and for its final holding that foremen were under the protection of the Act. Clearly that was a basic issue of policy on which decision should be made by Congress rather than by the Board. Without discussing the issue, it may be said here that the later majority of the Board seems to have been right in giving the protection of the Act to foremen, since they were "employees" under the definitions of the Act and had not been excluded by Congress from the protection provided for concerted activities. The hasty reversal of policies by a new majority of the Board in 1943 was a disservice to the Board and to the war effort, since foremen were left with only the weapon of strikes in their effort to obtain bargaining rights at a time when many felt the need for them. Cf. also *infra*, n. 17.

11. *Supra*, ch. 6, pp. 196–200.

12. *Ibid.*, pp. 174–89.

13. There was also a widespread impression in the later years that the Board was unduly reluctant to make findings of discrimination. This is an issue as to the facts in each case and very difficult to check sufficiently for any sure generalization.

effective. Company practices which interfered with the rights of employees, or union habits which ran counter to the basic premise of democratic free choice of bargaining representatives, could not be left undisturbed when they came before the Board. Nothing in the experience under the Act leads us to doubt the wisdom of these requirements. On the whole, the Board acted with reasonable self-restraint in applying these policies. In so far as it was successful in obtaining informal adjustment of complaint and representation cases, it avoided unnecessarily detailed regulation of industrial affairs. Its refusal to intervene when matters were properly subject to determination by grievance machinery was sound. Reliance on collective bargaining history as an important indication of the appropriateness of bargaining units was a similarly wise exercise of discretion.

Inevitably, however, the Board found itself pressed further into deciding details. When employers, as often happened, or unions, insisted on formal decision by the Board, sometimes for obstructionist and delaying purposes, the Board was forced to decide many details as to units and other issues. And as it developed standards on such matters, they tended to become rigid and to be applied perhaps without adequate attention to the particular situation. Exclusion or inclusion of certain fringe groups in collective bargaining units was, for instance, a source of friction in some industries. When the Board began to consider the objectives of strikes, it opened the possibility of more detailed intervention in labor relations than had been intended when the Act was passed. Such a basic matter of policy should be decided by Congress rather than by the Board, however. Unnecessary resort to the Board was encouraged by a late tendency to treat with more respect the status of a certified union than of one which had won recognition without such formalities. Whenever either unions or employers relied on the Board unnecessarily, also, they encouraged the perhaps inevitable tendency of intervention to expand beyond its original intent and to bring on regulation of matters which might more satisfactorily be determined by those directly concerned. The Board through most of its history, however, had exercised sound restraint on these matters, avoiding unnecessary intervention where collective bargaining could better work out problems within the framework of the principles of the Act. Similarly it avoided intervention in local industries where there was no sufficient reason for an extension of federal power, especially in view of the limitations of the budget. The Act itself was limited, intending only to clear the way for collective bargaining. Perhaps a case could be made for further intervention on a few carefully defined points. Criticisms of excessive interference by the Board itself find less support in the record than does the opposite charge that the Board failed effectively to enforce the law, to which we now turn.

WEAKNESS AND INEFFECTIVENESS

Labor organizations, despite their strong support of the policies of the Act and their recognition of the accomplishments of the Board, and despite their sometimes unwisely intemperate criticisms of particular policies, always made as their major complaint the claim that the Act was not adequately enforced and that labor never received the full protection of the rights guaranteed by the Act. To a considerable extent this was the fact. Delay and failure to obtain full compliance were all too common in the history of the Act's administration.

Inadequate appropriations were a major factor. The Board was always handicapped in its efforts to administer the Act fairly and effectively by the inadequacy of funds and staff. Never did it have more than $4.5 million to spend in any year. The result was serious delay in handling cases during much of the life of the Board. At some periods there were intensive efforts to setttle cases in order to clear the docket, with the result that less than full compliance was accepted. Lack of funds and staff was a reason for failure to enforce orders promptly, sometimes with drastic results upon the efforts of employees to obtain their rights under the Act. The problem of obtaining compliance with Board and court orders was never fully solved. The increase in the proportion of complaint cases withdrawn or dismissed in the later years, also,[14] must have reflected inability of the Board to handle all the cases filed, as well as certain changes in Board policy. Delays in handling representation petitions were a major criticism of the Board in the later years, as well as at some earlier periods. Delays in handling complaint cases toward the end were so great that many unions thought it useless to file them, except in the most flagrant instances. The smaller proportion of unfair labor practice cases in later years was partly a result of the feeling that more was obtained by concentrating on elections than by trying to use the Board to eliminate violations of the Act. When to the inevitable delays resulting from inadequate appropriations was added occasionally hesitation to move decisively on an issue which had become politically important, as was charged with some basis in later years, unions

14. *Supra,* ch. 3, pp. 81–83.

had strong grounds for their claim that they never received full protection of the rights guaranteed by the Act.

In an occasional case the Board hesitated or failed to apply general policy vigorously and promptly, and so was open to criticism on this ground. This was especially true in later years as the Board became more sensitive to criticism and tended to "keep its ear to the ground," notably for congressional reactions. Perhaps the Kaiser case[15] which led to the "Frey rider" would have resulted better if the Board had spent less time in consultation with the parties and other agencies and had moved more promptly with the normal procedures. Other instances of long delay, where unions believed that pressure from another union or from influential members of Congress affected the Board's action or failure to act, discredited the Board. The California canneries fiasco was a major late example.[16] In several important instances on major policy, also, the timing of the decision gave support to criticisms that the highly controversial decisions were in part politically motivated.[17] When the new membership of the Board in the last two years, and especially after November, 1946, chose to rethink and revise certain policies, numerous commentators observed that the Board was trying to "beat advocates of amendment to the draw" or, more politely, was "alert to the mood of Congress."[18]

Whatever the fact in any particular instance as to whether the Board's action was made entirely on the merits of the case or was motivated by political or other considerations, certain observations can be made. Whenever it appeared that any members of the Board

15. *Supra*, ch. 6, pp. 207–9.
16. *Ibid.*, pp. 224–32.
17. The Maryland Drydock Co., decision, 49 NLRB 733 (1943), which reversed earlier holdings that foremen were under the protection of the Act, was issued when a new member of the Board joined Mr. Reilly against the Chairman. The decision was issued in haste, on May 12, 1943, without allowing the Chairman time to prepare his dissenting opinion. Rumor had it that the majority wished to forestall action by the House Military Affairs Committee which was at the time considering a bill to exclude foremen from bargaining rights; the Board was also to appear shortly before the House Appropriations Committee to discuss the appropriation for the following year. The American News Company decision, 55 NLRB 1302 (1944), equally controversial, was issued by the same majority on April 14, 1944, just one week before the annual appearance of Board members before the Appropriations Committee, and at a time when the public was concerned over an increase in strikes. *Supra*, ch. 6, pp. 196–200.
18. *Labor Relations Reporter*, 19, Analysis 75 (March 3, 1947); *Business Week*, March 8, 1947, pp. 5–6. But cf. the Board's statement, U.S. House of Representatives, Committee on Education and Labor, *Hearings, Amendments to the National Labor Relations Act*, 80th Cong., 1st Sess., 1947, Pt. 5, pp. 3090, 3109–12, cited as House Committee on Education and Labor, *Hearings, 1947*.

were susceptible to pressure, naturally the pressures increased. The only protection was fearless decision on the merits in accord with well-thought-out general policy. If the modifications of policy in the last years were to any extent motivated by belief that critics could thus be satisfied, experience shows that appeasement, here as in other historical instances, failed to work. "Pulling of punches" and less vigorous protection of the rights of labor under the Act in the last years, whether primarily due to hopeless inadequacy of funds and staff, or to a belief that it might protect the Act from attack, failed to stem the tide.

This is not to say that reconsideration of policy was improper. The Board should and did study its experience and make revisions when it considered them necessary, and, in so doing, over the years on the whole it strengthened its body of policies. It was proper to adjust policies to the needs of changed conditions, too, as unions grew strong and collective bargaining became more stable. It was proper to meet any fair criticisms. There was a question, however, whether the personal predilections of individual Board members should lead to upsetting established and well-accepted doctrines. Certainly great self-restraint was desirable, as "the Board" came to be an institution which was in a real sense more than the three men who constituted its membership at any one time. Their leadership and ultimate responsibility had to rest on the body of well-tested doctrine which had been built up in the past with the help of a skilled and experienced staff. There was a difficult problem, also, as to whether policies should shift in response to apparent changes in public opinion. The extent of the changes in the late period, when Congress was considering amendment, inevitably raised the question whether the Board was not going farther than it properly should, when its responsibility was to administer the Act as given to it, not to amend it.

The Board, like other independent agencies during this and other periods, had the problem of whether it could maintain its independence when the political climate was changing. The NLRB was the object of bitter attack from the start, and it never was sure how long its support from Congress would continue. Its relations with the congressional appropriations committees were always difficult, to say the least. It never solved the problem of getting such understanding and approval of its work that it could obtain adequate funds. The improvements in administration in the middle years did not solve the problem of relations with Congress. And if there were better personal relations later as a result of more attention to the thinking on "The Hill," this gave no protection ultimately to the Act itself. Also, while any indications of weakening the protections of the Act only increased the pressures, they discredited the Board with those for whose protection the Act had been written, and thus weakened its support at crucial times. It would seem to have been more sound to continue a fearless policy of administering the Act as written, with all the improvements in administration and in policy which came from experience, and to have appealed on that record for adequate funds and for added power where experience indicated a need. Whether the outcome would have been different will never be known. But it would have lessened some of the just criticisms by labor that the Act was never fully enforced.

INEQUALITIES UNDER THE ACT

Criticisms so far considered were directly specifically against the administration of the Act, though often they were based upon dislike of the Act itself. Others were more direct charges against the Act. Employers frequently complained that the Act was unequal as between employers and unions and that it was concerned with the rights of unions at the expense of rights of minorities and of individual employees. First, the charge of inequality. The Taft Report[19] in 1947 spoke of "the one-sided character of the Act itself, which, while affording relief to employees and labor organizations for certain undesirable practices on the part of management, denies to management any redress for equally undesirable actions on the part of labor organizations." To what extent was this charge justified? When it was made so sweepingly as in effect to protest against restraint of employers' antiunion activities, although pronunion activities by union representatives were permitted, or against lack of limitation on the right to strike, although employers' use of their economic power against organization was restricted, it was a denial of the basic purpose of the Act. Experience has made a clear case for such restrictions on employers. The Act was of course unequal in that it meant to protect labor's right to organize and restrict employers' interferences with that right which had been so widespread and which still continued at some points in 1947. As Dr. Leiserson has said:

What gives the employers the impression that the law favors labor is that it is not impartial as between individual and collective bargaining. Just as a court must be partial to property rights against those who do not believe in

19. U.S. Senate, Committee on Labor and Public Welfare, *Federal Labor Relations Act of 1947*, Report No. 105, 80th Cong., 1st Sess., April 17, 1947, p. 2, cited as *Taft Report*.

246

such rights, so the NLRB must be partial to collective bargaining as against individual bargaining where the employees want unionism and collective dealing.[20]

Critics went beyond this, however. They complained that coercion by employers was outlawed, while the Act did nothing about coercion, intimidation, and violence by unions in organizing or on the picket line. There was still a strong case for the original plan of the Wagner Act, nevertheless, that policing of employees' activity in such cases was better left to the ordinary courts and state law-enforcement authorities than to the slow administrative process of a federal agency.[21] Employees were already in jeopardy of jail and other penalties for such illegal actions; while no employer was ever so punished for violations of the Wagner Act, nor could he be unless he put himself in defiance of a court. Moreover, the Board did in fact act against misconduct by refusing to protect from effective discharge strikers who were guilty of serious violence.

Employers pointed out more convincingly, however, that the Act prohibited interference by employers with the right of free choice by employees but did not specifically and effectively prevent such interference by unions, when, by boycott, strike, or other show or threat of economic power, they attempted to coerce employers to violate the Act. Some unions were so powerful that they could and sometimes did coerce employers, especially small employers, and their employees, by these methods rather than following the democratic process of organizing people and proving their right to recognition as majority representative. This was an especially serious problem in some areas, as California, and with some unions, as the Teamsters, and at times when delay in processing cases by the Board gave incentive to use quicker methods. Instances of such coercion contrary to the rights of a certified union or the majority of the employees occurred frequently enough to cause real concern and were properly criticized.[22] The Board dealt with these problems indirectly by its orders to employers.[23] But power to issue orders against the unions themselves, backed in an occasional case by the possibility of obtaining injunctions against such action, would have been more direct and more effective than the methods under the Act as it was. Here there was a strong case for an "equalizing amendment."

20. William M. Leiserson, in Louis G. Silverberg, *The Wagner Act: After Ten Years* (Washington: Bureau of National Affairs, 1945), pp. 119–20.
21. *Supra*, ch. 6, pp. 191–93 and ff.
22. *Ibid.*, pp. 203–33.
23. *Infra*, pp. 256–57.

Employers frequently complained also that restrictions on their freedom of speech were inequitable when unions were unlimited in their freedom to say whatever they pleased. The Board however did set aside elections or refuse credence to union evidence of majority if union actions had interfered with the employees' right of free choice. But such interference with employees' rights was more often possible as a result of employers' actions.[24] Experience showed little if any evidence of unreasonable restraint of employers by Board decisions and considerable evidence of abuse of "free speech" by employers, even in the later years. A limited and reasonable free-speech amendment, nevertheless, might eliminate some misunderstanding and remove a grievance of employers, thereby promoting a healthy atmosphere where employers were in fact accepting collective bargaining and not attempting to interfere with the rights of their employees.

Another complaint was that employers were required to bargain collectively in good faith but that there was no parallel specific obligation upon the union. In fact, the possible need of such a statutory obligation would hardly have occurred to the writers of the Act, since its purpose was to protect the exercise of the right to bargain by the representatives of the employees against its denial by employers. Experience indicated that occasionally unions were remiss in their obvious duty to bargain in good faith. Often this meant an attitude in negotiations implying that the obligation to bargain rested entirely on the employer. Sometimes, rather, a union was trying to induce an employer to accept the standard contract which by prior collective bargaining had set basic conditions to stabilize and standardize competitive conditions in the area or industry. While the Board did consider union actions as among the factors pertinent in deciding cases against employers, there was something to be said for "equalizing" the law at this point, declaring the parallel duty of both parties to bargain collectively for the solution of their difficulties, since a "take-it-or-leave-it" attitude from either side was contrary to the spirit of the Act.

Was it inequitable, also, as often claimed, that the Act did not provide for a right of employers to petition for representation elections? There were sound administrative reasons at first for denying this right to employers, when before the rights under the Act were well established it might have been used to interfere with the right of employees to organize. But later the Board recognized that sometimes an employer needed the right to petition if he and his employees were to

24. *Supra*, ch. 6, pp. 174–89.

be protected from coercion by a union which preferred not to submit to the test of an election in rival union contests. Even when only one union was involved, there were similar situations, when to permit the employer to invoke the Board's election processes would protect the democratic right of free choice. Of course a representation dispute under the Act was considered, and properly so, one over whether the majority of the employees, not the employer, wanted a union. But the dangers in permitting employer petitions could be safeguarded against by the Board, given discretion. On the whole the experience pointed toward the desirability of further extension of this right to employers, to remove one of the points of criticisms and to give actual relief in an occasional case.[25]

Finally, the charge of inequality in the treatment of independent and affiliated unions by the Board lacks support in the evidence, unless interference by employers in union organization was thought to be entitled to protection. The Act itself required that the Board investigate the fact as to whether an "independent" charged with "company domination" was in reality tainted by such illegal interference; and, if so, it could not be given "equal treatment" comparable to that of the bona fide union. This was essential if "free unionism" was to be protected. The experience with elections and with dismissal of charges of company domination and refusals to "disestablish" in many cases refutes the charge of unfair treatment of bona fide independents.[26]

The sweeping charges of inequality made against the Act by some critics are clearly not supported by the evidence. Even the cases of union coercion to force violations of the Act, which most clearly needed restraint in the interest of equality, apparently occurred less frequently than was generally supposed, although they were serious in some areas and industries. Other points on which there was some validity in the claims of inequality could be and for the most part were being handled administratively and in practice were of less significance than the attention which they received would imply. But in the interest of good relations and equality of responsibility for sound, democratic, and responsible ways in industry, amendments on these points seemed to be desirable. Dangers there might be in giving possible weapons to those employers who still looked for all means to delay and obstruct the organization of employees and the processes of the Board. Yet these, given good administration, might be counterbalanced by greater acceptance of the Act as fair and equitable.

25. *Supra*, ch. 5, pp. 160–63.
26. *Supra*, ch. 4, pp. 109–10; ch. 6, p. 207.

From the Wagner Act to Taft-Hartley

INDIVIDUAL AND MINORITY RIGHTS

Frequently it was claimed that individual and minority rights suffered under the Act. Congressman Hartley, who felt that there was need for a new "bill of rights for the American workingman," drew a black picture of the years during which, he claimed, "as a result of labor laws ill-conceived and disastrously executed, the American workingman has been deprived of his dignity as an individual. . . . In short, his mind, his soul, and his very life have been subject to a tyranny more despotic than one could think possible in a free country."[27] We must consider seriously whether union rights were protected to the detriment of the rights of individuals, and whether there was a real problem of many being "unionized against their will."[28]

This attack in the name of interest in the individual worker was an attack upon the whole principle of collective bargaining upon which the Wagner Act was built. Under this principle, the majority of the employees if they wish, choose a collective representative who speaks for the whole group in determining the basic conditions of employment and in administering the collective agreement. This is the democratic process in industry. It assumes that individuals engage in group action because they find this a way to increase their real freedom.[29] It assumes that the minority accedes to the democratically arrived at decision of the majority. It assumes also that the members of the minority are protected in their efforts to influence decisions and perchance in due time to become the majority. Did it work so in practice?

In fact the Act as it was administered gave protection to employees in their right to have a union or not, whichever the majority chose, and to change their bargaining agent if they so desired. Secret, free elections, safer than using evidence of signed cards, assured that employees could express their free choice. Prohibition of exclusive or

27. U.S. House of Representatives, Committee on Education and Labor, *Labor-Management Relations Act, 1947*, Report No. 245, 80th Cong., 1st Sess., April 11, 1947, p. 4.

28. Cf. T. R. Iserman, House Committee on Education and Labor, *Hearings, 1947*, Pt. 4, pp. 2723–25, 2731–32.

29. This was officially noted as early as 1902 in the *Report of the Industrial Commission* to Congress. Speaking of the idea that the individual freedom of the worker was lost under collective agreements, the *Report* said: "The union brings him a sense of greater liberty. . . . The union is a democratic government in which he has an equal voice with every other member. By its collective strength it is able to exert some direct influence upon the conditions of employment. As a part of it, the individual workman feels that he has a voice in fixing the terms on which he works." U.S. House of Representatives, Industrial Commission, *Final Report*, Doc. No. 380, 57th Cong., 1st Sess., 1902, p. 807.

closed-shop contracts with minority unions, limitation upon discharge for dual unionism, and the willingness of the Board on petition of rival unions at proper times to hold new elections, all gave important protections to the right of employees to have what the majority decided. The employer was entitled at the end of contract periods, also, to cease recognition of a union if in fact, and without his interference, the union had ceased to represent the employees. There is no protection of unions at the expense of the rights of individuals in all this.

But what of the nonunion minority? True as it is that in the twelve years of the Wagner Act more than a million and a half workers voted against unions, more than six million voted for union representation. The records do not disclose the number voting against the unions which won elections. Nevertheless, it is the democratic system that majority rules. When many of these democratically chosen unions then entered into closed-shop or union-shop agreements, the minority were coerced into helping support the union chosen by the majority. But later evidence in the overwhelming favorable majorities in the union-shop elections conducted under the Taft-Hartley Act[30] give no support to any assumption of large dissatisfied minorities under such agreements. Supporters of unions found to be company dominated and therefore not permitted on representation ballots, also, were denied any right to vote for those unions, but this was essential unless an "unfree unionism" was to be perpetuated. Individuals who for any reason were dissatisfied with depending upon the union to take up their grievances could present them to the employer themselves and be present during their negotiation.[31] All this does not accomplish the impossible desired by Senator Taft, of "assuring complete freedom of choice to employees who do not wish to be represented collectively as well as those who do."[32] But protection of nonunion minorities further than this would undermine the system of collective bargaining. Only if individual bargaining is more to be protected than collective bargaining, and individual rights are more important than the rights of the group, is there cause for complaint in all this. Such an assumption was emphatically, and we think wisely, rejected by the Wagner Act.

And what of minority unions? They had a right to raise a new question of representation if they thought they could muster a majority, at appropriate times. The one real question was when a majority in a small unit which desired to have separate representation was not

30. *Infra,* ch. 16, p. 613.
31. *Supra,* ch. 4, n. 66.   32. *Taft Report,* p. 3.

permitted to do so. Some felt that this was a serious invasion of rights. But the right of the majority of the large group was entitled to consideration also, and there could be no absolute answer as to which right was entitled to prevail. The Board struggled with this extremely difficult problem, and it tended over the years to give increasing weight to the desires of the smaller group. Rarely is there any real basis in this experience for protest against violation of rights of minorities.[33]

The Act thus in its terms and in Board policies supported the right of majority choice but gave reasonable protection to minorities. There were, nevertheless, limits to this protection, and some problems remained unsolved. There were possibilities of abuse under closed-shop and other union-security agreements, which were beyond the power given the Board by the Wagner Act. There were still instances of collusive contracts. The "Frey rider,"[34] which made it impossible for the Board to proceed against wartime closed-shop contracts made without evidence of the choice of a majority of the employees, protected "compulsory unionism" on a large scale. When the Board in other circumstances held contracts to bar proceeding to elections, occasionally injustice may have been done and the will of a majority thwarted for an unreasonable period. The most extensive and serious violations of the "dignity" and rights of individual employees, nevertheless, must have been in the cases, of which there were unfortunately many, in which the Board did not succeed in effectively protecting employees from discrimination or other interference with their rights or from refusal of employers to recognize and bargain with the union which they, with the majority of their fellow-employees, had chosen as their representative.

THE ACCOMPLISHMENTS

Leaving the analysis of the commonly made criticisms of the Board and the Act, with their occasional elements of truth in a mass of exaggeration and misrepresentation, we come to the question of what was accomplished during the life of the Wagner Act. Were the results those intended by the Act? Were they in accord with sound public policy?

CHANGES IN EMPLOYERS' POLICIES

A comparison of the American industrial relations scene in 1947 with that in 1935 cannot attribute all the changes observed to the Wagner Act. Without it undoubtedly union organization and collective bargaining would have increased during the war as it had during

---

33. *Supra*, ch. 5, pp. 138–55.   34. *Supra*, ch. 6, pp. 207–10.

World War I. The mass-production industries were "ripe for organization" in the thirties, and unions would in all probability have attempted to expand their organization there, but at the cost of considerably more strife than actually developed in the early years of the NLRA. Yet it is inconceivable that, without the change in national labor policy which protected the basic right to organize, the changes could have been so far-reaching, have been achieved so peaceably, or have shown such signs of stability. Despite the inadequacy of the NLRB's funds and staff, and failure at some points to achieve vigorous and complete enforcement, the Act made an enormous impression on the climate of opinion and practice in industrial relations. By 1947 the openly antiunion activities which had formerly been common in major corporations as well as in less well-established concerns had largely been eliminated from common practice in industrialized areas and to some extent in others. The labor spy, "yellow-dog contracts," espionage, discrimination, violence against organizers, and bitter violence on both sides in organizing strikes were no longer usual. It could come as something of a shock to those not participants or observers of these events to find that such practices still occurred in the South and occasionally in other areas.[35] Mass discrimination cases no longer turned up frequently in the Board's cases, and discrimination when it occurred was more carefully executed and harder to prove. Meantime union membership had nearly quadrupled, and more than two-thirds of the employees in manufacturing and nearly half of all in occupations where unions were actively seeking to organize were covered by union agreements.

To a large extent collective bargaining had been accepted. Some employers accepted it as permanent; others by force of the law and the compulsion of events, but hoping that it was only temporary. Some still fought it actively. But the difference was highly significant between the bitterly fought and violent postwar strikes of 1918–19 and the peaceful though determined strikes over wage issues in 1945–46 with no apparent effort by employers to smash the unions.[36] Large groups of employers under the Wagner Act had found collective bargaining not an impossible way of handling labor relations and were

35. Cf. *supra*, ch. 4, pp. 125–27. The CIO reported in 1947 that twenty CIO organizers and local union leaders had been physically assaulted during the southern organizing campaign and that "a large portion of the textile industry engaged in wholesale violations of the Wagner Act." Congress of Industrial Organizations, *Final Proceedings of Ninth Constitutional Convention*, October, 1947, p. 77.

36. Cf. B. M. Selekman, *Labor Relations and Human Relations* (New York: McGraw-Hill Book Co., 1947), p. 193.

working out its problems. But there was need for continuing protection by law of the basic rights of labor if the clock was not to be turned back toward the old struggle for survival and recognition. Too many employers still, notably in the South and in rural areas, had not accepted collective bargaining or recognized the right to organize as appropriate and necessary and felt no compunction about violating a federal law protecting these rights.[37]

EFFECTS ON UNIONS

The representation machinery of the Board had provided a sure, democratic, and orderly means by which unions could demonstrate whether or not they were entitled to recognition. Strikes for recognition in the industries under the Board's jurisdiction should have disappeared entirely, and many were prevented by the thousands of elections. But inadequacy of funds and staff and long delays in handling cases at many periods, as well as reluctance of some employers to grant bargaining rights even after a majority was demonstrated, gave incentives to unions to continue to use their economic strength where it offered a prospect of a more prompt success.[38] Similarly, unremedied unfair labor practices sometimes led to strikes instead of or as accompaniment to resort to the Board, when the Board's processes were too slow and uncertain to meet the urgently felt need for protection of employees' rights. More could have been accomplished had the Board received adequate support from the congressional appropriations committees so that it could have handled cases more promptly. But the holding of nearly 37,000 elections, many of them covering thousands of workers, in the twelve years, contributed substantially to peaceful and democratic ways in industry rather than settlement by force. The contribution made by the Board during the war in thus settling disputes which might otherwise have interrupted vital production can hardly be overemphasized. The marked decline in strike violence which had been so characteristic of major industrial disputes for many decades, also, indicated that, once the federal power to prevent interference by employers with the right to organize was clearly established after 1937, a major source of bitterness and violence was eliminated.

The elections themselves, also, were a democratic experience—for some of the more than seven million who voted in them over the

37. Cf. statement of a southern lawyer, *supra*, ch. 4, p. 127. For further discussion of the attitudes of employers see *infra*, ch. 8, pp. 292–95.
38. *Supra*, ch. 3, pp. 91–93.

twelve years undoubtedly the first such experience with casting a ballot in a self-determination election. These elections, in the great majority of cases peaceful and orderly processes, must have been an education in democratic ways. Campaign propaganda, extremes of electioneering sometimes from one or all sides, the psychology of conflict bitter when there was strong opposition—these were often present; yet, all in all, workers must have learned much of issues, conflicts, and ways of working together. Some of this needed to be unlearned later, after labor organizations were accepted and the more prosaic process of collective bargaining went on;[39] still a basis was laid for vital and self-governing organization which could and often did become a force for democracy in the community as well as in industry.

Union habits were influenced at many points by the orderly processes and the standards provided by the Board.[40] These influences were heavily weighted in the direction of democratic, responsible action. The majority-rule principle, the Board's elections, and the outlawing of collusive contracts with minority unions all established the *obligation* of unions to organize the employees whom they wished to represent, not just to sign contracts with employers, as had not infrequently been done in the past—and sometimes continued to be done. Responsibility of the union toward its constituents was promoted, something of which there had in some instances been marked need. Numerous local unions under the challenge of representation petitions filed by a rival were stimulated to renewed activity so that grievances were adjusted and collective bargaining was more effectively conducted, and the members became content to remain with their old union. It was arguable whether at some points the Board did not unduly restrict the freedom to shift affiliation. On the other hand, perhaps the extent of this freedom unduly encouraged raids and instability. A fairly reasonable balance was struck which provided a peaceful means of settling bitter disputes between rival unions and which promoted democratic unionism with proper relationships of control and responsibility between the union and rank and file. The influence of Board policies and practices ran strongly against the hold of racketeering unions and old, inefficient, undemocratic unions.

Union structure and the structure of collective bargaining were both influenced by the Board's decisions on the unit appropriate for collective bargaining. The industrial units needed by the newly organized mass-production unions, and multi-plant and association-

39. Cf. Selekman, *op. cit.*, *passim.*   40. *Supra*, ch. 5, pp. 170–72.

wide units needed for the broader bargaining which was sometimes feasible as organization increased, were both accepted by the Board, sometimes over the protests of old-line unions. Necessarily the Board decided case by case, since it had no mandate, or desire, to establish any one principle of organization as predominant; and it necessarily was guided realistically by the experience in the industry as well as by the desires of employees. In the extremely difficult situation created by the frequently conflicting desires of different groups, it struck what must be considered a fairly reasonable balance. Toward the end, however, its greater willingness to permit small groups to pull out of established industrial units encouraged instability and raiding and the breakup of well-established bargaining on a broad basis, to the detriment of employers and workable collective bargaining.[41] Governmental decisions on units inevitably affected the labor movement. In a time of irrational and troublesome competition between unions, probably more workable adjustments were made by the Board than could have been done by any rigid rule. The flexible administrative process was best suited to deal with the problem, if the unions were unable to resolve their conflicts themselves.

As union strength expanded under the protection given by the Act, inevitably some abuses arose. Unions differed in the ability, responsibility, and democratic habits of their leadership. Issues as to the extensive strikes of which a strong labor movement was capable in a time of great stress were outside the scope of the NLRB's authority and functions, though they raised question as to whether there was need for strengthening the government's methods of promoting peaceable settlement of such disputes. In a number of other respects, however, union actions came within the Board's province, since they affected the rights under the Act.

Regulation of the internal affairs of labor organizations was not included under the Wagner Act, since Congress was attempting to deal only with the specific problem, most urgent at that time, of the right to organize. Nevertheless, the Board in considering unfair labor practices of employers and determining disputes over representation inevitably came to a number of quite specific restraints upon union actions which ran counter to the policies of the Act. This was in addition to the broad influence on union habits and thinking which we have noted. Most of the specific regulations of union action have been indicated earlier, also. Several had to do with coercion by unions which in various ways might interfere with the right of employees

41. *Ibid.*, pp. 138–55, 172.

256

to a free choice of bargaining representative. First, coercion by unions in the signing of cards undoubtedly occurred, though how extensive it was no one knows. The Board guarded against the possibility of such coercion affecting the result, when, as in most instances in the later years, it required elections rather than accepting the evidence of signed cards as conclusive.[42] Second, elections[43] were set aside or postponed when it appeared that union coercion interfered with the free expression of the desires of employees.

Third, union coercion of employers and employees in jurisdictional disputes or other rival union conflicts was prevented in so far as the Board had power or used its power. The right of employers to file petitions for elections in rival union cases, the setting-aside of contracts resulting from coercion or collusion, and the clear policy that union coercion was no defense against charges of violation of the Act were all useful in these cases.[44] A fourth important type of case in which unions were forced to meet certain standards in accordance with the policies of the Act involved use of closed-shop contracts to interfere with the right of employees to free choice of their representative. The Board was able to give substantial protection to the right to choose or to change bargaining representatives by establishing policies which limited discharges under a union-security contract for activity in behalf of a rival union at appropriate times when a question of representation could be raised.[45] Nevertheless, the Board did not always succeed in eliminating coercion in rival union conflicts of these kinds, when a powerful and determined union defied the democratic processes provided by the Act. Partly this resulted from delays and reluctance to proceed vigorously in a controversial situation, partly from lack of power to act directly and quickly against the union itself.

Fifth, the Board exerted at least a limited influence against racial discrimination by unions. It refused to find units appropriate for collective bargaining if based on distinctions of race. The Board held that it had no authority to consider membership qualifications of unions, but it could insist upon the duty of a union to give equal representation to all in the unit for which it was statutory representative. It warned, therefore, that, on a showing that such non-discriminatory representation had been denied, it would withdraw its certification.[46]

42. *Ibid.*, pp. 133–34.   44. *Ibid.*, pp. 160–62; ch. 6, pp. 204–7, 216–20.
43. *Ibid.*, p. 164.   45. *Ibid.*, pp. 210–16.
46. *Tenth Annual Report*, pp. 17–18; *Eleventh*, p. 11.

Sixth, charges that unions had refused to bargain, although not explicitly provided for in the Act, were naturally considered by the Board in judging whether employers had refused to bargain, and cases were dismissed when the Board found that a union's ultimatum or other action in negotiations made impossible a test of the employer's willingness to bargain in good faith.[47] Finally, in a series of cases involving discrimination against strikers, the Board and the courts put certain types of violent or other unlawful conduct outside the protection of the Act.[48]

Inevitably, therefore, a law designed primarily to prevent unfair labor practices by employers and protect the right of workers to organize and bargain collectively through their own representatives resulted in some correlative regulation of union behavior. It raised the question whether it might not be preferable to have the law itself specific on some of these points, especially where union actions could seriously interfere with the rights of employees under the Act.

EFFECTS ON INDUSTRIAL RELATIONS

The great influence of the Wagner Act and the NLRB during these twelve years in making possible the extension of union membership and of collective bargaining, and promoting responsible and democratic ways, came about not through detailed regulation of labor relations but by attempting to create basic conditions under which free collective bargaining could grow as a method of industrial life. The Board was never meant to act as a substitute for or regulator of collective bargaining. Did it in fact help the parties in industry to work out their own problems, or did it result in unnecessary intervention of government in the details of labor relationships?[49] The Act and the Board functioned primarily through laying down and defining in case-by-case decisions certain broad standards of conduct, a democratic code of ethics for industrial relations—noninterference by employers with the right of workers to organize, free choice of bargaining representatives, exclusive recognition of the majority representative in an appropriate unit, bargaining in good faith. Informal cases were then handled in line with these standards, and they affected widely the standards of action in innumerable situations which never had reason to come before the Board. It was entirely normal that, once a group of employees had organized and been recognized by their employer, there might never be further relationships with the

47. *Supra*, ch. 4, pp. 116–17.
48. *Supra*, ch. 6, pp. 189–203. 49. Cf. *supra*, pp. 241–43.

Board—if there had been any—or concern with the Act. If a question of representation was raised by another union, it might be handled by the informal processes of the Board or, if certain issues could not be agreed on, by formal decision. Employers who were willing to work out problems with their employees by collective bargaining often were little affected by the Board or the Act. Many had no contact whatever. There were after all only some 100,000 cases of all sorts filed in the twelve years of the Act, and only a little more than 3,000 formal decisions in complaint cases and 11,000 in representation cases. This was the reason why the Board with relatively little money and a staff which in no year reached as high as 1,000 members, was able to exert so wide an influence. Reasonable standards were set in the Act and by the Board, and these standards received increasing acceptance, although acceptance was never complete.

No picture of a complex scene, full of life and contrasts, with here and there such conflicts that lines are not entirely clear, can be drawn in simple and sharp outlines of black and white. Nevertheless, judged by tests of democratic self-government and sound industrial relations, the Wagner Act must be said to have made a great contribution to the democratic bases of American life. During its time unionism and collective bargaining had been accepted, and attitudes toward industrial relations on this basis had changed to an extent which most employers would not have thought possible fifteen years earlier. Millions of workers and their representatives, with their employers, were living under a more democratic system of industrial relations and working on the problems of responsible and efficient relations in industry on this basis. Millions of workers were engaged in an experiment with self-government from which they often learned democratic processes and possibilities, as well as sometimes extreme difficulties and possible failure. This is not to deny that some unions, perhaps many, were undemocratic; but there can be little doubt that on balance in the period of the Wagner Act unions were a training school for democracy. Effects upon community life and political life were to be seen in all parts of the country. Nevertheless, there were still many areas, industries, and individual companies and plants, and some unions, where the principles of the Act were not yet accepted; and there was doubt whether without the protection of the Act these principles could prove to have been permanently accepted in some others. The job of establishing the federal policy was not yet completed, as cases filed in 1947 in every regional office showed.[50] To a

50. Cf. *supra,* ch. 4, pp. 124–27.

large degree, however, democratic rights had been defended and democratic ways in industry furthered. By 1947 it was time to consider whether the Act needed change or supplement in order further to meet public needs as they had become clear by that time.

WERE AMENDMENTS NEEDED?

Study of major aspects of the experience of twelve years under the Wagner Act points strongly to the conclusion that valid criticism was due not for bias, or unfair or unreasonable administration, or abuse of power, or, with some exceptions, inequality under the Act, or overriding of the rights of individuals—although the Board was human at all times and made mistakes. The most important deficiency was that the sound and democratic rights under the Act were never fully protected. Partly this resulted from lack of adequate financial support from Congress so that the job could be done. In addition, time was necessary to achieve a revolutionary change in industrial practices, and the Board could not move too fast or expect too sudden a change. The division of the labor movement added enormous difficulty to a task difficult at best. But it still must be said also that both early and later there were instances where the Board failed vigorously to push for enforcement and compliance with the Act. Particularly in the later years, faced with a growing attack upon the Act, the Board became less militant in carrying out the purposes of the Act as it had been written. Finally, there was increasing evidence that the Board needed additional power against unions themselves, when they acted in such a way as to thwart rights of employees under the Act.

Several points have been suggested at which amendments to the Wagner Act appeared desirable, in the interest of removing inequalities where that complaint was valid and of giving additional power to the Board where it was needed in order to carry out the policies of the Act. They may be summarized: First, a carefully drawn free-speech amendment which would have assured employers that they had a right to discuss any matters of common interest with their employees so long as the speech was not made coercive by a context of other unfair labor practices or by implied threats or promise of benefits contained within itself. Second, an expanded right of petition by employers in case of a dispute over representation where one or more unions were demanding recognition, the Board being free to decide as in all representation cases whether the purposes of the Act would be promoted by holding an election. Third, a positive duty laid upon the union as well as upon the employer to bargain in good faith.

Fourth, power in cases of dual union discharges to find a union as well as the employer guilty of an unfair labor practice and, in the discretion of the Board, subject to liability for back pay to "make whole" the discharged employee. Fifth, and most important, power to find a union guilty of an unfair labor practice when it attempted to induce an employer to violate the law, contrary to his obligation to recognize a certified union or other union representing a majority of the employees in an appropriate unit and to refuse exclusive recognition or union-security agreements to minority unions. In addition, the Board's power to petition a circuit court for a temporary restraining order needed to be specifically extended to this kind of situation, where a union defied the orderly processes of the Board and engaged in coercion to force violation of the rights of employees and employers under the Act.

None of these suggested amendments, if carefully drawn and well administered, would have seriously weakened any rights under the Act. They would have promoted acceptance of the Act as equitable. And they would have given added power at the one point where the Board had been seriously limited in the weapons it needed to deal with infringements upon the right freely to organize and choose representation for bargaining purposes.

No change in the statute was needed as to administrative organization.[51] The record appears conclusive, when carefully studied, that problems had been solved administratively and that the organization was sound and efficient for operation in the spirit of the administrative process. Centrally determined, unified policy; separation of functions and delegation of authority; decentralization of much of the administration, with emphasis on informal settlements; proper care for the independence of hearing officers, careful review of records, and thorough consideration by the Board in making final decisions in formal cases—all these had been achieved even before the standards adopted by Congress in the Administrative Procedure Act. It was very unlikely that any drastic change in plan could bring as effective and fair administration as had been achieved by the National Labor Relations Board over the years.

Finally, other questions could be asked as to whether there was need for additional law to deal with the problem of strikes and with

51. Possibly an increase in the membership of the Board would have been desirable. It would increase the difficulty of reaching agreement on difficult cases but would expedite the handling of the more routine cases by a panel system. It might also have the advantage of more continuity of policy, since a change of one member would have less effect than the change of one in three.

government activities to promote prompt and peaceable settlement of disputes over wages and other issues of the terms of collective agreements or with alleged abuses of power by unions in a variety of situations. Except as to certain problems which have been discussed above, these matters are outside the scope of the Wagner Act, and its particular experience throws no light on the problem. This is not to say that there was no need for further analysis and determination of sound public policy on these matters, possibly with further legislation.

PUBLIC OPINION AND THE ATTACK UPON THE ACT

The National Labor Relations Board and the Wagner Act which it administered emerge from this study with an appearance different in most respects from that pictured in congressional committee reports, much of the testimony in congressional hearings, and the accounts of many vigorous critics. Over the years as the Board improved its administration, as it met criticisms where they appeared sound, as it worked out thoroughly considered solutions for the extremely difficult problems which came before it, and toward the end as it appeared somewhat less vigorous in protecting the rights guaranteed by the Act and more eager to reassure employers that their parallel rights were not contravened, it is a paradox that the attack upon the Act did not decrease but rather rose to its climax in the legislation of 1947. Some of the factors in the movement for amendment of the Act and the history of the efforts which culminated in 1947 will be analyzed later, but here a few questions may well be posed.

Public opinion polls in so complex a field as this are of doubtful value, but some of them are at least suggestive on certain aspects of our problem.[52] First, a Gallup poll[53] in January, 1947, reported that only 19 per cent of the population had a generally correct idea of the provisions of the Wagner Act, 12 per cent gave completely wrong answers, and 69 per cent said that they simply did not know. Nevertheless, asked whether the Act should be left "as is," changed, or done away with, more than a third, 36 per cent, wanted no change. The proportion who advocated some change in the law had increased from 43 per cent in 1938 to 53 per cent in 1947; but those who wanted the Act done away with had decreased from 19 per cent in 1938 to 11 per cent in 1947. A considerable body of general support for the

52. See the valuable analyses of recent public opinion polls, under the editorship of C. Wright Mills, in *Labor and Nation*, 2 (November–December, 1946), 11–13; 3 (March–April, 1947), 25–28, 48; 3 (November–December, 1947), 8–12.

53. *Ibid.*, 3 (November–December, 1947), 8.

idea of the Wagner Act was indicated, with a decreasing minority who were completely opposed, and a small majority who felt sufficient dissatisfaction that they approved the idea of change. But the most impressive aspect was the ignorance of the law itself.

The question is raised, therefore, as to why the Board was unable to get more public understanding and confidence, if by and large it did as good a job as the record seems to show. Possibly answers could be found in part in the generally hostile press. The influence of major associations of industry which led the attack upon the Act, rather than promoting acceptance of the basic purposes of the Act and working for sound law and administration to maintain those purposes, was important. The influence of many lawyers played an important part, first in attacking the constitutionality of the Act and encouraging refusal of employers to accept the policies of the Act in its first years; and later by their advice stirring up and keeping alive many employers' inclination to fight rather than to learn to live within the Act and with the unions of their employees. Bitter attacks by labor groups, when their own practices were affected by the administration, gave very useful ammunition to those who wished to destroy the protections which the Act had given to the rights of employees. The congressional investigations, for the most part conducted under control of men avowedly hostile to the basic purposes of the Act, proved a useful sounding board for attacks based upon partial presentation of the evidence and emphasis of "horrible examples" at the expense of a rounded picture. Public irritation at major strikes and at known abuses in the operation of some unions also strengthened the vague and poorly informed support for change in the laws.

Back of all the propaganda, charges, and countercharges was the basic fact that power in industry had been shifted by the development of a powerful labor movement. The shifts of power created possibility of abuse. Strong unions, in some instances far more powerful than the small employers with whom they dealt, and sometimes disregardful of rights of individual employees and the public, by their actions created a strong case for legislation to check certain abuses of power by unions. But, in addition, groups who resented a lessening of their power were active in the effort not merely to redress real abuses but effectively to change the law so as to weaken the protection of the right to organize and bargain collectively. All these and other influences need study as background for the sweeping legislation of 1947 which came despite the fact that large groups of employers had accepted the policies of the Wagner Act and wanted only minor amendments.

Could the administration of the Act have been further strengthened or any devices used in order to obtain more public confidence? In retrospect one wishes that the first Board, with all its brilliance in building the legal basis for the work, had been equally wise in personnel administration and organization. Some of the early frictions might have been avoided by more skill in that area in the first years. One wonders too whether, after the constitutionality of the Act was established, it would have been possible by any means to invite and obtain the co-operation of law-abiding employers and the different union groups for the most satisfactory administration of the Act. The practice of holding public hearings on proposed important changes of rules or policy, which began in 1943,[54] and later of annual conferences of attorneys to discuss Board policies, were generally approved and seemed useful. Perhaps they would have been even more useful in 1938 and 1939.

The great failure of the Board was its failure to achieve public understanding of its work, even after twelve years. Had it not been so swamped with the struggle to enforce the Act against bitter opposition in all the earlier years, it might have found ways of promoting understanding and co-operation among the increasing number who had accepted the purposes of the Act. It might then earlier have accepted criticism which was well founded and made changes to meet it. There is a real question, too, whether the Board on the basis of its experience with the Act should not have proposed amendments where they appeared needed. Possibly this might have been done had it not been for the war, which for five years made it unwise to open such issues. Any such initiative on the part of the Board would of course have opened it to attack from the unions; but a courageous and reasonable proposal for moderate amendment at an earlier date might conceivably have helped avoid the more serious attack upon the Act. On the other hand, the more politically minded, cautious administration in the later years, while rewarded with occasional words of approval from employers and Congress, did not prevent the attack, nor did it, apparently, secure any larger degree of understanding and approval from the public. The history of this Board poses the unanswered question of whether it is possible for such an

54. *Supra,* ch. 2, p. 62.

agency in a controversial field to obtain an informed public understanding of its work. Even at its strongest the NLRB never succeeded in this.[55]

Twelve crucial years under the revolutionary national labor policy expressed in the Wagner Act left an imprint upon American life which would not easily be erased. Unions and employers could learn from this experience, and many of them had done so, the wisdom of so managing their affairs that government would not find it necessary to step in. Abuses by employers brought the Wagner Act. Abuses by unions under the protection of that Act brought a need for certain checks upon union activities. The wisdom of accepting responsibility and working out problems democratically, within unions and through collective bargaining, was clear to many, although others in various parts of the country still failed to accept such democratic ways in industrial life. It was clear, too, that government control once entered upon tended to grow and that the best way to maintain freedom from excessive control was to settle problems at home, since government

55. In connection with this question of public opinion and amendment of the Wagner Act, it is of interest that Dr. Millis, after his year as a member of the first National Labor Relations Board under the NIRA, and after his return to Chicago, wrote to President Roosevelt on June 21, 1935, urging him when approving the Wagner Act "to give out a public statement in order to lessen the exaggerated fears of industrialists and to improve the chances of successful operation under the measure." Parts of the letter deserve quotation here:

"The Wagner Bill as it stands is a needed next legislative measure, but not a complete labor code. In the long run it will need to be amended in the light of experience. If employers are required to recognize the duly selected representatives of their employees and to make a reasonable effort to agree with them on the terms and conditions of employment, the labor unions have moral responsibilities which have not been incorporated into law. One of these is to present proper requests in a proper manner and to give the employer sufficient time to consider and act upon them. All too frequently, newly established unions have made exorbitant demands in anything but a strategic way and all too frequently they have quickly resorted to economic pressure. Indeed, many unions have given employers little or no opportunity to engage in the collective bargaining process imposed upon them. Sooner or later it may be necessary to impose time limitations on strikes and lockouts, but that cannot be said publicly at this time. My thought is, however, that a statement calling attention to the importance of collective bargaining and the necessity for a cooperative, intelligent use of new rights by organized labor would be helpful in allaying the fears of industry and in minimizing the misuse of its rights by organized labor. Many unions, and almost as many employers, must learn to respect labor agreements entered into. There must be a cooperative attitude and respect for contracts. Possibly, experience will call for the registration of agreements or for other devices in order to temper the situation."

265

regulation at best meant distant control and slow, somewhat cumbersome processes that at times would interfere with the working-out of the most satisfactory local arrangements in industry. For both industry and labor the minimum of control which would insure reasonable basic standards of behavior without unnecessary government intervention was to be desired. But, so far as members of either group failed to act responsibly and democratically, they cast their weight on the side of an expansion of control over their affairs.

The experience of this Board, operating in a new and difficult field, was illuminating also on a number of governmental problems. It illustrated the great merit of administration by an independent agency, through the flexible administrative process, of basic regulation in such a complex field. The whole history of the Board, as it struggled with a large degree of success to solve the problems of administration and of policy, showed the need for flexibility, unified control of policy, sound understanding of the problems of the field, and a strong Board. It demonstrated also the need for constant self-appraisal by the Board on the basis of its experience and of the results of its policies. Experience points out, also, though the Board never completely solved the problem, the need to be in touch with the opinions and criticisms of those with whom it dealt, as well as of "the public" and Congress, but yet to maintain the independence upon which the full performance of its function depended. The extremely difficult demands of such a job as that of Board member called for intelligence, integrity, courage, imperviousness to special pressures, as well as knowledge of the field of industrial relations and of labor law, and common sense in dealing with people. The NLRB over the years to a large extent met these tests. It was more vigorous early than later. Its history showed shifts of emphasis, from interest in legal principles, to sound and workable industrial relations, and again toward legalism. There were differences over the years in the administrative skill shown. There were also differences over the years and among the members of the Board in strength and independence. Yet the record of the Board and its staff by and large stands high as an example of effective and devoted public service. They failed during this period to obtain official recognition of their contribution, but perhaps they had some reward in the knowledge of the sound work that had been done, although it was still incomplete when the Wagner Act came to an end.

For national labor policy, experience indicated that those who wrote the Wagner Act built soundly in establishing the basic protections of the civil rights of labor in industry which are needed for a democratic system and an administrative structure which could develop effective and fair administration. There is much evidence to indicate that the great majority of American workers in the basic industries and many others had come to believe in and desire unions and collective bargaining. Effective protection of their right to so choose was necessary if bitter strife over this basic issue was to be avoided. The provision for peaceful and orderly settling of representation disputes was an essential accompaniment of the protection of the right to organize and would be expected finally to remain the major activity of the Board after violations of the rights guaranteed by the Act for the most part had become a historical anachronism.

No law, especially in so new and controversial a field, could be perfect, however, and there was need for continuing review and at some points change with experience. The growth of a labor movement, very powerful in many sections of the economy although still new and weak in others, changed the balance of forces to some extent and called for reconsideration of policy, so that the wholesome purposes of the Act, to promote greater equality of bargaining power and sound collective bargaining, could be maintained in the varied situations apparent by the mid-forties. In addition, the increased possibilities of large-scale strikes, when labor organization was strong, raised issues as to how the federal government could further the prompt and peaceable settling of such disputes without undercutting basic liberties. Careful study was needed of these problems. Within the limited scope of the Wagner Act's interests, however, the needs of public policy as they appeared in 1947 were for continued effective protection of the rights of labor against unfair labor practices of employers; power to prevent interferences by unions with the rights of employees under the Act; a strong and expert Board to administer the Act; a unified and effective administration which would continue to emphasize flexible adjustment to needs and the informal handling of as much as possible of the work; adequate financing so that the job could be well and promptly done; and self-restraint by the Board and by the law-writers to avoid unnecessary intervention by government, when issues might better be worked out by employers and labor themselves within the healthy basic standards set by law.

The principles of the Wagner Act were as sound in 1947 as they were in 1935. They needed only to be supplemented and extended so that the democratic purposes of the Act could be maintained under all the conditions which had arisen during twelve years' experience.

From the Wagner Act to Taft-Hartley

Any limitation upon labor's freedom to act, if found necessary for protection of the rights under the Act or other public interests, needed to be carefully drawn to meet very specific problems. But any weakening of the basic protection of workers' right to organize and bargain collectively when they so desired would mean an undercutting of one of the major supports of a democratic way of life.

PART II

How the Taft-Hartley
Act Came About

CHAPTER 8

THE BACKGROUND OF THE TAFT-HARTLEY ACT. I. LABOR, EMPLOYERS, AND GOVERNMENT

IN THE Labor-Management Relations Act of 1947 national labor policy turned sharply toward the "right," after fifteen years of following the road marked by the Norris–La Guardia and the Wagner Acts. Although inevitably modified in some respects during the war, the major reliance for working out problems had been upon free collective bargaining, once the inequality of bargaining power which had resulted from the employers' economic position and from court restrictions on union activities had been reduced. In contrast with congressional attitudes in 1935 when the Wagner Act met little serious opposition in Congress, in 1947 the Taft-Hartley Act was passed by an overwhelming majority in the House of Representatives and by the two-thirds necessary to override the presidential veto in the Senate. The new legislation not only met the clear need for limited amendments to the Wagner Act but also went much farther into detailed regulation of labor relations. Drastic changes were made not only in the Wagner Act but also in the basic law of labor. The dramatic shift in the climate of opinion in Congress, and in state legislatures also, reflecting changes in public attitudes, needs more analysis than we can give here. Nevertheless, some major factors in the extremely complicated situation out of which the new legislation came can be indicated. The next two chapters will then consider the development of legislation in the states and in Congress from 1935 to 1947.

During the fifteen years from the depth of the depression, organized labor had grown greatly in membership and power. It had added some twelve million members to its rolls, under the influence of the protection afforded by the Wagner Act along with new methods and attitudes in organizing and the expansion of industry and shortage of labor accompanying the defense, war, and postwar periods of

271

prosperity and full employment. Many organizations survived which might not have survived under the old "bare knuckles" order. And collective bargaining, although some of it the result of "shotgun weddings," had become more and more the general fact in most important fields of industrial endeavor. There were more big unions —Teamsters, Steelworkers, Automobile Workers, Mine Workers, and others—as well as the building crafts, railway workers, and others whose power had not essentially changed during these years. Unions powerful in terms of members and financial resources could in time of stress conduct huge strikes with paralyzing effects upon large sections of the economy and drastic repercussions in the press and upon attitudes of much of the public. The unions for the most part survived the test of the major 1945–46 strikes and reconversion stresses and were continuing strong in the second postwar year. This was in marked contrast to 1920, when two years after the Armistice a number of major strikes had been broken, and a well-organized open-shop offensive was already under way and showing its effects in many industries and many sections of the country. Changes in the balance of power in many sectors of industrial life had become very clear by two years after the close of World War II. Those who sought to curb union power therefore turned to the legislative field.

Most of the arguments for changes in the labor laws, both federal and state, from 1939 on, can be summed up in three major points: (1) under existing laws organized labor had come into a dominant position in industry; it had too much power and there was need to effect a balance; (2) many of the unions had not developed a necessary sense of responsibility to industry and the public, or to individual employees and union members, correlative to their protected rights; and (3) labor organizations should be under the same or equivalent limitations and responsibilities as rested upon employers; the need was for a national labor policy which would "equalize" the law and insure "equitable" administration of laws. In the name of equalization, also, some would relieve management from at least a part of existing limitations under federal law or weaken the administration of that law where it was thought to rest too heavily upon employers.

First, a few preliminary comments on these points are needed. The word "power" needs to be defined in meaningful terms. Does it mean power to question management rules or certain of those rules adopted in nonunion days? Does it mean power to press seriously for bargaining about practices which have become the accepted rule in other plants or industries? Does it mean power of a single union dealing with many small employers to get standardized wages, hours, and other conditions and make them common to all firms in the market, to the exclusion of substandard conditions and firms? Does it mean power to close down the operations of the many plants of a huge corporation or to close down an industry crucial in a locality or the nation? Or, to change the drift of the question, does it mean power greater than is possessed by the employer with whom the union deals? Situations vary. There may be powerful unions and associations of employers, as in Pacific Coast shipping; strong unions facing great corporations in mass production; division among unions as they face nation-wide operations such as those of Western Union; unions in many areas in the early stages of dealing or trying to deal with large chain-store companies; strong unions like the Teamsters, in highly strategic position as they deal with thousands of employers, many of them small; a great union and associations of small employers organized in order to meet the union on a more equal footing; great textile mill chains in many of whose mills unions have never achieved even a precarious hold; and many other combinations and permutations of power relationships. In spite of the impressive over-all figures indicating union strength, the disparities are very great, with the balance on this side here, and the other side there. No indiscriminate weakening of the power of unions could be expected to do justice or promote equality.

With respect to irresponsibility, experience with arbitration and in the National Labor Relations Board shows many instances of deficient sense of responsibility both among officers and members of labor organizations and among employers. On the other hand, most experienced men have a sense of fairness when they come to know the facts. It must be noted too that for responsibility, both union and employer must have sufficient power to maintain their organization and perform their functions. The problem is then how to make a sense of fairness and responsibility more general. What will assist in effectuating and what will militate against this end?

"Equalizing the law" is an old plea, increasingly used in the later years. Much of it was sales talk with little basis in fact. Some, though not all, of the proposals to "equalize the Wagner Act" were unrealistic, based on misunderstanding of the facts or seemingly with other objectives behind them. Yet the slogans were highly appealing and received a great deal of support. The need was for careful analysis and carefully drawn legislation to remedy any situations lacking a

273

proper balance between organized labor and management from the standpoint of public interest. Much of the attack upon the Wagner Act with its demand for restrictive legislation, however, in spite of the slogans was in reality aimed simply at reducing the power of unions. It reflected a struggle over industrial and political power.

Turning from these generalities, we consider some factors in actions of unions, employers, and government which contributed toward the 1947 "legislative climate" and the new framework for the relations of labor and employers.

UNION FACTORS

Organized labor and collective bargaining on the whole had functioned well when the essentials of the Wagner Act and the assumptions underlying it had been complied with. Certainly during the years of preparedness and war the great mass of unions were very loyal, minimizing strikes and slow-downs, consenting to longer hours of work, relaxing working rules, and seeking intensive individual application by those on jobs, so that more was accomplished and more goods and weapons turned out than had been thought possible. Union and worker attitudes and efforts made their great contribution to the result, along with technological advance and management efficiency.

While the general labor record was an excellent one during the perilous years of 1941–45, there were "quickies" and stoppages, most of them officially disavowed and sometimes the leaders disciplined. Some stoppages and slow-downs will inevitably occur, especially when most unions are still young, when many of their members have not yet become union men at heart, and many if not most of their officers are inexperienced. Management, from top management to supervisors, likewise was frequently inexperienced in collective bargaining, immersed in solving its production problems, and sometimes not possessed of the best judgment. Management sometimes caused impatience and low morale by saying to workers, "Of course you should have more money, but the War Labor Board bureaucrats won't let us give it to you." Sometimes, too, manpower was being wasted, at least temporarily, and foremen said, "What's the hurry?" But the most troublesome factor where there were "quickies" or stoppages or bad morale appears to have been failure to recognize the importance of good grievance machinery and its timely and considerate use. Sometimes this was due simply to inexperience on both sides. Not infrequently, however, it reflected failure of management fully to accept collective bargaining and the need for working out

274

as many issues as possible at home. Instead, too often it was said, "Take it to the Labor Board." And delays in the government's handling of cases added to the widespread unrest. During the war the immediate responsibility for stoppages and slow-downs seems to have rested about equally upon management and upon the unions in organized trades. The War Labor Board in some cases penalized unions for irresponsibility in violating the no-strike pledge. In a number of important cases during or after the war, management and unions worked out "union responsibility" and "management security" clauses in an effort to meet this problem.[1] But some thought that the solution was to be found in new legislation "to make unions responsible."

Wartime federal agencies which necessarily were established to handle industrial relations problems on the whole functioned well. Yet it became necessary, or at any rate advantageous, for both management and unions "to run to Washington" for aid in resolving their problems or for authoritative settlements. Indeed, some strikes were designed to get cases acted on quickly or favorably. Suggestions or directives from Washington extensively replaced collective bargaining, especially where union-managment relations were new. For the war years, therefore, the lessons concerning normal procedures and the sense of responsibility which develop with collective bargaining experience failed to be learned by many managers or by many union officials and the rank and file. On V-J Day there were large "awkward squads," who had still to a considerable extent to learn these lessons.

In occasional cases, also, unions both young and old engaged in behavior which gave some basis for the frequent claim that unions failed to "bargain in good faith." Sometimes it was the inexperienced official of a new union, sometimes the rather arbitrary demand of an old and strong union, which brought forth this comment. An occasional union negotiator acted as though the obligation to try to reach agreement was all on the other side of the bargaining table. When a powerful union laid down its contract with a "Sign here" ultimatum, even though this was the standard contract established by collective bargaining in the area, the employer's resentment was understandable. When such a union was prepared to back its ultimatum by a boycott, although it had not always been careful to organize a majority of the employees first, the employer's resentment was thoroughly justified. When the International Typographical Union in-

1. Cf. the Ford and Kaiser agreements. *New York Times,* January 10, 1946; February 25, 1946; May 21, 1946.

sisted that its international laws, some of which dealt with working conditions, were not subject to negotiation or arbitration, its action was more appropriate to an earlier time when only the workers were organized and working conditions were decided by union action than to one of modern collective bargaining.

Another source of friction and considerable grief to employers and the public as well was found in the active division of the labor movement. Some of this was inevitable during the phenomenal expansion in union membership and collective bargaining which followed the rise of the CIO and its stimulus to the older unions. More and more money was spent on organizing campaigns. Some of the increasing number of paid organizers were of limited and short-range vision. The major part of the efforts, at least in earlier years, was devoted to organizing the unorganized. But as the larger plants and the major industries were increasingly brought within the fold, the temptation to expand by annexing the other fellow's members was substantial, and considerable energy was expended in such efforts. Competition between rival unions and the possibility that workers could shift their affiliation from one union to another exerted considerable influence for democratic, honest, and effective unionism. But the competition and raids created difficulties also. Lasting agreements not to raid were the exception; promises with respect to wage advances, job security, and improved working conditions all too frequently greatly exceeded what could reasonably be expected; shortcomings of management at times were exaggerated in the unions' propaganda; and a premium was placed on secessions from one organization and signing up with another; needed discipline was frequently sacrificed by militant unions. Factionalism and the left-right struggle, within and between unions, frequently intensified the conflicts. Related problems arose from the expansion of the jurisdictions of many of the international unions. Frequently these jurisdictions seriously overlap, even among unions within the same national federation. This caused more jurisdictional disputes. Many an employer willing to do the "right thing" found himself "in the middle."

Such disputes were commonly solved by elections conducted by the NLRB. Nevertheless, they were not always "solved." Unless the results of an election were really conclusive and the losing organization lost hope of a "comeback," it frequently renewed its organizing efforts and then petitioned for a new election, when an existing contract did not clearly constitute a bar, and sometimes when it did. The Board, of course, developed rules under which these petitions were processed or dismissed. But, in any event, bargaining for the new contract was held up while the question of representation was being settled. There was delay of some weeks, frequently, even for a consent election, and of many months for a hearing and ordered election. In a minor but increasing number of cases still more time was required to investigate and rule on challenges and objections to elections. Frequently "stalling" entered in. All this inevitably had an influence on the morale and efficiency of the workers and on production. Then, if a new organization became the representative of the employees, the new contract had to be thrashed out and new representatives dealt with. This rivalry between competing unions all too frequently became a management "headache." A divided, competitive labor movement, in spite of its indications of vitality, levied a heavy tax on management and on public understanding.

Nor is this the entire story. Important unions sometimes used their power by strikes, picketing, or boycotts to force employees to join the union, or to change their union affiliation, regardless of the results of elections or other evidence of their free choice, or while a representation issue was still unsettled.[2] The problem of such coercion by a union to force an employer to violate the law, by recognizing a union other than one representing the majority of his employees, had found no complete solution under the Wagner Act. A New York State court, however, held that picketing by a defeated union of an employer who had entered into a contract with a certified union could be enjoined.[3] The NLRB in many cases sought, by setting aside collusively made contracts, to protect its authority in representation cases and the freedom of workers to choose their bargaining representative. But the breakdown of jurisdictional lines, extreme competition for members, and the willingness of a minority of powerful unions to turn from the election process to persuasion supported by picketing or boycotting in some cases wrought serious damage to the rights of employees under the Wagner Act and to the sense of justice of employers who were willing to live in accordance with the law. Jurisdictional disputes over work assignments when these resulted in strikes also seemed to employers and the public a particularly unjustifiable kind of strike.

Abuses under closed-shop contracts, too, in rival union situations, gave the labor movement another black mark. Occasionally the incumbent union used its contract to try to perpetuate itself in power, regardless of the desires of its members as to affiliation, by expelling

2. *Supra*, ch. 6, pp. 216–33.   3. *Infra*, ch. 12, pp. 457–58.

and then demanding the discharge of any who wished to advocate a change to a different union.[4] This occurred even or perhaps especially when the origin of the closed-shop contract was somewhat questionable. Here again the failure of the union movement to eliminate these abuses gave support to the demand for regulation by law.

Picketing and boycotting took various forms and frequently led to charges of irresponsibility against the unions. Some of the criticized practices occurred in connection with rival union disputes, some merely in an effort to extend organization in unorganized sectors. Some of them were clearly beyond the bounds of reasonable action from the standpoint of public interest or that of employers and of other employees.

Most picketing was still of an old simple type with a few employees stationed near a struck plant to apprise workers of the fact that a strike was in effect and to persuade them not to work as "scabs." It might be accompanied only by trivial remarks, or it might involve serious "intimidation," "coercion," or even "violence" as these terms are used by the courts. For some years, however, with rapid organization and with many large plants involved in strikes, and with considerable protection of picketing under the Norris–La Guardia Act, much was heard of mass picketing, by very large groups, running up to hundreds or even thousands on occasion, with the aid of large numbers of supporters normally employed elsewhere and of sympathetic members of the community. Sometimes access to the plant was denied to management and to clerical and other employees not directly involved in the dispute. If the plant tried to operate— less frequently done under the Wagner Act than when unionism was less strong—there was danger of violent clashes between strikers and strikebreakers. In the "stay-in" strike, considerably used in the early years of rapidly expanding organization as an improvement on picketing, management was locked out and kept off the job, of course without sanction at common or statute law. While strike violence apparently decreased during the life of the Wagner Act in direct ratio to the extent to which the right to organize was accepted, coercion and violence are more likely to occur when picketing is on a large scale. Mass picketing has been widely condemned as coercive.

Boycotts are of a great variety. They had been used in recent years more widely than at any time since the 1880's when both the AFL and the Knights of Labor tried to bring them under control. Their increased use is to be explained partly by the rivalry between AFL

4. *Supra*, ch. 6, pp. 210–16.

and CIO, partly by the fact that labor was "on the march," largely by the effect of the Norris–La Guardia Act in limiting the issuance of restraining orders by the federal courts, and seemingly by a rather general feeling that any behavior not enjoinable under that Act, as interpreted by the Supreme Court, had been made lawful. Some unions attempted to organize retail outlets of various sorts, by picketing and boycotting restaurants and small stores, rather than by directly organizing the workers themselves; when successful they often obtained closed shops without regard to the desires of the employees. Teamsters frequently used their power of refusing to haul materials in or out, either to support efforts of other unions to organize certain plants or stores or to induce employers and employees to accept and sign contracts with the Teamsters. Boycotts of "nonunion" materials and tools were frequently used in many different situations. A retailer might be picketed because he sold a product of a nonunion manufacturer who paid substandard wages. Or members of one union might refuse to work on material hauled or delivered or processed by nonunion men, this again in an effort to protect workers in the industry from substandard labor conditions in unorganized plants. Another type important particularly in New York was a boycott against products made elsewhere, sometimes even under contract with unions affiliated with the same international, in order to protect local employers and craftsmen from any outside competition from products manufactured and sold at lower prices. Such well-known attempts at "balkanization of the market" as that of AFL Electrical Workers and employers in New York City illustrate this much-criticized practice.[5]

Even such summary discussion as this indicates differences among these situations and in the extent to which they might be justified by efforts of a union to organize and eliminate substandard conditions which threaten the welfare of its members. But it is clear that certain unions were much criticized, and open to criticism, for unjustifiable actions in this area. Some of their methods were coercive of employees, employers, and the public and contrary to the rights of others under the Wagner Act as well as of other public interests. They gave support to the frequent arguments that "union monopolies" were endangering the public interest.

Another set of union actions which led to serious criticism had to do with the internal affairs of unions. Although many unions, probably the great majority, are democratic in government and responsible

5. Allen Bradley Co. v. Local Union No. 3, IBEW, 325 U.S. 797 (1945).

toward their membership, well-known abuses of a minority created much unfavorable publicity. Thus certain unions capitalized on war conditions and charged excessive dues to war workers under closed-shop contracts.[6] The fact that "there is no evidence that dues are generally exorbitant . . . and relatively few unions charge exorbitant initiation fees, and not many workers are affected by them"[7] was less well understood by the public than the fact that abuses did exist. Most unions also make financial reports to their members, and many publish them so that they are available to the public, but some unions have been lax.[8] Although the problem of racketeering in unions had apparently decreased greatly from its heyday in the 1920's and 1930's, glaring instances of financial dishonesty of union officers still appeared in the courts. In addition, the admission requirements of some unions were open to criticism, when they still discriminated on racial grounds, or when they used their closed-shop provisions with restriction on membership to limit entrance to the industry. There were also enough complaints that rights of individual members were sometimes abused by arbitrary union discipline, expulsions for vague offenses or for "political" purposes, and by undemocratic "union bureaucracies" to arouse feeling for governmental regulation in this area.

Union leadership was fully aware of these serious problems in its own house. Behind the scenes there were discussions of whether labor could work out its own "bill of labor rights and duties." But individual union autonomy, lack of unity in the labor movement, fears of internal opposition and of giving encouragement to antiunion forces, all prevented any proposal from labor itself to deal with the admitted abuses.[9] All this made it easier for others to obtain support for rather drastic revisions of the laws, when more constructive solutions might have been found in law or otherwise, had labor leadership taken more responsibility on these points.

Finally, probably most important of all in supporting the wide im-

6. This is however to be blamed partly on the government, which early in the war permitted unions with few members to collect dues from all new workers. Later the situation was to some extent rectified under government pressure.

7. Philip Taft, "Dues and Initiation Fees in Labor Unions," *Quarterly Journal of Economics*, 60 (1946), 231–32.

8. The Hod Carriers Union in 1941 made its first financial report in thirty years, covering over-all totals of monthly receipts and expenditures for each year. American Civil Liberties Union, *Democracy in Trade Unions* (New York, 1943), pp. 59–60.

9. Cf. "The Congress, the Public, the Unions," *Labor and Nation*, 1 (February–March, 1946), 23–26; A. H. Raskin, "Labor Missed the Boat," *Labor and Nation*, 1 (June–July, 1946), 29–30; *Business Week*, March 1, 1947, p. 6.

pression that unions were too powerful and irresponsible were wartime strikes by a few unions, notably the United Mine Workers, and the great strike wave in the reconversion year of 1945–46. But before these matters can be discussed we need to turn to factors on the employers' side of the picture and to things done and not done by government itself, which by 1947 helped to bring about the crisis over labor laws.

EMPLOYERS AND EMPLOYER ASSOCIATIONS

Employers no more than labor organizations can be spoken of as all reflecting the same views, influenced by the same customs and experience, and motivated in the same way, either at one time or at all times throughout a twelve years' history. With few exceptions employers who were vocal from the introduction of the Wagner Bill to its enactment into law expressed opposition. From then on the major associations in industry followed a fairly consistent line of opposition, although this necessarily took somewhat different form after the basic principles of the Wagner Act appeared rather thoroughly established in law. Individual employers varied extensively among themselves and over the years. Their attitudes were affected by experience and by other factors in the environment; but many of them came to a much greater degree of acceptance of the Wagner Act and of collective bargaining than seemed to be true of major spokesmen for the business community.

EMPLOYER ASSOCIATIONS

The National Association of Manufacturers, with its affiliated and co-operating organizations, led the opposition to the Wagner Act from the start until sweeping amendment was achieved in 1947.[10] It fought the passage of the Act, organizing pressure against it in 1934–35.[11] After the failure of this effort the NAM argued that the Act

10. In 1947 the NAM reported a membership of 16,500, and affiliation through the National Industrial Council with 347 other employers' associations with over 40,000 members, in 35 state associations, 185 trade associations, and 150 local associations. Carroll E. French, *The Role of Employers' Associations in Industrial Relations* (New York: Industrial Relations Counselors, Inc., 1948).

For an analysis of NAM history and policy, criticizing it for "extreme conservatism" and "rationalization of narrow group self-interest," and claiming that, led by representatives of a very small number of large industrial firms, it was not truly representative either of its membership or of American industry as a whole, see Alfred S. Cleveland, "NAM: Spokesman for Industry?" *Harvard Business Review*, 26 (1948), 353–71. Cf. also "Renovation in N.A.M.," *Fortune*, 38 (July, 1948), 72–75, 165–69.

11. U.S. Senate, Committee on Education and Labor, *Violations of Free Speech and Rights of Labor, National Association of Manufacturers*, Report No. 6, Pt. 6, 76th Cong., 1st Sess., 1939, pp. 75–122, cited as *La Follette Committee Reports*.

could not be applied to manufacturing industries and that the majority-rule principle was unconstitutional, and for some time it encouraged an attitude of noncompliance on the part of its members. In December, 1935, it recommended repeal of the Act.[12] Prominent members of the NAM were among those whose injunction suits to prevent the NLRB from holding hearings were effective in interfering with the administration of the Act in its first two years.[13] Some of them were large users of labor spy systems during this period.[14] Other associations, too, played their part in the opposition, prominent among them the National Metal Trades Association, which told its members that the Act was unconstitutional and unenforceable. The Liberty League's report, to the same effect, had wide publicity.[15]

When to the great surprise of the business community the Supreme Court in April, 1937, upheld the constitutionality of the Wagner Act, a shift in the character of the opposition was necessary. But, to say the least, the attitudes expressed by the major spokesmen of business toward the new national labor policy were negative and grudging. The Chamber of Commerce of the United States late in April, 1937, began a campaign for amendment of the Act to add regulation of certain "unfair labor practices" of employees.[16] It pointed out that, while the Act was constitutional, issues as to the wisdom of the policy were still open. It gave no indication of full acceptance of the policy of the Act but emphasized the lack of control over labor activities. It suggested that employers should secure the advice of counsel as to "the extent of their obligations, if any, under the statute," and that they should raise the question of jurisdiction and enter "a vigorous and complete defense" if a complaint were filed. A resolution adopted by the Chamber on April 29, 1937, made no mention of collective bargaining and recommended "equalizing" amendments to the Act and state and federal legislation to regulate union activity.[17] The NAM, shortly after the Supreme Court decisions, distributed for bulletin-board use an analysis of the Act which conspicuously failed to emphasize the positive rights provided for employees or the parallel duties of employers. It argued that employee representation plans

12. *Ibid.*, pp. 122–32.

13. *Supra*, ch. 2, p. 39.

14. *La Follette Committee Reports, National Association of Manufacturers*, pp. 130–32, 142–53.

15. *Infra*, p. 295.

16. *New York Times*, April 28, 1937. The Chamber was reported in 1946 to have some 2,500 affiliated local Chambers of Commerce.

17. Chamber of Commerce of the United States, *Federal Regulation of Labor Relations* (Washington, D.C., May, 1937), esp. pp. 13, 19–20.

were not outlawed and distributed suggestions on how to transform them into "independent unions." In May, 1937, it adopted a labor relations program which indicated preference for individual bargaining and went only so far as to say that, if this became impossible, then there should exist "means of cooperative collective negotiation between individual employees and managements." The board of directors approved suggestions for amendment of the Act and voted "its opposition to the primary basis of government efforts to prevent labor disputes by stimulating union recognition."[18] The amendments proposed included a provision against "coercion from any source," restriction of the right to be recognized as bargaining agent to organizations which met given tests, and restriction on certain types of strikes. Concern was expressed for the rights of those who did not want unions and should be free from coercion to join.[19] It is understandable that to the NAM, long committed to an "open-shop" program, the walls of its world must have appeared shaken when the Supreme Court permitted the government to interfere with old antiunion practices, and when in the mass movement of the 1937 strike wave the CIO encroached on the strongholds of antiunionism. The General Motors agreement with the UAW–CIO, following the sit-down strike, had been signed in February, 1937, and the Carnegie-Illinois Steel agreement with the Steel Workers Organizing Committee, CIO, in March.

The drive for amendment of the Act then began in earnest, as part of a real power struggle. The NAM had begun in 1937 a long-range program to influence public opinion. It attempted by various types of publicity and by working with various community groups to promote understanding of industry and of the free-enterprise system as the sponsors understood it. This propaganda campaign in its earlier years was described in some detail in reports of the La Follette Committee. Using radio, news, cartoons, editorials, advertising, leaflets, and other devices, often with their source not disclosed, the "educational program" reached every important industrial community. It was summarized thus by the La Follette Committee:

Its message was directed against "labor agitators," against governmental measures to alleviate industrial distress, against labor unions, and for the advantages of the status quo in industrial relations, of which company-

18. *La Follette Committee Reports, National Association of Manufacturers*, pp. 135–37, 140–42; cf. also U.S. Senate, Subcommittee of the Committee on Education and Labor, *Hearings, Violation of Free Speech and Rights of Labor*, 75th Cong., 3d Sess., Pt. 17, pp. 7624, 7628, 7645–65, and 76th Cong., 1st Sess., Pt. 35, pp. 14071–76.

19. *New York Times*, April 22, 1937; July 1, 1937.

dominated unions were still a part. Antiunion employers and local employers' association executives used the propaganda material . . . to combat the organizational drive of unions in local industrial areas.[20]

How the belligerent employers' associations in some of the states encouraged antiunionism, organized resistance to collective bargaining even after the passage of the Wagner Act, and promoted anti-closed-shop and other restrictive state legislation is shown in the La Follette Committee's reports on employers' associations in California.[21]

By 1938–39 both the Chamber of Commerce[22] and the NAM[23] had approved detailed programs for amendment of the Wagner Act, and they supported the moves in Congress for investigation of the Board and revision of the Act. Both groups argued that the Act had increased strife and created new inequalities in industry. It must be said also, however, that by this time the American Federation of Labor, disturbed by Board policies which in some instances supported CIO unions against the AFL, was proposing amendments too, and thus gave considerable aid to the employers' drive against the Act.[24] In June, 1940, after the House had passed the Smith Bill amending the Act, the NAM called on the Senate to act promptly, in order to enable industry "to make its maximum contribution to national defense." It stated without qualification—for the first time so far as we have seen—that the NAM "does not oppose collective bargaining," but it sought

20. *La Follette Committee Reports, National Association of Manufacturers*, p. 218, chs. 5, 6.

21. For a summary, see *La Follette Committee Reports, Employers' Associations and Collective Bargaining in California, General Introduction*, Report No. 1150, Pt. 1, 77th Cong., 2d Sess., 1942.

For a brief account of some of the numerous local and sectional organizations which later carried on antiunion and prorestrictive legislation propaganda, often with support from large corporations, see Victor H. Bernstein, "The Antilabor Front," *Antioch Reveiw*, 3 (1943), 328–40. A study under way at the University of Chicago by Professor Avery Leiserson on "Public Opinion and National Labor Policy" will throw light on these matters. A brief analysis of the later policies and legislative campaign by the NAM appears in Clark Kerr, "Employer Policies in Industrial Relations, 1945–47," in Colston E. Warne *et al.* (eds.), *Labor in Postwar America* (Brooklyn: Remsen Press, 1949), pp. 43–76.

22. Chamber of Commerce of the United States, *Amendment of the National Labor Relations Act* (Washington, D.C., March 23, 1939); *New York Times*, April 2, 1939.

23. National Association of Manufacturers, *Why and How the Wagner Act Should Be Amended* (New York, June, 1939); *New York Times*, March 26, 1939, October 21, 1939. For the major changes proposed by business groups at this time see *infra*, ch. 9, pp. 349–50.

24. *Infra*, pp. 347–49, 351–53.

284

"to correct unsound legislation so that it may operate for the social benefit of the whole people."[25]

The 1938–40 drive for abridging, corrective, "equalizing," or emasculating amendments failed, because of lack of merit or because the Senate Committee on Education and Labor was opposed to them, at any rate at that time. Perhaps the revelations by the La Follette Committee, with its discrediting evidence on antiunion activities of employers and employer associations, helped to defeat the move. But there must have been some correlation between this drive and the fact that the movement for restrictive legislation got well under way in the states in 1939, with the first laws extensively regulating union activities adopted in four states, two of which had earlier enacted "Baby Wagner Acts."[26]

With the war came a respite in attempts to amend the Wagner Act, as employers and Congress turned their attention to other matters. The needs of full production in a time of great shortage of labor was sufficient explanation. The NAM in 1943 published two pamphlets which were quite straightforward accounts of major governmental policies in regard to labor relations, with suggestions as to how to make collective bargaining work effectively.[27] But by 1943 a coal strike brought to a head growing agitation for antistrike legislation. When the Smith-Connally War Labor Disputes Act was under consideration, the NAM announced its support. The passage of this bill over the presidential veto in June, 1943,[28] gave warning that antiunion feeling was growing in Congress and might become a force to be seriously reckoned with later. The NAM published an address of one of its leaders in January, 1944, in which suggestions were made in rather general terms for amendments of the NLRA.[29] And in 1943 and

25. *New York Times*, June 17, 1940. In 1942 the NAM quoted with approval as still its position a statement in its 1935 platform to the effect that harmonious co-operation in industry required that "employer and employees be free to bargain collectively or individually in such forms as are *mutually satisfactory to them* [italics ours] without coercion from any source." National Association of Manufacturers, *Employer-Employee Cooperation* (New York, 1942), p. 30.

26. *Infra*, ch. 9, pp. 318–21.

27. National Association of Manufacturers, *Collective Bargaining, a Management Guide* (New York, July, 1943), *Collective Bargaining, Management Obligations and Rights* (New York, November, 1943).

28. *Infra*, pp. 298–99. The adoption of the "Frey rider" to the Board's appropriation, in July, 1943, at the request of the AFL metal trades unions, also reflected at least an anti-Board and anti-CIO feeling; *supra*, ch. 6, pp. 207–9.

29. H. W. Prentis, Jr., *Government's Place in Postwar Labor-Management Relations* (New York: National Association of Manufacturers, 1944).

1944 the movement for restrictive legislation in the states made considerable headway, especially in the West and South.[30]

During 1945, as the war moved swiftly toward its close, there were many signs of trouble ahead on both the industrial and the legislative fronts. An effort was made under the leadership of Eric Johnston, then president of the Chamber of Commerce of the United States, to secure agreement by industry and the major union federations on a charter of principles to promote full production and industrial peace. A statement of principles initialed late in March by Johnston, and by Philip Murray and William Green for the CIO and the AFL, was ratified by the boards of these three organizations. It was hoped that the NAM would join, but that organization held back lest it interfere with its efforts to obtain new legislation. NAM members on the Automotive Council for War Production were reported as especially opposed. The CIO had headlined the agreement "It's Industrial Peace for the Post War Period," but the high hopes collapsed, and no meeting was held of the joint committee planned to implement the charter. The final blow was given when the AFL Executive Council, under pressure from the Carpenters and others, decided that it would not sit with the CIO in joint sessions.[31] Meantime it had been disclosed that a joint NAM–Chamber of Commerce Committee was working on a program of restrictive legislation. It was clear that there was dissent from the Johnston approach in the Chamber of Commerce as well as in the NAM. An NAM publication in March, 1945, suggested that it was "time for management to act," assuming that much of industry would continue to deal with organized labor but that law could establish rules which would provide an atmosphere more conducive to "mutual respect and equality of bargaining strength."[32]

The Ball-Burton-Hatch Bill, introduced in the Senate in June, 1945, was the first step in the final serious attempt to revise the federal laws. Labor papers began to point to signs of a rising antiunion drive like that which followed World War I and to charge conspiracy on the part of big employers to foment strikes in preparation for a legislative drive. They found some support in the widely quoted and distributed pamphlet by John W. Scoville, economist for Chrysler, which after an attack on all collective bargaining as monopolistic and there-

30. *Infra*, ch. 9, pp. 322–26.
31. *New York Times*, March 29, 1945; April 24, 1945; May 6, 1945; June 10, 13, 15, 1945; *CIO News*, April 2, 1945, May 21, 1945.
32. National Association of Manufacturers, *Labor Relations Today and Tomorrow* (New York, March, 1945).

fore against public interest, declared: "As industrial turmoil increases, more and more people will see the evils generated by collective bargaining, and we should look forward to the time when all federal labor laws will be repealed."[33] The active drive for legislation waited upon the outcome of the Labor-Management Conference in November[34] and the new congressional session. But the comment of *Business Week* on the tenth anniversary of the Wagner Act was significant:

> The fact remains that industry still is not reconciled to what it believes is a one-sided statute against industry's interests. It seems safe to predict that unless they succeed earlier, more than another decade will go by before employers give up their attempt to amend or repeal the law. . . . The more impressive the Board's record, the more heated that argument will become, for behind every case that NLRB closes in favor of employees is an employer who has had to change his personnel practice.[35]

The propaganda campaigns continued. The NAM in February, 1946, began a series of newspaper ads in which among other points it called for "establishing a labor policy that will treat labor and management exactly alike, and above all be fair to the public."[36] The great postwar strikes of early 1946 gave occasion for extensive, full-page newspaper ads by "struck" corporations, and answering ads by the unions. The American Iron and Steel Institute and the United States Steel Corporation, for example, carried on a campaign in the country newspapers during the steel strike by "canned" stories and editorials and advertising.[37]

Influential groups in industry in 1946 still wanted to seek repeal of the Wagner Act,[38] but both the Chamber of Commerce[39] in May and the NAM[40] at its December meeting defeated such proposals. Apparently the policy was to be to accept collective bargaining but to attempt to curb union power. The Chamber called for extensive "equal-

---

33. John W. Scoville, *Collective Bargaining*, address before Kiwanis Club, Detroit, August 8, 1944, distributed without charge by Newspaper Statistical Service, Detroit. A sheet inclosed urged that the reader inform his congressmen of his views.

34. *Infra*, pp. 306–11.

35. *Business Week*, July 14, 1945, pp. 97–98.

36. National Association of Manufacturers, *The Challenge and the Answer* (New York, 1947), p. 6.

37. P. Alston Waring and Clinton S. Golden, *Soil and Steel* (New York: Harper & Bros., 1947), pp. 34–40.

38. The National Founders Association put itself on record favoring repeal. *New York Times*, November 9, 1946.

39. *Ibid.*, May 5, 1946. Chamber of Commerce of the United States, *Policy Declarations, Industrial Relations in America*, adopted May 2, 1946.

40. *New York Times*, December 6, 1946; December 23, 1946.

izing amendments" and for legislation against monopolistic practices of unions and various types of strikes. It suggested that other states consider the experience of those with labor relations laws. In the NAM a minority argued strongly for complete repeal of the Wagner, Norris–La Guardia, and Wage and Hour Acts. But the program adopted was a more moderate one for amendments to the Wagner Act and legislation to restrict strikes and promote union responsibility, similar to that presented in the massive two-volume work on *The American Individual Enterprise System*, published by the NAM in 1946.[41]

The year of reconversion crises came to an end with the only new federal labor relations legislation the Lea Act, directed against the Musicians, and the Hobbs Act, directed against the Teamsters.[42] The Case Bill had failed of passage when the House mustered only 255 votes against 135 for overriding the President's veto.[43] But in several more states in 1945 and 1946 restrictions upon unions had been added to the books by statute or constitutional amendment.[44] And a new Republican Congress was about to meet, with a "mandate" from the people, although not a clearly defined one.

In 1947 as the final chapter was written in congressional hearings and committees and conference rooms and on the floor of both houses, the propaganda campaign was continued. We can only guess at all its ramifications as it was carried on through state and local organizations directly or indirectly affiliated with the national associations, through the local and trade press and radio, and by contacts with women's clubs, education, farm leaders, and other groups. The NAM frankly described its public relations methods in a pamphlet published in 1947. The "targets" were: "The great, unorganized, inarticulate, so-called 'middle-class'; The younger generation...; and The opinion-makers of the nation."[45] Its ads which appeared in the

41. National Association of Manufacturers, Economic Principles Commission, *The American Individual Enterprise System* (New York: McGraw-Hill Book Co., 1946), Vols. I and II, esp. I, pp. 215–24; cf. also National Association of Manufacturers, *The Public and Industrial Peace* (New York, 1946). This work had called the Norris–La Guardia Act class legislation which should be repealed or substantially modified, along with amendments to the Wagner Act.

42. *Infra*, ch. 9, n. 51.

43. *Ibid.*, pp. 360–62. The cut in NLRB appropriations had also been significant.

44. *Ibid.*, pp. 326–28.

45. National Association of Manufacturers, *The Challenge and the Answer* (New York, September, 1947), p. 3. This was published in connection with a drive for three million dollars to carry on the program. It described in detail the extent and nature of its activities. Among those directed to the public was its

New York Times indicated the character of the campaign. In January, 1947, a full-page ad headlined "For the good of all," called for co-operation and a "fair" program for industrial harmony. It asked for equality of obligation upon unions and employers, prohibition of monopolistic practices by either, freedom to strike except under certain conditions, freedom from coercion, prohibition of compulsory union membership and of any requirement that employers bargain collectively with foremen, and for "impartial administration of improved laws primarily designed to advance the interests of the whole public while still safeguarding the rights of all employees." It said also: "The preservation of free collective bargaining demands that government intervention in labor disputes be reduced to an absolute minimum."[46] The general tenor of later ads, in April and May, can be seen from their headlines: "How about Some Pro-Public Legislation?"; "Industry-wide Bargaining is No Bargain for You"; "The Road to Freedom for the American Worker"; "Who Wants the 'Closed Shop'?"[47] The ads were made up for the most part of appealing slogans, with little detail. They were designed to appeal to any anti-union sentiment in the name of fairness and equity, the interests of individuals, the "right to work," and equality. In addition, the *NAM Law Digest* by detailed analyses of state regulation of unions and its

---

newspaper ad campaign, starting in January, 1947, with full pages in 73 metropolitan dailies, and continuing in April and May with five ads appearing in "287 daily newspapers in 193 key industrial centers, having a combined total of 38 million readers"; "Views were presented constructively, not argumentatively, and 'in the *public* interest'" (italics and quotation marks in original). *Ibid.*, p. 11. Weekly transcribed programs, supplied free, were used by more than 350 radio stations. A press service clipsheet went to 5,665 weekly newspapers and 2,500 trade and employee publications. Monthly periodicals specially prepared for each group went to 40,000 teachers, 40,000 club women's leaders, 20,000 farm leaders, and 25,000 clergymen. "In all this work the NAM reaches the people whose opinions in turn influence many millions of Americans in every walk of life." *Ibid.*, p. 16. Labor legislation was a major point of emphasis in 1946–47. The pamphlet suggested, "For the box-score to date, check this three-point program against the record to date." *Ibid.*, p. 6.

Cf. also a headline in the *NAM News*, January 25, 1947, "Congress Will Pass Effective Labor Legislation Only If Firmly Reassured by Staunch Public Support," and the statement, "If the majority of the people think strong labor legislation is essential—and let Congressmen know their views—the chances are that the people will get what they want." Quoted from Kerr, *op. cit.*, p. 59. Later numbers of the *News* indicated considerable resentment at the barrage of labor opposition to which congressmen were subjected. The NAM pamphlet, *Americans Won't Stand for Monopolies* (New York, April, 1947), received wide distribution. For a comment on the unions' counterpropaganda campaign see *infra*, pp. 294–95.

46. *New York Times*, January 8, 1947.
47. *Ibid.*, April 28 and 30, 1947; May 11, 1947; June 1, 1947.

constitutional basis, and of proposals under consideration in Congress, encouraged its members and affiliated associations to work on the legislative front.[48]

Meantime, the Chamber of Commerce adopted at its May, 1947, meeting a program going far beyond its earlier ones. It now put major emphasis on protecting the public from interruption of operations, called for limitations on strikes, for the outlawing of any coercion and of compulsory union membership, for control of monopolistic practices of unions, exclusion of foremen from bargaining, accountability at law for any injurious conduct by employees and unions as well as by employers, and in general for "equality" of the laws and equitable administration. It called on the states as well as the federal government to act on these and other points.[49] The program was in generalities, some unexceptionable, some debatable. No one could object to the statement of the need for continuing improvement of legislation and for "intensive study" of problems by the state and federal legislative bodies. But details were still to be worked out, and some of them would be a far cry from the Chamber's stated desire for "that minimum of control that will encourage voluntary rather than government-imposed settlement of labor disputes."

To summarize, over the years the major national associations of employers, with the NAM in the lead, had started with outright opposition to the Wagner Act and obstructionism, and only belatedly came to accept, verbally at least, the right to collective bargaining through majority representatives and its protection by law. But from 1937 on they continued to talk of the "unfairness" of the law and to call for amendments. And after V-J Day they went much further, relying on a public reaction aroused against unions by the postwar strike wave and inflamed by continuous publicity attacks. The campaigns were made not in the name of the interests of employers, so much as in the more appealing name of the interests of the public and of individual employees. The fact that they involved primarily a struggle over industrial and political power was concealed only from the uninitiated. The long propaganda campaign was directed in part at real problems on which experience clearly showed need for new legislation. But it went much beyond that; it used typical propaganda methods of appealing slogans, half-truths, misinterpretation and possibly known

48. "State Regulation of Labor Union Practices and Affairs," *NAM Law Digest*, 9 (December, 1946); "Pending Labor Legislation," *ibid.*, January, 1947, Supplement No. 2.

49. Chamber of Commerce of the United States, *Policy Declarations, Industrial Relations in America*, adopted May 1, 1947.

misrepresentation, as well as failure to disclose real motives; and by these means it prepared the way for seriously weakening the protection of the right to organize against the many employers who were still antiunion, of the freedom of unions to function in the interest of their members—and of the freedom of employers and unions to work out their own problems by collective bargaining—as well as for restraints upon abuses of power by some irresponsible unions.

It may be asked whether all this was not the normal and to be expected opposition and propaganda of those who disapproved of the Act. But its significance is the influence of a well-organized and very well-financed group who did not necessarily represent fully either the opinions or the long-run interests of the majority of employers. The long campaign was successful only when other elements in a complicated situation made the times propitious for the final drive. Nevertheless, it appears that a large share of the responsibility for the character of the 1947 legislation is to be attributed to this organized movement, which history may say overreached itself.

A word should be said about other groups who did not follow the line of the NAM. The American Management Association, with its background of interest in scientific management and personnel administration, in its annual meetings considered rather practically matters of how to deal sensibly with problems which arose under the new national policy, and much good advice was given by experienced men. While different points of view were expressed, the net effect must have been to promote acceptance of collective bargaining and a realistic consideration of the needs of the future. Somewhat similarly the Committee for Economic Development in its statement on national policy early in 1947 put emphasis on ways of making collective bargaining work better on a voluntary basis. It presented a limited program for legislation to supplement existing policy by supporting free collective bargaining, outlawing interferences with it, and outlawing such union activities as jurisdictional strikes, strikes to compel violation of laws, and union monopolies which are clearly evasions of the antitrust laws.[50] But it is doubtful whether these organizations had as much influence upon employers, or certainly upon the public, as did other groups with their extreme campaigns for a change in national labor policy.

50. Committee for Economic Development, Research and Policy Committee, *Collective Bargaining: How To Make It More Effective* (New York, February, 1947).

INDIVIDUAL EMPLOYERS

If these were the attitudes and policies of the major associations which acted as spokesmen for employers, what of the attitudes of individual employers themselves? In attitudes and activities employers formed several different groups; and, as a result of legal decisions and changing labor market conditions, union policies, and personal and group experience, in many instances employers shifted from one group to another.

Always there was a minority of employers opposed "on principle" to the Wagner Act *in toto*. They thought in terms of personal government rather than of representative government in industry. They usually avoided any dealings, or at least any effective dealings, with unions. Some of these were employers whose personal experience, as they interpreted it, or the experience of others which had come to their attention, was unfortunate, so that they thought in antiunion terms. At the other extreme were many who from the start accepted and practiced rather carefully whatever was called for by law. There were also many, perhaps a majority, who were converted by experience, brought to dealing with the unions by pressure of the law and union strength, but who found collective bargaining not too difficult a way of handling labor relations, sometimes even with some advantages. Some of this moderate group were not frightened by any issue of power and had few, if any, fears of things to come as they worked out problems with the unions. Many of these, however, had reservations: they feared that unions might get too much power; they wanted the Wagner Act "equalized" and perhaps that certain union practices should be eliminated by law. A final group gave at least lip service readily enough but were prone to avoid the law and to "cut second base" in so far as they thought they could succeed; they evidently did not accept either existing national labor policy or union strength as permanent and requiring complete adjustment to the needs of a new relationship. These would follow the militant leadership of the NAM when conditions were propitious, or under other conditions go along with the more moderate group.

When employers' attitudes changed, this reflected many factors, such as particular experiences with labor organizations and collective bargaining. Changes in the market for the product and for labor and problems of manpower during conversion and then postwar reconversion had their effects, too, on employers' minds. Postwar fears of depression stiffened the resistance of many. Many employers in

292

their attitudes reflected the widespread opposition to any part of the "New Deal." Many were influenced in addition by the campaigns for restrictive legislation and adopted those attitudes as their own even when they got on well with their own unions.

The points most on the minds of employers in 1947 as they thought of their experience under the Wagner Act and of the possibility of new legislation are shown by testimony from many, though somewhat selected, employers before the congressional committees in 1947 and from numerous others in interviews. Most frequent of all were the problems of boycotts and strikes to coerce violations of law, or against the desires of employees, or in jurisdictional disputes. Very frequent was dislike of union security, either on "principle" or because it increased union strength. A great many employers were at least somewhat concerned over the "free-speech issue," especially because of uncertainty as to the extent to which they were limited. A considerable number were concerned, particularly as they thought of the past, over what seemed unfair administration of the Act. Many were worried over problems of union responsibility and stoppages, and some over "union refusal to bargain," especially in connection with industry-wide bargaining or the influence of the international unions in local situations. Many were worried, too, about "management prerogatives" and the scope of collective bargaining required by law. To some the issue of bargaining by foremen was important. But, in spite of all this, many were not greatly worried about the laws and did not expect to be particularly affected by any change. The temper of most in individual discussion was rather more dispassionate than was the growing heat of the public campaign for amendments.

Later trends in NLRB cases suggest a changed psychology on the part of at least a fraction of the employers after V-J Day. Certainly some labor spokesmen thought that this was so, and their attitudes were affected by that conclusion. Reconversion, with expanded organizing drives especially in the South, again brought changes in the character of the work of the NLRB. The number of representation cases continued to increase, but the relative increase in complaint cases was even more. The change was in part to be expected. But the increase in charges of refusal to bargain collectively was probably significant. This was no doubt affected somewhat by the fact that the War Labor Board was no longer available, and by the fact of a large number of union representatives who had become unused to collective bargaining and to the need for presenting carefully considered demands if that process was to be effective. Yet many employers apparently came to be of the same mind in their relations with the unions as most were following World War I. The increased number of complaint cases and the decreased proportion that could be adjusted informally indicated a stiffening of resistance by employers in the last three years of the Wagner Act. The same was true of the increasing effort of a large fraction of employers to influence representation elections.

The experience with Board elections may be regarded as something of a barometer of employers' thinking and behavior, whether based upon "principle," experience, or fear. Especially after the "free-speech" decision in the American Tube Bending case it became not at all exceptional for an employer to act as though he were "running against the union," going beyond merely answering any misleading and exaggerated statements made by the union in its campaign.[51] In the later years more and more companies became active in these elections. To say the least, the inference was that these employers objected to such representative government as was in prospect, if not to all such representative government, and would prevent it if possible, even though they might accept it if an election were won. The steadily declining proportion of elections won from 1944 on must have been related to these activities.

All these indications of opposition by employers, even though a minority, to the basic purposes of the Wagner Act or to the increase in union power, or both, along with the growth of the propaganda for basic changes in the governmental labor policy, both state and federal, made a deep impression on the minds of workers and union officials and affected their actions. Increasingly in 1946 and 1947 union papers charged that there was a "conspiracy" led by big employers, comparable to the open-shop drive after World War I, to provoke strikes, stimulate antiunion organizations and sentiment throughout the country, and provide a pretext for the passage of antiunion legislation.[52] The unions countered through their own

51. Cf. *supra*, ch. 5, pp. 166–69; ch. 6, pp. 174–89.

52. Cf. James A. Brownlow, "This Is Not the 1920's," *American Federationist*, 54 (May, 1947), 15–17; Ruben Levin, "Take Heed America," *Machinists Journal*, 58 (April, 1946), 86–87; Philip Murray, statement in *CIO News*, June 3, 1946, p. 1; editorial, *ibid.*, pp. 4–5.

That some of these fears were felt by others, too, is shown in an address by Gerard D. Reilly in May, 1946, while still a member of the NLRB, to the Southern Labor Conference, AFL, in Asheville, N.C. The text, as given in an NLRB release, May 11, 1946, stated: "As I see it, in the very near future the acceptance and practice of collective bargaining in certain areas may well be put to as severe a

papers and later through ads and the radio. But their access to the "public" was never as extensive as that of the organized employers. Also, it was too largely in terms of slogans to bring about much real understanding of issues. And its countereffectiveness must have been limited by the fact that the unions failed to admit and offer solutions for the real abuses in parts of their own field which made them vulnerable to attack. The press was of course generally hostile to the unions and the Act.[53] And in 1947 the drive of employer groups, with considerable support from "the general public," to impose substantial legal curbs upon unions, was successful to varying degrees in some thirty states and in Congress.

A word must be added on the influence of lawyers in all this. The widely distributed report in late summer of 1935 on the "unconstitutionality" of the Wagner Act by the National Lawyers Committee of the American Liberty League, signed by fifty-eight lawyers, many of them eminent members of the Bar, had great influence on employers' attitudes and practices.[54] Some of this group continued to be among the most active and determined opponents of the work of the NLRB. Throughout the country the influence of individual attorneys could be seen in the patterns of conduct which many of their clients followed in relation to the Act and the Board.[55] Many became known as masters of obstruction, delay, and subtle violations of the spirit of the Act which were difficult to prove. Some of them were largely responsible for the continuing resistance of groups of employers who fought the law and the unions with all the weapons available to them, rather than devoting constructive efforts to working out problems with the representatives of their employees. Certainly many found a profitable business in encouraging employers' resistance. The "free-

---

test as any of our other institutions have had to face. Let us not forget what happened after World War I, when the 'Open Shop Plan' swept certain areas and left a wake of disrupted unionism. . . . All concerned should be careful lest, either through ignorance, anxiety to do away with strikes or to put one over on the other team, they surrender irreplaceable and basic liberties."

53. For an analysis of the treatment in the periodical press from April 1, 1947, through January 31, 1948, of the issues involved in the Taft-Hartley Act see Philip Ash, "The Periodical Press and the Taft-Hartley Act," *Public Opinion Quarterly*, 12 (summer, 1948), 266–71. "The viewpoints of organized labor, presented in positive terms, did not appear in any of the major periodicals of wide circulation . . . the viewpoints of management and related groups that favored the Act appeared frequently . . ." (p. 271).

54. For the list of signers and the report, see U.S. House of Representatives, Committee on Labor, *Hearings, Proposed Amendments to the National Labor Relations Act*, 76th Cong., 1st Sess., 1939, Vol. 8, pp. 2241–87.

55. Cf. *supra*, ch. 4, pp. 121, 127. Every Regional Director could cite instances.

speech" campaigns of course showed the hand of counsel who found employment in the preparation of employers' campaign literature. To the credit of the profession it must be said that many attorneys, and an increasing number, counseled a sensible attitude of acceptance of the purposes of the Act and attempts to solve problems by collective bargaining. But there were too many who either "on principle" or for less creditable motives encouraged at least part of industry in the failure ever fully to accept the basic policies of the Wagner Act. Advice of counsel must have been influential both in individual businesses and in the decisions of the NAM and other associations which carried on the long fight, even while the larger group of employers, probably the large majority, were accepting the national labor policy. And the law which resulted in 1947 was above all the handiwork of lawyers.

PERFORMANCE AND NONPERFORMANCE BY GOVERNMENT

Policies and actions of the federal government, both the Administration and Congress, in relation to industrial disputes in the war and postwar periods, also played their part in developing the complicated situation out of which came the new legislation of 1947. Failure to prepare adequately and wisely for postwar problems and the resulting instances of "crisis government" were of major significance in bringing about the bitter strikes of the postwar years, which made possible the drastic 1947 legislation.

The chief reliance for industrial peace and uninterrupted production during the war was upon the no-strike pledge which the unions voluntarily gave the nation after Pearl Harbor. But there was need for adequate machinery to settle disputes. The National Defense Mediation Board, established by the President in March, 1941, to supplement the work of the Conciliation Service, came to an end in November, 1941, in a conflict over the United Mine Workers' demand for a union shop in the "captive mines" of the steel corporations. It had been handicapped by the lack of agreed-upon principles as a basis of its work, although such principles might have been established had the opportunity for an early representative conference been grasped. After Pearl Harbor the President called a conference of industrialists and labor leaders, from the NAM, the United States Chamber of Commerce, the AFL, and the CIO. They agreed readily on a no-strike, no-lockout policy for the duration of the war, and for the establishment of a new agency to settle disputes, but they failed to agree on policy as to union security. The unions were unwilling to freeze the status quo as was done in the last war, and employers opposed any extension of the closed shop. Instead of insisting upon a resolution of this issue, the President rather abruptly announced that agreement had been reached on policies to avoid interruption of operations and that a National War Labor Board would be established to handle labor-management disputes which the parties failed to settle by other means. On January 12, 1942, an Executive Order established a tripartite twelve-man Board, with power to determine *all* disputes certified to it by the Secretary of Labor. Developing its principles on a case-to-case basis and refusing to consider disputes until strikers went back to work, and decentralizing as much as possible of its work through regional boards, the Board had a large degree of success in settling disputes which the Conciliation Service had been unable to resolve. Despite some serious clashes of interest and opinion within the Board, it held together with its management, labor, and public membership and was able to carry on its important public service all through the war years.[56]

The issue of union security was one of the War Labor Board's most difficult problems in view of the lack of agreement between industry and labor. The "maintenance-of-membership" compromise proved a workable solution, although employer members were never reconciled to it; and it prevented strikes which otherwise might have occurred over this issue. During the war closed-shop and union-shop agreements increased only a little in the proportion of workers covered, but "maintenance-of-membership" agreements covered nearly three in ten of workers under agreement by 1945. With the end of the war and a return to "free collective bargaining" unions sought to obtain the stricter forms of union security, and by 1946 closed-shop and union-shop clauses covered nearly 7.5 million workers, half of those under agreement.[57] This effort of the unions to extend union security, especially strong because of their fears of an antiunion campaign, was one of the factors leading to the increased drive for anti-closed-shop legislation, which again accentuated the unions' feeling of insecurity.

56. For a valuable analysis of this experience see George W. Taylor, *Government Regulation of Industrial Relations* (New York: Prentice-Hall, 1948), chs. 3 and 4. The official history is National War Labor Board, *Termination Report* (Washington, 1947); cf. also E. E. Witte, "Wartime Handling of Labor Disputes," *Harvard Business Review*, 26 (1947), 169–89; Dexter M. Keezer, "Observations on the Operations of the National War Labor Board," *American Economic Review*, 36 (1946), 233–57.

57. *Monthly Labor Review*, 64 (1947), 767.

From the Wagner Act to Taft-Hartley

THE WAR LABOR DISPUTES ACT AND STRIKES

While the number of employees and the proportion covered by collective bargaining agreements rose greatly during the war years, the great majority of agreements resulted from bargaining by the parties without any intervention of government agencies. And the great majority of all agreements and dispute settlements were reached without strikes. Time lost by strikes dropped sharply in the first war year, but in 1943 it increased, with the result that antistrike legislation began to receive serious consideration in Congress. The issue came to a head with the coal-mine stoppages in May and June. AFL and CIO unions reaffirmed their no-strike pledge.[58] Nevertheless, although the legislation was opposed, as no solution for strikes, by the Secretaries of Labor, War, and the Navy, the WLB, and the Chairman of the War Production Board, both House and Senate passed the Smith-Connally War Labor Disputes Act and on June 25 overrode the President's veto.[59] The Act gave statutory authority to the War Labor Board and authorized the President to seize and operate struck plants; the latter had of course already been done under the existing war powers, but now instigating a strike in such a plant was made subject to penalty. Most controversial were the provision for thirty days' notice of a labor dispute which might interrupt war production, and provision for a secret ballot by the NLRB on the thirtieth day thereafter, if the dispute had not been settled, on the question whether the employees wished to permit an interruption of production over the issue involved. Anyone failing to meet the requirement as to strike notices might be held liable for damages incurred as a result of a strike in which the required notice had not been given. There was also a provision, entirely irrelevant to the stated purpose to prevent strikes but giving insight into underlying attitudes, prohibiting political contributions by labor organizations in connection with a national election, with penalties of fine and imprisonment.

The President's veto had been directed especially at the provision for strike votes which, he pointed out, ignored the no-strike pledge and might in effect encourage strikes. It is worth while to consider the experience under this provision. Strikes did not decrease; rather, with ups and downs the generally upward trend continued through the war, reflecting increasing tensions. The provision for notice and strike-vote elections proved expensive and disrupting. It was difficult

58. *New York Times*, May 15 and 18, 1943.
59. 57 U.S. Stat. 163 (1943). Cf. *infra*, ch. 9, pp. 354–56.

for union leaders, most of whom were loyally trying to maintain the no-strike pledge, to explain to their members that the government, which was providing the machinery for a strike vote, had not meant to make strikes legal or proper. Strike notices were filed in large numbers as a means of bringing disputes effectively to the notice of government agencies and putting pressure on them and on employers for a settlement. Sometimes this stirred up strike sentiment and made it more difficult to control. The thirty-day waiting period, especially where a strike vote was actually conducted, served more for "boiling up" than "cooling off." The unions naturally used the strike notice and ballot as an organizing and bargaining device. In general, in the strike polls they won a large vote in favor of striking —but then did not strike. Most strikes which occurred during this period were regardless of the provisions of the Act. Where polls were held the votes in favor of a strike rose from 68 per cent in 1943 to 72 per cent in 1944 and to 84 per cent in 1945. But work stoppages followed such favorable votes only in 34 out of 102 cases in 1943, in 69 of 271 in 1944, and in 213 of 1,249 in 1945.[60]

After V-J Day and the end of the no-strike pledge the unions made more use of the system both as a bargaining device and for protection against any charge of illegality, since the Act was still on the books. The NLRB was swamped by the necessity of conducting these votes,[61] some of them on a nation-wide basis, as in the cases of the Ford, General Motors, and Chrysler employees and the steelworkers in November, 1945. Faced with the problem of a stoppage of administration of the NLRA because of concentration on strike polls, and the enormous cost involved, Congress finally ordered the Board to expend no more funds on such polls, effective December 28, 1945.[62]

This experience indicates that when governmental intervention in a labor dispute takes the form of asking workers publicly to support or repudiate their leadership, they tend strongly to do the former. The comment of John L. Lewis was significant, after the bituminous coal vote which cost the government over $160,000, in March, 1945, when he expressed his pleasure at receiving an "overwhelming vote of confi-

60. *Monthly Labor Review,* 58 (1944), 941; 60 (1945), 970; 62 (1946), 734. The complete figures on cases filed under the War Labor Disputes Act are reported by the NLRB. Polls were held in 1,571 cases, or 2,168 separate units, of which 1,850 voted for a strike. Nearly two million votes were cast; 26,630 separate employers were involved. *Eleventh Annual Report,* pp. 68–69, 91.

61. Cf. *supra,* ch. 2, p. 61.

62. Until the Act expired in June, 1947, however, unions continued to file the notices, and in increased numbers, probably chiefly to avoid the possibility of damage suits in a time of increased conflict. By May a total of 4,159 had been filed during 1947. *New York Times,* June 11, 1947.

dence."[63] Altogether the Act had relatively little total effect on war-time labor relations, but what it had was more often hurtful than constructive, although it was a very expensive experiment. The damage-suit provision was little used, apparently.[64] The provisions as to the powers of the WLB and of the President in seizing struck plants were helpful to some degree. But the punitive antiunion approach was not calculated to promote an atmosphere in which disputes could most easily be settled.[65]

A summary picture of the trends of industrial disputes—strikes and lockouts—is needed since they were so significant a factor in building up the complicated situation out of which came the 1947 legislation.[66] This resulted partly from the great number of persons involved or affected, in part from the great sensitivity of most people to industrial disputes, and in part from Washington policy.

For some fifteen years the number of disputes had been considerably larger than it was during the 1920's and the early 1930's when unionism was at low ebb. The number in each year 1944–46 (4,750 or more) and in 1937 (4,740) exceeded the previous high of 4,450 in 1917; and strikes were almost as numerous in 1941. As to the number of employees directly involved, however, no years until 1945 with 3,470,000 and 1946 with 4,600,000 were at all comparable to the previous peak of 4,160,000 in 1919. The number of employees directly involved in strikes might be expected to grow as the number employed, and especially the number of union members, increased greatly over the years. But the proportion of all employees who were involved in strikes in the year in 1943 and 1944 was only slightly above that of the earlier war, and even in 1945 with 12.2 per cent involved in strikes, and 1946 with 14.5 per cent, this was far below the 1919 peak of 20.8 per cent. Thanks to more and better machinery for the conciliation and arbitration of disputes, to the strong pressure exerted by public opinion as war approached and then became a reality, also to the

63. *Ibid.*, March 30, 1945.

64. Dr .Witte reports that some cases were pending in 1947, but there had been no recovery by that time. Witte, *op. cit.*, p. 182. A settlement out of court in a suit against the Teamsters for $500,000 damages for losses in a strike in which no notice was filed, was reported in the *Baltimore Federationist*, March 9, 1945, according to an *NLRB Press Release*, March 14, 1945. One group of miners was prosecuted and sentenced for a strike while the mines were under government operation, but only one of the miners was actually imprisoned, when he violated his probation by instigating work stoppages, according to the *New York Times*, June 2, 1945.

65. For other appraisals cf. Witte, *op. cit.*, pp. 181–83; Taylor, *op. cit.*, pp. 165–69.

66. Full details are available in the annual reports by the U.S. Bureau of Labor Statistics. Cf. *Monthly Labor Review*, 64 (1947), 782.

no-strike pledge, the average length of stoppages was much less than
it had previously been. Even in 1945 the average length of strikes
increased only to 9.9 days, from a little more than half as many in
1944; and not until 1946, when the great strikes of the winter brought
the average duration up to 24.2 days was it at all comparable to the
late twenties and thirties. The index of man-days lost as a direct result of stoppages increased, however, from 1935–39 as 100, to 224 in
1945 and to 684 in 1946, as against only 25 in 1942, the first year of
the War Labor Board, and 136 in 1941. The previous high, from 1927
when this series began, was 1937, a year of great organization drives
and of efforts to "up" wages when business had improved. The percentage of estimated working time that was lost directly by strikes
for the entire period of World War II was only 0.11, although for
the first postwar year it rose to 1.62 per cent.[67]

The years 1945 and 1946 were therefore relatively bad strike years,
in terms of the annual figures. Yet they should not be considered as a
whole. V-J Day in August, 1945, brought considerable change in the
trend. Man-days idle in industrial disputes had been rising through
the spring months as workers became more restive over "frozen
wages." But it was not until after V-J Day, when no-strike pledges
were considered no longer binding—some had of course thought this
earlier—that the figures really jumped. Then as the great strike wave
of winter and early spring developed, man-days lost rose to seemingly
astronomical figures in January and February, 1946, nearly 23 million
in the latter, then declined and for the last half of the year remained
around the level of September, 1945. In 1947 again they decreased,
until the coal, telephone, and maritime strikes sent them soaring in
April, May, and June.[68] Even at the peak in February, 1946, the

67. *Ibid.*, 63 (1946), 883. For calendar year 1945 it was 0.47 per cent; for
1946 it was 1.43 per cent.
68. The monthly figures of man-days lost in strikes were as follows, in thousands:

Month	1945	1946	1947
January	199	19,700	1,340
February	388	22,900	1,230
March	775	13,800	1,100
April	1,470	14,300	8,540
May	2,220	13,700	6,730
June	1,890	4,580	3,960
July	1,770	3,970	3,970
August	1,710	3,900	2,520
September	4,340	4,880	1,970
October	8,610	6,220	1,780
November	6,930	4,980	829
December	7,720	3,130	590

(*Monthly Labor Review*, 64 [1947], 789; 66 [1948], 483).

percentage of estimated time lost directly by the strikes had been only 4.19. This, however, was little measure of the disruption of the economy by the strikes in basic industries.

This, then, was the immediate background of the demand for anti-strike legislation which rose in Congress in 1946 and resulted in the vetoed Case Bill in June of that year, as well as other proposed anti-strike measures. But several things need to be said. The first is that the record for the war period was relatively good in comparison with World War I, when union membership was far less general and the number employed much less. The second is that for every stoppage there were scores of peaceful settlements. In other words, strikes were a decided exception to the general rule, especially during the war, but also even during the difficult reconversion period. The third point relates to the causes behind the strikes. Careful consideration of policies, procedures, and causes as well as the results of strikes is needed, in addition to the bare facts of their numbers.

In most years for which we have data, wages or wages and hours have been the largest and generally the dominant cause of strikes and lockouts.[69] Though "fringe issues," such as maintenance of membership, travel time, seniority rights, and the like, became more and more important causes of disputes during the life of the War Labor Board, the cause of causes was still to be found in wages and hours. And most dramatically was this true in the great strikes of the first postwar year. In strikes involving 1,000 or more workers from V-J Day to June 30, 1946, with a total of nearly 4 million workers involved and more than 104 million man-days lost as a direct result, wages and hours were the major issue for over 77 per cent of the strikers and nearly 86 per cent of the lost time.[70] We shall return to these postwar strikes after a consideration of certain factors in governmental and industrial policy which were significant in bringing them about.

RECONVERSION ISSUES

The end of the "shooting war" brought industrial relations problems incidental to reconversion that were as difficult as, perhaps more difficult than, those involved in prosecuting the war. Events during this period, and especially what government did and failed to do before and during those crucial months, weighed perhaps even more than factors discussed earlier in the final decisions as to new federal

69. Harry A. Millis and Royal E. Montgomery, *Organized Labor* (New York: McGraw-Hill Book Co., 1945), pp. 699–702.
70. *Monthly Labor Review*, 63 (1946), 886.

labor policy in 1947. In our view, certain things of fundamental importance failed to be recognized and appropriately acted upon.

War had greatly changed the industrial situation and the modes of thought of many groups of people. But neither the Congress nor the Administration developed before V-J Day or later a well-thought-out, well-co-ordinated and comprehensive reconstruction policy. President Truman announced immediately after V-J Day that controls should be removed as soon as possible. The War Labor Board was to be terminated, although no plans had been made for government's role in the inevitable labor conflicts during reconversion to "free collective bargaining" as well as to a postwar "free economy."[71] Wages and purchasing power must be kept up, the Administration said repeatedly, but a large part of any increased labor cost could and should be absorbed by business; any necessary price adjustment would be considered when the need became evident. In no event must there be inflation with its natural offspring of deflation, depression, and unemployment.[72] Labor and certain others agreed, fearful of a specter of serious unemployment; not so some other powerful groups. The concerted drive to eliminate or emasculate price control was largely successful within the first year after V-J Day and almost complete a few months later. Congress, also, presumably under the same pressures as those which wanted the end of war controls, failed to accede to the President's request for expansion of the unemployment insurance system, retention of federal control over the employment service at least during reconversion, or an increase in the minimum wage under the Fair Labor Standards Act. Action on the urgent problem of housing also was hesitant. It was the same at most points on the domestic situation and the problems of reconversion.

The details of all this need not detain us. The immediate point is that lack of consistent and constructive consideration of problems and neglect of causes breeds fear and bad industrial relations. It also breeds narrow, selfish groups. So it was in the two postwar years in America. In this situation each group in the population tended to develop pressure tactics to promote or to protect its own nearsighted interest, and all—industrial organizations, farmers, real estate groups, among others—employed methods not dissimilar to those for which unions were then being criticized. Many of the pressure groups obtained at least a part of what they desired. Certainly the barrage of

71. Cf. discussion in Taylor, *op. cit.*, pp. 196–206.
72. See especially the President's statement after V-J Day and his September message to Congress, *New York Times*, August 17, 1945; September 7, 1945.

propaganda and counterpropaganda left the people more confused, bewildered, and divided than enlightened. At the same time some who were neither confused nor bewildered, and who "knew the ropes," could turn the situation to their advantage. All this was unfortunate, for the people of the country faced perhaps the greatest problems in their history and needed to find their way out with some degree of unity and good will. In this confused situation in which emotions ran high, there was the rash of strikes which we have seen, and organized labor lost greatly in prestige. It became more difficult to make necessary accommodations in many sectors of industry, and the opportunities for normal growth in collective bargaining were sacrificed in considerable part. The Labor-Management Conference of November, 1945, was one effort, with only a limited success, to cope with some of these problems.

The dominant immediate issue in industrial relations in the first postwar year was that of wages and their relation to prices. In the background of course were issues as to power, with growing resistance to the unions by important sections of industry, and increasing fear and insecurity on the part of organized labor. For more than two decades organized labor had held the doctrine that wages must increase in step with industrial advance, the standard of living must be improved in good times and must not be permitted to sag in time of unemployment, in terms of wage rates relative to the cost of living. In contrast to some other countries, no exception has been made willingly even during a war when it was difficult to maintain the standard of living already attained. Thus demands for wage-rate increases were insistent during the life of the National Defense Mediation Board even though workers were being paid for more hours per week, some of this at overtime rates, and the number of wage-earners per average household was increasing. The same was true in the earlier days of the War Labor Board until the adoption of the Little Steel Formula, which permitted a 15 per cent cost-of-living increase in wage rates over those of January 1, 1941. Under the Stabilization Act of October, 1942, the Little-Steel Formula continued as an effective brake, although increases were permitted by the War Labor Board to remove inequities and substandard wages. Also, because of manpower shortages and employers' desire generally to "hold labor" or "attract labor" by increasing wages, indirect ways of accomplishing the result were frequently resorted to by granting holiday pay, vacations, merit increases, incentive pay, and other "fringe" items.[73] As a consequence, increases in the basic wage-rate structure were held to moderate proportions, and for many important industries general increases were little more than 15 per cent. But in addition selective adjustments to individuals and small groups raised the average of rates. And hourly and weekly earnings increased sharply as a result of longer hours of work, overtime rates, shifts to higher-paid industries, upgrading, incentive systems, and other factors. The contents of the weekly pay envelope increased on the average considerably more than the cost of living, although increased taxes and social security deductions, plus War Bond deductions widely made, left actual "take-home" pay for many individuals only a little, if any, larger in purchasing power than before 1941.[74] Union attacks upon the validity of the Department of Labor's cost-of-living index and attempts to obtain the abandonment of the Little Steel Formula failed to bring about modification of wage policy during the war period.

With the end of the war and the cancellation of war orders, the favorable earnings situation was threatened by reduced hours, less overtime, shifts to lower-paid industries, downgrading, and a decrease in the number of wage-earners per family as many, young women especially, withdrew from the labor force. In addition, there was a reappearance of the problem of unemployment, fears of which were very real in both official and unofficial circles at the time. By October, 1945, average weekly earnings in manufacturing industries had decreased to $41.04 from April's $47.12, or 12.9 per cent, while the cost of living was drifting upward.[75]

Accordingly organized labor, especially in the durable goods industries where there were the greatest cutbacks, demanded increases in wage rates so that with the shorter hours there would be little if any sacrifice in take-home pay. Increasing wage rates and keeping down the cost of living by maintaining effective governmental control of prices were regarded as equally necessary in order to insure purchasing power to support full employment against the specter of mass unemployment. Wage questions, therefore, were the central issue which had to be settled in collective bargaining in the recon-

73. National War Labor Board, *Wage Report to the President on the Wartime Relationship of Wages to the Cost of Living, February 22, 1945* (Washington, 1945), pp. 4–11.

74. *Monthly Labor Review*, 62 (1946), 538; "Spendable Earnings of Factory Workers, 1941–43," *ibid*, 58 (1944), 477–89.

75. *Ibid.*, 62 (1946), 290, 304, 343; see also "Workers' Experiences during Reconversion," *ibid.*, 62 (1946), 707–17.

version year. A large degree of freedom of action was given by the Executive Order of August 18, 1945, permitting voluntary wage increases when possible without increases in prices; and later relaxations of the stabilization policies permitted price relief following wage increases under some circumstances. The assumption was, as the President indicated in his address of October 30, 1945, that "there is room in the existing price structure for business as a whole to grant increases in wage rates." It was inevitable that disputes over wages would be difficult. But the War Labor Board was in process of dissolution, and, while its stabilization functions were turned over to a National Wage Stabilization Board, there was no adequate plan for solving the serious disputes which should have been foreseen.[76]

THE LABOR-MANAGEMENT CONFERENCE

Collective bargaining in the fall of 1945, therefore, in its first crucial test after the war, had to deal with a wage problem made more difficult because it was involved in national price policy. The problem would not be settled until political decisions were made on a national scale. In addition, there were controversies over contract clauses such as those on union security, union responsibility, and "management prerogatives" which needed to be worked out now that the War Labor Board was no longer available to settle such disputes and collective bargaining was once more free from wartime controls. Fears and resentments on the part of both labor and management growing out of wartime experience and the economic uncertainties of the future also complicated the situation. Increasingly talk was heard in many circles of a coming "showdown."

There had been some little discussion as much as a year before V-J Day of the desirability of a labor-management conference to seek agreement on some of the problems which would face labor and industry as well as government upon the end of the war, but nothing had come of it. Early in 1945 the effort by a liberal group of the Chamber of Commerce to obtain agreement of employer and labor groups on ways to promote peace and co-operation also had fallen

76. For useful summaries of this period, see "Wage Policy and the Role of Fact-finding Boards," *Monthly Labor Review*, 62 (1946), 537–49; "Money and Real Earnings during Defense, War and Reconversion Periods," *ibid.*, 64 (1947), 983–96. By June, 1946, there had been a decrease from April, 1945, of 8.1 per cent in average weekly money earnings and 12.4 per cent in real earnings; from June, 1946, to February, 1947, money earnings increased 9.2 per cent, while real earnings decreased 4.7 per cent, as the consumers' price index showed its steepest rise in history. *Ibid.*, pp. 989, 996.

by the wayside. Finally the idea of a labor-management conference under government auspices, which had been "in the air" for some time, was crystallized by a suggestion of Senator Vandenburg to the Secretary of Labor, and the plan for such a conference was approved by the major organizations of both groups. The President announced the plan, but it was not until early September that a representative committee went to work on the plans,[77] and not until November 5 that the Conference convened. By that time the strike crisis was already well under way, and it was too late; at any rate, the Conference failed to avert the major immediate conflicts. The emphasis was upon long-term "major causes of industrial strife and the methods of reducing them." The immediate problems of conflicts over wage-price issues, or of a solution when negotiations failed to bring agreement, were not on the agenda.

The Conference, which met on November 5, 1945, consisted of eighteen delegates representing the AFL, CIO, the United Mine Workers and the Railroad Brotherhoods, with alternates; eighteen representing the NAM and the Chamber of Commerce, again with alternates; the Secretary of Labor, the Secretary of Commerce, Chief Justice Walter P. Stacy of the Supreme Court of North Carolina, chairman, and George W. Taylor, secretary. The public members were without vote. The delegates constituted an able, fairly representative, and responsible conference group. Marked differences within each group, however, both among the labor representatives and between the liberal management attitude represented by the president of the Chamber of Commerce and the more militant attitude represented by the NAM, were a hindrance to the most effective work.

President Truman in his opening address called upon the Conference to provide a "broad and permanent foundation for industrial peace and progress." He stressed the imperative need to avoid industrial strife and his conviction that if labor and management were to approach each other with the realization that they had a common

---

77. A committee of six, with Major Paul H. Douglas as chairman representing the Secretary of Labor and others representing the Secretary of Commerce, the AFL, CIO, U.S. Chamber of Commerce and the NAM, agreed upon plans which were unanimously approved. The membership of this committee and of the conference itself is available in "Labor-Management Conference on Industrial Relations," *Monthly Labor Review*, 62 (1946), 37–42; U.S. Department of Labor, Division of Labor Standards, *Summary and Committee Reports, The President's National Labor-Management Conference, November 5–30, 1945*, Bulletin No. 77, 1946. The complete documentation of the conference, in processed form, is available also in most university and other leading libraries.

goal they could find a way to resolve their differences without stopping production. And he warned them: "If the people do not find the answers here, they will find them some place else. For these answers must and will be found."

The Conference committees, each of them bipartisan, worked diligently and reached agreement on a number of important problems; on others their agreements and disagreements clarified issues between management and labor representatives. But on major immediate problems which were behind the growing strike crisis they found no basis for an agreed solution.

The first of these issues was that of wages. Philip Murray for the CIO early introduced in the executive committee a resolution pointing out that collective bargaining had broken down over this issue, and calling on labor and management to engage in genuine collective bargaining in an effort to resolve the question within the framework of the President's recent message in which he had held wage increases imperative in order to "cushion the shock" of reconversion and sustain adequate purchasing power. Other labor groups objected to the particular formula, although they supported immediate increases arrived at by collective bargaining. Management held that wage increases could not be given without price increases. No agreement was reached, and opportunity, perhaps necessarily so at this late date, was provided for the bitter struggles over the wage-price issue which followed.

A second major question was as to what could be done when collective bargaining broke down. On one point at least the Conference seemed to be in complete agreement—its opposition to anything approaching compulsory arbitration. Great public interest was evident at this time in the possibility of some form of public fact-finding with compulsory "cooling-off periods" in critical disputes, but this matter was not definitely assigned to any of the working committees, and there appeared to be marked reluctance to tackle the issue. The executive committee discussed the matter at length but never reached agreement, and so made no report, and there was no Conference action on the matter. Clearly both sides were fearful of increasing government intervention in collective bargaining, although the president of the NAM stated frankly that it was an aim of the management group "to attempt to reduce strikes to the minimum," and that a cooling-off period would help attain that result. So the Conference failed to find a solution for the immediate problem of the great and paralyzing

308

strikes which were threatened and in fact already under way before its adjournment on November 30.

Greater progress was made on matters of procedures and attitudes which would make collective bargaining work better in the long run. Three committees made unanimous reports which were adopted by the Conference. Two of them wrote sound and constructive statements of established good bargaining practice, the first as to the making of initial agreements, the second, on existing collective agreements. Both emphasized the role of conciliation and, *"where mutually agreed to,* arbitration." Compulsory arbitration, however, not agreed to by the parties, was opposed.

The third committee which reached unanimous agreement and whose report was adopted by the Conference was that on conciliation services. It recommended that every effort be made to establish the U.S. Conciliation Service as "an effective and completely impartial agency within the U.S. Department of Labor," with a representative Advisory Committee from labor and management; the parties to disputes should make every effort to settle them by collective bargaining before requesting conciliation services, and as far as possible disputes should be settled at the plant level. This report also specifically rejected compulsory arbitration.

On the other hand, three committees, on collective bargaining, on representation and jurisdictional disputes, and on management's right to manage, agreed on some phases of the problems before them but disagreed on others. Accordingly separate reports were submitted by the labor and management members and no action resulted by the Conference. The disagreements were due in part to the complexities of the situation facing labor and management and the fact that the Conference was held in the midst of conflicts rather than a year earlier when some of the problems might have been resolved in advance. But they reflected also basic cleavages in atttitudes toward collective bargaining. In all these committees, nevertheless, there was partial agreement which added something to the accomplishments of the Conference. In fact, as a whole there may have been more agreement than disagreement between the labor and management members on these committees.

The committee on representation and jurisdictional disputes was in sharp disagreement. Management wanted jurisdictional disputes eliminated by law if the unions failed to resolve these disputes by their own machinery; strikes, boycotts, or lockouts over representation questions should be eliminated by being made unfair labor practices; employers should have a right to petition the appropriate agency for an election when in doubt as to a union's claim to represent a majority of the employees; multi-plant bargaining units were opposed except where agreed to by employers or established by prior bargaining practice. Labor representatives, on the other hand, opposed any amendment of the Wagner Act or any limitation on the right to strike, although they recommended that unions should set up and abide by the results of determinations by their own jurisdictional dispute machinery; no union should strike or boycott against the result of voluntary noncollusive recognition agreements or determinations by federal or state agencies of representation disputes. But they thought that the management proposals would be subject to abuse by antiunion employers and that management sought crippling legislation for the purpose of weakening unions.

In the important committee on collective bargaining there was agreement on many points as to the meaning and process of bargaining in good faith. But management insisted that there was need for guaranties of responsibility and legal enforcement of contracts, along with protection against unlawful acts and control of union activities. Labor, on the contrary, thought that good relations and responsibility could better be promoted by voluntary means and co-operation and refused to agree to any legal regulation of these matters.

As might be expected, "management's right to manage" brought the greatest disagreement. Management, fearing an extension of union power, wished to have areas of management control defined, though recognizing that at certain points the union had a right to raise questions under the grievance procedure. Labor, on the other hand, knowing of much variation in customs and experience, and perhaps wishing to extend collective bargaining in many instances into new fields, held that it was impossible to define such areas, and strongly opposed management's defensive plan. Labor, here, as at other points, emphasized co-operation and mutual confidence based on experience, while management tended rather to want definitions and limits set to the evolving institution of collective bargaining.

The Conference adjourned with a feeling of deep disappointment on the part of many, and its members went out, many of them at least, to lead the bitter conflicts already starting. Nevertheless, agreement had been reached on long-run methods for making collective bargaining work, to an extent that was highly significant. While this Conference was unable at that late date to solve the extremely difficult problems that then faced labor, industry, and government over collective bargaining disputes, it stayed together until it had formulated substantial areas of agreement and clarified at least some of the issues on which there was basic conflict. All this showed a substantial change in climate since the 1919 conference, which broke up on the issue whether employees had a right to claim recognition of national unions as their bargaining representatives.[78] In 1919 management representatives after the failure of the conference began their big "open-shop" drive. In 1945, however, somewhat comparably, some of the management representatives said as they left that they were convinced of the need for legislation on certain points where no agreement had been reached. The failure of labor and management to reach agreement on many of these issues prepared the way for the 1947 legislation which was to impose new restrictions upon unions and upon collective bargaining itself, as well as for the bitter and paralyzing strikes which were already beginning.[79]

POSTWAR STRIKES

Almost immediately after the Conference adjourned, President Truman on December 3 sent a message to Congress asking for legislative provision for fact-finding with cooling-off periods in major disputes in key industries. Opposition developed immediately, both from the unions who objected to the cooling-off period, and from General Motors and others who objected to the right to subpoena "the books." A number of antistrike bills[80] were promptly introduced and received serious consideration as the trial by combat continued in the industrial field. But already without waiting for new legislative authority fact-finding panels had been appointed for the oil dispute and in the General Motors and the steel disputes, the latter two directly by the President.

The strikes themselves were of a sort to arouse extreme public interest and concern—large strikes in key industries affecting huge groups of employees and sometimes the consuming public very directly. On a smaller scale but with great emotional impact were strikes of public utilities, electric power, or local transportation systems. The effect is frequently not indicated at all adequately by the mere figures, limited to what happens in struck plants. In such con-

---

78. Cf. *supra*, ch. 1, p. 17.
79. For a more extensive and very valuable analysis of the Conference and its accomplishments and failures see Taylor, *op. cit.*, ch. 5.
80. *Infra*, ch. 9, pp. 356 ff.

spicuous strikes as those after V-J Day emotions are aroused also by much information and misinformation disseminated in the public press and over the radio. This was true in the case of the corporation-wide General Motors strike, which began before the November Labor-Management Conference adjourned; of the earlier coal strike of September–October over the organization of foremen; of the CIO Electrical Workers' strike against General Electric, General Motors, and Westinghouse; of the packing-house strike; of the nation-wide steel strike which began in January; and again of the bituminous coal strike starting in April. The coal strike ran into May, when the country-wide railway stoppage occurred because of refusal of the Trainmen and Engineers to accept a settlement agreed to by other unions. The General Motors strike led to chaos in the motor industry, partly because of relations between the large manufacturers and the smaller companies which supply parts. Worse still in its effects was the steel strike, which sooner or later interfered with industry after industry dependent upon steel for its raw materials. The coal strike which ran for several weeks caused short hours and layoffs in plant after plant and "dimouts" and "brownouts." This stoppage inevitably involved hundreds of thousands who were not on strike but were affected as consumers or as employees of other industries by its effects on transportation and industry generally. Though fortunately short, the stoppage by the Trainmen and Engineers halted practically all rail transportation throughout the country, and from the point of view of industry, employment, and the whole population, was, while it lasted, much worse than the Shopmen's strike of 1922.[81]

It must not be forgotten that during these months thousands of new agreements were being negotiated peacefully, most of them with wage increases. To what extent the failure to do the same in the basic industries meant that collective bargaining was made more difficult by a real challenge to union strength, and by answering resentment and resistance by the unions, no one can be sure. Without such an issue as to future power, even this difficult wage-price conflict might have been more quickly resolved. But in some of the major cases strikes could not, or would not, be settled until a national "wage pattern" was set and a new national wage-price policy established. The General Motors strike lasted 113 days, that of General Electric

81. Accounts of these strikes and their settlements are available in "Postwar Work Stoppages Caused by Labor-Management Disputes," *Monthly Labor Review*, 63 (1946), 872–92; "Wage Policy and the Role of Fact-finding Boards," *ibid.*, 62 (1946), 537–49.

58 days, of Westinghouse 115 days. Unions considered their demands for wage increases to maintain take-home pay, as well as other issues involved, worth fighting for, and their wartime treasuries were well enough stocked to make a fight possible. Many corporations stood on principle in refusing increases of the extent demanded until price relief was available. Moreover, they could offset losses to some extent by refunds from the Treasury on portions of their wartime excess profits taxes.

The "wage pattern" on which most of the strikes were settled was evolved from reports of fact-finding panels and the President's own intervention in the steel strike, but not until after the President on February 14, 1946, by Executive Order, permitted the National Wage Stabilization Board to approve any wage increases consistent with the "general pattern" of increases which had been established in the industry or area by that date, thus giving a basis for price relief. The major disputes were settled in the next month or two on approximately the same basis as the first one, in steel, with its 18½-cent wage increase and price relief. There was some skepticism about the awards of the various fact-finding panels, with suspicion of influence by persons in high places; and certainly there was too much expression of opinion by them while panel work was in process. In several cases the recommendations were rejected by one or the other party to a dispute. However, the rough formula arrived at, largely through government action, was regarded by many if not most men experienced in industrial relations as "about right." In any event, the pattern set by big industry exerted great influence on wage adjustments in other industries.

It was the coal and railroad strikes that put the final touches on the acute case of nerves from which the public and the government were suffering. The coal strike was settled on May 29, after the government took over the mines, by agreement between the Secretary of the Interior and the United Mine Workers for an 18½-cent increase and a 5-cent per ton levy for a health and welfare fund. Meantime, the railroad crisis had come and gone, during which President Truman had asked Congress for emergency legislation permitting him to take over an industry, providing for injunctions against strikes and for criminal penalties against union leaders for violating the provisions, for loss of seniority rights by strikers, and for drafting strikers. But the strike was settled almost simultaneously with the President's appearance before Congress on May 25. The President's proposed bill was passed immediately by the House, but on later consideration its drastic provisions were not approved by many. With this background, however, the Case Bill was revised and passed by both houses, although it failed to be carried over the President's veto on June 11. The President called for further study before permanent legislation. But the public agitation resulting from this wave of strikes had come very near to putting a hastily drawn and very drastic anti-strike bill on the lawbooks. Part of this bill was separately passed as the Hobbs Anti-racketeering Bill, directed against the Teamsters, and was signed by the President on July 3, 1946.

During the next twelve months strikes were at a somewhat lower level, but there were enough newsworthy strikes causing inconvenience to substantial groups of the public to keep the flames alive. As price control was emasculated and finally killed, prices rose and wage demands with them. Wage stabilization came to an end in November, 1946, and the "second round" of wage increases was for the most part achieved without major strikes. But there were maritime strikes in September and October; the coal strike of November in a dispute with the government which led to the injunction and the finding of Mr. Lewis and the United Mine Workers in contempt of court; a New York City trucking strike; a Pittsburgh light and power strike; and then in April, 1947, another coal stoppage; and in April–May the nation-wide telephone strike, with all its inconvenience to the public; and in June again a maritime strike and another coal walkout. Meantime, the election had brought in the new Congress, and the campaign for amendment of the laws and control of union activities had gone on. And June 23, 1947, saw the passage of the Taft-Hartley Act over the President's veto.

CONCLUSIONS

The industrial conflicts of the first year of reconversion played a major part in creating a climate in which the 1947 legislation could be accomplished. If, as we think, better long-range planning on the part of the Administration and Congress could have avoided the necessity of forging postwar wage-price policy in the heat of industrial battle, then we might have seen long-range legislation developed with less heat and anger and more real statesmanship. The administration's emergency proposals made little contribution toward a sound program. And back of that immediate situation which put the match to an inflammable mixture were the other factors which had prepared the fuel.

Actions by some unions had made all unions vulnerable to attack and aroused irritation, fear, and resentment; and the labor movement, unfortunately too little sensitive to public opinion about strikes and other union actions, was adamant against any revision of the Wagner Act and failed to propose solutions for problems on which the public was with some justice aroused against labor. The hostile press of course contributed. The public naturally assumes that the union is responsible for a strike, without inquiring whether management is in some cases equally or even more responsible because of failure to seek a reasonable basis of settlement. In addition, while the National Labor Relations Board had in reality met most of the reasonable criticisms by improving its administration, perhaps at some points going even too far in response to criticisms, the Administration had been slow to admit issues on which amendment of the NLRA was desirable. Administration, labor, and other supporters fought a defensive battle to preserve the Wagner Act, rather than by positive constructive proposals cutting some of the ground from under the feet of those who wanted legislation for other purposes. And much of the credit, if it be such, must go to the long, patient, persistent campaign for amendment and change of the national labor policy by groups who feared, resented, and fought the shift of power resulting from a strong union movement. It was a campaign astute in its effort to lead and remake public opinion, changing its line in some respects with changing conditions, but never losing sight of basic objectives. Its success was made possible by the events and conditions in the two years after V-J Day which aroused extreme resentment against labor.

In the name of equalizing the laws and protecting the public interest and free enterprise, rather than repealing the Act which had received an increasing amount of acceptance through the years, legislation was finally achieved which effectively revised the basic law of labor and the framework of collective bargaining. This revision included far more than the changes on which there was an objective case for new law. The extent to which it relieved antiunion employers from their obligations under the former law, and set unions back into an earlier type of restrictive environment, in addition to bringing government further than ever before into peacetime collective bargaining, would only become fully apparent when it had been tried out and tested in the courts, and if a time of less than full employment gave opportunity for its maximum use, should industry so choose, to weaken the union movement.

CHAPTER 9

THE BACKGROUND OF THE TAFT-HARTLEY ACT. II. STATE LEGISLATION AND ATTEMPTED LEGISLATION IN CONGRESS

DEVELOPMENTS IN THE STATES, 1937–47

BEFORE turning to the attempts in Congress from 1937 to 1947 to amend or drastically to change the national labor policy expressed in the Wagner Act, significant developments in the states must be noted.[1] The Wagner Act, "designed to give more nearly equal rights to management and to labor by limiting the activities of the former when they transgressed the rights of the latter,"[2] left to the common and statute law of the states matters of policing external relations of the unions or regulating their internal affairs, except in so far as the regulation of interstate commerce and the granting of restraining orders by federal courts were concerned. Yet the regulation of employers' "unfair labor practices" inevitably served as an invitation to regulate unions. Such regulation was proposed when the Wagner Act was under consideration in 1935 and was rejected then and on several occasions later. But the factors which led to these proposals in Congress were operating in the states even more directly, and their effects were seen first in state legislation. The fights for restrictive legislation in various states affected also the congressional election campaigns and were carried over into Congress. The correlation between these campaigns in the states and in Congress was marked, and success in the states helped then to bring results in Washington.

1. Much of the material here appeared first in H. A. Millis and H. A. Katz, "A Decade of State Labor Legislation: 1937–47," *University of Chicago Law Review*, 15 (1948), 282–310, and in H. A. Millis and R. E. Montgomery, *Organized Labor* (New York: McGraw-Hill Book Co., 1945), pp. 533–35, 547–54, 616–20.
2. Millis and Katz, *op. cit.*, p. 282.

The Background of the Taft-Hartley Act

With the main features of the Wagner Act declared constitutional and New Deal philosophy not yet worn thin, it was expected in 1937 that many states would adopt similar legislation, but only five did so in that year. They were New York, Wisconsin, Massachusetts, Pennsylvania, and Utah. The trend of state legislation in the decade following, contrary to what was expected, was chiefly one of increasing efforts to regulate unions in various respects, while at the same time weakening or omitting protective features found in the National Labor Relations Act. In addition, the new legislation frequently provided for the establishment of new or further machinery for the conciliation and settlement of industrial disputes. The years 1938 and 1939 saw attempts on the Pacific Coast to restrict union activities through local antipicketing ordinances and drastic state laws limiting strikes and picketing sponsored by open-shop associations. And in four states in 1939, the year when the first serious attempt to amend the Wagner Act got under way, omnibus labor relations acts were passed which imposed restrictions upon unions as well as upon employers. Wisconsin and Pennsylvania amended or replaced their "Baby Wagner Acts" by this new type of "equalizing law," and new laws were adopted by Michigan and Minnesota. In 1941 Rhode Island put itself on the list of states with "Baby Wagner Acts," and there was only a little restrictive legislation in other states. But by 1943 resentment against the Wagner Act and the growth of union strength accompanying the wartime growth of industry, especially in the South and Southwest, brought an active campaign for restrictions upon unions; and in that year a total of twelve states wrote into their laws restrictions, many of them drastic, upon union activities. The new laws in the South and West were for the most part simply restrictions upon unions without correlative obligations upon employers. Colorado, however, wrote a comprehensive labor relations law of the "equalizing" sort. The Kansas law, primarily restrictive of labor, included a few unfair labor practices of employers but did not establish any administrative agency to enforce the law. In addition, the drive to outlaw the closed shop put through "right-to-work" constitutional amendments in two states, Arkansas and Florida, in 1944, a statute in South Dakota in 1945, and constitutional amendments in Arizona, Nebraska, and South Dakota in 1946. In 1945 one more industrial state, Connecticut, adopted a "Baby Wagner Act," while a handful of states tightened existing restrictions upon unions or adopted new laws. And in 1947 the active drive for such restrictive legislation, spearheaded by the National Association of Manufac-

317

turers and the Chamber of Commerce,[3] as we have seen, bore fruit in a flood of legislation adding further restrictions upon union activity in some thirty of the states.

There is no need here to analyze this state legislation in great detail. Its significance for present purposes is how it reflected the problems and pressures which finally brought revision of federal labor policy, and how it contributed to the development of the new policy. Much of what appeared finally in the Labor Management Relations Act of 1947 had already been written into the law of various states, as well as having long been on the program, more or less specific at different dates, of the National Association of Manufacturers and other employer associations.

LABOR RELATIONS ACTS, 1937 AND 1939

The "Baby Wagner Acts" as adopted originally in 1937 in five states, and in 1941 and 1945 by two other industrial states, differed in relatively few and unsubstantial respects from the federal pattern.[4] All these laws were procedurally of the administrative type, with "preliminary investigation by state employees, the encouragement of settlements between the parties consistent with the policies of the acts, the winnowing out of weak or frivolous cases which might otherwise be pressed to hearing by over-zealous private litigants, the elimination of protracted hearings wherever possible, and the evolution of a unified governmental policy on labor relations."[5] By 1947 only New York, of the original group, with Rhode Island and Connecticut, still had laws of the Wagner Act type, limited to the protection of labor's right to organize against interference by employers. The others had all replaced or amended their laws by the addition of restrictions upon "unfair labor practices" of employees and unions.

The second chapter in labor relations legislation began to be written in 1938. Among the earlier rumblings against a liberal labor policy were those on the Pacific Coast, and especially in California, where the articulate organized fruit growers and processors and the open-

---

3. *Supra,* ch. 8.

4. The New York and Wisconsin acts made it an unfair labor practice by discrimination "to encourage membership in any company union," thus apparently leaving the employer free to encourage membership in a bona fide labor organization. The New York Act limited the Board's discretion by requiring it to find craft units appropriate for collective bargaining when the majority of the employees of a craft so desired.

5. Paul M. Herzog, "The Labor Relations Acts of the States," *Annals of the American Academy of Political and Social Science,* 224 (1942), 22.

shop associations sought city and county ordinances and state legislation as well as amendment of the Wagner Act.[6] Drastic ordinances
to control picketing were enacted in such places as Los Angeles and
the county of Shasta, only to be declared invalid.[7] Attempts were
made also in the three Pacific states to secure adoption by popular
vote of highly restrictive laws based more or less directly on the Los
Angeles restrictive picketing ordinance. All these states had been torn
by controversies "incidental to the attempts of workers to organize,
by the awkward and questionable activities of newly established
unions, by the activities of alleged racketeers, by the stopping off of
work by unions contesting for power, by hostile employers' associations not at all inclined to share power with labor or to observe in
good faith the National Labor Relations Act, and by farmers angered
by labor activities of almost any kind."[8] The referendum votes in
California and Washington failed, but Oregon in November, 1938,
adopted by substantial majority an extremely restrictive measure.
It outlawed all strikes, picketing, and boycotting except in disputes
directly relating to wages, hours, and working conditions where a
majority of the employees of an employer were involved. Any interference with transportation, manufacturing, processing, and marketing of agricultural and other products was made unlawful. The courts
were given a free hand in restraining any such activities. The acts
prohibited were also punishable as misdemeanors. There were limitations also on union dues. No limitations were put on management
activities. This Act was promptly invalidated in 1940 by the Oregon
Supreme Court in a five-to-one decision.[9] But during its brief life
it had considerable effect in hampering the activities of labor organizations and weakening their bargaining position.[10] Moreover, it was
more or less influential in shaping labor legislation in other states,
especially in 1939.

Four industrial states in 1939 adopted the policy of imposing restraints upon both employers and unions. In Wisconsin the La Fol-

6. For details on the drive on the Pacific Coast see U.S. Senate, Committee on
Education and Labor, *Violations of Free Speech and Rights of Labor, The Organization of Resistance to Collective Bargaining in California, 1935–39*, Report No.
398, Pt. 1, 78th Cong., 1st Sess., 1943, esp. pp. 771–75.

7. People v. Gidaly, Superior Court of Los Angeles, July 18, 1939; Carlson v.
California, 310 U.S. 106 (1940).

8. From H. A. Millis and R. E. Montgomery, *Organized Labor* (1945), p. 617.
Courtesy of McGraw-Hill Book Co.

9. AFL v. Bain, 106 P. 2d 544 (1940).

10. For a discussion of its operations and effects see Herbert Harris, *Labor's
Civil War* (New York: A. A. Knopf, 1940), pp. 215 ff.

lette period was at an end, and farmers were in revolt against its policies. There had been serious strikes which disturbed the public. The 1939 legislature repealed the Labor Relations Act and adopted in its stead an Employment Peace Act. Pennsylvania, also, the scene of bitter conflicts during the adjustments necessary to the new national labor policy, drastically amended its Labor Relations Act. Michigan and Minnesota approached the problems differently. They both had seen bitter and violent strikes and now adopted measures which emphasized the conciliation and mediation of disputes, with notice and waiting period before strikes, but included also prohibition of certain unfair labor practices on the part of both employers and labor. Wisconsin and Pennsylvania modified enforcement of their acts by making the boards essentially courts of first resort to hear charges rather than administrative agencies which investigate and attempt to obtain voluntary settlements. Prevention of violations became matters of private right rather than of public interest to be protected by an administrative agency. Michigan and Minnesota relied upon the courts for the prevention of unfair labor practices, the former by making violations misdemeanors, and the latter by providing injunctive relief. Representation procedures were included, except in Michigan, with the employer having the right to petition for an election, and craft units mandatory if a majority of the craft so desired.

The protection of labor against unfair labor practices by employers in these states was somewhat diluted. Thus Wisconsin eliminated the word "interference" from its list of banned activities by employers. Wisconsin and Minnesota denied the benefits of their acts to anyone violating their provisions, and Pennsylvania provided that unfair labor practices by the opposing party should be a complete defense to a complaint against one of them. Wisconsin and Minnesota specified what was always implicit—the right to refrain from concerted activities.

The limitations placed upon labor activities under the name of unfair labor practices were rather extensive. With differences among the states, they included such prohibitions as that of coercion or intimidation of workers in connection with their right to join or refuse to join a union; coercion of an employer to violate the law, as by a strike against a certified union; picketing or boycotting except when a strike had been called by a majority of the employees concerned, or after following the required procedures set up in Minnesota and Michigan; mass picketing; sit-down strikes; secondary boycotts; and, in Wisconsin, strikes in violation of an agreement. Wisconsin also limited closed-shop agreements by requring a three-fourths vote of the employees in the unit. Thus in two industrial states the little Wagner Acts had been modified and "equalized," while two others had enacted measures which likewise provided only a somewhat diluted version of protection of the "right" of workers to organize when they so desired. All these measures were designed to protect the "rights" of individual workers, farmers, creameries, employers, and the public quite as much as, if not more than, the right of employees to organize.[11] In addition, Wisconsin and Pennsylvania amended their anti-injunction laws to relax somewhat the previous limitations on injunctions in labor disputes. Only two states, Connecticut and New Mexico, passed new legislation limiting such injunctions.

1941 AND 1942

The next two years saw only a little industrial relations legislation, but some of it showed which way the wind was blowing. In 1941 Rhode Island adopted a Labor Relations Act of the Wagner type, and New Jersey adopted an anti-injunction law and established a State Mediation Board. North Carolina also established a conciliation service. But Texas passed a very drastic antipicketing law—known as an "antiviolence" law—making it a felony for anyone by force or violence or threat to attempt to prevent any person from engaging in any lawful occupation, or to assemble near a place where a labor dispute existed and attempt to prevent persons from working. California passed its Hot Cargo Act, subject to referendum vote in 1942, prohibiting secondary boycotts or refusal to handle "hot cargo."[12] Maryland prohibited sit-down strikes; Georgia required thirty days' notice to the employer before a strike except in seasonal industries; Minnesota among other amendments added violation of contracts by employee or employer to its list of unfair labor practices. Colorado re-enacted provisions of its 1915 law making strikes in industries affected with a public interest unlawful until after investigation by the Industrial Commission. Arkansas required persons soliciting advertising for labor publications to post a $5,000 bond to assure that they would perform any contracts entered into; this was supposedly

11. For more detailed summaries of this legislation, Millis and Montgomery, *op. cit.*, pp. 547–53; Millis and Katz, *op cit.*, pp. 285–90.

12. The Act was adopted by referendum, but finally in 1947 the "hot cargo" provision was held unconstitutional by the California Supreme Court. *Ex parte* Blaney, 184 P. 2d 892 (1947).

for the protection of those who deal with the labor press, but no other group was similarly protected.[13] The political and industrial climate of the southern and southwestern states which adopted most of these new restrictions showed the desire to encourage their expanding industry, including "runaway plants" from the North, by maintaining freedom from unionism so far as possible.

In 1942 only a few legislatures were in session, and the country was preoccupied by war problems. State Labor Relations Acts were amended in New York to permit petitions by employers, as in Wisconsin, Minnesota, and Pennsylvania; and in Rhode Island an amendment permitted court review of certifications as well as of cease-and-desist orders. Mississippi adopted an antipicketing statute similar to that adopted in Texas a year earlier, with its drastic limitations and its provision for punishment of violations as felonies.

1943 AND THE CAMPAIGN IN THE SOUTH AND SOUTHWEST

The year 1943 was more prolific of state labor legislation than any other year to that time. Proposals for union regulation were introduced in nearly all the state legislatures, and twelve states passed new statutes or amended existing ones in this field. By this time the great wartime expansion of industry into the South and Southwest, as well as into the nonindustrial hinterland of other states, and with it the increase in union organization and actual and impending extension of collective bargaining, brought to new activity the latent forces of opposition to the policy of permitting or even protecting union activities. Unreasonable use of the new power of some unions contributed to the basic opposition of those who feared expansion of unionization as a threat to the desired industrialization of their states or localities or to the power of management. Many unfair labor practice cases filed with the National Labor Relations Board attested to the fact that the expansion of unionism was not accepted without stiff opposition in many quarters. Frequently farmers joined with business in efforts to stop the "menace." The wartime strikes which brought demands for antistrike legislation in Congress increased the pressures in many states for restrictive legislation. And in many areas state, local, and sectional associations participated actively in the drive to put such legislation on the books. Some of those which had been described by the La Follette Committee in its study of California a little earlier were still active, especially in southern Cali-

13. U.S. Department of Labor, Division of Labor Standards, *Digest of State and Federal Legislation, 1940–41,* Bulletin No. 48.

fornia,[14] and there were others with headquarters in the North whose propaganda efforts were far-reaching. While little specific information is available, the evidence suggests the influence of organizations working across state lines and promoting certain types of bills. Thus the Texas laws served as a model for attempted legislation in many other southern states. Registration bills of the Texas type were introduced in at least fifteen states in 1943. Its 1941 model "antiviolence" law, which was adopted in Mississippi in 1942, was enacted in Arkansas and incorporated into the law enacted in Alabama in 1943. This bill, sponsored by the "American Christian Association" with headquarters in Houston, Texas, had been introduced in at least eight other legislatures where it was defeated that year.[15]

It was significant that most of the regulatory legislation of this year came not from the great industrial states of the East and Middle West but from the heretofore nonindustrial areas of the nation. The legislation was only incidentally, if at all, protective of labor's rights. Principally the acts imposed limitations on the right to organize and function through unions and to conduct union affairs without undue outside interference. And in 1943 for the first time extensive regulation of the internal affairs of unions was established in a number of states, along with restrictions upon unions' external activities.[16]

The most comprehensive statute was that of Colorado, modeled largely after the Wisconsin Employment Peace Act. It declared the right of employees to organize or to refrain from so doing. It included both a list of unfair labor practices of employers and a longer list directed against activities of employees. Engaging in a "slow-down" or requiring a "stand-by" not needed by the employer were additions to the proscribed activities of employees. A three-fourths vote was

14. Cf. *supra*, ch. 8, pp. 283–86, esp. nn. 18 and 21.

15. *Monthly Labor Review*, 56 (1943), 941–42; Victor H. Bernstein, "The Anti-labor Front," *Antioch Review*, 3 (1943), 328–40. The so-called "Women of the Pacific," organized in 1938 with headquarters in Los Angeles, was mentioned the next year as active in the California drive for anti-closed-shop and other restrictive legislation, along with the Associated Farmers and other organizations. At that time, however, the move was opposed by the State Chamber of Commerce and the San Francisco Employers' Council as one that threatened to cause disunity in wartime. *New York Times*, September 17, 1944; December 27, 1944. The "Women of the Pacific" were still functioning in 1947, when they published a pamphlet, *Workers! Do You Know Your New Rights under the Taft-Hartley Law?*

16. For summaries of the legislation see U.S. Department of Labor, Division of Labor Standards, *Digest of State and Federal Labor Legislation, 1942–1943*, Bulletin No. 63; cf. also E. Merrick Dodd, "Some State Legislatures Go To War— on Labor Unions," *Iowa Law Review*, 29 (1944), 148–74.

required for an all-union agreement. Failing to give thirty days' notice of a strike if agricultural products were involved, or twenty days' in other cases, also was proscribed. This was of course a continuation of the Colorado system adopted in 1915 of a required waiting period and an investigation and attempt to settle an industrial dispute by the Industrial Commission. In addition, the Act put many requirements on unions: compulsory incorporation with the right to sue or be sued, reasonable dues, annual examination of union books by the Commission, detailed financial reports to members, provision for secret ballot on important matters, majority vote by secret ballot before a strike could be called, and no use of funds for political purposes.[17] Charges of violation were to be heard by the Industrial Commission, as in the Wisconsin and Pennsylvania acts, but violations were also misdemeanors and subject to injunctive relief.

Another sweeping law was that of Kansas. Its list of unfair labor practices of employers was extremely limited, there was no provision for a board to administer the Act, and its list of unfair labor practices by employees was the most extensive of any state; it was therefore primarily a restrictive law directed at labor organizations. As in Colorado, the right to refrain from organization was stated. Union business agents were required to be licensed by the state, and unions were required to file certain documents, including financial reports, with the secretary of state. Violations were punishable as misdemeanors, and the license of any business agent violating the Act could be revoked by the court. A Federal District Court in 1945, however, found unconstitutional the provisions banning jurisdictional strikes and refusal to work on nonunion goods and requiring licensing of business agents.[18]

Minnesota, which in 1939 had pioneered with Wisconsin in regulating union methods, adopted a "Labor Union Democracy Act," regulating union elections and requiring unions to make financial reports to their members. It also amended its 1939 statute by outlawing jurisdictional strikes, such disputes to be settled where necessary by a referee appointed by the governor, and made any strikes without the required notice or without a secret vote of a majority of the employees voting, or in violation of an agreement, unfair labor practices. It was also made an unfair labor practice to interfere with the production, marketing, or processing of agricultural products. Other states adopt-

17. The provisions regulating internal affairs of unions were, however, invalidated when the related compulsory incorporation provision was held unconstitutional by the state supreme court. AFL v. Reilly, 155 P. 2d 145 (1944).
18. Stapleton v. Mitchell, 60 F. Supp. 51 (1945).

ing more extensive regulation of union internal affairs were Florida, Texas, and Alabama. Texas required all union organizers, and Florida all business agents, to obtain a card or license from the state. Texas and Alabama required the filing with the state of certain information, including financial reports. Texas also regulated union elections, controlled expulsions of union members, and limited union fees; and it banned political contributions by unions. Heavy penalties were provided as well as enforcement by injunctions. Alabama prohibited fees for work permits, political contributions, strikes without majority vote, and refusal to work on nonunion materials.[19] It prohibited also inclusion of executive, supervisory, or professional employees in a union including other employees. Violations were made subject to fine or imprisonment or both. Florida included many of the unfair labor practices found in the Kansas statute, but none directed against employers. It banned jurisdictional strikes, strikes without majority vote, secondary boycotts, mass picketing, and picketing beyond the area of the industry in which the dispute arose. Violations were made felonies. An anti-closed-shop amendment to the state constitution was to be submitted to the voters. The drastic "antiviolence" provisions adopted by Alabama and Arkansas, on the Texas model, have been mentioned above. Massachusetts, also, added its first restriction upon unions by prohibiting the requirement of fees for work permits. Pennsylvania banned political contributions by any corporation or unincorporated association.

The constitutionality of much of this body of regulation of union affairs was of course questionable. Courts invalidated the restrictions upon certain union methods in the statutes of California, Colorado, Kansas, and Oregon, in whole or in part.[20] The Supreme Court in 1945 found the Texas "identification card" provision unconstitutional when it was applied to a speech for the solicitation of union members.[21] It found the Florida licensing requirement invalid, also, as in conflict with the National Labor Relations Act.[22] Certain other provisions of the acts in Texas and Alabama were invalidated by state courts.[23]

19. It appeared to forbid union-security agreements, also, but a 1947 decision of the Alabama Supreme Court held otherwise. Hotel and Restaurant Employees International Alliance v. Greenwood, 30 So. 2d 696 (Ala., 1947), cert. den., 332 U.S. 847 (1948).
20. *Supra,* nn. 12, 17, 18.
21. Thomas v. Collins, 323 U.S. 516 (1945).
22. Hill v. Florida, 325 U.S. 538 (1945).
23. AFL v. Mann, 188 S.W. 2d 276 (1945), in the Court of Civil Appeals of Texas; Alabama State Federation of Labor v. McAdory *et al.*, 18 So. 2d 810 (Ala. Sup. Ct., 1944).

Fears by agricultural interests in several states brought also the enactment of statutes designed to protect agriculture from interference by unions. Idaho prohibited secondary boycotts where applied to agricultural products, banned picketing of agricultural premises or the entry upon such premises by union agents without the consent of the owner, and required complete financial statements to be filed annually by all unions with the secretary of state. Violation was made a misdemeanor. A similar law was adopted in South Dakota. Both of these were held unconstitutional in whole or in part.[24] Minnesota also added to its laws provisions designed to prevent interference with the transportation of agricultural products, and Michigan adopted a somewhat similar provision affecting both farm and commercial products.

Thus the 1943 state legislation, especially the very drastic regulations and restrictions imposed by six southern and southwestern states, gave a preview of the types of restriction on labor desired by many articulate groups in industry and agriculture. As Professor Dodd has said:

> Many of the new statutory provisions are unmistakable signs of the deep cleavage which exists between labor unionists and other elements in the population with respect to the legitimate functions of labor organizations and the extent to which they should be permitted to operate as self-governing bodies. . . . Many of the provisions . . . will inevitably be regarded by organized labor as a whole and not merely by its leaders as war legislation in a very sinister sense—legislative declaration of war against unions.[25]

The unions were worried but not yet sufficiently to establish a united and effective counteroffensive.[26]

THE POSTWAR DRIVE: ANTI-CLOSED-SHOP AND OTHER RESTRICTIONS

The last two years of the war saw relatively little further restrictive or regulatory legislation in the states, although the drive for "right-to-work" or anti-closed-shop legislation continued and made some headway in the South and West. Florida and Arkansas banned the closed shop by constitutional amendment in 1944, as did South Dakota by law in 1945 and by constitutional amendment in 1946. In the latter year also Arizona and Nebraska adopted constitutional

24. AFL v. Michelson, 9 CCH Lab. Cas. 67,064 (1944); AFL v. Langley, 168 P. 2d 831 (1946).
25. Dodd, *op. cit.*, p. 174.
26. Cf. the account of an attempt to set up a "legislative coalition" by the AFL, CIO, and railroad brotherhoods in February, 1943. *New York Times*, February 6, 1943.

amendments against the closed shop. "Right-to-work" proposals, banning virtually every type of union-security agreements, were introduced in almost identical form in at least eleven legislatures in 1945. But the major success was not to be achieved until 1947. Minnesota in 1945 amended its labor relations law to prohibit any strike, boycott, or picketing designed to interfere with the right of a certified representative to function during the effective period of the certification. Wisconsin reduced to two-thirds the vote required to authorize an all-union agreement. But Connecticut, contrary to the trend in state legislation, enacted a Labor Relations Act of the Wagner Act type.[27] The New York and New Jersey acts of 1945 forbidding discrimination in employment based on race, creed, or color, and providing for enforcement, should also be mentioned. In 1946 Massachusetts and in 1947 Connecticut also adopted fair employment practice laws with teeth.

In 1946 only eleven states held regular legislative sessions, but restrictive legislation was adopted in several.[28] The "right-to-work" constitutional amendments in three states have already been noted. Resentment at the postwar strikes helped to bring new restrictions in some of the states. Louisiana and Virginia joined the list of southern states with restrictive laws. Louisiana prohibited "wildcat" strikes in violation of collective agreements, sit-downs, and violence, force or threats around a plant in connection with a labor dispute, thus apparently banning mass picketing. It also made unlawful a conspiracy in restraint of trade between management and a union. Violations were made misdemeanors as well as subject to injunctive restraint. Virginia banned mass picketing, "stranger" picketing, the use of force or intimidation, and any interference with the right of another to work. Violations were a misdemeanor. New Jersey added to its Mediation Act the provision that the governor might seize and operate any public utility where one of the parties to a dispute refused to accept the recommendations of a fact-finding panel appointed by the Mediation Board. And in Massachusetts, following a popular referendum,[29]

27. U.S. Department of Labor, Division of Labor Standards, *Digest of State and Federal Labor Legislation, 1943–44,* Bulletin No. 71; *1944–45,* Bulletin No. 75.
28. "State Labor Legislation in 1946," *Monthly Labor Review,* 63 (1946), 754–59.
29. Cf. Commonwealth of Massachusetts, *Report of the Governor's Labor-Management Committee,* House of Representatives No. 1875, March 18, 1947. The Committee included representatives of labor, management, and the public. Following the referendum it made proposals as to what limited information

a law was enacted requiring unions to file annual statements showing names and addresses and salaries of all officers, their scale of dues, the dues and other amounts charged members, and receipts and expenditures.

In 1947 came the real flood of state legislation restricting union activities. Postwar conflicts had aroused resentment and set the stage for the successful drive for legislation.[30] The campaigns of the National Association of Manufacturers and the United States Chamber of Commerce, with their affiliated associations and others in all parts of the country, rose to a climax.[31] And the harvest came in "equalizing" or more often merely restrictive legislation in at least thirty states, as well as in the federal Labor Management Relations Act of 1947.[32]

The most comprehensive enactment was the Delaware Union Regulation Law, including one of the most extensive lists of unfair labor practices of employees; it made closed-shop agreements contrary to public policy and unenforceable, made any interference with "the right to work" unlawful, and made strikes unlawful except after a majority vote; political contributions by unions were banned. In addition, unions were required to register and file annual financial reports and came under regulation as to their fees and elections. Injunctions, damage suits, and penalties of fine or imprisonment were provided for enforcement.

Two of the original states with "Little Wagner Acts" in 1947 added unfair labor practices of employees to their statutes. Massachusetts banned interference by employees with the right of employees to choose or reject representatives for collective bargaining, and strikes or boycotts to induce the commission of an unfair labor practice. It also declared the obligation of a recognized union to bargain collectively. Utah specified several unfair labor practices of employees, including intimidation, sit-down strikes, picketing in the absence of a majority strike vote, and secondary boycotts. Pennsylvania also tightened its prohibition of interference with employees in their choice as to joining or refraining from joining a union or their choice of representative.

---

should be required in the annual statements to be filed. Substantial sections of the report are reprinted in *Industrial and Labor Relations Review*, 1 (1947), 110–28.

30. *Supra*, ch. 8, pp. 311–14.

31. *Ibid.*, pp. 287–91.

32. "State Labor Legislation in 1947," *Monthly Labor Review*, 65 (1947), 277–84.

Anti-closed-shop legislation was the type occurring most frequently in 1947. Twelve states, four of which already had constitutional amendments, prohibited closed shops, or in most cases any other type of union-security agreement; three others limited them in one or another way, and New Mexico proposed a constitutional amendment to be voted on at the next election. Twelve states imposed further limitations upon picketing or other strike activity; eleven prohibited secondary boycotts; six restricted jurisdictional disputes; eleven states provided for the regulation of disputes in public utilities; seven states banned strikes of public employees. Delaware, New Hampshire, and North Dakota required registration and the filing of financial reports by unions.

It was significant that the major part of this legislation in 1947 still came from the South and Southwest, and from the largely agricultural states of the Midwest and Far West. Restrictions upon strikes by public or public utility employees, however, came in four northern states—New York, New Jersey, Ohio, and Indiana. And greater or less restrictions upon union activities were added in Delaware, Massachusetts, Connecticut, Pennsylvania, and Michigan, as well as in Maine and New Hampshire.

SUMMARY

In summary, by the fall of 1947 state legislation on industrial relations and the rights and obligations of employers or employees, or both, on major points was about as follows:[33] Comprehensive labor relations acts of the Wagner Act type, protecting the right of labor to organize and putting obligations explicitly only upon employers, were to be found in only three states, New York, Rhode Island, and Connecticut. Seven other states had to a greater or less extent included unfair labor practices of employees or unions, in an "equalizing" law; these were Colorado, Massachusetts, Michigan, Minnesota, Pennsylvania, Utah, Wisconsin. Four others—Alabama, Delaware, Florida, and Kansas—had extensive lists of unfair labor practices of labor, the last with some quite limited restrictions also upon employers. Closed shops, and usually all other types of union-security agreements, were banned by constitutional amendment or statute or both in thirteen

33. The count of major types of legislation follows Millis and Katz, *op. cit.*, with a few additions as checked from other sources, especially Charles C. Killingsworth, *State Labor Relations Acts* (Chicago: University of Chicago Press, 1948), Appendix A, and E. Merrick Dodd, "Trends in State Legislation Relating to Unions," *Proceedings of New York University First Annual Conference on Labor* (Albany: Mathew Bender & Co., 1948), pp. 497–535.

states,[34] all of them predominantly agrarian, nonindustrialized states with relatively little experience with collective bargaining or union-security provisions. Four others—Colorado, Kansas, New Hampshire, and Wisconsin—permitted such agreements only after vote of the employees; three—Delaware, Louisiana, and Maryland—declared them, as well as nonunion contracts, against public policy and so unenforceable, while Nevada made both types unlawful; and six states provided some measure of protection against unreasonable expulsion or refusal of membership in unions with union-security contracts.[35] Check-off arrangements were controlled by nine states;[36] work permit fees were banned by eleven states.[37]

Although the Supreme Court in cases involving antipicketing statutes and ordinances had held that picketing is protected as a form of free speech,[38] many states continued efforts to restrict picketing and boycotts. Some of these as we have shown above had already been invalidated. While the validity of the entire body of such restrictions continued to be in doubt, the statutes remained on the books as threats and sometimes actual weapons used against union use of economic power. At least eighteen states[39] by 1947 banned intimidation of nonunion workers, ten of them by the drastic antiviolence laws of the South and Southwest. Mass picketing was specifically banned in thirteen states.[40] Five states permitted picketing only if a majority of the employees had voted for a strike;[41] these and seven others[42] made strikes themselves illegal in the absence of such a vote. Secondary boycotts were banned in more or less sweeping fashion in fourteen

34. By constitutional amendment in Arizona, Arkansas, Florida, Nebraska, South Dakota; New Mexico also had such an amendment to be voted on at the 1948 election; others by statute, Georgia, Iowa, Maine, North Carolina, North Dakota, Tennessee, Texas, Virginia.

35. Colorado, Delaware, Massachusetts, New Hampshire, Pennsylvania, Wisconsin.

36. Arkansas, Colorado, Delaware, Georgia, Iowa, Pennsylvania, Rhode Island, Texas, Wisconsin.

37. Alabama, Delaware, Georgia, Iowa, Massachusetts, New Hampshire, New York, North Carolina, Tennessee, Texas, and Virginia.

38. Thornhill v. Alabama, 310 U.S. 88 (1940); Carlson v. California, 310 U.S. 106 (1940).

39. Alabama, Arkansas, Colorado, Delaware, Florida, Georgia, Kansas, Louisiana, Michigan, Minnesota, Mississippi, Nebraska, Pennsylvania, South Dakota, Texas, Utah, Virginia, Wisconsin.

40. Colorado, Delaware, Florida, Georgia, Kansas, Louisiana, Michigan, Minnesota, South Dakota, Texas, Utah, Virginia, Wisconsin.

41. Colorado, Delaware, North Dakota, Utah, Wisconsin.

42. Alabama, Florida, Kansas, Michigan, Minnesota, Missouri, Oregon.

states.[43] Strikes, picketing, or boycotts to upset valid certifications and induce violations of the labor relations laws were outlawed in six states—Colorado, Delaware, Massachusetts, Minnesota, Pennsylvania, and Wisconsin. Jurisdictional strikes were banned or subject to greater or less control in thirteen states.[44] Strikes in violation of contracts were either unfair labor practices or unlawful and subject to injunctions or damage suits in eleven states.[45] Strikes of public employees in addition were forbidden by eight states,[46] and in eleven[47] restrictions were imposed upon strikes in public utilities.

Regulation of the internal affairs of unions had gone less far than attempts at control of strikes and picketing and other methods used by labor organizations. Twelve states, however, had adopted requirements for registration and filing of certain information by unions.[48] Union elections were regulated by statutes adopted in Minnesota, Texas, and Delaware. Florida, Texas, and Kansas had required union agents to obtain a license, but each of these laws had been invalidated at least in part. Political contributions had been banned by five states—Alabama, Colorado, Delaware, Pennsylvania, and Texas—but in the first two the provisions had been invalidated.

It is not our purpose here to report on all details or to pass judgment on this body of state legislation regulating and restricting union activities in addition to the specific protection given in a minority of the states to labor's right to organize. Some of it, as in Massachusetts, was rather carefully designed to deal with real abuses and problems. Some of it was highly debatable in purpose, such as the sweeping prohibitions of union-security clauses. Some of it was of the sledgehammer sort meant to beat down effective methods of the use of economic power by unions. Some provisions had already been declared unconstitutional, and more would in all probability be invalidated. Much of it opened the way for an increase in intervention by the courts such

43. Alabama, California, Colorado, Delaware, Idaho, Iowa, Minnesota, Missouri, North Dakota, Oregon, Pennsylvania, Texas, Utah, Wisconsin.
44. California, Colorado, Delaware, Florida, Iowa, Kansas, Massachusetts, Michigan, Minnesota, Missouri, Oregon, Pennsylvania, Wisconsin.
45. California, Colorado, Delaware, Louisiana, Minnesota, Missouri, North Dakota, Pennsylvania, South Dakota, Texas, Wisconsin.
46. Michigan, Missouri, Nebraska, New York, Ohio, Pennsylvania, Texas, Virginia.
47. Florida, Indiana, Massachusetts, Michigan, Missouri, Nebraska, New Jersey, Pennsylvania, Texas, Virginia, Wisconsin. Minnesota prohibited strikes in any charitable hospital.
48. Alabama, Colorado, Delaware, Florida, Idaho, Kansas, Massachusetts, New Hampshire, North Dakota, South Dakota, Texas, Utah.

as had not been seen since the Norris–La Guardia Act set standards of judicial restraint in labor disputes. Only the test of experience would show the real effect of the legislation upon union strength and collective bargaining and upon political developments. The major significance for our present purposes is in how this history paralleled and influenced the efforts to obtain more or less similar enactments in Congress. At the end the developments in the states, even though the greater part of that experience came from the agricultural and semi-industrial states which were still in the early stages of the establishment of labor organization and collective bargaining, strengthened the hands of those who desired a comprehensive revision of federal labor policy.

DEVELOPMENTS IN CONGRESS, 1936–46[49]

Scarcely had the ink dried on the President's signature establishing the National Labor Relations Act as part of our national policy when bills to repeal or amend the Act began pouring into the congressional mill. Despite numerous proposals, only two major pieces of legislation substantially affecting national labor policy passed both houses of Congress between 1935 and the passage of the Labor Management Relations Act in June, 1947. The War Labor Disputes Act[50] became law in 1943 over the veto of President Roosevelt. While from the point of view of the Wagner Act it was restrictive, it did not approach either some of the earlier legislative proposals or the later Case Bill as far as fundamental changes and revisions in national labor policy were concerned. The Case Bill failed of passage over a presidential veto in June, 1946. One other bill of major importance was approved by the House, although it never came to a vote in the Senate. This was the Smith Bill passed by the House in 1940 after the preliminary report of the Smith Committee to investigate the NLRB.[51]

49. This section was written by Seymour Z. Mann.
50. 57 U.S. Stat. 163 (1943); *supra*, ch. 8, pp. 298–300; *infra*, pp. 354–56.
51. *Infra*, pp. 350–54, 360–62. Other bills pertaining to national labor policy which were acted upon in some manner during these years were as follows: an amendment to the Byrnes Anti-strikebreaking Act of 1936, Public Law 779, 75th Cong., 3d Sess., amending 40 U.S. Stat. 1899; S. 1970, the Oppressive Labor Practices Act, sponsored by Senators La Follette and Thomas (Utah), which passed the Senate, 76th Cong., 3d Sess.; H.R. 4139, reported from the Naval Affairs Committee, and providing for the investigation and mediation of disputes in naval construction, passed by the House, 77th Cong., 1st Sess.; the Lea Act (60 U.S. Stat. 89), April, 1946, banning royalty payments to the union in the making of phonograph records; H.R. 653, the Hobbs Bill, approved by the House, 78th Cong., 1st Sess., later included in the vetoed Case Bill, then separately passed

The Background of the Taft-Hartley Act

In the ten years covered by this analysis, 169 bills relating to national labor policy were introduced in Congress. If we add those introduced in the Eightieth Congress before the passage of Taft-Hartley, but excluding the original Taft proposal (S. 1126) and the original Hartley Bill (H.R. 3020), we find a total of 230 such bills introduced. If we consider also the more important of the resolutions which if acted upon could have resulted in policy changes, we find that between 1937 and 1947 more than 50 other legislative proposals could be added to this total.[52] It is extremely difficult to assess accurately the meaning of these sheer numbers. Some bills were omnibus measures that would have legislated on labor relations matters from A to Z. Others might contain only one specific proposal. And a further complication results from duplicate bills being introduced by the same or different congressmen, even during the same session of Congress. Nevertheless, this does constitute a significant number even for a Congress that often works in terms of tens of thousands of bills awaiting or praying for legislative action.

One is impressed in examining these legislative proposals with the

---

and signed as the Hobbs Act (60 U.S. Stat. 420), July, 1946, removing labor union exemption from the Federal Anti-racketeering Act; and H.R. 6578, 79th Cong., 2d Sess., passed by the House to meet the railroad emergency but not acted on by the Senate.

52. The information for this section was obtained as follows: The proposals we are concerned with include only those having a major impact on national labor policy. They do not include legislation on wages, hours, social security, etc. Also excluded are riders to appropriation legislation or other measures alluding only indirectly to labor relations matters. The primary sources of information used were the Index and Legislative History volumes of the *Congressional Record* for each session of Congress, the Digests prepared by the Legislative Reference Service of the U.S. Library of Congress, and copies of the bills and resolutions proposed.

The bills considered and the more important resolutions were classified into seven major categories. They dealt with proposals on: (1) NLRB procedure, organization, and jurisdiction; (2) problems of representation; (3) limitations upon the scope and procedures of collective bargaining; (4) unfair and oppressive labor practices; (5) limitation and regulation of self-help activities; (6) employer-union regulation and the imposition of legal obligations and responsibilities; and (7) the settlement of disputes. Anyone familiar with these matters realizes the impossibility of developing hard-and-fast categories for such a classification. There is much overlapping, and some classifications are undoubtedly arbitrary. In each of the bills or resolutions the specific suggestions contained were analyzed and classified. Many miscellaneous proposals were intentionally omitted from the tabular analyses. What follows, then, cannot be presumed to be statistically exact; enough materials were evaluated, however, to establish certain trends and conclusions.

fact that the attack upon the principles of the Wagner Act, and in essence this is what the largest portion of these proposals meant, was consistently conducted by a small minority continually harping on a few points. This minority was successful finally in winning enough people to their point of view to develop into a successful majority. It is obvious, when these legislative proposals are broken down into their component parts and classified, that all the major proposals put forward during the years were finally acted upon in some way in the revisions and additions to national labor policy contained in the Labor Management Relations Act of 1947.

1. *Problems of NLRB organization, procedure, and jurisdiction.*— A first major group of these proposals related to Board jurisdiction and power, or to the size, organization, and makeup of the Board, or its procedures. It was the Seventy-sixth Congress, in 1939–40, that was most preoccupied with these problems. During 1939 and 1940, also, Congress was concerned with charges of bias and unfairness on the part of the NLRB. Added momentum was given these charges by the raging dispute between the divided camps in the labor movement. The proposals advanced[53] ranged from reducing the jurisdiction of the Board to shearing it of its unfair labor practice duties. A large number of the bills would have excluded agricultural activities and supervisors and other persons from the application of the Wagner Act. Every proposal made on these matters in the Seventy-sixth Congress was repeated in substantially the same form during the three succeeding Congresses. At least fourteen bills introduced would have changed the size or organization of the Board, some going as far as the abolition of the Board and the creation of independent judicial and prosecuting agencies. Eleven would have limited the Board's discretion in the application of remedies. Such proposals appeared in every Congress from the Seventy-sixth through the Seventy-ninth. There were twenty-seven proposals as to unfair labor practice procedures, and thirty-one for revision of representation procedures. Again demonstrating the trend, well over half of both of these occurred during the Seventy-sixth Congress.

While the total number of proposals included here was large, they did not necessarily all differ from one another. Very often the suggestion made in the earliest Congress was sponsored over and over again in substantially the same form by the same congressman or group of congressmen. Four of Representative Hoffman's bills, for

53. More than 25 such proposals, contained in 18 major bills, were classified. At least 15 of these were advanced in 1939 and 1940.

example, introduced in each session from 1939 through 1946, were for all practical purposes duplicates of each other. These bills all contained similar provisions limiting the jurisdiction of the Board, requiring certain case procedures, restricting Board uses of personnel, or affecting the remedies to be applied by the Board. This constant repetition of proposals reflecting charges against the Board is quite typical of the kinds of legislation introduced during these ten years.

When we examine this legislative history from the point of view of what was finally enacted into law by Taft-Hartley, it can be seen that the most important of the proposals were legislated upon, although the most extreme changes suggested over the years did not find place in the congressionally approved 1947 legislation. Among important changes made by Taft-Hartley in this area, which had been proposed many times in the preceding ten years, were the separation of the judicial from the administrative and prosecuting functions, changes in the Act's provisions as to evidence and the scope of judicial review, exclusion of supervisors, and a number of changes in procedure and rules of decision. Proposals as to the position of Trial Examiners were largely handled by the Administrative Procedure Act.

2. *Problems of representation.*[54]—Again it can be said that the Seventy-sixth Congress more than any later one was concerned with these problems. This, too, resulted largely from the AFL-CIO split and the ensuing controversy over the craft-unit question. Almost half of the proposals in this area attempted to amend the Wagner Act to assure craft-unit representation where desired. One of the Burke bills introduced in 1939 would have eliminated completely the majority-rule provisions of the NLRA. Many kinds of bans were advanced on multi-employer or multi-plant units, as well as other requirements as to the representation units allowed. The craft-unit question was acted upon in the Taft-Hartley Act. Perhaps the Communist affidavit requirements of the 1947 Act, also, can be compared to the suggestions occasionally put forward to prohibit subversives from serving as bargaining representatives.

3. *Limitations upon the scope and procedures of collective bargaining.*[55]—Almost all the proposals analyzed here restricted collective bargaining in some manner. Some matters, the closed shop and others,

54. We exclude here any proposals already noted under procedural questions in representation matters. Eighteen major proposals are included here.
55. Such proposals were sponsored at least 40 times, in 28 major bills. This grouping is not all inclusive of collective bargaining matters since many issues relating to this topic were classified under union-employer regulations, or under limitations upon self-help activities.

were to be completely removed as proper subjects of collective bargaining. Other proposals removed the "bargaining" from collective bargaining by legally requiring the inclusion of certain provisions, such as specified procedures for the settlement of disputes, or adjustment boards for grievance controversies. Many of these restrictions placed unions under the antitrust laws by preventing their entering into contracts, conspiracies, or combinations having as their object some of the items banned, and making such actions subject to injunction.

The Seventy-ninth Congress, of 1945–46, led with the most specific proposals in this area. This was accounted for in part at least by the growing belief that inequality between unions and employers was then stacked in favor of the former. The large number of major disputes occurring in the postwar period added to the argument that something had to be done to curb union power. Such limitations could be accomplished in part through legislation affecting the scope of the collective bargaining process.

In the Taft-Hartley Act we find sections limiting collective bargaining in ways similar to those previously suggested. Among them were limitations on the closed shop and union shop, on the check-off, on royalty payments and welfare funds, the prohibition of featherbedding practices, and the sixty-day-notice requirement for terminating or modifying a contract.

4. *Unfair and oppressive labor practices.*—Here again many matters that could fall into this area have been classified elsewhere. An attempt has been made to distinguish between propositions referring to "unfair" labor practices and those referring to "unlawful" labor practices. The latter are in most cases treated under limitations on self-help activities. The Oppressive Labor Practices Bill introduced in every session of Congress since the early La Follette Committee made its report is placed here because of the similarity to activities designated as employers' unfair labor practices, although some of these practices would have been declared unlawful. Unfair labor practice proposals, found in twenty-one major bills, ran the whole gamut from the complete exclusion of unfair labor practices as subjects of national legislation to redefining small parts of them to benefit special groups. Most of the proposals attempted in some way to bring unions and employees under their purview. This was accomplished by making persons other than employers subject to the prohibitions against certain unfair labor practices under the Wagner Act; by adding special

prohibitions to apply to union and employee conduct; or by the creation of altogether new unfair labor practices to apply to unions, employers, and employees alike. Here too the greatest concern with proposals of this kind was in 1945 and 1946, reflecting the argument over union-employer equality which gained in momentum until the adoption of the Taft-Hartley Act. For the 1947 law legislated quite extensively in this area. Its list of unfair labor practices to apply particularly to labor organizations and their agents was typical of the bans suggested often during the preceding ten years.

Brief mention must be made of the Oppressive Labor Practices Act, first proposed in the Senate by La Follette and Thomas in the Seventy-sixth Congress, in 1939. It would have banned the use of strikebreakers, strikebreaking agencies, labor spies, the use of private guards armed with dangerous weapons, the use of industrial munitions during strikes, and the like. This was the result of one of the most intensive and extensive investigations ever conducted by any governmental agency, the La Follette Committee investigation on violations of free speech and the rights of labor, instituted pursuant to a resolution in the Seventy-fourth Congress and extended through 1943.[56] Aside from the original passage by the Senate in 1940, this bill never received further action other than being placed in the legislative hopper in both the Senate and the House. The treatment of such proposals demonstrates the changing attitudes prevalent in Congress after 1935. Occasionally bills in the spirit of the Wagner Act originated from the Senate. If they received favorable action there, they were usually not considered by the House. Bills contrary to the spirit of the Wagner Act occasionally received House approval or consideration. These were never able to get favorable, if any, attention by the Senate committee dealing with labor matters. The strongly supported bills for an Oppressive Labor Practices Act were consistently ignored, although a growing number of congressmen were ready to consider "restrictive" legislation with only superficial investigation.[57]

5. *Limitation and regulation of self-help activities.*—As would be

56. Senate Committee on Education and Labor, Subcommittee on Senate Resolution 266, Robert M. La Follette, Jr., Chairman. Measures referring to strikebreaking activities were included in the Byrnes Act and its later revisions. See *supra*, n. 51.

57. For discussion of the Smith Committee investigations, cf. *infra*, pp. 350–52; *supra*, ch. 2, pp. 49–50. Its methods were the subject of considerable criticism and controversy.

expected, most of the changes sought here[58] were limitations upon the concerted activities of labor groups. They ranged from flatly prohibiting strikes, as in one Hoffman measure,[59] to some minor procedural requirements that strikers had to meet before striking, as in several bills. In between there were proposals that dealt with every phase of every kind of concerted activities that unions or unorganized employees might undertake. A large number of these restrictions stemmed from bills dealing with procedures for the settlement of disputes, which included various kinds of cooling-off periods, strike ballots, notice requirements, and a host of other miscellaneous provisions. The defense and war period naturally brought forth many of them. Some of these were written into the law when the Smith-Connally War Labor Disputes Act received legislative sanction.[60] The total number of proposals was swelled also by demands for making strike participation treason.[61] Many restrictive measures meant to deal specifically with defense and war industrial activities were later introduced in practically their identical form, merely dropping all war or defense phraseology. The Smith Bill, H.R. 4875, introduced in the Seventy-ninth Congress, was a chief example. It had been introduced twice previously as a measure applying to the special defense and war situation.[62]

Among the more important proposals seeking to limit concerted activities was the oft-repeated attempt to revise the Norris–La Guardia Act and the Wagner Act by defining "labor dispute" so as to include only those who stood in proximate relationship of employee and employer. Such a limitation was included in at least seven of the bills examined. Outright repeal of the Norris–La Guardia Act was suggested by Senator Moore during the Seventy-ninth Congress.

These limitations and regulations on concerted activities fell mainly into two classes. There were first those that prohibited certain activities at the risk of losing rights and status under the NLRA as amended. Certain of these proposals would have prevented violators from receiving such federal benefits as social security or unemployment compensation. Second, there was a very large number of proposals re-

58. One hundred and seven important proposals contained in 62 major bills or resolutions were classified.
59. H.R. 1407, Seventy-seventh Congress.
60. See *infra*, pp. 354–56.
61. As in H.R. 4223, 5929, and 6057 in the Seventy-seventh Congress.
62. H.R. 6149, 77th Cong., 1st Sess., and H.R. 2124, 78th Cong., 1st Sess. Much of the latter measure of course was included as part of the War Labor Disputes Act.

stricting strikes, boycotts, picketing, and other activities by declaring them unlawful. In most cases jurisdiction over violation was given to the district courts, and the bulk of these activities previously protected by the Norris–La Guardia Act were to be opened to the injunction remedy. There were also many proposals relating to union security and to coercive activities, proposals regulating the use of property in self-help activities, and others. Self-help activities would also have been severely limited by numerous suggestions to make unions liable and suable for damages resulting from concerted activities or contract violations.[63]

Great preoccupation with these matters of limiting and regulating self-help activities is found in the Seventy-seventh and Seventy-ninth Congresses. This is probably explainable for the former, since such matters were assuming more importance as the defense period gained momentum. Moreover, 1941 was a record strike year. The attention given such matters in the Seventy-ninth Congress can be attributed to the postwar strikes and to the growing pressure to curb labor union power as the months of 1945 and 1946 progressed.

Many of the self-help limitations and regulations put into the legislative mill during this ten-year period were included in one form or another in the 1947 law. Organizational, jurisdictional, and sympathetic strikes, boycotts, picketing, contract violations, featherbedding, coercive, violent and destructive activities, Norris–La Guardia Act limitations, and others all received Taft-Hartley attention.

6. *Regulation of employers and unions; imposition of legal obligations and responsibilities.*—It was quite apparent that most of these legislative proposals were directed at unions. Only a few suggestions dealt with regulation of employers in regard to labor matters. Of course, much of the legislation was predicated on the idea that employers and businesses were already sufficiently controlled and circumscribed by adequate legal regulations and responsibilities. The argument most often advanced in favor of the type of union regulatory legislation here considered was based on the notion that unions and their activities were similar enough to ordinary business activities to bring them under the same kinds of legal requirements as those imposed on business and industry. Over one-fourth of these proposals[64] would have required union incorporation or registration of one kind or another. More than two-fifths of them attempted in some

63. These are classified in our next group. Such proposals were contained in 12 major bills.

64. More than 85 proposals were advanced in 50 significant bills or resolutions.

manner to regulate internal union affairs. Many of these called for specific kinds of election procedures within unions; some would have regulated details of dues and assessments; many would have specified who could serve as union officers; some would even have legislated concerning the internal decision-making processes of labor organizations. Many would have made unions liable and suable at civil law for damages resulting from concerted activities or contract violations. A number included prohibitions on political contributions and activities.

Pressure for such legislation mounted from 1937 to 1942. With the Seventy-eighth Congress it subsided considerably, probably because of our entrance into the war and the passage of the War Labor Disputes Act in 1943, which naturally acted to cut off further legislative proposals for a short while. But, as the postwar situation developed during the Seventy-ninth Congress, these matters received increasing attention. Such pressure passed over into the Eightieth Congress and came to a head with the inclusion in law of much of the essence of the proposals made over these ten years. The 1947 labor law included extensive requirements for registration and filing of certain documents by unions before they could use the facilities of the NLRB and imposed extensive legal obligations and responsibilities in the way of suability and liability for a variety of causes. A ban on political contributions and expenditures was included, as well as clauses removing in some ways protections unions had previously enjoyed against application of the antitrust laws.

7. *The settlement of disputes.*—Methods for the settlement of labor disputes were not within the province of any of the basic federal labor laws other than the Railway Labor Act. Although for many years the Department of Labor maintained its Conciliation Service, there was no legislation on mediation and conciliation procedures. There were many proposals, however, to limit strikes in some manner or to provide for their prompt settlement. Especially was this true for public utility disputes, or disputes in industries where stoppages could have serious repercussions on the health, safety, or vital interests of the nation. Most of the thirty-five important bills containing suggestions in this group provided for boards, panels, or tribunals for the settlement of various kinds of disputes in a variety of industries. They ranged from the suggestions offered as far back as the Seventy-fifth Congress to give mediation and conciliation functions to the NLRB to the setting-up of procedures similar to those of the Railway Labor Act for maritime labor. Steps to be used in the settling of disputes

ranged from mere legislative urging that mediation and conciliation facilities be first used to procedures to be followed in case strikes continued in plants or mines that had been seized by the government in order to prevent or end a work stoppage. In between such extremes were cooling-off or status quo provisions, conciliation and mediation, adjustment boards for disputes arising over contract interpretations, fact-finding, arbitration, and government operation. Under many of these proposals violators might have lost status under the NLRA, had their violations enjoined or restrained by the courts, or have been subjected to criminal penalties.

Understandably the greatest activity over measures of this kind occurred during 1945 and 1946. In the light of the peculiar postwar conditions,[65] the major work stoppages then occurring, the attitudes of business and the public, and the congressional political realignments, such concern in Congress is easily explained. While none of the extremes of these proposals were adopted, the most important of them are contained in Title II of the Taft-Hartley Act.

This ten-year survey shows the range and character of the legislative proposals that preceded the Taft-Hartley Act. Merely from a review of the subjects covered one can discern the pressures for amendatory legislation that were mounting during this period. An examination of other elements in the legislative background of the 1947 Act will give added meaning to these growing pressures.

PERSONS, PARTIES, AND REGIONS[66]

Personalities, parties, and regions are of interest in relation to this mass of labor legislation proposed from 1937 to April, 1947. For the 200-odd bills and resolutions analyzed there were some 100 senators and representatives who had assumed the responsibility for sponsoring such measures. This was not a one-man-one-bill affair. Some 66 representatives were responsible for the 161 major House measures introduced. Many bills were, of course, plurally sponsored, but credit was given for a bill or resolution to each man sponsoring the proposal. The variation between the number of sponsors and the number of bills offered is accounted for primarily by the activity of a few

65. *Supra,* ch. 8.
66. The ten-year legislative period for this chapter has covered the period from the opening of the Seventy-fifth Congress in 1937 to the opening of the Eightieth Congress in 1947. For this section we have extended the period to include the first four months of the Eightieth Congress so that measures proposed in the House before the introduction of the Hartley Bill and measures proposed in the Senate before the introduction of the Taft Bill could also be examined.

men. Representative Hoffman in the House with thirty-four bills to his credit is the extreme example. Smith of Virginia follows with nine. A few representatives had five or six bills to their credit. More than a score sponsored from two to four bills. It must be remembered, of course, that many of these were merely reintroductions of similar measures not acted upon earlier. Even some bills introduced in the same session by the same person were, for certain strategic reasons, duplicates of each other, or were parts of omnibus bills put into the hopper earlier during the session—if not on the same day. Yet the actual numbers of these proposals introduced serve as an index to the activity and concern exhibited over labor policy at any given session. Such raw numbers alone, also, give important clues to the intentions and motivations of the sponsoring congressmen, for it was not unusual to find very restrictive proposals, less restrictive proposals, and occasionally even nonrestrictive proposals offered by the same man at a single congressional session. What can one assume when one notes a bill which proposes to repeal the Wagner Act, offering no amended version or substitute version of a national labor law, accompanied or followed by various proposals to amend the Act in one fashion or another? Is it unfair to suppose that repeal would have been preferred to amendment had such repeal been possible?

Taking first all the legislation offered in the House, without any reference as to whether its over-all effect or intent were restrictive or nonrestrictive, well advised or ill advised from the point of view of policy expressed in the Wagner Act, the breakdown by party of proposed legislation was as follows: 40 Democratic representatives, 25 Republicans, and one Progressive participated in the sponsorship of these measures. Until the Eightieth Congress there was a Democratic majority in the House. When Republicans became the majority in the Eightieth Congress, there was a noticeable upturn in the number of Republicans participating in these proposals for labor legislation. When we exclude legislation, however, which could be considered as favorable to labor, or in the spirit of the NLRA, or bills for settlement of disputes with few regulatory or restrictive provisions, or those bills introduced at the behest of the President (especially during the Seventy-ninth Congress), we can exclude at least 11 Democrats from the original 40 participating. Of the 29 remaining Democratic representatives, at least 15 who can be termed southern Democrats were responsible for a large amount of the restrictive type of proposals. Turning to the 25 Republican representatives, over half had made no previous labor legislation proposals before 1945. Of this half only

2 had been in Congress at the time of the passage of the Wagner Act, while 4 other Republicans who had made such proposals had served continuously since 1935. More than one-half of the 25 did not enter Congress until 1943.

During the Seventy-ninth Congress in 1945 and 1946 and in the first four months of the Eightieth Congress in 1947 there were 73 bills related to labor policy introduced in the House. Republicans whose first legislative proposals on such matters came in 1945 or later were responsible for more than two-fifths of the 73 proposals. These measures, sponsored for the most part by delegates from northeastern states, could be classified as restrictive in nature. Some nine Democrats who had not previously sponsored any labor legislation put into the hopper during this period bills that were in some manner restrictive. These Democratic restrictive proposals represented less than one-fifth of the total of 73 bills, and most of these were introduced by southern representatives. Of all restrictive measures, then, introduced in the House during the Seventy-ninth Congress and the first months of the Eightieth Congress, more than three-fourths were introduced by Republican members; most of the remaining measures were sponsored by southern Democrats.

These figures corroborate general observation. The pressure for restrictive legislation in the House as it mounted came from the traditionally conservative regions and representatives: from the South, always Democratic and usually conservative on labor questions, and during this period vexed by the growth and challenge of unionism in the South stemming from the war and postwar period; and, second, from significant numbers of eastern and midwestern Republican representatives. Even without detailed analysis, when debate and committee work are considered as well as the activity of other members who did not directly sponsor legislation, these trends become even more patent.

Taking the over-all picture in the Senate, we find that for the 68 major proposals in the Senate in the ten years there were 33 senators involved. Democrats accounted for 17 of this total, Republicans for 15, and there was 1 Progressive. As in the House, there were also in the Senate plural sponsorships, repeated proposals, and inconsistent proposals. Fewer men, however, had large numbers of proposals to their credit, although Senator O'Daniel (D.) of Texas with 19 legislative proposals and Senator Ball (R.) of Minnesota with 8 stand out somewhat, considering that the total number of proposals in the Senate was of course less than in the House. The Senate accounted for only one-third of the total bills and resolutions. Excluding the nonrestrictive bills in the same way as in our discussion for the House, we can exclude at least 9 Democrats, 2 of whom were southern Democrats. There were a total then of 5 southerners among the 8 Democratic sponsors, of whom O'Daniel and Byrd loom large as supporters of restrictive labor measures. Members from the Republican side of the Senate, on the other hand, sponsored 38 measures here considered, all restrictive in one way or another, out of the total of 68.

The increased concern of the Senate on these matters in the Seventy-ninth and Eightieth Congresses is very evident. Until 1943 there were only 25 measures introduced in the Senate, and a good number of these were not restrictive in any sense of the term. From January, 1946, until April of the following year 45 measures, almost twice the number of the previous eight years, were introduced in the Senate. The absence of large amounts of amendatory legislation in the earlier Congresses reflects the usual prolabor attitude exhibited in the Senate until the Seventy-ninth Congress. The increase commencing with 1945 reflects the growing number of Republicans entering the Senate who felt disposed to take an active part in the shaping of national labor policy; of the 15 Republican senators included in this activity, over half did not enter the Senate until 1942. Of these Republicans, only Senator Vandenberg was a member of Congress at the time the Wagner Act became law.

The same general trends as to attitudes, pressures, and proposals found in the lower chamber of Congress were also indicated by the activity in the upper chamber.[67] The Senate, however, until the Seventy-ninth Congress was much less disposed to extreme restrictive action, or any action at all for that matter, than was the House. Southern Democrats were active in the Senate as in the House, although there are proportionately fewer names involved, and there are some notable exceptions of men who stood against the traditions of the region they represented. The importance of Republican representation from the eastern and midwestern states is significant in the

67. It should be noted that quite often attempts were made on the part of congressmen interested in restrictive labor legislation to get their bills referred to other committees than the House and Senate labor committees. Many bills whose passage would have been of major importance for labor activities were referred to the military committees, judiciary committees, or others. Outstanding, of course, are the examples of the 1940 Smith Bill gaining consideration through Rules Committee action. The Smith-Connally Act in 1943 emanated from the House Military Affairs Committee largely, and the Case Bill in 1946 was a substitute measure written by Representative Case and allowed as a substitution by the Rules Committee of which he was an important member.

Senate. There was perhaps greater participation by western state representatives on these matters in the House. Lastly, we note the profound impact of newer Republican members in the Senate such as Ives of New York, Morse of Oregon, Ball of Minnesota, Ferguson of Michigan, and McCarthy of Wisconsin.

STATE TRENDS AND NATIONAL TRENDS

Significant relationships are to be noted between the development of labor legislation in the states during this ten-year period and activity in the national legislature at the same time. In 1935 Congress led with the Wagner Act, and those states which were to adopt its principles in legislation of their own followed only after the NLRA had become law. After that time, however, it was the states which first adopted or attempted to adopt various kinds of amendments or changes in labor policy. Legislation coming to the House and Senate for consideration, or pressing for consideration there, very often had been previously suggested in state legislatures in various parts of the country; or it may even have been adopted and put into practice in one or several of the states.

By 1947 more than thirty-five states had legislation which was to some degree restrictive of labor or union activities and practices.[68] It is true that a number of these states had basic legislation of the Wagner Act type and that certain restrictions were additions or amendments to their basic protective-type acts. On the other hand, a goodly number of these states had no previous experience with labor legislation of this kind, and their original activity in industrial relations statutes was all restrictive or regulatory in content. These states represented to a large extent the southern and southwestern states experiencing new problems as war and defense industries spread to their regions, and along with such industrialization labor unrest and labor organization of a magnitude they had not before known. Such states, for example, as Alabama, Arizona, Arkansas, Georgia, and Texas could be so classified. As the pressure for revision of policy at the national level increased, the activities of congressmen from these same states are very noteworthy. O'Daniel of Texas and many of his colleagues in the Senate and the House give good examples of attempts of state representatives to get action at the national level along the lines of patterns adopted in their own states. Other significant examples are not wanting.

When proposals and their sponsors are analyzed in detail by states,

68. *Supra*, pp. 329–32.

one finds that on at least forty occasions legislation on national labor policy was introduced into the House or Senate by representatives or senators immediately following activity on labor policy legislation in their own states. In many cases the suggested legislation followed quite closely that adopted by the state legislatures.

The extraordinary amounts of restrictive and regulatory legislation adopted in the states in 1945 and 1946 accompanied the very strong pressures evident in Congress during this time, and they preceded, of course, the adoption of any legislation at the national level, although both houses of Congress approved the Case Bill in June, 1946. That there is some relationship between the trends in the states and the pressures at the national level seems obvious from the number of states active during the years of the Seventy-ninth and Eightieth Congresses who had representatives in Congress active on the same or similar kinds of proposals there.[69]

THREE CRUCIAL PERIODS IN TAFT-HARTLEY BACKGROUND

Three particular phases of legislative activity in Congress deserve special mention in any account of the ten years of developments which preceded the approval by the Eightieth Congress of the new labor act. The first concerns the attempts to amend the Wagner Act during 1939 and 1940; they came to a temporarily unsuccessful climax when the Senate failed to approve the Smith Bill, upon which the House had acted favorably. The next important phase centered about the adoption of the Smith-Connally War Labor Disputes Act in 1943 over the veto of President Roosevelt. Finally, there was the activity during the Seventy-ninth Congress, climaxed by the House and Senate acceptance in June, 1946, of the Case Bill. During each of these significant sessions bills were proposed, hearings were held, debate occurred, and the measures were accepted in part and rejected in part by one or both of the houses. While there was not the detailed investigation of many of the phases of the 1947 Act which numerous citizens would have preferred, the action taken by Congress in the spring of

69. We may cite such states and representatives as Indiana with Landis and Jenner; Maine with Hale and Smith; Massachusetts with Herter and Hesselton; Michigan with Dondero, Ferguson, Woodruff, and Hoffman; Minnesota with Ball; Missouri with Bennett and Slaughter; Nebraska with Miller and Wherry; New Jersey with Hartley, Auchinschloss, Case, and Smith; Pennsylvania with Muhlenberg; South Dakota with Case; Texas with O'Daniel; and Virginia with Byrd, Smith, and Randolph. The list of states and congressmen is only partial, and additions are certainly possible.

1947 in large part echoed and re-echoed attempted and successful legislative action in these three significant preceding periods.

The treatment of these developments which follows seeks to describe systematically some of the more important pieces of legislative history which give meaning to the acceptance of Taft-Hartley by the Eightieth Congress. An over-all legislative survey has already been made. The basic reasons for these recurring campaigns to change our labor policy have been shown in chapter 8; and, what is more, the materials dealing with the specific charges hurled at the Board and the Act it administered have formed the basic subject matter in the first seven chapters.

1. *1939–40—the Seventy-sixth Congress.*—While the first major attempts to amend the Wagner Act came in the sessions of the Seventy-sixth Congress, indications of pressures to be felt by Congress appeared in the latter half of 1938.[70] The AFL at meetings early in that year and from time to time through President Green, John P. Frey, and AFL legal counsel had begun to talk and prepare resolutions along the lines of the Walsh Bill, soon to be introduced; but it was in October, 1938, at its Fifty-eighth Annual Convention that the AFL adopted its important proposals for amendments[71] that were to set the stage for a good portion of the legislative history to ensue during the following twenty-four months. These proposals were, of course, largely designed as an attack against the Board itself in retaliation for alleged bias and unfairness in matters of collective bargaining units and the invalidation of contracts, which the AFL had been consistently claiming since the split with the CIO had occurred.[72] They aimed toward gaining an advantage for the AFL in its interunion quarrels with the CIO. This division in the labor movement was a most important factor behind the drives for amendment to the Act and the defenses of the Act made during this period. The CIO during this pre-Congress period, as well as during the 1939

70. Much help in ideas and background material for this section came from Millis and Montgomery, *op. cit.,* pp. 534–47, and the news items and documentary materials in the *Labor Relations Reporter,* Vols. 2 through 7, as well as the original analysis by the writer.

71. They included amendments to favor craft units, to curtail the power of the Board to invalidate contracts, set specific qualifications for trial examiners. . . . "Some are wholly incompetent and unfit to serve in that capacity . . ," liberalize rules as to subpoenas, end secrecy of the Board's files, permit intervention by interested parties as a matter of right, set time limits for the holding of elections and the making of decisions. American Federation of Labor, *Report of the Proceedings of the Fifty-eighth Annual Convention,* October, 1938, pp. 344–45.

72. Cf. *supra,* ch. 5, pp. 143–44; ch. 6, pp. 204–7.

session, opposed amendments of all kinds and vowed to support the opposition with all its resources.

Industry was active, too, in this drive for legislation. Senator Burke had delivered an address at the annual meeting of the Chamber of Commerce of the United States in March, 1938, which portended all the proposals he was to embody in the bills introduced in the Senate during the Seventy-sixth Congress. These proposals were, short of repeal, all those for which the major business and industry associations and spokesmen had begun to work. Their demands for amendments were to increase as the months rolled on toward the opening of the new Congress. Both the NAM and the Chamber of Commerce, as well as other important groups, continued this barrage of proposals and pressures during the whole of the Seventy-sixth Congress.[73] With minor modifications, and in some quarters with greater belligerency and daring, it was the same program that the major employer groups followed in pressing for legislation in 1946 and 1947.

Of some twenty significant bills introduced during the Seventy-sixth Congress, we stress eleven whose impact was very strong in 1939 and 1940 and which for the most part retained their significance for the next eight or nine years.[74]

These proposals fall into three broad groups. First are those of the Lea and Logan types broadly redefining agricultural labor so as to exclude from the application of the Act certain workers otherwise covered. A second group somewhat modified Board procedure and jurisdiction but not the form or spirit of the Act itself. Into this group fall most of the AFL proposals which sought to strengthen its position against the CIO. The Walsh, Barden, Hartley, and Norton bills, and to an extent the Smith Bill as passed, are the prime examples. The third group would have radically modified Board procedures and structure as well as other important aspects of the Wagner Act. These were the bills receiving the strong support of the various business and industry groups. The Burke, Hoffman, Anderson, and Holman proposals and the Smith Bill as introduced are outstanding here.

73. Cf. *supra*, ch. 8, pp. 283–85.

74. All except two of these were introduced during the first session. Two, the House Labor Committee Norton Bill and the Smith Bill resulting from the Special Committee Investigating the NLRB, came during the third session. In the Senate we are interested in the Burke, Holman, Walsh, and Logan bills, and in the House in the Barden, Hartley, Hoffman, Lea, Anderson, Norton, and Smith proposals. The Barden and Hartley bills were duplicates of each other; the Logan and Lea bills were substantially similar and represented a host of proposals of the same nature also introduced. Respectively, S. 1264, S. 1392, S. 1000, S. 1550, H.R. 4749, H.R. 5231, H.R. 4990, H.R. 4400, H.R. 2761, H.R. 9195, and H.R. 8813.

The details of each proposal are not of great significance at a post–Taft-Hartley date. We can summarize, however, the major aspects of these three kinds of bills. The first group are self-explained. They are important because of their number, because of the continued strong sentiment behind such bills all the way through the Seventy-ninth Congress, and because of the intent shown to remove jurisdiction in as many areas as possible from the Board. The remaining two groups in large measure set the general framework for most of the significant proposals that were to follow until the adoption of Taft-Hartley.

The second group of bills, that would have made less than major modifications of national labor policy but contained the changes desired by the AFL, generally included some or all of the following most significant modifications:

1. Limited the discretion and the jurisdiction of the Board by removing its authority in jurisdictional disputes or in designating multi-plant or multi-employer units and by requiring craft units whenever desired by a majority of the craft employees.
2. Changed the concept of employer neutrality under the NLRA by allowing the employer to interfere in employee choice of unions but not to "restrain or coerce" employees; by giving employers the right to freedom of expression when not accompanied by acts or threats of discrimination; by not holding employers responsible for acts of supervisors not vested with the right to hire or fire.
3. Created a new five-man Board or enlarged the Board from three to five members.
4. Required notice to all parties who might be adversely affected and provided for labor organization intervention in complaint cases where a showing of interest could be made.
5. Set new rules in representation cases, by permitting employers to petition for elections; giving district courts power to order the Board to act in conformity with hearing or elections; requiring the Board to hold hearings on representation questions; requiring elections when requested by a labor organization; establishing a one-year rule for new elections or certifications.
6. Required independent, fair, and impartial trial examiners for complaint and representation questions and provided for disqualification for bias on a charge by one of the parties.
7. Prohibited the Board from impairing agreements between employers and representatives of employees except under specified conditions; redefined requirements as to evidence.

Bills of the third kind, supported by business groups and containing primary changes in national labor policies, were for the most part restrictive and regulatory of labor union activities. They included more or less of the following:

349

1. Defined collective bargaining to make it mean less than under the NLRA; specified that employers or unions were not required to make counterproposals or reach collective bargaining agreements.
2. Changed the concept of employer neutrality by permitting employers to "counsel and advise" in matters of organization (this not qualified by prohibition of restraint and coercion of employees).
3. Changed or modified the Board in makeup, organization, and function or abolished it completely and created new agencies in its place; all would have separated the judicial and prosecuting functions of the Board in some manner.
4. "Equalized" the NLRA by proscribing unfair labor practices of unions and employees; provided that the commission of an unfair labor practice on the part of an employee was a complete defense for the commission of same by employers.
5. Prohibited filing complaints more than thirty days from the time the act was committed; required thirty-day notice to employees or employers of complaints to be filed; provided for the removal to the proper district courts of complaint cases within twenty days.
6. Permitted employer petition for elections in case of dispute between unions; required determination of representation issues at the request of an employer; eliminated the majority rule provisions of the NLRA.
7. Prohibited the appointment of aliens to any position.
8. Defined disputes as current only until normal production was resumed; provided penalties for striking without written demands and without allowing time for demands to be answered, and for striking in violation of agreements or participating in sit-down strikes; required registration of unions; provided that union officers or employee representatives could not be subversives.

Extensive hearings were conducted by the labor committees of both houses, starting in April and May, 1939, and running until late July or August. As the hearings commenced, the Board itself, in a lengthy memorandum submitted to the Senate committee, came out strongly against amendments. On four points already under discussion, however, it declared itself open-minded: on permitting employer petitions under proper safeguards; on statutory guidance as to the determination of bargaining units; on additional safeguards for contracts, although the power to invalidate contracts should not be removed from the Board; and on a time limit for the opening of hearings after issuance of complaints. When the House committee was in its twelfth week of hearings, the House voted 254 to 134[75] to approve the resolution presented by Howard Smith of Virginia for a special committee to investigate the NLRB. While the resolution was opposed by most of the members of the House committee, it was supported by the AFL. The growing temper of the House was clearly

75. *Cong. Rec.*, 84:9592.

shown in the debate, the action taken, and the character of the committee appointed.[76]

Shortly after the completion of the hearings of the regular committees of both houses the CIO also announced itself as critical of the NLRB, contrary to its expressions during the weeks of hearings.[77] The CIO claimed that the Board was attempting to meet criticisms and to placate the AFL, by decisions permitting the carving-out of craft units and the breaking-up of company-wide units by separate plant elections despite successful organization and collective bargaining on a broad basis.[78] Before the 1940 session of Congress convened the CIO declared in favor of certain amendments to the Wagner Act. Two of these would have added further penalties for violations of the Act by employers, but the third was designed to check the tendency to permit carving-up of established CIO industrial units.

The AFL continued its stand for amendments, although with some uncertainty since internal opposition developed at the 1939 con-

76. Mrs. Mary T. Norton, chairman of the House Labor Committee, urged that the Labor Committee be permitted to finish the job it had started, and asserted: "He [Mr. Smith] is the last man in the world to pass on labor legislation. . . . I have yet to find a single labor bill for the benefit of the workers of the country that he has ever voted for." *Cong. Rec.*, 84:9583. Mr. Smith disclosed that he had voted against the Wagner Act on the ground that it was unconstitutional. "But time has changed the Supreme Court and the Supreme Court has changed the Constitution," he said. *Ibid.*, 84:9582. Representative Cox, stating that the AFL supported the resolution, said, "If we are to wait here until the Committee on Labor takes action to restrain the Labor Board in its maladministration of the law, then we will be here until Gabriel blows his horn." *Ibid.*, 84:9591. At a later point in the debate Representative Smith answered Mrs. Norton's charge by citing bills beneficial to the workers for which he had voted. *Ibid.*, 84:10235-10236. The members appointed to the Committee were Smith (D., Va.), chairman; Healey (D., Mass.), Murdock (D., Utah), Halleck (R., Ind.), and Routzohn (R., Ohio). Two members had been previously committed to amendment, two appeared favorable to labor, according to their past action in the House, and one had been a former general counsel for an AFL union. Chairman Smith was a member of the Rules Committee and not of the Labor Committee.

77. A summary of the testimony before the two regular committees showed the following. Of 160 witnesses before the Senate Committee in its seventeen weeks of hearings, 108 favored amendment to the NLRA. The CIO's 15 witnesses opposed any change. Among those supporting amendments were 52 employers' representatives, most of them favoring the Burke amendments; 11 of the 15 AFL speakers, indorsing the Walsh bill; 15 farm representatives indorsing the Logan Bill; 23 of 27 representatives of independent unions. Of 55 witnesses before the House Committee in its thirteen weeks of hearings, 25 favored amendments and 30 opposed. Six CIO representatives opposed; of 10 AFL representatives, 7 supported amendments. Others favoring amendment included 8 employers and 2 independent unions. *Labor Relations Reporter*, 4 (August 7, 1939), 873.

78. *Ibid.*, p. 949. For discussion of some of the controversial decisions of this period, cf. *supra*, ch. 5, pp. 138–44, 148–49, 151–52.

vention. Business groups continued their ever strengthening line of attack. Meantime the Special Committee for the Investigation of the National Labor Relations Board carried on its extensive hearings and investigations.[79] In March, 1940, before completion of the hearings and before any report from the House Labor Committee after its protracted hearings of the first session, the majority of the Smith Committee issued an Intermediate Report[80] and introduced H.R. 8813, the Smith Bill. The Intermediate Report and bill were strongly opposed by the Healey and Murdock minority.[81] The AFL declared in favor of those proposals meeting its earlier suggestions for amendment but opposed others which it felt "invaded the basic principles of the Act."[82] The CIO vigorously opposed the bill. As was to be expected, the Chamber of Commerce and the NAM approved but called for further amendments.

The House Labor Committee finally in April presented the Norton Bill, including only four amendments, even these opposed by seven members of the Committee. It would have added two members to the Board, required craft-unit designation by the Board when such a desire was indicated by a majority of the employees of a particular craft, permitted employer petitions where competing unions were involved, and protected certifications of representatives for one year. The NAM called this a red herring and pressed for the Smith amendments; the AFL gave full approval, and the CIO offered vigorous opposition. As had been threatened by the Rules Committee, the Norton Bill was quickly sidetracked when it came up for consideration in June, by a rule which permitted the substitution of the Smith Bill intact. A letter from President Green giving AFL approval to the latter if certain modifications were made was read into the record, and the bill was shortly passed with these changes.[83]

79. For comments on its work, cf. *supra,* ch. 2, pp. 49–50. Its proceedings were published in thirty volumes, covering hearings from December, 1939, to December, 1940.

80. U.S. House of Representatives, Special Committee To Investigate the National Labor Relations Board, *Intermediate Report,* Report No. 1902, 76th Cong., 3d Sess., Pt. 1, March 29, 1940.

81. *Ibid.,* Pt. 2, April 11, 1940.

82. American Federation of Labor, *Report of the Executive Council to the Sixtieth Annual Convention,* November, 1940, pp. 75–76.

83. The four changes made eliminated the following: a change in the statement of national labor policy to omit reference to encouraging collective bargaining; a definition of collective bargaining to relieve the employer of the duty to make counterproposals; a clause barring certifications where competing unions failed to agree on the unit; and a limitation of back pay for discharged employees to six

In the Senate Committee very little was done with the Smith Bill. Senator Thomas pleaded the long study necessary and procedural complications because of the passage of the Walter-Logan Bill with its code of procedure embodying some of the suggested NLRA amendments for all administrative agencies.[84] Besides it was reported that despite his letter President Green did not support the bill; the letter was claimed to have been a tactical move to get the bill passed and on to the Senate where objectionable portions could be eliminated. By November it was clear that there would be no action in the Senate and consequently no change in national labor policy during 1940.

These 1939–40 attempts at amendment set the pattern for the continuing efforts almost until Taft-Hartley.[85] The passage of the Smith-Connally Act was the first success. The postwar crises brought new opportunity. When a Republican majority began to assume control in 1946 and 1947, their proposals pushed so vigorously followed the pattern of the bills introduced in 1939–40.

The employer associations and business groups whose appetites for change had been whetted continued their support of the basic and far-reaching amendments, adding new ideas as circumstances indicated or allowed. Only the AFL had had its fingers burned in attempting to get the kind of amendments it wanted. It soon joined the CIO in the safer strategy of opposing most legislation that would tamper with the Wagner Act. If we are to see the same ideas pressing for consideration through the years, we also see many of the same faces pressing for the original ideas they had presented during this period, or other ideas of the same amendatory and restrictive spirit. We need but mention the names of Barden, Hartley, Hoffman, and Smith to realize the import of Senator Wagner's remark, made during this time: "Based on more than thirty years' experience as a legislator, I am willing to set down as a first principle that, while all great social legislation needs to be perfected over the years, no great social

months (a twelve-month limitation was accepted). The Act as passed included most of the points listed in our analysis of the second group of bills, *supra,* p. 349.

84. Senator Taft for the minority stated flatly that no action was taken because the majority simply refused. He thought a committee vote should have been taken.

85. Ex-Chairman Hartley of the House Labor Committee of the Eightieth Congress in his book expressed this Committee's indebtedness to the important contributions of Howard Smith personally and of the Smith Committee. Fred A. Hartley, Jr., *Our New National Labor Policy* (New York: Funk & Wagnalls Co., 1948), pp. 14–15.

legislation has ever been genuinely perfected except by its true friends."[86]

2. *The Smith-Connally Act.*—The next critical period occurred in the midst of the war during the 1943 session of the Seventy-eighth Congress. For the first time since the passage of the Wagner Act both houses of Congress approved a bill contrary to the spirit of that Act. The War Labor Disputes Act became law on June 25, 1943, when very substantial majorities voted to override the veto of President Roosevelt. All the provisions of the Smith-Connally Act had previously been suggested in one form or another in the years 1941 and 1942. Some of the proposals were contained in the bills in the Seventy-sixth Congress just discussed. Representative Smith had introduced a bill immediately after Pearl Harbor which included all and more than the adopted legislation contained. Difficulties had arisen and emotions had run high as a result of the crises in the bituminous coal industry. The concurrence of the Senate in this Smith-Connally type of legislation in 1943 so shortly after the vigorous stand the same majority in the Senate had taken on the various proposals offered in the Seventy-sixth Congress, and despite the very good record labor as a whole was making on its no-strike pledge, attests to the emotion and public disfavor aroused by the increased number of strikes during this period. We need not repeat our discussion of the merits or demerits of the Smith-Connally Act, or its record in preventing or engendering strikes during the years it remained on the statute-books.[87] Its significance here is in the extent to which it gives added perspective to the actions of the Eightieth Congress.

The original Connally Plant Seizure Bill (S. 796) was passed by the Senate early in May. It provided for presidential seizure of plants, strong prohibitions against any attempts to interfere with production in a seized plant, subpoena power for the War Labor Board, rules of procedure for the WLB, and court review of WLB decisions in relation to matters of law.

More important for our purposes are the amendments offered to the bill during its consideration but not adopted. These included allowing the federal courts to enjoin violations, thus extensively modifying the Norris–La Guardia Act. Such proposals had begun to appear in the two years previous. In these proposals we find evidence of a growing sentiment which reached a climax in the proposed Ball-

86. *Cong. Rec.,* 86:2775 (March 13, 1940).
87. Cf. *supra,* ch. 8, pp. 298–300.

354

Taft amendment during the Senate's discussion of S. 1126 in the Eightieth Congress; this would have again opened the injunction remedy to private parties. Some modifications of Norris–La Guardia were of course included in Taft-Hartley as adopted. A cooling-off period suggested by Taft in the Senate in 1943 was also defeated.

When the bill reached the House, a much more drastic measure based for the most part on the Smith proposals of the current and past Congresses was adopted. Its final form as passed by the House included the following provisions: statutory authority and subpoena power for the WLB; government seizure, with strong penalties for interference with production in such seized plants; a thirty-day cooling-off period and a prohibition of strikes after that period without a favorable secret ballot; registration requirements for unions; and prohibition of union political contributions.

Here, too, the clauses which were omitted after debate, although recommended by the committee, are significant. For the first time the whole House actually considered measures that would have forbidden jurisdictional strikes and violent picketing and would have authorized the Attorney-General to seek antistrike injunctions in the federal courts. Other provisions considered by the committee, but not reported to the whole House, would have banned sympathy strikes and boycotts. These also are significant in portending the future and indicating the pressures being exerted in regard to national labor policy.

The final version agreed upon by Senate and House conferees contained four major provisions: (1) requirement of a thirty-day strike notice in private plants, the NLRB to conduct a secret ballot on the thirtieth day after notice; (2) provision of statutory authority for the WLB; (3) prohibition of strikes in government-held plants or mines; and (4) prohibition of political contributions by unions in federal elections. Criminal penalties were provided for interference with government operation, and there was liability for damages resulting from strikes in violation of the provisions for notice and cooling-off period. The strike-notice requirement and the cooling-off provisions were of course to appear in almost all the bills for settlement of disputes that poured in on Congress in the postwar period of 1945 and 1946. The ban on political contributions was written into the Taft-Hartley Act despite the protests made when this was first introduced in the War Labor Disputes Act and the little discussion given to it in the Eightieth Congress.

Though it was a special situation that precipitated the War Labor Disputes Act, and though the warnings of the President concerning its probable effects went unheeded, it remained law even through a part of the postwar period. In its various forms it foreshadowed the Case Bill to follow three years later and, through it, the Labor Management Relations Act of 1947.

3. *1945–46—the Seventy-ninth Congress.*—Changing attitudes of the public, the continuing demands of the labor and business groups and their tactics, and the labor unrest and work stoppages during the postwar period formed the background for the activities of the Seventy-ninth Congress.[88] It remains here to summarize the legislative history of the 1945–46 period. Attention will be paid chiefly to several major bills representative of the more than fifty which this Congress had before it on the matter of national labor policy. We do not aim to discuss the vital issues these proposals raised. This is the task of the chapters analyzing Taft-Hartley itself, for by the time of its consideration the issues were essentially the same. Almost all these proposals offered in the Seventy-ninth Congress were pointed to, and colored by, the very difficult industrial relations situation during these years.

In June, 1945, the Ball-Burton-Hatch Bill was introduced into the Senate. The introduction of this bill which had been preceded by a considerable amount of fanfare elicited strong responses both negative and affirmative from various elements in the country. The legislative proposals which followed it were indeed written in the shadow of Ball-Burton-Hatch. For purposes of organization it will be discussed not in chronological order but in conjunction with the modified version introduced as the Ball-Hatch Bill. The next major bill was introduced by Senator McMahon on September 20, 1945. Shortly after this the Labor-Management Conference, called at the invitation of the President, met for almost four weeks and ended in agreement on some matters but great disagreement on others.[89] Immediately after the close of this conference the President requested emergency fact-finding legislation. His suggestions were incorporated in the Ellender-Norton proposal.

At this juncture, another measure was introduced by Congressman Smith on December 3. This was a very different measure, akin to the Smith Bill of 1939 and also those of 1941 and 1943 passed by the House but not acted upon as such by the Senate. It had been incorpo-

88. Discussed *supra*, ch. 8.
89. Cf. *ibid.*, pp. 306–11, for a discussion of the Conference.

rated in a limited manner in the Smith-Connally Act. The Ball-Hatch Bill was introduced on December 10 as a substitute for the Ellender-Norton proposal. A fifth measure was the Case Bill, which was introduced in the House as a substitute measure and, after revisions, passed on February 7. After considerable revision in the Senate, the bill was accepted by the House. This amended bill was vetoed by the President in June, 1946, and the veto was narrowly sustained.[90] With this over-all view of the important occurrences we can examine these major proposals individually.

The McMahon Bill.[91]—This was a measure not objectionable to labor because of any compulsion, or cooling-off period, or strike limitations, for all these were carefully guarded against. Nor would it have amended federal labor law. In a sense, it was a rival of the labor-opposed Ball-Burton-Hatch Bill, which had been introduced the preceding June. It provided for conciliation functions such as had been performed by the Conciliation Service, but now to be under a Conciliation and Mediation Division headed by an administrator and located in the Department of Labor. There was also provision for the appointment of boards of inquiry to investigate disputes and to report to the public the position of each party, but to refrain from making any recommendations. In addition, a United States Board of Arbitration was to be established as an independent agency, to aid in setting up voluntary arbitration.[92]

The Ellender Bill.[93]—On December 3, 1945, upon the close of the Labor-Management Conference, the President in a message to Congress proposed legislation to cope with the then pressing problem of labor disputes. This statement of the President's marks a turning point in the history of labor legislation, for this was the first time since the Wagner Act that a chief executive had favored, or called for the passage of, legislation that would affect the law of labor in this country. This marks the Seventy-ninth Congress as different from the four that had preceded it, and it undoubtedly had its effect on the pattern of proposals and counterproposals which stands out as a feature of this period. The proposals he made at that time were embodied in the Ellender Bill, providing for fact-finding panels to be

90. The House majority vote to override the veto fell five votes short of the necessary number.

91. S. 1419, also sponsored by Senators Hayden, Tunnel, and Thomas (Utah).

92. The McMahon Bill, as well as others to be summarized, authorized the Bureau of Labor Statistics to maintain a file of copies of agreements resulting from conciliation or arbitration, etc.

93. S. 1661, similar to the Norton proposal, H.R. 4908, in the House.

appointed by the President when a dispute in progress, or a threatened dispute, seriously affected the national interest or interstate or foreign commerce. These panels were to have power to make recommendations as well as the responsibility of making the facts in a dispute available to the public. A mandatory cooling-off period was provided. There were no specific penalties for violations of the status quo requirements, but injunctions could be obtained to prohibit such actions. The recommendations of the panel were purely advisory, and neither of the disputants was bound to accept the recommendations.

Ball-Hatch.—Some background is needed in order to make clear the peculiar origin of the Ball-Hatch Bill through the original Ball-Burton-Hatch proposals. In the spring of 1943 a group of men met in Philadelphia to consider needed federal legislation relating to industrial relations. Others were recruited and in February, 1944, the group took the name of "Committee To Promote Industrial Peace." Though among them were some very able and liberal businessmen, such as Mr. Samuel S. Fels and Mr. Arthur N. Whiteside, and several lawyers, neither business, management, nor labor as such were represented. In other words, the Committee regarded itself as representative of the public, not of the different interested groups, although it was said that outside contacts were made in order to draw upon experience in industry and to test out ideas. The chairman, Donald R. Richberg, played a leading role.[94] In the course of time, the Committee drafted a legislative proposal, which was submitted to an additional group with invitations to join in sponsorship. Following this, conferences were held with certain members of the Senate Committee on Education and Labor. These conferences led to substantial revisions in the draft which were mutually agreeable to the committee and to the three able and active senators, Hatch of New Mexico, Burton of Ohio (later an Associate Justice of the Supreme Court), and Ball of Minnesota, who became sponsors of the revised draft. This draft was introduced in the Senate in June, 1945, as S. 1171, and referred to the Committee on Education and Labor, which held no public hearings

94. Richberg had at one time served as counsel for the railroad brotherhoods and in NRA days had served closely with General Hugh Johnson, head of that organization. After his service in the government he again practiced law, with offices in Washington. For his account of the origins and work of the committee, with the names of the original members and of those who accepted and did not accept the invitation to sponsor the measure (there were finally twelve signers, seven of them lawyers), see Donald R. Richberg, "The Proposed Federal Industrial Relations Act," *Political Science Quarterly*, 61 (1946), 189–204.

on it. Reduced to pamphlet form, it was widely circulated and was made known to the public through speeches and radio.[95]

The Ball-Burton-Hatch Bill was an extremely complex and broad measure. It was largely based on the Railway Labor Act with its concept of the obligation to bargain collectively, but contained also provisions drawn from other sources such as the Minnesota Labor Relations Act of 1939.[96] All the possible devices to prevent or allay industrial disputes were included: cooling-off periods, adjustment boards for the handling of grievances, conciliation, mediation, voluntary arbitration, and fact-finding boards with power to recommend settlements. And in stoppages that would work severe hardship on the public the fact-finding boards could be vested with special powers for compulsory arbitration at the discretion of the Federal Labor Relations Board created by the Act. Violation of such arbitration awards could be enjoined by the courts, when action was instituted by this Board; and provision was made for access to the courts for recovery of damages by parties injured as a result of violations.

Controversies were divided into four classes or groups: (1) those over representation for the purposes of collective bargaining; (2) those over the making of agreements; (3) those arising out of grievances; and (4) other labor controversies. All these were within the jurisdiction of the Federal Labor Relations Board which was to replace the National Labor Relations Board and to which also were to be transferred the functions of the United States Conciliation Service. A separate semijudicial agency, the Unfair Labor Practices Tribunal, was to be set up to handle charges of unfair labor practices. Thus representation questions were to be handled in connection with disputes over the substance of agreements, rather than by the agency handling the often closely related unfair labor practice issues. Orders in connection with representation questions, however, were to be reviewable by the courts.

In addition, the Ball-Burton-Hatch Bill would have amended the federal law of labor by "equalizing" changes in the unfair labor practice provisions. These would have been applied to employees and unions as well as to employers and, by extensive additions, would

95. The bill was received with bitter criticism by labor groups both for what was contained in it and for the manner in which it was prepared. See, for example, the editorial, "Proposed Federal Industrial Relations Act," in the *Pattern Makers Journal*, July, 1945. For a critical analysis of the bill see Herbert R. Northrup, "A Critique of Pending Labor Legislation," *Political Science Quarterly*, 61 (1946), 205–16.

96. *Supra*, pp. 319–21.

have imposed substantial restraints upon concerted activities of labor.

The Ball-Hatch Bill, introduced on December 10, 1945, as a substitute for the Ellender Bill, eliminated the more drastic of these changes. The Wagner Act as such was to be left untouched. The substitute provided for a Federal Industrial Relations Board, concerned only with mediation, voluntary arbitration, and fact-finding with a thirty-day waiting period in public interest cases. It was empowered to seek injunctions in the federal courts without the limitations of the Norris–La Guardia Act.

The Smith Bill of 1945.—This bill (H.R. 4875), introduced on December 3, 1945, was also very different from the Ellender Bill both in scope and in concrete proposals. Not only did it concern itself with the mediation, conciliation, and voluntary arbitration of industrial disputes, of course with cooling-off periods, but it also contained provisions relating to the organization of unions, their internal operations, annual reporting, and the like, as well as far-reaching restrictions on strikes, picketing, and boycotting. Such proposals and procedures have been summarized in discussing the earlier Smith bills. The settlement procedures except in detail were similar to earlier proposals.

The Case proposals.—On these four important measures (including Ball-Hatch as part of the larger Ball-Burton-Hatch proposals) were built the three discernible forms in which the Case Bill appeared in the Seventy-ninth Congress. These four measures, of course, were in themselves not new but represented the accumulation of almost ten years of suggestions at the national level and a considerable amount of actual achievement along these lines in state legislation.

It has been charged that the original Case Bill presented to the House as a substitute measure for the President's proposals embodied in the Ellender-Norton bills was carefully prepared by certain members of the Committee on Rules.[97] There were conferences, or something resembling such, outside of the Committee. The substitution was made on January 30 at a time when hearings on fact-finding had been temporarily suspended. This measure with amendments made on the floor became the House version of the Case Bill.

This version was referred to the Senate Labor Committee, then passed on February 7. The Senate committee majority reported out a very much watered-down bill early in March, which removed all the House provisions for penalties imposed on unions for violations of the

97. See, for example, Philip Murray's letter, urging President Truman to veto the Case Bill. *New York Times,* June 3, 1946.

would-be Act and all clauses which would have actually amended the Wagner Act. This was the second version of the bill. The minority in the committee, spearheaded by Ball and Taft, who were to become the major figures of the new committee majority when the Eightieth Congress opened, offered amendments which would have retained these provisions, clarifying them somewhat and making them less drastic than the House had conceived them. The procedures for settlement of disputes advocated by the minority would also have involved basic changes in the law of labor not included in Senator Murray's majority proposals.

The third and final version of the Case measure is the bill as it was finally passed by the Senate and accepted by the House.[98] The reflection of the earlier measures is clearly seen in the main points of this bill:

1. Creation of a Federal Mediation Board to encourage the making and maintenance of agreements and to aid the parties in settling disputes.
2. Provision for a sixty-day cooling-off period.
3. Provision for enforcement of the cooling-off period by administrative remedies against employers and deprivation of Wagner Act rights for employees.
4. Provision for fact-finding commissions in major labor disputes involving public utilities, to make recommendations, and with extension of the cooling-off period until five days after the report of the commission.
5. Imposition of stringent penalties against "whoever" interferes by violence or extortion, or conspiracy to do so, with the movement of goods in interstate commerce.
6. Proscription of employer contributions to welfare funds administered exclusively by unions.
7. Exclusion of "supervisors" from the Wagner Act's definition of "employee" but not prohibiting union membership to them.
8. Provision for damage suits against unions for violation of contract.
9. Provision for action against "wildcat" and rival union violations of collective bargaining contracts by deprivation of Wagner Act rights for employees involved.
10. Outlawing of secondary boycotts by making them unlawful under the antitrust laws, and removing the limitations of the Norris–La Guardia Act on the use of injunctions in labor disputes in such cases.[99]

98. It was in the midst of the consideration of the Case Bill by the Senate that the President asked Congress for emergency legislation to deal with the existing railway emergency. See *supra*, ch. 8, p. 313. After the House acceptance and the Senate rejection of this legislation, on the same day both houses passed the Case measure with minor amendments, on May 25, 1946. On June 11 the President's veto of this final form of the Case measure was sustained.

99. Cf. *Labor Relations Reporter*, 18 (June 3, 1946), Analysis 17. Point No. 5 of the Case Bill was later adopted as the Hobbs Act. The President's veto message

From the Wagner Act to Taft-Hartley

The relationship is clear between the contents of this bill and its legislative history and what was to follow in 1947 when the Labor Management Relations Act was passed, based on the extreme Hartley Bill in the House and the less restrictive, though definitely amendatory, Taft Bill of the Senate.

CONCLUSIONS

On the basis of this analysis several observations can be made: first, there were few major provisions in Taft-Hartley which did not find counterparts in legislation previously introduced; second, a relatively small number of points in the NLRA and its administration were severely and consistently criticized by a minority of representatives and senators during the ten-year period; third, important members of this minority were the same members who consistently proposed restrictive amendments that would have changed the basic law of labor; fourth, it was the views of this minority, substantially unchanged, which became the predominantly accepted view of the Congress as a new Republican majority joined hands with diehard southern Democrats; and, lastly, despite the lengthy hearings of the Senate and House labor committees at two widely separated times, and the investigation by the highly controversial Smith Committee in 1939–40, there was never any systematic, nonpolitical study or investigation authorized or undertaken by Congress before it acted on many complex and technical matters about which it had relatively little accurate information.

---

on June 11, 1946, included many arguments which crop up later in the criticism of the Taft-Hartley Bill by the President and the Democratic minority. The major points may be summarized: The bill would not have prevented or shortened the great postwar strikes; the cooling-off period was inequitable in its penalties and might provoke strikes and hamper mediation; fact-finding was inexplicably limited to public utility disputes; the Mediation Board would deprive the Secretary of Labor of many of his responsibilities, without being fully responsible either to him or to the President; welfare fund questions should not be removed from the scope of collective bargaining; the bill did not fairly handle the question of supervisors; the boycott provisions might eliminate certain evils but would make remedies available against recognized legitimate activities of labor; the labor injunction should not be permitted as a weapon of the private employer except with the careful restrictions of Norris–La Guardia; there was need for careful study preparatory to long-range legislation. *Cong. Rec.*, 92:6674-78 (June 11, 1948).

CHAPTER 10

TAFT-HARTLEY AND THE
EIGHTIETH CONGRESS

O N THE day that the Eightieth Congress convened no less than seventeen bills dealing with labor policy were dropped into the hopper of the House of Representatives.[1] This showed that the tremendous pressure demonstrated in the preceding Congress had gained even greater momentum when the congressional elections of 1946 made clear that the "mandate of the people" was to be carried out by a Republican majority in Congress. As bills to change national labor policy continued to appear in the early weeks of the session and as President Truman himself requested labor legislation in his January State of the Union Message, it was obvious that this Congress would place the passage of some labor legislation high on its agenda. This problem was probably *the* major concern of Congress until Taft-Hartley became law in June. For the first six months of 1947 the formulation of this labor legislation and the course of the legislative strategy which led to its ultimate embodiment in the law of the land occupied a large share of the time of the chief majority and minority members in the new Congress.

CHRONOLOGY OF THE LEGISLATIVE HISTORY

It is difficult to establish the precise moment when the legislative history of this Act begins. The drive for revision of our national labor policy which met success in 1947 actually was begun immediately after the passage of the Wagner Act in 1935. Despite the numerous bills which the labor committees in both houses of Congress had before them when they opened their hearings in the early months of 1947, it can be said with little reservation that there was not much in these suggestions that had not been presented in the national legisla-

---

1. This chapter was written by Seymour Z. Mann.
For a rather detailed survey of the legislative proposals before the Eightieth Congress see John A. Fitch, "New Congress and the Unions," *Survey Graphic*, 36 (1947), 235.

ture previously. They were all variations on old and well-worn tunes that a small minority had been playing constantly.

Perhaps the real legislative history in the Eightieth Congress itself commenced with the President's State of the Union Message on January 6. Mr. Truman asked for action to prevent jurisdictional disputes, to prohibit secondary boycotts with "unjustifiable objectives," to provide for machinery to help solve disputes arising under existing collective bargaining agreements, and to create a temporary joint commission to investigate the whole field of labor-management relations and to report their recommendations by March 15. The President's proposals were embodied in bills sponsored in both houses. Needless to say, his proposals were very much weaker than congressional inclinations on these matters, but they did, in a way, set the stage for the legislative history to follow. With even the President suggesting legislation it was a foregone conclusion that this new Republican Congress would act on labor policy.

On January 23 the Senate Committee on Labor and Public Welfare opened hearings on these problems. These lasted until March 8. On February 5 the House Committee on Labor and Education opened its hearings which continued some six weeks until March 15. It was obvious when these hearings opened that there would be no action on the bills and resolutions to establish the oft-suggested temporary joint commission for thorough study of labor-management relations before any general legislation. By the time committee hearings opened the chairmen of the House and Senate labor committees had both signified that their committees were going ahead to prepare bills, and at these early dates they had indicated the major outlines of their proposals. The Republican Policy Committee in the Congress early had announced that a new version of the Case Bill would be introduced in the House.

Before April 11, when H.R. 3020 was favorably reported from the House Committee, and before April 17, when S. 1126 was likewise reported to the Senate by its Labor Committee Chairman, Mr. Taft, these committees had over sixty major bills to consider. Although the House hearings ended somewhat later than the Senate hearings, the House committee was ready to present its bill for action first. Four days after the Hartley Bill was reported in the lower chamber it was decided overwhelmingly to limit general debate on the bill to but six hours. This was on April 15, and two days later, almost at the same time that Mr. Taft was reporting S. 1126 to the Senate, the House passed and sent to the Senate H.R. 3020. The Senate, on the other hand, had the Taft measure under the scrutiny of debate almost continuously from the time the minority report of the Labor Committee was introduced on April 22 to its passage as amended on May 13. This contrast to the six hours given in the House on what was a much more difficult and complicated piece of legislation seems significant despite the customary limitation on debate in the lower chamber.

Since the House disagreed with the amendments to its H.R. 3020 as passed by the Senate, a Conference Committee was appointed which met from May 15 through May 29. On June 3 the Conference Report was introduced in the House, and the following day, after a one-hour general debate, it was accepted by the lower chamber. In the Senate the same report was submitted on June 5 and debated that day and the next before passage.

The President's veto message was received by Congress on June 20. In the House, without any debate and discussion, the successful vote to override was taken immediately after the reading of the message. In the Senate the vote to override occurred on June 23 after two days of debate.

The character of the committees and their hearings, the course of the general debates, the Conference Committee and the debates which followed its report, and lastly the presidential veto and the action of Congress thereupon remain to be described and analyzed.

COMMITTEES, HEARINGS, AND DEBATES—THE HOUSE

The service records of the members of the House labor committees since 1935 are significant. In the Eightieth Congress there were twenty-five members of the House Committee on Education and Labor.[2] Fifteen of them were Republicans and ten were from the Democratic side of the House. Of the fifteen Republicans, ten had not served on the Labor Committee prior to the Eightieth Congress. Excluding any service before 1935, the five experienced members of the committee had a total of twenty years' service. Only one member,

2. The members of the House Committee on Education and Labor were: Fred A. Hartley, Jr., New Jersey, *chairman;* Gerald W. Landis, Indiana; Clare E. Hoffman, Michigan; Edward O. McCowen, Ohio; Max Schwabe, Missouri; Samuel K. McConnell, Jr., Pennsylvania; Ralph W. Gwinn, New York; Ellsworth B. Buck, New York; Walter E. Brehm, Ohio; Wint Smith, Kansas; Charles J. Kersten, Wisconsin; George MacKinnon, Minnesota; Thomas L. Owens, Illinois; John Lesinski, Michigan; Graham A. Barden, North Carolina; Augustine B. Kelley, Pennsylvania; O. C. Fisher, Texas; Adam C. Powell, Jr., New York; John S. Wood, Georgia; Ray J. Madden, Indiana; Arthur G. Klein, New York; John F. Kennedy, Massachusetts; Wingate H. Lucas, Texas; Carroll D. Kearns, Pennsylvania; and Richard M. Nixon, California; with W. Manly Sheppard, *clerk.*

the Chairman, Mr. Hartley, had ten or more years of experience on the committee.[3] Of the ten Democrats, only four were without previous service on the Labor Committee. The six remaining members accounted for thirty years of experience since 1935, with one, Mr. Lesinski, having been in continuous service since the Seventy-fifth Congress. Of the ten Democratic committee members, four did not join with their fellow party members in supporting the minority report of the committee submitted to Congress.[4]

Open hearings before the House committee were held for six weeks. During this period five volumes of testimony were accumulated, totaling some 3,873 pages. While this mass of material is included in the printed record of the hearings, not all of it was heard at the hearings themselves. Much of the testimony consists of formal statements, letters to the committee or its various members, and exhibits of one kind or another given to the committee for inclusion in the completed record. These materials, not made public at the hearings themselves, were always on file in the committee offices for inspection of the various members. It is impossible to know the quantity or quality of the evaluation these records were accorded by committee members. There were allegations on the floor of the House that many members were unaware of much that was in the testimony. Certainly many representatives rightly proclaimed that the mass of testimony was so complicated and so great that there was little time between the conclusion of the hearings and the vote on the committee bill to give adequate attention to this record.

More than a hundred and thirty witnesses were heard or had testimony inserted in the record in the six weeks of hearings. Fifty-five of

3. Mrs. Norton, former chairman of the House Committee on Education and Labor, gave as her reason for resigning from the committee the following: "... I regret to say I have no respect for the present chairman of the Labor Committee. And I could not serve with a chairman for whom I hold no respect. My reason for that is that during the 10 years I was chairman of the Labor Committee, the gentleman from New Jersey, who is now the chairman of the Labor Committee, and who comes here before you and talks about labor as if he knew something about it, attended exactly six meetings in 10 years. That was my reason for leaving the Committee on Labor." *Daily Cong. Rec.*, 93:3542 (April 15, 1947). Mr. Hartley, in a book published in the fall of 1948, mentions Mrs. Norton's charge but does not specifically refute it. Fred A. Hartley, Jr., *Our New National Labor Policy: The Taft-Hartley Act and the Next Steps* (New York: Funk & Wagnalls Co., 1948), p. 26.

4. These were Messrs. Barden (North Carolina), Fisher (Texas), Wood (Georgia), and Lucas (Texas). Three of these representatives voted for passage of H.R. 3020, while one (Wood) did not vote. As the debates testify, this left an effective minority of six members.

these represented employers or employer associations, while twenty-seven represented labor or labor organizations. Twelve congressmen were heard, mostly testifying on bills they had proposed. Public officials, including Secretary of Labor Schwellenbach and Paul M. Herzog, Chairman of the NLRB, accounted for five witnesses. Representing themselves, the public, or public institutions were some fourteen witnesses. Four of these testified as experts, including two representatives of the Brookings Institution. Of two listed as professors, only the testimony of Professor Slichter of Harvard seemed important. Six of these witnesses were lawyers appearing independently. Among the witnesses who supposedly represented a public or expert point of view were some large corporation lawyers. Included among the lawyer witnesses was Theodore Iserman, who was later said to have done much of the writing of the committee bill.[5] Among other institutions or organizations represented were the Committee for Economic Development, the Federal Farm Bureau, the Committee for Constitutional Government,[6] engineering societies, the Institute of Architects, and others.

Only a minute analysis of these hearings would indicate whether a satisfactory representation of public and private viewpoints was made. It is even more difficult to know whether important persons who wished to testify or should have testified remained uninvited. Despite bitter and caustic personal comments against committee members from both sides of the House, both majority and minority statements during debate attested that the hearing aspect of the committee's work was conducted ably and fairly.[7]

One outstanding criticism can be made. From the many employers, representatives of employer associations, and the corporation labor lawyers, as well as from some of the supposedly neutral experts on the matter, there were constant and often bitter criticisms of the NLRB and its work in the administration and interpretation of the Wagner Act. Certainly over half the witnesses voiced serious dissatisfaction

5. Cf. *infra,* p. 370.

6. This committee sponsored the anti-collective bargaining *Labor Monopolies—or Freedom* (New York, 1946), written by John W. Scoville, formerly with the Chrysler Corporation, and charged on the House floor with influencing strongly the committee bill.

7. Representative Klein of New York, a member of the Committee, however, stated in a speech delivered before a meeting of labor unions in New York that a great majority of the management witnesses who appeared before the House committee were employers who had been cited by the NLRB and the courts for unfair labor practices. *New York Times,* March 5, 1947.

with Board practices or the Act the NLRB was administering. Certainly more than half of the total hours of testimony were along this line. To answer such charges publicly, to correct many errors that appeared in the record, and generally to explain or defend their actions in the administration of the Act they knew so well, representatives of the Board were given relatively little time in contrast to other witnesses who had equal or even more time.

Chairman Herzog's testimony came toward the end of a long day of committee hearings, most of which had been given over to the examination of Secretary Schwellenbach. Late in the afternoon when Mr. Herzog was called to the stand, the committee chairman announced that, since many committee members had previous evening engagements, there would be insufficient time for cross-examination of the witness, but that an hour might be spared the next morning. After some discussion it was agreed that members would as far as possible refrain from questioning in view of the shortness of time and that some opportunity would be given in the morning for further cross-examination. Chairman Herzog then indicated that the whole Board had to appear at 10:00 A.M. the next day before the deficiency committee of the Appropriations Committee. It was made clear that there would be no other time available for further Board testimony after that morning but that the committee would release Mr. Herzog by 10:00 A.M. Chairman Herzog's time before the committee did not total more than three hours.

This lack of time was an obvious handicap to the witness, despite his statements of appreciation for the extreme courtesy of the committee. There were many gaps that had to be left in his prepared testimony, questions could not be answered fully, and much important testimony had to be inserted in the record without comment but with a hope for later reading. Particularly in the case of the Board's testimony these forced omissions from the direct presentation were unfair and dangerous. This procedure was unfair, since a large portion, which was directed as rebuttal to previous testimony, was not heard directly by the committee and was not subject to as good press coverage as otherwise.[8] Such a procedure prevents direct questions and answers which might bring out important information, and which would have allowed the witness to defend his statements. Any charges made later against the Board or its testimony by committee members

8. For example, the *New York Times* of March 12, 1947, carried only a brief paragraph on the Herzog testimony, at the end of its report on the Schwellenbach testimony.

who read the unheard portions of testimony could only be answered by letter or further insertions in the record. In contrast it can be noted that Mr. Iserman, a bitter foe of the Board, was heard for more than four hours, he was not rushed, and most of his testimony was given fully and directly without the necessity of merely inserting much of it in the record.

As to the writing of the committee bill itself charges of a serious nature were leveled at the majority of the committee. The signers of the House Minority Report said that H.R. 3020 was not a committee bill, since no general meetings of the committee were held to consider the bill. Some support for the charge is available merely from the chronology. Committee hearings were concluded on March 15. It was said that no meetings were called for two weeks, but the bill was introduced in the House by Representative Hartley on April 10. The following day it was reported favorably by the majority of the committee.[9] The minority members were handed their copies of the bill on April 10, the day the bill was introduced, with a request to have any minority report prepared by the twelfth.[10]

Further allegations were made during the course of the debate that the bill was written before termination of the committee hearings. Representative Klein charged this openly on the floor and even maintained that its writing began before the hearings opened.[11] The charge seems to receive some support from a statement made by Chairman Hartley himself. As early as January 29, before committee hearings opened, he was reported as saying that the committee would propose an omnibus labor reform bill which would be ready for consideration not later than March 15. All the issues which he then stated the committee would consider appeared in the bill introduced on April 10.[12]

9. U.S. House of Representatives, Committee on Education and Labor, *Labor-Management Relations Act, 1947*, Report No. 245, 80th Congress, 1st Sess., April 11, 1947, cited as *Hartley Report*. The *Minority Report* is in the same document, pp. 64–112.

10. *Ibid.*, p. 64.

11. *Daily Cong. Rec.*, 93:3530. Cf. also Representative Powell's statement, *ibid.*, 93:3584. A convenient source for the congressional committee reports and debates in connection with the formulation and adoption of Taft-Hartley is the *Legislative History of the Labor Management Relations Act, 1947*, published by the National Labor Relations Board (Washington, 1948), Vols. 1 and 2. We cite the committee reports individually, and the debates by reference to *Daily Congressional Record*, which was used in the *Legislative History*, and the paging of which differs from that of the bound volumes of the *Record*.

12. *New York Times*, January 30, 1947. Describing his legislative strategy and defending the actions of his committee at a later date, Hartley admitted that the

From the Wagner Act to Taft-Hartley

Also appearing frequently was the charge that H.R. 3020 as reported was written with the help of prominent employer and industry spokesmen. Such allegations were made from the first days of the debate and continued even after the final conference measure was passed over the President's veto. This charge was made most specifically by Representative Klein, and it was echoed and re-echoed in the House.[13] It was said also that, no matter what one could say about who wrote it, comparison of the bill with the 1946 legislative proposals of the NAM showed amazing similarities. A point-by-point comparison was introduced into the debate by Representative Blatnik on April 17.[14]

---

measure was worked out "behind closed doors" but defended it by saying: "Nevertheless, a certain measure of secrecy was essential. There were many differences of opinion within the Committee on particular legal phraseology, and on the best method of tackling individual problems. Had these differences of opinion become known to the labor leaders here in Washington the well-organized propaganda forces at their disposal would have exploited such differences to defeat the purposes of the legislation, and to make our task even more difficult." Hartley, *op. cit.*, p. 50. Hartley indicated that a measure acceptable to majority committee members was worked out first. This was considered by the full committee. The legislation was then taken to the Republican caucus of the House, where further changes were adopted, and finally back to the full committee where it was further amended. *Ibid.*

As to the charges of aid by industry in the writing of the bill, he reviewed the legislative background of the Hartley Bill especially in relation to the old Smith Committee proposals and the Case Bill of the former Congress, and concluded that "it would appear ridiculous for the labor bosses and their spokesmen in Congress to attack the legislation as hastily conceived or worked out behind closed doors by representatives of business organizations." *Ibid.*, p. 60.

13. Klein's statement is quoted: "The new House labor bill was not written with the help of the Democratic members of the committee. In fact, they were not consulted and no full committee meetings were held to discuss it. The bill was actually written with the help of several industry representatives and some lawyers from the National Association of Manufacturers and the United States Chamber of Commerce. [He named William Ingles, T. R. Iserman, and Jerry Morgan, with their industrial connections.] This group of high-priced lawyers quietly worked up the most vicious bill yet produced. The Democratic members were ignored. For 2 weeks no committee meeting was called." *Daily Cong. Rec.*, 93:3530.

See also the remarks of Mr. Powell, *ibid.*, p. 3584. "The tragic thing about it is that we, the Representatives of the people, meaning the gentlemen on both sides of the aisle, did not write this bill. Not only did we not write it but we did not even see it, and right now not one-half of the Members, both Republican and Democrat, of this Congress have read the bill. This bill was written on the fifth floor of the Old House Office Building, written by over a score of corporation lawyers, paid not by the Government of the United States, not by even small business, but paid by big business, monopoly business."

14. *Ibid.*, pp. 3732–33. The CIO and AFL made the same charges. See *New York Times*, April 17, 1947. The NAM thought enough of these charges to later make a specific denial in a mimeographed statement made available to the public,

The tone and pattern which the House debates were to follow were set by the statements of the majority and minority in their reports on the Hartley Bill. Before analyzing their positions, the chronology of the debate should be noted.

While the general debate did not actually commence until after the adoption of the six-hour rule for debate, there was discussion of the bill on the day previous, and an important debate about the bill on April 15 when the rule to govern debate was being considered in the House. This rule allowed six hours for general debate on the measure and a very restricted time, under a five-minute rule, for the proposing and consideration of amendments. In any event there were not more than three sittings of the House given over to debate on the measure, for the bill was passed on April 17. Nine major amendments were offered which would have softened the bill somewhat but were overwhelmingly rejected. Three slight alterations accepted in the final stages of debate would have strengthened existing restrictions on labor activity or added new ones. The final vote for passage of the measure, after a motion to recommit was soundly beaten, was 308 to 107. Only 22 Republicans voted against the bill, while 93 Democrats stood with the 215 Republicans voting in the affirmative.

The bill presented to the House for debate was long and complicated. It covered some sixty-six pages of text with many sections that could not be understood without constant reference to other sections. The majority presented this bill as a "labor bill of rights." In his opening remarks in the report Chairman Hartley listed twenty major points that the bill would accomplish. Each of these would-be accomplishments was stressed as a boon to labor, as an aid to smooth labor-management relations, and as giving privileges and protections to individual workers that most working people desired and had not been able to achieve under the Wagner Act. It was contended also that the then present period of industrial strife and unrest was a result of abuses within the "House of Labor" that would be cured by the suggested bill and that the result would be industrial peace. The proponents of this bill, and especially the majority members of the committee, were called the real friends of labor, the real champions of

---

Who Wrote the Taft-Hartley Bill?, January 13, 1948. One gets the impression from some remarks of Congressman Blatnik that each representative had received a leather-bound copy of the NAM booklet, *Now Let's Build America,* with his name inscribed in gold on the cover. This booklet contained the NAM legislative proposals formulated at the Fifty-first Annual Congress of American Industry. *Daily Cong. Rec.,* 93:3600.

the public, for they had considered all the interests involved and not only industry's or labor's alone. This strategy was followed by the majority throughout the debates. The opening gun, a speech by Mr. Smith of Ohio on the day before the bill was called up for debate, reiterated the theme that the Wagner Act "does not bestow upon wage-earners the benefits claimed."[15] That the NLRA was not the Magna Carta of labor, but that H.R. 3020 was a fair bill and would protect the rights of workers, was woven into the web of the majority argument in every major defense made of the bill; the Hartley Bill was not harsh; it was not restrictive; it was, on the contrary, as fair and as unbiased as the Wagner Act had not been in its intent, its interpretation, and its administration. These remarks must be borne in mind for contrast with what was said during and after the Senate and House conference.[16] Another tune played in many ways and at all times was that Congress by the return of Republicans to a majority in that body had received a "mandate from the people" to enact reform labor legislation.

The minority in their report on H.R. 3020 attacked these premises vigorously and made the essential points that were to set the pattern for the opposition on the floor of the House. The Hartley Bill, they argued, was not truly representative of public interests. The bill was one-sided, giving all to the interests of business and industry; furthermore, the wishes of employers expressed during the hearings had been given full satisfaction while labor appeals were ignored.[17] They bitterly condemned the majority favoring the bill for covering themselves with the cloak of ostensible friendliness to labor. They argued that

15. *Daily Cong. Rec.*, 93:3471–75.

16. Cf. *infra*, pp. 384–87.

17. The minority had some difficulty with this argument, for the failure of labor representatives to propose any suggested legislation of their own, or admit that there were perhaps some abuses which could stand legislative treatment, was an outstanding factor in the committee hearings and deliberations. Mr. Murray and Mr. Green both finally agreed that jurisdictional strikes were morally unjustifiable, although they both indicated they could be solved without legislation. Mr. Green for the AFL thought that perhaps employers could be guaranteed extended free-speech rights. Nor did labor in general, and the CIO in particular, endear itself to Congress by direct and indirect assertions that Congress was incapable and not prepared to act on labor legislation. Cf. testimony of Van A. Bittner, U.S. House of Representatives, Committee on Education and Labor, *Hearings, Amendments to the National Labor Relations Act*, 80th Congress, 1st Sess., 1947, pp. 2361–2465, cited as House Committee on Education and Labor, *Hearings, 1947*. Mr. Hartley writing at a later date stresses this point and is insistent that labor's nonco-operative attitude during the course of the hearings had some effect on the final provisions included in the bill. Hartley, *op. cit.*, p. 48.

some of the most bitter foes of labor organization in this country were leaders in the formulation and fight for this bill. In addition, they contended that the majority was ignoring the basic economic and social issues of the day—such matters as inflation, housing shortages, and the lack of congressional action on minimum wages and the extension of social security. Placing the onus on labor abuses was merely a political device for covering up failures on the most significant problems of the day. They denied the "mandate of the people" refrain by insisting that the election results were really indicative of aroused public feeling over these more basic matters; furthermore, the Republicans in their 1944 platform and in the major pronouncements of party leaders did not campaign on the kind of national labor policy now proposed.

The opposition protested too that the President's suggestions were given no heed. It was asserted that at least the proposal for joint study should have been accepted, since many of the matters included in the bill were areas of ignorance for the congressmen as well as for the country at large. The majority was attacked in particular for forcing a measure of great complexity to a vote before it could be given adequate study by individual representatives and the House as a whole. It was argued that House members were swayed by their emotions and prejudices to such an extent that they were prepared to act on a momentous piece of legislation although most of them had not even read the bill in its entirety and certainly did not understand its full meaning and impact. There was severe criticism of the undue haste with which the measure was being considered.[18] Finally, it was said that the Republican policy-makers had decided that labor legislation of this nature must be passed; no matter what the members of the Labor Committee did or did not believe, they were forced by the Republican organization to report the kind of a bill that did emerge.

While the House debates at times became very caustic, personal, and bitter, on the whole they seemed dispirited. The majority was confident of victory from the time the measure was introduced, and charges were never seriously or fully answered. At the same time, the opposition through such stalwarts as Lesinski and Sabath admitted in the opening discussions and continued to lament throughout that there was nothing they could do to stem the tide in the House, and it was almost useless trying. Some matters received no attention or very scant attention, although they represented new departures in labor policy. Among these were the provisions relating to the reorganization

18. Congressman Sabath spoke of the "indecent rush" to pass the Hartley Bill. *Daily Cong. Rec.*, 93:6545.

of the NLRB, to craft units, to prehearing elections, to the use of temporary injunctions, to suits for breach of contract, to the banning of political contributions, and to the prohibition of strikes by government employees. This is only a partial list, but for some of these crucial items there are not even passing references recorded in the journal of the debates.

We are forced to conclude that the House proceedings did not do credit to that body in terms of adequate and relevant analysis of the important issues presented. Whether because of the shortness of time, the lack of information on the part of many members, or the sense of defeat harbored by the opposition, relatively few persons participated, and their contributions were on the whole neither brilliant nor penetrating.

COMMITTEES, HEARINGS, AND DEBATES—THE SENATE

The membership of the House Committee on Education and Labor as a whole was relatively inexperienced in so far as congressional service was concerned. The same cannot be said for the Senate Committee on Labor and Public Welfare. Of the thirteen members on this committee, eight were Republicans and five were Democrats.[19] Two of the eight Republicans had not previously served on the committee. Of the remaining six Republicans, the chairman, Mr. Taft, had served seven years, two others had served six each, and the three others had each served two years. All five Democratic members had seen previous service on the Labor Committee. Four had accumulated two or more years of service, and the other was a member for nine years previously. The six Republicans, then, had a total of twenty-five years' accumulated service, while the five Democrats had among them served more than forty-nine years. Two Republican Senators, Morse and Ives, also, had long experience in labor relations prior to their entry into the Senate.

In the Senate, as in the House, the members of the minority party did not act as a unit in the reporting and consideration of the committee bill. Senators Ellender and Hill did not join with their colleagues in the minority report. In the vote on S. 1126, the Taft Bill, Ellender was recorded for passage, while Hill voted against the

19. The members of the Senate Committee on Labor and Public Welfare were: Robert A. Taft, *chairman;* George D. Aiken, Vermont; Joseph H. Ball, Minnesota; H. Alexander Smith, New Jersey; Wayne Morse, Oregon; Forest C. Donnell, Missouri; William E. Jenner, Indiana; Irving M. Ives, New York; Elbert D. Thomas, Utah; James E. Murray, Montana; Claude Pepper, Florida; Allen J. Ellender, Louisiana; and Lister Hill, Alabama; with Philip R. Rodgers, *clerk.*

measure. In the Senate committee, however, unlike the House, there was sharp and serious disagreement between some Republican members. Senators Morse and Ives stood out as opposed to important restrictions that their colleagues favored. Senators Taft, Ball, Donnell, Jenner, and Smith all signed supplemental reports supporting in whole or in part amendments that would have made the final bill more restrictive. Only Morse, however, voted against his colleagues when the Senate bill was passed. There was what might be termed a "conservative-liberal" split in the committee majority. The bill as finally accepted by the Senate included most of the provisions desired by Senator Taft, who represented the conservative views on the committee.

According to a statement of Taft in the majority report, the committee heard some 83 witnesses. Our own count in the hearings of all testimony available to the committee included some 97 witnesses. Labor and labor organizations were represented by 31 witnesses, while employers and employer associations had 41 spokesmen. Three congressmen were heard on their proposed bills, and 5 public officials, including former Governor Stassen of Minnesota, presented testimony. Nine miscellaneous witnesses recorded their views, including one individual, Cecil B. DeMille, who also testified before the House, representatives of engineering societies, architectural associations, the Foreman's Association of America, the Farm Bureau, the American Nurses' Association, and the NAACP. The professors testifying as experts, Wolman of Columbia and Slichter of Harvard, were not an altogether representative cross-section of the expert views available. Among the lawyers, prominent corporation labor lawyers were in a majority.

The Senate hearings proceeded much more slowly than did those in the House, having begun on January 29 and ending two days earlier than the House hearings on March 13. The printed record includes four volumes, totaling 2,424 pages. There were almost daily sessions during this time, and these were followed by four weeks of executive sessions held almost daily in which all members of the committee, according to their own word, participated. On the day that the House passed the Hartley Bill, April 17, Senator Taft introduced S. 1126 in the Senate. The contrast seems obvious.

The committee bill was as lengthy as the House measure, covering some 68 pages of text. It was, however, much better organized than H.R. 3020. This is not to say that it was not complicated. The final bill which became law was based on the Taft Bill, and, as the analysis in the succeeding chapters will demonstrate, its complicated structure, its maze of technicalities, and its difficult language often couched in negative terms, did not make it a model of clarity, conciseness, and simplicity. Both sides of the Senate realized this, and while the supporters of the measure blamed it on the difficulty and technicality of the subject matter the legislation treated, it was used as ammunition by the opposition. The bill was, nevertheless, a better-designed measure technically and structurally than was the Hartley Bill of the other body.

The criticism leveled at the House committee as to the conduct of the hearings and the writing of the bill could not be leveled at the Senate committee. Perhaps general criticism could be made of the method of the hearings and the committee procedure in general, but this is true for many of the congressional committees. All members of the committee stated publicly that the bill that resulted, even with the minority report, represented a genuine committee effort. It was reported out by an eleven-to-two vote.[20] All members agreed that, while very conflicting viewpoints were represented on the committee, these were ameliorated and mitigated to the extent that "a fair and conscionable compromise"—the mark of a true legislative product—resulted. Contrary to the feeling of some members of the House, the Senate felt that on the whole the committee conduct of the hearings did make possible a true sample of views that should have been heard.[21] In a way this was demonstrated by the fact that both majority and minority members in the reports of the committee and in the debates were able to turn to the hearings for evidence to support their various points of view. The minority, of course, insisted that while the hearings were perhaps long enough and thorough enough, an even better result would have been obtained if the President's proposal for an impartial and more nonpolitical body to make a prelegislation survey had been followed.

Veiled or open assertions that bitter enemies of labor wrote the

20. Senator Thomas voted to report out the bill, although he also signed the minority report. He felt it was a committee measure and ought to be considered by the Senate.

21. See as a good example of this attitude the remarks of Senator Morse, made on March 10 after the hearings were concluded and on April 17 when the Taft Bill was introduced. *Daily Cong. Rec.*, 93:1884, 3786. Chairman Herzog of the NLRB in his testimony for the Board did intimate that too many of the employer witnesses did not have good bargaining relations with their employees. U.S. Senate, Committee on Labor and Public Welfare, *Hearings, Labor Relations Program*, 80th Cong., 1st Sess., 1947, Pt. 4, p. 1852, cited as Senate Committee on Labor and Public Welfare, *Hearings, 1947*.

Senate bill in its entirety were never vigorously made in the Senate as in the House. Largely it was not necessary, since most of the help the committee received was an open and acknowledged fact. Gerard D. Reilly, a former member of the NLRB who had aided Senator Ball in the formulation of some of his measures, was employed by the majority of the committee to help in the writing of their bill. Mr. Reilly, of course, was known as a proponent of Wagner Act revision, not only from past statements and activities and the views which he shared with Senator Ball; he had clearly make known his opinion when he appeared as witness before the committee on the last day of its public hearings. It is reported that his engagement as a consultant by the committee was by a divided vote.[22] Similar complaints of possible bias and partiality against Thomas E. Shroyer, who was selected as staff adviser on labor relations to the committee, were also heard. The appointment of Shroyer, who had been an NLRB regional attorney in Cleveland, was announced by Taft shortly after the public hearings opened.[23] No matter what grounds these charges had or what the influence of Reilly and Shroyer on the outcome of the measure may have been, the issue did not assume the importance either in the debates or the labor press that alleged committee help in the House did.

As in the House the various reports of the committee set the tone and the framework for the discussions that followed in the eleven days of major floor debate preceding the passage of S. 1126 on May 13.[24] The majority report said: "The Committee bill is predicated on our belief that a fair and equitable labor policy can best be achieved by equalizing existing laws in a manner which will encourage free collective bargaining."[25] This was the keystone of the majority strategy, and it was voiced over and over again at every critical point in the proceedings. Senator Taft commenced the hearings with that

22. *Daily Labor Report,* No. 49:AA–1, March 11, 1947. President Murray of the CIO in a letter to Taft demanded the removal of Reilly, stating among other things that he was widely denounced by "the entire labor movement as biased and partisan." *CIO News,* March 24, 1947, p. 16.

23. *Daily Labor Report,* No. 21:A–15, January 30, 1947.

24. U.S. Senate, Committee on Labor and Public Welfare, *Federal Labor Relations Act of 1947,* Report No. 105, 80th Cong., 1st Sess., April 17, 1947, cited as *Taft Report.* Part 2, *Minority Views,* is dated April 22, 1947. Also included in Part 1 were a separate report by Senator Thomas, supplemental views containing the suggested amendments of Senators Taft, Ball, Donnell, and Jenner which they were to offer to the committee bill, and the views of Senator Smith, who was concurring with reservations to the supplemental views of the four other majority members.

25. *Ibid.,* Pt. 1, p. 2.

idea stated publicly, and he reiterated it at the conclusion of the conference that produced Taft-Hartley and even after the bill had become law. Unlike the House, however, not so little was made of the Wagner Act. Rather, stress was placed on the fact that the Wagner Act and the Norris–La Guardia Act were experimental in nature, and that the experiment, though not entirely unsuccessful, showed that changes were necessary; moreover, the Supreme Court in its interpretation of the Anti-injunction Act and the Clayton Act placed those who were protected by the NLRA beyond the reach of federal antitrust law; and, furthermore, a poor and biased administration of the Wagner Act, in part stemming from the one-sided character of the Act, had played such havoc with the Act and permitted so many abuses to develop that only additional legislation could rectify the situation. The majority in the Senate did not stress as strongly the claim that they were carrying out the "mandate of the people" as had been done in the House. They did, of course, insist that this was a fair bill and not harsh or restrictive. It was in the Senate that Republican colleagues of the House majority called the other body's bill vicious and harsh. The argument was stressed that the equitableness of the Senate proposals would have to be accepted in order to meet the threat of a presidential veto. Naturally, as in the House, every exposition or defense of the bill insisted that the measure provided exactly the formula needed to solve the kinds of strikes occurring at the time; the bill would bring industrial peace.

These same arguments were used by the right wing of the committee to support their four major amendments: (1) making it an unfair labor practice for employees or unions to interfere with or coerce employees in the exercise of their rights to join or refrain from joining a union or engaging in organizational activities; (2) placing important restrictions on industry-wide bargaining; (3) placing important restrictions on welfare funds; and (4) allowing direct action against secondary boycotts and jurisdictional strikes by declaring them unlawful, permitting injunctions on petition of private parties, and providing that injured parties could sue directly in the courts.

The opening paragraph of the minority views read as follows:[26]

This bill is designed to weaken the effective program of labor legislation which has been, with great pains, built up over the years. It would be destructive of much that is valuable in the prevention of labor-management conflicts. It contains many barriers, traps, and pitfalls that can only make more difficult the settlement of disputes. Its principal results would be to create misunderstanding and conflict, and to aggravate the imbalance between wages, prices, and profits which already endangers our prosperity.

26. *Ibid.*, Pt. 2, p. 1.

It can be seen that this was substantially similar to the opposition arguments in the lower chamber. Even more in the Senate did the minority fall back on the original proposals of the President in his State of the Union Message and score the majority for giving these no heed. They attacked the Republican majority's attempt to slough off all blame for postwar industrial unrest on labor abuses instead of attempting to find solutions for the basic social and economic issues of the day. With the help of Senator Ives, they continually contended that the forcing of an omnibus measure on the Senate was unjust; that this, as well as other things, showed that the Republicans were ordered to follow this procedure by their policymakers, although many Republican senators felt that on many things included there was no need for legislation at all.

That the area of disagreement between the majority and the minority in the Senate was less than in the House is shown by the number of proposals in the committee bill which the minority members and other opposition members on the floor stated they would agree with if the bill went no further. Such an area of agreement was obviously absent from the more vituperative statements and discussions in the House.[27]

On April 23 the general debate on the Taft Bill in the Senate commenced. While only nine actual days were given over to major debate on the bill, it was not until May 13 that the final vote was taken. Many more major amendments were suggested and discussed than in the House. And, at the same time, amendments adopted by the Senate as a whole were much more significant than the relatively minor changes instituted by the lower chamber on their bill. Among the more important of the changes accepted by action of the whole body were included: (1) making coercion of employees by unions an unfair labor practice; (2) the Ball amendment relating to restrictions on payment to employee representatives; (3) part of the Taft amendment making unlawful the boycotts, jurisdictional strikes, and sympathy strikes which were already made unfair labor practices, and providing for direct suits in the courts by any injured party for injunctions or damage suits; (4) an amendment prohibiting certification of unions whose officers were members of the Communist party; and (5) the McLellan amendment providing for "free speech" for employers and employees. Important amendments offered but rejected included the following: (1) an amendment that would have restricted industry-wide bargaining; (2) that part of the Ball and Taft amendments on unlawful activities that would have opened up the use of the

27. *Ibid.*, pp. 40 and 41.

injunction remedy to private parties; (3) the Ball-Byrd amendment to outlaw the union shop; and (4) the O'Daniel amendment to restrict drastically the application of union-security provisions. These rejected amendments stand out as a mark of a Senate attitude in contrast to the feeling in the house, which had already included the more important of the rejected proposals in their H.R. 3020.

The question of individual measures for special problems in place of the proposed omnibus measure reached the floor of the Senate for a vote when Senator Morse proposed that S. 1126 be recommitted to the Labor Committee in order that the various titles could be reported out as separate measures. A vote was taken on this proposal on May 7 during the fifth day of debate and narrowly missed being adopted; the vote was 44 to 43. In contrast to the House a substitute measure embodying the principal views of the minority was presented to the Senate. This measure, introduced by Senator Murray on May 9, received some discussion. On May 13, the next legislative day on which the Senate again considered the Taft Bill, it was defeated by a vote of 73 to 19. On the same day the Taft Bill as amended passed the Senate with 68 yeas and 24 nays. Twenty-one Democrats joined with the forty-seven Republicans on the affirmative side as contrasted to the three Republicans (Morse, Langer, and Malone) who voted with the remaining Democrats opposing the measure.

Absent almost entirely from the general Senate debate were the caustic and bitter interchanges of a highly personal nature that marked much of the discussion in the House. This difference seemingly resulted from the different way in which the two committees went about their work of conducting the hearings and writing the bills. This is not to infer that the Senate body was beyond criticism for its methods of work, but its methods were very different from those of the House committee, if only a part of the allegations made by the minority members in the lower chamber are believed. Also absent from the Senate debate until the conference report was the defeatist attitude of the minority. While relatively few members of the minority party in the Senate took an active part in the debate, they were certainly not "lying down on the job" in attempting to show fallacies in the approach of the majority party and their proposed legislation.

The very serious omission of topics from discussion that we noticed in many instances in the House debates did not occur to such a great extent in the Senate. Again, it must be remembered that the Senate had more time, and there were fewer members to be heard in the time available; nevertheless, some important problems that it would seem deserved the full consideration of the Senate received little time. Often during the debate over these matters, even where time was given to them, the remarks consisted of explaining again and again what this or that provision would or would not do; but at the same time there was an absence of discussion dealing with the essential questions of whether the proposal made was the best possible or the best designed to meet a particular problem. And often when such statements or answers were sought by opposition members from supporters of the Taft Bill they were given in return a further explanation of the mechanics of the questioned proposal and what it was intended to accomplish. Among important issues which received this kind of "debate" or meager treatment were the following: craft units, prehearing elections, union-shop elections, the precedence of state anti-closed-shop laws, the changes proposed for the mediation service, the handling of disputes involving national emergencies, provisions on breach of contract, bans on political contributions and expenditures, strikes by government employees, and the provisions creating the joint committee for further study. Many of these matters which received inadequate treatment during the debates were the subject of much controversy in the early administration of the Taft-Hartley Act.

The whole Senate debate, despite this criticism, was on a much higher plane than the discussion in the House. There was much more of an attempt to get questions answered and to discuss real issues clearly. This procedure was not always successful, for while the answers of Senator Taft and his colleagues on particular issues were much more reasoned and full than the meager answers of their counterparts in the other body, there was still much to be desired. The controversy arising within the first year of the Act as to what some of the legislative history meant in the interpretation of the Act bears out this point. The Senate with its ninety-six members, and operating under a much less restrictive time limit than the House, naturally produced a much fuller debate. Speeches and colloquies were longer and contained much more of the philosophy and the reasoning and attitudes behind the arguments of the various participants. The Senate debate was open and full and compares favorably with similar debates on other important issues of national policy. Yet one has the feeling that it still did not match the difficulty of the subject or the needs of the times.

From the Wagner Act to Taft-Hartley

Almost a month after the House had passed its bill, that measure and the Senate proposal went to a conference of House and Senate appointed managers, who were to work out a compromise acceptable to both chambers. Both the House and the Senate bills passed their respective bodies with more than the two-thirds vote necessary to override a presidential veto. This veto factor had been much in the minds of senators as their work on their own bill had progressed. There was a strong feeling that a bill such as the House measure, often called "tough" and "harsh" on the Senate floor even by majority members, would not be accepted by the President. Ives, Morse, and Aiken at times had opposed the strengthening of the Taft Bill as it came from committee, often on the ground that amendments of the Ball-Taft variety would not be countenanced by the President. There was division of opinion as to the political wisdom of getting a bill passed in the first session of the Eightieth Congress by making it a "safe" one, or whether the better strategy would not have been to design a bill the President could not sign, so that the Republicans could make political hay of the issue in 1948 and serve notice what the 1948 Republican intentions would be labor-wise. Important in the background of the conference was the veto possibility, coupled with speculation that perhaps a veto might be upheld in the Senate, where it was expected that some of the twenty-one Democrats who had supported the Taft measure might, in the event of a veto, switch to the support of their own party.

Appointed as managers from the House were Chairman Hartley and Representatives Landis, Hoffman, Lesinski, and Barden. The latter two were minority members, although Barden had generally supported the majority of the committee, and his advocacy of change in basic labor policy was old and well known. From the Senate side the managers were Chairman Taft and Senators Ball, Ives, Murray, and Ellender. The latter two represented the minority party. Murray was of course opposed to the Taft Bill as passed and naturally even more strongly opposed to the House version. Senator Ellender, on the other hand, had not joined with his Democratic colleagues in the minority report on the Senate committee bill. He had, in fact, introduced some legislation of his own that had gone far beyond the suggestions of his party leader, the President.

By the time the conference managers began their work on May 15 the House bill had generally become known through constant press reference as a "tough" or "harsh" measure. The Senate bill, on the other hand, was considered "soft" and "mild"—at least in comparison to what the House had accepted in the Hartley Bill. A brief summary of the essential differences and similarities in the two bills is necessary in order that the task of the Conference Committee can better be understood. Significant similarities in the two bills, though not all particulars were identical, were:

1. Certain unfair labor practices of unions, including union coercion of workers, were prohibited.
2. Employer "free-speech" rights were extended.
3. The closed shop was outlawed, but the union shop under certain restrictions permitted.
4. Involuntary check-offs were prohibited.
5. Supervisors were removed from coverage of the law.
6. Bargaining rights were denied to unions with Communist officers.
7. Government injunctions were provided in "national emergency" disputes.
8. An independent agency for mediation and conciliation was set up outside of the Department of Labor.
9. Federal district courts were opened for suits for damages for unlawful concerted activities and violation of collective bargaining agreements.

The most essential differences were these:

1. The House bill abolished the NLRB and created a board for hearing cases and an agency for prosecuting cases under an administrator. The Senate bill provided only for minor alterations in the organization of the Board.
2. The House bill had a long and detailed list of unlawful concerted activities by unions and brought unions under the antitrust acts. The Senate bill had a shorter section making boycotts and certain jurisdictional and other strikes unlawful.
3. Injunctions against unions on petition of *employers* were permitted by the House for unlawful concerted activities. The Senate bill provided for injunctions on petition of the *Board* in unfair labor practice cases, such injunctions being mandatory in certain types of cases against unions.
4. Economic strikes were permitted by the House bill only after a vote of approval of employees concerned and after notice and cooling-off periods. Such procedural limitations on strikes in the Senate bill were restricted to "national emergency" disputes.
5. Mass picketing was made unlawful in the House bill.
6. The House bill outlawed entirely employer payments to any union or joint health and welfare funds. The Senate regulated them only.
7. Industry-wide bargaining was greatly limited by the House.
8. Detailed regulation of internal union activity was provided for by the House bill. The Senate bill provided little regulation.

9. The House bill banned strikes by government employees.
10. The House bill banned political contributions or expenditures by unions in national elections or primaries.
11. The Senate bill called for a joint committee to study labor-management relations.

The importance of the omnipresent possibility of a presidential veto that might be sustained was indicated in the early reports concerning the conference. The attitude of the majority of the conferees from both the House and the Senate showed this as the conference opened. While some of the House conferees were more moderately inclined than the tone of their whole bill, they had, nevertheless, supported the general strategy of calling the Hartley Bill fair and just. Their first major concession was the admission early in negotiations that something similar to the Taft measure would have to be achieved to meet the veto possibility. As the conference progressed, they became more and more conscious, at least for public purposes, of the concessions they were making to the Senate. Taft in reporting to the press the daily accomplishments of the conference had early listed each day the concessions made by the House. These seemed more numerous than Senate concessions to the House. These outlines of the give and take were later soft-pedaled after Mr. Hartley made several statements that he was "catching it" in the House. A complete news ban was finally placed on the activities of the conference, and a *New York Times* story intimated that the censorship was imposed at the request of the House conferees.[28] The House conferees generally answered their critics in the House by asserting that the Senate bill as passed was more restrictive than it would otherwise have been if the early House measure had not set an example; and, second, that if it had not been for the early and firm decision of the House leaders to push through an omnibus bill, the final legislation sent to the President would have been in piecemeal form and subject to piece-by-piece destruction by the veto.[29]

28. *New York Times,* May 26, 1947. Our account of the conference depends a great deal on the news stories and by-line articles in the *Times.*
29. *Ibid.,* May 27, 1947. This statement of the "early example" intent of the House seems contrary to Hartley's statements as early as February 12 when he indicated the intention of House leaders to wait with their bill until the Senate acted first. This was based on previous congressional history when the House had on occasion produced restrictive labor measures only to see them refused or emasculated by the Senate. At that time Hartley was reported as anxious to re-establish the prestige of the House labor committee. *Ibid.,* February 13, 1947.

Hartley indicates in his book that he was at first in agreement with the idea of waiting for developments in the Senate before the House prepared its bill, because

Certain remarks of Mr. Hartley made at the conclusion of the conference seem to indicate that the House leaders were not sincere in their original defense of their measure or that they had changed their minds somewhat in the intervening month between the passage of the Hartley Bill and the Senate acceptance of the Taft Bill. He said: "Confession being good for the soul, I can say now that we deliberately put everything we could into the House bill so we would have something to concede and still get an adequate bill in the end."[30] Thus on May 29 the "compromise" measure was ready to be returned to the respective chambers.

On June 3 the conference report on H.R. 3020 was given to the House.[31] The following day the conference measure was agreed to by the House after a one-hour general debate. The vote was 320 to 79, a total of 217 Republicans and 103 Democrats affirming the bill. Opposing it were 66 Democrats, 12 Republicans, and 1 American Laborite.

Most members of the House did not have access to the conference report until the morning of June 4. Despite this fact the report almost missed being read in its entirety to the House. Mr. Hartley himself thought this was not necessary. In his opening remarks defending the bill Hartley tried to minimize the concessions the House had made to the Senate and at the same time to intimate that the bill was still a strong measure.

of the likelihood that the Republican senators would get out an acceptable measure, and the fact that the Senate was organized before the House and had already begun hearings. "As time passed, however, it became more and more apparent that once again the House would have to take the initiative." Hartley, *op. cit.*, p. 34.

As to the early plan of passing an omnibus measure Hartley said: ". . . It was my decision to wrap all the provisions that appeared desirable into a single package and to put the entire weight of the Republican Party and the southern Democrats behind it.

"In this decision we ran afoul of a different plan of operation developing in the Senate. Over in the other body, the leaders had proposed a series of different bills. In forcing the Senate to take the omnibus labor bill we sent them, the House of Representatives made its greatest single contribution to the rapidly developing labor legislation." *Ibid.*, p. 35.

30. *New York Times*, May 30, 1947. Hartley suggests in his book that the technique of deliberately and consciously making the House bill appear stiff and harsh at many points was part of the design for the over-all legislative strategy. He said: ". . . We did include among its original provisions several that could easily have been omitted without sacrificing any of the basic philosophy of the original bill.

"Our method was simple but not easily understood. We merely provided several different remedies for the same offense." Hartley, *op. cit.*, p. 67.

31. U.S. House of Representatives, *Conference Report, Labor-Management Relations Act, 1947*, Report No. 510, 80th Cong., 1st Sess., June 3, 1947. The same report was the official report in the Senate.

Just what really basic concessions did the House conferees make? We conceded on the ban of our bill [o]n industry-wide bargaining. We conceded on the ban in our bill on welfare funds. We conceded on the question of injunctions to be obtained by private employers and on the provisions making labor organizations subject to the antitrust laws.

I call your attention to what is left in this bill, because I think you are going to find there is more in this bill than may meet the eye and may have been heretofore presented to you.[32]

The general line of argument for the measure was that a good bill accomplishing the original intentions of the House had been achieved, and yet it was a measure of the type that the President could not morally veto. Some Republicans in the House thought that the bill was not strong enough. The spokesman voicing such sentiments was Hoffman, who maintained the bill was a gift to the labor leaders of the country. The House, he claimed, had given way completely to the Senate in conference; furthermore, he made point of the fact, as did the minority, that things happened so fast in the conference that no one knew rightly what was taking place at any particular moment. Early in the debate, on a point of order, he attempted to have the conference report thrown out because it contained language and treated matters not in either of the original bills.

The opposition argued that this bill was a grave matter, yet most of the representatives were acting without knowing or understanding the bill. They pleaded with the House to consider its action. They naturally took as an argument in their favor contentions of the majority conferees that House concessions had not made the bill less restrictive or harsh than it had originally been. According to Lesinski,

32. *Daily Cong. Rec.*, 93:6540. Speaking of the conference strategy, Hartley said: "Our strategy at that time was so simple as to be almost transparent.

"We had to retain as much of the House measure as we could without jeopardizing the final two-thirds majority in the Senate.

"As the situation developed the conference became a battle of nerves and, more than that, a battle of public relations.

"We had to create the general impression that most of the original Hartley bill had been discarded by the conferees in favor of the so-called milder provisions of Taft's bill." Hartley, *op. cit.*, p. 75. And at an earlier point he wrote: "We knew what was known to few persons outside of Washington at that time . . . the discrepancies between the Taft bill and the Hartley bill were more fancied than real." *Ibid.*, p. 73.

One item in Senator Taft's Foreword to Hartley's book seems to intimate that the strategy noted here was perhaps what Hartley thought it was, and not necessarily what Taft thought it was. He says: "There is a suggestion in Mr. Hartley's book that various desirable changes were omitted from the Senate bill simply to get enough votes to pass the bill over the President's veto. Of course, this was a consideration, but fundamentally the difference[s] with the House were brought about by differences of principle." *Ibid.*, p. xi.

strong evidence indicated that the House measure had been purposely touted as harsh and the Senate measure as soft in order to confuse the final outcome, although most of the severer points of the Hartley measure were really included in the conference bill.[33]

The Senate began its consideration of the conference measure on June 5. It concluded its debate on the following day and passed the measure by a vote of 54 to 17. Favoring the bill were 37 Republicans and 17 Democrats. Against it were 15 Democrats and Republicans Morse and Langer. Of the absentees whose views were announced, 15 would have been in the affirmative and 7 would have been opposed. Here as in the House more than the two-thirds necessary to override a veto had been attained.

Senator Taft opened the debate in the Senate with a defense of the conference report and a statement that the conference bill represented a victory for the Senate, since it was substantially the same as the version of S. 1126 sent to the conference:[34]

> . . . I think that as a general proposition I can say that the Senate conferees did not yield on any matter which was the subject of controversy in the Senate; certainly not on any important matter. The bill represents substantially the Senate bill. Concessions as to language were made here and there. We made concessions on some matters which were not perhaps dealt with in the Senate bill at all. The only major additions to the bill, as I see them, deal with matters which the Senate has approved in other measures.

The two major concessions the Senator referred to were the bans on political contributions and expenditures and on strikes of government employees. He listed a third possible major change, the featherbedding provisions taken over in part from the House. Among minor concessions made Taft included the acceptance of portions of the House bill on "free speech." The summary and analysis that Mr. Taft later offered for the record, however, of the differences between the House measure and the Senate measure and the inclusions of each in the conference bill showed many other important changes and concessions. This was not read or discussed by him in the Senate.[35] On this general position of Senator Taft was based the whole of the majority defense of the conference bill. Summed up, it said that this bill was still fair and just and represented workable solutions to the pressing labor relations problems of the day, since it was for all practical pur-

33. This was spelled out more in detail in a speech delivered to the House on the day previous to the President's veto message. *Daily Cong. Rec.*, 93:7493. The CIO made a similar charge. See *New York Times*, June 5, 1947.

34. *Daily Cong. Rec.*, 93:6593.   35. *Ibid.*, pp. 6598–6603.

poses the same bill which the Senate had originally agreed to and which had been based on these premises of equitableness and workability.

The stand of the minority was similar to that taken in the House but much more detailed and thoroughly presented. Here too the Senate majority was assailed for retreating from the stand it had taken on its own legislation before the conference. The opposition said that none of the concessions were minor; they were all major changes that made the bill restrictive, vicious, and unfair. The strategy of the minority seemed to be that of attacking the bill at every major point and pointing out the difficulties and problems that would arise from its acceptance. They hit very hard, of course, the previous stand of the bill's supporters in the Senate that the Wagner Act was only being amended while its essential principles and ideas were being retained. The opposition contention was that the conference "compromise" measure effectively repealed the whole of the NLRA.

Perhaps the opposition arguments were best stated and summed up, although in a more moderate form than some of the extreme statements, by Republican Senator Morse in his long speech against the bill on June 5. Two pertinent quotations follow:

I shall vote against this bill that has been reported by the conference committee because, after careful study, I am completely convinced that the amendments added in conference make it an impracticable and unadministrable law. Virtually every amendment which has been made threatens the legitimate rights of the American workingman; the net effect is to discourage and stifle collective bargaining and to impede, if not make impossible, effective enforcement of the National Labor Relations Act.

. . . .

Mr. President, this conference report is a far cry even from the Senate bill. It is unfair, it is destructive of legitimate labor rights, and administratively it is unworkable. I think it will cause, rather than prevent, labor disputes. It must, and I believe it will, be opposed by the working people of America. I think it makes a disastrous contribution to the Nation's economic health and well-being.[36]

THE VETO AND FINAL PASSAGE

On June 20 the Congress received the President's veto. President Truman had been subjected to very strong pressure to veto in the interim between the Senate and House passage of the bill and his return of the measure as unacceptable. Labor delegates poured into Washington, the White House mail in favor of a veto was very heavy, and all over the country gigantic rallies were staged by the

36. *Ibid.,* pp. 6608, 6614.

labor organizations. In New York the bill even stimulated AFL-CIO co-operation to the point that the CIO used the same banners the AFL had used at their rally in Madison Square Garden a week previous. Both organizations promised strong political programs to defeat the supporters of this "slave labor" measure. Needless to say, the prominent employer associations and the leaders in the House and Senate declared again and again during this interlude that the bill should be approved, as it represented a fair and workable solution to the labor-management relations problems facing the nation.

The President had about fifteen days to consider the measure finally approved by the Congress after the conference. Early during this period the Cabinet was reported as split over the matter of a veto. Some of the department heads felt that it would be a useless gesture in view of the almost certain overriding a veto would get in both houses. Others felt that perhaps a veto would have been proper had the nation not been faced with the threat of another coal walkout on July 1.[37] Likewise the inner-circle White House advisers were reported as divided. Of the former group, the views of Secretary Schwellenbach were definitely known as favoring a veto. Of the latter group, Clark Clifford, one of the chief Truman advisers, also supported a veto. During most of the time between his veto message and the passage of the conference measure the President was away from the White House. Before his departure he had left instructions for the kind of analysis he wanted with his aide John Steelman, and during his absence a large staff worked on the preparation of the analysis of the bill for the President. It was reported that no bill in the President's career had received the minute analysis given the Taft-Hartley Act. Cabell Phillips in the article here referred to maintained that the veto came only after the advice of a dozen of Truman's closest advisers and the final unanimous agreement of the Cabinet.[38]

From the point of view of organization and articulateness the

---

37. *New York Times,* June 8, 1948.

38. *Ibid.,* June 22, 1947. This article described the following procedure used for analyzing the bill: Secretary Schwellenbach had the major job of over-all analysis; the legal aspects were examined by the Attorney-General, who assessed the possibilities for litigation under the Act; the Secretary of Commerce gave his views on the industrial implications; Secretary Krug of the Interior Department (the then custodian of the coal mines) gave his views of the bill's effects on the coal situation; Chairman Herzog, of the NLRB, studied the administrative problems; presidential counsel Clark Clifford generally guided the conferences and particularly studied the legislative history of the bill and the many committee reports. The message itself was written by the President with the help of Clifford and Press Secretary Ross.

President's message was a good one. It covered the whole bill systematically, and yet for a message so momentous it was not lengthy or overburdening. The President first stated his conviction that there were abuses that could have been met by legislation. Had Congress followed his original January proposals concerning those abuses, and delayed further legislation until study by the proposed joint commission, he could have gone along with them. He subjected the bill to four general tests: (1) would it result in more or less intervention by the government in economic life; (2) would it improve human relations between employers and employees; (3) was it a workable bill; (4) was it a fair bill? On all four tests Mr. Truman found the bill wanting. He listed and discussed in detail nine major objections which covered practically all the sections of the bill. In almost every portion of the bill the President found objectionable items that made it unacceptable. These nine general objections were as follows:

1. The bill would substantially increase strikes.
2. The area of collective bargaining is restricted by deciding against the workers issues which were normally the subject of collective bargaining.
3. The bill would expose employers to numerous hazards by which they could be annoyed or hampered.
4. The bill would deprive workers of vital protection which they then had under the law.
5. The bill abounds in provisions which would be unduly burdensome or actually unworkable.
6. The bill would establish an ineffective and discriminatory emergency procedure for dealing with major strikes affecting the public health and safety.
7. The bill would discriminate against employees.
8. Unanimous convictions of the Labor-Management conference were ignored or upset.
9. The bill raises serious issues of public policy which transcend labor-management difficulties.

Mr. Truman at the end of the detailed analysis then stated the very general and fundamental objections which caused him to return the measure unsigned:[39]

The most fundamental test which I have applied to this bill is whether it would strengthen or weaken American democracy in the present critical hour. This bill is perhaps the most serious economic and social legislation of the past decade. Its effects—for good or ill—would be felt for decades to come.

I have concluded that the bill is a clear threat to the successful working of our democratic society.

39. *Daily Cong. Rec.*, 93:7503. This same message though in more general form was carried to the nation in a radio broadcast by the President on the same evening.

Without debate or discussion the House immediately after hearing the veto message voted to override, by a total of 331 to 83. This was 55 more votes than the two-thirds needed to override the veto. The Senate did not proceed immediately to vote. Debate followed that evening. Senator Taylor of Idaho gained the floor about 10:00 P.M. and commenced a "talkfest" with the objective of delaying the vote until the following Monday in order that the sentiment of the country over the President's message might reach the Congress. He was joined by Senators Morse, Pepper, and Murray, and, despite majority assertions to the contrary, it would seem that their objectives were achieved when the Senate agreed to postpone the final vote until 3:00 P.M. of June 23.

The majority arguments against the veto followed the pattern of Senator Taft's radio address to the nation immediately following the address of the President on June 20.[40] Taft attacked the President for misrepresenting the bill to the nation and finding no good in it whatsoever. He remonstrated with him for being able to examine the whole bill and find nothing in it that met with his approval and for not giving due credit to the time and study that was put into the bill. And, lastly, the Senator indicated that the President had not really given adequate time to the study of a measure many months in the process of completion, since most of the time the bill was available to him he was not even in the White House. These criticisms were, of course, repeated on the floor of the Senate by Taft and others. It was even insinuated that the President's message followed a CIO memorandum prepared by Lee Pressman, the CIO's general counsel. The insinuation was acidly retorted to and denied by Pepper. The main line of arguments used by the majority and indicated previously was followed to the very end of the debate. Perhaps, however, there was more tendency after the veto to admit that the bill was not perfect though it would be workable with a good administration and that it could be amended if necessary.

The minority and opposition arguments on the floor followed quite closely the President's message. The veto message itself was substantially similar to the pattern of the attack the minority had conducted after the conference. Perhaps such a strategy had been worked out beforehand. Pepper led the attack, and while the debate on the veto was ably conducted, the bipartisan support of the bill in the Senate simply overwhelmed him and his followers. At the last moment an urgent message from the ailing Senator Wagner, the father of the

40. For a text of this address see *ibid.*, p. A3232.

NLRA, was read urging the sustaining of the veto. As a final element, the minority leader, Senator Barkley, read a letter from the President addressed to himself which commended those who fought against the measure and urged the others to sustain the veto. Such procedures were to no avail. Senator Aiken, the first senator on the roll call and one of the doubtful Republicans, cast the first vote in favor of the measure and everyone then knew the veto would be overridden. It was, by a final Senate vote of 68 to 25. Thus, the Labor Management Relations Act of 1947 became law.

A final word is necessary concerning the strategy of the minority in the final days preceding the overriding of the President. One of the bitterest foes of the measure and a key figure in the Senate, Senator Thomas of Utah, was not present at the last vote. Many felt that he should have been there to bolster the minority. There is some indication that he was willing to fly from Switzerland, where he was on official business, to be present at the final vote. Indecisiveness and misunderstanding some place in the Democratic hierarchy prevented his coming. It was later said that it would have been a useless gesture, since it would not have affected the outcome. Thomas himself told this to Phil Murray via transatlantic phone. There is some question as to whether or not the President did his utmost to influence doubtful congressmen to uphold his veto. It was not until the day of the veto that he called some thirteen senators, all except one of whom had voted for the measure, to a luncheon at the White House to explain his views. As party leader perhaps the President should have done more in this respect.

The veto message itself, despite its general worth, could perhaps be criticized. Possibly the President should have been somewhat more conciliatory toward a Congress which had exhibited such majorities in favor of the vetoed bill. Perhaps he could have achieved the better legislation he ostensibly sought by recognizing and complimenting the work Congress did on the measure and by pointing out the good or better aspects of the bill and indicating that such legislation, despite his specific January proposals, he would have accepted. There was much rumor around Washington at the time to the effect that this would have been a more desirable and successful procedure. There are, of course, many political connotations difficult to assess accurately.

This is the legislative history which preceded the final adoption of the Taft-Hartley Act—a dramatic and important history, which illuminates many details of this complex legislation.

PART III

The Taft-Hartley Act

CHAPTER 11

THE TAFT-HARTLEY ACT: IN GENERAL AND ADMINISTRATIVE PROCEDURES

THE Wagner Act was a product of time and circumstance. After twelve years, under different circumstances and with many interpretations, correct and incorrect, of the experience with it, it was extensively amended and supplemented by the Labor Management Relations Act, 1947.[1] While substantial parts of the Wagner Act were retained, the amendments were far-reaching as to legal rights, controls, and administrative machinery and procedures. Very important, also, the 1947 law went far to substitute new basic labor law. The 1935 law had left comparatively untouched the limited federal statutes affecting the basic law of labor. It was assumed in 1935, also, that the general industrial relations law found in the states and localities should not be affected except in so far as necessary to accomplish the limited purposes of the Wagner Act. The 1947 law extended federal control, to some extent over management, and much more over union rights and activities, as well as to some degree over internal affairs and political activities of labor organizations. Moreover, on behalf of the public interest and the general welfare, the new law relocated the federal mediation machinery outside the Department of Labor and provided new special treatment for "national emergency" strikes. Incidentally, it prohibited strikes by federal employees. Though conceived as an incomplete code, perhaps with more limitations and controls to be added later, the Taft-Hartley Act was an "omnibus" measure and involved a great extension of federal power.

The complexity of the Labor Management Relations Act appears from a mere listing of its major sections. Following a statement of

1. 61 U.S. Stat. 136 (1947). "An Act to amend the National Labor Relations Act, to provide additional facilities for the mediation of labor disputes affecting commerce, to equalize legal responsibilities of labor organizations and employers, and for other purposes." For a note on the *Legislative History* published by the NLRB, a convenient source for the congressional committee reports and debates, see *supra*, ch. 10, n. 11.

policy its four main titles deal with (1) amendment of the National Labor Relations Act; (2) conciliation and national emergency strikes; (3) suits by and against labor organizations, welfare funds, boycotts and other unlawful combinations, restrictions on political contribution and expenditures, and strikes by government employees; and (4) creation of a Joint Congressional Committee to study the operation of the Act and other problems. It is not to be assumed, however, that these are unrelated parts of the Act. Interrelated parts must be brought together for an understanding of the Act. In general, however, we shall follow the organization employed in this Act and first of all treat it as an amendment of the Wagner Act.

It is a rather general practice to begin an Act with a statement of findings and policy. The Taft-Hartley Act contained two such statements, one which applied to the entire Act and emanated from the House, the other, in Title I, coming from the Senate and bearing directly on the amendments to the NLRA.

As its general declaration of policy,[2] the Taft-Hartley Act states:

Industrial strife which interferes with the normal flow of commerce and with the full production of articles and commodities for commerce, can be avoided or substantially minimized if employers, employees, and labor organizations each recognize under law one another's legitimate rights in their relations with each other, and above all recognize under law that neither party has any right in its relations with any other to engage in acts or practices which jeopardize the public health, safety, or interest.

It is the purpose and policy of this Act, in order to promote the full flow of commerce, to prescribe the legitimate rights of both employees and employers in their relations affecting commerce, to provide orderly and peaceful procedures for preventing the interference by either with the legitimate rights of the other, to protect the rights of individual employees in their relations with labor organizations whose activities affect commerce, to define and proscribe practices on the part of labor and management which affect commerce and are inimical to the general welfare, and to protect the rights of the public in connection with labor disputes affecting commerce.

As would be expected by one familiar with the House hearings and the formulation of this measure, these paragraphs were designed to stand in contrast to the faith and policy set forth in the introduction to the Wagner Act and retained with additions in the statement coming from the Senate. In this second statement of "Findings and Policy" the significant additions to that of the Wagner Act are the limiting words "some"—always of course assumed—in the first sentence, and the important fourth paragraph.[3]

2. Sec. 1(b).
3. Title I, Sec. 1. Italics indicate additions to Wagner Act statement.

General and Administrative Procedures

SECTION 1. The denial by *some* employers of the right of employees to organize and the refusal by *some* employers to accept the procedure of collective bargaining lead to strikes and other forms of industrial strife or unrest, which have the intent or the necessary effect of burdening or obstructing commerce by (*a*) impairing the efficiency, safety, or operation of the instrumentalities of commerce; (*b*) occurring in the current of commerce; (*c*) materially affecting, restraining, or controlling the flow of raw materials or manufactured or processed goods from or into the channels of commerce, or the prices of such materials or goods in commerce; or (*d*) causing diminution of employment and wages in such volume as substantially to impair or disrupt the market for goods flowing from or into the channels of commerce.

The inequality of bargaining power between employees who do not possess full freedom of association or actual liberty of contract, and employers who are organized in the corporate or other forms of ownership association substantially burdens and affects the flow of commerce, and tends to aggravate recurrent business depressions, by depressing wage rates and the purchasing power of wage earners in industry and by preventing the stabilization of competitive wage rates and working conditions within and between industries.

Experience has proved that protection by law of the right of employees to organize and bargain collectively safeguards commerce from injury, impairment, or interruption, and promotes the flow of commerce by removing certain recognized sources of industrial strife and unrest, by encouraging practices fundamental to the friendly adjustment of industrial disputes arising out of differences as to wages, hours, or other working conditions, and by restoring equality of bargaining power between employers and employees.

Experience has further demonstrated that certain practices by some labor organizations, their officers, and members have the intent or the necessary effect of burdening or obstructing commerce by preventing the free flow of goods in such commerce through strikes and other forms of industrial unrest or through concerted activities which impair the interest of the public in the free flow of such commerce. The elimination of such practices is a necessary condition to the assurance of the rights herein guaranteed.

It is hereby declared to be the policy of the United States to eliminate the causes of certain substantial obstructions to the free flow of commerce and to mitigate and eliminate these obstructions when they have occurred by encouraging the practice and procedure of collective bargaining and by protecting the exercise by workers of full freedom of association, self-organization, and designation of representatives of their own choosing, for the purposes of negotiating the terms and conditions of their employment or other mutual aid or protection.

These somewhat contrasting statements occur in different parts of the new Act and consequently might be expected to differ somewhat. Yet attitudes and outlooks indicated are significant. More concern with and faith in collective bargaining was apparent on the part of the Senate than of the House. The emphasis upon protection of "the rights of individual employees in their relations with labor organizations," in the introductory declaration fathered by the House, is meaningful. In general, the conference bill which became law over the President's veto seems to emphasize a congeries of legal requirements to be observed, as over against responsible representative government through democratic organization and collective bargaining, which much of management, unions quite generally, and most "outsiders" familiar with the matter, have stressed. Of course law is basic, but it can easily be carried too far. What management and labor have become accustomed to, elasticity, adaptability, and considerable discretion at many points, are among the things to be emphasized in a quest for the best road to industrial peace and representative government. Taft-Hartley, on the contrary, is widely regarded as too much a technical lawyer's act, which it in reality is, too little a product of men who know what makes the wheels go round in industry and what motivates management and workers in the very real world in which they live and work. Taft-Hartley was not a "slave labor law," but it was too much a strait-jacket, a strait-jacket which, we believe, proved a misfit at many points.

AMENDMENTS OF THE WAGNER ACT: SOME DEFINITIONS, INCLUSIONS, EXCLUSIONS

The Taft-Hartley Act contained a number of definitions, and much else, which left doubt as to their exact meaning or which changed the law in substantial respects and affected the handling of unfair labor practice cases. The definitions of "employer" and of "agent" are in point.[4] They apparently did not change the law as to the responsibility of an employer for the acts of his supervisors or other agents, although litigation on this issue was expected.[5] The Board might however be prevented from finding Chambers of Commerce or other local organizations guilty of unfair labor practices when carried on "in the interest of" an employer.[6] Just what "agent" meant in regard to charges against unions and liability to suits for damages was uncertain.[7] Other definitions or analyses open to serious objection are those of "sympathetic strikes," "boycotts," and "featherbedding."[8]

Several changes were made in the coverage of the law. As in the

4. Secs. 2(2), 2(13).
5. Some excellent lawyers believed that this might be a source of serious difficulty. Cf. Archibald Cox, "Some Aspects of the Labor Management Relations Act, 1947," *Harvard Law Review,* 61 (1947), 13–14.
6. *Supra,* ch. 4, pp. 125–26; ch. 5, pp. 168–69.
7. Cf. discussion *infra,* ch. 12, pp. 443–44; ch. 13, p. 502.
8. *Infra,* ch. 12, pp. 455–71, 476–80.

Wagner Act, an individual employed as an agricultural laborer or in the domestic service of any family or person at his home, or any individual employed by his parent or spouse, remained outside the coverage of the Act.[9] The definition of "agricultural laborer" had been warmly contested for many years, but the courts had sustained the demarcations made by the Board between farm work, not under the Act, and industrial employment in packing sheds and other plants engaged in processing farm products.[10] Employers engaged in packing and processing fruits and vegetables sought a limiting definition which would have removed part or all of the controls over their operations. But Taft-Hartley finally omitted any such definition and left Board and court decisions undisturbed. The exemption of railway labor continued with slight change in the new Act. But a new exclusion from the definition of "employee" was that of "independent contractors," thus reversing the old Board and the Supreme Court's decision in the Hearst case,[11] where newsboys had been held to be protected by the Act; apparently numerous unions of truckers and others therefore fell outside the protection and control of the amended NLRA. The exclusion also of any nonprofit hospital, as the organized medical fraternity had desired all the while, nullified a decision in a Washington, D.C., hospital case, which had been upheld on appeal.[12]

Of greater consequence was the exclusion of foremen and supervisors[13] whose organization had presented a thorny question to the

9. Sec. 2(3). In a long and bitter recognition strike of agricultural laborers on the DiGiorgio Fruit Corporation ranch, the issue was raised whether such laborers who could not obtain the protection of the Act were subject to its restraints. After the union's attempt to obtain an NLRB election had failed, the General Counsel sought and obtained an injunction, in June, 1948, against picketing and boycott by the Farm Labor Union and Teamster locals. The Trial Examiner in April, 1949, recommended dismissal of the charges against the agricultural labor organizations, holding them not subject to prosecution under the Act. Cases No. 21-CC-26, 27, 29, 34, 40.

10. The leading case is North Whittier Heights Citrus Association v. NLRB, 109 F. 2d 76 (C.C.A.9, 1940), cert. den., 310 U.S. 632 (1940). A rider incorporated in the appropriation acts from 1946 on defined "agricultural laborer" as in the Fair Labor Standards Act, and required no substantial change in Board policies.

11. NLRB v. Hearst Publications, 322 U.S. 111 (1944). For decisions in which the Board held that the amended Act required it to apply "the ordinary tests of the law of agency" in distinguishing between employees and independent contractors see Kansas City Star Co., 76 NLRB 384 (1948); Southwestern Associated Telephone Co., 76 NLRB 1105 (1948); Morris Steinberg, et al., 78 NLRB 211 (1948).

12. NLRB v. Central Dispensary and Emergency Hospital, 145 F. 2d 852 (C.A.D.C., 1944), cert. den., 324 U.S. 847 (1945).

13. Secs. 2(3), 2(11), 14(a). The latter reads: "Nothing herein shall prohibit any individual employed as a supervisor from becoming or remaining a

NLRB, with diverse opinions among its members. Though foremen were left free to join unions if they wished to do so, and employers might bargain collectively with them outside the restrictive provisions of the law, foremen could make no use of Taft-Hartley to obtain bargaining rights, nor could they seek redress for discriminatory treatment.[14] Except for railway labor, the prohibitions applied even to a considerable part of industry—printing, water shipping, and several other fields of employment—where there had been a long and well-known history of collective bargaining covering foremen. For more than half a century in these industries foremen had increasingly become members of unions and then been covered in collective bargaining contracts. All this was swept aside by Taft-Hartley, disregarding history and past practices. The new policy regarded foremen only as a necessary and integral part of management, not "employees" under the protection of the Wagner Act. It is based on what we regard as a false assumption, that there are only "management" and "rank-and-file employees" in industry. This was considered necessary if management was to retain or secure the loyalty of supervisors. But might it not on occasion have an opposite effect? In fact, the organization of foremen had stimulated management to take stock of foremen's problems and to seek to give them new status and security. Would there be a reversion, now that threat of organization was lessened under the revised law?

More than offsetting these exclusions is the extension of federal controls by changes in the law and its administration. New types of cases were provided for, such as union-shop and other new types of elections and unfair labor practice cases filed against unions. In addition, the jurisdiction of the Board was in effect greatly extended. The law itself made no change in the definition of industries "affect-

---

member of a labor organization, but no employer subject to this Act shall be compelled to deem individuals defined herein as supervisors as employees for the purpose of any law, either national or local, relating to collective bargaining."

14. The Supreme Court had upheld the decision by a majority of the Board that foremen were "employees" under the old Act and protected by its provisions. Packard Motor Car Co. v. NLRB, 330 U.S. 485 (March, 1947). After the passage of the new Act, the Supreme Court in remanding a case to the circuit court for further consideration in light of the amended Act, held that a company could still be required to reinstate and "make whole" a foreman discriminated against in 1944 in violation of the old Act. NLRB v. Edward G. Budd Manufacturing Co., 332 U.S. 840 (December, 1947). But an order to bargain with a union of foremen, though valid when issued, could no longer be enforced. L. A. Young Spring and Wire Co. v. NLRB, 163 F. 2d 905 (C.A.D.C.), cert. den., 333 U.S. 837 (1948).

ing commerce" which are covered by the Act.[15] The old Board as a matter of policy did not seek to extend coverage to border-line industries unless the cases were really important in view of the numbers involved and the effects upon commerce—this due partly to doing first things first and limitations of staff and time. Many cases were dismissed as a matter of discretion for jurisdictional or budgetary reasons. Few cases were filed from the construction industry because of its widespread unionization and the nature of collective bargaining prevailing, and the Board had no desire to extend its operations into that field. But a conspicuous place for this industry under Taft-Hartley was clearly intended, as was shown by the concern of Congress for jurisdictional disputes, secondary boycotts, and other union methods which had wide notoriety in building construction. Charges against unions on such matters, and applications for restraining orders in building and other industries, as well as union-shop elections, could be expected to alter considerably the work-load of the Board under the new Act.

It was unclear, however, to what extent it was the duty of the Board to assert its jurisdiction in fields which formerly for budgetary or policy reasons it was inclined not to enter. The General Counsel held that jurisdiction should be asserted "to the full extent that the Act will permit,"[16] but the Board was not inclined to go so far. In several early cases the majority of the Board took jurisdiction over relatively local industries[17] such as a retail truck company, and a local building supplies concern, but later the trend turned toward declining to assert jurisdiction where the effect upon commerce was "insubstantial" or the industry "essentially local."[18] It was far from

---

15. Secs. 2(6), 2(7), and 501.

16. The difference of opinion between the Board and the General Counsel was aired before the Joint Congressional Committee on June 11, 1948. U.S. Congress, Joint Committee on Labor-Management Relations, *Hearings, Labor-Management Relations*, 80th Cong., 2d Sess., Pt. 2, pp. 1131–37, 1155–66. This Committee was commonly known as the "Ball Committee," and its hearings and reports are cited as *Ball Committee Hearings* and *Reports*. The House Committee on Executive Expenditures sharply criticized the policy of extending the jurisdiction of the Act over small business. U.S. House of Representatives, Committee on Expenditures in the Executive Departments, *Twelfth Intermediate Report, Investigation To Ascertain Scope of Interpretation by General Counsel of National Labor Relations Board of the Term "Affecting Commerce" as Used in the Labor Management Relations Act, 1947*, 80th Cong., 2d Sess., House Report No. 2050, May 26, 1948.

17. Liddon White Truck Co., 76 NLRB 1181 (April, 1948); Central Sash and Door Co., 77 NLRB 418 (April, 1948).

18. Cf. Duke Power Co., 77 NLRB 652 (May, 1948); J. E. Stone Lumber Co., 78 NLRB 627 (July, 1948); Midland Building Co., 78 NLRB 1243 (August,

clear, however, what industries and businesses were covered, and dissatisfaction was aroused both in small-business circles and in Congress.[19] Extension of jurisdiction over business hitherto considered essentially local in order to carry out the apparent intent of Congress to deal with certain problems inevitably would considerably increase the work of the Board and extend its control. Another factor of some importance is that the Board was no longer as free as under the old Act to make agreements with state Boards, leaving them jurisdiction over essentially local enterprises. The 1947 Act permitted such limitation of federal jurisdiction only if the state Act was consistent with the federal,[20] and no such agreements proved to be possible during the first year.

One countervailing factor which was for the first months at least to substantially reduce the number of certain types of cases filed and processed was the requirement that before petitions or charges could be filed by unions, or complaints issued on charges filed by unions, the union must have filed certain information with the Secretary of Labor, and its officers must have filed non-Communist affidavits.[21]

THE REVISED BOARD AND THE GENERAL COUNSEL

The National Labor Relations Board under the 1947 Act ceased to be an administrative agency of the traditional form, a unified agency with control of policy by the Board members and proper delegation of functions and decentralization of operations for efficient administration. Instead there was an experiment with a totally new type of administrative structure, a bifurcation into two authorities, the Board itself and the General Counsel, in addition to the Trial Examiners' Division, which even before the 1947 Act was largely independent.

More or less similar proposals to separate the judicial from the other functions of the Board had long been proposed—as far back as 1939. It is not worth while to debate here how much fact, how much fiction, how much misunderstanding were behind many of the statements

---

1948). However, in the Watson's Specialty Store case, 80 NLRB 533, late in November, 1948, involving a boycott on a local remodeling job, the majority of the Board took jurisdiction, although the Chairman and Mr. Houston questioned the exercise of federal power in so local and "diminutive" a controversy.

19. U.S. Senate, Joint Committee on Labor-Management Relations, *Labor-Management Relations*, Report No. 986, 80th Cong., 2d Sess., Pt. 3, December 31, 1948, pp. 11–15, cited as *Ball Committee Report*. See also chapter 16, n. 28.

20. Sec. 10(a). See discussion *infra*, ch. 15, pp. 586–93.

21. Secs. 9(f), (g), (h); *infra*, ch. 14, pp. 537–60; ch. 16, pp. 643–44.

that were made. Much of what has been commonly said in criticism is refuted by any careful examination of the Board's record.[22] Congress itself, only in 1946, after more than ten years of study of the administrative agencies by congressional committees and other authorities, had adopted the Administrative Procedure Act.[23] The organization and procedures of the NLRB had been found to be open to little criticism, and the Board quickly made the minor changes in its rules and regulations which were required to conform fully to the standards of this Act for the governance of all the federal administrative agencies.

Nevertheless, critics of the Wagner Act and of the NLRB, especially in the House, were insistent upon special treatment for this agency. Some members of the Senate Committee also expressed little faith in the "administrative" process, and the Senate finally joined the House in the far-reaching changes in the organization, procedures, and functions of the NLRB. The underlying idea was that the Board should be primarily a court, more even than the other regulatory agencies, with more of its rules and procedures specified, and some of its former practices banned. Thus the NLRB was made the sole exception to the general rule established for the federal agencies by the Administrative Procedure Act.[24]

The Board itself was increased from three to five members and authorized to delegate any or all of its powers to any panel of three of its members. The functions of the Board concerned only general policy and the making of decisions on election and complaint cases,

22. Cf. *supra,* ch. 2, esp. pp. 49–50, 66–75; ch. 7, pp. 237–43.
23. 60 U.S. Stat. 237 (1946); *supra,* ch. 2, pp. 63–64.
24. It may be noted that few of the amendments made by Taft-Hartley had the approval of the three members of the Board, all of whom were continued when the membership of the Board was increased from three to five. The underlying theory behind many of the provisions appeared in S. 360, which was drafted and explained in an "Analysis of S. 360" by a former Board member who first acted as counsel for the committee minority led by Senator Ball, and then for the new committee majority in 1947. U.S. Senate, Committee on Labor and Public Welfare, Hearings, *Labor Relations Program,* 80th Cong., 1st Sess., 1947, Pt. 1, pp. 301–7, cited as *Senate Hearings, 1947.* It appears that no evidence was taken on some of the matters involved, and some of the "facts" are stoutly questioned by other Board members conversant with them, including the writer, who, as Chairman of the Board, had a large hand in the revamping of organization and procedures in 1941, in an effort to achieve the best operation both in the field and in the decision-making process. It has also been admitted that the bifurcation of the Board was urged in part in order to remove the Director of the Field Division from office. U.S. Senate, Committee on Labor and Public Welfare, *Hearings, Confirmation of Nominees for National Labor Relations Board,* 80th Cong., 1st Sess., July 23, 1947, p. 2, cited as *Senate Confirmation Hearings, 1947.* Cf. also *supra,* ch. 2, pp. 53–56.

with some power on appeal in representation cases. Over against the Board was a General Counsel—an "administrator"—appointed by the President, subject to approval by the Senate, for a term of four years. His position was substantially different from that of the former General Counsel appointed by the Board to serve as its legal adviser as needed, to direct litigation matters, and to supervise the lawyers on the staff other than Trial Examiners. Taft-Hartley gave to the General Counsel very extensive powers. By law the investigation and prosecution of complaint cases, in the field and in Washington, was his concern alone. The Act provided:

The General Counsel of the Board shall exercise general supervision over all attorneys employed by the Board (other than trial examiners and legal assistants to Board members) and over the officers and employees in the regional offices. He shall have *final authority*, on behalf of the Board, in respect of the investigation of charges and issuance of complaints under Section 10, and in respect of the prosecution of such complaints before the Board, and shall have such other duties as the Board may prescribe or as may be provided by law.[25]

While it was clear from the legislative history that Congress intended the Board to act primarily as a court, the Act did not specify all details of the division of functions between the Board and the General Counsel. Nothing was said as to authority in administering representation cases or in postdecisional litigation; and other than the final authority given the General Counsel in the section quoted above, all the powers of appointment and of carrying out the work of the Act stood in the name of the "Board." As a practical matter, however, it was necessary to make workable arrangements. The Board decided that it would not be feasible, with the General Counsel exercising complete authority in the regional offices over the handling of complaint cases as well as "general supervision" over those offices, to have the Board itself responsible for representation cases or for the appointment of field staff. Accordingly the Board delegated[26] to

25. Sec. 3(d). (Italics ours.) The new appointments on the Board were Abe Murdock of Utah, who had served six years as senator and eight years in the House of Representatives, and who had been a minority member of the Special Committee To Investigate the NLRB in 1940; and J. Copeland Gray of Buffalo, N.Y., who had served as an industry member on the Regional War Labor Board in New York and on the National Wage Stabilization Board. The new General Counsel was Robert N. Denham, who had been a Trial Examiner for the NLRB since 1938.

26. The Delegation Agreement, adopted on August 21, 1947, by the Board, with the provision that the delegated powers might be revoked by the Board at any time, is available in *Ball Committee Report*, Pt. 3, December 31, 1948, pp. 101–4.

him practically all the authority vested in the Board outside its judicial functions. He was given control of all the administrative functions of the agency, appointment and control of personnel other than the staff directly attached to the Board itself, and responsibility in the various types of representation and other noncomplaint cases, for investigation, hearings and conduct of elections, and for administrative decisions at the informal stages. The Board, however, reserved to itself the right to hear and decide appeals from the General Counsel's actions on these matters. The General Counsel also received the responsibility on direction and in behalf of the Board to seek compliance with its orders and to conduct any court litigation for that purpose. He was also to exercise "full and final authority and responsibility, on behalf of the Board," in any injunction proceedings. He was put in control of some 80 per cent of the Board's staff, of the budget, and of perhaps 85 per cent of the work of the agency.

Thus by congressional intent expressed in the Act and in its legislative history, and by administrative agreement going further than the Act itself required, there was established what was described as

two independent and separately functioning, but not uncoordinating, parts—the Board and the Office of the General Counsel. . . . [The latter] is primarily the prosecuting and administrative arm of the Agency, with exclusive and final jurisdiction in his area of activities. The Members of the Board. . . constitute the judicial arm of the Agency, with the Trial Examiners acting as their Hearing Officers of first instance. The Board members have no voice in whether an unfair labor practice shall be prosecuted or how it shall be prosecuted. They have [by delegation] no voice in selecting the personnel or directing the activities of the Regional Offices, where investigations are made and prosecutions carried out. That, exclusively, is the field of the General Counsel who, with finality, determines whether, when, and how a charge of unfair labor practice will be prosecuted. He also . . . directs all the administrative operations of the Agency.[27]

And, in addition, "this segregation of authority—and responsibility— is complete and definitely unique in government structure of administrative boards."[28]

Taft-Hartley in this way gave its answer to the widespread though, we think, all but empty criticism that the Board had issued complaints, tried them, and then decided the issues. Although the actual separation of functions under the old Act had avoided possibility of abuse while insuring unity in basic policies, still there might be some

27. Address of General Counsel Robert N. Denham before the Conference of Circuit and District Judges of the Fifth Judicial Circuit, New Orleans, June 4, 1948.

28. Address of General Counsel, April 19, 1948.

advantage in the new arrangement so far as it ended one basis of criticism and propaganda against the Act. If it increased "public confidence" in the Board, this might facilitate the work. The division of authority also contained the possibility of saving time and attention given by the Board to administrative matters, some of it probably unnecessary in the past, and made this available for decision-making. The use of panels, which were authorized for the enlarged Board and were put into effect in January, 1948, also would expedite the decision of at least routine cases and free time for the consideration by the whole Board of cases involving important issues. On the other hand it would take more time for a Board of five to debate and reach agreement on difficult cases than was true when only three men were involved.[29]

The final answer as to the wisdom of this separation of functions, contrary to the otherwise general system approved in the Administrative Procedure Act, would be given by how the device worked.[30] A number of problems, however, required solution before the experiment could be called a success. The first major question was whether, with such division of authority and with the work in the field under the separate control of the General Counsel, emphasis on informal disposition of cases, the essence of the administrative process, could be maintained. The success of the Board depends in large measure on what happens at the source of its cases—out in the field. Taken as a group, Board decisions can scarcely average better than the field investigations made and the conferences and trials there conducted. Amicable settlements during investigation, dismissal or withdrawal of cases, sometimes voluntarily but frequently reluctantly, as well as the securing of compliance after Board decision—these are of extreme importance in the actual administration of industrial relations law and the meaning it has in practice. The informally handled cases, as against those that went to hearing and Board decision, constituted the great bulk of cases under the Wagner Act.[31] The question was whether the "administrative" approach could be maintained, or whether the emphasis would be upon prosecution and full legal procedure.[32]

29. Possibly a seven-man board would permit more effective use of panels, as Mr. Houston suggested in U.S. Senate, Subcommittee of the Committee on Appropriations, *Hearings, Labor-Federal Security Appropriation Bill for 1949*, 80th Cong., 2d Sess., March 24, 1948, p. 203, and as had been provided in the Senate bill.

30. For a discussion of the experience, 1947–48, see *infra*, ch. 16, pp. 618–29.

31. *Supra*, ch. 2, pp. 66–67; ch. 3, pp. 80–83.

32. Possibly significant of attitudes on this was the statement of the General Counsel, in a speech in which he sensibly urged personnel men to settle contro-

The second closely related problem was whether unity of policy could be achieved with such a division of authority. On representation cases the Board maintained its authority to decide appeals from action of the General Counsel, but under the law the latter had final authority on all action on complaints until they reached the Board for decision. The Board continued presumably to be the policy-making body, but since the great bulk even of complaint cases are withdrawn, dismissed, or settled in some manner—that is, if anything like the old methods continued—a right of appeal to the Board on these also was needed. Otherwise in case of difference of opinion the General Counsel might be reversed perhaps months later in a formal decision; while in other cases which never come to the Board the action might be contrary to the policies of the Board itself. Such right of appeal would protect the Board in case of differences of opinion between the Board and the General Counsel. It would also protect the latter from "heat put on him" by parties to dismissed cases, if the expected harmony should not prevail at all times. Naturally the Board and the General Counsel conferred and referred questions one to the other in an effort to achieve a close working relationship and unity of policy in spite of the theory of "complete separation" between them, as was understood would be the fact by the congressional committee.[33] But issues could still arise and result in serious delay.[34] Such possibilities could be avoided only by real efforts on the part of both parts of this bifurcated agency to work in full unity of purpose and policy. But there are many questions in this complex field on which reasonable men can disagree. Accordingly the absence of complete authority on the part of the Board to decide matters of basic policy when they arose, even in early stages in the field, in contradistinction to decision on the facts of particular cases, created more problems than it solved.

With this extensive separation of work and authority under the Act, the General Counsel was frequently referred to as a "czar," with the Board reduced to a more or less subordinate position. While such possibilities were present under the 1947 law, and while the authority

---

versies whenever possible without recourse to the Board: "No labor controversy is ever as well disposed of as by settlement without recourse to the agencies *before whom they must otherwise be litigated.*" (Italics ours.) Address, May 17, 1948. Of course this position is in harmony with the position of all the Boards under the Wagner Act, which handled most cases without "litigation" in the strict legal sense.

33. *Senate Confirmation Hearings, 1947,* esp. pp. 2, 11.

34. Cf. Northern Virginia Broadcasters, 75 NLRB 11 (October 7, 1947), *infra,* ch. 14, p. 547.

of the former was too extensive and final, the Board retained a sufficient area of authority to make the charge not entirely warranted.[35] Nevertheless, there is still serious question whether any one man should have the final responsibility for so many decisions on important matters of policy. It seems inevitable that many questions would be decided by subordinates, for lack of time for adequate consideration by the General Counsel, or else by "off-the-cuff" decisions. Criticism on this score might have more basis than the similar complaints against the old three-man Board. The location of ultimate responsibility in the Board members themselves, with the right to delegate authority as seemed wise, on the other hand, had the advantage of clear centralization of basic authority for the sake of unity of policy; and it gave some protection against mistakes and against pressures from special interests, by the broader base upon which responsibility rested.

A further serious question was that of selection, training, and direction of the staff, which by delegation was the responsibility of the General Counsel, except for the legal aids and others attached directly to the Board itself, and the Trial Examiners. The old Board had built up an able, experienced, and conscientious staff, including many nonlegal administrators, Regional Directors, and field examiners.[36] But the General Counsel, as was expected, set up his own new organization in Washington to handle relations with the work in the field.[37] Policy as to appointments was talked about with considerable concern, both within the staff and among at least some of the Board's clients, during the first months of the new regime.

Only experience would tell, therefore, whether the bifurcated agency could achieve a unified, efficient, and fair administration of a law which would be even more difficult to administer well than was the Wagner Act. Much depended upon the General Counsel and his policies as to appointments and as to problems and methods of operation in the field and in Washington. But approval of this arrangement on the ground that the Board could act as a court and the General Counsel as a "district attorney"[38] reflected a serious miscon-

35. The main support for such a charge might be found in certain comments of the General Counsel in *Senate Confirmation Hearings, 1947*, esp. pp. 2–4, and in the conference late in 1947 between a committee of the NLRB union and the General Counsel. On the latter see Paul Klein, "Mr. Denham Plays God," *Nation*, 165 (1947), 640–41, and *New York Times*, November 29, 1947.

36. See *supra*, ch. 2, pp. 53–60.

37. *Infra*, ch. 16, pp. 619–20.

38. *Ball Committee Report*, Pt. 1, March 15, 1948, p. 8.

ception of the nature of the work in administering such a law as this.

The Board itself, by the Act and by delegation of other powers, employed only an executive secretary and a solicitor to act as legal adviser, a group of legal assistants for the individual Board members, and the necessary secretarial assistance. All other employees, except for the independent Trial Examiners, were employees of the General Counsel.[39] The Board acted only upon appeals on representation case action in the field and on formal cases requiring decision after hearing.

HEARINGS AND REPORTS: THE TRIAL EXAMINERS' DIVISION

For representation and other election cases Taft-Hartley provided that the hearing officer should not make any recommendations.[40] For some years the Board as a matter of economy had in most cases used attorneys or examiners in the regional offices rather than Trial Examiners for hearing representation cases, and this was permitted to continue. The record, when it came to the Board, was ordinarily accompanied by a brief report or statement by the hearing officer. This the Board found useful, since sometimes with relatively inexperienced representatives of the parties participating in the hearing, the record might not make clear some of the information needed or the main issues. The reports were expected to assist in obtaining an adequate record and in clarifying the issues. Perhaps the same values can be obtained without "recommendations," but it is important that the Board be able to get as much aid as possible from the hearing officers in clarifying issues and evaluating evidence, in order to deal efficiently with the large volume of cases which it must decide. A representation hearing, unlike a hearing in an unfair labor practice case, is not an adversary proceeding but a part of a field investigation. There is no need therefore to attempt to isolate the Board in this manner from any possibility of influence from those who conducted the investigation. The Board of course makes its own decision, as it always had in the past.

39. A rather curious limitation upon the power to appoint is that none might be appointed for "economic analysis." Sec. 4(a). The Act of course in many provisions—back pay, featherbedding, jurisdictional disputes, union dues, among others—required detailed and technical analysis, by whatever name, of industrial practices and experience, in relation to particular cases being handled. The provision was apparently aimed to prevent re-establishment of a Division of Economic Research, abolished in 1940. Cf. supra, ch. 2, pp. 51–52. There had been for many years disavowal of any interest in such a program, although the Board had for several years beginning in 1942 provided for studies of its own experience in important aspects as an aid to good administration. *Ibid.*, p. 60.

40. Sec. 9(c).

For complaint cases the Trial Examiner system was changed in some respects. No Trial Examiner's Report was to be reviewed, before or after publication, except by a member of the Board or his legal assistant; and no Trial Examiner might advise or consult with the Board in regard to exceptions taken to his findings, rulings, or recommendations. In addition, if no exceptions were filed after service of his report and recommended order upon the parties, the recommended order becomes the order of the Board.[41] Trial Examiners, as a result, were completely on their own, subject to no review, and had complete independence, responsibility, and authority through all stages of their work. The prohibitions of review and consultation with the Board, which came from the Senate, reflected a fundamental misconception of previous practice.[42] It was believed that there were abuses in that the reports of Trial Examiners were not their own but had frequently been revised or influenced by supervisors in the Trial Examiners' Division. In fact,[43] the Trial Examiners had long been independent and not subject to "dictation," although they had the assistance when needed of an associate attorney—frequently an examiner in training—to read first drafts and check back on the record, and there were conferences with the Chief Trial Examiner or other supervisor on the draft reports. In addition, there were meetings of Examiners and their supervisors to review major developments in Board and court decisions. All this was important for the training of new Trial Examiners and to aid in keeping up on policy, and for checking as to accuracy and adequacy, as well as to phraseology, such as any worker on a complex problem is more likely than not to find helpful. The strict prohibition of any review seemed likely to create difficulties. It hindered the training of new men in the details of a highly specialized job, requiring knowledge of Board and court decisions on policy, as well as careful legal craftsmanship. Reports published before any check by others might give rise to confusion as to policy or be in conflict with law as laid down by court decisions, when a conversation almost universally desired by Examiners would avoid slips at once recognizable by a supervisor, though he is not a "dictator." The proper independence of the Trial Examiner in judging the evidence and making his recommendations does not,

41. Secs. 4(a), 10(c).
42. Cf. U.S. Senate, Committee on Labor and Public Welfare, *Federal Labor Relations Act of 1947*, Report No. 105, 80th Cong., 1st Sess., 1947, pp. 9–10, 20, cited as *Taft Report;* also "Analysis of S. 360," by counsel for Senator Ball, *Senate Hearings, 1947*, Pt. 1, p. 303.
43. *Supra*, ch. 2, pp. 46–47, 56–57.

realistically, require such arbitrary prohibition against any review as that provided by the 1947 law.[44]

The congressional committees and their counsel also believed that there had been serious abuse in the attendance of a Trial Examiner at Board sessions when "his" case was being decided. It was apparently thought that a Trial Examiner was permitted to defend his position in general. In fact,[45] he was there to answer Board questions as to why he had disposed as he had of any issue of credibility of witnesses testifying in conflict with one another. Credibility is a difficult question in many of the cases decided by the Board, and the opportunity for the Board to discuss this matter with the Trial Examiner was frequently very useful. Any possibility of abuse as a result of his presence is of course prevented by the new prohibition. Possibly sufficient attention to credibility by Trial Examiners in their Reports could avoid most of the disadvantage, although occasionally this limitation upon the Board's discretion would be a hindrance to a sure judgment on controverted evidence.

Beyond these points, Taft-Hartley made no change in the Trial Examiners' Division. The complete independence of that Division had already been assured by the Board's own policy and by the Administrative Procedure Act, which necessitated only minor changes in the Board's own procedures.

THE PROCESS OF DECISION-MAKING

A more important change was the abolition of the Review Section and its replacement by a group of legal assistants for each individual Board member to review transcripts of hearings and prepare drafts of opinions.[46] It was apparently believed in both the Senate and the House that Board members had not "done their own deciding" because of the delegation to a central Review Section of the reviewing of records, Trial Examiners' Reports, and briefs and exceptions, and the preparation of memoranda on cases for the Board by the review attorneys. It was thought that, by giving each Board member whatever legal assistants were needed, the Board could function more in the manner of the courts, and perhaps that the Board member personally would review the record and write draft opinions.[47] The record of consideration of this problem unfortunately shows little

---

44. Cf. *infra*, ch. 16, pp. 622–23.   45. *Supra*, ch. 2, p. 57.   46. Sec. 4(a).
47. Cf. *Taft Report*, pp. 8–9; U.S. House of Representatives, Committee on Education and Labor, *Labor-Management Relations Act, 1947*, Report No. 245, 80th Cong., 1st Sess., 1947, p. 25, cited as *Hartley Report; Daily Cong. Rec.*, 93:3953, 4267, 4720.

if any understanding of the function of review attorneys or legal assistants to Board members or of the actual process by which decisions were made and of the safeguards provided by a carefully developed procedure for handling a great volume of cases.[48]

Under the review system as it was developed by the Board especially from 1941 on,[49] the review attorneys and their carefully selected, able supervisors studied the Trial Examiners' Intermediate Report, briefs, exceptions, and the record of oral argument, if any, before beginning review of the record of the hearings to check as to the accuracy, adequacy, and correctness in law as well as in fact, of the Intermediate Report. The review memoranda were to make clear in detail any disagreement with the Trial Examiner. These reports, along with the Intermediate Report, briefs, and exceptions, went to each member of the Board, who with the aid of his legal assistant was expected to give special attention to any conflicting parts of the documents, going back to the record if need be. The results were then assumed to give a sound basis for each Board member's judgment as to the facts and issues, and what the essentials of the decisions should be. A memorandum covering this was expected to be drafted by the member and circulated to the other Board members. The much more numerous, though usually less complex, representation cases were handled in approximately the same way. Finally, after conference and discussion by the Board, the decision was made and directions were given for drafting an opinion. The drafts were frequently revised and rewritten by the members, until finally there was agreement, or sometimes dissenting opinions were issued. The decisions were made *by the Board* through a constructive process of conference and accommodation of views, though independence of judgment was reflected both in the frequent reversals of Trial Examiners in part or sometimes in whole and by dissents and separate concurrences by individual members.

Taft-Hartley abolished this system, developed and tested by experience and apparently approved by all members of the Board under the Wagner Act save one, and substituted instead a group of legal assistants of whatever number needed, ten to fifteen or more, for each

48. The *Taft Report,* for instance, indicates that Review Supervisors reviewed the attorneys' memoranda for the Board on cases without having seen the transcripts or familiarized themselves with briefs and exceptions. This is contrary to the fact. The *Minority Report* by Senators Thomas, Murray, and Pepper states: "The hearings are completely lacking in evidence of any abuse arising out of the present structure." *Taft Report,* Pt. 2, *Minority Views,* p. 32.

49. Cf. *supra,* ch. 2, pp. 47–48, 57.

Board member—in effect five little review sections to be supervised and directed by the members themselves. The Board member himself was expected to be responsible for the report on a case to the panel, with the analysis and report prepared by his legal assistants, and thereafter for a draft decision prepared by his legal assistants[50] for further consideration by the panel.

A number of important problems were inherent in this system of decentralized review under individual supervision by Board members rather than by a centralized review system responsible to the Board as a whole. Whatever the organization, each Board member would be expected to be responsible to the Board. Why should not the review attorneys also work for the entire Board, under supervision chosen by the Board, and with always the possibility of check by individual Board members by use of their own legal assistant? The problem of supervision is a major one. With cases assigned to separate groups of legal assistants under each member, would not the member necessarily assign an attorney to act as supervisor for him? What is a new member to do, and how long would it take him to learn the Board's job well enough to do his primary job and be an efficient supervisor of his group, whether he had been a judge, a lawyer, an industrial relations man, or whatever else? No one appointed to the Board would be as efficient to start with as he would be expected to become. Not all members are lawyers, nor should they be; hence in spite of the contribution that an able and experienced man makes to the Board, he may not be experienced in the technicalities of reviewing a record and judging evidence, and hence not the best qualified to supervise that technical job.[51]

Or suppose that there were occasional honest differences of view on law or policy, how would the different members of the Board get an equal opportunity to learn the given case? The member to whom the case was originally assigned would have the "whip hand" in determining the eventual decision. Members would naturally tend to appoint legal assistants of their own way of thinking, and review memos might turn out to be quite different depending upon whether

50. *Ball Committee Report*, Pt. 1, March 15, 1948, p. 7. The *Report* states: "Since each Board member always personally studies the trial examiner's report and exceptions and briefs filed by the parties, an adequate check upon the memoranda prepared by the legal assistants is provided." This was of course assumed to be the case also under the former system. For discussion of the experience in the first year see *infra*, ch. 16, pp. 623–26.

51. In fact the Board reported in the *Thirteenth Annual Report*, p. 5, the names of the five chief legal assistants who supervised the work of the five separate staffs of legal assistants.

they came from the legal assistants of one or another Board member. There might be differences in ability between the different groups of legal assistants, also. If for any reason any other member felt uncertain of the adequacy of a report, it might be embarrassing to ask for an opportunity for his own legal assistants to look at the record; in contrast, there was no hesitation under the old system for members to insist upon further study of the record by the Review Section or by their own assistants. Moreover, it might become known that a given case was being handled by such and such member of the Board, with the result that a party to the case or his counsel might try to "see" this member. The protection from such improper pressure in individual cases through an anonymous review process and Board rather than individual responsibility at all points has considerable practical value.[52]

The analogy to a court where each judge has his own legal assistants disregards the character of the work of the Board, its great volume, and the fact that Board members are not ordinarily chosen for training and experience which would qualify them as, for instance, circuit court judges. No appellate court approaches the Board in the volume of its work.[53] Moreover, when cases reach the appellate courts, ordinarily the issues have been narrowed, and briefs and legal arguments tend to be of such quality that decisions can be made without detailed study of lengthy records. Ordinarily, after discussion by the judges, one of them is assigned to write the opinion. For Board decision, on the other hand, the record of the hearing, which in important complaint cases in the past sometimes reached thousands of pages, must be analyzed carefully for a check on the report of the Trial Examiner or the Hearing Officer. In June, 1948, in cases awaiting decision by the Board testimony to be studied reached a total of 175,000 pages.[54]

The problem is how to insure that the review of records is done in such a way as to make decisions as nearly "foolproof" as possible. The system which had been evolved by the Board on the basis of its experience worked well, in our opinion. Decisions of the Board, fol-

52. Cf. *supra*, ch. 2, pp. 74–75.

53. The Board in 1945–46 issued 1,248 decisions in contested cases, while the six judges of the Second Circuit Court of Appeals turned out 296 decisions, and terminated 154 cases without hearing or submission; and the Supreme Court disposed of only 218 cases by opinion, plus denying certiorari in 943 cases. *Eleventh Annual Report*, p. 81; *Annual Report of the Director of the Administrative Office of the United States Courts, 1946*, pp. 73–74.

54. *Ball Committee Hearings*, Pt. 2, p. 1121.

lowing review under fully trained and able supervisors, were a joint product based on thorough consideration by the individual Board members and accommodation of views through the constructive process of group consideration of facts, law, and policy. The core of decision-making is, of course, becoming informed on the facts and issues. On this, Board members faced with a huge volume of cases need all the help possible in getting and analyzing the information on the basis of which *they* make decisions. It would seem very difficult, if at all possible, to obtain as good review reports and as thoroughly considered decisions under the changed system as was achieved with the central review section. It is doubtful whether there could be assurance of as good supervision in all instances, by Board members or by supervisors in five separate little review sections, as there was in the earlier consolidated section, with centralized responsibility in the hands of the most capable supervisors whom the Board could find. The changed system could undoubtedly be made to work, but some loss appeared inevitable both in efficiency and in economy. One must ask whether it is wise for Congress to legislate on such a detailed matter of administration, rather than leaving to the discretion of the Board the problem of finding the most efficient machinery, within the general limits laid down by the Act it was to administer and the Administrative Procedure Act.

Taft-Hartley did not solve, even with the increase in the membership of the Board, the problem of how to handle quickly and efficiently as well as justly a heavy load of cases requiring formal decision. There was need for reconsideration of ways to reduce the load and to handle the work most effectively.[55] Unified policy, centrally decided, was still essential, but there was need for every encouragement to handle cases informally in the regional offices whenever possible. Perhaps more delegation of authority to Regional Directors would be possible. Ways might be found by the Board, permitted discretion, to streamline procedures without undercutting the need for careful consideration of cases and of policy. Possibly more delegation to state boards should be permitted. Proposals made in some quarters to relieve the Board by turning over some of its work to district courts or to special labor courts, however, disregarded the nature of the cases and the desirability of handling as many of them

55. The Ball Committee in its final report noted with concern that the problem of delay in case handling had become "a greater problem under the Taft-Hartley Act without any apparent justification by volume of cases being considered." *Ball Committee Report*, Pt. 3, December 31, 1948, p. 11.

as possible by informal administrative means rather than by litigation. Taft-Hartley did not end the need for good administration, which means careful handling of each case, unity in policy, and the avoidance of unnecessary reliance upon formal decision by government. The informed judgment of the Board itself as to practical solutions of these problems might better be allowed more scope than was done in the 1947 Act.

RULES OF DECISION, EVIDENCE, AND COURT REVIEW

Whether any substantial changes were made by the amendments as to the conduct of hearings, the rules of evidence for such hearings and for the Board's findings of fact, and the character and extent of court review of Board orders, is a matter upon which experts—and others—disagree. Perhaps the most that can be said pending decisions in many cases and final word by the Supreme Court is that changes in the text of the Act created uncertainty and thereby promoted litigation as well as possibly encouraging some to go further in actions which might or might not finally be held violative of the Act. There is no doubt that many in both houses of Congress wanted the Board bound more strictly by technical rules of evidence and wanted the scope of court review broadened. But the question here is as to what was actually embodied in the amended law, and whether it meant to provide a system different from that under the Administrative Procedure Act already in effect covering the NLRB as well as all other federal administrative agencies.

In place of the Wagner Act's provision that the rules of evidence prevailing in courts of law or equity were not to be controlling, Taft-Hartley provided that unfair labor practice proceedings "shall, so far as practicable, be conducted in accordance with the rules of evidence applicable in the district courts of the United States,"[56] in effect therefore providing for the use of the rules of evidence prevailing in the civil courts of the state in which the hearing is conducted. The Board was to make its findings of fact and issue its orders upon "the preponderance of" the testimony;[57] the Wagner Act said "all the testimony." And upon petition for enforcement or review of Board orders, the findings of the Board "*with respect to questions of fact* if supported by *substantial* evidence *on the record considered as a whole* shall be conclusive."[58]

There had been much criticism of the Board for alleged failure to follow the rules of evidence and dissatisfaction with the scope of

56. Sec. 10(b).   57. Sec. 10(c).
58. Sec. 10(e). Additions to the Wagner Act text in italics.

court review.[59] But the conferees for the Senate and the House disagreed as to whether, or to what extent if any, the law was actually changed on these points.[60] On the matter of rules of evidence, Board hearings had long followed in the main the established principles, as was found by the Attorney-General's Committee,[61] and with the qualification in the Act, "so far as practicable," there might be little difference in effect. The courts had long held, also, and the Board acted upon that rule, that "evidence" in the Wagner Act meant "substantial evidence." The Board had of course considered "the record as a whole" and "the preponderance of the testimony" in making its findings of fact. The major question is whether the courts were given greater scope to review the Board's findings of fact, or whether the Act merely restated the "substantial evidence" test of the Administrative Procedure Act, as indicated by the Senate Committee. The interpretation by the House conferees, who thought that the scope of review had been materially broadened, differed from that of the Senate Committee, which was responsible for the provision. Professor Cox,[62] pointing to discrepancies between the text of the Act and the reports of the conference committees, commented:

... To follow the statement of the House Managers would seem to require accepting the conclusion that legislation not suggested by the bill may be written in a committee report ... it is becoming increasingly common to manufacture "legislative history" during the course of legislation. The accusations of outside participation made in Congress, and the elaborate interpretations in some passages in the committee reports, suggest the danger that this occurred during consideration of the Taft-Hartley amendments. Judicial exposition of the way in which the balance is struck between these opposing considerations would offer an interesting lesson in the techniques of statutory construction.

Those who accept as sound the traditional principles of administrative law continued to hope that the system whereby the agency, expert in its field, makes the findings of fact, would not be upset by permitting the courts to go behind such findings if they are supported by substantial evidence, viewed in the light of the record as a whole.[63]

59. *Supra*, ch. 2, pp. 72–73.
60. *Daily Cong. Rec.*, 93:6602; U.S. House of Representatives, *Conference Report, Labor Management Relations Act, 1947*, Report No. 510, 80th Cong., 1st Sess., June, 1947, pp. 55–56; Cox, *op. cit.*, pp. 38–44. Cf. also Gerhard P. Van Arkel, *An Analysis of the Labor Management Relations Act, 1947* (New York: Practising Law Institute, 1947), pp. 14–20.
61. *Supra*, ch. 2, p. 73.   62. Cox, *op. cit.*, p. 44.
63. In the first court decision on this point the Seventh Circuit Court held that in effect the scope of review "is only immaterially changed." NLRB v. Austin Co., 165 F. 2d 592 (C.C.A.7, 1947).

Two other provisions in connection with matters of evidence threatened to make difficulties. One is the "free-speech amendment," to be discussed later in other aspects.[64] But here it must be noted that the protected "views, argument or opinion" were not to "be evidence of" an unfair labor practice.[65] This was incorporated on the insistence of the House. It meant apparently that the Board was barred "from even considering such statements in weighing the significance of other conduct by employers and unions,"[66] a most unusual limitation put upon the the Board and the courts, contrary to the common practice of considering statements as evidence of motive in judging the nature of an action. How serious the limitation would prove to be could not be known in advance of a considerable number of decisions. To some extent it unquestionably made more difficult the enforcement of the prohibitions against unfair labor practices both of employers and of unions.[67] This limitation on the use of speech as evidence would in all probability be significant especially in regard to protection against antiunion discrimination. The Act provided that the Board might not require reinstatement or back pay for any individual "suspended or discharged for cause."[68] In judging motive, inevitably an important part of the proof in such cases, the prohibition against using "views, argument or opinion" as supporting evidence might make difficulty. But again only experience would tell the extent to which enforcement of the Act was weakened by this provision going beyond the needs of reasonable protection of employers' rights.

Finally, in line with the numerous points indicated above where the Board's discretion was limited by the new Act, there was a series of more or less specific rules for decision on particular points. Some of these may be mentioned here as illustrations of the basic attitudes in Taft-Hartley toward the administrative process. Thus, for example, the Board was enjoined to treat unions alike, regardless of whether or not they are affiliated, the rule on its face completely ignoring the difference between "company-dominated unions" and "independent unions"; only one election a year might be held, although in occasional circumstances the purposes of the Act might better be achieved

64. *Infra*, ch. 12, pp. 422–25; ch. 16, pp. 631, 639, 647–48.
65. Sec. 8(c).
66. Chairman Herzog, in address, April 23, 1948.
67. Some union attorneys were of opinion that the changes in rules such as those as to evidence, agency, free speech, etc., might be of more benefit to unions charged with unfair labor practices than to employers. It is a paradox that an Act which attempted control over certain union activities at the same time by changes in the rules made it more difficult to enforce the provisions.
68. Sec. 10(c); discussed *infra*, ch. 12, p. 429.

by a relaxation of the general rule; in determining whether a unit is appropriate, the extent to which employees have organized was not to be controlling, thus in some instances postponing collective bargaining, although a group for whom bargaining is feasible were organized and desiring such joint action; employees on strike were not eligible to vote in any Board election if "not eligible to reinstatement," a question exceedingly difficult to determine during a strike.[69] Some of the specific rules are easily defensible, others doubtful or wrong in the view of many informed people. But the issue here is as to the wisdom of laying down such specific directions rather than leaving to the discretion of the administrative agency the details of how best to effectuate the general policy established in the Act.

Taft-Hartley thus gave numerous indications of a basic distrust of the administrative process. While many of the changes noted here were in answer to frequently repeated criticisms of the Wagner Act and the Board, it is impossible to find in the record of congressional hearings, reports, and debate adequate factual support for them, or justification for making the NLRB the sole exception to the system approved by the Administrative Procedure Act. Few of the changes were supported by members of the Board or by other informed persons. On the whole the amendments on administrative aspects restricted the power of the agency to develop the most efficient machinery for handling its work or to adjust policy to shown needs in the light of its own experience. The possibility that court review had been broadened encouraged litigation. Assuming, as we must, that Congress meant what it said in its statements of policy and wanted the law well and fairly administered, we think it doubtful whether the elaborate prescriptions of machinery and policy, and the changes as to evidence and court review, were well calculated for that purpose, although they removed some of the bases of widespread criticism. Only experience would tell whether a bifurcated and in many respects strait-jacketed agency would be able to provide an efficient and fair administration of this Act, which was in essence a new and drastic experiment both in administration and in detailed regulation of practices of unions and management.

69. Cf. discussion of these and other rules in chs. 12 and 14.

CHAPTER 12

UNFAIR LABOR PRACTICES
UNDER TAFT-HARTLEY

THE Wagner Act, centered in the protection of workers against
unfair labor practices by employers and the determination of
representatives for the purposes of collective bargaining, included no *explicit* corresponding control of the practices of organized
labor. The Act was therefore described as a "one-way street." There
was said to be need for "equality of treatment of management and
labor organizations" and for restraint upon the power exercised by
labor, in order to develop a sense of responsibility, protect the American way of life, and safeguard the public interest. "Unfair labor practices" by unions as well as by management, accordingly, were prohibited by the 1947 Act.

MANAGEMENT UNFAIR LABOR PRACTICES

It has frequently been said that the Taft-Hartley clauses relating
to management unfair labor practices are essentially the same as the
five found in the Wagner Act. But this is somewhat misleading. Some
of the clauses were expressly changed. Others differed from the point
of view of remedy for the victims of unfair labor practices. In addition,
the effectiveness of such provisions in protecting the rights of labor
depends largely upon their administration and upon matters of proof,
evidence which can be used, and the character of court review. On
all these points changes were made. The tendency inevitably would
be for a somewhat less full protection, partly because of innumerable
opportunities given by an extremely complex law for delays that
might frustrate the achieving of employees' rights. Significant of the
intent of the law, also, is the fact that certain of the charges of unfair
labor practices against labor were required to receive priority in handling over all other cases.[1] An unusually short "statute of limitations,"
in addition, providing that no complaint might be issued based on

1. Those arising under Sec. 8(b)(4)(A), (B), and (C); Sec. 10(l).

420

any unfair labor practice occurring more than six months before the charge was filed,[2] might in an occasional case make the prevention of violations by employers more difficult. The Board had administratively discouraged the filing of stale charges; but in a rare case the difficulty of obtaining evidence, or the concealment of the unlawful actions for a considerable time, made it desirable to proceed on a case beyond the usual period.[3] No evidence was presented justifying such a limitation upon the Board's discretion. It seems another indication of a desire for less effective protection against unfair labor practices. The limitation of course also applied to charges against unions.

The statement of the fundamental rights of employees guaranteed by the Act remained as in Section 7 of the Wagner Act, except for a significant additional clause, here italicized.

SEC. 7. Employees shall have the right to self-organization, to form, join, or assist labor organizations, to bargain collectively through representatives of their own choosing, and to engage in other concerted activities for the purpose of collective bargaining or other mutual aid or protection, and *shall also have the right to refrain from any or all of such activities except to the extent that such right may be affected by an agreement requiring membership in a labor organization as a condition of employment as authorized in section 8(a)(3).*

Such remaining aloof from a union connection is not new as a matter of law. The new language only made explicit what had been implicit and always so regarded by the NLRB, except under valid contracts requiring union membership. Nevertheless, the insertion served to advertise that fact and to ease the conscience of individual workers who did not respond to appeals that they should join in a common cause, or assist in paying the bills incidental to the work of a union, ordinarily serving all those in the same group. Naturally, the insistence upon the additional clause is regarded as one instance of antiunion feeling on the part of the lower house, from which it emanated.

Five management unfair labor practices were recognized and retained in Taft-Hartley. Except for the ban on the closed shop and limitations on other union-security contracts, substituted for the for-

2. Sec. 10(b).
3. The General Counsel held that the limitation did not apply retroactively, so that charges of unfair labor practices under the Wagner Act could be processed if filed during any time until six months after the effective date of the new Act, August 22, 1947. He stated: "This does not necessarily mean that we will process stale charges where there is no excuse for the long delay in filing, but there are many such charges in which good reason existed for not filing them earlier." Address by General Counsel, May 17, 1948.

mer proviso in Section 8(3), the clauses *read* precisely as before. But the context must have consideration. For example, the definitions of "employer" and of "agent" to an extent not entirely clear might relieve some persons from charges of illegally interfering with the rights of employees. Most important for its effect upon the interpretation of the words of Section 8(a)(1), "to interfere with, restrain, or coerce employees in the exercise of the rights guaranteed in section 7," however, undoubtedly was the "free-speech" amendment, which affects many other sections of the Act also.[4]

"FREE SPEECH" AND INTERFERENCE WITH THE RIGHTS OF EMPLOYEES

The "free-speech" amendment, Section 8(c), which went far beyond the constitutional protection of free speech, ran as follows:

> The expressing of any views, argument, or opinion, or the dissemination thereof, whether in written, printed, graphic, or visual form, shall not constitute or be evidence of an unfair labor practice under any of the provisions of this Act, if such expression contains no threat of reprisal or force or promise of benefit.

Thus in response to the widely held and frequently repeated opinion that the Board had limited employers in the exercise of their constitutionally guaranteed right of free speech, Taft-Hartley incorporated a sweeping restriction upon the Board. Not only were statements of "views, argument or opinion" in the absence of explicit threats or promises not to be considered in the light of their context— the Senate's qualifying phrases, "under all the circumstances" and "express or implied" were omitted—but instead only the expressions themselves standing alone. In addition, such statements could not be used as *evidence* of any unfair labor practice, this upon the insistence of the House, unless in themselves they contained threats or promise of benefit. The intent was to prevent decisions in which statements were found to be unlawful because they were integral parts of a "context of unlawful conduct" or in which they were used as an indication of employers' motives, on the basis of which, among other things, the character of actions can be judged.

All this went far beyond what the Supreme Court had required in its decisions[5] which had guided the Board from 1941 on. The Board had of course accommodated its policies to these decisions of the

4. Cf. *supra*, ch. 11, p. 418; *infra*, ch. 14, pp. 526–28.
5. NLRB v. Virginia Electric and Power Co., 314 U.S. 469 (1941); 319 U.S. 533 (1943); Thomas v. Collins, 323 U.S. 516 (1945); discussed *supra*, ch. 6, pp. 177–79. For the Board's policies and discussion of the problems under the Wagner Act see *ibid.*, pp. 174–89.

courts. Never did the Supreme Court overturn a Board decision when a speech or communication contained a threat of reprisal, or where there was a significant background of other unfair labor practices. For the Supreme Court had said that, in determining whether there actually was interference, "the Board has a right to look at what the Company has said as well as at what it has done."[6]

Congress, however, less realistic about how things work in industry, incorporated a much narrower rule. Under Taft-Hartley "freedom of speech" could be practiced by employers to defeat unions in their attempts to organize and win representation elections considerably more than was permissible under the Wagner Act, at least until the later months. Until late 1946–47, probably at least a majority of the Board, like the writer, had taken full cognizance of the statement of policy of the Wagner Act and thought that unionism and collective bargaining were to be encouraged and were not to be discouraged by management in plants where efforts were being made by the employees to organize. In other words, efforts to organize and to have the advantage of representation elections were considered under the Act primarily the concern of the workers and not of management, who possess a natural advantage when they make battle by speeches or letters or both on the eve of an election. Naturally, the management had a right to correct misstatement, and to present its statement of the pertinent facts, but not to make threats, *explicit* or *implicit*, of economic losses to follow unionization. But it is very questionable, from the standpoint of good industrial relationships, and from that of completely free choice of employees, whether management should enter as an active participant into such election campaigns.

In the last six months or so of the Wagner Act the Board had tended not to use employers' speeches and letters to employees as freely as it had before, as part of the evidence to be weighed in deciding whether there had been interference or discrimination. Chairman Herzog in fact held that the first part of the 1947 free-speech amendment would have little effect, since the Board "had not, for some time before the law was amended, held uncoercive anti-union statements by employers to be violations of the Wagner Act."[7] The matter of *evidence* had greater effect, however.

Board decisions were most clearly affected when the "compulsory audience" theory of the Clark Brothers[8] case was rejected. As the

6. 314 U.S. 469, 478 (1941).
7. Address of Chairman Paul Herzog, April 23, 1948.
8. *Supra,* ch. 6, pp. 184–85.

Board pointed out in the Babcock and Wilcox case,[9] this was the intent shown by the legislative history. Any coercion arising simply from the employer's control in the plant, permitting him access to employees more easily than was possible to the union, was no longer to be considered. Even in a context of other unfair labor practices, employers' extensive campaigns of statements or letters were held to be privileged.[10] When a speech included a direct threat of closing the plant, however, it was held unlawful.[11] And in the important General Shoe Corporation case[12] the majority of the Board set an election aside, finding the employer's campaign so extreme that they could not assume that "the election results represented the employees' own true wishes." The Board pointed out that the free-speech amendment applied specifically only to unfair labor practice cases. It did not find the campaign in question an unfair labor practice, but held that the Board was under a duty to protect the employees' opportunity for a free election.

Such a distinction, if it could be maintained, could avoid some of the worst effects of the amendment in extreme cases at least, though it is doubtful whether this was in accord with the intention of the proponents of the clause, at least in the House. The amendment, in the view of the writer, went entirely too far in permitting employers, even with a background of interferences with their employees' rights, to play an active part in resisting organization. A limited free-speech amendment,[13] however, perhaps along the lines of the Supreme Court's statement in the Virginia Electric and Power Company decision, might serve a useful purpose by reassuring employers as to the right of free discussion in the absence of coercion or promise of benefit, without inviting an increase of antiunion activity and of litigation as was done by the clause adopted.

Prohibition of the use of statements as *evidence* is completely unjustifiable, as was well pointed out in Senate debates.[14] The Board had not abused its discretion on this point, though statements were of course used as one indication of motive as is generally done in

9. Babcock and Wilcox Co., 77 NLRB 577 (May, 1948). Cf. also Merry Brothers Brick and Tile Co., 75 NLRB 136 (1947).

10. Cf. Wrought Iron Range Co., 77 NLRB 487 (1948); Tygart Sportswear Co., 77 NLRB 613 (1948).

11. Alliance Rubber Co., 76 NLRB 514 (1948). But cf. Mylan-Sparta Co., 78 NLRB 1144 (1948), where the statements in question were held to be only a prophecy of the effect of unionization, not a threat.

12. 77 NLRB 124 (April, 1948), discussed *infra*, ch. 14, pp. 527–28.

13. Cf. discussion *supra*, ch. 6, pp. 187–89.

14. *Daily Cong. Rec.*, 93:6604, 6610, 6656.

many types of litigation. How extensive the limitation would prove to be was uncertain. Senator Taft said that "statements which are acts in themselves or contain directions or instructions—of course, could be deemed admissions and hence competent under the well-recognized exception to the hearsay rule."[15] But even the NAM, expressing doubt as to the meaning and effect of the provision, said that a literal construction "obviously . . . would impose a harsher rule of evidence even than existed under common law rules in criminal cases."[16] By the fall of 1948 no decisions had discussed the limitation in detail. In practice, testimony was taken on allegedly coercive statements in order that the Board might have opportunity to pass on the evidence, but in several cases the Board excluded privileged statements from use as evidence of motive.[17] One Intermediate Report commented on the paradox that according to the law statements not associated with threats or promise of benefit could not be used as evidence of an unfair labor practice, although they could be used as evidence of their absence, "odd as such a result may appear to the lay mind." The Trial Examiner carefully based his finding of unfair labor practices on other evidence, not the antiunion speech.[18] However the clause was interpreted, the task of preventing interferences with the rights of labor under the Act had been made more difficult, perhaps even in some instances impossible. The fact that the same difficulties were created in cases against unfair labor practices of unions[19] was hardly a mitigation of the other problem. As Professor Cox said, the free-speech clause erected "another legalistic obstruction to the protection of freedom of organization and will reduce the effectiveness of the Board."[20]

COMPANY-DOMINATED UNIONS

Likewise, Section 8(a)(2) read precisely as its corresponding clause of the Wagner Act, forbidding an employer "to dominate or interfere with the formation or administration of any labor organization or contribute financial or other support to it. . . ." But, again, later sections

15. *Ibid.*, p. 7002.
16. *NAM Law Digest*, 9 (1947), 66.
17. Cf. Fulton Bag and Cotton Mills, 75 NLRB 883 (1948), Carpenter Steel Co., 76 NLRB 670 (1948). For the General Counsel's instructions that evidence on any statements that "might conceivably be found coercive" should be introduced at the hearings, see Bureau of National Affairs, *The Taft-Hartley Act—after One Year* (Washington, 1948), p. 162.
18. Greensboro Coca Cola Bottling Co., 82 NLRB No. 67 (1949).
19. *Infra*, n. 151.
20. Archibald Cox, "Some Aspects of the Labor Management Relations Act, 1947," *Harvard Law Review*, 61 (1947–48), 1–49, 274–315, at 20.

threatened to undermine the protection against an "unfree unionism" in which the Wagner Act had functioned well. Section 9(c)(2) read, in part: ". . . in no case shall the Board deny a labor organization a place on the ballot by reason of an order with respect to such labor organization or its predecessor not issued in conformity with section 10(c)." And Section 10(c) provided "that in determining whether a complaint shall issue alleging a violation of section 8(a)(1) or section 8(a)(2), and in deciding such cases, the same regulations and rules of decision shall apply irrespective of whether or not the labor organization affected is affiliated with a labor organization national or international in scope."

"Discrimination" by the Board against "independent unions" had been widely charged and was apparently believed by both houses.[21] It was said that there was need to prevent disparity of treatment between "independent unions" and those affiliated with a larger organization. The case made involved misuse of the English language, for never had the Board in a representation case made any distinction between the great mass of *unquestioned independents,* on the one hand, and affiliated unions, on the other. Hundreds of true independents were on the ballot in each of the later years.

The Board with reason had proceeded on the assumption that unlikes were involved when complaint cases concerned, on the one hand, company-dominated, unaffiliated, local unions and, on the other hand, employer-assisted or dominated unions affiliated with genuine international unions. It assumed that the affiliated union was subject to the influence and control of the international and would be freed from "company domination" or assistance and quickly become a "free union" once its character became known. This was the reason for an order requiring only the withholding of recognition "unless and until certified" in such cases, and permitting these unions to appear on the ballot in a free election.[22] In the other case of the unaffiliated company-dominated union, the order of disestablishment had the effect of depriving company unions of an opportunity to appear on the ballot—which would have tended strongly to beget company-

21. Cf. "Analysis of S. 360," in U.S. Senate, Committee on Labor and Public Welfare, *Hearings, Labor Relations Program,* 80th Cong., 1st Sess., 1947, Pt. 1, pp. 305–6, cited as *Senate Hearings, 1947.* For other citations see *supra,* ch. 4, p. 109, n. 41. For discussion of the Board's policies and practices cf. *ibid.,* pp. 106–10, and ch. 3, pp. 89–90.

22. The Board may have assumed, too, that it was not expected to "disestablish" an affiliated union, although its experience indicated that its remedy was not entirely adequate in all such cases. Cf. *supra,* ch. 6, pp. 206–7.

dominated unions and encyst them in the labor movement. Of course employees were free if they chose to organize a *real independent* after a company union was disestablished, and such independents were on the ballots in Board elections in large numbers.[23]

The Board, perhaps sensitive to criticisms, had for many years scrutinized the complaints of company domination and in many cases had held that the company assistance did not go so far as to make complete disestablishment necessary. In such instances the order was the same as that where an affiliated union was involved.[24] The Board had carefully distinguished in its treatment what in its best judgment on all the evidence were "likes" and "unlikes." Relatively few charges were entertained or company unions disestablished in the later years. Possibly it would have been wiser for the Board, however, earlier than it did, to have given more attention to the history and activity of an "independent union," and somewhat less to its original establishment or domination or its failure to meet a strict test based upon "fracture."

Taft-Hartley, however, instructed the Board to make no distinction between affiliated and unaffiliated unions and not to deny a place on a ballot to any union by reason of an order not in conformity with the above precept. Was the intention to permit company-dominated unions on the ballot in Board elections? Or was it to require stricter treatment than in the past of an affiliated union which was beneficiary of the employer's influence and favor? The former seems more probable at least in the House.[25] The Act, however, gave the Board a choice, and the Board made the sensible decision. In the important Carpenter Steel Company case,[26] where a disestablishment order was issued against an employee representation committee in March, 1948, it declared its policy. As Chairman Herzog later summarized it:

From now on the Board will disestablish unions only when there is compelling proof of employer *domination;* this remedy will be applied identically to affiliated as well as unaffiliated unions. If, on the other hand, the record only supports a finding of employer assistance, the Board will

23. For examples see *supra*, ch. 4, pp. 107–9.
24. *Ibid.*, p. 109, n. 42.
25. U.S. House of Representatives, Committee on Education and Labor, *Labor-Management Relations Act, 1947*, Report No. 245, 80th Cong., 1st Sess., April, 1947, pp. 33, 42, cited as *Hartley Report*, and *ibid., Minority Report*, pp. 85, 89; U.S. House of Representatives, *Conference Report, Labor Management Relations Act, 1947*, Report No. 510, 80th Cong., 1st Sess., June, 1947, pp. 48, 54–55, cited as *House Conference Report*.
26. 76 NLRB 670 (1948). Cf. also Hershey Metal Products Co., 76 NLRB 695, where only a "withhold recognition" order was issued.

merely order that the employer cease such assistance in the future—again regardless of whether the labor organization is affiliated or unaffiliated.[27]

In succeeding weeks a number of disestablishment orders were issued, and several "withhold recognition" orders, all against unaffiliated unions. Possibly the facts would never sustain a charge that an affiliated union is "company-dominated" to an extent requiring disestablishment. Pessimistic predictions had frequently been made of the return of the company union, but these did not appear to be borne out by events. Perhaps it would be more difficult to find a "successor union" company-dominated, but the Board had already, perhaps with sufficient reason, relaxed its requirements in cases of independents with a *substantial* history of independent action even if their origins were of a "shady" character. Perhaps effective administration would be possible under the new clauses—unless the inability to use statements as evidence proved too hampering.

One further clause needs mention, although the intent cannot have been to strengthen the penalties against company support and domination of a union. Title III, Section 302(a), made it unlawful "for any employer to pay or deliver . . . any money or other thing of value to any representative of any of his employees. . . ." Penalties of heavy fine or imprisonment were provided. While the severity of the penalties is explainable by the fact that the section, and the debates on it, largely concerned "trust funds" or "welfare funds"—shades of John L. Lewis and Petrillo—there can be little doubt that the words applied also to financial contributions in connection with aid to a company union. The NAM took the possibility seriously and warned its members to exercise "extreme caution."[28]

DISCRIMINATION AND UNION-SECURITY PROVISIONS

"Discrimination in regard to hire or tenure of employment or any term or condition of employment to encourage or discourage membership in any labor organization" was prohibited by Section 8(3) of the Wagner Act except under valid closed-shop agreements permitted by a proviso to that section. The wording of the leading clause on discrimination is the same in Taft-Hartley, but the *proviso* was changed into an invalidation of the closed shop, while permitting a "union shop" or "maintenance of membership," but only under certain conditions.

27. Address by Chairman Herzog, March 18, 1948. See also NLRB, *Thirteenth Annual Report*, pp. 51, 53–55.
28. *NAM Law Digest*, 9 (1947), 73–74.

Whether or not the remedy for discriminatory suspension or discharge, namely, reinstatement with or without back pay, could still be effectively used was in some doubt because of later provisions of the new Act. The difficulty arose from the phrase "discharged for cause," found in Section 10(c): "No order of the Board shall require the reinstatement of any individual as an employee who has been suspended or discharged, or the payment to him of any back pay, if such individual was suspended or discharged for cause."

The House had complained of NLRB policy which distinguished between major and minor derelictions in deciding whether an employee was entitled to reinstatement, though this had been done many times by both courts and arbitrators; and its conferees held that a new policy was required by the Conference Agreement. The Senate conferees had accepted the House language almost verbatim.[29] Yet Mr. Taft, leader of the Senate conferees, stated:

Under provision of the conference report, the employer has to make the proof. *That is the present rule and the present practice of the Board.* The Board will have to determine—and it always has—whether the discharge was for cause or for union activity, and the preponderance of the evidence will determine that question. The mere fact that there may be a little cause or real reason would not in any way lead the Board to refuse to give the employees reinstatement and back pay.[30]

In the view of the General Counsel, no real change was made in the law on this point, since the Board always had to decide whether a discharge or refusal to hire or reinstate was for a *real* "cause" or for a discriminatory purpose. This was a question of fact to be determined in each case. "But pretext cannot be substituted for cause any more today than it ever could."[31] Motive, however, as Professor Cox points out, is "an elusive subject of inquiry," and the warning to the Board, along with the possibly broadened scope of judicial review, might give an additional safeguard against error.[32] An increase in litigation was expected to result and perhaps antiunion discrimination to be encouraged for a time at any rate. An important decision of the Second Circuit Court, however, upheld the Board's interpretation of this clause as merely declaring the existing law and not limiting the Board's discretion to determine whether in fact a discharge was for valid cause or for union activity.[33]

29. *House Conference Report*, pp. 38–39, 55; *Daily Cong. Rec.*, 93:6600.
30. *Daily Cong. Rec.*, 93:6678. (Italics ours.)
31. Address of General Counsel Denham, May 17, 1948. Cf. also *supra*, ch. 4, p. 102.
32. Cox, *op. cit.*, pp. 21–22.
33. NLRB v. Sandy Hill Iron & Brass Works, 165 F. 2d 660 (C.C.A.2, 1947).

From the Wagner Act to Taft-Hartley

Other provisions of the Act on unfair labor practices of unions, strikes within the sixty-day notice period at the end of a contract, national emergency strikes, and unlawful activities, in all probability considerably extended the types of activities which would be held to justify effective discharge and permit later refusal to reinstate.[34] Considerably more risk was put into striking, as was clearly intended.[35] Some of this might promote more responsible action by unions; but some of it was likely to unreasonably restrict their right to engage in activities for mutual aid, free from reprisals. This was especially true in view of many uncertainties as to the meaning of the law.

The changes made by Taft-Hartley as regards "union security" were among the most important of all, except for those in basic labor law, for such union-security clauses had for various reasons found place in most joint agreements in industry. According to the United States Department of Labor, 78 per cent of the workers under collective agreements in 1946 were covered by union-security clauses; about 4.8 million of them were covered by closed- or union-shop provisions with preferential hiring, almost 2.6 million by union-shop clauses without reference to hiring, and 3.6 million by maintenance-of-membership clauses.[36]

The proviso in Section 8(3) of the Wagner Act was inserted in order to change as little as possible the state statutes and court-made law, at a time when the law differed from one state to another but was, in large measure, based either upon that of New York State or

34. Secs. 8(b), 8(d), 208(a), 303(a). Cf. also discussion of problems of discrimination against strikers, *supra*, ch. 6, pp. 189–203. In a case filed under the Wagner Act the Board decided in April, 1948, that local union leaders could be discharged because of their responsibility for and participation in mass picketing which, though peaceful, unlawfully barred access to the plant. International Nickel Co., 77 NLRB 286 (1948). An employers' attorney interpreted this to mean that "in the case of mass picketing, the employer may select leaders and more active pickets for discharge." T. R. Iserman, "NLRB Rulings under the Labor-Management Relations Act," in American Management Association, *Personnel Series*, No. 122 (September, 1948), p. 17. Cf. *Thirteenth Annual Report*, pp. 55–58.

35. The right to strike was of course specifically limited by these and other provisions, and some immunities were removed from strikers. Cf. Section 13: "Nothing in this Act, *except as specifically provided for herein*, shall be construed so as either to interfere with or impede or diminish in any way the right to strike, or *to affect the limitations or qualifications on that right.*" (Italics ours.) The *House Conference Report*, p. 40, stated that "many forms and varieties of concerted activities which the Board, particularly in its early days, regarded as protected by the act will no longer be treated as having that protection, since obviously persons who engage in or support unfair labor practices will not enjoy immunity under the act."

36. *Monthly Labor Review*, 64 (1947), 766–67.

upon the more restrictive law prevailing in Massachusetts.[37] It provided only that nothing in the Act precluded an employer from making an agreement requiring union membership as a condition of employment, so long as the union was not one illegally established, maintained, or assisted, and so long as it represented a majority of the employees in an appropriate unit when made.[38]

Closed-shop cases became more and more numerous after unions were more general and after the CIO was organized and the competition between it and the AFL grew more strenuous. They were also of an increasing number of types. In a large percentage of these cases decided by the Board, management was found to be in violation of the Wagner Act because there had not been the required majority at the time the contract was made, whether the purpose had been collusion to shut out another union, or relief from a threatened organizing boycott, or other; therefore, workers discharged in conformity with a closed-shop clause were ordered reinstated. Other cases were decided similarly where workers had been deprived of employment under closed-shop contracts because of their desire to exercise their right of free choice in self-organization at an appropriate time, as in the Rutland Court case and the Wallace case.[39]

All in all, while the proviso served well to protect the rights of workers, along with the elections at appropriate times to settle issues as to their choice of representative, the decisions were against management, the union losing nothing more, if anything, than its defective contract and assumed "rights" under the law. No unfair labor practice charges against unions were provided in the Wagner Act, and no order could be issued against a labor organization. That law, our experience showed, needed to be amended appropriately so as to deal more effectively with such closed-shop abuses.[40] The writer, from his experience and his knowledge of restrictive initiation fees or closed books and abuses of the power of discipline, has long been aware of problems in the closed shop which called for appropriate solution. Nevertheless, a substantial case has been found for the closed shop itself, which should not therefore have been cast out altogether as Taft-Hartley did.

While the intent of Taft-Hartley was to proscribe, in due course,

37. The status of the law of some years ago was discussed by the writer in H. A. Millis and R. E. Montgomery, *Organized Labor* (New York: McGraw-Hill Book Co., 1945), pp. 560–65.
38. See *supra*, ch. 6, pp. 203–16, for the interpretations of this clause.
39. *Ibid.*, pp. 212–14.
40. *Ibid.*, pp. 215–16.

the closed shop generally, the "union-shop" and "maintenance-of-membership" contracts also were recognized, but conditionally. Specific limitations were prescribed in order to protect management's "right" to *hire* in an "open market" (but without discrimination between union and nonunion workers), to protect the individual worker in independent action, and to make for fluidity in the work force—perhaps also to weaken unionism and its power. In general, the union shop differs from the closed shop, in which only union members are *hired*, in that all those hired must join the union before or at the end of a probationary period—not less than thirty days under Taft-Hartley. If the individual worker retains his employment, he is generally required to remain in the union for the duration of the contract, or until the union loses its position under the rules as to representation cases. But, as indicated, conditions precedent were prescribed.

Taft-Hartley thus invalidated any joint agreement to require the *hiring* of union members only, from or through the union, or through the business agent, or through a union hiring hall such as has been operated in ocean shipping on the Pacific Coast.[41] However, if only union help was available, the hiring of union men only was not prohibited; but to protect the individual's "right to work" whether he be union or nonunion, and management's freedom to hire, all discrimination on the basis of unionism or nonunionism was proscribed. To discriminate in hiring on such a basis was made an unfair labor practice on the part of management and to cause or attempt to cause such discrimination was an unfair labor practice on the part of a union.[42] The worker discriminated against could file a charge against the *guilty* party. In short, closed-shop agreements such as commonly found in many industries—shipping, printing, building and other construction, electrical industries, and many others—and even though

41. When Sec. 8(a)(3) and Sec. 102 are taken together, it is evident that most closed-shop contracts in effect did not become invalid at once, for they were made prior to the enactment of Taft-Hartley in June, 1947. They remained effective for a year or until their termination date. Some agreements made in anticipation of the law were for two years, a few for five years. A contract entered into after the effective date of the Act and contrary to the provisions of this section was held not to act as a bar to a new determination of representatives. The case involved a union-shop clause with no provision for a Board election, held to be an illegal provision. C. Hager & Sons Hinge Manufacturing Co., 80 NLRB 163 (November, 1948).

42. Sec. 8(a)(3); 8(b)(2). In the first Board order assessing back pay against a union and an employer for a discriminatory lay-off, they were made "jointly and severally liable" without deciding the division between them. H. M. Newman, 85 NLRB No. 132 (August, 1949).

432

long practiced and generally acceptable to the contracting parties, were placed under a ban.

A test of the issues involved began early in the much-publicized cases against the International Typographical Union and the National Maritime Union. President Randolph of the ITU testified that one of the "essential traditional rights" of ITU members which the Act threatened to destroy was the right of only union members to work in printing shops; "the closed shop had been a practice 'for all time past' in the ITU."[43] Whether an injunction could be obtained against a union charged with discriminating or seeking to cause an employer to discriminate against nonmembers was answered in the affirmative when a temporary injunction was issued restraining the ITU from such actions, among others.[44] The Board in its first decision, in a maritime case, held that the union had refused to bargain and had sought to induce employers to discriminate by insisting upon retention of the hiring hall which as operated in the past had involved discrimination. Similarly a strike for a closed-shop clause was held a violation of the Act.[45]

Union-shop contracts, requiring as a condition of employment union membership after thirty days (or lesser forms of union-security arrangements such as "maintenance of membership"), were not precluded, however, if certain conditions were met. One was that the union must be the recognized bargaining agent of the employees in the unit concerned. Then, upon petition by a minimum of 30 per cent of the employees, a special election must be held by the NLRB and the union must obtain authorization by the favorable vote of a majority of all the workers concerned, not merely of those actually casting ballots.[46] But such authorization was merely *permissive;* the

43. Intermediate Report, April 20, 1948, International Typographical Union and Graphic Arts League, Case 5-CB-1. For an interesting analysis by the union of its experience under the Act, and its discussion of issues, see *Typographical Journal,* 114 (1949), 68–75.

44. The injunction was issued under Sec. 10(j) by Judge Luther M. Swygert, March 27, 1948. Charges had been filed by the American Newspaper Publishers' Association. Evans v. International Typographical Union, 76 F. Supp. 881 (S.D. Ind.). In this and other similar cases Intermediate Reports found the union guilty of refusal to bargain and attempting to induce employers to discriminate, for their insistence on clauses which were held in effect to be designed to maintain closed-shop conditions. Cf. *infra,* ch. 16, pp. 616–17, 627–28, 636–37, 641–42.

45. National Maritime Union and Texas Co., 78 NLRB 971 (August, 1948); Amalgamated Meat Cutters and Butcher Workmen and The Great Atlantic and Pacific Tea Co., 81 NLRB No. 164 (March, 1949). The maritime order was enforced by the Second Court of Appeals on July 5, 1949, and the case was expected to reach the Supreme Court.

46. Sections 8(a)(3), 9(e).

employer might refuse, or he might be induced to enter into such a contract by persuasion or exercise of economic power. A strike to secure a union shop was, however, lawful if a majority of the employees had voted for it.[47] "Deauthorization" elections also were provided for on petition of at least 30 per cent of the employees alleging that they wished to rescind authority to enter into a union-shop agreement. But not more than one election in a year was to be held on these questions.

An important further limitation upon the "union shop" was imposed by a second proviso to Section 8(a)(3):

Provided further, That no employer shall justify any discrimination against an employee for nonmembership in a labor organization (A) if he has reasonable grounds for believing that such membership was not available to the employee on the same terms and conditions generally applicable to other members, or (B) if he has reasonable grounds for believing that membership was denied or terminated for reasons other than the failure of the employee to tender the periodic dues and the initiation fees uniformly required as a condition of acquiring or retaining membership. . . .

To the same effect is the second union unfair labor practice, in Section 8(b)(2). The most general rule, therefore, was that, while the union could talk about its member workers to management, it might not require the discharge of an employee if he had paid his initiation fee and had kept his dues paid up. Incidentally, initiation fees, but not dues, came under the jurisdiction of the Board but only if the union was party to a union-security contract.[48] In other words, the Board received only this limited control of initiation fees, which are frequently charged with being too high even in the absence of a closed shop. Nor did the Act provide for any control of qualifications for union membership[49] or of union discipline. Only arrears in payment

47. The United Mine Workers in July, 1948, struck the "captive mines" in an effort to force them to sign an agreement similar to that which the commercial mines had accepted, continuing a union-shop clause without an election, pending adjudication by the Board and the courts. An injunction was sought under 10(j), but was withdrawn after the parties, urged by Justice T. Alan Goldsborough, had negotiated and signed the agreement with the understanding that the complaint against the union would be prosecuted. The Board in May, 1949, held the clause illegal and ordered the union to cease giving effect to it. United Mine Workers and Jones & Laughlin Steel Corp., *et al.*, 83 NLRB No. 135. Cf. also *infra*, ch. 15, p. 584.

48. Sec. 8(b)(5).

49. A proviso to Sec. 8(b)(1) specifically reserved to a labor organization the right to prescribe its own rules with respect to the acquisition or retention of membership. Taft-Hartley is not a "Fair Employment Practices Act." This was

of initiation fee or dues required the employer to discharge upon union complaint.[50] If a worker was suspended or expelled from the union, say, for dual union activity or for defaming the organization, or for serving as a spy, or as a "Communist," it mattered not. Nor need an employer discharge a nonunion worker after the thirty-day period, if he had reason to think that the man had not been admitted to the union on the usual and appropriate terms.[51]

It is clear, therefore, that a union shop under the 1947 Act was very different from what it, or the closed shop, often so similar in practice, had traditionally been. It was primarily a dues-collecting device, without the provisions for maintaining union discipline which have generally been held to be very important, though they have been subject to some abuse.

Finally, the relation of these provisions in Taft-Hartley to the more restrictive laws in some of the states[52] must be noted. If *greater* restrictions relating to union security obtained in a state law, such *greater* restriction was to prevail over federal law. Section 14(b) read: "Nothing in this Act shall be construed as authorizing the execution or application of agreements requiring membership in a labor organization as a condition of employment in any State or Territory in which such execution or application is prohibited by State or Territorial law." This is in contrast to another provision of the Act, Section 10(a), which permitted the Board to cede jurisdiction to state boards only if the state law was consistent with the federal law. On the matter of union security, however, it was the clear intent not to interfere with the greater restrictions recently imposed by many states.[53]

Many problems were inevitable under these union-security provi-

---

added to make explicit that there was no intent to regulate internal affairs of unions.

50. Dues might possibly be interpreted to include assessments also, under an opinion of the Department of Justice to the effect that "initiation fees and assessments, being incidents of membership, should be considered as falling within the classification of 'membership dues.'" The opinion was issued in answer to a query as to the legality of check-off of initiation fees and assessments as well as "periodic dues" under Section 302. *Daily Labor Report,* 96:A-1 (May 17, 1948). Question may be raised as to fines also. But the General Counsel held, in an address on June 4, 1948, that refusal to pay fines or assessments would not justify a discharge.

51. U.S. Senate, Committee on Labor and Public Welfare, *Federal Labor Relations Act of 1947,* Report No. 105, 80th Cong., 1st Sess., March, 1947, pp. 5–7, 20, cited as *Taft Report;* also *Minority Views* of Senator Thomas, ibid., Pt. 2, pp. 9–10.

52. Cf. *supra,* ch. 9, pp. 326–30.

53. Resulting problems are discussed *infra,* ch. 15, pp. 588–90.

sions, only some of which would reach the Board and the courts for decision. The constitutional question was apparently settled when the Supreme Court upheld state anti-closed-shop acts.[54] An immediate problem, which greatly affected the administration of the Act in its **first year, was the overwhelming** volume of union-shop election petitions.[55] Admittedly this was one point where the Act did not work as expected. The basic philosophy behind the Act was a belief that individual employees needed protection from the union, and given an opportunity would in many if not most cases vote against compulsory union membership requirements. Experience was quite to the contrary. Overwhelmingly large proportions of the employees voted—and voted for the union shop. No support was given to the theory that employees themselves who wanted union representation were to any large degree opposed to union security.

The provisions of Taft-Hartley—with their bans, restrictions, and controls—were intended to be far-reaching. They were denounced by most union officers, and perhaps the views expressed were shared rather generally, yet not always, by the rank and file as well. Nor, it is interesting to note, did all the criticism come from organized labor. Indeed, many employers, for one reason or another, have gone along with or frequently gladly granted the closed shop or the *heretofore* closely related union shop. This fact raises the pertinent question, why?

In building and related construction work, where the closed shop has been prevalent, the contractors, assembling and using crews of craftsmen for a limited period of time, have generally appreciated a definite source of labor upon which to draw and are usually glad to turn to the business agent of the union for needed help. They likewise appreciate the partial guaranty of efficient help found in an apprentice system and its requirements, which have increasingly been brought under joint control. And they appreciate a relatively stabilized crew, teamwork and understanding among the employees, and a degree of protection of labor costs during the life of a contract. Adapting Taft-Hartley to the building trades would be an exceedingly difficult, if not impossible, task, and at best the result would be in contrast to that in other branches of industry.[56]

In ocean shipping, with the rapid changes in crews, and employees

54. Lincoln Federal Labor Union v. Northwestern Iron and Metal Co., 335 U.S. 525 (1949).
55. Cf. *infra*, ch. 16, pp. 611–13, for details.
56. See *infra*, ch. 14, pp. 536–37; ch. 16, pp. 635–36, for the experience.

usually sailing with a different carrier at the completion of a voyage for which they had signed, the shippers prefer to have a closed-shop contract if they deal with unions at all. It is not surprising that on the Pacific Coast a contract was entered into after Taft-Hartley became effective, between the Association and President Lundberg, of the seamen, which was designed, apparently, to effect a *closed shop with a union hiring hall as its source of needed help.*[57] Hiring halls were a major issue in the threatened strike of the CIO National Maritime Union in June, 1948, and the September strike of the Pacific Longshoremen. The issue was well stated in a *New York Times* editorial which said:

Impartial observers agree with operators who point out that the old hiring terms are outlawed by the Taft-Hartley Act, and with seamen who say the union shop, permissible under certain conditions under the Act, is unworkable for the merchant marine, unless one is willing to accept destruction of the union security for which maritime labor struggled so long.[58]

In newspaper publication and in large segments of commercial printing, contracts have for decades and in some localities for more than half a century provided for the closed shop. The nature and details of the work are such that these contracts appear to be favored by many, if not most, managements who deal with unions. The various printing crafts, except for one with its subordinate Mailers, sought successfully, within or contrary to Taft-Hartley, to make with their employers adjustments such that Taft-Hartley would cause little or no changes in the essentials of their relationships. The International Typographical Union, on the other hand, was bitterly opposed to the requirements of Taft-Hartley, and strikes and other conflicts were widespread in newspaper publishing and commercial printing during the first year. In the wordy struggle, with Chicago as an important testing point, the spokesman of the Chicago Newspaper Publishers Association in public testimony referred to the local record in collective bargaining with general approbation and officially stated that the Publishers were satisfied with the closed shop but could not enter into closed-shop contracts in violation of the present law.[59]

57. Whether this contract met the requirements of the new law under which it was made raised a question. The chairman of the Senate Committee, who had personal contact with the parties concerned, was reported to have said that it did; the chairman of the House Committee that it did not. Here, it has been observed, "the doctors do not agree."

58. *New York Times*, June 16, 1948. For further discussion of the issues in these industries cf. *infra*, ch. 15, pp. 584–85; ch. 16, p. 642 and n. 51.

59. At a hearing in Chicago, an active member of the House Committee lauded the ITU and expressed surprise that Taft-Hartley at any point would affect that organization. Cf. *supra*, p. 433.

In the manufacture of ladies' and men's garments, the preferential shop, adopted at the suggestion of the late Justice Brandeis more than thirty-five years ago in New York, was later used successfully by the Amalgamated Clothing Workers of America in Chicago and elsewhere. For more than twenty-five years that union has conducted in Chicago a model employment office devised by Bryce Stewart which has been much appreciated by the industry. A great burden theretofore involved in obtaining a new and balanced crew each "season" was lifted from the manufacturers, and preference to those at the top of the list has been satisfactory to the membership of the union at large. Perhaps the instances cited are typical of at least a large minority of those in management having bargaining relations with unions.

The union position with reference to union security, and especially under the union closed shop, deserves comment. The craft unions well know the significance of the closed shop, including the usually temporary union shop of the past—very different from that under Taft-Hartley. The unions say that they ordinarily provide trained labor, give at least partial guaranty of efficiency, stabilize employment in the plant, and stabilize labor costs for a period. Again, the closed shop or union shop makes for harmony among the workers, eliminates "free riders," assists in maintaining needed discipline, makes possible more assumption of responsibility by the union, and protects against spies and other undesirables.[60]

But why, with discrimination by employers made unlawful by the Wagner Act and by Taft-Hartley also, and with workers granted the right to select a new representative at an appropriate time, should there nowadays be such a thing as a closed shop or union shop in most industries? As to the first of these facts, the "closed shopper" would correctly say that the protection from discrimination given by the Wagner and Taft-Hartley Acts provided only a check, and certainly not always an effective one. To the second, he may reply that the closed-shop agreement may give protection against inroads by a rival union, especially when there is an active, divided labor movement and another union may make trouble by attempting to "organize the organized." In other words, the closed shop may give protection against a rival, not to say a raiding, union as well as against a feared

60. For a well-argued union case for the union shop see Clinton S. Golden and Harold J. Ruttenberg, *The Dynamics of Industrial Democracy* (New York: Harper & Bros., 1942), ch. 7.

employer. The competitive, divided labor movement has without question increased the demand for "union security."[61]

Assuming that restrictions on admission to the union are reasonable, a matter which with its complexities cannot be discussed in these pages, and with such safeguards of the individual worker as are found in Taft-Hartley, but without overstressing the "rights" of the *individual* against those of the *group*, as the 1947 Act did, the writer sees no good case for outlawing the closed shop. The problem is to prevent its misuse. If unions are open, we see no reason to fear "monopoly of the labor market," nor any case for attempting to break down the traditional unwillingness of loyal union members to work with non-unionists. In any event, a careful study should have been made of closed-shop problems before Taft-Hartley was adopted, and the law should have dealt only with clear abuses. "Evils" connected with the closed shop might be brought under control in ways analogous to some of those accompanying the union shop under Taft-Hartley. Four states, among them Wisconsin, had by 1947 permitted closed shops only after a vote of the employees. Six states also, by 1947, had provided some measure of protection against unreasonable expulsion or refusal of membership in unions with closed-shop agreements.[62] The protection provided under the Wagner Act against dual union discharges might have been extended by giving the Board power to hear charges of other types of unreasonable union discipline which led to discharge or refusals of employment.

Organized labor objects also to trimming-down of the union shop. Perhaps the requirement of an election to legitimatize the making of a union-security agreement would not meet serious objection, if the union or closed shop were not too much restricted, and if management's "freedom of speech" were not carried too far. There are some advantages in a democratic election procedure to determine whether the employees wish to require union membership, though a requirement of a majority of all employees in the unit, rather than of those voting, as in Taft-Hartley, is counter to our usual democratic processes. Expense and delay not justified by existence of a real question, however, as well as the possible disruption of relations by an election

61. The Typographical Union has argued also that the closed shop is necessary to protect the craft against employers who break down and parcel out parts of the work.

62. *Supra*, ch. 9, p. 330. For a very interesting discussion of this problem see Commonwealth of Massachusetts, *Report of the Governor's Labor-Management Committee*, House Document, No. 1875, March 18, 1947.

campaign, could be avoided by requiring authorization elections only where there had not previously been a union-security contract.[63]

Organized labor's main objection to the provisions relating to the union shop, however, seems to be that they might seriously affect necessary union discipline. The Minority Report presented to the Senate by Senators Thomas of Utah, Murray, and Pepper stressed this danger:

> . . . an employee could with impunity completely defy the union. He could defame it, he could betray confidential union information, he could seek to wreck it, attempt to bring it into disrepute, act as a spy or stool pigeon or strikebreaker, be a racketeer or a grafter, and yet the union would have no effective sanction against him. If he pays or offers to pay his dues and initiation fees, the employer need not fire him and any attempt by the union to persuade the employer to do so would be an unfair labor practice on the part of the union. The union would be completely shorn of effective power to discipline its members for good cause.
>
> If these provisions are merely designed to outlaw the closed-shop closed-union arrangement and to permit union-security agreements not based on the closed-union practice, they have gone far beyond what is needed to achieve that purpose.[64]

Direct knowledge of experience under union-management agreements gives support to this view. Occasional abuses of the rights of individuals under closed-shop or other similar agreements were checked to a considerable degree under the Wagner Act, and such protection could have been extended by providing standards and the right of appeal to the Board against unreasonable exclusion from a union. But the sweeping modification of well-established and on the whole well-functioning systems of working relationships could only contribute to instability, insecurity, and distrust. Interpreted with reason as designed to weaken unions, rather than merely to eliminate recognized abuses, they made for a psychology of conflict and for bad relationships.[65]

OTHER UNFAIR LABOR PRACTICES OF MANAGEMENT

Discrimination for filing charges or testifying under the Act, the fourth prohibited practice for management, read exactly as before.

---

63. The Board and the General Counsel recommended the elimination in whole or part of the union-shop election procedures. U.S. Congress, Joint Committee on Labor-Management Relations, *Hearings, Labor-Management Relations,* 80th Cong., 2d Sess., Pt. 1, pp. 51, 62, May 24, 1948, cited as *Ball Committee Hearings.*

64. *Taft Report,* Pt. 2, *Minority Views,* April 22, 1947, pp. 9–10; cf. also Cox, *op. cit.,* pp. 291–99.

65. *Infra,* ch. 16, pp. 635–37, 641–42.

Its enforcement was subject to the same influences as those discussed above in connection with 8(a)(3), in so far as change was made by the rules as to proof and discharge for "cause."

The fifth unfair labor practice also, refusal to bargain, read as before. A definition of collective bargaining, in Section 8(d), was largely a restatement of Board and court principles in decisions on the meaning of bargaining in good faith. Certain details as to negotiations upon the expiration of contracts, the settlement of disputes, and a considerable number of other limitations and proscriptions, however, would make collective bargaining somewhat different from what it was before. Since unions also came under a requirement not to refuse to bargain, discussion of these matters may better be postponed until they are reached in our consideration of the new unfair labor practices of unions.

UNFAIR LABOR PRACTICES BY UNIONS
AND THEIR AGENTS

Far-reaching legal restraints were imposed upon union activities by the new unfair labor practices incorporated in Taft-Hartley. On the other hand, the restraints imposed upon management under the NLRA were on the whole weakened by the changes in the Act. But by no means were all the restraints and bans against labor new, for many of them had been found in court-made and state laws, with state and local administration here strict, there weak. Moreover, some of them had found place in NLRB decisions having to do with union abuses which came within the Board's jurisdiction, as in the misuse of the closed shop, or union interference with free elections.[66] Now, however, important provisions relating to union behavior appeared over against the five listed management unfair labor practices. Some of these union unfair labor practices corresponded to those imposed by the Wagner Act upon the employer, but others did not. The most outstanding facts are that Taft-Hartley federalized the law and turned the clock back in the field of what we have called "basic labor law."[67]

66. *Supra*, ch. 5, p. 164; ch. 6, pp. 203–16.
67. We have in mind Senator Taft's objective stated when discussing the Case Bill, on May 25, 1946, *Cong. Rec.*, 92:5696–97. He said that the Case Bill would have "done no more than restore the law as it was after the passage of the Clayton Act for many years before the decisions of the present Supreme Court." The general policy and labor law of that period to which the Senator would have us return was high-lighted and developed rather consistently from the majority decisions in *Duplex, Bedford Stone,* and related court cases decided in the 1920's. Cf. *supra*, ch. 1, pp. 11–13.

From the Wagner Act to Taft-Hartley

The sections relating to unlawful practices by labor organizations or their agents must be quoted. Section 8(b) read as follows:

(b) It shall be an unfair labor practice for a labor organization or its agents—

(1) to restrain or coerce (A) employees in the exercise of the rights guaranteed in section 7: *Provided,* That this paragraph shall not impair the right of a labor organization to prescribe its own rules with respect to the acquisition or retention of membership therein; or (B) an employer in the selection of his representatives for the purposes of collective bargaining or the adjustment of grievances;

(2) to cause or attempt to cause an employer to discriminate against an employee in violation of subsection (a)(3) or to discriminate against an employee with respect to whom membership in such an organization has been denied or terminated on some ground other than his failure to tender the periodic dues and the initiation fees uniformly required as a condition of acquiring or retaining membership;

(3) to refuse to bargain collectively with an employer, provided it is the representative of his employees subject to the provisions of section 9(a);

(4) to engage in, or to induce or encourage the employees of any employer to engage in, a strike or a concerted refusal in the course of their employment to use, manufacture, process, transport, or otherwise handle or work on any goods, articles, materials, or commodities or to perform any services, where an object thereof is: (A) forcing or requiring any employer or self-employed person to join any labor or employer organization or any employer or other person to cease using, selling, handling, transporting, or otherwise dealing in the products of any other producer, processor, or manufacturer, or to cease doing business with any other person; (B) forcing or requiring any other employer to recognize or bargain with a labor organization as the representative of his employees unless such labor organization has been certified as the representative of such employees under the provisions of section 9; (C) forcing or requiring any employer to recognize or bargain with a particular labor organization as the representative of his employees if another labor organization has been certified as the representative of such employees under the provisions of section 9; (D) forcing or requiring any employer to assign particular work to employees in a particular labor organization or in a particular trade, craft, or class rather than to employees in another labor organization or in another trade, craft, or class, unless such employer is failing to conform to an order or certification of the Board determining the bargaining representative for employees performing such work: *Provided,* That nothing contained in this subsection (b) shall be construed to make unlawful a refusal by any person to enter upon the premises of any employer (other than his own employer), if the employees of such employer are engaged in a strike ratified or approved by a representative of such employees whom such employer is required to recognize under this Act;

(5) to require of employees covered by an agreement authorized under subsection (a)(3) the payment, as a condition precedent to becoming a member of such organization, of a fee in an amount which the Board finds excessive or discriminatory under all the circumstances. In making such a

finding, the Board shall consider, among other relevant factors, the practices and customs of labor organizations in the particular industry, and the wages currently paid to the employees affected; and

(6) to cause or attempt to cause an employer to pay or deliver or agree to pay or deliver any money or other thing of value, in the nature of an exaction, for services which are not performed or not to be performed.

RESTRAINT OR COERCION

In the first unfair labor practice prohibited to unions or their agents, the major question concerns the meaning of the words "restrain or coerce." But two other matters need mention. The first is the proviso added to make explicit that there was no intent to regulate union internal affairs or rules as to union membership.[68] A union could refuse admission or expel a member as freely as before, although under the union-shop provisions it could not require an employer to discriminate against any involuntary nonmembers. The second is Subsection (B), which protected an employer in the selection of his agent for collective bargaining or grievance handling, corresponding to the freedom of workers to choose their representatives. Senator Taft thought this might be useful in some cases where unions objected to certain negotiators or even to a foreman; and, perhaps more important, it would not permit the union to insist that an employer bargain through an employers' association, this being the only section of the bill which touched nation-wide collective bargaining, he said.[69] Problems might arise under this section in connection with efforts of unions to standardize conditions in a competitive area, although in general there is little reason to object to the provision.

The prohibition against restraint or coercion of employees by unions or their agents is a somewhat limited form of the "coercion from any source" clause long desired by many.[70] It related, however, only to what a union or its "agent" directed or approved, not to what a mere member did on his own, for which he could be disciplined by management, or perhaps arrested. But what is an "agent"? As in the case of agents of employers, "the question of whether the specific acts

68. *Supra,* pp. 434–35.
69. *Daily Cong. Rec.,* 93:1012. But cf. also the related Sec. 8(b)(4)(A), where a strike or boycott to force an employer or self-employed person to join any labor or employer organization is forbidden. The first use on record of Sec. 8(b)(1)(B), curiously, was against the United Mine Workers, when a charge was filed that they violated this section as well as refused to bargain, by refusing to negotiate with Southern Coal Producers Association. On petition of the Board, Justice T. Alan Goldsborough issued an injunction against the union, on June 4, 1948. Madden v. United Mine Workers, 79 F. Supp. 616 (D.C. D.C.).
70. Cf. *supra,* ch. 1, p. 28; ch. 6, p. 191; ch. 9, pp. 338–39.

performed were actually authorized or subsequently ratified [is not] controlling,"[71] but still "agency" had to be proved. A clear intent was to replace the rule of the Norris–La Guardia Act under which unions and their officers and members were not held responsible or liable for unlawful acts of officers, members, or agents, except upon clear proof of actual participation in or authorization of such acts.[72] Senator Taft explained that "agent" meant "an agent under the ordinary rules of agency, an agent of the labor union . . . as such. The fact that a man was a member of a labor union . . . would be no evidence whatever to show that he was an agent."[73] But this still left the matter open. What of illegal acts by union members on a picket line? And is the union responsible for an unfair labor practice and liable for damages in case of a "wildcat" strike in violation of contract or for an illegal purpose? What of the respective liabilities of a local union and its international? Many decisions would be required to make clear the extent to which unions might be held responsible for unlawful actions of members, as well as of officers, official organizers, stewards, or others who were unquestionably acting as authorized agents of the union.[74]

What then was the real intent of this prohibition of restraint or coercion? As one of the "equalizing" amendments, paralleling the prohibition of interference, restraint, or coercion by employers, it was, its proponents said, meant to protect the rights of individual employees under Section 7 to engage in *or refrain from* self-organization and concerted activities. But though the Senate debates were sharp and prolonged,[75] no adequate definition of the words "restrain" or "coerce" is to be found. These words could be given precise meaning only by the Board and the courts in their decisions, case by case, as was true under the Wagner Act as applied to management unfair labor practices. One would expect parallel treatments here, though the limitations could not be identical because the one related to management behavior, the other to that of the union, union officers, and agents, who, differently circumstanced, do not do precisely the

71. Sec. 2(13). Cf. *supra,* ch. 11, p. 398.

72. *Infra,* ch. 13, pp. 487, 502.

73. *Daily Cong. Rec.,* 93:4561; cf. also 93:6680.

74. There was difference of opinion among Trial Examiners in early cases as to whether unions were to be held responsible for actions of pickets. In spite of some differences also among Board members, the Board began to develop its theory of agency, and found labor organizations responsible for "coercive" activity by pickets, in the first decisions on this point. Sunset Line and Twine Co., 79 NLRB 1487 (October, 1948); Perry Norvell Co., 80 NLRB 225 (November, 1948); Smith Cabinet Manufacturing Co., 81 NLRB No. 138 (February, 1949).

75. *Cong. Rec.*: Senate, April 25 and May 2, 1947, for example.

same things. We look to the debates, therefore, for statements of *intent*. Concern was expressed over "the coercive and restraining acts of the union in its effort to organize unorganized employees"[76] and "coercive acts of unions against employees who did not wish to join or did not care to participate in a strike or a picket line."[77] Threats, violence, mass picketing, were clearly meant to be covered. However, as Senator Taft said, "It would not prevent anyone using the strike in a legitimate way, conducting peaceful picketing, or employing persuasion. All it would do would be to outlaw such restraint and coercion as would prevent people from going to work if they wished to go to work."[78] It was recognized that the right of free speech would protect many statements, although Senator Ball thought that under some circumstances misrepresentation and false promises would be held coercive.[79] The words "interfere with" had been omitted on Senator Ives's motion, lest the broader language be interpreted to prevent efforts to persuade others to join a union. Senator Taft made clear that a union organizing drive "by persuasion, by propaganda, so long as it has *every legitimate purpose*," could not be held an unfair labor practice.[80] Nevertheless, he said also that the elimination of the words would not make any substantial change in the meaning of the clause.[81]

Possibly more meaningful are some positive statements as to types of actions which were meant to be covered, although some of the looser interpretations were repudiated at other times. A statement by Senator Taft[82] can be summarized as follows, with our parenthetical comments at points:

1. Threats to raise initiation fees if employee fails to join in time. [Not an infrequent practice in union organizational efforts, for unions frequently make special arrangements to favor new members for a brief time. Nor is such treatment limited to labor organizations alone.]
2. Threat to get a closed shop and prevent the employee from holding his job. [Such a threat would of course be unlawful under the Taft-Hartley ban on the closed shop.]
3. Threat to beat up a worker or his family if he did not join. [Which is contrary to law in every state.]
4. Actual violence preventing a man from working. . . . [It is to be noted that the law was not directed to unfair labor practices by *employees*, but by unions and their agents.]

76. Senator Ball, *Daily Cong. Rec.*, 93:4559.
77. Senator Taft, *ibid.*, p. 7001.
78. *Ibid.*, p. 4563. The next sentence is not quoted, since clearly the Senator was under a misapprehension as to the Byrnes Act.
79. *Ibid.*, pp. 4137, 4560.   81. *Ibid.*, p. 4398.
80. *Ibid.*, p. 4560. (Italics ours.)   82. *Ibid.*, p. 4562.

5. Preventing employees from entering or leaving plants by mass picketing or other means. [Already contrary to state law.]

Additions by Senator Ball[83] included these:

1. Coercive organizing by union "goon squads."
2. False electioneering statements by unions . . . such as statements that unaffiliated unions are not recognized by the NLRB; that the union has won wage increases at other plants of a company, and such is not the case. [Of course the NLRB had held that under the Wagner Act a company had a right to answer such misrepresentations of fact if it did not threaten reprisals.]
3. Defamatory articles and statements by unions directed at opponents or company officials. [The NLRB's practice under the Wagner Act was to give the company the right to answer such statements with facts, if coercive language was not used.]
4. Threats of violence or reprisals, etc., in an organizational campaign or perhaps in an organization strike.

Fears felt by Senator Morse and others that this section would prove "a tremendous handicap to legitimate strikes and legitimate organizational activities" were denied by the proponents. Senator Taft admitted that the law might encourage local law-enforcement agencies to act, but he did not see any duplication of state laws except in cases involving actual violence.[84]

It is evident that the provision is vague and uncertain and could be expected to promote litigation and sometimes delay the settling of disputes. Much of the behavior aimed at was unlawful already under state laws, so far as individuals are concerned. Though any intention of having federal policing of such matters was disavowed, the law was federalized. Superimposition of federal law also means that multiple penalties or remedies are made available for the same conduct.[85] The most effective remedy for violence or other actual coercion would still be prompt police action, or possibly injunctions under Section

83. Especially *ibid.*, pp. 4136–37, 4558–59. These were summarized in Bureau of National Affairs, *The New Labor Law* (Washington, 1947), pp. 35–36.

84. *Daily Cong. Rec.*, 93:4563.

85. In addition to the possibility of arrest and punishment of individuals for violation of local laws, there is the threat of federal injunction and possible contempt action, as well as the slower process of obtaining cease-and-desist orders against unions; also the possibility of suits for damages. Individuals concerned might also lose protection against selection by the employer for discharge. *Supra*, n. 34. The establishment of federal standards on these matters is not necessarily bad, of course. But the vagueness of the standard and the possibility of abuse in putting unreasonable restrictions on union action is to be questioned. The law might stimulate better local policing, or it might encourage abuses by local police or courts against strikers; there were some indications of the latter in the first year. Cf. *infra*, ch. 13, pp. 495–96; ch. 16, pp. 640–41.

10(j). The Board's cease-and-desist order, perhaps a year after the incidents in question, with the posting of the required notice by the union—"We will not restrain or coerce the employees, etc."—would be a weak remedy for the actions Congress sought to eliminate. Some deterrent effect upon violent and coercive methods which have been used by some unions would be a valuable result of this section; but against this was the uncertainty as to what is legitimate and the use of the new weapon by antiunion employers to delay and fight organization and strikes.

In the first cases decided the Board reversed Trial Examiners and found specific instances of violence and intimidation on picket lines and mass picketing coercive and violations of this section.[86] Peaceful picketing by one man at a store, however, was held to be protected by the free-speech amendment.[87] In other cases Intermediate Reports went far in holding unions responsible for actions found to be coercive on picket lines. Attempted defenses by unions which could not file charges because they were not in compliance with the filing requirements of the Act, that their strikes had resulted from unfair labor practices of employers, were not accepted.[88]

86. Cited *supra,* in n. 74.

87. Watson's Specialty Store, 80 NLRB 533 (November, 1948); but cf. *infra,* n. 151.

88. Cf. Smith Cabinet Manufacturing Co., decided February, 1949, 81 NLRB No. 138; Cory Corp., 84 NLRB No. 110 (July, 1949); Colonial Hardwood Flooring Co., 84 NLRB No. 69 (June, 1949). The minority report of the Ball Committee, U.S. Senate, Joint Committee on Labor-Management Relations, *Labor-Management Relations,* Report No. 986, Pt. 2, *Minority Views,* 80th Cong., 2d Sess., April 1, 1948, p. 20, held that there were dangers in a too broad interpretation of "coercion" by the General Counsel in these cases. It said: "It is no answer to suggest that they may subsequently be corrected by action of the Board or of the Trial Examiner. The mere issuance of a complaint, which after all rests upon a judgment that there is a substantial basis for believing that there is a violation of the law, exerts a tremendous effect upon the course of a labor dispute."

A theory accepted in some of the early Intermediate Reports, rejected in others, was that unions coerced employees or their own members by insisting upon or striking for objectives which were found to be violative of the Act, as in some of the cases involving closed-shop issues. Such an argument was rejected by the Board in National Maritime Union and Texas Co., 78 NLRB 971 (August, 1948). Cf. comment of Arthur J. Goldberg, General Counsel of the CIO, in *Ball Committee Hearings,* Pt. 2, p. 690: ". . . The theory that a union coerces its own members when it promulgates legitimate and time-honored union rules relating to such matters as crossing picket lines or working upon struck work is a profound insult to the group loyalty, good sense, and unity of American working men and women. It rests upon the ridiculous assumption that unions are held together by fear and intimidation and that union members never act toward a common objective through democratically arrived at means but rather are forced to do so by a threat of reprisal." Cf. also *ibid.,* Pt. 1, p. 291.

447

The second unfair labor practice of unions, related to discrimination against nonmembers, has been considered above in our discussion of union security. Nor is it necessary to make further reference to the fifth, which prohibited excessive initiation fees, under union-security contracts, and thus gave the Board a limited control over union fees.[89]

REFUSAL TO BARGAIN, THE MEANING OF COLLECTIVE BARGAINING, AND THE SETTLEMENT OF DISPUTES

A legal duty to bargain collectively, corresponding to the obligations laid upon management under both the Wagner Act and Taft-Hartley, was imposed by section 8(b)(3) upon a union representing employees.[90] And a definition of collective bargaining was provided in section 8(d). The law as to the duty to bargain has been well summarized as follows:

Presumably the Board will test the obligation of the union to bargain by the same standard of "good faith" as it applies to employers. Proposals and counter-proposals must be made although concessions need not be granted. Unions will not be permitted to submit contracts to employers on a "take it or leave it" basis. Both parties must approach the bargaining table with a sincere desire to negotiate. It is probable that the refusal of one party to bargain will excuse the failure of the other party to meet his legal bargaining obligations.[91]

It should be noted at the start that it has been management far more than unions which has balked at and attempted to thwart collective bargaining. In fact, many instances of this still remained to be coped with, cases in which counsel advised resistance to recognition of a union and bargaining with it[92]—a fact which received little attention in the Eightieth Congress. On the other hand, unions are organized primarily for the purpose of collective bargaining. Of

89. *Supra,* p. 434.

90. Certain limitations upon the scope of the duty to bargain were established by exclusions from the coverage of the Act and qualifications for use of the facilities of the Board. The most important group excluded are the supervisors. *Supra,* ch. 11, pp. 399–400. In addition, unions but not employers could file petitions and charges with the Board only if they had qualified by filing certain information and "non-Communist affidavits." *Infra,* ch. 14, pp. 537–58. A noncomplying union, if the representative of a majority of the employees in an appropriate unit, still had a right to be recognized for the purpose of collective bargaining, apparently, and a duty to bargain in good faith, but its "right" could not be implemented by filing a charge of refusal to bargain or obtaining an unconditional bargaining order from the Board. *Ibid.,* pp. 555–56 and n. 114.

91. Burton A. Zorn and Howard Lichtenstein, *The More Important Provisions of the Labor-Management Relations Act, 1947* (Chamber of Commerce of the State of New York, 1947), pp. 5–6.

92. Cf. *supra,* ch. 4, p. 121.

course instances occur in which a union adopts the policy of "take this proposed contract or else." Sometimes also, unfortunately, unions have insisted upon contracts made unlawful in some part by Taft-Hartley, but this largely to protect their asserted legal rights in court. An outstanding fact has been that unions have desired collective bargaining "in good faith." The numerous complaints to the contrary arise very largely from differences as to the ends in view. Unions generally wish to standardize wages and conditions of employment in the industry, locally or otherwise, and to avoid diverse arrangements which may protect inefficiency in management, to the disadvantage of "fair" competitors. For the most part, minimum wage laws or the Fair Labor Standards Act have had a similar end in view. There are, of course, cases of hold-up unions here and there. But most of the complaints, we think, come from those employers who wish an agreement, if any, not in line with an agreement signed by other managements. We do not say that there is no problem, only that its size is exaggerated. Indeed, if a stated obligation to bargain is administered in the light of the pertinent facts and in an application of the element of "good faith" as the NLRB tried to apply it to cases against employers under the Wagner Act, there is no objection in principle, and it might contribute to responsible bargaining. Any real objection lies in other but related parts of the Act.

The fact is that subsection 8(b)(3) is not entirely new.[93] Though complaints against unions for "refusal to bargain" were not envisaged by the Wagner Act, what the union had done in a given case was considered as well as what management had done in deciding whether management had refused to bargain. Unless there were an unequal administration of the law—and this was not to be expected—the new specific requirement that unions also must not refuse to bargain, standing alone, carried only the same obligation as was implicit in the Wagner Act. The difference was that the law had been "equalized," with the result that a considerable number of countercharges would be filed by management against unions. Equalization of the law at this point is sound in principle. But difficult legal questions arose in some of the earliest cases when unions were charged with refusal to bargain because of their attempts to obtain union-security or other clauses which were held illegal.[94] The major problems and any case against this section come from other parts of the law which unions did

93. *Ibid.*, p. 116.
94. *Supra*, p. 433; *infra*, ch. 16, pp. 641–42.

not consider fair or proper, and therefore sought to test.[95] These other, related provisions in the 1947 law and especially in the "basic labor law" must be carefully scrutinized. Many of them we regard as unsound or unnecessary, adopted without adequate information or not meeting the requirements of a proper industrial relations policy.

Before further specific discussion of the unfair labor practice of "refusal to bargain," it is necessary to consider some very basic questions of public policy toward collective bargaining. A question raised by many employers, by unions generally, and by most industrial relations experts is that of how far should government regulation extend, as against freedom of contract between management and a labor organization. Presumably, were the labor-management conferees of 1945[96] reconvened, they would once more strongly espouse freedom of contract, with only such government implementation as required to further this, to avoid any abuses, and to safeguard the public and further the public peace. The Conference of 1945 was adamant against any extensive regulation and was fearful that, with one thing leading to another, we might move far in the direction of compulsory arbitration. Outstanding industrial relations men have felt that Taft-Hartley went too far in its "musts," restrictions, and bans. Many foresee danger of industrial control getting into politics and begetting political activity which might be exceedingly unfortunate. The Congress perhaps thought so, as shown by the limitation imposed on union contributions and expenditures for political purposes.[97]

The sponsors of Taft-Hartley stated again and again that industrial relations must rest chiefly upon clean, effective, free, collective bargaining.[98] That was properly said to be the appropriate road to travel. However, articulate union officials and many others assert that a great many things in Taft-Hartley had a contrary effect, that collective bargaining and freedom of contract were weakened. This position calls for an examination of several important parts of the new Act.

Of course Taft-Hartley in unequal degrees affects management and union "rights." The net effect could adequately be established only after unclear provisions had been ruled upon by the Board and the courts, when the attitudes and behavior of both management and

95. Dr. Taylor makes an additional point that any such legal requirement of employers and unions tends to lead to regulation of the bargaining itself. George W. Taylor, *Government Regulation of Industrial Relations* (New York: Prentice-Hall, 1948), pp. 282–84.

96. *Supra,* ch. 8, pp. 306–11.

97. Sec. 304, discussed *infra,* ch. 15, pp. 593–98.

98. Cf. Senator Taft's statement, *Daily Cong. Rec.,* 93:4563.

labor became fairly clear, and when more was known of the administration of the Act. Some good amendments were made to the Wagner Act, to encourage collective bargaining, beget a greater feeling of responsibility in industrial relations, and here and there eliminate things generally recognized as undesirable. But discussion is needed of other provisions of the law which affected the scope and nature of collective bargaining and procedures to be followed by management and labor and by the General Counsel, and changed the basic law generally. Taft-Hartley was assumed to impose equal obligations upon unions and employers to bargain, under certain conditions. For either to fail to meet this obligation was an unfair labor practice, which, when found by the NLRB, was to be restrained through cease-and-desist orders. Authority was provided also, in cases against management as well as labor organizations, for the General Counsel, on behalf of the Board, to seek a restraining order from a district court.[99] In some types of cases against unions such petition for an injunction was mandatory.

"Equalization" is sound in principle if and when it equalizes in fact. On the face of the 1947 law the obligations were mutual. But important questions of law arose in early cases brought against unions under this section of the Act, and others undoubtedly would arise. One central question is, where does a "right" leave off? For example, does a union have a right to demand a uniform "scale" for all competitors in a local or wider area, or must it make concessions because an employer is differently circumstanced than some of his competitors? Can an employer insist upon the "right" under this section and Section 8(b)(1)(A) to require the union to bargain with him separately? Can an employer stand on his contract rigidly and refuse to negotiate even though a change in conditions has created problems which in the interest of sound relationships need to be faced? Must a union give up practices, deeply imbedded in union mores and well established in industrial practices, "from time immemorial" so far as union history goes, such as the refusal of union men to work with nonunion or to work on "struck work"—a refusal certainly thought by such men to be a "right"?

"Freedom of contract," moreover, as it has been understood in collective bargaining, was restricted by numerous points in Taft-Hartley. As Professor Cox points out, in some matters commonly the subject of collective bargaining "Congress undertook to settle for the benefit of one side specific issues heretofore resolved by collective bargaining

99. *Infra*, ch. 13, pp. 489–96.

and the interplay of economic forces."[100] Examples are the prohibition of closed shops and preferential hiring arrangements, including "hiring halls"; permitting union shops only in a form with extreme limits upon traditional powers of union discipline, and only after a time-consuming and expensive election process of which in perhaps most cases the result was known from the start and which was open only to a union willing to file the required statements; prohibiting "featherbedding," without clear definition; and prohibiting with heavy penalty any payments of money to any representative of the employees—both of these being uncertain enough to raise in countless negotiations questions as to whether numerous well-established clauses in old contracts could legally be continued; and outlawing without distinction or qualification the self-protective devices of refusal to work on nonunion materials where an "object" is to force an employer to cease using or dealing in such materials or doing business with any other person. These and other points differ in the extent to which they limited the freedom of employers and unions to work out acceptable arrangements. Some were in the name of protecting the public or individual employees, but we think without adequate evidence of need. Most of them gave a new weapon to an employer who wished to use them in bargaining. These are not "equalizing," but restrictive, amendments, some of them restricting employers as well as unions, when they would prefer to work out problems as experience indicates.[101] We consider them unwarranted interferences with collective bargaining.

Bargaining in "good faith" was defined in Section 8(d). It declared first of all essentially the principles worked out by the Board in cases decided against employers under the Wagner Act. Both the negotiation of an agreement and of any question arising thereunder are included; the signing of any agreement arrived at, if requested by one party or the other, was required; and the "obligation does not compel either party to agree to a proposal or require the making of a concession." So far there was nothing new except to make it clear that the obligation was mutual upon management and union. But, to this leading sentence, Taft-Hartley added a proviso relating to the extension or renewal of an agreement, and provided that such an agreement could not be terminated or changed during its term without

100. Cox, *op. cit.,* p. 288.

101. An occasional management representative has made similar statements, among them Nathan W. Shefferman, retired industrial relations director for Sears Roebuck, according to reports of an industrial relations conference at the University of Minnesota, in March, 1948. *Minneapolis Star,* March 30, 1948.

mutual consent. No party to such contract might terminate or modify it, unless that party served written notice upon the other sixty days before the expiration date or the proposed date of termination or modification, offered to meet for negotiation of a new contract or the proposed modification, notified the Federal Mediation and Conciliation Service and any state mediation agency within thirty days if no agreement had been reached by that time, and continued the old contract in full effect, without resorting to strike or lockout, for the period of sixty days or until the expiration of the contract, whichever was later. This provision, making contracts in effect binding and laying down procedural rules, was intended to make for stability. But it might have the contrary effect by bringing short-term contracts or many "opening clauses." Taft-Hartley assumed that collective bargaining is not something requiring adjustments as conditions change. Thus another sentence in this section read:

. . . and the duties so imposed shall not be construed as requiring either party to discuss or agree to any modification of the terms and conditions contained in a contract for a fixed period, if such modification is to become effective before such terms and conditions can be reopened under the provisions of the contract.

The fact is that when changes occur amendments may be necessary in order that satisfactory relationships continue.[102] We see no occasion for federal law on this matter. In the natural course of events contracts remain binding until changed by mutual agreement, and normally contracts themselves provide means for handling violations. But Taft-Hartley added these prescriptions and provided also:

Any employee who engages in a strike within the sixty-day period specified in this subsection shall lose his status as an employee of the employer engaged in the particular labor dispute, for the purposes of sections 8, 9, and 10 of this Act, as amended, but such loss of status for such employee shall terminate if and when he is reemployed by such employer.[103]

The effect was to deprive such strikers of protection against reprisals, or of a right to vote in any election under the Act, unless and until rehired. Thus the employer was given a weapon, distinct from the provisions in the agreement itself for its enforcement and the prevention of violations. But litigation is unlikely to be a satisfactory answer to problems arising during the term of a contract.

Another limitation upon collective bargaining which presented

102. Cf. *infra*, ch. 13, pp. 505–8.
103. Injunctions and damage suits were also possible. Cf. discussion *infra*, ch. 13; ch. 16, p. 638.

danger to the integrity of collective bargaining and majority rule was the provision for individual grievance handling. The Wagner Act had provided, in order to protect an individual should the union be unfair in its treatment of his grievance, that any employee or group of employees should have "the right at any time to present grievances to their employer." But Taft-Hartley added the following:

... and to have such grievances adjusted, without the intervention of the bargaining representative, as long as the adjustment is not inconsistent with the terms of a collective-bargaining contract or agreement then in effect: *Provided further,* That the bargaining representative has been given opportunity to be present at such adjustment.[104]

The addition reflected, as did so many others of the amendments, distrust of collective bargaining and the feeling that individual employees need to be protected against their union, rather than, except in rare cases, finding their strength increased through collective action.

Under the Wagner Act the Board had interpreted the proviso as meaning this:

... that individual employees and groups of employees are permitted "to present grievances to their employer" by appearing in behalf of themselves—although not through any labor organization other than the exclusive representative—at every stage of the grievance procedure, but that the exclusive representative is entitled to be present and negotiate at each such stage concerning the disposition to be made of the grievance.[105]

But Taft-Hartley made the right of the bargaining agent less clear and gave encouragement to dissident minorities to insist on separate settlement of their grievances. Although Section 8(d) recognized that collective bargaining includes settlement of questions arising under the contract, here it appeared to be assumed that individuals have a right separate from or superior to that of the majority bargaining representative, for the settling of grievances. While in an exceptional case some provision of this sort for the protection of an individual may be important, this clause goes too far. It is contrary to sound relationships to encourage unnecessarily such individual action, which may run counter to the interests of the entire group of employees who have chosen a collective bargaining representative.[106] Any employer who hoped to undermine the union would find this provision a useful one for his purposes.

104. Sec. 9(a).
105. Hughes Tool Co., 56 NLRB 981 (1944), modified and enforced in 147 F. 2d 69 (C.C.A.5, 1945). Cf. *supra*, ch. 4, n. 66.
106. Cf. Cox, *op. cit.*, pp. 299–303; Gerhard P. Van Arkel, *An Analysis of the Labor-Management Relations Act, 1947* (New York: Practising Law Institute, 1947), pp. 39–41.

Title II of the Act, which deals with the Mediation and Conciliation Service and with national emergency disputes, starts with an excellent statement of national policy emphasizing the importance of voluntary methods for settling labor disputes. There is also a sound statement of the duty of employers and the representatives of employees to exert every reasonable effort to make and maintain agreements, and to confer and attempt to settle disputes expeditiously.[107] But the detailed provisions here and elsewhere do not at all points square with these sound principles.

The provisions of Taft-Hartley, therefore, imposed "equal" obligations upon labor and management to bargain in good faith and set certain standards and procedures which, along with the aid of the Federal Mediation and Conciliation Service, should promote this desirable end. Yet the bargainers were hobbled at a number of points, to the detriment of the constructive dealing with problems as they arise which is of the essence of true collective bargaining. And in the main the hobbles were tighter upon the unions and weakened their bargaining position. On the other hand there was in the first year considerable evidence of efforts of employers and unions to work out other solutions which would avoid the restrictions of the law. It is to be questioned whether provisions which make such efforts necessary or inevitable, and greatly increase litigation, square with the claimed belief in the values of free collective bargaining.

STRIKES AND BOYCOTTS: SECTION 8(b)(4)(A, B, C)

In the provisions outlawing certain types of strikes, and boycotts broadly defined, along with later provisions[108] for injunctions and for suits for damages as well as other penalties of one kind or another, Senator Taft and his colleagues succeeded in turning back the hands of the clock, as had been sought in the Case Bill in 1946.

The Wagner Act had scarcely changed what we here call "basic labor law." That was then regarded as primarily a state and local province, and many still regard it so. There was, in 1935, much state and local legislation and a large body of more or less varying court decisions applying the common law. Of federal legislation there was the Sherman Antitrust Act of 1890 and the Clayton Act of 1914, though this had been deprived of much value by the Supreme Court in *Duplex* and other related decisions; and there was the Norris–

---

107. Secs. 201, 204. Provisions of this Title are discussed *infra*, ch. 15, pp. 569–86.
108. Secs. 10(j) and (1), 303, discussed *infra*, ch. 13.

La Guardia Act of 1932, effective as regards the "yellow-dog" contract and the labor injunction, both of which had been widely practiced especially during the decade and a half preceding the enactment of this far-reaching measure.[109] Taft-Hartley changed the legal framework rather drastically, though it was considerably less drastic than several other measures proposed. It federalized the law within the wide limitations of federal power and reversed federal policy at important points. Numerous questions of interpretation and constitutionality needed answers before one could be sure just how far and at what points the hands of the clock were turned back. Yet it was clear that under Taft-Hartley they were turned back so as to give the federal government a substantially different labor policy from that adopted in the 1930's, one much less acceptable in many respects.

Perhaps before turning to our attempt to analyze as realistically as possible the important Section 8(b)(4),[110] the core of the unfair labor practices banned to labor organizations and their agents, it may be helpful to try to state in everyday language the meaning of this extremely complex, technical, and difficult section, despite the danger of less than complete accuracy. In general, unions were forbidden to engage in or to induce employees to engage in strikes or concerted refusal to work or boycotts—refusal to use, process, or handle certain goods or materials—when *an object* is one of the four prohibited by clauses A through D. The first prohibited object is forcing or requiring an employer or self-employed person to join any organization, or, more important, forcing or requiring anyone to cease using the products of, or doing business with, any other person—thus banning "secondary boycotts," very broadly defined. The second is to force recognition by *any other* employer of any union unless certified, thus preventing pressure in behalf of what may be a minority union. The related (C) bans pressure against *any employer* to recognize a particular union when another has been certified as the representative of the employees in an appropriate unit. And (D), the fourth, bans economic pressure in a jurisdictional dispute. All of this needs to be spelled out further, for the benefit of readers who are not technical lawyers well versed in American labor law. And these sections must be considered along with related parts of the Act, especially as to the remedies provided.

Some forms of union behavior which were under attack in Congress are not found among the proscriptions in Taft-Hartley. It remained

109. *Supra*, ch. 1, pp. 9–15.
110. Quoted *supra*, pp. 442–43.

lawful for a union to strike[111] against an employer's unfair labor practices, to strike in prosecuting demands for wages, hours, seniority, and the like, to strike for recognition unless there was another certified representative, or to strike for a union shop for which a majority in the appropriate unit had voted but which the employer declined to grant. But the intent of the Congress was to proscribe many types of union behavior designed to obtain labor's objectives, save for those relating to wages, hours, and the like.[112] A list of things remaining lawful is not too significant. A list of things forbidden would be helpful, but uncertainty prevailed pending application of the law to many different cases. Very significant was the substitution by the Conference Committee of the clause "where an object thereof is" for the words in the Senate bill, "for the purpose of," in Section 8(b)(4). The words "the purpose" had sometimes been interpreted as indicating "primary" or a main objective. The substitution of "an object" has the technical effect of saying "where any one of the objectives" is proscribed. This was expected to "button up" the proscriptions and leave no loopholes.[113] It would make for uniformity in interpretation but would also be more restrictive.

A number of the proscriptions of union behavior found in 8(b)(4) and related sections of Taft-Hartley we regard as acceptable, but others are at least questionable—unless one desires by law to limit the power of unions and to weaken them, or is not interested in mere "equalization" of power and rights. Clauses (B) and (C) seemed likely to give a welcome remedy in some types of cases which were troublesome under the Wagner Act.

Union abuses gave the NLRB considerable difficulty. In the first place, there were instances of boycotts and picketing by minority unions when firms had entered into collective bargaining with the majority union certified by the NLRB or by one of the state boards. Of course such action was in defiance of the policy manifest in the

111. Subject of course to the sixty-day provisions in 8(d) and any restriction in a "national emergency" under Secs. 206–10.
112. The limitations on "union security" have been discussed, *supra*, pp. 428–40. For limitations on welfare funds, see *infra*, ch. 15, pp. 561–68. The Board held, however, that pensions are a proper subject of bargaining. *Ibid.*, p. 568.
113. As Senator Taft expressed it, "Obviously the intent of the conferees was to close any loophole which would prevent the Board from being blocked in giving relief against such illegal activities simply because one of the purposes of such strikes might have been lawful." *Daily Cong. Rec.*, 93:7001. Van Arkel, *op. cit.*, p. 48, correctly says: "An intent is evident to define in the broadest possible language the terms 'strike' and 'lockout' to cover *any* union activity designed to achieve ends prohibited by the Act."

Wagner Act or state law, or both,[114] and such defiance worked injury to the unions which represented the majority of the employees and to the employers concerned. Although in a number of cases courts threatened unions with the possibility of being held in contempt of court, such orders of the court were tardy; quick handling was needed if justice was to be done and respect for the law developed on the part of organizations which, at the same time, were using government agencies when this met with their desires and plans. Taft-Hartley in Section 8(b)(4)(C) seemed to meet this problem.

Frequently also various unions failed to respect the requirements of the closed-shop proviso in Section 8(3) of the Wagner Act. Some of them continued to act as they had in the past, and sometimes, under threat of boycott and picketing, sought closed-shop contracts though they had few or no members in the unit covered by the contract presented for signature.[115] There was no quick and effective way in these cases of securing observance of the Wagner Act, especially in states which limited injunctions by laws based upon the Norris–La Guardia Act. Taft-Hartley provided more effective protection under the law by its prohibition in Section 8(b)(4)(B) of pressure upon "any other employer" to recognize a union unless it had been certified.[116] The same is true of the problem presented in the California cannery conflict. Whatever may be said concerning the processing of these cases, the NLRB's findings were widely flouted for some two years or more.[117] The incumbent organization won its place by exercise of power, bolstered perhaps by the jurisdictional "rights" accorded by the parent and co-operating organizations. Power given the Board by clauses (B) and (C) of this section and related parts

114. *Supra*, ch. 6, pp. 216–20, 222–24; cf. Florsheim Shoe Store Co. v. Retail Shoe Salesmen Union, 288 N.Y. 188 (1942), where the court held picketing by a union defeated in a State Board election to be illegal. The first Board order under this section came in the New York department stores controversy. Oppenheim Collins & Co., 83 NLRB No. 47 (May, 1949).

115. *Supra*, ch. 8, pp. 277–79.

116. A by-product of these clauses (B) and (C) was to increase the value of Board certification, since the protection afforded against raids and pressure by or in behalf of a minority union seemingly went only to a "certified" union, not to one validly recognized as representing a majority, without Board action. It was unfortunate thus to encourage resort unnecessarily to the Board's election process when there was no real dispute over the facts as to a union's right to recognition. But many unions were expected to file petitions in order to obtain this protection against raids. The majority of the Board indicated in Advance Pattern Co., 80 NLRB No. 10 (October, 1948), that it would accept petitions for representation elections even where the union was already recognized, in order not to deny the union the certification which acted as a protection against raiding.

117. *Supra*, ch. 6, pp. 224–33.

of the Act could be effective against such misuse of power by unions.

Another type of abuse, outside the authority of the old NLRB, we may refer to as the "balkanization of the market." This was not limited to the electrical industry in New York, out of which the Allen-Bradley case developed.[118] Whether or not there had been collusion in that instance between electrical manufacturers and contractors and the Electrical Workers in refusing to instal or to use electrical goods purchased outside the New York area, be they union-made or nonunion, need not concern us here. The final decision was that there had been an infraction of the Sherman Antitrust Act, and the injunction was upheld. However, an incidental statement made in the course of the decision was to the effect that, had this same thing been done by the union alone, the decision would have been different.[119] But what difference should it make whether such a monopolistic practice resulted from collusion or from the exercise of union power alone? Is not unlicensed monopoly monopoly in any event? We think such monopoly properly restricted under the otherwise too sweeping prohibition of boycotts in Section 8(b)(4)(A).

Perhaps these Taft-Hartley clauses provided the more effective remedy needed against these and other real abuses. But the question must be raised: Do these prohibitions unduly restrict legitimate, non-abusive economic self-help by unions? We turn therefore to the more difficult "core" in the provisions relating to boycotts, sympathetic strikes, "direct" strikes as very broadly defined in Section 501(2) and jurisdictional disputes and featherbedding. The issues raised must be candidly examined because, as everyone knows, when persuasion and adjustment at the bargaining table fail, the union must and does rely on economic pressure through strikes, boycotts, and picketing as important weapons in protecting its members from loss of what they have had or, much more frequently, in obtaining some part or all of the gains they desire. We discuss boycotts, sympathetic strikes, direct strikes and other union behavior in order, though many cases may be spoken of as the one or the other.

118. Allen-Bradley Co. v. Local 3, IBEW, 325 U.S. 797 (1945); cf. *supra*, ch. 8, p. 279.

119. For a similar conclusion as to the effect of the Clayton and Norris–La Guardia Acts see U.S. v. Hutcheson, 312 U.S. 219, 232 (1941). Justice Frankfurter, speaking for the Court, said: "So long as a union acts in its self-interest and does not combine with non-labor groups, the licit and the illicit under sec. 20 are not to be distinguished by any judgment regarding the wisdom or unwisdom, the rightness or wrongness, the selfishness or unselfishness of the end of which the particular union activities are the means."

From the Wagner Act to Taft-Hartley

A study of common-law boycott decisions[120] shows that there has been considerable difference in the use of the terms "primary" and "secondary," when any such distinction has been made. These terms were appropriately omitted from Taft-Hartley because of the wide differences in court decisions and in state laws. Perhaps, too, there was concern as to the bearing of "freedom of speech." In any event, Taft-Hartley seemed to forbid all boycotts and attendant picketing not protected by "freedom of speech."[121] An effect was, of course, to extend the proscription so as to forbid under the federal jurisdiction even the boycott said to be a primary one by the law in New York and in other more liberal states.

Such a study of common-law cases also shows much difference of view on the part of judges. In their rulings on "secondary" boycotts most of the judges seem not to have considered the possibility or the significance of justification for the union's action, circumstanced as the workers were because of a "common interest," or a "unity of interest," or whatever this element may have been called. Nevertheless, an increasing proportion of the judges found adequate justification in the behavior of labor as against the element of injury to the employer or to those whose business relations with him were inconvenienced or interrupted, even when a breach of contract had been involved. Professor Charles O. Gregory,[122] among other outstanding students of the law, has been impressed with the presence of real but conflicting interests which need consideration if justice is to be done by proper treatment of boycotts in their different settings in a real world. But, in spite of this approach by some courts, a majority of decisions under the common law remained to the effect that "secondary" boycotts were unlawful. That, however, is not an election return. The question remains as to what exceptions should be made in drafting a labor relations law. Does the boycott ever have justification?

New York State courts have been highly respected for the caliber of their decisions and the liberality of their point of view, and many of their decisions became leading precedents. An important case from New York is *Goldfinger* v. *Feintuch*. The union involved had not succeeded in organizing the poorly paid workers of a New York firm manufacturing meat products. It therefore picketed retail distribu-

120. Cf. *supra*, ch. 8, pp. 277–79. An unpublished manuscript from one of the federal agencies analyzes court decisions in an application of common law in a dozen rather important types of boycott cases.

121. Cf. *infra*, n. 151.

122. See his interesting discussion of cases in *Labor and the Law* (New York: W. W. Norton, 1946), chs. 5 and 6.

tors—but not the entire business of these stores. The manufacturer failed to secure an order restraining this picketing; one distributor, Goldfinger, then sought to do so, but was denied relief. The New York Court of Appeals, in upholding the lower court, said:

Within the limits of peaceful picketing . . . picketing may be carried on not only against the manufacturer but against a *non-union product* sold by one in unity of interest with the manufacturer who is in the same business for profit. Where a manufacturer pays less than union wages both it and the retailers who sell its products are in a position to undersell competitors who pay the higher scale, and this may result in an unfair reduction of the wages of union members. . . . Where the manufacturer disposes of the product through retailers *in unity of interest with it,* unless the union may follow the product to the place where it is sold and peacefully ask the public to refrain from purchasing it, the union would be deprived of a fair and proper means of bringing its plea to the attention of the public.[123]

In this case the boycott was regarded as a *primary* boycott, for only the "Ukor" meats were advertised as unfair. Had the boycott been compounded by extension to the entire business, the court stated it would have been unlawful.

The view of the New York Court of Appeals in this Goldfinger case has been followed in a few other states, as Illinois,[124] Louisiana,[125] and Pennsylvania.[126] Indeed, the New York courts have gone far in legalizing the "secondary" boycott, as this term is generally used. Not only have they sanctioned such a boycott as on nonunion lumber by carpenters who claimed jurisdiction over millwork as well as construction work;[127] they have also sanctioned the boycott by building tradesmen of materials serviced by nonunion teamsters[128] and by dockworkers of freight hauled by nonunion drivers.[129]

California courts, however, have probably taken the most liberal view of boycotts. In one important early case,[130] Parkinson conducted a hardware and supply store and also a building materials mill. His relations with one of the unions were none too happy, and he became a leader in the Citizens' Alliance. The carpenters and other unions then boycotted both the store and the mill products. The courts decided that the refusal to use Parkinson's building materials, though

123. 276 N.Y. 281, 286 (1937). (Second italics ours.)
124. Wagner v. Milk Wagon Driver's Union, 50 NE 2d 865 (1943).
125. Johnson v. Milk Drivers and Dairy Employees Union, 195 So. 791 (1940).
126. Alliance Auto Service v. Cohen, 19 A. 2d 152 (1941).
127. Bossert v. Dhuy, 221 N.Y. 342 (1917).
128. Willson and Adams Co. v. Pearce, 264 N.Y. 521 (1934).
129. N.Y. Lumber Trade Association v. Lacey, 269 N.Y. 595 (1935).
130. Parkinson Co. v. Building Trades Council, 154 Cal. 581 (1908).

already contracted for, was lawful. In the Fortenbury case,[131] decided much later, the pickets carried banners which called a distributor "unfair." In reversing a lower court order for an injunction against such picketing, the California Superior Court held that labor may exert any economic pressure against employers, provided that peaceful means are used and the purpose is one reasonably related to labor conditions. The court pointed out that the distributor could not claim to be an innocent third party. Buying nonunion goods, produced with lower wage costs, placed him at a competitive advantage, and he therefore became an ally of the manufacturer in whose goods he dealt. Nor, it was said, could he claim to be helpless in bringing about a conclusion of the dispute. Refusal to purchase the products of a "disputed employer" would remove the pickets from his establishment and bring pressure on the manufacturer to settle the controversy.

Admittedly, the illustrative cases cited in which "unity of interest," "common interest," or what Mr. Teller calls "a beneficial economic relationship" was recognized never became the most general rule in court decisions and statutes.[132] Rather, the predominant consideration was of management's interest and in what might happen to the business interests of firms supplying that firm with materials or buying, transporting, or using its product. The concern of the union in a real world was given less, if any, consideration. Usually only the infrequent "primary boycott" prevailed, based upon persuasion and not attended by inconvenience or by violence and coercion imposed upon others. This attitude is reflected in Taft-Hartley, which in Section 8(b)(4)(A) banned any boycott activity having as "an object" the "forcing or requiring . . . any employer or other person to cease using, selling, handling, transporting, or otherwise dealing in the products of any other producer, processor, or manufacturer, or to cease doing business with any other person."

The Labor Management Relations Act of 1947 was born in the shadow of the decisions of the Supreme Court in *Duplex, Bedford Stone*,[133] and other cases decided under the antitrust laws between 1908 and the enactment of the Norris–La Guardia Act in 1932, and the great change made in the constitution of the Supreme Court somewhat later in the days of the New Deal. The Duplex Company manu-

131. Fortenbury v. Superior Court (S.F.), 106 P. 2d 411 (1940).
132. Ludwig Teller, *A Labor Policy for America* (New York: Baker, Voorhis & Co., 1945), p. 147 and elsewhere.
133. Duplex Printing Press Co. v. Deering, 254 U.S. 443 (1921); Bedford Cut-Stone Co. v. Journeymen Stone Cutters' Association, 274 U.S. 37 (1927).

factured printing presses that were marketed in competition with the products of three other unionized companies. These complained of unequal competition due chiefly to substantial differences in wages and hours at Duplex. The Machinists, therefore, called an organization strike against the Duplex Company. Only eleven of some two hundred workers employed in the plant, in Battle Creek, Michigan, and three road men, responded to the strike call. Members of the union in New York and elsewhere then came to the strikers' assistance. They refused to instal or repair Duplex presses, warned a trucking firm not to haul them, and threatened an exposition company with a strike if it exhibited them. The Court, in a divided decision, held that under the Sherman Act and the Clayton Act this behavior could be enjoined, since the privilege of concerted action was limited to those who are "proximately and substantially concerned." Past, present, or prospective employees of the Duplex Company had such interest, but other members of the union, in New York or elsewhere, did not. This was the narrower common-law rule. The Court was of the view that, properly interpreted, Section 20 of the Clayton Act, which limited the granting of restraining orders, "had in mind particular industrial controversies, not a general class war."[134] The law remained just as it had been.

Justice Brandeis, Justice Holmes, and Justice Clarke dissented from the majority decision, which reversed the rulings of the lower courts. They expressed the view that in application of the common law many courts, with "better appreciation of the facts of industry," had recognized a *wide common interest* among the workers.[135] So had the Congress in the Clayton Act. The refusal of the Duplex Company to deal with the Machinists' Union and to observe its standards threatened the interest of all members of the unions employed by plaintiffs, competitors, and by others whose more advanced standards the plaintiff was, in reality, attacking. The parties restrained in this case had justification in *self-interest*. "They have injured the plaintiff, not maliciously, but in self-defense."[136]

The Bedford decision of 1927 has been called "the capstone of the long development in the application of the Sherman Act to labor."[137] In 1921, marked by the open-shop drive and reductions in wages, a conflict broke out over the negotiation of a new contract in the limestone quarrying and cutting district of Indiana. Relations were broken,

134. 254 U.S. 443, 472 (1921).   135. *Ibid.*, p. 482.   136. *Ibid.*, p. 480.
137. Edward Berman, *Labor and the Sherman Act* (New York: Harper & Bros., 1930), p. 179.

the unions went on strike, and the firm set up organizations of their "scab" employees. In 1924 the Journeymen Stonecutters' Association of America, with jurisdiction over both stonecutting and the installation of stone on buildings, began to enforce a provision of its constitution prohibiting its members from handling stone "cut by men working in opposition" to it. As a result, in an effort to bring pressure to bear upon the stone companies, building operations were interrupted in various parts of the country. With the major part of their product finding a market outside Indiana and with sales more or less diminished because of the fear of building contractors of difficulty with their workmen, the companies sought a restraining order. The Supreme Court finally, by majority decision, held the companies entitled to such an order.

The union contended that its sole purpose was to organize the workers at the quarries. The Court conceded that such organization was the ultimate end in view, but ruled that its accomplishment was sought by unlawful means of restricting interstate commerce. The Court said:

These strikes, ordered and carried out with the sole object of preventing the use and installation of petitioners' product in other states, necessarily threatened to destroy or narrow petitioners' interstate trade by taking from them their customers. That the organizations, in general purpose and in and of themselves, were lawful and that the ultimate result aimed at may not have been illegal in itself, are beside the point. Where the means adopted are unlawful, the innocent general character of the organizations adopting them or the lawfulness of the ultimate end sought to be attained, cannot serve as a justification.[138]

Justice Brandeis dissented, with the concurrence of Justice Holmes. He pointed out that the Court in Standard Oil, American Tobacco, and other cases had held that only *unreasonable* restraints of trade were prohibited by the Sherman Act. The union's action in this case, Justice Brandeis thought, had been reasonable. The workers, acting under a provision of their constitution to which they had subscribed when joining the union, had in different localities only refused to set stone purchased from their industrial enemy. This was their only

138. 274 U.S. 37, 55 (1927). Cf. Loewe v. Lawlor, 208 U.S. 274 (1908) and other cases. Cf., however, Apex Hosiery v. Leader, 310 U.S. 469 (1940), in which the majority greatly narrowed the application of the Sherman Act to labor cases. The decision was to the effect that the only restraints prohibited by the Act in such cases are those "which are so substantial as to affect market prices." The non-access of Apex Hosiery to the interstate market was not intended to and had no effect upon prices of hosiery in that market. See critical analysis in Gregory, *op. cit.*, pp. 256 ff.

means of self-protection against a combination of militant and powerful employers. To restrain the union from doing these things, he said, "reminds of involuntary servitude."

Duplex and *Bedford Stone* are significant for our discussion of the boycott, for the real issue is at bottom very much the same, namely, labor's "common interest," or "unity of interest."[139] As would be expected, these and other main rulings of the federal courts for more than a decade and a half caused a rapid increase in the number of federal injunction cases.[140]

An outcome of all this was the adoption of the Norris–La Guardia Act in 1932[141] with the approval of President Hoover. It banned the granting of restraining orders by the federal courts in labor disputes unless specified conditions had been complied with, and, stated broadly, unless fraud or violence were involved. Moreover, and more important, the term "labor dispute" was much more broadly defined than it had been by most of the courts. It now was to include disputes involving persons with *"direct or indirect interest* therein," and *"regardless of whether or not the disputants stand in the proximate relation of employer and employee."*[142]

As interpreted by a "reconstructed" Supreme Court, Norris–La Guardia gave the United States a new labor policy, one recognizing the concept of "common interest" which in general had been made clear by the few earlier court decisions specifically noted above.[143] However, all this became largely historical in 1947. For the provisions of Taft-Hartley to a considerable degree replaced those of the Norris–La Guardia Act. But the real question is: Was this in line with a sound labor relations program?

No doubt the President had in mind the issues we have raised here when he presented to the Congress his message on the State of the Union on January 6, 1947. He said:

139. A "beneficial economic relationship" or "unity of interest" between separate business concerns such as manufacturer and distributor is naturally one of the factors relating to "common interest" or "unity of interest" among workers.

140. Cf. *supra*, ch. 1, pp. 8–14.

141. 47 U.S. Stat. 70 (1932). The act, with some modifications, followed a draft made by a subcommittee of the Senate Judiciary Committee with the aid of several liberal legal scholars—Frankfurter, Oliphant, Richberg, Sayre, and Witte.

142. Sec. 13. (Italics ours.) It is to be noted that the latter phrase was kept in the Taft-Hartley definition of labor dispute, in Sec. 2(9), but in the context of other parts of the Act this would not have the same effect as in Norris–La Guardia. The Act is considered in more detail *infra*, ch. 13, pp. 485–89.

143. *Supra*, pp. 460–62.

Not all secondary boycotts are unjustified. We must judge them on the basis of their objectives. For example, boycotts intended to protect wage rates and working conditions should be distinguished from those in further-ance of jurisdictional disputes. The structure of industry sometimes requires unions as a matter of self-preservation to extend the conflict beyond a particular employer. There should be no blanket prohibition against boy-cotts. The appropriate goal is legislation which prohibits secondary boy-cotts in pursuance of unjustifiable objectives, but does not impair the union's right to preserve its own existence and the gains made in genuine collective bargaining.[144]

With this statement we are in agreement. But not so the Congress, which in adopting the omnibus Taft-Hartley Act intended to ban all "secondary boycotts." Senator Taft explained that in weeks of hear-ings the committee "never succeeded in having anyone tell us any difference between different kinds of secondary boycotts";[145] there-fore all were banned. But sweeping definitions do not square with the decisions of many able jurists who in applying the common law had displayed what many think a keener analytic ability and understand-ing than did some very influential members of the Eightieth Congress. Or was it perhaps a difference in basic philosophy that was displayed? In any event the analysis upon which the outlawing of all secondary boycotts was based is open to criticism. There are boycotts and boy-cotts, as well as sympathetic strikes and sympathetic strikes, and varieties of jurisdictional strikes, featherbedding, and other kinds of concerted activity. We think distinctions might better have been made, taking into account the real economic interest of organized workers in the unionization of a market if they are to protect what they have gained or to add to their effectiveness in securing further gains; but interference with the equal rights of other workers under the Act could and should be prevented.[146]

Only two boycott cases were decided by the NLRB in the first fifteen months under Taft-Hartley. Both were clear under the law. One involved boycott pressure upon distributors of Schenley prod-

144. *Cong. Rec.*, 93:136.

145. *Daily Cong. Rec.*, 93:4323. It should be noted, however, that among a number of witnesses who proposed significant distinctions was Secretary of Labor Schwellenbach, who, on request of the Committee, submitted a proposed bill which would have defined and outlawed two types of secondary boycotts, to fur-ther a jurisdictional dispute or to compel an employer to commit an unfair labor practice. *Senate Hearings, 1947*, Pt. 4, pp. 1937–38. For another suggestion on distinctions that should be made, cf. "Labor's Economic Weapons and the Taft-Hartley Act," *University of Pennsylvania Law Review*, 96 (1947), 88–92.

146. Cf. *supra*, pp. 457–59; also ch. 6, p. 233. It is not our purpose or function to make detailed proposals in this technical field, but we think reasonable, fair, and workable definitions and proscriptions could be worked out in conference.

ucts, in support of a strike over conditions of employment at a Schenley subsidiary, by members of the same international union. The dispute had been settled before the Board issued its decision finding the union guilty of an unlawful boycott.[147] The other involved a strike of carpenters against the use of nonunion men by a subcontractor on a local remodeling job. The Board found this an illegal attempt to compel the builder to cease doing business with the nonunion contractor, and hence a violation of Section 8(b)(4).[148] Of other cases in which Intermediate Reports had been issued, about half involved strikes or boycotts of building craftsmen against working with nonunion men; some others involved "struck work." The net was wide and caught a variety of instances of concerted activity. Probably some of them were clearly unjustifiable. Most such instances were apparently cleared up promptly. But some of those under the ban of the law involved such community of interests among workers that we find no sound reason in public policy for banning them.[149] The restriction was sharply criticized as unreasonable by union spokesmen in many different industries.[150] The extent to which any of these activities were protected by the free-speech amendment was by no means clear.[151]

147. Schenley Distillers Corp., 78 NLRB 504 (1948).
148. Watson's Specialty Store, 80 NLRB 533 (1948).
149. In one early case in which a complaint was issued and an injunction sought the District Court denied the injunction on the ground that the secondary employer, a subcontractor whose volume of work greatly increased during the strike, was not an "innocent bystander, or a neutral." Douds v. Metropolitan Federation of Architects, 75 F. Supp. 672 (D.C. N.Y.). *Thirteenth Annual Report,* p. 93. The Trial Examiner recommended dismissal of the boycott charge, and this part of the case was dropped.
150. *Ball Committee Hearings,* May–June, 1948, Pt. 1, pp. 115–16, 257; Pt. 2, pp. 771, 1044. *Ball Committee Report,* Pt. 3, Dec. 31, 1948, pp. 24–27; see also *infra,* ch. 16, p. 649.
151. The dilemma arising from the clear conflict between the free-speech amendment and the sweeping prohibition of boycotts by Sec. 8(b)(4)(A) was not faced by the Board until February, 1949, when during the Senate hearings on the bill to replace Taft-Hartley the Board issued its divided decision in United Brotherhood of Carpenters and Joiners and Wadsworth Building Co., 81 NLRB No. 127. The majority, Chairman Herzog concurring separately, held that the free-speech clause was not to be applied when Congress had clearly meant to outlaw all secondary boycotts; therefore peaceful picketing and "We Don't Patronize" lists in furtherance of such a boycott were prohibited. Mr. Herzog felt constrained to agree with this interpretation of the congressional intent in spite of his grave doubts as to the constitutional question. Mr. Houston and Mr. Murdock dissented, considering that the antiboycott provision was to be enforced "up to the barriers imposed by constitutional principles and by Congress itself in section 8(c)." The difficulty arises in our view from a free-speech clause so sweeping as to make difficult a reasonable enforcement of the intent of Congress; and from a prohibition so unwisely broad as to limit needed and reasonable concerted activities. We would think proper a limitation on picketing in the interest

In discussing the boycott we have already considered the most important legal question involved in the "sympathetic" and for that matter in many "direct" strikes. Many disputes have been called both "boycotts" and "sympathetic strikes." In fact, these are frequently twins. Under the 1947 law every sympathetic strike was apparently made unlawful by Section 8(b)(4)(A).[152] Moreover, Section 303 made it, like the boycott, unlawful and subject to suit for damages. But anyone familiar with industrial relations knows that in reality there are different sorts of sympathetic strikes, as has been recognized by courts and more frequently by arbitrators.

Now and then a union or a number of unions may lay down their tools for a day or so or indefinitely in sympathy with another striking group in a different industry when they have no tangible common interest. This the courts have held to be unlawful, and properly so, for there are more important things at stake. This is admitted to be correct by almost anyone not inclined to regard just any strike as for a good purpose. Rather generally the unions in a building trades council strike along with a given union when it goes out on strike over wages or for other lawful objectives. But can this be thought lacking in justification when the relationships in the industry are recognized? Certainly were the craftsmen organized into an industrial union, they would be one and act as one in case of a controversy

---

of objectives which should reasonably be prohibited, such as we have suggested *supra*, pp. 457–59.

In several early boycott cases the General Counsel held, and obtained favorable action in district courts, that picketing was not protected either by the First Amendment or by Section 8(c) of the Act. In two of them, Trial Examiners took an opposite position. As the General Counsel put it: "Where the Trial Examiners part company with the General Counsel's Office, is upon the question of whether, in the light of present day realities, a picket sign of a union, whether one to which an employee belongs or not, is not such as to put the employee in fear of his standing with his own union, or his fellow members, or his fellow workers as the case may be, so as, in effect, to coerce his will." Address of General Counsel before the Conference of Circuit and District Court Judges of the Fifth Judicial Circuit, June 4, 1948. One may ask, however, whether the General Counsel was not setting up tests as to union actions which had been excluded by the Board in applying the "free-speech" amendment to employers' behavior.

For two pertinent circuit court decisions upholding injunctions in boycott cases cf. United Brotherhood of Carpenters and Joiners v. Sperry, 170 F. 2d 863 (C.C.A.10, 1948); Printing Specialties and Paper Converters Union v. Le Baron, 171 F. 2d 331 (C.C.A.9, December 13, 1948). In the latter case the Board reversed the Trial Examiner and held that a union violated Section 8(b)(4)(A) when its pickets followed the products of a struck employer to the premises of other employers. Sealright Pacific, Ltd., 82 NLRB No. 64 (March, 1949).

152. Note also the sweeping definition of "strike" in Section 501 (2); *infra*, pp. 470–71.

in which they were not immediately or directly concerned. Another and frequent form of sympathetic strike is found when workers refuse to process strike-bound goods which are being added under "contract" to their usual work because of another firm's dispute with the same or a sister-local. Printing crafts have long incorporated in their contracts a statement of their right to refuse to work on "struck work." Such instances are not by any means as frequent in the clothing trade as they used to be, but there were many of them in the days of only partial union organization. Certainly, law or no law, the "people" will usually balk at doing any "unfair" work an employer may, as a favor, or as a contractor, take into his shop; and union employers frequently recognize their right to do so.

One more case may be cited, that of *Iron Moulders Union* v. *Allis-Chalmers Co.*[153] Approximately forty years ago a dispute over lawful objectives arose at Allis-Chalmers, and, after a time, the management contracted out molding work to be performed by other companies, its competitors in the industry, many of whose employees were union molders. These workers refused to work on the "unfair" patterns. A restraining order against the international was obtained, but then set aside on appeal to the higher court. This court declared that the local union calling the original strike was just as free to solicit and receive aid from the other locals of the same union in its economic tussle with the employer as the employer was to seek the aid of other plants in getting out its orders.[154]

How can one escape the conclusion that Taft-Hartley is unrealistic and too drastic in its treatment of sympathetic strikes, as it is of boycotts? The "struck work" clause was a source of conflict and a bitter feeling of injustice among union members in many industries in 1947 and 1948. It was one of the issues in the many ITU strikes and Board cases. In the Chicago newspaper strike Typographical Union members in numerous instances were required in commercial shops to work on newspaper ads, thus undercutting their striking brothers. Some quit in preference. The legality of a solution through a statement of intent by the employers in their contracts to accept only "normal account" jobs was challenged in one of the Intermediate Reports.[155] The case in which union machinists were required to

153. 166 Fed. 45 (C.C.A.7, 1908).
154. Cf. comment by Gregory, *op. cit.*, p. 126.
155. International Typographical Union and Union Printers Section of Printing Industry of America, Case No. 2-CB-30 (May, 1948); but other Intermediate Reports held that insistence on a clause to protect the union was not illegal, since employers were entitled voluntarily to make such an agreement. Cf. Chicago

work on jobs sent to their shop by another plant in which machinists were on strike was typical of situations which caused bitter resentment in many industries.[156]

Much has already been said incidentally in these pages concerning the "direct" strike. We have noted with approval several provisions in Taft-Hartley which restrict strikes as well as boycotts.[157] Of course the strike and attendant picketing are linked with the boycott in Section 8(b)(4). Very important here, and we think unfortunate, is the implicit limitation of a lawful dispute to those in the employ of any—that is, "an"—employer, disregarding the very real "unity of interest" frequently found in wider groups of employees. There is also the ban on strikes and lockouts for the sixty-day notice period before termination or modification of a contract, and the longer "cooling-off" period designed to assist in the settlement of national emergency disputes.[158] Taft-Hartley thus established extensive control over organized industry; and this control involved for the most part regulation of union behavior. Many strikes remained lawful—over wages, hours, seniority, management unfair labor practices, and the like. But many others would fall under the bans of Section 8(b)(4). Strikes in violation of contract were not specifically made unfair labor practices but were subject to suit for damages under Section 301(a). And picketing could be expected to be restricted, both under the prohibition of coercion and by findings of illegality of the object sought. The extent to which picketing was protected, on the other hand, both by the "free-speech" clause and the constitutional right, was a crucial issue raised in early cases.[159]

The very inclusive definition of "strike" in Section 501(2) is important in relation to much that has been said above. It read:

> The term "strike" includes any strike or other concerted stoppage of work by employees (including a stoppage by reason of the expiration of a collective-bargaining agreement) and any concerted slow-down or other concerted interruption of operations by employees.

What bearing this had on proscribed union behavior remained to be seen. The inclusion of "or other concerted stoppage of work by em-

---

Typographical Union and Chicago Newspaper Publishers Association, Case No. 13-CB-6 (August, 1948). For a statement of the union case for this method of protecting against substandard work cf. *Ball Committee Hearings*, Pt. 1, pp. 287–89, 301–2, 384.

156. Cf. *Ball Committee Report, Minority Views*, April 1, 1948, pp. 13–14. See also case cited *supra*, n. 149.

157. *Supra*, pp. 457–59.

158. Secs. 8(d) and 206–10; *supra*, pp. 452–53; *infra*, ch. 15, pp. 574–75.

159. *Supra*, n. 151.

ployees (including stoppage by reason of an expiration of a collective bargaining agreement)" was designed among other things to cope with the coal situation.[160] "Quickies" also were included, though management already had a remedy in discharge or other discipline such as fines and other penalties employed widely in mining and other industries under terms of collective agreements. But all these concerted activities, along with boycotts, came under the ban of the Act when "an object thereof" was one of those prohibited by this section. There were of course saving clauses having to do with the right to strike. One was the incidental clause to protect the constitutional right of an individual employee to quit his job.[161] The other is found in Section 13[162] on "the right to strike," but this is significant chiefly in indicating that, contrary to the Wagner Act, Taft-Hartley did in various important respects limit and qualify that right. The effect of the final proviso of Section 8(b)(4), which applied to all the union unfair labor practices, is by no means clear, although the Senate Committee said it meant that "refusing to cross a picket line or otherwise refusing to engage in strikebreaking activities would not be deemed an unfair labor practice unless the strike is a 'wildcat' strike by a minority group."[163]

JURISDICTIONAL DISPUTES

Among the strikes and boycotts properly banned by Section 8(b)(4)(A), (B), and (C), many concerned jurisdictional disputes of one sort or another. More suitable means are available to determine these conflicting claims as to representation, with protection of the right of free choice of all employees under the Act. Clause (D) related to a different kind of jurisdictional dispute. It made economic

160. Contrary to the finding of the President's Board of Inquiry, in April, 1948, President Lewis took the position that there had been no "concerted stoppage"; rather that there was only a letter calling attention of the locals to the fact that no plan for the payment of miners' pensions had been adopted, and placing the blame on the operators; and that thereupon miners individually stopped work. The government, however, obtained a restraining order against the union. *New York Times*, April 4, 1948.

161. Sec. 502.

162. Quoted *supra*, n. 35.

163. *Taft Report*, p. 23; cf. also Van Arkel, *op. cit.*, pp. 52–54. This clause is one of numerous examples of sections written negatively so that their intent and effect are exceedingly obscure. For a more detailed discussion of uncertainties, complexities, and problems arising under Section 8(b)(4) in "the hodge-podge of compromise, horsetrading and bad draftsmanship known as the Labor Management Relations Act of 1947," cf. William L. Dennis, "The Secondary Boycott," *Proceedings of New York University First Annual Conference on Labor* (Albany: Matthew Bender & Co., 1948), pp. 359–418.

pressure by a union in regard to work assignment an unfair labor practice.

With active division in the organized labor movement, formation of overlapping internationals, enlarged jurisdictions claimed by many unions, and changes in materials and methods of work as technology changed, "jurisdictional disputes" grew substantially in number and became a problem of increasing importance in spite of not a little serious effort in the unions to settle such differences without stoppage.[164] The Congress, and the President likewise, regarded use of economic pressure in these disputes as unjustifiable and requiring legislation.

"Jurisdictional disputes" involving issues as to which union should proceed with organization and the resultant clashes as to which should serve as the representative of the employees for the purpose of collective bargaining have in large part been solved by NLRB elections. But such representation disputes were not always worked out successfully.[165] Under Taft-Hartley, however, elections might be expected to be used with more success in the difficult cases, since economic pressure was banned by Section 8(b)(4)(C) when another union had been certified.[166]

A different type of jurisdictional dispute is found among crafts, strictly or loosely defined, for the most part with the same general affiliation, over which of them is to perform certain work. Such disputes are familiar to everyone through conflicts between Carpenters and Sheet Metal Workers over which should hang metal doors and instal metal window frames, and many others. These have been in the past entirely outside the field of the NLRB. Such disputes have been found most conspicuously, although not alone, in the building trades. Perhaps they find their origin in differences in practice based on varying customs followed in different places; each union may have precedents for its view. Or the origin may be found in the contractor's or other management's efforts to obtain the best price from the groups available, or in a matter of personal favoritism—not a negligible factor but seemingly finding no place in the analysis basic to 8(b)(4)(D). But, whatever the causal factor, most of such contests have been adjusted without serious difficulty. Not infrequently, however, stoppages of work occur in spite of the efforts of the parent-organizations or of the local machinery established to prevent them, and affect de-

164. *Supra*, ch. 6, pp. 220 ff.; ch. 8, pp. 276–77.
165. Cf. *supra*, ch. 6, pp. 199–200, 224 ff.
166. Cf. *supra*, pp. 457–58.

pendent parts of the productive process. Note the machinery developed and the efforts at times put forth in the building trades and also in the metal trades and elsewhere. But note, also, that the best intentions have at times been balked by one or more large labor organizations or by combinations into cliques.[167] Most of these disputes involve technical problems, problems which few persons outside of immediate management and craftsmen know at all well. Any arbitration must recognize this fact if settlements are to be well made.

Under Section 8(b)(4)(D) it was made an unfair labor practice for a union to engage in strikes or boycotts to force or require "an employer to assign particular work to employees in a particular labor organization or in a particular trade, craft, or class rather than to employees in another labor organization or in another trade, craft, or class, unless such employer is failing to conform to an order or certification" made by the Board. In other words, a "management prerogative" was accepted in the assignment of work in dispute, except where this had been limited by the Board. Economic pressure by the union in this connection, like the boycott in general and the sympathetic strike, was made unlawful per se. Cease-and-desist orders could be issued as in other cases of unfair labor practices, with the possibility of injunction proceedings—these being at the discretion of the General Counsel, not mandatory as in boycott cases—and suit for damages. When violation of subsection (D) by strike or otherwise was charged, the Board was to hear and to decide the dispute itself—and not through an arbitrator's award as had been proposed in the Senate bill—unless, within ten days after notice that such charge had been filed, the parties to the dispute "submit to the Board satisfactory evidence that they have adjusted, or agreed upon methods for the voluntary adjustment of, the dispute."[168]

The sponsors of Taft-Hartley hoped that this provision would stimulate settlement of jurisdictional disputes outside the Board and that provisions for such adjustment would extend from industry to industry. While the Act provided for compulsory arbitration of such work disputes resulting in actual or threatened strikes, this was designed to be employed only as a last resort. This was a fortunate approach

167. Cf. Millis and Montgomery, *op. cit.*, pp. 271–79, for a somewhat detailed discussion of jurisdictional disputes.

168. Secs. 10(k) and (1); Sec. 303. According to the Board's rules, if its award was not complied with and the disputants failed to settle the dispute, there would then be a further hearing on the charge of unfair labor practices, which would normally result in a cease-and-desist order, enforceable in circuit court. *Rules and Regulations Effective August 22, 1947*, Subpart E.

based on sound principles. Settlements "at home" are much better than Board decisions, for many reasons, especially the fact that most "work disputes" involve highly technical matters better decided by those directly involved. Early experience indicated that frequently the possibility of Board action was enough to bring about the settlement of the dispute and the withdrawal of the charge.[169] In addition, a stimulus was given to the setting-up or strengthening of systems for the settlement of disputes within industry. One such was reported in the motion-picture industry in New York in August, 1947.[170] And a nation-wide system of adjustment was set up for building and construction, effective May 1, 1948.

The National Joint Board for the Settlement of Jurisdictional Disputes in the building and construction industry was established with the encouragement of the NLRB, by the Associated General Contractors of America and the AFL Building and Construction Trades Department. Provision was made for a "labor and industry pool" of twenty-four members, twelve from each of the contracting parties, and for a board of trustees of eight. This board selected the impartial joint board chairman and approved the selection of two men from each side, not from the crafts in dispute, to serve with him on a board of five which decides any jurisdictional dispute referred to it. Any earlier decisions or agreements made in the course of years, *and a matter of record in the construction industry,* were to be binding; the National Joint Board hears and decides other claims only, and this only upon the failure of mediation in conference called by the president of the Building and Construction Trades Department.

All this apparently related to the far-reaching disputes and to such local disputes as might be appealed. It was expected that local machinery in Chicago, New York, and elsewhere would be used in the first instance to bring about settlement in the ordinary, local cases. However, any such local settlement or agreement applied only to the

169. An example was a case involving carpenters and iron workers at a Ford Motor Company plant in New Jersey, over installation of a conveyor system. The preliminary "nonadversary" hearing was adjourned to permit the parties to reach a private settlement, which they did; but the case was held open so that, should the dispute break out again before the job was completed, hearing could have been quickly resumed, to lead to a work-award certification. *Daily Labor Report,* 251:A-9 (December 24, 1947). Other cases were reported as adjusted informally without notice of hearing. The first use of the power to obtain a temporary restraining order in a jurisdictional dispute case was in August, 1948, when the AFL stagehands were restrained from interfering with a television première in connection with its dispute with an independent union. BNA, *The Taft-Hartley Act—after One Year,* p. 101.

170. *New York Times,* August 28, 1947.

particular dispute in question, and an appeal could be taken directly to the Joint Board by any of the parties. Decisions made under the agreement were to be binding, and there was to be no stoppage of work arising out of any jurisdictional dispute. It was especially provided that members of the unions "shall continue to work on the basis of their original assignments, provided no employer will assign employees to perform work contrary to decisions or agreements of record."

This plan was based largely on plans adopted and commonly used in the building trades in the preceding thirty years. Such plans accomplished much, but on more than one occasion they fell short of what had been expected of them, chiefly for the reason that powerful unions refused to accept a decision and withdrew co-operation. The best thing about Section 8(b)(4)(D) was that it removed some of the weaknesses found in the past; in the vernacular, it could be said to add by implication the words "or else." But a great majority of cases might be local, and the decisions local in their application. Problems might arise because of past, but still effective, decisions. Care was needed to avoid conflicts in decisions. Nevertheless, this plan on the whole promised a good experiment, and it was hoped that it would prove not to be a disappointment.[171]

The best hope was that, under the prospect of otherwise having a decision by the NLRB, the parties to disputes would make their own adjustment systems work, so that few if any cases need come to the Board. But this "solution" might be accompanied by serious delays in getting things done at the proper time. Most jurisdiction troubles arise when contracts are being made for specific construction work. If the disputes failed to be settled by the parties, the NLRB could not intervene in advance of the charge alleging a strike or boycott. Delays in handling cases could create problems, although the injunction procedure was available when needed. Moreover, most work disputes

171. An "active insider" was quoted to the effect that the plan was fine and might be expected to last until the first big case arose, or until it was decided. By September 1, 1948, the National Joint Board was reported to have received some forty disputes and to have disposed of about half of them. *Ball Committee Report*, Pt. 3, Dec. 31, 1948, p. 58. All decisions had been unanimous. A conference of contractors and building trades representatives in January, 1949, voted to continue the plan indefinitely. There was apparently some feeling, even among the union representatives, that "the club in the closet" in the form of the injunction had helped in obtaining acceptance of decisions. *New York Times*, January 31, 1949. A few months later, nevertheless, the unions voted to scrap the joint board; but by midsummer, 1949, it appeared probable, since Taft-Hartley was still on the books, that a revised joint board would be continued in the hope that disputes could be settled without decisions by the NLRB.

present technical problems. The Senate Committee at one time had provided for use by the NLRB of arbitrators, whose decisions would be final and binding just as Board decisions are, except for the fact that Board decisions are subject to appeal to the courts. The staff men could have included the best qualified help, both in technical bent and in experience. But this Senate provision was eliminated. Neither Trial Examiners nor the Board could be expected to be expert in the technical problems involved in such cases. If cases were not settled by the voluntary machinery, the Board would have a new type of case for decision, perhaps with union officials as witnesses at somewhat prolonged hearings. And there would be the usual right to litigate decisions made by the Board.

Nevertheless, if the stimulus to voluntary settlement worked at all as well as early signs indicated, this section would be one of the more successful parts of the 1947 Act. If unions feared the delays and possibly technically inadequate decisions under the Board's procedures, the alternative solution was in their own hands. In the first year relatively few charges were filed under this section, but the filing was enough, most typically, to bring about a settlement. Meantime there seemed to be a large degree of protection against a type of strike very difficult to justify, which had with reason been "bad medicine" in the eyes of the public.[172]

"FEATHERBEDDING"

The sixth union unfair labor practice is commonly referred to as the "featherbedding" clause.[173] This made it an unfair labor practice for

172. The first decisions by the NLRB in jurisdictional dispute cases showed unforeseen difficulties. Thus in one the Board, holding that the respondent union was not entitled to require the company to assign work to its members, said that they were not by this action to be regarded as "assigning" the work in question to the Machinists. "Because such an affirmative award to either labor organization would be tantamount to allowing that organization to require Westinghouse to employ only its members and therefore to violate Section 8(a)(3) of the Act, we believe we can make no such award. In reaching this conclusion we are aware that the employer in most cases will have resolved, by his own employment policy, the question as to which organization shall be awarded the work. Under the statute as now drawn, however, we see no way in which we can, by Board reliance upon such factors as tradition or custom in the industry, overrule his determination in a situation of this particular character." See Los Angeles Building and Construction Council and Westinghouse Corp., 83 NLRB No. 76 (May, 1949), and three earlier cases cited therein. This was the first case which went on to a hearing on a charge of unfair labor practices and an Intermediate Report. The Trial Examiner found the Council and the Carpenters guilty of violation of Section 8(b)(4)(D), in September, 1949.

173. Sec. 8(b)(6); *supra*, p. 443. Sec. 8(b)(5), which prohibited a requirement of excessive initiation fees under a union-shop agreement, has been commented on above, p. 434.

a union or its agent "to cause or attempt to cause an employer to pay or deliver or agree to pay or deliver any money or other thing of value, in the nature of an exaction, for services which are not performed or not to be performed." It is fairly clear that attempts to persuade as well as to coerce were outlawed. In addition to the usual cease-and-desist orders, the Board might seek a restraining order at its discretion in a specific case, under Section 10(j).[174]

"Featherbedding" is a very loose term, for as popularly used it may be limited in its scope to generally recognized abuses such as in connection with trucking produce to certain markets—New York City and certain other places—or some practices of the Musicians, also the old "reproduction law" long applied by the ITU in many places and requiring the typesetting, proofreading, correction, and then destruction of the whole after printing from papier-mâché forms and the like.[175] These are one extreme; at the other the term is used for almost anything an employer's spokesman happens not to like. If it is employed in the latter sense, there are endless cases of featherbedding in hundreds of industries, and new ones develop with changes in materials, machinery, and new techniques, and even the amount of employment. In printing, for example, there are questions concerning the size of crews on old and new presses, operated under excellent conditions or under conditions much less good. In the textile industry we find very frequently the issue of speed-up which may be real and of limitations on production derived from custom or desire to avoid unemployment or possibly to "take it easy" on the other. Then there frequently is a question of speed in assembly lines in mass production. And there may be substantial differences in what management expects or is wont to require, for no obvious reason. Early in the century a strike was lost in the copper-mining industry in northern Michigan over the issue of whether one miner or two should man a heavy pneumatic drill, bringing it through the underground passageways, placing it on the wall—frequently wet and insecure—then holding it in place while operating it; though the accident rate was high, the operator frequently saw no one except perhaps a roving inspector in the course of a workday.

174. Possibly any actual payment or receipt of payment of a sort banned by this unfair labor practice would also come under the ban of Sec. 302(a) and (b), subject to criminal penalties. Cf. *infra*, ch. 15, pp. 561–62.

175. The latter was among the issues in some of the widely publicized Typographical Union cases in the first year. Trial Examiners did not find that demand for inclusion of the clause was a violation of the Act. For a full discussion see Intermediate Report, International Typographical Union and American Newspaper Publishers Association, Case No. 9-CB-5, August 6, 1948.

These are only a few instances of "featherbedding," if it is broadly defined. One is impressed with differences in motives, in situations varying widely from plant to plant, in changes of equipment, materials, and the techniques used and the quality of output required. In most cases a practical man is much impressed also with the many technical aspects involved, to be commanded by a Board or a court if it is to make good decisions.

Another aspect should be recognized. Not all "featherbedding" is or has been the product of labor's action. For example, a large clothing manufacturer before there was any union in its plants had rules limiting height of lays and mixture of fabrics in the cutting of suits and overcoats, rules worked out and applied by a former superintendent. These rules were accepted by the union for more than twenty-five years; then some ten years ago it was agreed to abolish most of them in the interest of greater production at lower labor costs. It is our information that no work rules or limitations have been introduced by union action in this market, but, rather, the union accepted the varying rules, when any, found in the different "houses." During World War II, also, there were many instances of featherbedding practiced in the use of labor under government cost-plus contracts, motivated largely by desire to maintain a reservoir of labor upon which to draw when it might be needed.

This Taft-Hartley clause was a substitute adopted by the Conference Committee for a very inclusive provision in the House bill which would have made strikes or other efforts to force employers to engage in featherbedding practices, broadly defined, unlawful coercive activities. That was a Lea Act "watered down" somewhat, perhaps because of the cloud hanging over that law at the time,[176] but extending the control over all industry within the scope of the Act. The chairman of the House Committee had said: "When any question arises as to whether or not a union demands more people than are 'reasonably required' to do certain work, industrial engineers and time-study people can, and constantly do, resolve the question by reliable, scientific methods."[177] But one might note more faith on the part of the congressmen in the accuracy of time study than the "timers" ordinarily have, and he would wonder whether such studies would always be impartially made and applied by "timers" hired and paid by managements and subject to separation from a job. The Senate Committee

176. The Lea Act (or Anti-Petrillo Act) had been declared unconstitutional by a district court but was subsequently upheld by a divided Supreme Court. U.S. v. Petrillo, 332 U.S. 1 (1947).

177. *Hartley Report*, p. 25.

originally included nothing on featherbedding, since it was thought to be impracticable in most cases to give a court or a board "the say" as to how many workers are needed. As Senator Taft properly observed in Senate debate on the clause finally adopted by the Conference Committee, to do more than was proposed in the compromise adopted would require a determination of facts in hundreds of cases which might arise, with all of their variations and technicalities. He did, however, defend the provision which was adopted and indicated that it would apply only to clear and well-recognized abuses. And after the Conference bill had been passed by the Senate, he again insisted that 8(b)(6) did not proscribe any legitimate union activity. "The use of the words 'in the nature of an exaction,' make it quite clear that what is prohibited is extortion by labor organizations or their agents in lieu of providing services which an employer does not want."[178] But Senators Murray and Pepper raised questions as to what might be considered proscribed behavior. Senator Murray summarized his fears as follows: "The chief danger in the provision is that it may restrict labor organizations in their attempts to combat speed-ups, to protect the safety and health of the workers, and to spread the burden of unemployment. These considerations suggest that the solution of this problem could better be left to the collective bargaining process."[179]

In our opinion Senator Taft's approach to the problem was correct. Clearly, there have been unjustifiable exactions which should be treated as unfair practices. It would be very unfortunate should the featherbedding clause be applied to more than these. Other issues, equally with complaints of "speed-up" or "stretch-out," should be left to be settled in the negotiation of contracts or to be treated as grievances under properly drawn work contracts containing arbitration clauses as is now common practice.[180] They would then ordinarily

178. *Daily Cong. Rec.*, 93:7001–2; cf. also 6601, 6603.
179. *Ibid.*, p. 6662.
180. The absence of clear definition in this clause, even though the intent of Congress was fairly clear, was a source of irritation and delay in negotiations, according to many reports. *Infra*, ch. 16, pp. 638–39. The first major formal case, on which Intermediate Report was awaited at time of writing, was one brought against the Musicians. In another case a Trial Examiner recommended dismissal of a charge of violation of this section when an attempt was made to apply it to a demand of a union for a day's pay for an unemployed union driver after the company had used a nonunion driver in violation of its closed-shop contract which was still valid under the law. International Brotherhood of Teamsters and Henry V. Rabouin, d/b/a Conway's Express, Case No. 2-CC-14, June, 1948. The first Board action on a charge under this section was an order based on agreement of the parties for repayment by a local union of money exacted by four employees

receive due consideration at the hands of management and union representatives with the experience and technical knowledge required to make the best decisions in the general run of cases. If collective bargaining and proper grievance procedure constitute a sound method to be employed in organized industry, and we are assured in Section 201 of Taft-Hartley that they do, this should not be undermined by too much court action. If court action is to be of frequent occurrence in industrial relations, the question arises: Would not compulsory arbitration at the hands of a court selected for that purpose be preferable? Yet almost all persons in American management and organized labor are opposed to that, and we are strongly of that view.

CONCLUSIONS

Before we can draw conclusions as to the "equalization" attempted by Taft-Hartley, we must consider the remedies provided for the various proscribed practices of management and unions or their agents, and whatever evidence is available in the first year of experience as to how it all worked. But perhaps some summary of the changes in the law as to unfair labor practices is in place here, along with statement of some of the major questions raised.

Management unfair labor practices stood for the most part proscribed in the same words as before, except for the new union-shop proviso to the antidiscrimination clause. But many other parts of the Act, notably the free-speech amendment and possibly the changes as to evidence and court review, changed the result and, on the whole, although to unknown degree, weakened the protection of workers in their right to organize and bargain free of interference or denial of these rights by employers. The same might to a degree result from an administrative system less unified and effective than the old. And the fact that certain union unfair labor practices received priority of handling suggests the relative weight given by Congress to the violations by employers as against those by unions. On the other hand, the possibility of obtaining injunctions against employers could in some extreme instances result in more prompt and effective action against an employer.

Against this are the sweeping restrictions put upon unions by the new unfair labor practice provisions. In part these dealt with real abuses and might be expected to promote responsible collective bargaining and to discourage union practices in organizing which have

---

for services they did not perform. Cement Finishers Local No. 627, AFL, and R. H. Parr & Son, Case No. 21-CB-69, August, 1948.

sometimes disregarded rights of other workers, and employers, and real public interests. But, beyond this, the restraints were extensive and too little discriminating, as well as unclear. There was real danger that they would restrict unions in the use of weapons needed if they are to perform their function of protecting legitimate interests of the workers in standardizing and improving labor conditions and that they gave a weapon to an antiunion employer with which he could harass and weaken the union that sought to deal with him. Not just union abuses, but the bargaining position of unions in general, was weakened by many of these provisions. Moreover, the extensive restrictions and limitations meant an interference with the freedom of the collective bargaining process at many points, adding uncertainty, confusion, and instability, contrary to the spirit of a free collective bargaining which we believe to be the better road for the solution of industrial relations problems.

CHAPTER 13

REMEDIES UNDER TAFT-HARTLEY

TAFT-HARTLEY was not intended alone to amend the Wagner Act, though that it did very much. It was also designed to give the United States a new and substantially different labor policy. Most of our policy with reference to basic labor law—except under the Railway Labor Act, Norris–La Guardia, and the Wagner Act with its limited scope—had found expression in the common law as applied by the courts and in varying state statutes and local ordinances. Real effort at enforcement of the latter enactments was far from universal. While Taft-Hartley contained little not already found here or there in state law, it federalized large parts of basic labor law. And procedures and penalties were provided to make that Act effective law, under very wide federal jurisdiction as defined by the Supreme Court in 1937 and subsequently. This federal law as a result could mean much more in reality than at any earlier time when there was not the degree of uniformity now to be expected, in view of the Act's "musts" and "must nots" and penalties designed to supply a fairly complete "set of teeth." We are interested here chiefly in these "teeth" provided to make the legislative regulations substantial reality. Although we shall be interested chiefly in the labor injunction and suability for damages sustained, we shall first deal briefly with penalties.

PENALTIES

Penalties provided under Taft-Hartley were of four kinds. The first of these is "remedial orders designed to make the position of wronged parties the same as before the commission of a wrong."[1] Such remedial orders by the Board were to run against both employers and unions found to have engaged in unfair labor practices. These are the so-called cease-and-desist orders which are generally applied to unfair labor practices when cases are not adjusted by informal means. As regards employers, they included posting of notices prom-

1. Our summary in part follows and quotes that of Bureau of National Affairs, *The New Labor Law* (Washington, D.C., 1947), pp. 15–16.

ising discontinuance of these practices, the disestablishment of dominated organizations, reinstatement of employees found to be discriminated against, payment of back wages for time lost, orders to bargain, and other requirements which the Board finds appropriate. Corresponding to these were cease-and-desist orders directed at unions found guilty of unfair labor practices. Payment of back wages was in the past the most effective remedy, in effect a penalty, and now *unions* as well as employers were made subject to such orders when found responsible for a discriminatory discharge.

The second kind of penalty is found in criminal sanctions, of fines and imprisonment. Such penalties were provided for four offenses: (1) for violation of restrictions on the check-off, welfare funds, and other payments by employers to union representatives, a fine of $10,000 or a year in prison or both was provided;[2] (2) for violation of a ban on political contributions and expenditures, the penalty was a fine of $1,000 or a year in prison or both;[3] (3) falsification of a non-Communist affidavit made by an officer of any local union or an officer of its international, if any, was subject to a fine up to $10,000, ten years in prison, or both;[4] and (4) for wilful interference with Board agents a fine of $5,000 or a year in prison or both might be imposed as under the Wagner Act.[5]

Third are the penalties imposed by courts for contempt of an injunction or a restraining order. Injunctions or restraining orders might be issued under Taft-Hartley in four types of situations: (1) to restrain "unlawful" strikes or boycotts by unions;[6] in such cases the General Counsel, in whom the Board vested its statutory authority, was *required* to seek an injunction if, after the preliminary investigation, which had priority over all other cases in the office except those of like character, it appeared that a union was engaging in such unlawful activity; jurisdictional strikes were excepted, as a separate procedure was provided for them; (2) as restriction upon other unfair labor practices, by either employers or unions, the General Counsel—this by Board action—might seek a restraining order requiring compliance with the law while the Board decided a case, but he was *not required* to do so;[7] (3) after issuance of a final order, the Board might seek what amounts to an injunction from a circuit court of appeals, enforcing its order as heretofore;[8] and (4) the Attorney-General was

2. Sec. 302.
3. Sec. 304.
4. Sec. 9(h) and Sec. 35(A) of the Criminal Code.
5. Sec. 12.
6. Sec. 8(b)(4)(A), (B), (C); Sec. 10(1).
7. Sec. 10(j).
8. Sec. 10(e).

empowered to seek an injunction to restrain a "national emergency" strike or lockout.[9]

The fourth kind of penalty is *loss of employee rights.* The rights of employees under the law might be revoked for striking before the end of the sixty-day waiting period required in the negotiation of contract renewals.[10] Government employees who strike, in violation of the Act, were to be discharged and forfeit their Civil Service status and not to be eligible for re-employment by the United States for three years.[11] In addition, unions lost their rights to file complaints or petitions with the Board or to be certified as bargaining representative if they failed to register and to file financial statements as required, or if the officers failed to execute affidavits denying that they are Communists or the like.[12]

Assessment of damages against a union or employer, on private suit, while not strictly a "penalty," may be added to the above list as a fifth important type of "teeth" provided in the Act, in case of violation of contract, or the banned boycotts and other unlawful concerted activities.[13]

As has been seen, Taft-Hartley, aside from the new sections relating to the settlement of industrial disputes and "national emergencies," had the effect of weakening here and there the obligations which rested upon employers under the Wagner Act; and also, on the other hand, it greatly extended the obligations resting upon labor by adding unfair union practices and changing the basic law in numerous respects. The priority given to certain of the charges against unions is significant. Though the penalties provided generally applied to both management wrongs and labor wrongs, unions would be the chief sufferers from the new provisions. Indeed, some of them applied to labor alone, as in the case of strikes by federal employees, the requirements of periodic reporting to the Secretary of Labor and the distribution to each union member of an annual financial statement, and the penalties connected with contributions and expenditures for political purposes. Naturally, most of these requirements which involved substantial outlays on necessary staff and incidental expenditures by unions did not apply so much to management. In addition, suits at law were expected to rest more heavily on unions than they had, for such suits could be more readily brought against unions than heretofore in some states. As a result, many of the activities prohibited to

9. Sec. 208.
10. Sec. 8(d).
11. Sec. 305.
12. Secs. 9(f), (g), (h).
13. Secs. 301, 303. *Infra,* pp. 496 ff.

unions or their agents under the 1947 law were subject to multiple remedies, cease-and-desist orders, damage suits, injunctions, and in some instances loss of employee rights. These were in addition to criminal penalties under federal, state, and local law for some of the types of behavior outlawed by Taft-Hartley. The hazards were heavy for violations of the provisions of the Act, which imposed new, sweeping, and often not clearly defined restrictions upon unions.

With the government a more important figure in industrial relations than in the past, the outlay on union legal staffs for salaries, subsistence, traveling expenses, and cost of records made were complained of bitterly by at least some labor organizations.[14] With much increased costs and necessarily expanded services, unions complained that they were forced to restrict organizational effort and time devoted to collective bargaining, including the handling of grievances arising under work contracts. If, as we have seen, the new Act placed more "hobbles" on labor organizations than they had under federal and state law before August, 1947, and there was the more vigorous administration of law now expected, the "hobbles" might be expected to be much more extensively "riveted on" than formerly. This should not be objected to as such. Any restrictive policy requires penalties to be vigorously applied, and this is especially true in view of the fact that the new policy was not entirely clear on many points and certain parts of it could not be expected to become generally self-enforcing without such vigorous application for at least some time.

INJUNCTIONS

Our greatest interest here, however, lies in the labor injunction and suits for damages to which Congress devoted much attention when framing Taft-Hartley. Both of these are prominent among the proceedings provided for in the 1947 Act. First, then, the labor injunction, as it was under the Norris–LaGuardia Act and then under Taft-Hartley.

The Norris–La Guardia Act of 1932[15] was designed to cope with the

14. Cf., for example, the detailed statement by the International Association of Machinists on its increased expenses as a result of the law, published as Appendix D in U.S. Senate, Joint Committee on Labor-Management Relations, *Labor-Management Relations*, Report No. 986, Pt. 2, *Minority Views*, 80th Cong., 2d Sess., April 1, 1948, cited as *Ball Committee Report, Minority Views*. It concluded: "This expense must ultimately be borne by the membership itself and therefore results in an increased cost for the right of representation under the law and a decrease in the actual service to the union's membership. The law has caused a terrific increase in the union's operating overhead."

15. 47 U.S. Stat. 70 (1932).

"labor injunction" which had reached its zenith here and which was almost peculiarly an American problem.[16] American courts departed from the English conception of property, closely limited to tangible physical things of value, and "property" came to include a right to do business as well, without interference by union activities regarded as unlawful. Early in this century, when a growing labor movement was reacted against by most managements as running counter to the business interests of the day, the increasing protests by labor unions were thought to have been met by the Clayton Act.[17] This, however, lost most of its expected effect in a series of Supreme Court decisions:[18] in *Hitchman Coal and Coke*,[19] which protected the employer's rights in yellow-dog contracts but neglected labor's right to organize for mutual support; in *Duplex*,[20] which limited labor's lawful activities to those employees who had a proximate interest in a given plant; in *Bedford Stone*,[21] which held it unlawful to refuse to lay stone quarried in another state by nonunion workers who had taken the places of union men on lawful strike over the renewal of an expired contract; in the *Shopmen's* case,[22] where the court had enjoined a long list of union activities; in the Chief Justice's observation in *American Steel Foundries*,[23] followed in some later cases, that under the facts of that case picketing by more than one picket at each place of ingress or egress would not be peaceful and therefore could be enjoined. Scores upon scores of injunctions, in large cases and small, were issued in this period centering in the 1920's, the number mounting each year.[24] Some of those granted by the lower courts were appealed to the higher courts, and some were modified or reversed; but usually strikes or picketing and other activity had by then ended, and any such reversal was too late to give unions any protection in the cases directly involved. The harm had already been done.

All this and more—including a partially changed conception of law applied more generally to union activity, questionable procedure used by a large majority of the courts, and many instances of important differences between courts of the same community, as in Kansas City,

16. Cf. *supra*, ch. 1, pp. 7–15.
17. 38 U.S. Stat. 730 (1914).   18. Cf. *supra*, ch. 1, pp. 11–13.
19. Hitchman Coal and Coke Co. v. Mitchell, 245 U.S. 229 (1917).
20. Duplex Printing Press Co. v. Deering, 254 U.S. 443 (1921).
21. Bedford Cut Stone Co. v. Journeymen Stone Cutters' Association, 274 U.S. 37 (1927). This and Duplex are discussed *supra*, ch. 12, pp. 462–65.
22. 283 Fed. 479 (1922), 290 Fed. 978 (1923).
23. American Steel Foundries v. Tri-City Central Trades Council, 257 U.S. 184 (1921).
24. For Dr. Witte's data on recorded injunctions, see *supra*, ch. 1, p. 8.

Missouri—entered into the injunction problem of the time.[25] Protests against labor injunctions became more numerous and more emphatic. Nor did these emanate solely from labor unions and their officers. Others in increasing numbers, including some businessmen, were of the opinion that a real problem had developed which called for congressional action. The Norris–La Guardia Act was designed to solve this problem.[26] Some of its provisions must be noted here.

Section 5 of the Norris–La Guardia Act proscribed the issuance of any restraining order upon the ground that any of the persons participating or interested in a labor dispute constituted or were engaged in "an unlawful combination or conspiracy" because of the doing in concert of any of a series of acts enumerated as not to be enjoined. Section 6 provided that no officer or member of any organization participating or interested in a labor dispute should be held "responsible or liable in any court of the United States for the unlawful acts of individual officers, members, or agents, except upon clear proof of actual participation in, or actual authorization of, such acts, or of ratification of such acts after actual knowledge thereof." This was directed against the "blanket injunction" including "all persons generally," though they were not of course personally served with notice. Section 7 provided that no court of the United States should issue a temporary or permanent injunction in any case involving or growing out of a labor dispute—except after hearing testimony of witnesses in open court,[27] with opportunity for cross-examination in support of the allegations of a complaint made under oath, and testimony in opposition, if offered, and except after findings of fact by the court, to the effect—

(a) That unlawful acts have been threatened and will be committed unless restrained or have been committed and will be continued unless restrained, but no injunction or temporary restraining order shall be issued on account of any threat or unlawful act excepting against the person or persons, association, or organization making the threat or committing the unlawful act or actually authorizing or ratifying the same after actual knowledge thereof;

(b) That substantial and irreparable injury to complainant's property will follow;

(c) That as to each item of relief granted greater injury will be inflicted

25. For an excellent summary statement of the problem as it developed, see Charles O. Gregory, *Labor and the Law* (New York: W. W. Norton & Co., Inc., 1946), pp. 95–104.

26. Cf. *supra*, ch. 12, p. 465.

27. Provision was made under certain conditions for the granting of restraining orders without such hearing, etc., but any such order was limited to five days.

upon complainant by the denial of relief than will be inflicted upon defendants by the granting of relief;

(d) That complainant has no adequate remedy at law; and

(e) That the public officers charged with the duty to protect complainant's property are unable or unwilling to furnish adequate protection.[28]

A further, meaningful limitation is found in Section 8, which reads:

No restraining order or injunctive relief shall be granted to any complainant who has failed to comply with any obligation imposed by law which is involved in the labor dispute in question, or who has failed to make every reasonable effort to settle such dispute either by negotiation or with the aid of any available governmental machinery of mediation or voluntary arbitration.

Even more important was Section 13, which greatly limited the use of restraining orders and injunctions, for it changed the then usual concept of "labor dispute" and brought under the protection of the Act the large majority of such disputes which in the development of court-made law previously had not been recognized as legitimate. Indeed, this was a most important change in legal concepts. Section 13 reads as follows:

When used in this Act, and for the purposes of this Act—

(a) A case shall be held to involve or to grow out of a labor dispute when the case involves persons who are engaged in the same industry, trade, craft, or occupation; or have direct or indirect interests therein; or who are employees of the same employer; or who are members of the same or an affiliated organization of employers or employees; whether such dispute is (1) between one or more employers or associations of employers and one or more employees or associations of employees; (2) between one or more employers or associations of employers and one or more employers or associations of employers; or (3) between one or more employees or associations of employees and one or more employees or associations of employees; or when the case involves any conflicting or competing interests in a "labor dispute" (as hereinafter defined) of "persons participating or interested" therein (as hereinafter defined).

(b) *A person or association shall be held to be a person participating or interested in a labor dispute if relief is sought against him or it, and if he or it is engaged in the same industry, trade, craft, or occupation in which such dispute occurs, or has a direct or indirect interest therein, or is a member, officer, or agent of any association composed in whole or in part of employers or employees engaged in such industry, trade, craft, or occupation.*

(c) *The term "labor dispute" includes any controversy concerning terms or conditions of employment, or concerning the association or representation of persons in negotiating, fixing, maintaining, changing, or seeking to*

28. Note "(c)" and "(e)" particularly.

arrange terms or conditions of employment, regardless of whether or not the disputants stand in the proximate relation of employer and employee.[29]

This Act of 1932 was rather revolutionary, and it scarcely needs be said that it had the effect of reducing the number of labor injunctions granted by the federal courts to a small fraction of what they had been. Moreover, it substantially affected the federal labor law as it was applied by the courts. Taft-Hartley, however, changed *practically all* of this to fit into its other provisions, which imposed extensive restrictions upon what unions may do.

Under Taft-Hartley a very important provision for use of the injunction was in "national emergency"[30] cases such as that which reappeared in coal in 1948. After the President had found from the report of a duly established board of inquiry that such an emergency existed, he was empowered to direct the Attorney-General to petition a district court for an injunction, with Norris–La Guardia made inapplicable. Subject to modification or reversal by a superior court on appeal, the injunction would remain in effect pending settlement during the prescribed eighty-day "cooling-off" period.[31]

Of course the NLRB was authorized, as before, to seek an injunction by a federal court in securing compliance with its orders.[32] But, in addition, Taft-Hartley vested the Board with additional powers to seek an injunction from an appropriate federal district court in unfair labor practice cases in advance of its hearing and decision.[33] Moreover, in cases involving the strikes and boycotts banned by the sweeping Section 8(b)(4)(A), (B), and (C), it was made *mandatory*, when the preliminary investigation gave "*reasonable cause to believe*" that the charge was true and that a complaint should issue, to seek an injunction pending final decision by the Board. The preliminary investigation of these cases against unions, also, was to receive priority over other types of cases. By the Act and by delegation of the Board,[34] in the discretionary as well as the mandatory injunction proceedings under Sections 10(j) and (1), the General Counsel exercised full and final authority and responsibility. The mandatory injunction provisions, Section 10(1), must be quoted:

(1) Whenever it is charged that any person has engaged in an unfair labor practice within the meaning of paragraph (4)(A), (B), or (C) of section 8(b), the preliminary investigation of such charge shall be made forthwith and given priority over all other cases except cases of like charac-

29. Italics ours.
30. Title II, Sec. 208.
33. Sec. 10(j).
31. Discussed *infra*, ch. 15, pp. 574–86.
32. Sec. 10(e).
34. *Supra*, ch. 11, pp. 404–5; see also NLRB, *Thirteenth Annual Report*, p. 90.

ter in the office where it is filed or to which it is referred. If, after such investigation, the officer or regional attorney to whom the matter may be referred has reasonable cause to believe such charge is true and that a complaint should issue, he shall, on behalf of the Board, petition any district court of the United States (including the District Court of the United States for the District of Columbia) within any district where the unfair labor practice in question has occurred, is alleged to have occurred, or wherein such person resides or transacts business, for appropriate injunctive relief pending the final adjudication of the Board with respect to such matter. Upon the filing of any such petition the district court shall have jurisdiction to grant such injunctive relief or temporary restraining order as it deems just and proper, *notwithstanding any other provision of law:*[35] *Provided further,* That no temporary restraining order shall be issued without notice unless a petition alleges that substantial and irreparable injury to the charging party will be unavoidable and such temporary restraining order shall be effective for no longer than five days and will become void at the expiration of such period. Upon filing of any such petition the courts shall cause notice thereof to be served upon any person involved in the charge and such person, including the charging party, shall be given an opportunity to appear by counsel and present any relevant testimony: *Provided further,* That for the purposes of this subsection district courts shall be deemed to have jurisdiction of a labor organization (1) in the district in which such organization maintains its principal office, or (2) in any district in which its duly authorized officers or agents are engaged in promoting or protecting the interests of employee members. The service of legal process upon such officer or agent shall constitute service upon the labor organization and make such organization a party to the suit. In situations where such relief is appropriate the procedure specified herein shall apply to charges with respect to section 8(b)(4)(D) [jurisdictional disputes].

These provisions relating to injunctions and restraining orders had finally been agreed upon by the Conference Committee after sharp differences between the House and the Senate. The House bill was evidently designed to reinstate the old injunction practices of the 1920's. Norris–La Guardia was not repealed, but it would have been left without much effect. A number of questions had arisen in the framing of the Senate bill. A rather general although not universal feeling was evident in the Senate that the injunction was needed for successful administration to prevent the prolonged delays which frequently occurred under the Wagner Act. One of the stronger statements for injunctive relief was made by Senator Taft in his report of April 17, 1947:[36]

35. Italics ours. This of course means the Norris–La Guardia Act and the Clayton Act.
36. U.S. Senate, Committee on Labor and Public Welfare, *Federal Labor Relations Act of 1947*, Report No. 105, 80th Cong., 1st Sess., p. 27, cited as *Taft Report.*

Experience under the National Labor Relations Act has demonstrated that by reason of lengthy hearings and litigation enforcing its orders, the Board has not been able in some instances to correct unfair labor practices until after substantial injury has been done. Under the present act the Board is empowered to seek interim relief only after it has filed in the appropriate circuit court of appeals its order and the record on which it is based. Since the Board's orders are not self-enforcing, it has sometimes been possible for persons violating the act to accomplish their unlawful objective before being placed under any legal restraint and thereby to make it impossible or not feasible to restore or preserve the status quo pending litigation.

Though there were several shades of thought, only two main positions were advanced in Senate debate in regard to injunction proceedings. A considerable number of senators, led by Mr. Ball, wished to reintroduce the injunction after the pattern of the twenties. Over against these were Senators Morse, Ives, Smith of New Jersey, Pepper, Thomas of Utah, Murray, and others, with a substantial majority following, who opposed a return to the earlier pattern in which private parties were petitioners before the district courts. The first three of these, at least, desired to lodge the filing of petitions in the hands of the NLRB, as was finally done. Senators Pepper, Thomas, and Murray objected strongly to the mandatory injunction provision, but it was not entirely clear to what extent they would have accepted the injunction petition by the Board if more discrimination had been made as to the types of activity banned. As we have seen, it was made mandatory in cases arising under 8(b)(4)(A), (B), and (C), as soon as preliminary investigation indicated that a complaint should be issued, for the Board—that is, General Counsel—to proceed at once to petition for an injunction from the appropriate court. In cases of disputes over work jurisdiction, (D), the same procedure might be used, but the filing of a petition was not required. In any event, upon a petition for injunctive relief the judge had wide discretion to decide under what conditions and precisely how he would exercise his judicial authority.[37] The district judge in these cases, it is important to note, acts largely as an agent for the enforcement of federal statute law, and his decision is in a sense subject to review by the Board in the eventual decision.[38]

37. He was apparently free of the limitations of the Norris–La Guardia Act in the mandatory injunction cases, although not explicitly so in those under Section 10(j).

38. The General Counsel held in early cases, however, and district courts agreed with him, that only a prima facie case need be presented, and the court needed only to "determine whether there is a reasonable probability that the allegations of the complaint in the principal case before the Board will be estab-

While the Senate's position with reference to petitions for restraining orders and injunctions prevailed in the Conference Committee, some have thought that this authority was not lodged exclusively with the Board (General Counsel). However, the record with minor exceptions[39] indicates clearly that injunctive relief on petition of private parties was not contemplated under the Act.[40] Nevertheless, doubt remained in the minds of some as to whether under Taft-Hartley private parties as well as the Board could not petition a district court for a restraining order. In fact, a number of such petitions were filed. Some judges denied them on the ground that they could be filed only by the Board (General Counsel), but other judges accepted them and issued affirmative orders.[41] On April 1, 1948, however, the Fourth Circuit Court of Appeals, a very able court, rendered a unanimous decision which clarified the issues, in the Amazon Cotton Mill case.[42] The district court had granted an order on the union's petition, requiring the company to bargain with the union. An affirmative order would of course have been to interfere with the normal work of the Board in unfair labor practice cases, hence the Board joined the com-

lished." General Counsel Denham in address, June 4, 1948. As Judge Brennan stated in Douds v. International Longshoremen's Association (Cargill, Inc.), October 2, 1947, N.D. N.Y., 20 *LRRM* 2642, "This Court does not decide which litigant is ultimately entitled to prevail.... A showing of a *prima facie* case for equitable relief satisfies the statute." See also Douds v. Local 294, International Brotherhood of Teamsters, 75 F. Supp. 414 (D.C., N.Y.) and other cases cited in NLRB, *Thirteenth Annual Report*, pp. 86–87. Unions complained as a result that they were denied opportunity to defend themselves. U.S. Congress, Joint Committee on Labor-Management Relations, *Hearings, Operation of Labor Management Relations Act, 1947*, 80th Cong., 2d Sess., Pt. 2, p. 694.

39. Chairman Hartley of the House Committee in his report on the action of the Conference Committee admitted that the House conferees had conceded to the Senate on this point, *Daily Cong. Rec.*, 93:6540; but he held that the power of the Board under this provision "will not affect the availability to private persons of any other remedies they might have...." U.S. House of Representatives, *Conference Report, Labor-Management Relations Act, 1947*, Report No. 510, 80th Cong., 1st Sess., June, 1947, p. 57.

40. Cf. Gerhard P. Van Arkel, *An Analysis of the Labor Management Relations Act, 1947* (New York: Practising Law Institute, 1947), p. 63. He noted, however, a possible exception, in that Section 302, dealing with restrictions on payments to employee representatives, granted power to the district courts to restrain violations of that section without regard to the Norris–La Guardia Act or Sections 6 and 20 of the Clayton Act.

41. Cf. Longshoremen v. Sunset Line and Twine Co., petition by union for injunctive relief and damages, dismissed April 7, 1948, 77 F. Supp. 119 (D.C., Cal.); Dixie Motor Coach Corp. v. Street, Electric Railway and Motor Coach Employees of America, injunction granted January 16, 1948, against picketing to support a secondary boycott. 21 *LRRM* 2193.

42. Amazon Cotton Mill Co. v. Textile Workers Union, 167 F. 2d 183 (C.C.A.4, 1948).

pany as appellant. The circuit court reversed the district court and upheld the exclusive jurisdiction of the Board. Judge Parker speaking for the court held that the Act gave limited jurisdiction to district courts by specific language at a number of points, but no general grant of concurrent jurisdiction with the Board in unfair labor practice cases could be read from these limited grants. The intent of Congress was clear to maintain the system of initial determination of the issues by the specialized administrative agency. Any other conclusion would be disastrous to successful administration and result in great confusion, with more than two hundred local agencies open to employers or unions with cases before the Board. Moreover, Congress could not have meant that unions which could not go to the Board for relief, because of their failure to file the required documents, could obtain such relief from the courts.

Judge Parker's several points were well taken. Under all the circumstances a different decision might have meant a return to what Senator Ball and others had fought for so vigorously. In our view, to open the right to petition for injunctions to private persons would play havoc with the administrative process and make it impossible for a consistent policy to obtain.

Yet of course the injunction, in any event, whether it is on petition of the Board or of a private party, whether it serves as a deterrent, as it does in most cases, or as a method of procedure, falls with tremendous weight upon unions and their agents as compared with management. Under Taft-Hartley this weight upon unions resulted most of all, however, from the substantive provisions of the new law. We have taken issue particularly with Section 8(b)(1) on the ground of its lack of clear definition of "restraint and coercion," and the fact that it enacted federal police regulation on matters that are better handled by state and local legislation; and with Section 8(b)(4)(A), (B), and (C) on the ground that the analysis and the conception of the problem are too narrow. We have argued[43] that many boycotts, many sympathetic strikes and other union weapons placed under a ban, are adequately justified by a unity of interest which should be recognized in our basic labor law. However, this position has been made clear and nothing more needs to be said.

Complaints and problems were inevitable under the arrangements made for the administration of the injunction. For example, many labor attorneys felt that they were handicapped with the Board (in fact, the General Counsel) as the petitioner for the restraining order;

43. *Supra,* ch. 12, pp. 459–71.

any government agency is ordinarily able to get what it wants from a district court, and they (labor attorneys) would perhaps get a "better break" if petitions were made by one or the other private parties involved. Moreover, the restraining orders, which might be in effect for months before final decision of the case, were issued without any consideration of the union's defense.[44] There was also some feeling that the Board itself might in a measure be placed behind the "eight ball," first by the statutory independence of the General Counsel in what he sought from the court, and then by the necessity of passing judgment on the court's action when the Board eventually decided the case.[45] No doubt "hot spots" would be found in the very unequal number of injunctions against unions as compared to those against employers. It was probable that some complaints issued, on which injunctions were sought and secured, would not be sustained by the Board. But in such cases union action would have been restrained, ending their use of weapons perhaps needed under the circumstances, although later—too late for the particular dispute—their right to use them might be sustained by the Board. Especially is this important, and danger of injustice results, in view of the fact that injunction petitions were made mandatory when a complaint was issued in certain boycott and other cases. No discretion was permitted the administrative agency to decide whether circumstances warrant such drastic action. Thus in a close case of this type, it was not possible under the law for the General Counsel to litigate the case and seek a Board decision on the issues before the government entered on the employer's side of the dispute through the injunction procedure. A district court might of course occasionally decline to go along with the petition filed by the General Counsel[46] when it did not consider injunctive relief "just and proper." But is the district court the best equipped to make such a decision, and should such action be taken on only a prima facie case, when it may be a matter of life and death to a union involved in a particular dispute?

An important question is as to the effect of the injunction procedures and the federal proscription of "restraint and coercion" by

44. Cf. *supra,* n. 38.
45. Cf. the ITU injunction and contempt cases, *infra,* ch. 16, pp. 627–28.
46. Through February, 1949, 42 petitions for injunctions were filed. Of those in which the court had issued orders, petitions against employers were granted once and denied once; those against unions were granted in 21 cases and denied in 6. Senate Committee on Labor and Public Welfare, *Hearings on S. 249, Labor Relations,* 81st Cong., 1st Sess., Pt. 4, pp. 1713–14. See also *infra,* ch. 16, pp. 616–18.

unions on the policing of strikes.[47] If coercion occurs on a picket line, action by the local police is the obvious and prompt remedy. Clearly the slow process of Board investigation and ultimate cease-and-desist order is an ineffective remedy in such matters; hence the pressure from employers for injunctions. Fortunately in this type of case a petition for injunction was discretionary. Action at this point might be crucial as to the outcome of the strike, and injustice might result from an injunction issued on only a prima facie case, without consideration of the union's defense. Yet to the unions the filing of charges and investigation by the Board's agents, even without seeking an injunction, is a strikebreaking process. Charges of coercion might be filed and the case brought to hearing by the General Counsel on the basis of minor disorders on the picket line for which there were not even any arrests.[48] Would the vague definition of coercion and the possibility of federal intervention lead to better or poorer local policing? Would it stimulate more attention to methods of insuring justice to all parties in industrial disputes, or would it encourage a return to the abuses of governmental intervention on the side of the employer? Charges have been made that the Act "stimulated a wide variety of lawless acts and attitudes on the part of state and municipal authorities,"[49] as well as an increasing number of injunctions obtained by private employers in state courts. We question whether solution of the very real problems involved in the policing of strikes when feelings run high is to be found in federal action. Considering the difficulties involved in drafting appropriate law on this subject which would permit justice to be done to all parties, and the administrative difficulties of industrial policing, this is an appropriate field for state and local legislation. And with the propensity of the law-enforcement authorities to place different interpretations on such laws and ordinances, and frequent maladministration, moreover, more than laws and ordinances are involved if justice is to be done and a desired respect for law is to be more fully developed.[50]

The possibility of injunction proceedings, either mandatory in the "boycott" cases, or discretionary in jurisdictional disputes and other

47. Cf. *supra*, ch. 12, pp. 446–47.

48. In two early cases Trial Examiners recommended dismissal of charges of coercion in connection with strikes, but the Board held otherwise. Perry Norvell Co., 80 NLRB 225 (November, 1948); Sunset Line and Twine Co., 79 NLRB 1487 (October, 1948).

49. *CIO News*, June 21, 1948, p. 8; cf. *infra*, ch. 16, p. 640.

50. The question of policing of strikes was discussed at some length in Harry A. Millis and Royal E. Montgomery, *Organized Labor* (New York: McGraw-Hill Book Co., 1945), pp. 667–89.

cases against unions or employers, clearly had a useful deterrent effect against some of the unjustifiable actions by unions to which we have referred. But is there not danger of going too far and "unequalizing" bargaining positions of unions in their efforts to function? The basic labor law was changed, as we have seen, by proscribing some concerted activities which we consider justifiable because of the common interests of groups of workers. In addition, the procedural safeguards of the Norris–La Guardia Act appear to have been largely removed. No longer, for instance, was the question to be raised whether an employer came into court with "clean hands" or had made reasonable efforts to settle the dispute before the government came to his aid by giving him temporary injunctive relief in specified types of cases. Moreover, the injunction proceedings were mandatory in the "boycott" types of cases against unions, regardless of the judgment of the administrative agency as to the relative significance or insignificance of such a case in comparison with others against employers which might be crucial to the life of a union involved. And there was a lack of clear standards to guide the courts in the issuance of injunctions.[51] The possibilities of abuse were grave.

However carefully the new unfair labor practice and injunction features of Taft-Hartley were administered, and of course excellent administration was very important, feelings were inevitably aroused which militated against the conditions necessary for sound industrial relations and the best service of the general interest. And to this must be added the danger of excessive litigation which such proceedings place in the path of healthy industrial relations.

DAMAGE SUITS

The damage-suit provisions in Taft-Hartley were presumably designed largely to equalize the law of labor as it applies to employer and union, to promote the sense of responsibility in management and unions, and to provide a method of obtaining compensation for economic losses resulting from unlawful behavior or breach of contract. Title III, Section 303, concerned loss from "boycotts and other unlawful combinations," while Section 301 concerned breach of collective bargaining agreements.

The damage suit had been employed against unions here and there for some forty-five years before the labor injunction came into vogue

51. For a valuable discussion of this point see "The Labor Management Relations Act and the Revival of the Labor Injunction," *Columbia Law Review*, 48 (1948), 759–72.

in the 1880's. Yet it has been employed in relatively few cases. Indeed, it has not been a ready instrument and has no doubt been threatened, successfully or otherwise, more frequently than actually used. In the more than three hundred cases noted by Professor Witte in 1932, in at least a third, he found, the plaintiff asked both for damages and for an injunction to prevent future injury. But not all of these were brought by employers. Many of them were filed by nonunionists or expelled union members, and a few by third parties injured by union activities.[52]

The fact is that serious suits for damages have been few as compared to the number of labor injunctions. The explanation is to be found in a number of factors. The first is that the injunction for decades was the widespread method used to check or prevent loss, since it was more effective than the slow process of the damage suit, when employers wanted quick relief. This was widely effective until Norris–La Guardia was enacted in 1932 and quickly followed, with adaptations perhaps, in a very considerable number of the states. A second factor is found in the peculiar situation in industrial relations. Production must be largely a co-operative process, with management and employees working together. Suits, when more than threats, are therefore likely to be avoided by practical men unless the individual employee or union and management are engaged in something closely akin to divorce proceedings. Damage suits may well wreck the working situation and seldom do they pay, especially when, under law, labor has the right to organize and, when it properly qualifies, to bargain collectively with management about wages, hours, and working conditions. Still another, and greatly emphasized, factor has been in the procedural situation which was chiefly a matter of state concern until Taft-Hartley. The Sherman Antitrust Act was an exception under federal law, though increasingly used in the federal courts—in Danbury Hatters, Coronado, and other cases decided during a quarter-century preceding 1932. But of course suits might otherwise be brought in the federal courts, provided a diversity of citizenship obtained and the sum involved was not less than $3,000—limitations which were excised by Taft-Hartley. And in federal suits matters procedural were controlled by the law of the state in which the given case arose. Hence in the case made for damage-suit legislation, emphasis was placed on variations in and inadequacies of state law or rules relative to suits against labor organizations.

52. E. E. Witte, *The Government in Labor Disputes* (New York: McGraw-Hill Book Co., 1932), p. 138.

Such variations and inadequacies have been great from the point of view of effective suit, and, though laws have been extensively amended here and there, the problem has continued. Some states remained under the common law; voluntary associations are not, in their collective capacity and name, recognized at common law as having any legal existence apart from their members. The funds are the property of the members, and suit must be brought against the members joined. A number of states, among them New York, Ohio, Rhode Island, Washington, and Wisconsin, have statutes permitting a union to be sued by bringing action against its officers or selected members as representatives of the entire membership. A still larger number adopted statutes or have court decisions under which suit may be brought against unincorporated associations in the common name. In addition to procedural matters such as these, the problem arises of establishing and defining the responsibility of the union or its members. Does mere membership establish responsibility, or is something more required? And what is the responsibility of the union in the event of unlawful picketing? But the maze of variations and inadequacies cannot be pursued further. Suffice it to say that most state laws were more or less uncertain and unsatisfactory, that labor nevertheless found much fault with them, and that the situation was usually unsatisfactory to employers and regarded as unduly restrictive by them, and especially by those employers more or less hostile to unionism.

Drives for greater legal responsibility on the part of unions have occurred notably at times when unions were in disfavor and perhaps faced active "open-shop" campaigns. Early in the century there was a strong management demand that labor organizations should be required to become incorporated and assume the full responsibility connected therewith. This demand reappeared some thirty years ago with the extensive revolt by much of management against unions during or following World War I; but it largely disappeared as it became clear that incorporation could not be required because such incorporation is a voluntary act and practically all unions have for a half-century or more been opposed to incorporation, for reasons good and otherwise. Incorporation had been sponsored particularly by the League for Industrial Rights, so active during the "American Plan" movement in the 1920's for the "open shop" or in considerable part no contracts with unions at all. This League also sponsored a bill "For a Better Protection of Public Welfare against Unwarranted Strikes and

Lockouts,"[53] a very restrictive bill which was enacted into law in Alabama alone.[54] It was not unrelated to some of the later restrictive "antilabor" measures which have been discussed in these pages; and it was a factor in some states in securing legislation relating to suability for damages resulting from unlawful union behavior. Pressure for greater financial responsibility on the part of labor organizations brought some legislative results. Nevertheless, the situation was unsatisfactory to the sponsors of Taft-Hartley and to many others.[55]

Suits for damages in federal district courts, without regard to diversity of citizenship or the amount involved, were permitted by the two Sections 301 and 303. Section 303 provided for suits *against labor organizations only,* brought by anyone who had sustained damages from "boycotts and other unlawful combinations," that is, from union practices proscribed by Section 8(b)(4), unlawful strikes, boycotts, picketing, and jurisdictional disputes, which are repeated in this section. These practices, where "commerce" is involved—that is, as a matter of law now in almost all economic activities[56]—were subject to cease-and-desist orders by the Board, mandatory or discretionary injunctions on petition by the Board, and now also by this section to suits for damages in federal courts. Senator Ball also, as noted earlier, wished to open them to injunction on private suit, but this was defeated.

It will be noted that Section 303 runs only one way—against unions. Managements *may* to an extent do things to help other employers which are closely analagous to some of the proscribed labor boycotts—which unions had heretofore entered upon in an effort to promote a common economic interest of the workers concerned. Co-operative relations may exist among employers, by contract or by mere lend-a-hand arrangements, to accept each other's strikebound work, so that union employees are required to proceed with such work. Such co-operation among employers made no difference whatever in the union's liability under Taft-Hartley should it balk at such strike-breaking activity, in the absence of specific contracts binding the employer not to accept or process strikebound materials. Many sympathetic strikes arise in just this way. Damage suits against unions may then result from co-ordinated activities which arise as a defense to such co-ordinated antiunion activities by employers permitted by

53. Quoted in full in Millis and Montgomery, *op. cit.,* pp. 659–60.
54. Alabama Code (1928), Secs. 5723–28. 55. Cf. *Taft Report,* pp. 15–18.
56. Of course rail transportation, agriculture, and certain other activities are excluded; but a broad construction of "affecting commerce" was to be expected in cases under Section 303. Cf. *supra,* ch. 11, pp. 400–402.

the Act. Under Taft-Hartley the threat of such a damage suit was sometimes enough to force workers to refrain from refusal to work on "struck work" or from other activities closely related to a union's need to survive and make gains for its members.[57]

The possible impact of Section 303 upon cases against unions under the Sherman Antitrust Act is not entirely clear. The intent to restore the law as declared in the Duplex and Bedford cases was explicit, yet only single damages were provided as remedy for injuries rising from violations of this section, not the triple damages of the Sherman Act. While the antitrust acts were not specifically mentioned or amended, perhaps it can be said that in effect the Sherman Act was made available to millions of individuals, for the right to sue was federalized and open to anyone "injured in his business or property by reason of any violation of these provisions." As Van Arkel has stated,[58] a new statutory framework was created into which Antitrust Act decisions must be fitted, and it was to be expected that the changes in the labor statutes would have substantial results.

In any event, Section 303 provided further strong sanction against the boycotts and other combinations which it was desired to stop. While some of these activities, in our view, should be proscribed, the sweeping and undiscriminating character of these proscriptions make this sanction, however justified in some cases, open to abuse and a threat to unions when they engage in effective action reasonably related to the performance of their function of protecting the interests of their members.

Section 301 dealt with a related, yet rather different and perhaps more important matter—suits by and against labor organizations for violation of contracts, which may be brought in any appropriate district court as under Section 303. Section 301(b) reads:

> Any labor organization which represents employees in an industry affecting commerce as defined in this Act and any employer whose activities affect commerce as defined in this Act shall be bound by the acts of its agents. Any such labor organization may sue or be sued as an entity and in behalf of the employees whom it represents in the courts of the United States. Any money judgment against a labor organization in a district court of the United States shall be enforceable only against the organization as

57. Cf. *supra*, ch. 12, pp. 469–70; *infra*, p. 512.
58. Van Arkel, *op. cit.*, p. 63. Cf. also statement of Professor R. A. Lester in *Ball Committee Hearings*, Pt. 2, pp. 975–76, that Sections 8(b)(4) and 303(a) made secondary boycotts, "regardless of the union's purpose in engaging in them, unfair labor practices and unlawful in a way that is practically equivalent to pr[o]scribing them under the anti-trust laws except for the triple damage penalty."

an entity and against its assets, and shall not be enforceable against any individual member or his assets.

Section 301(e) should also be quoted because of the peculiar significance it may have:

For the purposes of this section, in determining whether any person is acting as an "agent" of another person so as to make such other person responsible for his acts, the question of whether the specific acts performed were actually authorized or subsequently ratified shall not be controlling.[59]

Thus the law was federalized so as to make any joint agreement binding and violations subject to suit for damages provided "commerce" is present, and, as noted below, provided further that this suability is not eliminated by a provision of the agreement itself.[60]

Section 301 was an improvement upon some of the state laws in that it provided for and made it clear that any money judgment against a labor organization in a district court should be enforceable only against the *organization as an entity* and against *its assets,* and not against any individual member or his assets.[61] This brought the federal statute into accord with the modern theory of the legal nature of a collective agreement, by providing for the limited liability of the labor representative. This protects against such a decision as was made in the Danbury Hatters' case, *Loewe* v. *Lawlor,*[62] in which *mere membership* in the union carried responsibility for damages extending to all of one's possessions, though some of the members knew nothing of the boycott found to be unlawful. Indeed, some of such members had not even attended a meeting of the union in years, yet lost everything they owned. The boycott had not been approved by the members in advance or later. But the main point lies not in such facts as these but in the theory of union versus membership responsibility. The best and increasingly accepted theory is that an ordinary collective agreement is between the employer and the labor bargaining agency as such. Ordinarily the latter can reduce wages or make other changes in an agreement adverse to its members during the life of the contract without legal right of redress to complaining members. As has been stated,[63] "the courts are developing an appropriate theory that collective agreements neither confer indefeasible rights nor im-

59. This incorporates the words of Sec. 2(13); cf. *supra,* ch. 11, p. 398.
60. *Infra,* pp. 510–12.
61. This applies also to suits under Sec. 303.
62. 208 U.S. 274 (1908), *supra,* ch. 1, p. 9.
63. From H. A. Millis and R. E. Montgomery, *Organized Labor* (1945), p. 665. Courtesy of McGraw-Hill Book Co.

pose duties upon individual workers. Under this theory, the obligations created by the collective contract are neither the individual property nor the individual burden of each union member. A true collective contract grants neither rights to, nor exacts obligations from, the individual employee; his protection is obtained through the union which can, within the limits of its constitution and by-laws, change the terms of an agreement and modify the worker's tenure."

Important also is the fact that Section 301 did not, as did the vetoed Case Bill,[64] a closely related measure, contain any provision depriving one who strikes in violation of a contract of his protection as an "employee" under the Act. No doubt the Act left discipline by discharge, suspension, or otherwise to be exercised by management, under Section 10(c), which provided that "no order" of the Board should require reinstatement of any individual or the payment to him of any back pay if he was suspended or discharged "for cause."[65] By contract provisions, on the other hand, quite frequently such matters of discipline and the right of appeal through the grievance machinery have been agreed upon.

A third point concerns the meaning of "agent." Employers and unions were to be bound by the acts of their agents, and "the question of whether the specific acts performed were actually authorized or subsequently ratified" is not to be controlling. But what is an agent, in connection with liability for damages? The Norris–La Guardia limitation under which unions were liable for unlawful acts of officers, members, or agents only upon clear proof of actual participation in or authorization of such acts was given up for "the ordinary rules of agency."[66] But this still left great uncertainty. Stewards and committeemen in a plant under contract deal with grievances as a part of their work. Are they agents? Is the union responsible, and liable for damages, if a strike is held to be in violation of contract? And what of the respective liabilities of a local union and its international? Much litigation would be necessary to clarify the effect of the changed definition on union liability for damages.

Taft-Hartley thus for the first time brought suability for violation of agreements under federal law and the jurisdiction of the district courts. The result of this and also of many of the state laws is in striking contrast to what obtained a little less than a generation ago.[67] As is well known, in Britain, where modern unionism had its birth,

64. *Supra*, ch. 9, p. 361.
65. For significance of the word "cause," see *supra*, ch. 12, p. 429.
66. Cf. *supra*, pp. 487–88, and ch. 12, pp. 443–44.
67. Cf. Millis and Montgomery, *op. cit.*, pp. 661–67.

collective agreements have generally been only moral obligations,[68] not contracts at law. On the continent of Europe, on the other hand, collective agreements generally in the course of time became binding contracts in a mass of government regulations, until "free unions" were extensively placed under a ban with the growth of fascism. In the United States prior to 1920 the situation was roughly the same as in Great Britain then and now. In that year, however, a New York Supreme Court held that an agreement between the manufacturers and the Ladies' Garment Workers was a contract at law, and the three-year contract which had been signed by the parties and then widely violated by the employers was reinstated by court order for the remainder of its term.[69] Beginning in that way, the courts in state after state, but not in all, came to hold that joint agreements were enforceable contracts at law, as in cases involving "runaway shops" and unlawful strikes. The consequence was that joint agreements were given legal validity by the courts in many states and by statute in some others, as in California, Minnesota, Wisconsin, and Colorado. Only a small minority of the states had not fallen into line before 1947. But, of course, the difficulties and inadequacies to which reference has been made had application in breach of contracts as well as in the general field of legal liability.

Suability in federal courts for breach of collective bargaining contracts was agreed upon in the Conference Committee, but the section was in a sense a product of the vetoed Case Bill of 1946 and of the bill introduced early in 1947 by Senator Ball, acting for Senator Taft and other minority members of the Senate Committee of the Seventy-ninth Congress. The aim was described in the report on the Senate bill in April. Collective bargaining contracts were to be equally binding and enforceable on both parties. In the judgment of the committee, breaches of collective agreement had become so numerous that the aggrieved party should have a right of action in the federal courts, in addition to making such breaches unfair labor practices under the Act as was proposed but finally not done. Such a policy was considered completely in accord with the purpose of the Wagner Act, which, as the committee paraphrased a Supreme Court decision, was "to compel employers to bargain collectively with their employees to

68. Under exceptional circumstances the Taff Vale precedent of 1901 permitting damages against a union for breach of contract might be used under the Trade Union Act of 1927. *Ibid.*, pp. 495–97.

69. Schlesinger v. Quinto, 192 N.Y.S. 564 (1921) affirmed 201 App. Div. 489 (1922).

the end that an employment contract, binding on both parties, should be made."[70]

But Senator Taft pointed out the procedural difficulties, that the laws of many states "make it difficult to sue effectively and to recover a judgment against an unincorporated labor union. It is difficult to reach the funds of a union to satisfy a judgment against it. In some states it is necessary to serve all the members before an action can be maintained against the union. This is an almost impossible process." In addition, the Norris–La Guardia Act and similar laws in many states "insulated labor unions, in the field of injunctions, against liability for breach of contract." Federal and state courts had held that strikes in breach of a collective agreement involved a "labor dispute" under these Acts so as to make the activity not enjoinable except under very limited conditions.[71] Moreover, in the absence of federal laws giving either an employer or even the government itself "any right of action against a union for any breach of contract, . . . there is no 'substantive right' to enforce, in order to make the union suable as such in Federal courts."

On the problem of violation of contracts Senator Taft appropriately quoted the President's statement to the Labor-Management Conference of 1945, that: "Contracts once made must be lived up to. . . . If we expect confidence in agreements made, there must be responsibility and integrity on both sides in carrying them out." The Senator continued:

> If unions can break agreements with relative impunity, then such agreements do not tend to stabilize industrial relations. The execution of an agreement does not by itself promote industrial peace. The chief advantage which an employer can reasonably expect from a collective agreement is assurance of uninterrupted operation during the term of the agreement. Without some effective method of assuring freedom from economic warfare for the term of the agreement, there is little reason why an employer would desire to sign such a contract.
>
> Consequently, to encourage the making of agreements and to promote industrial peace through faithful performance by the parties, collective agreements affecting interstate commerce should be enforceable in the Federal courts. . . .
>
> It is apparent that until all jurisdictions, and particularly the Federal Government, authorize actions against labor unions as legal entities, there will not be the mutual responsibility necessary to vitalize collective-

70. *Taft Report,* pp. 15–18; H. J. Heinz Co. v. NLRB, 311 U.S. 514, 525–26 (1941).

71. Citing Wilson & Co. v. Birl *et al.,* 105 F. 2d 948 (C.C.A.3, 1939); Nevins v. Kasmach, 279 N.Y. 323; Bulkin v. Sacks, 31 Pa., D and C 501.

bargaining agreements. The Congress has protected the right of workers to organize. It has passed laws to encourage and promote collective bargaining.

Statutory recognition of the collective agreement as a valid, binding, and enforceable contract is a logical and necessary step. It will promote a higher degree of responsibility upon the parties to such agreements, and will thereby promote industrial peace.

The report emphasized that the bill provided for suits by unions and against unions as legal entities in the federal courts in disputes affecting commerce but that

only the assets of the union can be attached to satisfy a money judgment against it; the property of the individual members of the organization would not be subject to any liability under such a judgment. Thus the members of the union would secure all the advantages of limited liability without incorporation of the union.

Several of the Senator's points are questionable, notably his assumption that the problem can primarily be solved by liability in the courts, also his assumption as to the extent of the problem, and the implication that violation of contracts occurs more frequently on the part of unions than of employers. In addition, though the Senator apparently assumed that employers always have a legal liability, the Taft report was directed specifically at unions. Of course, that assumption was not always true and especially in those states where, in 1947, collective agreements had not by statute or court decision become enforceable contracts. In some cases employers had as much freedom under the law to breach contracts as had labor organizations. The writer, however, is of the opinion that in view of American developments and problems, collective bargaining agreements should be enforceable contracts if and when the basic labor law is appropriately equalized. Yet he feels very strongly that suits for damages should be avoided except as a last resort and after certain other proceedings had been complied with, lest such suits should tend to make collective bargaining more difficult and add to its problems and perhaps undermine representative government in industry. We turn to a discussion of issues and possible problems which should spell "caution."

Problems arise with most collective bargaining contracts and especially in plants in which unions are new and awkward or in which management is inclined to think too much in terms of prerogatives based upon what it had done in nonunion days and is not inclined to make such adjustments as may be necessary in successful industrial relations. Frequently one hears the argument from technical lawyers and others that real estate contracts, insurance contracts,

505

ordinary business contracts, and contracts generally are regularly binding and enforceable in the courts; why, then, should not collective bargaining contracts be likewise binding for the term and when breached give basis for suits for damages? But it should be noted that not all "contracts" are alike or lend themselves to the same treatment, including enforcement in the courts. The usual commercial contract defines a limited relationship. A collective bargaining agreement is different. During every working hour, every workday, every week, every month in a contract period, management and employees must be in the mine, mill, or factory and work together for better or for worse and perhaps under changing conditions. Management is the chief administrator and necessarily makes many decisions which may affect the wages or working conditions of employees. The union, under an agreement, is usually entitled only to present grievances—except on a new bargaining day when the contract can be "opened" under specified conditions and new terms perhaps then agreed upon. Of course the union may charge explicitly that management has violated the agreement. Appeal then is made to the grievance machinery, which is a regular part of the contract in most cases, and should be in absolutely all, including provision for final determination of any disputes on the interpretation and application of the agreement.[72] But in any event most grievances are naturally charged against management as the chief administrator in the mine or factory in the day's work. And not always are grievances handled promptly or consistently or according to the written contract. Breaches of agreements are not committed by labor alone.

Uppermost in difficulties which arise under contracts are day-to-day things calling for adjustment in some way or other. But, in addition to these, there are occasionally lockouts and more often strikes in violation of agreements. Yet the strikes are more often "stoppages" in a department or an occupational group or by dissident groups than by the employees generally. Some of these have cause, some of them not. "Slowdowns" may occur, but not infrequently in such cases workers have been required or think they have been required to work faster than formerly or normally, or with different materials and with newly introduced mechanical devices which may affect earnings and number of jobs substantially. Or better quality on quotas or on piece work may have been called for. With change more or less normal in most industries, such problems are to be ex-

72. This was the unanimous recommendation of the Labor-Management Conference of 1945. *Supra*, ch. 8, p. 309.

506

pected. Most of them call for quick adjustment as grievances by union and management in a spirit of decent co-operation and by developing understanding and toleration. Only experienced management and seasoned union officials can know of the importance of change in the course of time covered by one-, two-, or three-year agreements. Recall, for example, changes in the cost of living, in rates of wages and hours of work around about in industry or a community, or in the availability of labor. These called for many changes by agreement or by War Labor Board order during World War II. Recall also the introduction of bonuses, welfare funds, or other things by even unorganized industry. Certainly in many respects a collective bargaining contract is quite frequently unlike other business contracts, in which suits at law may provide a fitting remedy in case of violation.

Indeed some competent authorities, not relatively inexperienced persons or mere technical lawyers, have said that a collective bargaining agreement is not a contract in the full legal sense.[73] The element of truth in this must be recognized. This element differs, however, between agreements of different types. There are at one extreme those, as in the Chicago clothing industry, which may begin with a preamble and statement of policy, set a few explicit standards relating to wages and hours, provide a system of consultation on problems and perhaps establish a Trade Board or a Board of Arbitration to fill in a lot of detail as cases arise in which agreement has failed between the "house" and union representatives. Compare the first Hart Schaffner & Marx agreement of 1911 and a relatively few amendments or additions made by the firm and union by 1919, with the sizable booklet of the latter year which combined with these explicit things much "common law" made chiefly by decisions of the Trade Board and Board of Arbitration. Near the other extreme, take the agreement between General Motors and the UAW which covered explicitly what should be the rule on many points and provided for an umpire who in settling disputes should not add to or subtract from the printed page or make any decision not based directly and explicitly upon the language of the little "Green Pamphlet." In some industries agreements have been spelled out even in greater detail. Some of them are all but statutes effective in the plant or the larger bargaining unit.

Most agreements contain provision for grievance machinery as a minimum, and only less so some provision for voluntary or for self-imposed compulsory arbitration of disputes arising. But Taft-Hartley

73. Cf. Gregory, *op. cit.*, p. 381.

contained no explicit provision for the use of such machinery as a condition of filing suit for damages for breach of contract. Should it not have done so in the furtherance of collective bargaining? The courts could first of all see that the grievance machinery had been used, or else refer the case back to the principals involved. But would it then be too late in the specific case? An additional step should also receive consideration. Should not the acceptance or spurning of official attempts to mediate and the acceptance or rejection of arbitration of certain types of disputes have found place in Section 301?[74] Taft-Hartley left all such matters to be disposed of by collective bargaining, or, it may be, to the discretion of the courts.

Suits for damages for violation of collective agreements were to be heard under Taft-Hartley by an appropriate district court. The question has been raised whether the decisions should be made by district courts, heavily committed as they are, with a great variety of questions to decide and seldom well fitted to hear and decide labor-management cases.[75] The 1947 Act opened their doors to damage suits, however small. If breach of contract cases are to be litigated, the question should be raised whether such cases should rather be heard and decided by specialized labor courts, established and with judges appointed for that specific purpose. Attention may be directed to the "labor courts" established in Germany and other European countries when collective bargaining agreements were recognized and made binding at law. This has been seriously advocated here.[76] Such a development could well be expected if suits multiplied and government played an increasing role in these matters. What then as to the effect of the new provisions for suits in federal courts on the volume of litigation?

The question raised cannot as yet be answered with any degree of certainty, though it seemed to be the view of the sponsors of Taft-Hartley that Section 301 would beget an increased sense of responsi-

74. This would be in harmony with the statement of policy in Sec. 201 in regard to the desirability of settling issues through the processes of conference and collective bargaining, with the aid where desirable of governmental facilities for mediation, conciliation, and voluntary arbitration. Cf. *infra*, ch. 15, p. 569; cf. also the provision of Sec. 8 of the Norris–La Guardia Act denying injunctive relief to any complainant "who has failed to make every reasonable effort to settle such dispute either by negotiation or with the aid of any available governmental machinery of mediation or voluntary arbitration."

75. An interesting discussion of this and related matters may be found in *Taft Report*, Pt. 2, *Minority Views*, submitted by Senator Thomas on S. 1126, for himself and Senators Murray and Pepper, esp. pp. 12–15.

76. Cf. Ludwig Teller, *A Labor Policy for America* (New York: Baker, Voorhis & Co., Inc., 1945).

bility in relationships and make for industrial peace. But immediate attitudes on the part both of management and of organized labor, and any changes in behavior resulting, do not lead yet to any sure conclusions on such matters. It must be acknowledged that organized labor generally resented Taft-Hartley because, in some respects with reason, it regarded that law as antiunion. Moreover, had some of the change effected been accomplished in a different manner, the adverse reaction would have been less. In the industrial field, however, there was some evidence of changes in union behavior, but much of this was explainable chiefly by the feeling that labor was on the end of a very short stick and needed to find ways out of its plight.

On the other side of the struggle there was considerable elation on the part of that fraction of management which has been approximately an equal cause of difficulties in the field of industrial relations. Some desired to exercise fully any new "rights" under a very much changed law which, in our opinion, contained much that is not desirable. Yet it is quite evident that some, if not most, of the leaders who had much to do in realizing a large part of what they had desired through amended law, in the first year were strongly advising management to be very careful, in order to "sell" what had been secured from the Congress and to keep in mind an election year. The evidence is clear and widespread. The year 1948, therefore, meant little as compared to what might be fact in 1949 and the years to follow.

We doubt very much whether these more ready and extended suability provisions would long be of great importance, even to those lawyers who devote much of their time to practicing labor law. No doubt Section 301 could mean much in some concrete cases, but it was not likely to be resorted to widely or for long.[77] The chief reasons for this belief are two: that many suits which might be brought against unions simply will not pay out in the case of those who are in business and wish to remain there to make a profit; and that there are too many ways for labor organizations to avoid any great financial responsibilities placed upon them by law.

On the first point, we must emphasize again that industrial relations have to do with problems involved in living and working together. Sound, friendly relations between labor and management for the greater part must be worked out in the plant rather than sought through litigation. Litigation should be avoided in nearly all cases which do not justify resort to a divorce court were they marital prob-

77. Cf. *infra*, pp. 512–13.

lems. Losses in court fights in the field of industrial relations may not, indeed frequently do not, end with the close of damage suits. To emphasize this point an extreme case may be cited. This occurred in an eastern city under an excellent trade agreement, providing for good grievance procedure, and, in event of failure of the grievance committee to solve a problem, recourse to the services of a standing arbitrator, who was authorized to impose penalties for damages. The agreement was between an association and a union of men whose work involved the handling of incoming and outgoing freight and parcels. One of the members of the association felt that more than a tolerable number of mistakes had been made in handling his wares. Under the contract, the issue of fact went finally to arbitration. The award found for the "house" and imposed damages in the sum of $3,000. This sum was promptly paid, and without official objections or protest. After some weeks the union official who had signed and transmitted the check received a note from the manager of the plant stating in effect, "Why not let bygones be bygones? Find inclosed your check for $3,000." Our guess is that there had been an increase in the number of mishandlings of freight and parcels but each such case appeared as a natural one—"due to accident." Of course, we do not know which party had actually been in the right. Our point is only that in industrial relations human nature is involved. Anyone who thinks largely in terms of proscriptions, and some sponsors of Taft-Hartley seem to do so, might profit from a study of the record of compulsory arbitration in New Zealand and Australia. Whether or not compulsory arbitration has made for industrial peace is still argued there, but, we think, the case for it has not been made out. Experience in Canada under the Industrial Relations Acts also deserves attention, before and after the approach to cases was altered, and mediation, with discretion, emphasized by the administrators of the "compulsory investigation" system.[78]

Our second point relates to a very large number of changes in agreements in the months after the new Act became effective, in order to avoid or limit union liability under suits at law. Unions felt a very real threat to their treasuries and therefore to their ability to survive and function under the law. This attitude and its basis was perhaps rather typically expressed in a personal letter from a responsible union official, which may be quoted:

The real and present danger of suits designed to weaken the unions and to break their treasuries because of real or fancied violations, and the gen-

78. Cf. discussion in Millis and Montgomery, *op. cit.*, ch. 14.

eral atmosphere in which this power is given to employers, plus—and this is the determining factor—the fact that trade unions are deprived by Taft-Hartley of the power to discipline their members, and plus the fact that the Taft-Hartley Law creates, in effect, a new law of agency, wherein unions may be held responsible for the acts of persons construed to be their agents whether such acts are authorized or not, all these things combine to make a "no-strike clause" a civilized luxury which a union can no longer afford in the labor relations jungle planted by Messrs. Taft, Hartley, et al.

A statement by a CIO spokesman to the Joint Congressional Committee also is in point:

> The damage suit provisions . . . jeopardize the mature development of the grievance-arbitration mechanism. Moreover, these provisions place in the hands of antilabor employers a means of blackmailing a union. Damage suits are typically instituted not to make an employer whole for a claimed breach of contract, but to bleed a union and destroy its treasury.
>
> Because damage suits pose such a tremendous threat to the very existence of the labor organizations they embitter industrial relations. Where a strike is accompanied by a damage suit, as is not infrequently the case, the striking union is forced to prolong its contest with the employer until adequate provision is made for the settlement of the damage suit.[79]

Whether, or to what extent, such fears were justified, many unions adopted a policy that they would sign "no-strike" agreements only with clauses clearly limiting their liability to suit. The International Harvester and the Ford agreements in August, 1947, were the first widely publicized "limited liability" agreements.[80] The Ball Committee[81] commented that clauses in which a union's responsibility in the event of an unauthorized strike was clearly defined and its liability to suit limited were becoming quite common. On these clauses Professor Cox,[82] an eminent legal scholar, said:

> There can be little doubt of the effectiveness of these methods of guarding a union against a potentially crushing liability. The practice of including

79. *Ball Committee Hearings,* Pt. 2, p. 704, June 4, 1948.

80. Discussed *infra,* ch. 16, pp. 637–38. Cf. discussion *supra,* ch. 6, pp. 193–96, of cases under the Wagner Act involving discharge of strikers where the strike was found to be in violation of the contract. In 1946–47 as a result there were signs of reluctance of unions to sign no-strike agreements, and the beginning of a movement to define and limit liability. The United Mine Workers' bituminous agreement of July, 1947, provided for the elimination of any "no-strike" or penalty clauses and stated that the agreement covered employment in the bituminous coal mines "while such persons are able and willing to work."

81. *Ball Committee Report,* Pt. 1, March 15, 1948, p. 38.

82. Archibald Cox, "Some Aspects of the Labor Management Relations Act, 1947," *Harvard Law Review,* 61 (1947–48), 308–12. For another discussion of the probable legal effects of such clauses cf. "Union Escape Clauses and the Taft-Hartley Act," *Columbia Law Review,* 48 (1948), 105–19.

"no strike" clauses in collective bargaining agreements was by no means universal when Section 301 was enacted, and although Congress undoubtedly assumed that the practice would spread, rather than diminish, Section 301 does not require their inclusion in any form. The question was raised specifically before the Senate Committee, which concluded that the inclusion of such a clause was "a point to be bargained over" in collective negotiations. The same reasoning would appear to sustain the validity of an exculpatory clause or covenant not to sue.

We may add that in some instances Section 301 served a useful purpose in forcing management and unions to face up to the problem of their joint responsibility for discipline and sound relations and resulted in an effort to design a more workable system which would protect the legitimate interests of all concerned. And some unions may have seen the wisdom of increased effort on the matter of their responsibility to prevent "quickies." But against this was the addition of another difficult point to be threshed out in negotiations at a time when suspicions were rife, on the one side of intent to evade the law, and on the other of intent to use the Act to weaken or break unions. And more serious was the invitation to those of management who had not yet learned how to get on with a union in day-to-day dealings to resort to the courts for a solution of difficulties which could finally be solved only by the parties themselves.

Experience under Taft-Hartley emphasized the significance of these questions. There is no way of knowing how often threat of suit under Sections 301 or 303 brought more responsible efforts to settle issues by collective bargaining, or how often they restrained action which unions should have been free to use. Unions complained bitterly of friction, interference with collective bargaining, and unreasonable restraints upon union activities as a result.[83] Relatively few suits were filed in the first year. A number of suits against unions for very substantial sums were initiated, according to newspaper reports, in the first months after Taft-Hartley became effective, but some of them were withdrawn after the dispute was settled. The Ball Committee in its final report[84] stated that approximately fifty-seven suits had been brought under Sections 301 and 303; thirty-seven were brought by employers against unions, nineteen by unions against employers, and one by an employee against an employer. In no case so far as the committee knew had damages been recovered, although more than a third were still pending. The great majority were brought for vio-

83. Cf. *Ball Committee Hearings*, Pt. 2, pp. 703–4, 800, 1044. See also *infra*, ch. 16, pp. 637–39, 646–47.

84. *Ball Committee Report*, Pt. 3, December 31, 1948, p. 31.

lation of contract; frequently a strike was involved, and when the strike was settled the suit was dismissed by agreement. Of all the cases, twenty-one were dismissed by agreement and nine by the court. The committee believed that the suits to date showed that "neither party desires to recover money damages from the other, but that the very presence of this remedy has encouraged employees and unions alike to act with a deeper sense of responsibility"; and "the most pronounced effect of the two sections has been restraint." Our interpretation is that they were used as bargaining weapons; and they may have encouraged resort to the courts rather than promoting responsible efforts for the expeditious settlement of disputes at home.

While we find merit in the general principle incorporated in Section 301, we have experienced a dwindling faith in suits at law in the field of industrial relations. This is explained by experience at home and elsewhere. But most of all we feel that any deficiencies in Sections 301 and 303 as adopted are relatively unimportant compared to what we regard as more essential matters—an unacceptable basic labor law, proscriptions such as those on welfare funds and union security and other matters which theretofore had been left to collective bargaining, and an indicated desire to weaken unions and their control of nonmembers in collective bargaining units,[85] while talking in terms of increased responsibilities for the observance of contracts. The chief objections are not found in Sections 301 and 303 themselves so much as in other parts of Taft-Hartley which provide the setting in which these sections are found.

85. See *supra* concerning the handling of grievances of nonunion members, ch. 12, pp. 453–54.

CHAPTER 14

REPRESENTATION AND ELECTIONS
UNDER TAFT-HARTLEY

UNDER the Wagner Act the provisions for determining the representatives of employees, when a majority chose to engage in collective bargaining, were of central importance for achieving the purposes of the Act. Through the years, as these purposes received increasing acceptance, more and more of the time of the Board and its staff was devoted to the handling of representation cases, which cleared away disputes over recognition and made it possible for the parties to proceed with collective bargaining. Taft-Hartley, in its Section 9, continued the basic system of majority rule and the provisions for settling disputes over recognition. But again the net result was somewhat different because of changes in the context and the addition of new provisions which reflected different assumptions from those of the Wagner Act. Here and there, both in limiting the discretion of the Board and in provisions for new types of elections, the benefit of any doubt seemed to be given to those who oppose collective bargaining rather than to those who want it and believe it sound public policy to encourage its acceptance. Some of the changes made were minor and created no serious difficulty. Some of them met criticisms which possibly had some foundation, or at least were widely believed to have. But others threw their weight against recognition of unions and collective bargaining as a stable, more or less permanent institution. Their influence was for instability, and therefore we think tended to bring insecurity, fear, and bad industrial relations, unless employers exercised self-restraint and took a farsighted view.

The basic policy is indicated in Section 9(b), where the Board was instructed to decide the unit appropriate for collective bargaining "in order to assure to employees the fullest freedom in exercising the rights guaranteed by this Act." These rights are the rights guaranteed by Section 7, to engage in or *to refrain from* engaging in organization, collective bargaining, or other concerted activities. The right to refrain was of course implicit in the Wagner Act, except as it was limited by majority rule established in free elections and by closed-shop contracts entered into by majority representatives. But the Wagner Act set as the standard for the Board in its Section 9(b) "in order to insure to employees the full benefit of their right to self-organization and to collective bargaining, and otherwise to effectuate the policies of this Act." Taft-Hartley in Title II of course carried a statement of faith in collective bargaining as the most satisfactory way to "sound and stable industrial peace and the advancement of the general welfare." But here the emphasis is different. There was great concern in the Eightieth Congress, especially in the House, with giving additional guaranties, "recognizing and protecting . . . the rights and interests of individuals and minorities."[1] The assumption seemed to be that the rights of individuals are trespassed on or denied in many connections by unions or under collective bargaining arrangements. One gets the impression from many of the provisions adopted that individual bargaining is the natural thing and preferable to collective bargaining. This is a question of majority rule and its relation to the rights of individuals and of the group, which appears in any democratic relationship, whether in "public life" or in a narrower field. The issue is whether proper protection of individual rights is to be obtained through the democratic process of fair and uncoerced elections leading to collective bargaining when the majority so choose, with specific protections for individuals or minorities at some points where a need is shown; or whether, on the other hand, it should be sought by encouraging dissenters, nonunion minorities, and antiunion employers. Taft-Hartley was of two minds on all this, but too often, we think, chose the latter approach.

Five types of elections to be conducted by the Board were provided for. First is the basic election for choice as to representation, on petition by unions or employees, or on petition by employers under somewhat broader conditions than had been permitted by the Board under the old Act. Next is an election on petition of a group of employees to "decertify" a union which has been their bargaining representative. Third is the election to authorize a union to make a union-shop agreement; and fourth, on petition of a group of the employees covered, a vote on the question of rescinding the authority previously

1. U.S. House of Representatives, *Conference Report, Labor-Management Relations Act, 1947*, Report No. 510, 80th Cong., 1st Sess., June 3, 1947, p. 47, cited as *House Conference Report*. Cf. discussion of issues as to individual and minority rights under the Wagner Act, *supra*, ch. 7, pp. 250–52.

given to make such agreements. Finally, there is the provision for a vote on the employers' last offers in national emergency cases.

RULES OF PROCEDURE IN REPRESENTATION CASES

A number of changes were made as to procedure. The change in administration, under which by delegation from the Board the General Counsel was responsible for the handling of the representation cases in the field, has been discussed earlier.[2] Fortunately for the interest of unified policy, the Board reserved to itself the right to decide any appeals from the General Counsel's action on representation cases in the regional offices. When cases could not be handled by informal procedures, and formal hearing was necessary, the Hearing Officer was to report to the Board without any recommendation. This is a specific regulation of procedure for which we can find no justification in the record. Elections held by consent of the parties, without hearing, were still permissible, thus enabling speedy handling of a great many cases. But the language of the Act no longer permitted agreements for a cross-check of union cards against pay rolls as a basis for informal determination of a representation dispute under Board auspices.[3] The Board had decided years before that in general the secret election was the safest and fairest way of determining whether employees wished a representative for collective bargaining; but, for the occasional case where consent cross-checks were used, certain safeguards were set up. The statutory restriction is of minor importance but an unwarranted limitation on the Board's discretion.

More important is the fact that prehearing elections also were excluded by Section 9(c)(1) and (4). This device, under which in simple cases an election was held before hearing, subject to the right of either party to challenge any voters and to request a hearing and Board decision on issues in dispute, was used with marked success in the last two years of the Wagner Act. It resulted in a substantial saving of time in many cases, to the advantage of all concerned.[4] But on the insistence of the House, for reasons not apparent in the record, this was excluded in conference, although it had been in the Senate bill. Senator Taft was clearly under a misapprehension as to the facts when he reported to the Senate that "its use has been confined to an

2. *Supra*, ch. 11, pp. 402–9, esp. p. 405.
3. Sec. 9(c)(4). For Wagner Act experience and policy cf. *supra*, ch. 5, pp. 133–34.
4. *Supra*, ch. 2, pp. 62–63.

516

inconsequential percentage of cases, and more often than not a subsequent hearing was still necessary."[5] Here again the Board was limited in its freedom to solve administrative problems at its own discretion in the light of experience. In addition, unnecessary resort to formal procedures was encouraged. Here we find another indication of "a technical lawyers' Act."

Another specific limitation upon the Board's discretion was the requirement in Section 9(c)(3) that no election should be *directed* in any bargaining unit within which a valid election had been held during the preceding twelve months. This was interpreted to include consent elections, also. The effect was to protect a union which won a representation election from attack by a rival union or from a petition for decertification for at least one year. On the other hand, if a union lost an election or a union was decertified, no second election could be held during that year even if the original union or another obtained support of a large majority within that period.

Under the Wagner Act the Board in the interest of stability had developed its one-year rule that normally a certification or a contract would bar another election for a year.[6] But when no union had been chosen and a later petition was filed even within a year, the Board considered all the circumstances, including the showing of representation made by the petitioning union, in deciding whether the purposes of the Act would be served by a new election. But Taft-Hartley laid down a rigid rule. Senator Taft considered that this limitation would "impress upon employees the solemnity of their choice" and avoid "a constant stirring up of excitement by continual elections."[7] But conditions change and exceptional circumstances arise as they did during the war and reconversion periods in which it is sound to hold an election and settle a representation question when it appears. If a substantial shift of union membership has taken place, it may be desirable to hold an election promptly in order to determine the desired representative in time to bargain at the end of the contract in effect. Most serious, however, is the question whether a lost election should foreclose the possibility of collective bargaining for an entire year. Here the right of collective bargaining was thought of less im-

5. *Daily Cong. Rec.*, 93:7002.

6. *Supra*, ch. 5, pp. 157–59. In some circumstances contracts of longer duration also were upheld as bars to elections.

7. U.S. Senate, Committee on Labor and Public Welfare, *Federal Labor Relations Act of 1947*, Report No. 105, 80th Cong., 1st Sess., April 17, 1947, p. 12, cited as *Taft Report. Daily Cong. Rec.*, 93:3954. In reality there were relatively few "repeat elections." *Supra*, ch. 3, p. 91.

portance than the right not to bargain and the desirability of avoiding agitation. But the question is whether the latter would be avoided by this rule should a strong movement for representation develop.

Dangers to the right of employees to organize and bargain were inherent also in the one-year rule in conjunction with the next sentence in Section 9(c)(3): "Employees on strike who are not entitled to reinstatement shall not be eligible to vote." Under the Wagner Act the Board had developed the policy that during a strike caused by unfair labor practices only the strikers were eligible to vote, since they were entitled to reinstatement; but in a strike over economic matters any replacements and those still on strike were eligible. In an "economic strike" of course the employer had the right to replace strikers if he could, but the Board held that it was impossible to tell during such a strike whether or not the strikers would return to their jobs.[8] Strikers who were found to have been validly discharged for improper conduct, however, could not vote.[9] Although it was possible under this policy for there to be more voters than jobs, this had seemed to the Board the most workable solution for an extremely difficult problem. Taft-Hartley, in spite of some feeling for a still stricter rule, declared only that strikers not entitled to reinstatement were not entitled to vote. Right to reinstatement, however, would be affected by the fact that the new unfair labor practice provisions extended the types of activities which might be held to justify discharge.[10] Even more important was the difficulty of deciding during a strike which strikers are not entitled to reinstatement because their places have been permanently filled; and the justice of the policy itself was questionable. The Board when it had to act on this problem decided to allow all strikers to vote subject to challenge. Should the challenged ballots affect the result of the election, the question as to which of them should be opened and counted would await "a further investigation concerning the employment status of the individual strikers and their replacements." In this first case the Board finally sustained the challenges of all the strikers' ballots and overruled the challenges of the striking union to the ballots of the replacements and of the prestrike employees who had returned to work. It held that the strikers had been permanently replaced. To the union's contention that to deny the right to vote to the strikers was to sanction a strikebreaking device and to place such hazards upon the exercise of

8. *Supra*, ch. 5, p. 136.
9. *Supra*, ch. 6, pp. 189–203.
10. Cf. *supra*, ch. 12, pp. 429–30.

the right to strike as to make it a nullity, the Board could only say that it was its duty to administer the Act as written.[11]

All this may appear a reasonable enough solution, since collective bargaining assumes that employer and union must be allowed to settle their economic dispute by the use of economic weapons when an impasse has been reached. But Senators Murray and Pepper pointed to danger that the antiunion employer was here given a weapon with which to break a union. As the latter said: "Under the bill all an employer has to do is to provoke his workers to strike, recruit replacements, and put them in permanent status, and call for an election, if there has not been an election in a year, and his new strike-breakers would elect new representatives, and the old union would be effectively disposed of."[12] And, in addition, should such a plan work and the old union be displaced, a full year would pass before it or another union could obtain another Board election. Thus "no-bargaining" was protected for a full year. This matter of strikers' voting was important in a number of bitterly fought struggles during the first year. The issue was posed whether this policy was sound or whether rather policy should not be to encourage prompt settlement of strikes. This provision promoted conflict.[13]

Another matter which had long troubled the Board was removed from its field of discretion by the requirement as to run-off ballots, in Section 9(c)(3). In the case of an inconclusive election involving two or more contesting unions, in the run-off election the ballot was

11. Pipe Machinery Co., 76 NLRB 247; 79 NLRB 1322 (1948). With 160 voters eligible, the union had challenged all 74 nonstrikers, and the company or the new independent union had challenged all the 74 strikers. For similar cases cf. Cory Corp., 78 NLRB 923 (1948), 84 NLRB No. 110 (July, 1949); Colonial Hardware Flooring Co., 76 NLRB 1039 (1948), 84 NLRB No. 69 (1949). Cf. also NLRB, *Thirteenth Annual Report,* pp. 32–33. U.S. Congress, Joint Committee on Labor-Management Relations, *Hearings on Operation of Labor Management Relations Act, 1947,* 80th Cong., 2d Sess., Pt. 2, pp. 1046–47, cited as *Ball Committee Hearings; infra,* ch. 16, pp. 631, 640–41.

12. *Daily Cong. Rec.,* 93:6686.

13. For an able and interesting analysis of the striker vote provisions see B. H. Levy, "Eligibility of Strikers To Vote Under the Taft-Hartley Act," *Personnel,* 25 (1948), 60–71. "This provision . . . will bring aid and comfort to those harassed employers who are saddled with a racketeering or otherwise corrupt union. . . . They may now battle with greater confidence of success. A responsible employer with a responsible union would doubtless not wish to upset his satisfactory and stable labor relations. Such an employer would doubtless close his plant during a strike and wait for it to subside. On the other hand, anti-union employers may wish to exploit this provision . . ." (p. 68). "The provision . . . is a concentration of 'atomic energy' which may be used for good or ill, depending on the wisdom of those endowed with the power to apply it in any given situation" (p. 71).

to provide a selection between the two choices which received the largest numbers of votes, whether two unions or one and a "no-union" option. Concern was expressed over the existing practice of the Board as to run-offs, finally adopted in 1943, which as the House Committee described it was "to compel employees, except in rare instances, to choose between the two leading unions unless, in the first balloting, the no-union vote was highest."[14] The solution chosen in the new Act had the obvious advantage of simplicity and apparent fairness. Yet it should be noted that representation elections are different from political elections. In the latter only one question is involved; in the other there are two: (1) Do we desire representation? (2) If so, by whom? The Board had found that no workable system could be devised that did not involve some assumptions as to what voters meant in such elections. Did a majority mean that they wanted collective bargaining, whatever the representative? Or that they wanted it only if their first choice was selected? It is impossible to know on the evidence of the first election. On the whole we consider the new rule acceptable; yet this solution gives the benefit of the doubt to the non-union minority rather than to the divided majority who voted for a representative, in the case where the no-union vote ran second. Here again the provision reflects a greater emphasis on minority rights than on the interests of those who want unionization and collective bargaining.

RULES OF DECISION IN REPRESENTATION CASES

Many of the major rules which the Board developed over the years for the handling of representation petitions were left unchanged, although at a number of points the Board's discretion was limited by a more or less specific rule incorporated in the Act. Early decisions indicated that the Board expected to continue such policies as those on the required showing of interest to be presented by a petitioning union, timeliness of petitions, and the conditions under which an existing contract constitutes a bar to an election.[15] The basic principle continued, of course, that the representative chosen by the majority of the employees is the exclusive representative of all the employees for collective bargaining purposes. But this was possibly weakened, to an extent not sure, by an addition to the Wagner Act

14. U.S. House of Representatives, Committee on Education and Labor, *Labor-Management Relations Act, 1947*, Report No. 245, 80th Cong., 1st Sess., April 11, 1947, p. 38, cited as *Hartley Report*. For discussion of the issues and the evolution of Board policy, cf. *supra*, ch. 5, pp. 134–35.

15. *Supra*, ch. 5; *Thirteenth Annual Report*, pp. 26–32.

proviso as to the right of individuals to present grievances, of the right to have them "adjusted without the intervention of the bargaining representative."[16]

Section 9(c)(2) required that in representation cases "the same regulations and rules of decision shall apply irrespective of the identity of the persons filing the petition or the kind of relief sought"; and in effect that no labor organization should be denied a place on a ballot by reason of an order which had discriminated against an unaffiliated union. This related of course to the rules of decision in company-dominated union cases, and the feeling that "independents" had been the subject of discrimination by the Board. The misapprehension as to what the Board had done and the issues involved have been adequately discussed earlier.[17]

THE APPROPRIATE UNIT

The most important changes in the rules of decision in representation cases had to do with collective bargaining units. Decisions on unit issues, like others, were to assure the fullest freedom of workers to engage in or to *refrain from* concerted activities. The rules were expected to result in "a substantially larger measure of protection" of "the rights and interests of individuals and minorities."[18] Here again the emphasis is to be noted; but should the interest of minorities have greater weight than that of a majority?

First we must note the complete exclusion of supervisors from the Act's definition of "employee" and therefore from any right to constitute an "appropriate unit" or to claim protection for collective bargaining purposes from the Board.[19] A related question was that of plant guards, whom the House wished similarly to exclude from the protection of the Act, for fear of "divided loyalty." The Senate accepted a compromise by which the Board was instructed not to include any guard in a collective bargaining unit of rank-and-file employees, or to certify any union as the representative for a unit of guards if it included or was affiliated with any organization which included the rank and file.[20] The Board's policy had been that militarized and monitorial guards could be represented only in a separate unit, but they could choose the same union as that representing production and maintenance employees. Nonmonitorial watchmen and

16. Sec. 9(a), discussed *supra*, ch. 12, pp. 453–54.
17. *Ibid.*, pp. 426–28.
18. *House Conference Report*, p. 47.
19. Secs. 2(3), 2(11), 14(a); *supra*, ch. 11, pp. 399–400.
20. Sec. 9(b)(3).

guards, however, could be included in units of production and maintenance employees. The Board's position was upheld by a divided Supreme Court[21] in May, 1947, while the Conference Committee was at work; but the conferees preferred the reasoning of the circuit court which had set aside the Board's order. Guards therefore could not be represented by any union affiliated with the AFL or CIO, even when collective bargaining had proceeded on the other basis without special problem.[22] The Board felt constrained to apply the section even in the case of ordinary watchmen having no disciplinary powers against other employees; but it raised question with the Ball Committee as to whether Congress desired the Board to enforce so strict a rule.[23] Professional employees also had special treatment, with the requirement that the Board might not include both professional and nonprofessional employees in a unit unless a majority of the former voted for inclusion. Such separate vote by the professional group had been usual in Board practice, and only rarely had real professionals been merged in units of other employees.

The long controversial craft-unit issue was the subject of the major amendment as to units. The House, with its interest in greater freedom of choice for smaller, separate groups of employees, had wished to require the Board to hold separate elections on request of any craft, or any other distinguishable group, and to include them in a broad unit only if a majority of the group so voted.[24] The Senate's more flexible clause was adopted, however, and the provision in Section 9(b)(2) provided that the Board should not "decide that any craft unit is inappropriate . . . on the ground that a different unit has been established by a prior Board determination, unless a majority of the employees in the proposed craft unit vote against separate representation."

The Wagner Act left the question of "the appropriate unit" to the discretion of the Board to be exercised in the light of the facts. But

21. NLRB v. Jones & Laughlin Steel Corp., 331 U.S. 416 (1947); NLRB v. E. C. Atkins and Co., 331 U.S. 398 (1947); *Daily Cong. Rec.*, 93:6601.

22. Cf. the statement of Louis S. Belkin, of the AFL Chemical Workers. Watchmen and guards had been included in 74 per cent of their bargaining units. He stated that the union would be compelled to change its policy toward work jurisdiction. "If we cannot represent and bargain collectively for watchmen, we must insist for the protection of our members that they shall do no work which comes within the duties of the production and maintenance workers whom we do represent. Thus, a successful, well-tried procedure satisfactory to both management and labor has been destroyed by misdirected legislation." *Ball Committee Hearings*, Pt. 1, pp. 250–51; cf. *infra*, ch. 16, p. 643.

23. *Ball Committee Hearings*, Pt. 2, p. 1126.

24. *House Conference Report*, p. 47.

the problem posed by the conflicts over craft versus industrial units by a very active, divided labor movement was perhaps the most difficult and complex problem with which the Board dealt.[25] Many employers in industries where bargaining on an industrial basis is well established are loath to find themselves forced to bargain with a number of separate unions. Undoubtedly in some cases the unity and strength of labor organization would be hurt by any extensive process of subdivision. Yet there are cases of small, compact, highly skilled groups of craftsmen who never acceded to bargaining through the industrial union, and for whom there is a strong case for the right to formal recognition for bargaining purposes. But what is a genuine "craft," and where is the line to be drawn, if it is attempted? And can the interests of such groups be protected without extending an invitation to much raiding by hosts of organizers of so-called craft and semicraft organizations which would extend their activities to "organizing the organized"?

After long and disappointing study it seems clear that the issue between the crafts and industrial unionism cannot approach a relatively satisfactory solution until irrational divisions within the labor movement have become a matter of the past. Then and perhaps only then would it be possible to solve the problem by such attitudes toward amalgamation and accommodation between craft and industrial unionism as have been accepted in Britain, Sweden, and other countries. This being true, we think the Taft-Hartley solution, which left the matter largely still to the discretion of the Board, a reasonable approach.

In spite of the widespread assumption that the Act made craft-unit elections mandatory on request, the Board did not find this to be the meaning of Section 9(b)(2). A key decision in a basic steel case held the only restriction to be that a prior determination by the Board or bargaining history "may not be the *sole* ground upon which the Board may decide that a craft unit is inappropriate without an election." In the steel industry, therefore, where there was a long industrial bargaining history, and a close integration of the work of bricklayers with the whole steelmaking process, the Board dismissed the petition for an election among that group of craftsmen. The employers as well as the CIO United Steelworkers had strongly opposed any craft severance in this industry.[26] The Board pointed out that in recent decisions it had been inclined "to exercise discretion in the direction of easing

25. Discussed *supra*, ch. 5, pp. 138–47.
26. National Tube Co., 76 NLRB 1199 (April, 1948).

the path of a union desiring severance of a craft unit." The Board, however, exercised its discretion to determine when true craftsmen should be permitted to break away from established units. "Globe elections"[27] were granted to such crafts as electricians, pattern-makers, operating engineers, machinists, and others, in spite of histories of industrial bargaining in petroleum, smelting, rubber, automobile, aircraft, paper, and other industries, sometimes in the face of objection by employers. But, as in the basic steel case, units of maintenance electricians were denied in assembly-line operations in the automobile industry.[28] In many other instances the Board dismissed craft or departmental petitions where it did not find the necessary conditions, such as "a high degree of skill acquired through a required apprenticeship in a particular field," homogeneity, and interests distinguishable from those of other employees, to justify separate representation. As it said in one case: "Only under these circumstances do we normally find that justification exists for disturbing established relationships; otherwise ever present minority groups of dissident employees would be continually tempted to upset established bargaining patterns, thereby impeding rather than promoting collective bargaining."[29]

Nevertheless, one of the results of the law was expected to be, and clearly was, an increase in attempts to carve out various groups from old established units. Raiding and rivalry were increased, certainly not all of it to the interest of the workers concerned[30] or of management either. The tendency to raiding was increased also by the fact that an industrial union which had not complied with the filing requirements of the Act would not be put on the ballot in a craft-union election, though it had a long history in the plant of contracts on a plant-

27. *Supra,* ch. 5, p. 140.
28. Ford Motor Co. (Maywood Plant), 78 NLRB 887 (August, 1948). Gerard D. Reilly, who had worked with the Senate Committee in writing the Act, is reported to have asked the Board to set off the entire chemical industry, also, and to refuse to permit craft severance there. *Daily Labor Report,* No. 166: A-3, August 25, 1948. In the case involved, Monsanto Chemical Co., 78 NLRB 1249 (August, 1948), the Board dismissed a petition for a unit of pipefitters, largely on the ground of the highly integrated character of operations and the long history of plant-wide collective bargaining, but made no comment on policy as to the industry as a whole.
29. Gulf Oil Corp., 79 NLRB 1274 (October, 1948); *Thirteenth Annual Report,* pp. 36–37.
30. The AFL, commenting on the fact that the Board was construing the craft requirement narrowly, said that, even if this amendment proved beneficial to the AFL, this was not enough "to overbalance the gross inequities of the other portions of the Act." *American Federationist,* 55 (April, 1948), 19.

wide basis. As one management representative pointed out, the provision "can be expected to have a disruptive effect upon many collective bargaining relationships . . . and can prove a major industrial headache." He foresaw possibility of "fragmentation of bargaining units [which] could work havoc to laboriously established wage plans," also jurisdictional disputes and complications between complying and noncomplying unions, along with the increased raiding which was made easier by the watering down of compulsory membership. Most employers, he said, were "alert to the danger but find themselves helpless before what one of them termed 'the balkanization of contracts by craft raids.' "[31]

A further limitation also reflected the concern of the House to protect the interests of those who choose to refrain from collective bargaining. Section 9(c)(5) provided that "in determining whether a unit is appropriate . . . the extent to which the employees have organized shall not be controlling." This, Chairman Hartley reported, "strikes at a practice of the Board by which it has set up as units appropriate for bargaining whatever group or groups the petitioning union has organized at the time."[32] The "extent of organization theory" which the Congressman considered so reprehensible had been based on a belief of the Board that

it is often desirable in the determination of an appropriate unit to render collective bargaining for the employees involved a reasonably early possibility, lest prolonged delay expose the organized employees to the temptation of striking to obtain recognition and permit unorganized employees engaged in other work tasks to thwart collective bargaining by those who have evinced an interest in selecting a representative.[33]

And the Supreme Court had upheld the Board on this.[34]

Senator Taft stated that this theory had been particularly bad when one union organized a small unit and later another came in to organize the remainder. However, he pointed out that the Board had numerous criteria of appropriateness, among them community of interest of the employees involved, which might justify the acceptance of small units.[35] The clause was a warning to the Board to be

31. E. H. Van Delden, "Management Experience under the LMRA," in American Management Association, *Personnel Series*, No. 115 (1948), p. 20. In a survey of management opinion, 40 per cent of 528 employers were opposed to permitting separate craft units where industrial bargaining was then in effect; 45 per cent of those with more than 250 employees were opposed. *Business Week*, August 21, 1948, p. 19.

32. *Hartley Report*, p. 37.   33. *Twelfth Annual Report*, p. 20.

34. NLRB v. Hearst Publications, 322 U.S. 111 (1944).

35. *Daily Cong. Rec.*, 93:7002.

sure that any small unit is justified by all the facts, not only by the extent of organization. This is reasonable and in general in accord with past practice, although the Board had sometimes been divided in its application of this theory. In a department-store case early in 1948 the Board dismissed a refusal-to-bargain complaint, when it decided that the unit of employees in the men's alteration shop set up in an earlier representation case should not have been found appropriate, even before the amendment of the Act. But in a similar case a few weeks later it held that the extent of organization was still one of the factors to be weighed in determining the unit.[36] The section nevertheless militated against the establishment of departmental units.[37]

From the standpoint of those who think collective bargaining should still be encouraged, or at least not discouraged, by government, Senator Pepper's comment is in point: "To deny collective bargaining in areas in which organization has been achieved is to deny it entirely."[38]

EMPLOYEES' FREE CHOICE AND EMPLOYERS' FREE SPEECH

Representation elections under the 1947 Act as well as the old presumably were meant to provide employees the fullest freedom to express their wishes as to whether or not to choose a representative for the purpose of collective bargaining. Always it was a problem for the Board to insure the integrity of elections, and the extent to which employers could enter into election campaigns without interfering with the free choice of employees was a difficult and controversial issue.[39] Under Taft-Hartley these elections were to be held in the context provided by the free-speech amendment, Section 8(c).[40] This section was written as a limitation upon findings of unfair labor practices, but it also affected representation cases. Employers were free to take sides in a pre-election campaign and to go far, even to the extent of requiring employees to listen to antiunion speeches in the plant in advance of the election.[41] The Board, however, still decided the limits beyond which an employer's statements become coercive

36. Carson Pirie Scott & Co., 75 NLRB 1244 (1948); Mandel Brothers, 77 NLRB 512 (1948).
37. *Thirteenth Annual Report*, p. 38.
38. *Daily Cong. Rec.*, 93:6611.
39. *Supra*, ch. 6, pp. 174–89.
40. *Supra*, ch. 12, pp. 422–25.
41. Babcock and Wilcox Co., 77 NLRB 577 (May, 1948), decided by a three-man Board.

because they contain threats of reprisal or promise of benefit. Thus in the case of a bank which told its employees in a letter the week before the election, "If you should join this union, you would find it difficult, if not impossible, to get a job with any other bank or financial institution,"[42] the Board set aside the election, holding the letter to have been "coercive in character and so related to the election in time or otherwise as to have had a probable effect upon the action of the employees at the polls."

In the General Shoe Corporation case[43] the majority of the Board went farther and held that Section 8(c) did not limit the discretion of the Board to set an election aside, in the interest of maintaining the integrity of elections, even if the employer's statements could not be held to be unfair labor practices. In this case, as summarized by the Board, the employer for two months preceding the election had engaged in a course of conduct consisting of "publication, through its supervisors, in letters, in pamphlets, in leaflets, and in speeches, of vigorously disparaging statements concerning the union, which undeniably were calculated to influence the rank and file employees in their choice of a bargaining representative." The statements, however, contained no threat of reprisal or promise of benefit and were considered to be protected by the Act, from the standpoint of an unfair labor practice case. But, in addition, on the day before the election the company's president had all the employees brought to his office in small groups of twenty or so and read to each group the same "intemperate antiunion address." The Board said:

> In our opinion, this *conduct*, and the employer's instructions to its foremen to propagandize employees in their homes, went so far beyond the presently accepted custom of campaigns directed at employees' reasoning faculties that we are not justified in assuming that the election results represented the employees' own true wishes.

The Board then stated its understanding of its function:

> In election proceedings, it is the Board's function to provide a laboratory in which an experiment may be conducted, under conditions as nearly ideal as possible, to determine the uninhibited desires of the employees. It is our duty to establish those conditions; it is also our duty to determine whether they have been fulfilled. When, in the rare extreme case, the standard drops too low, because of our fault or that of others, the requisite laboratory conditions are not present and the experiment must be conducted over again. That is the situation here.

42. LaFayette National Bank of Brooklyn, 77 NLRB 1210 (June, 1948).
43. 77 NLRB 124 (April, 1948).

Accordingly the election was set aside. Mr. Reynolds and Mr. Gray dissented, saying:

> If the expression or dissemination of views, arguments, or opinion by an employer is to be afforded the full freedom which the amended act envisages, it follows that the Board cannot justify setting elections aside merely because the employer avails himself of the protection which the statute specifically provides.

We agree with the majority of the Board that such conduct as found in this case clearly interferes with free choice by the employees and that such elections should not be accepted as a valid expression of the employees' desires. Whether such a distinction between unfair labor practice cases and representation cases was in accord with the intent of the proponents of the free-speech clause is less certain. The General Shoe decision was criticized in Congress and by some employer spokesmen.[44] In a later case, similar in many respects, the majority of the Board distinguished its facts from General Shoe as not so extreme as to warrant setting aside the election, although they considered the employer's conduct "regrettable."[45] Taft-Hartley thus increased the ever present difficulty of drawing a reasonable line, which must be drawn somewhere if free choice is to be protected. The major question, however, is whether it makes for good industrial relations to encourage employers to engage in campaigns against unionization, when the question arises in their plants. This was unquestionably done by Taft-Hartley, which here again promoted conflict rather than peace.

EMPLOYERS' PETITIONS AND DECERTIFICATION ELECTIONS

Important among the "equalizing amendments" were the provisions in Section 9(c)(1) for petitions by employers and for decertification petitions by employees. While the problems of the two are at least in some instances quite different, they were often grouped in discussion and apparently thought of as alternatives for some purposes, even by some employers in considering their own plans. Back of these provisions, again, on the part of at least some of their proponents, was an

44. U.S. Senate, Joint Committee on Labor-Management Relations, *Labor-Management Relations*, Report No. 986, 80th Cong., 2d Sess., Pt. 3, December 31, 1948, pp. 54–55, cited as *Ball Committee Report*.

45. Mallinckrodt Chemical Works, 79 NLRB 1399 (October, 1948). In some other cases where elections were set aside because of employers' interferences it was made very specific that the decision was based on actual unfair labor practices. Hinde & Dauch Paper Co., 78 NLRB 488 (July, 1948). Cf. *infra*, ch. 16, pp. 647–48.

exaggerated interest in dissenting groups, nonunion employees, and individual bargaining. These new types of petitions could be filed by:

(A) by an employee or group of employees or any individual or labor organization acting in their behalf alleging that a substantial number of employees . . . (ii) assert that the individual or labor organization, which has been certified or is being currently recognized by their employer as the bargaining representative, is no longer a representative as defined in section 9(a); or
(B) by an employer, alleging that one or more individuals or labor organizations have presented to him a claim to be recognized as the representative defined in section 9(a). . . .

If the Board upon investigation found "reasonable cause to believe that a question of representation . . . exists," it was to provide for a hearing, and when "a question of representation exists" to order an election.

These provisions were attacked by the minority in both Houses as tending to undermine stability of collective bargaining.[46] The House in fact would have permitted a decertification election at any time, regardless of a contract or the one-year rule. But the Senate form prevailed, and Senator Taft stated that neither of these amendments affected the Board's rules as to dismissal of petitions because of an inadequate showing of representation or the existence of an outstanding collective agreement.[47]

The provision for employer petitions, if properly used and carefully administered, may prove on the whole constructive. The fact that it removed one of the points on which there was widespread complaint of inequality is important.[48] In 1939 when the Board thought it safe to do so, it had opened the right of petition to employers faced with two labor organizations which sought recognition in the same unit or overlapping units. The right would in all probability have been further extended to at least some one-union cases after the war, had it not been for the imminence of congressional action on the matter. It is true that occasionally under the 1939 rule an employer was in an uncomfortable place when one union claimed recognition and tried to obtain it through use of economic pressure, by picket line or boycott, although it neglected to supply evidence of any right as a majority representative through a Board election. The 1947 Act permitted such an employer to petition for an election. In case the employees did not wish representation through the union in question, the employer

46. *Taft Report*, Pt. 2, *Minority Views*, pp. 11–12; *Hartley Report*, pp. 85–86.
47. *Taft Report*, p. 25.   48. *Supra*, ch. 5, pp. 160–63.

and the employees also had the protection of Section 8(b)(4)(B) against a boycott to force recognition of the uncertified union.[49] Thus the unjustifiable organizing tactics used by some unions should be effectively discouraged by these provisions.

An important safeguard is that a petition by the employer was permitted only after a union requested recognition. To thus discourage sometimes-used strategy of a request by a union for recognition before it is ready to prove its claim makes for orderly and responsible behavior, and we see no real objection. More serious is the danger that this extended right of petition would encourage an occasional antiunion employer in refusing to accept a stable unionism and collective bargaining in his plant, and would lead to harassment of the incumbent union and a continuing fight. At the end of a contract such an employer could raise question as to whether the union still had a majority and therefore refuse to negotiate unless there was a new certification. Senator Murray argued that there was a serious danger here:

The Board would not clearly have discretion to dismiss the petition if there was no reasonable basis in fact for the employer to doubt that the labor organization still represents a majority. Employers thus are given a useful device for delay. Moreover, unions would be compelled to engage in election campaigns at the close of each bargaining term and would be tempted to make unreasonable demands in order to retain the allegiance of the employees. Uninterrupted and stable bargaining relations would thus be impaired.[50]

Actually if a union had in fact lost its hold, or the employer was honestly in doubt, the employer's interests and those of employees who did not want the union were protected under the Wagner Act[51] by the fact that the employer at the end of a contract could simply refuse to continue bargaining; and the union, if it was in position to do so, could file a representation petition or a charge of refusal to bargain. The Board had some power to prevent misuse of this extended right of petition under Taft-Hartley, however, since an election was required only if "a question of representation exists." But how could the Board test that question on petition of an employer? In the case of a petition from employees or a union, the substantiality of the showing of representation, in the form of signed cards or signatures on a petition, is an indication of the existence of a question which needs to be answered. Should the Board find it necessary to proceed

49. *Supra*, ch. 12, pp. 457–58.
50. *Daily Cong. Rec.*, 93:6663.   51. *Supra*, ch. 5, p. 163.

on every employer petition, on the other hand, the dangers foreseen by Senator Murray might become real. Related was the fact that a lost election on an employer petition, as on others, foreclosed any further election for a year and that there were special dangers in the case of elections during strikes.[52]

A number of important safeguards in administration of employers' petitions were established by the Board. The rules as to conditions under which an existing contract would bar an election were assumed to continue as in other representation cases. The majority of the Board also decided that there was no "question of representation" when the union had withdrawn its claim to represent a majority of the employees. In a case[53] where after expiration of a contract the employer expressed doubt that the Machinists' union represented a majority, and he therefore filed a petition, the union disavowed any claim to represent the broad unit of production and maintenance employees. The Board accordingly dismissed the petition. Mr. Reynolds, dissenting, held that the employer's right of petition was thus emasculated, since a union was thus given an "unlimited veto" by the simple process of withdrawing a previous claim. The majority of the Board, on the contrary, pointed out that the employer had accomplished his object of determining that the union did not then represent the majority of all the employees. They said:

To force the Union . . . to an election in a unit which it does not claim to represent would result, not only in a futile act leading to a purely negative result, but also in depriving the employees of any opportunity to select any bargaining representative for an entire year after the election. The right of the Employer to seek an election is not a guarantee that it will secure one in every case, nor is it paramount to the right of the employees to designate a bargaining representative during the ensuing 12 months.

Since any other position would not only permit an employer in such a case to obtain release from an obligation to bargain with an incumbent union, but would also establish a year's interregnum before a new representative could be chosen in a Board election, should the employees so desire, we think this a reasonable exercise of the Board's discretion. There are those who disagree, however.[54]

52. *Supra,* pp. 517–19.
53. Ny-Lint Tool and Manufacturing Co., 77 NLRB 642 (May, 1948).
54. In a later case the majority refused to dismiss an employer petition when the union whose contract had recently expired failed to appear at the hearing. Mr. Murdock, dissenting, thought no election should be ordered unless the union presented a showing of interest. But the three-man majority held that to require such a showing would defeat the will of Congress to give employers confronted

Decertification petitions were provided for because of an apparent belief that substantial numbers of employees were the unwilling captives of unions which were not the freely chosen representatives of the majority. The House would have permitted petitions for such elections for decertification of an incumbent union by a group of employees at any time. But the one-year rule was kept for such elections as well as others.

Under the Wagner Act there was no provision for elections on petition of dissenters who raised a question of loss of majority in order to oust the certified representative and end collective bargaining. The Board interpreted the Act as being for the purpose of providing means for the selection of representatives for collective bargaining. Those who no longer wanted the certified representative could oppose it by organizing and petitioning for a new representative at the end of a certification period or by voting against the old union at a new election if the employer required a new certification as a condition of dealing with the union. The Board refused to accept a petition of employees who did not wish a representative, on the theory that their interests were sufficiently protected by the other regular procedures under the Act.[55]

Congress decided otherwise in 1947. Only experience would tell whether the values obtained would counterbalance the dangers. In an occasional early case where a union had organized and later neglected the interests of its members, the decertification petition apparently served a useful purpose in stimulating the union to serve its members and keep their loyalty or in freeing workers from a union they no longer wanted. Comparable in some respects were the elections held by the Board in early years in cases where unions claimed that closed-shop contracts were a bar to the election; in a substantial proportion of those cases where the question was raised the old union was repudiated and a new representative chosen.[56] The decertification procedure similarly could lead to a revival and new activity and renewed employee support in some cases or to the displacement of unions in others. It was used, too, in some cases where a competing union was not able to use the Board's representation procedures, since it had not met the filing requirements of the Act. Supporters of the new union

---

with a demand for recognition an opportunity for determination of the status of the union through an election. They did not interpret the union's failure to appear at the hearing as a withdrawal of its claim. Felton Oil Co., 78 NLRB 1033 (August, 1948); *Thirteenth Annual Report*, pp. 27–28.

55. *Supra*, ch. 5, p. 162.   56. *Supra*, ch. 3, pp. 90–91.

in the plant might "decertify" the incumbent union; then the rival was free to engage in a strike for recognition.[57]

Dissident factions, however, were likely to be encouraged by the decertification provision, especially where an employer was unwilling to settle down to bargaining with an established union. Dissension and turmoil could result, with weakening of collective bargaining as well as interference with production. There was considerable indication in early cases filed that a number of them were stimulated by employers, and this is to be expected. The large number of petitions which were withdrawn or dismissed suggests that many were not legitimate expressions of employee dissatisfaction, though in some the source of dissatisfaction was apparently removed after being brought to the front by the petition. It would, of course, be an unfair labor practice for an employer to stimulate the circulation of a petition for decertification, and filing of charges against employers was to be expected as a result in some cases. When a petition was filed by a foreman in behalf of a group of employees, this was properly dismissed, since a foreman, a management representative, was not entitled to file such a petition, nor could he act as representative of the employees.[58] The Board, following its usual procedures, refused to take evidence as to unfair labor practices alleged in a representation hearing; the question of motive in filing a petition is irrelevant in the absence of charges of unfair labor practices. But a decertification election would not be held while an unfair labor practice was pending against an employer. The decertification procedure was, however, a useful means at least of delay and harassment of a union. Especially was this useful to an employer who wished if possible to get out of his bargaining relationship with a union which failed to comply with the filing requirements of the Act and therefore was not in position to file charges against him.[59]

57. In two cases, where it was argued that decertification petitions were in fact filed in the interest of rival noncomplying unions, the Board found the contention without merit and ordered elections. Whitin Machine Works, 76 NLRB 998 (1948); Solvay Process Division of Allied Chemical & Dye Corp., 78 NLRB 408 (1948).

58. Clyde J. Merris and W. S. Monroe, 77 NLRB 1375 (June, 1948).

59. A decertification election was the one type of election in which a noncomplying union was placed on a ballot in a Board election. Harris Foundry and Machine Co., 76 NLRB 118 (1948). It is reported that noncomplying unions lost decertification elections in a larger proportion of the cases brought against them than did unions which were in compliance. A. Norman Somers, "The National Labor Relations Board from Wagner to Taft-Hartley," *Federal Bar Journal*, 9 (1948), 351.

Necessary administrative safeguards for the proper handling of decertification petitions were therefore very important, in view of the possibilities of abuse. The Board made clear, in accordance with its usual rules, that a showing of at least 30 per cent of the employees would be necessary on a petition for a decertification election. The same policies would rule as in other representation cases as to when a contract was a bar to an election. The majority of the Board decided also that there was no "question of representation" when a petition was withdrawn by the petitioners. It refused to consider the assertion of an employer that the union had coerced the employees into withdrawing the petition; if such were the case, the remedy lay in filing a charge against the union, and without such a charge the issues could not be investigated in a representation hearing. Two members of the Board, on the contrary, felt that, once a properly supported decertification petition had been filed, it should be carried through to determination of the issue by secret election.[60] Similarly, the majority of the Board refused to order an election when the union, though previously certified, renounced any claim to represent the employees.[61] Mr. Reynolds thought, on the contrary, as he did in similar employer petition cases, that the petition should be carried through to an election regardless of any disclaimer by the union. But the four-man majority held that

to direct an election despite the Union's disclaimer, would not only be a waste of Federal funds, but would also almost certainly mean, as the employer candidly argues in its memorandum to the Board, "that for a certain 12 month period it may safely" refuse to engage in collective bargaining, not only with this Union but with any other. It is nowhere asserted to be the purpose of the amended Act to facilitate such an objective.

Petitions were dismissed also, on the ground that the necessary conditions had not been met for a decertification election, when the unions in question had not been certified but had been recognized, and after the expiration of a contract the employer refused further recognition or bargaining. The appropriate remedy in such circumstances was a representation petition filed either by the employer or by the union.[62]

Questions also arose as to whether a small group could be "decertified" out of an existing broad unit. In the case of professional groups

60. Underwriters Salvage Co., 76 NLRB 601 (March, 1948). *Thirteenth Annual Report*, pp. 27–28.
61. Federal Shipbuilding and Drydock Co., 77 NLRB 463 (May, 1948).
62. Queen City Warehouses, 77 NLRB 268 (April, 1948).

the Board considered itself bound by Section 9(b)(1) to permit a vote of that group.[63] If other small groups were permitted to pull out of established units, a premium would seem to be put on dissension and instability. The Board decided, however, that it had to apply the same tests as in other representation cases, and, if the group desiring to cut itself out by a decertification election constituted an appropriate unit, an election would be ordered.[64]

Possible uses of decertification petitions in connection with attempts to break strikes were illustrated in a conflict of the CIO Furniture Workers with the Colonial Hardware Flooring Company. The union had not complied with the filing requirements of the Act and so could not file charges against the company, although it claimed the strike was one against unfair labor practices; and the union had made itself vulnerable by striking before the expiration of its contract. Upon a decertification petition the Board ordered an election, with replacements and strikers all eligible to vote subject to challenge as to the right to reinstatement. In addition, other provisions of the Act were used by the employer. An Intermediate Report, and the Board more than a year later, found the union guilty of coercion by its picket-line activity; and the company filed suit for damages for breach of contract and an illegal secondary boycott.[65] Regardless of the merits of the charges and countercharges in this case, it is clear that the employer's hand was strengthened by the provisions of the Act. Whether in all respects the influence was for more responsible action by all parties is, however, open to question.

The new employer and decertification petition procedures, thus safeguarded to some extent by the terms of the Act and by Board decisions, were apparently useful in occasional circumstances to prevent hardships to employers or groups of employees. On the other hand, they were subject to abuse in the entire context of the Act which gave the benefit of the doubt at so many points to those who prefer individual bargaining to collective bargaining. In view of the strong case made for these "equalizing" amendments it is somewhat surprising that the use of the new rights of petition was relatively small in the first year.[66]

63. Illinois Bell Telephone Co., 77 NLRB 1073 (June, 1948).
64. American Smelting and Refining Co., 80 NLRB 68 (October, 1948).
65. Colonial Hardware Flooring Co., 76 NLRB 1039 (March, 1948), 84 NLRB No. 69 (June, 1949); *Ball Committee Report*, Pt. 1, March 15, 1948, pp. 38–39. In the decertification election the vote was 39 to 35 in favor of the union, but the Board did not certify the union as it was not in compliance.
66. For the results see *infra*, ch. 16, pp. 613–14, 650.

From the Wagner Act to Taft-Hartley

Another new type of election provided was that upon petition of 30 per cent or more of the employees to authorize their majority representative to enter into a union-shop agreement or to rescind such authority.[67] Like other provisions, this was designed to give what was thought to be needed protection to the rights of employees against abuse by established bargaining agents. It was clearly assumed, as the General Counsel phrased it, "that if employees were given a chance to express themselves, compulsory union membership as a condition of employment could be expected to fall by the wayside."[68]

In fact the scales were tipped a bit against the supporters of the diluted form of union-security permitted, in that a majority vote of all the employees in the unit, not just of those voting, was required to authorize a union-shop agreement. Unions feared that the union shop might then be defeated by campaigns to refrain from voting. An absent vote could be considered, and in fact was counted, as a "No" vote, and those who voted might be assumed to have voted "Yes" and even be subject to reprisals. In any event there was a danger to the secrecy of the ballot as a result of this provision, which was contrary to the usual democratic practice.

In general, these dangers did not materialize. After some hesitation, unions began to file petitions, and a flood of union-shop election business nearly swamped the Board for some months in 1948. Unions as well as others must have been surprised at their overwhelming success in winning these elections. Very few were lost, although in a few cases the defeat stemmed from the small number voting, when a majority of the votes were for the union shop.[69] As the General Counsel said, "The closed shop may have been unpopular, but the union shop doesn't seem to be, if these figures mean anything."[70]

This experience raised question as to the wisdom of requiring such elections in order to validate union-security arrangements which were already so widespread in American industry by agreement. Especially in the building industry where the result was a foregone conclusion, and where the technical difficulties were enormous, it was question-

67. Sec. 9(e), discussed *supra*, ch. 12, pp. 433–34, 436, 439–40. One other type of election, that in national emergency cases, is discussed *infra*, ch. 15, pp. 575, 580–81.

68. Address of General Counsel Denham, April 19, 1948. A difficult question in the administration of this section arose when petitions were filed covering employees in states with anti-closed-shop laws. The policy adopted is discussed in connection with other issues in the relations between federal and state laws, *infra*, ch. 15, pp. 588–90.

69. For details see *infra*, ch. 16, p. 613.

70. Address of General Counsel, April 14, 1948.

able whether the procedure was worth its cost. It was proposed to
have several hundred area elections in large units, with the result by
area controlling, in contrast to other industries where the appropriate
unit was more frequently a single company or plant. A first "pilot
election"[71] in the road construction industry in western Pennsylvania,
on May 10, 1948, took three months of preparatory work by the
Board's staff, and on election day 25 mobile crews of 54 Board representatives. Of 18,000 possibly eligible, only 2,709 were actually working on the day chosen. They voted for authorization 10 to 1. And this
was considered a comparatively simple election as it included only
5 unions and some 100 contractors in 33 counties. After long preparation for a second "laboratory" election to be conducted in Detroit, the
plan was abandoned when one group, the Home Builders Association,
refused to participate in the general poll. Plans to poll building tradesmen were then suspended.[72]

In our view it is questionable whether there is sufficient value in
such elections to justify the expense, time, and necessary campaigning involved, unless possibly in a more narrowly defined set of circumstances where there is evidence of a real question.[73] Unions,
however, might be divided as to whether they would wish the repeal
of this one provision, if related parts of the Act were kept, since these
elections gave a useful demonstration of union solidarity at a time of
negotiations.[74]

PREREQUISITES FOR UNION USE OF THE
BOARD PROCEDURES

Before unions could file representation or union-shop petitions or
charges of unfair labor practices under Taft-Hartley they were required to file certain documents on financial and other matters, and

71. Address of Associate General Counsel Charles M. Brooks, May 12, 1948;
address of John W. McCaffrey, president, New York Chapter of the Society for
the Advancement of Management, to the Rutgers University Labor Institute, June
16, 1948.

72. *New York Times*, October 18, 1948. The Board and the General Counsel
had both recommended the elimination of the union-shop election, keeping the
"escape hatch" provision for "deauthorization elections," in *Ball Committee Hearings*, Pt. 1, pp. 51, 62, May 24, 1948; see also *Ball Committee Report*, Pt. 3,
December 31, 1948, pp. 46–49.

73. Cf. *supra*, ch. 12, pp. 439–40.

74. Cf. statement of Louis S. Belkin of the AFL Chemical Workers to the Ball
Committee. He advocated repeal of this provision on the ground of its "inexcus-
able extravagance" and the fact that it made it virtually impossible for the Board
to perform its essential functions. He said, however, "although the authors of the
legislation obviously did not intend the result, we have benefited greatly. . . . It has
given us an opportunity to reorganize our locals and to recement unity within
them. We have been given a stronger bargaining platform for negotiations with
management." *Ball Committee Hearings*, Pt. 1, p. 237.

"non-Communist" affidavits signed by their officers. These provisions, by reason of which at first many, and later a decreasing number of unions excluded themselves from using the facilities of the Board, created many problems in connection with representation cases and had far-reaching effects upon the operations of the Act and upon industrial relations in the first year. They affected unfair labor practice problems also, naturally, but the major impact upon representation cases is suggested by the fact that the requirement was written as a part of Section 9, on representations and elections.

The qualifying conditions set up in Sections 9(f), (g), and (h) applied to labor organizations only, not to employers or employer associations or to individuals. No investigation was to be made by the Board of a representation question, no union-shop election petition was to be entertained, and no complaint was to be issued on a charge filed by a union, unless the union and any national or international labor organization of which it was an affiliate had complied with these conditions. The first of the requirements was to file with the Secretary of Labor copies of its constitution and by-laws and report in accordance with Section 9(f):

(1) the name of such labor organization and the address of its principal place of business;

(2) the names, titles, and compensation and allowances of its three principal officers and of any of its other officers or agents whose aggregate compensation and allowances for the preceding year exceeded $5,000, and the amount of the compensation and allowances paid to each such officer or agent during such year;

(3) the manner in which the officers and agents referred to in clause (2) were elected, appointed, or otherwise selected;

(4) the initiation fee or fees which new members are required to pay on becoming members of such labor organization;

(5) the regular dues or fees which members are required to pay in order to remain members in good standing of such labor organization;

(6) a detailed statement of, or reference to provisions of its constitution and bylaws showing the procedure followed with respect to, (a) qualification for or restrictions on membership, (b) election of officers and stewards, (c) calling of regular and special meetings, (d) levying of assessments, (e) imposition of fines, (f) authorization for bargaining demands, (g) ratification of contract terms, (h) authorization for strikes, (i) authorization for disbursement of union funds, (j) audit of union financial transactions, (k) participation in insurance or other benefit plans, and (l) expulsion of members and the grounds therefor; . . .

In addition, the union had to show that it had

(1) filed with the Secretary of Labor, in such form as the Secretary may prescribe, a report showing all of (a) its receipts of any kind and the

sources of such receipts, (b) its total assets and liabilities as of the end of its last fiscal year, (c) the disbursements made by it during such fiscal year, including the purposes for which made; and

(2) furnished to all of the members of such labor organization copies of the financial report required by paragraph (1) hereof to be filed with the Secretary of Labor.

Section 9(g) required the union also to bring the above information up to date by annual reports, and to file with the Secretary of Labor and "furnish" to the members annually financial reports in the form and manner specified by the Secretary.

Third, a labor organization, but not employers, in order to qualify had to file with the Board, in accordance with Section 9(h), non-Communist affidavits signed by officers of any local concerned, and if affiliated, as most locals are, by the officers of its international union. The affidavit provision reads:

. . . an affidavit executed contemporaneously or within the preceding twelve-month period by each officer of such labor organization and the officers of any national or international labor organization of which it is an affiliate or constituent unit that he is not a member of the Communist Party or affiliated with such party, and that he does not believe in, and is not a member of or supports any organization that believes in or teaches, the overthrow of the United States Government by force or by any illegal or unconstitutional methods. The provisions of section 35 A of the Criminal Code shall be applicable in respect to such affidavits.

Several practical matters in the administration of these filing requirements must be considered first before we turn to more basic issues. What was necessary before a local union could file and have action on its petition for an election or a charge against an employer for, say, discrimination in connection with the union's organizing campaign? It filed with the Department of Labor a two-page form giving the name and address of its affiliated international union if any, the names, titles, and compensation of its own officers, and other information specified, with a copy of the union's constitution and of a financial report for the preceding fiscal year showing at least a minimum of specied information. The same was required of its international union. The local and the international then received compliance numbers from the Department of Labor, which they reported to the Board with the date to which they were valid; and they filed with the regional office and the Washington office, respectively, statements indicating how the financial reports were furnished to members. Acceptable methods were mailing copies to members, publishing in a paper distributed to members, and posting a copy at the local headquarters and meeting place with announcement at a regular meeting that copies were available for distribution. Finally, the local union also filed with the regional office of the Board, and its international with the Board in Washington, sworn affidavits listing the names and titles of all incumbent officers, with the expiration dates of their current terms. And these local officers and international officers filed, in the region and in Washington, respectively, sworn affidavits stating:

> I am not a member of the Communist Party or affiliated with such party. I do not believe in and I am not a member of nor do I support any organization that believes in or teaches the overthrow of the United States Government by force or by any illegal or unconstitutional means.

Note also that all of this needed to be kept up to date, the financial reports to be filed and furnished to members each year, and the non-Communist affidavits to be renewed annually. If the beginning of the fiscal year differed from the date for installation of officers, a union might "fall out of compliance" at either date if it did not complete its filing requirements in time.[75] Whenever any officer resigned or was replaced during the normal term, new filing was necessary before the union continued in compliance so that the Board could take action on its case. The amount of paper work involved in filing and keeping these records and checking upon their completeness and the "earliest expiration date," to be sure that the union was *still* in compliance before crucial actions were taken by the Board on the case, defies description. Note that local and international unions were involved, as well as the Department of Labor and the Washington and the regional offices of the Board. Note also the amount of detailed information required. A large proportion of the forms had to be returned because incomplete or incorrectly filled out in the early period, and the problem continued, especially with new local unions.[76] The Board suggested to the Joint Congressional Committee in June, 1948, in a carefully limited statement:

75. Because of inevitable delays in the availability of year-end financial reports, the General Counsel finally permitted a temporary ninety-day period of grace, during which the Board would continue to process a union's case, provided the union filed a statement of intent to renew its filing compliance.

76. In April, 1948, there were more than fifty employees in regional offices, more than twenty in the Washington office of the Board, and thirty in the Department of Labor, handling these reports. The processing of the reports through various stages by unions, the Department of Labor, and the regional and Washington offices of the Board required something like seven steps on national union filing, eleven on local union filing, and seven for refiling of the reports and four for refiling of affidavits.

540

The Board members' efficiency would also be enhanced if some changes were made in the administrative arrangements for handling information required to be filed pursuant to section 9(f), (g), and (h) of the amended act. All too frequently the issuance of decisions must be postponed because of a last-minute change in a union's compliance status and the fact that current information on the subject is not conveniently available.[77]

All this, involving substantial expense to the government and to unions, and delay in handling cases arising under the Act, and made unnecessarily complex by division of responsibility between agencies and rigid requirements which permitted too little discretion in administration, is of little importance if the provisions served a sufficient public purpose. To this more important point we now turn. Registration and financial reporting and the non-Communist affidavit are considered separately, as the issues are quite different.

REGISTRATION AND FINANCIAL REPORTS

Senator Taft's bill as reported by the Senate Committee had included the requirement of registering and filing financial and other information with the Secretary of Labor and furnishing financial reports to members, as a prerequisite for use of the Board by a union in either representation or complaint cases. But little was said in explanation of any need for the provision. Senator Taft spoke of the filing requirement as related to a public feeling that "one of the most important things . . . that should be done, is to make unions responsible." He went on, saying: "Such reports . . . are made in many unions today. Many unions favored the proposal. No man may longer conduct a union as his private concern and conceal from his members the salary he receives or the methods by which he disposes of their funds."[78] Later he reported that additions to the information required had been made at the insistence of the House.[79] The House, which went further than the Senate on these matters, intended this, according to Congressman Hartley, as part of a "Bill of Rights" for the workingman.[80] The Conference bill kept the Senate's approach to the ques-

77. *Ball Committee Hearings*, Pt. 2, p. 1124. On the difficulties in administration see also *ibid.*, Pt. 2, pp. 1153–54, 1169–72; *Ball Committee Report*, Pt. 3, December 31, 1948, pp. 41–44.

78. *Daily Cong. Rec.*, 93:3955.

79. *Ibid.*, p. 6602. After the Act was passed over the President's veto, Senator Taft inserted in the *Congressional Record* a series of questions and answers on the Act. Among other points he said that the requirement of giving full information to members would give them more freedom to express their opinions, especially in view of the fact that they would still be entitled to their jobs, even if the union should expel them. *Ibid.*, p. A3577–80 (July 8, 1947).

80. *Ibid.*, p. 3535.

tion, but it extended the requirement to apply to international unions as well as to local unions directly concerned, added further details as to information required, and made filing a prerequisite for union-shop elections as well as for representation and complaint cases filed by unions. Thus the regulation was considerably extended and its administration made much more difficult.

Questions must be asked on two points: whether there was a problem needing federal legislation; and whether the means chosen were well adapted to the end sought. On the first, everyone knows that there are cases of dishonest or undemocratic unions where the members do not have adequate knowledge of or control over the union finances.[81] There is no evidence indicating that these are more than a small minority of the whole, however. The only factual statement on this point which we find in the record was made by Senator Murray:

A study by the Department of Labor shows that 22 of . . . 26 internationals in the A.F. of L. provide for regular financial reports to the local unions or to the convention, and for regular publication of financial reports. Of 36 international unions in the CIO, 31 provide for regular financial audits by certified public accountants, 30 publish financial reports available to anyone, and 5 provide for financial reports to local unions or to members.[82]

No complete information was available on the wide variety of union financial practices or many other matters of internal union affairs. A later study reports that the large majority of international unions made detailed financial reports and provided for internal check and independent audit which compared favorably with those of corporations.[83] Anyone who has attended many local union meetings in different industries, also, can testify to the detailed reports of finances usually read at these meetings.

It is good public relations and an indication of proper responsibility to the membership when a union is willing, as so many of them are, to make its annual financial reports public. Yet it is questionable whether the needs of public policy require that every union, international or local, should do so. Even a financial statement distributed to the members may come to the employer's notice so that he will be better advised than he may now be as to the union's resources and financial strength. For a new, weak, or struggling union this may be important.

81. Cf. *supra*, ch. 8, pp. 279–80.
82. *Daily Cong. Rec.*, 93:6664.
83. George Kozmetsky, "Unions' Financial Reporting," *Harvard Business Review*, 27 (January, 1949), 13–23.

Corresponding knowledge of how an employer is circumstanced is not always known or available to the union. This is the traditional union argument against any requirement for publicity of union accounts. It has enough validity for the not-so-well established unions that any regulation should protect such unions from possibly harmful publicity. The Taft-Hartley provision, fortunately, did not make public the data filed with the Department of Labor. But even the requirement that financial statements be furnished to members or posted exposed new or weak unions to the risk that employers might thereby gain an advantage.

Taft-Hartley did not face directly the issue as to whether there was need for control over the finances or other internal affairs of unions. But here, as on some other points, by indirection it established a degree of control. All these and many of the provisions found in recent state statutes,[84] said to reflect interest in the individual workers, suggest that labor organizations, with constitutions and by-laws and supervision from an overhead national or international organization, are not considered democratic, responsible organizations. Yet little is said of other voluntary organizations most closely akin to labor organizations. The most eminent American student of union organization and democratic government has said that no one knows more than a fraction of what would be necessary to draft a proper broad trade-union code. This does not mean that no legislation on these matters should find place in state or national policy, but it does mean that investigation and consideration by representative groups should precede legislation.

The Eightieth Congress, however, aware of the existence of a problem, though with little actual information at its disposal, chose to deal with it by restricting access to the Board by unions which did not meet the requirements established. Opponents in both Houses pointed out the inequity in imposing such a requirement for detailed reports upon labor organizations but not upon employers' associations.[85] Moreover, a burdensome and expensive requirement was being imposed upon unions before they could use the Board, and upon the government to handle the administration. As Senator Thomas put it, "No abuse exists which these provisions will remedy."[86] It was noted also that unions were already required to file financial information with the Bureau of Internal Revenue, under the Revenue Act of 1943, and if desired the Revenue Act might be amended for that purpose,

84. Cf. *supra*, ch. 9.
85. *Daily Cong. Rec.*, 93:3589–90, 4897, 6664.   86. *Ibid.*, p. 4897.

543

"without confusing this problem with that of enforcing the National Labor Relations Act—with which it has nothing to do."[87] Most important was the point made in the minority report of Senators Thomas, Murray, and Pepper, and repeated in debate: "The effect of these provisions is to encourage resort to self-help by unions instead of encouraging them to resort to the procedures provided by the act. This is an inevitable result of erecting these additional obstacles to securing the relief the act is designed to provide."[88]

The means chosen to deal with the problem seem to us poorly related to their purpose. Perhaps some unions were stimulated to improve their financial methods, especially in the local unions. A number of internationals aided their locals to set up proper systems of accounting and reporting in order to qualify under the law.[89] But it may be doubted whether in the cases where there has been a real problem there was much effect. The financial data required was in such broad categories as to make the reports of little significance except for the totals of income, expenditures, and assets. The forms could be filed and the routine announcement made of availability of the reports with little or no effect in the extreme case of a "racketeering" union. Moreover, such unions might not care to use the Board's processes. The obstacle to use of the Board's processes and interference with its efficient performance of its main duties, also, might be more harmful to the public interest than any possible gain in increased democracy and responsibility.

If these matters need federal regulation, could not a better method be devised? In Great Britain, contrary to statements frequently made, registration of unions is entirely voluntary. Registered unions report annually to the Registrar of Friendly Societies, showing their financial status, but many unions are not registered.[90] It is in fact difficult to make a case for required registration of labor organizations, if employer associations are not similarly subject to regulation. The constitutionality of this provision, however, while subjected to attack, was never in much doubt, and was affirmed by the Supreme Court[91] in June, 1948.

87. *Ibid.*, p. 4157.

88. *Taft Report,* Pt. 2, *Minority Views,* p. 22. Cf. also *Daily Cong. Rec.,* 93:4157, 6656, 6658.

89. E. E. Witte, "An Appraisal of the Taft-Hartley Act," *American Economic Review,* 38 (May, 1948), 368–82, at 373. Cf. also *Ball Committee Report,* Pt. 3, December 31, 1948, pp. 34–35.

90. H. A. Millis and R. E. Montgomery, *Organized Labor* (New York: McGraw-Hill Book Co., 1945), p. 660.

91. National Maritime Union v. Herzog, 78 F. Supp. 146 (D.C., D.C., April 13, 1948), affirmed as to validity of Sec. 9(f) and (g), 334 U.S. 854 (June 21, 1948).

NON-COMMUNIST AFFIDAVITS

The "non-Communist affidavit" section, 9(h), had its origin in the House Committee's proposal to deny certification to a union with any officer who "is . . . or can reasonably be regarded as" a Communist.[92] The Senate bill originally had not included any such measure. After a rather brief debate the Senate rejected a proposal which would have permitted a union to expel a Communist and demand his discharge, but then without a record vote adopted the House provision with minor changes.[93] The Conference bill, however, substantially changed the clause. Senator Taft explained that it was thought impracticable and conducive to delays to have the Board investigate the character of the officers of a union before it could certify a bargaining agent. Hence it was decided to rely upon affidavits disclaiming Communist membership or the proscribed beliefs, subject to severe penalties of fines up to $10,000 or ten years' imprisonment.[94] In addition, the requirement was made to apply not only to representation cases as in the bills adopted by the two Houses but also to union-shop elections and to all charges filed by unions, as was done with the other filing requirements. Thus access to the Board's processes was closed to unions whose officers did not file the required non-Communist affidavits. No such restriction was put on employers or upon individuals who might file petitions or charges with the Board.

Members of both houses were much concerned over Communist infiltration into unions, and it was thought that the provision would aid and stimulate union members to get rid of Communist leaders. An inconsistency was pointed out between this approach and the union-security provisions which would not permit a union to expel a Communist and demand his discharge; but those who wanted the limitation on a union's power to require discharge prevailed.[95] Others, among them Senators Morse, Murray, and Pepper, argued that a provision putting obstacles in the way of peaceful resort to the procedures of the Board was an ineffective and self-defeating way to deal with the problem of communism in unions. Senator Morse's well-reasoned statement, which was never answered, deserves quotation at some length.

We all know that Communists feed their propaganda and thrive on strikes and industrial warfare. Under the terms of the bill, however, every local union will be denied all access to the peaceful machinery of the act if it has as an officer, or if its parent body has as an officer, a Communist

92. *Hartley Report*, p. 38.
93. *Daily Cong. Rec.*, 93:5081–86, 5095–96.
94. *Ibid.*, p. 6602.   95. *Ibid.*, pp. 3704–12, A2821, 5081–86, 5095–96.

or Communist sympathizer in fact or alleged. We do not help the patriotic membership of unions by requiring them to strike in order to protect the economic rights and benefits which other workers enjoy; and this provision does nothing to help them to purge their unions of Communist leadership. We merely play into the hands of the Communists in these organizations. They will capitalize, by way of their misleading and false propaganda, upon stirred-up tempers and emotions. They will capitalize on delays. . . .

That is not the way to handle communism in American labor unions. A much better way, it seems to me, is to give full protection to legitimate rights of American labor unions, to make clear to them that we are going to hold them responsible . . . , but that we are going to give them a continued opportunity to organize and bargain collectively in the interest of their legitimate rights. I fear that the provisions of the bill greatly hamper and injure those rights.[96]

The meaning and impact of the filing and affidavit provisions which were adopted can best be made clear by considering how they were applied. The extreme reluctance of many unions, led by the AFL and the CIO, to file the qualifying documents, and the necessity for the General Counsel to set up procedures and for the Board to decide its policies on a number of difficult issues, created an almost complete roadblock until late in October, 1947. This was removed gradually during the remaining months as the Board issued decisions and increasing numbers of unions brought themselves into compliance. Meantime, as the Chairman pointed out, "election cases filed by non-complying unions were completely blocked, and even unfair labor practice cases which they filed under the old law were thought to require some special treatment."[97]

The first issue was whether the officers of the national federations, AFL and CIO, were required to file affidavits, or only those of the international unions to which local unions were affiliated. This matter had not been discussed in either House, so far as the record showed. The General Counsel took the position that all top officers of the AFL or CIO must sign, before a union affiliated with one or the other, respectively, could qualify before the Board. Both federations at first refused and instituted a virtual boycott of the Board. By a ruling of the General Counsel all pending representation cases and unfair labor practice cases on which complaint had not yet been issued were to be dismissed if the unions did not comply by a certain date, later extended to October 31 to allow the AFL and the CIO to

96. *Ibid.*, p. 6612; cf. also p. 5290, where the Senator said: "Delay, stalling, litigation are the handmaidens of union-busting. Employers know that and that is why the pressure is so strong to pass this type of amendment."

97. Address of Chairman Herzog, April 19, 1948.

consider the matter at their annual conventions. Some 3,000 cases were in jeopardy. Several independent and AFL international unions filed shortly, and after the powerful International Association of Machinists filed, late in August, it was clear to many unions that they faced substantial competitive difficulties if they lacked access to the Board. But the flat refusal of John L. Lewis, a vice-president of the AFL as well as president of the United Mine Workers, made it impossible for the AFL to decide upon compliance, despite considerable pressure to do so from some unions. The CIO unions were more nearly in agreement on continuing the boycott, though some of them also filed at a rather early date.

In September the AFL Electrical Workers, whose international officers had filed, brought an appeal to the Board against the General Counsel's ruling. The union had been denied an election because the AFL was not in compliance. The Board by a four-to-one decision, on October 7, 1947, reversed the General Counsel and held that top AFL and CIO officers were not required to file the non-Communist affidavits before the affiliated internationals and their locals could qualify.[98] Admitting that the matter was not free from doubt, the Board decided that the words "national or international union" should be interpreted as commonly understood to mean the autonomous national or international unions in various crafts or industries, not the great national federations. They considered also that the congressional purpose would better be achieved by encouraging unions to resort to the Board than by permitting them to be barred by the failure of certain officers of the national federations to comply.

As a result the roadblock was broken. Increasingly unions which had at first refused complied with the requirements as they saw the very practical difficulties which they would otherwise meet. By October 31 a total of 110 international unions, 2,395 local unions, and 19,306 officers had complied. Then the numbers rose rapidly, and by June 30, 1948, there were in compliance 167 internationals, 7,917 locals, and 77,095 officers.[99] The major organizations still holding

98. Northern Virginia Broadcasters, 75 NLRB 11 (October, 1947). The delay of nearly two months before this fundamental issue was settled is a dramatic illustration of the disadvantage of the division in policy determination between the General Counsel and the Board.

99. From monthly press releases. The number of affidavits rose to a peak of 106,234 in November, 1948. The numbers then declined, but by mid-1949, as it appeared unlikely that there would be early repeal of the affidavit requirement, more unions brought themselves into compliance. In June, 1949, a total of 186 international unions had filed.

out were the United Mine Workers, the AFL Typographical Union, the CIO Steelworkers, and a group of "left-wing" unions, chief among them the CIO Electrical Workers, the National Maritime Union,[100] the International Longshoremen and Warehousemen, the Mine, Mill and Smelter Workers, and some others. The AFL meantime had changed its constitution to reduce the number of officers, and its officers had signed in order to permit directly affiliated locals to use the Board.[101] CIO top officials still refused to comply, although many of the CIO internationals had reluctantly given up the boycott and filed in order to use the facilities of the Board.

In the next several months as interpretations were made case by case, it was apparent that the Board meant to construe strictly the congressional intent as to the requirements for access of a union to the Board, and that a noncomplying union had "almost no rights under the statute except to be a defendant."[102] In representation cases the first general rule was that the Board could not investigate any question of representation on the petition of a noncomplying union; hence petitions were dismissed which were awaiting decision on the effective date of the Act,[103] or on which elections had been ordered but not conducted, or where elections had been inconclusive, or where objections to an election by a noncomplying petitioner were still pending.[104] Even when noncomplying unions had won elections, but had not yet been certified before August 22, the Board felt it necessary to "close the investigation" without certification, although it reported the fact of the union's majority. The Board held that certification was "a step, albeit the final step, in investigations

100. The NMU later after a referendum of its membership decided to comply, in November, 1948. By August, 1949, among other unions which had capitulated and filed were the Steelworkers, Fur Workers, Mine, Mill and Smelter Workers, Food and Tobacco Workers, Furniture Workers. In the latter three cases certain leaders announced that they had resigned from the Communist party. The Board accepted the affidavits and reiterated its policy that it was not the duty of the Board to investigate the truth or falsity of the affidavits. The General Counsel, however, referred several of the affidavits in question to the Department of Justice. NLRB Press Release, June 14, 1949; American Seating Co., 85 NLRB No. 49 (July, 1949); *New York Times,* August 21, 1949. In September, 1949, the CIO Electrical Workers voted to comply. *New York Times,* September 21, 1949.

101. As a result of Mr. Lewis' defeat on this matter, the United Mine Workers "disaffiliated" from the AFL.

102. As stated by Associate General Counsel Charles M. Brooks in address, May 12, 1948.

103. Rite-Form Corset Co., 75 NLRB 174 (November, 1947).

104. Monumental Life Insurance Co., 75 NLRB 776 (January, 1948); Hardwicke-Etter Co., 75 NLRB 992 (January, 1948).

conducted pursuant to Section 9(c). Despite some ambiguity, moreover, we believe that Sub-sections 9(f), (g) and (h), taken as a whole, reflect an intention on the part of Congress completely to debar non-complying unions from access to the Board's processes in representation cases."[105] Finally in an extreme situation where the Steelworkers had won an election two days before the Act became effective, but had not been certified, and the investigation had been closed as in the cases above, the Board held that the August election was not a "valid election" within the meaning of the Act. Another election could be held despite the one-year rule, on petition of the Machinists, who had held a contract for several years earlier. The Steelworkers, as a noncomplying union, could not appear on the ballot.[106] The Machinists won the votes of more than two-thirds of those eligible.

What were the rights, if any, of a noncomplying union which held a contract when a rival petitioned for an election? Such a union was permitted to "intervene" in the case but could not appear on the ballot unless in the meantime it had complied with the filing requirements.[107] The intervenor could present evidence as to its current contractual interest and any other issues,[108] and the usual rules continued as to when a contract was a bar to an election. If the contract had expired, however, even though the noncomplying union had been certified and had held contracts for several years, it was neither permitted to intervene nor to have its name on the ballot.[109] A noncomplying union or an individual not party to the proceedings had no standing to object to conduct affecting the result of the election. In the case of a decertification election involving a noncomplying union, however, when the union appealed to the Board against the Regional Director's dismissal of its objection to the election on the ground that

105. Myrtle Desk Co., 75 NLRB 226 (November, 1947). On the other hand, when a union had been certified only two days before the effective date of the Act, the Board dismissed the employer's petition for reconsideration, since the saving clause, Sec. 103, left unaffected for one year any certification issued under the old Act. The Board granted that it could not issue a complaint based upon such earlier certification, but it said: "If the employer should choose to bargain pursuant to the certification, and nothing in this order precludes its doing so, the problem would not arise." J. Freezer & Son, 75 NLRB 646 (December, 1947).

106. Nashville Corp., 77 NLRB 145 (April, 1948). Charges filed by individuals of discriminatory discharges of more than 140 employees were under investigation at the time. These employees were allowed to vote, subject to challenge.

107. Kinsman Transit Co., 75 NLRB 150 (October, 1947).

108. American Chain and Cable Co., 77 NLRB 850 (May, 1948).

109. Precision Castings Co., 77 NLRB 261 (April, 1948).

the company's interference had prevented a free election, the Board ordered a hearing.[110]

A dilemma was presented when an employer filed a petition after a request for recognition by a noncomplying union. The Board decided that such a union could not have a place on the ballot even under these circumstances, since, should it win the election, "a victory at the polls, even without later formal certification, would confer certain moral and practical advantages on the noncomplying union which the basic policy of Congress appears to discountenance."[111] The one situation in which the Board put a noncomplying union on a ballot was in a decertification election. Contrary to the case of the employer's petition, where the question of representation was raised in fact by the union's request for recognition, here the question was raised by the group who wished to displace a bargaining agent. Hence the Board held that it was not prevented by Sections 9(f) and (h) from conducting the election; otherwise noncomplying unions could "immunize" themselves against decertification proceedings by refusing to comply with the registration and filing requirements, and encouragement would be given to noncompliance, contrary to the congressional purpose.[112]

There was also the problem of what to do with the numerous unfair labor practice cases filed earlier, when complaints had been issued and the cases were pending at various later stages. The Board continued to issue remedial orders in these cases, although the unions were not in compliance. But in the important Marshall and Bruce case[113] it decided that no employer would be ordered to bargain in the future with a union which continued in noncompliance. The Board held unanimously that it had the power to issue the usual remedial order to bargain, upon a complaint issued long before the Act was amended. But the majority held that such an order would amount to a new certification of a union which was not eligible for certification, and that this would be contrary to the basic congressional policy. Mr. Houston and Mr. Murdock, dissenting, thought

110. The Board ultimately set this election aside. Univis Lens Co., 82 NLRB No. 155 (April, 1949). Cf. also Magnesium Casting Co., 77 NLRB 1143 (June, 1948); Oppenheim Collins Co., 79 NLRB 435 (September, 1948).

111. Herman Loewenstein, 75 NLRB 377 (December, 1947). For an argument that the union should have been put on a ballot in an election, and that if the union won it could be refused certification, or certification could be made contingent on its compliance with the filing requirements, see Gerard D. Reilly, "The Taft-Hartley Act," *Tennessee Law Review*, 20 (1948), 185.

112. Harris Foundry and Machine Co., 76 NLRB 118 (February, 1948).

113. 75 NLRB 90 (October, 1947).

that the filing requirements related only to procedures in new cases, not to remedial orders; they were meant "to affect *future* procedural rights, not substantive rights already vested before the new legislation became effective"; and they objected that the effect of the order was to "relieve this employer of the consequences of conduct no less a violation today than in 1945, and at the same time to nullify a right for which the public interest demands vindication today no less than when the right was infringed." The order issued was a conditional order to bargain, if and when the union had complied within thirty days of the order with the filing requirements of the Act.[114] On the other hand, in a discrimination case decided on the same day the Board unanimously ordered reinstatement and back pay for employees discriminated against, although the union which had filed the charge under the old Act was not then in compliance.[115]

Since noncomplying unions were so strictly limited in their use of the Board, it was to be expected that many cases would be filed by individuals. Were these individuals merely "fronting" for a union which could not have standing before the Board? Discrimination cases were accepted on individual filing,[116] but a refusal-to-bargain charge was not acceptable in the interest of a noncomplying union. In a representation case an individual who had recently resigned from a paid position as agent for a noncomplying union, but who claimed intervention as an individual, not in behalf of the union, was held to be acting for the union and denied a place on the ballot.[117]

114. It was somewhat anomalous that a noncomplying union found guilty of violating the Act was ordered to bargain. The Board granted that "such an order involves a recognition by the Board of the authority of the union to bargain, and thus, at least indirectly, may aid the bargaining position of the union." However, Sections 9(f), (g), and (h) were not meant to provide for a noncomplying union "a means of avoiding the obligation to bargain which Section 8(b)(3) imposes." Accordingly the Board ordered the union to bargain collectively *"upon request* so long as it is the representative of the Companies' employees, subject to the provisions of Section 9(a) of the Act." National Maritime Union and Texas Co., 78 NLRB 971 (August, 1948).

115. Pioneer Electric Co., 75 NLRB 117 (October, 1947).

116. No such cases were decided by the Board in the first year, but Trial Examiners in two cases found employers guilty of illegal discrimination against members of unions which were not in compliance. Augusta Chemical Co., 10-CA-118-139 (July, 1948); York & Foster, 6-CA-7 (October, 1948). In the former the Trial Examiner held that individual rights were involved and that it was not improper for the union, which was not in compliance, to help the individuals in preparing and filing charges. The Board ultimately agreed. 83 NLRB No. 7 (April, 1949). For an important case in which charges of illegal interference by the employer were dismissed administratively on the ground that the individual filers were agents of a noncomplying union see *infra,* ch. 16, pp. 628–29.

117. Campbell Soup Co., 76 NLRB 950 (March, 1948).

Questions arose also as to whether an international union could "front" for a noncomplying local. In the first case decided involving such a question, an election on petition filed by the international had been held before the effective date of the Act, and the union was certified. In later cases where the Board considered it improbable that the international's petition was in its own interest, rather than in that of the noncomplying local, the petition was dismissed.[118] Not until such locals came into compliance did the Board hold elections, with only the petitioning international on the ballot.[119] Except for individual discrimination cases, it was apparent that noncomplying unions were rather effectively excluded from obtaining any direct benefits from the Act.[120]

The constitutionality of this limitation upon access to the Board's procedures was challenged by a number of noncomplying unions, as was to be expected. In the first important case the National Maritime Union had complied with none of the requirements and challenged Sections 9(f) and (g) as well as (h), when it was denied a place on a ballot. The three-judge court of the District of Columbia decided unanimously that the registration and filing requirements were valid, and this was affirmed by the Supreme Court.[121] The majority of the three-man court held, to quote the summary of General Counsel Denham, that the requirement of the non-Communist affidavit was

a reasonable measure, justified by the evidence concerning the past activities of Communist-dominated organizations, to prevent subversion of the statute to purposes contrary to those for which it was enacted. Judge Prettyman, on the other hand, felt that although the portion of Section 9(h) which required an oath of non-belief in, and non-membership in an organization teaching violent overthrow of government was valid, the portion which required the disavowal of membership in a specifically named political party was not valid, in the absence of any specific finding concerning

118. Warshawsky and Co., 75 NLRB 1291 (February, 1948); Lane-Wells Co., 77 NLRB 1051 (June, 1948); United States Gypsum Co., 77 NLRB 1098 (June, 1948).

119. Lane-Wells Co., 79 NLRB 252 (August, 1948). The CIO Textile Workers had protested sharply against interference with the traditional bargaining system in this industry, whereby the international union, not the local, was the certified bargaining agent and party to the contracts. Letter of President Rieve of TWUA-CIO, *Daily Labor Report,* No. 153:A-4, August 6, 1948. The majority of the Board decided that it had no authority to limit this practice of some internationals, but should require the local to be in compliance in such cases.

120. An indirect benefit through obtaining decertification of a rival union, on individual petitions, has been mentioned above, p. 532. Protection of individual members against discrimination also was a help to such unions.

121. *Supra,* n. 91.

the nature and character of that organization, or any finding of a clear and present danger of the occurrence of the evils sought to be averted. . . .[122]

The Supreme Court, however, did not reach this point, since the union had not complied with the other requirements which were held valid. Several other cases raised squarely the issue of the non-Communist affidavit which would ultimately be decided by the Supreme Court. In one, a special three-judge court in New York upheld the validity of the section, although Judge Rifkind, dissenting, held that it "abridges the freedom of speech and the right of assembly without a showing of clear and present danger."[123] In the other, the Inland Steel Case, the United Steelworkers after registering and filing financial reports contested the validity of Section 9(h) alone, in appealing from the Board's bargaining order which was made conditional upon the union's compliance.[124]

Aside from the issue of constitutionality, questions must be raised on the other important matter of *policy*, on the basis of our analysis of the provision and of evidence as to its effects. First is the question whether the requirement was a means likely to be successful in its object of eliminating or reducing Communist influence in the labor movement. General Counsel Denham reported optimistically:

> It was not feasible to try to bar Communists from membership in unions, but it was feasible to rely on the solid Americanism of labor's rank and file to rid themselves of the Communistic influence, once it had been forcibly called to their attention. No more forceful way could have been devised, than to deny the valuable processes of the Board to those labor organizations whose officers were unable—or unwilling—to take [the required] oath. . . . The effect was almost instantaneous. Union members began to look around among their officers—and then—the affidavits began to flow in. Time went on—and then came the housecleaning in hundreds of unions that had not already thrown up protective barriers in their constitutions, until now—pretty well, the Communists in organized labor, can be clearly counted. Organized labor, in the main, has become Communist conscious.[125]

It seems to be true that, by bringing the matter into the open and to the attention of the members, the Act helped right-wing groups in

---

122. General Counsel Denham in address, June 4, 1948.

123. Wholesale and Warehouse Workers Union, Local 65 v. Douds, decided June 29, 1948, 22 *LRRM* 2276, 2278; American Communications Association v. Douds, decided at the same time, 22 *LRRM* 2276.

124. 77 NLRB 1 (April, 1948), enforced and constitutionality of Sec. 9(h) upheld, 170 F. 2d. 247 (C.C.A.7, September 23, 1948), cert. granted in Steelworkers, CIO v. NLRB, 335 U.S. 910 (January 17, 1949).

125. General Counsel Denham in address, April 14, 1948.

certain unions to "purge" Communist officials.[126] In some cases officials who were unable or unwilling to sign the affidavits resigned or were displaced, and the union then complied. This occurred, for example, in the Farm Equipment Workers and the United Packinghouse Workers in June, 1948. In some others, for example the United Shoe Workers, unions changed their constitutions to reduce the number of officers and so avoided the issue. Sometimes, however, former officers then went on the union pay roll as employees. In some left-wing unions, notably the Mine, Mill and Smelter Workers, and to a lesser extent the CIO Electrical Workers, dissension led to the splitting off of locals or groups of locals which remained independent or affiliated with other CIO unions. But perhaps rather typical, and also accurate, was the comment of a representative of the AFL Chemical Workers to the Ball Committee:

> We speak from our experience when we say that this legislation has not and will not drive communism from the labor movement. The Communist loves to operate from behind the scenes and to have others "front" for him. Since the passage of the Act some Communist-dominated organizations have changed their constitutional form so as to permit non-Communist officers to represent the organization and comply with the Act while the Communists remain in power. . . . At the same time the difficulties of complying with the Act have proven extremely burdensome. . . . [And] so long as individuals who maintain their membership in a labor organization by paying their dues and initiation fees may not be discharged, it is possible for Communists to infiltrate unions and foment discord by obstructionist tactics with impunity.[127]

A second important matter is the encouragement to raiding, since divisions between unions were accentuated and a kind of moral justification given for attacks upon another union, were that needed in the divided state of American unionism which is still more a collection of separate unions than a labor movement. In any event, unions which filed at an early date in a number of instances became very diligent in trying to "make hay while the sun shines" at the expense of noncomplying unions. The craft-unit amendment, while less far-reaching than some had hoped for, strengthened this trend. Unions which continued in noncompliance, whether left-wing or not, decidedly "felt the pinch" of raids from other unions. As time went on

126. Cf. the struggle for control in the National Maritime Union, which resulted finally in the filing of affidavits by the officers in November, 1948.

127. *Ball Committee Hearings*, Pt. 1, p. 255; cf. also *ibid.*, Pt. 2, pp. 701–2, 767–69. For a similar statement see International Association of Machinists, *The Truth about the Taft-Hartley Law and Its Consequences to the Labor Movement* (Washington, D.C., 1948), p. 23.

more and more of them felt it necessary to comply and did so. From the standpoint of the supporters of the affidavit requirements, supposedly it was a desirable result when a left-wing union found itself in such difficulty, or even broke up from such pressure. But against this was the conflict, upset, and instability in bargaining relationships which made trouble and perhaps was not worth the cost in all cases.[128]

A third point is the weapon given to an antiunion employer under contract with a union which failed to comply. If he chose, whether justifiably or not, to question the union's majority at the end of a contract, the union had no peaceable way to settle the issue. It could not of course file a charge or a representation petition, and the union would not be placed on a ballot upon a petition by the employer. On the other hand the Act still said, in Section 9(a), that "representatives designated ... by the majority ... shall be the exclusive representatives." When the issue was raised by Remington-Rand, of long history with the Board,[129] and the Board's regional office dismissed the company's petitions for elections, the General Counsel was reported in the press as having said that the company would act "at its own peril" if it proceeded to sign additional contracts with the union. This was later explained to mean only that the company might be subject to charges should it sign union-shop contracts or should some other union claim the right of recognition; and that the incumbent union could not file charges with the Board, though its contract would be valid for one year or until its maturity.[130] The company in the meantime had notified the union that it was severing relations.

A little later the Solicitor of the Department of Labor issued an opinion[131] to the effect that a noncomplying union was not barred by the Act from serving as bargaining agent, if it represented a majority. He implied strongly that the employer still had a duty to bargain with the union, although the duty was not enforceable through resort to the Board. The question then rose whether there was such a duty which was enforceable in the courts on petition of a noncomplying union. The Fourth Circuit Court, in the Amazon Cotton Mills case[132] held that there was no private right entitled to enforcement on peti-

128. The turmoil in the New York City retail stores in the summer of 1948 was a case in point.
129. *Supra*, ch. 4, pp. 98–100.
130. *New York Times*, December 5 and 8, 1947; *Daily Labor Report*, No. 248: A-2 (December 19, 1947).
131. *Daily Labor Report*, No. 16: AA-1, F (January 23, 1948).
132. *Supra*, ch. 13, pp. 492–93.

tion of a private party, under the amended Act any more than under the Wagner Act. In numerous cases in the first year of the Act there was conflict when employers refused to continue recognition of unions which failed to comply. Several long and bitter strikes involved this issue. Many employers felt, with considerable justification, that the law should have been explicit as to whether or not an employer should refuse to recognize a noncomplying union which appeared to be the majority choice of his employees. Congress by adopting this partial measure of denying access to the Board to noncomplying unions had given a weapon to employers who chose to use it and put the responsibility on employers of deciding whether or not to go farther than Congress itself had done. It was an unsatisfactory solution, from any standpoint.

In these and other cases, and this is our fourth point, unions were thrown upon the necessity of self-help to achieve recognition, since the peaceful procedures of the Board were not open to them. Strikes for recognition appeared to be increasing. On the other hand there were many cases where unions and employers turned to private sources for the conduct of elections to determine whether unions were entitled to recognition.[133] One management representative, also, reported that in a survey of 1,100 contracts signed after the amended Act became effective, 22 per cent were signed with noncomplying unions, most of them in continuance of an existing relationship. He said:

> While business men generally are in complete sympathy with the objectives of this provision, they do not believe that a restriction of this kind has any place in collective bargaining. . . . So long as the Communist Party is a legal political party . . . it seems inconsistent with our ideas of personal freedom to let a man's political affiliations affect the union which elected him an officer. . . . [Unless and until the Communist party is outlawed] many employers will continue to recognize and deal with non-complying unions wherever they legally are able to do so. . . . The instinct for self-preservation, as well as the fact that most of them have established relationships which they have no desire to upset, will keep them from climbing out on that well-known limb to which the saw is invariably applied.[134]

133. *New York Times,* September 27, 1947; October 5, 1947.

134. Van Delden, *op. cit.,* pp. 16–17. There was, however, considerable dissent from this position in the group to which he spoke. A National Industrial Conference Board survey of employer opinion reported a number of comments critical of the non-Communist affidavit requirement; a few suggested repeal, while 28 per cent suggested requiring executives as well as union leaders to file affidavits. *Personnel Management Record,* 10 (1948), 433–40. In a *Business Week* poll, 85 per cent indorsed the requirement. *Business Week,* August 21, 1948, pp. 19–20.

But where different attitudes prevailed, and employers refused to co-operate with unions which claimed a majority, though they had no access to the Board to prove it, there was conflict, bitterness, increased militance, and sometimes violence in strikes which brought the unions before the Board as defendants. Such conflicts were inevitable when unions were excluded from use of the peaceful procedures of the Board. The question must be asked whether the increase in strife was a cost worth paying for whatever was gained from the affidavit requirement.

The fifth point is the relation of such a limitation as this affidavit requirement to the great problem of preserving and strengthening our liberties. The point was well raised in the dissent of Judge Prettyman in the Maritime case when he said:

> It seems to me that the opinion proceeds as though the problem were merely what to do with the Communists. That might indeed be simple. But that is not the problem. The problem is how to deal with the Communists and at the same time preserve inviolate the freedoms of speech, press and assembly. It is not disposition of the Communists which creates the difficulty, it is the First Amendment.[135]

There is, however, a practical problem which must be faced in Communist influence in unions, where it can frequently be seen to be used for ulterior rather than for trade-union purposes. The international situation in 1947–48 of course heightened public concern over this problem. But this is a question on which more thorough consideration of the nature of the problem and of alternatives is needed. We question whether a labor relations statute should be used for such a problem. And to try to eliminate this influence by methods which drive it under cover or stir up emotions and conflict on which resentment feeds is unlikely to prove any solution. Is the use of undemocratic weapons the only protection of a democratic society against a possible enemy which uses the democratic process? Or is it better to rely on democratic processes within the labor movement itself for a solution? One thing should be kept in mind. An idea does not fold up and disappear as a result of nonconstructive attack or bans which trespass on freedom of thought. The way to correct unwanted ideas is to show a better approach and better ideas at work. Just contrary to what happens under Gresham's law that bad money drives out good, good ideas experienced in practice drive out the bad or less good

135. National Maritime Union v. Herzog, 78 F. Supp. 146 (D.C., D.C., April 13, 1948); *supra,* pp. 552–53.

ones. The Taft-Hartley approach, on the contrary, may create more dangers than it eliminates.

Finally, and applying both to the registration and filing requirements and to the non-Comunist affidavit, is the fact that they hampered easy access to the Board and prompt resolution of the various disputes which the Board was set up to eliminate as sources of industrial conflict. A heavy burden in money and time was put upon the unions to meet these requirements,[136] and the administrative difficulties put a burden upon the Board's staff which inevitably delayed the handling of cases. A substantial number of cases filed long before the Act was amended were dismissed without remedy for the unfair labor practices involved, or without resolution of representation disputes of long standing. And later such issues could not be brought to the Board by unions which as a matter of principle, or because of inability, had not complied. We question whether there is justification for all this in the needs of national security or other public purpose, or whether the best means were chosen to deal with existing problems.

These provisions, too, seemed to assume that it is a privilege for a union to use the Board and that this privilege may well be upon conditions set up by Congress. The assumption of the Wagner Act, on the contrary, was that the public has an interest in peaceful settlement of disputes and in the protection of the right of organization and collective bargaining and that this is served by encouraging resort to the Board rather than leaving disputes to be resolved by economic pressure. Did not this Taft-Hartley provision again reflect on the part of its sponsors doubt of the value to the public of the collective bargaining process, in spite of the statement of faith in Title II? They chose in these provisions, because of interest in other problems, to limit the use of the Board for the purposes which were considered so important to the public in the scheme of the Wagner Act.

IN CONCLUSION

As on other parts of the Act, questions must be raised as to the effects to be expected from the amendments on representation policies and procedures and the new types of elections provided. First, Taft-Hartley by its extension of the right of petition of employers, and by the new petition for decertification of a union by dissatisfied employees, removed one of the bases upon which the wide criticism of inequality in the old Act was founded. Perhaps public acceptance

136. Cf., for example, the statement of the Machinists cited *supra*, ch. 13, n. 14.

was promoted as a result, and at the same time the protection against abuses needed in occasional instances was given, and more responsible action by unions encouraged. The union-shop elections also may have served such purposes. But whatever values were obtained from these provisions were counterbalanced to some degree by misuse of the new rights for the delaying and antiunion purposes of a minority of employers.

Second are questions as to the rules of procedure and decision which limited the discretion of the Board. The specific rules in occasional cases made impossible the flexible adjustment of policy to needs of particular industrial relations situations that is essential for the best working of the administrative process in a highly complex, changing, and varied field such as this. Even a useful rule, such as the Board's one-year rule proved to be, would occasionally not fit the practical needs of a particular set of facts. We doubt the wisdom of the rigid limitations upon the Board's discretion by some of these amendments.

Third, the filing requirements as prerequisite to use of the Board by a union had some value in suggesting standards as to financial practices and reports to union members and in bringing to the attention of members the question whether their officers are Communists. The former, however, was a relatively ineffective and highly cumbersome and expensive type of approach to whatever problem exists in that area. It is at least subject to question, also, whether the latter had enough result in clarifying policies and attitudes of union leaders and strengthening the anti-Communist majority to counterbalance the increase in conflict and instability, the encouragement of raiding by other unions and of attacks by antiunion employers, and the danger to civil liberties, from this provision. The boycott of the use of the Board by a considerable group of unions, as a result of the qualifying conditions, put a substantial segment of industry back into the pre–Wagner Act jungle where issues as to union recognition and collective bargaining were decided solely on the basis of the strength of the parties. Were the gains enough to compensate? It is difficult to believe so.

Finally, while except for the filing requirements no one of the amendments considered in this chapter by itself is of great importance, the net result was considerably more than the sum of the parts. The encouragement to dissenting individuals and minorities and to those who wished to split off small units, the rule as to strikers' voting, the rigid one-year rule, especially with the greater freedom of employers to engage in pre-election campaigns against a union and with the possibility of charges and injunctions against unions under the vaguely defined but in some instances sweeping unfair labor practice provisions—all of these in net effect could be expected to weaken unions and collective bargaining if or when full use of all the possibilities was made. For employers and unions who had accepted each other and were seeking to solve their mutual problems by democratic and responsible collective bargaining, the encouragement of raiding and of dissenting minorities was sometimes a "headache."

On representation questions, as in its treatment of union unfair labor practices, we think Taft-Hartley went too far and was too little discriminating in its analysis of problems. Is it not at least as democratic to protect individual rights by a mutually acceptable collective action as by substituting for it a legislative protection? For the latter may act as a deterrent to the collective action individuals often seek as the *modus vivendi* for making their rights secure. This in itself is not only a denial of a fundamental right but a denial of man's capability for co-operative activity rationally chosen and voluntarily accepted. Taft-Hartley carried the possibility, whether intentional or not, that in its concern for the protection of individuals and minorities it seriously weakened the group action through which increasingly in modern industry individual workers seek to promote their common interests by joining with their fellows. If such possibilities developed, would it not provoke conflict rather than the "sound and stable industrial peace" which is desired?

CHAPTER 15

OTHER PROVISIONS OF TAFT-HARTLEY

OF THE remaining provisions of Taft-Hartley, some are quite closely related to the major problem of this study, the national policy expressed in the National Labor Relations Act and in other basic statutory or court-made law as to what unions and employers may lawfully do in connection with labor disputes. Some relate to the settlement of disputes; and one has extremely remote if any relation to the stated purposes of the amended Act. These provisions dealt, first, with restrictions on payments to employee representatives and regulation of welfare funds; second, with conciliation of labor disputes and national emergencies; third, with the relation of this federal legislation to state laws and administration; fourth, with restriction on political contributions and expenditures by labor organizations and corporations;[1] and, fifth, with "the joint committee to study and report on basic problems affecting friendly labor relations and productivity."

RESTRICTIONS ON PAYMENTS TO EMPLOYEE REPRESENTATIVES: WELFARE FUNDS

Section 302 made it unlawful for an employer to pay or deliver "any money or other thing of value to any representative of any of his employees," or to agree to do so, in an industry affecting commerce. Similarly it was made unlawful for any representative of employees to accept or agree to accept any such payment. Necessary exceptions to this sweeping prohibition were made, and the section excluded payment for compensation for services, or in satisfaction of a judgment of a court or an arbitration award or in adjustment of any claim or dispute "in the absence of fraud or duress," and payments in sale

1. Section 305 in Title III, also, made it unlawful for any individual employed by the United States or any agency thereof including wholly owned government corporations to participate in any strike. Any such individual who strikes "shall be discharged immediately . . . and shall forfeit his civil service status, if any, and shall not be eligible for reemployment for three years by the United States or any such agency."

or purchase of commodities in the regular course of business. Another clause permitted check-off of union dues, but only after authorization from each employee. Finally, payment to a trust fund for welfare purposes was permitted, but only under given conditions. Severe penalties of fine or imprisonment were provided for violations.[2] Violations were also made subject to injunction, without regard to the limitations in the Norris–La Guardia Act. The section, however, was not to apply to contracts in force, until after July 1, 1948; and the restrictions on trust funds were not to apply at all to those established by collective agreement before January 1, 1946.

This section stems from the Case Bill adopted but vetoed in 1946. The House would have gone further and made unfair labor practices any bribery by employers of an employee representative, any assistance to a union by checking off dues except on individual authorizations revocable *at any time* on thirty days' notice, and *any payment whatever* to a union trust or welfare fund. The attitude of the House Committee is seen in its statement: "Certainly, it is not in the national interest for union leaders to control these great, unregulated, untaxed funds *derived from exactions* upon employers. The clause forbids employers to *conspire with unions to mulct employees,* without their consent, of huge amounts that ought to go into the workers' wages."[3] A Case Bill type of limitation, to protect existing funds and permit contributions to welfare funds under certain conditions, was adopted by the Senate when it was offered as one of the Ball-Taft amendments. It was argued that this was needed to protect employees and employers against extortion and racketeering.[4]

Arrangements for the deduction of union dues by the employer under collective bargaining agreements were very widespread at the time Taft-Hartley was adopted, especially where there was a closed shop or union shop. According to the United States Department of Labor, in 1946 about six million workers, or more than 40 per cent of all under collective bargaining agreements, were covered by some form of check-off. Automatic deduction of dues was provided for more than half of these, while the others were under voluntary check-

2. *Supra,* ch. 13, p. 483.
3. U.S. House of Representatives, Committee on Education and Labor, *Labor-Management Relations Act, 1947,* Report No. 245, 80th Cong., 1st Sess., April 11, 1947, pp. 29–30, cited as *Hartley Report.* (Italics ours.)
4. For the formal statement of the proponents of the amendment see Supplemental Views of Senators Taft, Ball, Donnell, and Jenner, in U.S. Senate, Committee on Labor and Public Welfare, *Federal Labor Relations Act of 1947,* Report No. 105, 80th Cong., 1st Sess., April 17, 1947, pp. 52–54, cited as *Taft Report.*

off plans based upon individual authorization.[5] The method was efficient and avoided the necessity for individual collection of dues by union stewards or others. But there was a possible disadvantage that some employees under the automatic check-off might not know how much they were paying to the union or feel their personal responsibility. Perhaps also the union was thus missing an opportunity to keep in close touch with its members. Whether there was any actual abuse which called for federal regulation is doubtful. The minority in the committees of both houses thought not and argued against limiting the right of democratically chosen unions to work out such acceptable arrangements with employers through collective bargaining.[6] To Senator Taft, however, the check-off seemed "a device by which the employer pays into the union treasury, without the consent of the particular employees who have earned the money, a certain percentage agreed to in the . . . contract."[7]

Accordingly the amendment adopted prohibited the automatic check-off, but permitted a check-off upon written assignments by individual employees, not irrevocable for more than one year. The union then arranges for the signing of authorizations by the individual employees and repeats the process each year, unless by agreement an "escape period" is provided before automatic renewal. Additional work was put upon the union and perhaps even upon the employer to check upon these authorizations, as Senator Ives pointed out.[8] Use of the check-off tended to increase under Taft-Hartley, in spite of these difficulties. Many unions found in the early months under the Act that such a check-off was a relatively satisfactory substitute for a union shop or maintenance of membership and avoided the necessity for a union-security election. Noncomplying unions and other turned to the check-off instead.[9] The necessity of getting individual signatures gave an opportunity to see that each worker understood his relation to the union. A considerable amount of "reunioniza-

5. *Monthly Labor Review*, 64 (1947), 768–69.
6. *Hartley Report*, p. 78; *Taft Report*, Pt. 2, *Minority Views*, p. 24.
7. *Daily Cong. Rec.*, 93:4876.
8. *Ibid.*, p. 4878. Uncertainty as to what might lawfully be deducted continued to be a source of difficulty in negotiations, despite an opinion of the Department of Justice that initiation fees and assessments might be considered union dues for the purpose of check-off. Cf. *supra*, ch. 12, n. 50.
9. Thus a survey of 313 contracts signed after June 23, 1947, found that 70 per cent included check-off clauses; 17, or 5.4 per cent, appeared to be illegal, as they were automatic or involuntary and irrevocable. National Industrial Conference Board, *Union Contracts since the Taft-Hartley Act*, Studies in Personnel Policy, No. 94, August, 1948, pp. 11–13.

tion" undoubtedly went on, with a combination of education and social pressure, and perhaps some coercion, as unions tried to strengthen their positions against the real or expected dangers which might develop under Taft-Hartley.

Limitations upon union trust funds or welfare funds by Section 302(c) permitted contributions by employers only under specified conditions. The fund had to be for the sole and exclusive benefit of the employees and their families and dependents. The payments were to be held in trust for the purpose of paying for "medical or hospital care, pensions on retirement or death of employees, compensation for injuries or illness resulting from occupational activity or insurance to provide any of the foregoing, or unemployment benefits or life insurance, disability and sickness insurance, or accident insurance." The detailed basis for such payments had to be specified in a written agreement with the employer. Employers were to be equally represented in the administration of the fund, with provision for a neutral umpire in case of deadlock and for appointment if necessary of such an impartial umpire by a United States district court. An annual audit of the fund was required, the results to be available to interested persons. Finally, payments for the purpose of providing pensions or annuities were to be made to a separate trust which could not be used for any other purpose. Note that only funds for the purposes specified were permitted; provision for severance pay for members displaced by technological change, or pay for concerts by unemployed musicians, for example, would not be proper under the Act.

The case for these restrictions was argued by Senators Taft and Ball and their colleagues in their supplementary views in the Senate Committee Report.

The necessity for the amendment was made clear by the demand made last year on the part of the United Mine Workers that a tax of 10 cents a ton on coal be paid to the Mine Workers Union for indiscriminate use for so-called welfare purposes. It seemed essential to the Senate at that time, and today, that if any such huge sums were to be paid, representing as they do the value of the services of the union members, which could otherwise be paid to the union members in wages, the use of such funds be strictly safeguarded.

There is a serious question whether welfare funds of this character should be permitted at all unless the employees are willing to join such funds voluntarily and have their earnings diverted thereto. However, a number of such funds have been established, and we have no desire to interfere with their operation. One of the subjects for study by the joint committee proposed in S. 1126 is this matter of welfare funds and their relation to social security. In some way they should be integrated with social security, and the national assistance should not be broken up into a series of industry agreements. Pending that study, however, we believe it is imperative that where such funds are in existence or are agreed upon by collective bargaining, they should not be subject to racketeering or arbitrary dispensation by union officers. Without such restraints, employees would have no more rights in the funds supposedly established for their benefit than their union leaders choose to allow them. They may well become a mere tool to increase the power of the union leaders over their men, and even be open to racketeering practices.[10]

Union health and welfare funds set up by agreement of employers and unions were becoming of increasing importance. According to the Department of Labor, in 1945 about 600,000 employees were covered by such agreements, and by early 1947 the number had more than doubled, as coal-mining and some others had been added to the older plans, notable among which are those in the clothing and textile industries. Most of the plans were financed entirely by employers. In 1945 a little more than a third of the plans were administered jointly by employer and union, another third by insurance companies, and less than a third solely by the union. There was great variety in the funds as to both their support and their administration.[11]

Congress had become interested in this matter when the Mine Workers' demand for a health and welfare fund became the bottleneck in negotiations with the bituminous operators in the spring of 1946.[12] This demand had been renewed from two years before when no progress had been made, and in 1946 the Mine Workers insisted upon consideration first of all of "the principle" involved. This was objected to by the operators, some of whom stoutly opposed a tonnage tax on coal to finance such an undertaking. The resulting nationwide strike was finally settled only after the government took over the mines, and an agreement, to be effective during federal operation, was reached by John L. Lewis and the Secretary of the Interior. The agreement provided for a health and welfare fund, financed by a five-cents-a-ton levy on coal mines, and to be administered by three trustees, one each selected by the operators and the union, and the third to be chosen by these two. In the meantime the proposal had

10. Supplemental Views, in *Taft Report*, pp. 52–54. Cf. also Senator Ball's statement, *Daily Cong. Rec.*, 93:4805.

11. *Monthly Labor Review*, 61 (1945), 191–209; 64 (1947), 191–214. By mid-1948 the coverage had more than doubled again from 1947, to over three million workers. *Ibid.*, 67 (1948), 229–34.

12. *Supra*, ch. 8, p. 313; ch. 9, p. 361.

been made for the regulation of such funds, and this was included in the Case Bill, which failed of being carried over the President's veto on June 11, 1946. A year later, however, substantially the same provision became law in Taft-Hartley.

Opponents of the restriction, especially Senators Morse and Pepper, raised a number of important points.[13] One was the interference with collective bargaining, which had worked out a great variety of plans acceptable to the parties concerned and as to which there was no evidence of abuse requiring the intervention of the government. Moreover, the restrictions would tend to discourage a trend toward such supplementary welfare plans which were considered a healthy and desirable development and meeting a real need in coal-mining and other industries. The requirement that employers share in the administration was entirely unnecessary; many employers did not want to share responsibility in the administration of a fund which was for the benefit of employees and could appropriately be administered by their representatives. Finally, legislation should be postponed until there was available full information as to the funds, the extent to which they were subject to state laws, and the informed opinion in industries where they had been operating. Congressman Hartley had admitted that the status of the existing funds had not been thoroughly considered in his committee; and Senator Taft frankly said that this was stop-gap legislation, pending the needed thorough study.[14] But he felt that there was need for immediate restriction to prevent abuses in the face of such a tax on production as that in the coal industry, or a tax on phonograph records, which could easily become a racket.[15]

We agree with Senator Taft on the need for a thorough study of these matters, although we doubt whether the Joint Congressional Committee was the appropriate agency for the thorough and expert analysis needed of a highly technical problem. Anyone familiar with such matters will be sympathetic with health and welfare funds, also with the requirement that sound insurance principles and sound business principles shall be observed in connection with them. In a few instances where this had not been done, union insurance funds, like

13. For Senator Morse's statement, *Daily Cong. Rec.*, 93:4881–82; Senator Pepper, *ibid.*, pp. 4805–7.
14. *Ibid.*, pp. 3622, 4877.
15. Mr. Petrillo's royalty on phonograph records had already been outlawed by the Lea Act (60 U.S. Stat. 89), which became law on April 16, 1946, and was affirmed in U.S. v. Petrillo, 332 U.S. 1 (1947). The Musicians' Union banned the making of recordings by its members upon the expiration of its contract on December 31, 1947.

many other insurance ventures, had come to grief. Provided that sound principles are observed, one will be sympathetic with any solution for the many problems found in coal-mining communities. And since needed extensions of social security have not met much favor in Congress, and union after union is requesting that a health and welfare fund be incorporated in their collective contracts, it seems appropriate that employers and unions should be free by collective bargaining to decide upon plans to meet the needs felt in the particular industry, without undue restriction from federal laws. Nevertheless, a number of questions should be studied. Is it wise to rely for any substantial part of our "social security" upon industry plans, which will necessarily vary and result in inequities as between different groups of citizens? To what extent should industries be free to work out their own plans, and to what extent if any should limits be set, since the bills are paid ultimately by consumers? Should such plans be integrated with the national system? What kinds of safeguards are needed to avoid the possibility of unwise or even dishonest administration as the number of plans grows so that there is more danger of this sort? When appropriate safeguards are set up, should the older plans be completely exempted? These are real problems which in our view should have been studied before rather than after detailed restrictions were put upon plans worked out by collective bargaining.

The detailed restrictions on the funds and their administration led to controversy in a number of instances, for example, over the question whether plans set up before the deadline of January 1, 1946, could expand and bring other employers into the fund without changing their administration to conform to the new requirements. In the case of the coal welfare fund the March, 1948, strike related to the issues of whether under the Act benefits must be confined to employees of the contributing employers, as one trustee held. In the case of the Musicians, the ban on the making of recordings after the expiration of the agreement on December 31, 1947, continued until the companies and the union finally evolved a formula for continuance of a royalty on records which avoided the restrictions of Taft-Hartley. By agreement of the companies and the union the payments were to be made to a trustee who was selected by the companies and not a representative of the employees. The fund was to be used to pay unemployed musicians for concerts to be given free, as had been the plan under the former agreement. The new plan was put into effect in December, 1948, after the Attorney-General agreed with the Solicitor of the Department of Labor that the trust agreement did not conflict with the 1947 Act.[16]

The Joint Congressional Committee in its preliminary report in March, 1948, stated that the Act, so far as available evidence indicated, had not "operated to affect the rapid trend toward expansion in this field."[17] At the committee hearings in May and June, 1948, a number of employer witnesses urged that welfare funds and pensions should be excluded from the area of required collective bargaining. The issue had been brought to the fore by the Board's decision in the Inland Steel case, requiring the company to bargain on a pension plan,[18] and by the temporary restraining order obtained against General Motors to prevent its putting an insurance system into effect before determination by the Board of a charge of refusal to bargain on this matter.[19] It was argued before the committee that the areas of collective bargaining required by the Act should be defined, and these welfare matters excluded.[20] In our view, whatever difficult problems there may be in connection with bargaining over such matters, the interests of employees are so obviously involved that bargaining on them should not be excluded. These are problems best worked out by the parties through constructive use of the bargaining process.[21] But the important questions raised as to policy, techniques of administration, and whether or not there is a case for regulation of some points by the government need expert, objective, and thorough analysis before appropriate final answers can be given.

16. U.S. Senate, Joint Committee on Labor-Management Relations, *Labor-Management Relations,* Report No. 986, 80th Cong., 2d Sess., Pt. 3, December 31, 1948, pp. 97–98, 107–10, cited as *Ball Committee Report; New York Times,* December 14, 1948, June 16, 1949. The royalties of one-half cent to two and a half cents a record were expected to yield about one million dollars a year.

17. *Ball Committee Report,* Pt. 1, March 15, 1948, p. 42.

18. Inland Steel Co., 77 NLRB 1 (April, 1948), affirmed 170 F. 2d 247 (C.C.A.7, 1948), cert. den. as to the welfare fund issue, April 25, 1949, 336 U.S. 960. In September, 1949, a presidential fact-finding board recommended that the companies in basic steel incorporate social insurance and pension systems in their collective bargaining agreements. *New York Times,* September 11, 1949.

19. Bowen v. General Motors Corp. (D.C., N.Y., Civ. No. 44-674), January 29, 1948. The Board's order to bargain was issued February 18, 1949, 81 NLRB No. 126.

20. U.S. Congress, Joint Committee on Labor-Management Relations, *Hearings, Labor-Management Relations,* 80th Cong., 2d Sess., Pt. 1, May 28 and June 1 and 2, 1948, and Pt. 2, June 7, 1948, cited as *Ball Committee Hearings;* cf. also *Ball Committee Report,* Pt. 3, December 31, 1948, pp. 89–100.

21. Cf. discussion at Labor-Management Conference of 1945, *supra,* ch. 8, p. 310.

CONCILIATION OF LABOR DISPUTES

An excellent statement of national policy on collective bargaining introduces Title II of the Act. Its first two paragraphs deserve quotation in full.[22]

That it is the policy of the United States that—
(a) sound and stable industrial peace and the advancement of the general welfare, health, and safety of the Nation and of the best interests of employers and employees can most satisfactorily be secured by the settlement of issues between employers and employees through the processes of conference and collective bargaining between employers and the representatives of their employees;
(b) the settlement of issues between employers and employees through collective bargaining may be advanced by making available full and adequate governmental facilities for conciliation, mediation, and voluntary arbitration to aid and encourage employers and the representatives of their employees to reach and maintain agreements concerning rates of pay, hours, and working conditions, and to make all reasonable efforts to settle their differences by mutual agreement reached through conferences and collective bargaining or by such methods as may be provided for in any applicable agreement for the settlement of disputes.

Title II came in the main from the Senate bill rather than from the more extreme House bill, but the influence of the House was felt at several points in compromises made in conference. Committee reports and the debates in both houses showed that this part of the legislation, even more than others, was born in the shadow of the great strikes of 1945–46 and of the telephone, coal, and other strikes of the months of 1947 when the bills were under consideration.[23] A new Federal Mediation and Conciliation Service was created outside and independent of the Department of Labor, with its functions stated in detail. Special procedures and powers were provided for use in "national emergencies," but any matters subject to the Railway Labor Act were excluded from the application of these provisions.

The independent Mediation and Conciliation Service which replaced the old Conciliation Service in the Department of Labor took over its personnel and records and all the mediation and conciliation functions of the Secretary of Labor. The Service is under a Director appointed by the President with Senate approval. He has the aid of a National Labor-Management Panel, appointed by the President, six

22. The third has to do with governmental assistance to the parties in formulating for inclusion in agreements provisions as to procedures designed to prevent controversies, such as adequate notice of proposed changes, and means for final adjustment of grievances.
23. Cf. *supra*, ch. 8, pp. 300–302, 311–14.

from management and six from labor, with the duty, according to Section 205(b), "to advise in the avoidance of industrial controversies and the manner in which mediation and voluntary adjustment shall be administered, particularly with reference to controversies affecting the general welfare of the country." Upon request of parties in dispute, or upon its own motion, the new agency was to offer its services whenever a dispute "threatens to cause a substantial interruption of commerce." It could still establish fact-finding boards in particular disputes. The Director was required to avoid attempting to mediate disputes which would have only a minor effect on interstate commerce, if state or other conciliation services are available. If the Director was unable to bring the parties to agreement within a reasonable time, "he shall seek to induce the parties voluntarily to seek other means of settling the dispute without resort to strike, lock-out, or other coercion, *including submission to the employees in the bargaining unit of the employer's last offer of settlement for approval or rejection in a secret ballot.*"[24]

Handling of grievances arising under agreements was to be engaged in "only as a last resort and in exceptional cases." Rather, by Section 203(d) final adjustment by a method agreed upon by the parties is properly said to be the desirable method for settlement of grievance disputes. This sound provision is followed by another, also without "teeth" or bias. In order to prevent or minimize interruptions of the free flow of commerce growing out of labor disputes, Section 204(a) directed employers and employees and their representatives "to exert every reasonable effort to make and maintain agreements . . . including provision for adequate notice of any proposed change in the terms"; whenever a dispute arose to arrange promptly for conference and endeavor to settle the dispute expeditiously; and if the dispute was not settled by conference, to participate fully and promptly in any meetings arranged by the Service for the purpose of aiding in a settlement of the dispute. All this, of course, is much to be desired. In connection with this the earlier provision in Section 8(d) is important, requiring sixty days' notice of a desire to terminate or modify a contract, and after thirty days, if no agreement has been reached, notice to the Federal Mediation and Conciliation Service and also any similar state agency of the existence of a dispute.

Much of this is sound and in accord with practices which had been developed by the Conciliation Service and with recommendations of the Labor-Management Conference of 1945. Not all the provisions,

24. Sec. 203(c). (Italics ours.)

570

however, squared with those recommendations, and some of them should be questioned. First is the matter of why the Service was set up as an independent agency rather than continued in the Department of Labor. The 1945 Labor-Management Conference, made up of an able, representative, and hard-working group of employers and union leaders, *unanimously recommended* that the United States Conciliation Service should be reorganized "as an effective and completely impartial agency within the U.S. Department of Labor," with a representative advisory committee.[25] Other committee reports adopted then included statements of principles and procedures to make collective bargaining work effectively, some of them along the lines of the sound policies declared in Sections 203 and 204. But such an agreement as that on continuing the Service in the Department of Labor, made by representatives of the parties best informed and most immediately concerned with these matters, should not be taken lightly unless other considerations involved must be given more weight.

Much had been done in the year and a half after the 1945 Conference in reorganizing and strengthening the Conciliation Service along the lines recommended, although these efforts had met considerable opposition in Congress. An advisory committee from nominees by the AFL, the CIO, the National Association of Manufacturers, and the Chamber of Commerce, met monthly with the Director and shared actively in the policy-making process as the Service improved its organization, personnel, and procedures.[26] A group of special, part-time conciliators had been added to the staff to serve in connection with the most difficult cases and included outstanding men with experience in conciliation and arbitration. Experiments were under way also with conference groups to maintain and further industrial peace in special fields such as public utilities. All this meant progress and was being developed in close co-operation with industry and labor. And all this was reported on the floor of both houses,[27] where no clear case was made against continuing along the same lines. The case for making the Service an independent agency was stated simply by Senator Taft. "It was felt, rightly or wrongly, that as long as it was an agency of the Department of Labor it must necessarily take a pro-labor slant and therefore could not be as fair in mediating differences

25. Cf. *supra*, ch. 8, p. 309.
26. For an account of these developments by the then Director see Edgar L. Warren, "The Conciliation Service: V-J Day to Taft-Hartley," *Industrial and Labor Relations Review*, 1 (1948), 351–62.
27. Cf. *Daily Cong. Rec.*, 93:3538–41, 5102–4.

between the parties."[28] But such a question should be decided in the light of experience and the informed opinion of those most concerned. Is the abstract principle enough to counterbalance the advantages of continuity and of co-ordination within the Department of Labor of as many as possible of the functions relating to labor[29]—unless the decision reflects a wish to weaken the Department of Labor, as part of a desired "equalization" sought by the Act?

In fact, the matter of whether the mediation and conciliation functions are performed by an agency within or outside the Department of Labor is of far less importance than that the agency be well directed and well staffed and have proper policies, so that it can function effectively and impartially to assist the parties in making collective bargaining work. No one could doubt that a good start was made by the new agency under the able and universally respected new Director, Cyrus S. Ching, formerly director of personnel and public relations for the United States Rubber Corporation, and one of the "elder statesmen" of his field.[30] However, the new Advisory Committee appointed by the President, in place of the functioning Committee, was not set up and operating until the spring of 1948. The notice provisions served the useful purpose of stimulating the parties to begin negotiation early enough to allow time for adjustment before the deadline and of alerting the Service so that it was in position for the most effective mediation work when needed. The Service received 17,401 such notices in the year, but in about one-fourth jurisdiction was declined, others were settled by the parties, and in less than 5,000 cases did the Service take an active part.[31]

The House conferees had objected to specific mention of voluntary arbitration. Thus, if a dispute could not be settled by conciliation, the Director was to urge voluntary acceptance of "other means" of settlement, among them submission to the employees of the employer's last offer for approval or rejection in a secret ballot. Similarly Section 203(d) on settlement of grievances omitted the clause indicating a duty of the parties to an agreement to submit grievance disputes to

28. *Ibid.*, p. 7690; cf. also p. 3955.

29. It was pointed out on the floor of both houses by the minority that the Republican platform in 1944 called for placing all governmental labor activities under the direct authority and responsibility of the Secretary of Labor. *Ibid.*, pp. 3541, 5293.

30. For an account of the first year's operations see the valuable and interesting Federal Mediation and Conciliation Service, *First Annual Report, Fiscal Year Ending June 30, 1948.*

31. *Ibid.*, pp. 25–30.

arbitration. This of course was contrary to the unanimous recommendation of the Labor-Management Conference that agreements should include provision for "an effective grievance procedure with arbitration as its final step." Fortunately, however, the Service was free to use whatever devices were useful, and it urged and assisted employers and unions to develop means for peaceful settling of disputes, including assisting them to set up arbitration where desirable.[32]

The provision for a "last-offer" poll of employees was voluntary, although the House would have made it compulsory. This may be compared with the strike-vote provision of the War Labor Disputes Act, experience with which was disregarded.[33] This new provision assumed a need to protect the rank and file from union officers, and to assist in a return to work on terms of the employer's last offer, if the strikers had changed their minds. It apparently expected that strikers would repudiate their leaders, though experience shows that this is seldom done. The provision was susceptible of use in breaking strikes and had a discriminatory flavor.[34] It lacked realistic appreciation of the fact, also, that no "last offer" is final, and strikes are often settled with some further compromise after an offer is rejected. No provision was included as to how or by whom the vote should be taken. The Mediation and Conciliation Service held that in the absence of clear instructions from Congress the Service should not itself conduct such votes; and it instructed its conciliators to propose use of the device only in appropriate cases when efforts at settlement by other means had been exhausted.[35] In some circumstances the proposal would do more harm than good. The parties were then left to decide for themselves whether, if they agreed on such a poll, to have it conducted by an impartial third party, or under joint supervision, or even by the union. Clearly the proposal of such "last-offer votes" required great discretion on the part of the Service, if it was to maintain the needed impartiality and not throw its weight on one side or the other in a dispute.[36]

32. *Ibid.*, pp. 21–23.

33. *Supra*, ch. 8, pp. 298–300.

34. Cf. the provision, perhaps related in intent, that strikers not entitled to reinstatement were not entitled to vote in NLRB elections, *supra*, ch. 14, pp. 518–19.

35. Statement of Peter Seitz, General Counsel of the Federal Mediation and Conciliation Service to Joint Congressional Committee, June 11, 1948, in answer to the criticisms of George B. Christensen. *Ball Committee Hearings*, Pt. 2, pp. 1180–83; *First Annual Report*, pp. 19, 34–35.

36. The Service reported the first year's statistics of secret ballots on the employer's last offer, but indicated as its opinion that most of the so-called "last-offer ballots" were in fact only ratifications of agreements reached by employers

From the Wagner Act to Taft-Hartley

Many proposals had been offered in House and Senate relating to strikes in the area of public utilities or to such nation-wide stoppages as those in coal in 1946 and numerous earlier years, which remained fresh in the minds of congressmen as well as of users of coal generally. Fear of another national coal strike after June 30, 1947, when government operation of the mines seized in 1946 would come to an end with the lapse of the War Labor Disputes Act[37] gave a feeling of urgency to those who foresaw disaster unless the government were given new powers to deal with such an emergency. The proposals differed substantially between House and Senate, but in the compromise ironed out in Conference Committee the Senate version prevailed, with some modifications. Power to deal with "national emergency" cases was given the President, with provision for fact-finding, an eighty-day injunction, and, failing settlement, a report to Congress for its consideration and perhaps emergency legislation. "National emergency" was defined in Section 206:

Whenever in the opinion of the President of the United States, a threatened or actual strike or lock-out affecting an entire industry or a substantial part thereof engaged in trade, commerce, transportation, transmission, or communication among the several states or with foreign nations, or engaged in the production of goods for commerce, will, if permitted to occur or to continue, imperil the national health or safety, he may appoint a board of inquiry to inquire into the issues involved in the dispute and to make a written report to him within such time as he shall prescribe. Such report shall include a statement of the facts with respect to the dispute, including each party's statement of its position but *shall not contain any recommendations*. The President shall file a copy of such report with the Service and shall make its contents available to the public. [Italics ours.]

Any board of inquiry was to be constituted as determined by the President, and to "ascertain the facts with respect to the causes and circumstances of the dispute" and report them. It had power to subpoena witnesses and the production of records. The President could then direct the Attorney-General to seek an injunction from a district

---

and unions. The Service had proposed ballots in 734 instances, with 327 rejections, most of them by unions. Of 251 cases where the results were known, the offer was accepted in 139 cases and rejected in 112. *Ibid.*, p. 35.

37. For a summary of the rather turbulent history of the Mine Workers and their relations to the Coal Mines Administration, the injunction and contempt of court case, the March–April, 1947, stoppage in memorial to the 111 miners killed in the Centralia explosion, and the final agreement with the operators for a new contract including the welfare fund, on July 8, 1947, see *Monthly Labor Review*, 65 (1947), 211, 577.

court, regardless of the restrictions in the Norris–La Guardia Act, and if the court found that the threatened strike or lockout affected an entire industry "or a substantial part thereof" engaged in interstate commerce, and "if permitted to occur or to continue, will imperil the national health or safety, it shall have jurisdiction to enjoin any such strike or lockout, or the continuing thereof, and to make such other orders as may be appropriate."[38]

After the issuance of an injunction, it was the duty of the parties to make every effort to settle their differences, with the assistance of the Mediation and Conciliation Service, but neither party was under any duty to accept any proposal of settlement made by the Service. The President upon the issuance of the injunction was to reconvene the board of inquiry, and the board, if at the end of a sixty-day period the dispute remained unsettled,

shall report to the President the current position of the parties and the efforts which have been made for settlement, and shall include a statement by each party of its position and a statement of the employer's last offer of settlement. The President shall make such report available to the public. The National Labor Relations Board, within the succeeding fifteen days, shall take a secret ballot of the *employees of each employer* involved in the dispute on the question of whether they wish to accept the final offer of settlement made by their employer *as stated by him* and shall certify the results thereof to the Attorney General within five days thereafter.[39]

Finally, unless the dispute had been settled somewhere along the line, the Attorney-General was to ask for the discharge of the injunction, and the President was directed to submit to Congress a full report with any recommendations he might wish to make for consideration and appropriate action. It will be noted that provision was made for "cooling-off periods," lasting up to eighty days, and for use of a restraining order against strikes or lockouts in the interim. These are objected to by the larger part of organized labor. The somewhat related Canadian Act was similarly objected to at its inception forty years ago and at times in more recent years.[40]

Senator Taft, in explaining his bill to the Senate on April 23, 1947, made an important statement of the theory of the bill and especially of this section.[41] He said it was based on the proposition that "the

38. Sec. 208(a)(ii).
39. Sec. 209(b). (Italics ours.)
40. H. A. Millis and R. E. Montgomery, *Organized Labor* (New York: McGraw-Hill Book Co., 1945), pp. 783–92.
41. *Daily Cong. Rec.*, 93:3951–52.

solution of our labor problems must rest on a free economy and on free collective bargaining." He continued:

> That means that we recognize freedom to strike when the question involved is the improvement of wages, hours, and working conditions, when a contract has expired and neither side is bound by a contract. We recognize that right in spite of the inconvenience, and in some cases perhaps danger, to the people of the United States which may result from the exercise of such right. In the long run, I do not believe that that right will be abused. . . .

He went on to express opposition to compulsory arbitration or any steps which might lead to government wage-fixing and government price-fixing. Even for public utilities he held that "there is a right to strike and . . . labor peace must be based on free collective bargaining. We have done nothing to outlaw strikes for basic wages, hours, and working conditions after proper opportunity for mediation." For national emergency strikes the bill provided only for *delay*, through a board of inquiry, an injunction, further mediation efforts, and a vote of employees on the employer's last offer. "If they vote not to accept it, the injunction is dissolved and they are free to strike." And then:

> If there finally develops a complete national emergency threatening the safety and health of the people of the United States, Congress can pass an emergency law to cover the particular emergency.
>
> We did not feel that we should put into the law, as a part of the collective-bargaining machinery, an ultimate resort to compulsory arbitration, or to seizure, or to any other action. We feel that it would interfere with the whole process of collective bargaining. If such a remedy is available as a routine remedy, there will always be pressure to resort to it by whichever party thinks it will receive better treatment through such a process than it would receive in collective bargaining, and it will back out of collective bargaining. It will not make a bona-fide attempt to settle if it thinks it will receive a better deal under the final arbitration which may be provided. . . .
>
> [If we actually face an emergency,] eighty days will provide plenty of time within which to consider the possibility of what should be done; and we believe very strongly that there should not be anything *in this law* which prohibits finally the right to strike.[42]

This statement is in the main sound and shows very well the basic dilemma of a democratic society if faced by an industrial conflict which endangers public safety.[43] But a number of questions must be

42. Italics ours.
43. In this connection see the interesting colloquy between John L. Lewis and several senators on what Mr. Lewis called "the ordinary restraints" which operate

raised as to the particular formula for dealing with such problems which became law. It must be noted, too, that the Senate's plan was considerably broadened in conference when it was made to apply not only to disputes affecting an entire industry but also those affecting "a substantial part thereof." A number in both houses[44] felt that the provision was weak and that compulsory arbitration or sanctions of some sort should be added but that perhaps this was better than no law. The majority evidently hoped that it would be effective against the threats to the national economy which they feared. The minority, on the other hand, argued that no solution had been found for this very difficult problem and that there should be further study before legislation was enacted "which may be too far-reaching and which, in the end, may do more damage than good," especially since the special postwar situation which had engendered labor disputes would pass and more normal conditions return.[45]

Four major specific types of criticism were made of the provisions for dealing with national emergency cases. These were well stated by the minority of the Senate Committee and by Senators Murray and Pepper in debate.[46] One point of attack was the cumbersome and confusing diffusion of responsibility between different officials and agencies, ending with Congress, in the handling of a single dispute. A second difficulty was as to the boards of inquiry. Since their reports were preliminary to obtaining an injunction, the tendency would be to appoint such boards at an early stage in a dispute, when they might frustrate collective bargaining processes. As Senator Murray said:

Certainly they are valueless in the early stages of a dispute when they may completely block negotiation. . . . The use of the boards is important mainly to seek a reasonable ground for agreement and reliably to inform

in collective bargaining in the absence of compulsion. He defined them as "the restraints that animate you and me and every other citizen in our relationships with the others and with our Government; our obligations and our privileges— our privileges modified by our obligations. In other words, good, sound common sense." A bit later he said that the miners "would have gone to work before . . . if the President and his associates had not sought an injunction." U.S. Senate, Committee on Labor and Public Welfare, *Hearings, Labor Relations Program,* 80th Cong., 1st Sess., Pt. 4, March 7, 1947, pp. 1998–2000. This of course fails to note the important part played by the successive coal strikes in bringing about this legislation.

44. E.g., Congressmen Hand, Case, Javits, and Senator Hatch. *Daily Cong. Rec.,* 93:3582, 6437, 6450, 5138.

45. *Ibid.,* p. 5104.

46. *Taft Report,* Pt. 2, *Minority Views,* pp. 15–17; *Daily Cong. Rec.,* 93:5104, 5119, 6678, 6686.

public opinion of the issues and the equities for the purpose of inducing a fair and speedy settlement. It is a question for expert judgment as to when these stages are reached.[47]

The rigid limitation that they must only report the facts without recommendation, also, would limit their usefulness in some cases where the appointing officer might better be free to use his discretion as to the terms of reference to the board, in view of the needs of the particular case. Third, the system was unfair and one-sided, as all the coercion was against the union, by the eighty-day injunction. According to Senator Murray, the government "would abandon impartiality to throw its weight upon the employer's side of the bargaining table."[48] The wisdom of a return to "government by injunction" was sharply questioned. Finally, the requirement of a vote by employees on their employer's last offer was questioned as undesirable and ineffective. Experience with strike votes under the Smith-Connally Act demonstrated the ineffectiveness of such votes conducted by the government and showed that they "serve as an irritant to existing labor-management relations, creating an atmosphere that is harmful to the peaceful resolution of industrial disputes."[49]

On the whole we consider these positions well taken, and it is to be doubted, in spite of the sound approach to the problem which Senator Taft stated, whether Taft-Hartley had found a workable solution for the very real problem of major strikes which may endanger public health and safety. Possibly the problem is insoluble in a society which seeks to preserve both free enterprise and individual liberties. But some further comments must be made. Our first point is that if government efforts are to be successful in maintaining or restoring industrial peace generally, and perhaps especially in these most difficult situations which may create "national emergencies," causes and circumstances as well as machinery and procedures must receive careful attention. Prevention and avoidance of friction may well be more important than any system of handling disturbing industrial relations cases one after the other. Some of the basic factors in bringing about the great strikes of 1945–46 have been discussed earlier,[50] and it is clear that more than procedures were needed to solve the issues these involved. In their attempts to establish peaceful industrial relations, also, New Zealand and Australia did not begin nor have they ended

47. *Daily Cong. Rec.*, 93:5104.
48. *Ibid.*; cf. also Senator Pepper's statement, *ibid.*, p. 6686.
49. *Taft Report*, Pt. 2, *Minority Views*, p. 17; cf. *supra*, ch. 8, pp. 298–300.
50. *Supra*, ch. 8.

with compulsory arbitration. Rather has this been accompanied or followed by more extensive legislation, such as minimum or basic wage laws and social insurance.[51] Nor has Great Britain, while finding specific ways and means of coping with industrial disputes, been unaware of the importance of a strengthened social organization and an improved general standard of living. Among the circumstances important, too, is the matter of whether legislation and common law lay a secure basis for the kind of collective relationship we believe in and establish proper control of antisocial behavior. But, on the other hand, attempted controls may miscarry and have a contrary result. Labor may be put in a "strait jacket" and weakened in the exercise of rightful activities. If there is injustice, or if labor believes so, friction and industrial disputes may be multiplied. Indeed, it is possible that the real objective of some controls is merely to weaken labor, not to protect and further the public interest. The widespread belief on the part of union labor that Taft-Hartley was unfair created this kind of friction and worked against the possibility of resolution of disputes by a common-sense bargaining process.

Our second point, and all but relatively few persons would agree, is that collective bargaining in good faith must be the greatest reliance and must be cherished, not weakened or undermined. We agree with Senator Taft, and with the unanimous feeling among the representatives of labor and management at the 1945 Conference, in opposition to compulsory arbitration. Any acceptable system for dealing with "national emergency" disputes, therefore, must be designed to strengthen, not weaken, collective bargaining. And on this point Taft-Hartley is to be questioned. Instead of leaving the Mediation Service with responsibility to work with the parties and seek a settlement, in broadly defined "national emergency cases" the President might intervene at his discretion, however early in the case. During the eighty-day cooling-off period pressure upon the parties to settle the dispute was postponed, and bargaining might therefore be delayed or prolonged. Moreover, is the role of a board of inquiry simply a preliminary to obtaining an injunction, or is it to assist in reaching a settlement? Its work is quite different in one case than in the other. If it is merely "a whistle stop on the road to an injunction," as John L.

51. Millis and Montgomery, *op. cit.*, pp. 792–822. This is not to imply of course that we consider their systems successful. For a recent analysis which concludes that they have had no greater success in coping with the strike problem than either the United States or Britain, see Morris Weisz, "Conciliation and Arbitration in Australia and New Zealand: 2. An Analysis of Results," *Industrial and Labor Relations Review*, 2 (1948), 105–12.

Lewis called it, why is it needed at all, since the facts are presumably known to the Mediation Service which has been seeking a settlement and knows the progress of the dispute? If the latter, the fact that it has no power to make recommendations prevents its giving the most constructive aid possible. What function was played by the second investigation and report by the board of inquiry? Was the board expected to engage in mediation during the sixty days after the injunction, or what was its relation to the Mediation Service which was told to assist the parties in efforts to reach a settlement during the time? This procedure seems designed to decrease the prestige and effectiveness of the Mediation Service and to militate against its efforts to further successful collective bargaining. It would be preferable to put full responsibility upon the Service, with a right to appoint fact-finding boards when needed and to call upon presidential intervention only in the gravest case.

Note also that the coercion is all against the union which might otherwise strike, none of it against the employer to induce him to seek a reasonable basis for settlement before the expiration of the whole cooling-off period. The lack of recommendation by the board of inquiry is in point here, too. Labor had some justification for thinking this a one-sided system, designed to reduce the power of the union rather than to encourage a just settlement. The resulting distrust and resentment did not promote the accommodation necessary for the resolution of difficult issues at the bargaining table.

In addition, the provision for a vote of the employees of "each employer" on whether they wished to accept the final offer of their employer as stated by him was questionable. Is this a device to undermine the responsibility and authority of a national union? Is it intended to divide employees and set those of one employer against those of others and so break down "industry-wide bargaining"? It might well be interpreted as such. The United Steelworkers, for instance, called this an election "to determine whether the employees wish to repudiate their union by accepting the last offer of the employer."[52] Moreover, the experience with strike votes under the War Labor Disputes Act gives little support to any belief that many workers in such a crisis would repudiate their union. But here again the government appeared to be entering into the dispute to the aid of the employer,

52. United Steelworkers of America, *Legal Department Memorandum No. 3, Labor-Management Relations Act, 1947, Analysis of Provisions of the Act* (Pittsburgh, 1947), p. 11.

580

though in the guise of protecting the public interest. Moreover, as Professor Cox has said:

> Both sides will be forced to campaign actively for the employees' support, thus increasing antagonism and bitterness at a time when negotiations might result in a settlement. The emotional ardor and aggressiveness which union leaders must work up to a high pitch, in order to be sure that in the balloting the employees ratify their position, will later make it exceedingly difficult for the leaders to induce the same employees to accept a reasonable compromise.[53]

Altogether the question must be asked whether the types of intervention here provided did not take away part of labor's weapons, without effective action to promote resolution of the dispute by collective bargaining or to determine the issue by other means on an acceptable basis. Here again we meet the basic dilemma. Can compulsory arbitration be avoided? In any event a democratic society cannot for long maintain a system which seems basically unfair to a substantial and articulate group of citizens.

All this is not to imply that we see no case for fact-finding boards. The question is, however, how and under what circumstances they can be used to encourage, certainly not to discourage, responsible, representative government and the collective resolution of differences in industry by the disputants. It may be true, as labor generally feels, that too many boards, detailed requirements as to procedures, mandatory cooling-off periods, and penalties may discourage and weaken collective bargaining. Experienced men agree that such boards should be few, for, if there are many, they fail to achieve their purpose, either in influencing public opinion or in promoting the efforts of the disputants to settle their disputes. Moreover, there must not be an expectation at the beginning of negotiations that an investigation, with recommendation, is in the offing, lest the disputants feel "What's the use; let it go to a board." A fear of breakdown is frequently necessary to a willingness to make sacrifices, to pare down demands and reach agreements at the conference table, possibly with the timely assistance of an efficient mediator.[54] Moreover, mandatory cooling-off periods, with maintenance of the status quo or return to work on terms in dispute, are likely to operate unevenly and give rise to difficulties. When required under penalty they tend to change "cooling-

53. Archibald Cox, "Some Aspects of the Labor Management Relations Act, 1947," *Harvard Law Review*, 61 (1947–48), 287.
54. Cf. testimony of William H. Davis and of William M. Leiserson before U.S. Senate, Committee on Education and Labor, *Hearings, Labor Fact-Finding Boards Act,* 79th Cong., 1st and 2d Sess., 1945–46, Pt. 1, pp. 115 ff., 141 ff.

off" to "boiling-up," especially when a union feels that its case is a very sound one. Bad morale resulting may lead to violation of the injunction. Then there is the problem of what penalty may be effective. Experience in Canada and New Zealand and Australia is that penalties tend to become a dead letter and to be sparingly if ever used.[55] Only the injunction with possibility of contempt action is likely to have any significance. But the sense of injustice if this has much use works counter to the attitudes needed for co-operation and responsible collective bargaining.

Fact-finding boards, however, are useful in certain circumstances.[56] The problem of industrial breakdowns is not simple and uniform. There are strikes and strikes, most of which involve in no large degree the element of public interest or convenience or necessity. But on the other hand there are instances, as in coal or communications, in which the public interest and necessity is very great and in which fact-finding boards are therefore in order. There may be cases involving a power-seeking union leader, or unions with unacceptable policies, or managements addicted to power and not willing to bargain, in all of which a report by such a board may help to put on pressure for proper bargaining and adjustment. Cases may arise too in which there is need for examination by a competent body of issues of great importance, especially where agreements may set a pattern for substantial parts of the economy. Sometimes new matters, such as the annual wage, may be important in the unions' demands and need study by an expert board before the particular dispute can be settled. For these reasons there is need for fact-finding boards or boards of inquiry composed of able men with sufficient time to do a thorough job. But such boards should be few in number and created only for cases in which the repercussions of a stoppage would be so great that the public interest becomes an outstanding factor, or where novel and important questions are involved which are badly in need of thorough exploration and report. They will not serve the greatest use if fact-finding boards with an eighty-day cooling-off period mean simply routine prolongation of the collective bargaining process in such industries. While there is need for occasional boards of this sort, which the Mediation Service (or the Secretary of Labor) should have authority to establish, they need not and ordinarily should not be accompanied by mandatory prohibition of strikes. Nor should their establishment get into the political arena through the inter-

55. Millis and Montgomery, *op. cit.*, pp. 788–89, 801, 803.
56. Cf. *supra*, ch. 8, p. 308.

vention of the Chief Executive, save in the rarest and most serious of cases.

But the discussion cannot stop here. In the last analysis the sovereignty of the government should not be called in question by any private group. In rare contingencies a stoppage in coal or other basic industries might offer such a threat to the public safety that governmental action is essential.[57] As we have indicated, Taft-Hartley's provision for an injunction and eighty-day waiting period did not appear to offer a fair and constructive solution. What then are the alternatives?

Possibly in strictly limited cases the government should have the power, after mediation and the most effective use of fact-finding, to restrain a strike, or to seize and operate an industry until an emergency situation has been adjusted.[58] But the dilemma remains of how to accomplish this, even in such very rare cases, without undermining responsible collective bargaining. Here we think there is need for more study and an effort to find a plan which could be agreed on by those most competent to know what would work, those who deal constantly with the problems of collective bargaining. Such a study and attempt to find a solution could be successful only in an atmosphere somewhat different from that in which Taft-Hartley was written. Is it not possible that another Labor-Management Conference, with the constructive aid of men in government and industry experienced in these matters, who should be added to the labor and management representatives, might build upon the substantial accomplishments of the 1945 Conference, and carry their agreements further into this delicate field which they were not able to handle successfully in the

57. Cf. the injunction against a threatened railroad strike, made permanent by Justice Goldsborough in the District Court of the District of Columbia on July 2, 1948. The court held that even if the government had not taken over the railroads the permanent injunction would still have been proper, in spite of the Norris–La Guardia Act. In his oral opinion Justice Goldsborough held that unions can strike under the Norris–La Guardia Act even if it would cause great inconvenience and loss of production, "but they can't go to the point . . . however much right they have on their side . . . of adopting a process which will disintegrate society itself, and that is the situation here." U.S. v. Brotherhood of Locomotive Engineers *et al., Daily Labor Report*, No. 129:G-1 (July 2, 1948). The dispute was settled on July 8; but on the unions' request the court refused the government's request for dismissal of the injunction, in order to allow an appeal to the Circuit Court. *New York Times*, July 30, 1948.

58. For a summary of experience with seizure and a conclusion that it is preferable to compulsory arbitration for handling of crisis situations see Ludwig Teller, "Government Seizure in Labor Disputes," *Harvard Law Review*, 60 (1947), 1017–59.

heat and battle of 1945? We think this is the way by which solution might be found for this as yet unsolved problem.

Seven times during 1947 and 1948 the "national emergency" provisions were invoked—in an atomic-energy plant dispute, in meat-packing, twice in coal, and in long-lines telephone, maritime, and Atlantic longshore disputes.[59] In the first, in atomic energy, the injunction averted a stoppage, but the dispute was not settled until after the injunction was lifted, and then it was bargained out with the aid of the Federal Service, after a "last offer" had been rejected in an NLRB poll. In the meat-packing dispute the two-month strike continued after the report of the fact-finding board until the union was defeated; there had been violence at some plants and a bitter aftermath lasted. In the first coal case the injunction stopped the strike, but the dispute was not settled until legal issues involved in the administration of the pension fund were settled by court order. In the second the dispute was settled before the report of the board of inquiry, but only after the disposal of the legal issue of the first dispute, an injunction to compel the union to bargain with the representative of the southern operators, and acceptance by the operators of continuance of the union shop pending adjudication by the NLRB and the courts of its legality. In the telephone dispute the appointment of the board of inquiry served to induce the resumption of bargaining, which then brought agreement. In the maritime case the injunctions averted the threatened stoppage; and agreements were finally reached for the Atlantic and Gulf coasts just before the expiration of the injunction, but again only with the maintenance of the disputed hiring hall pending adjudication of its legality. On the Pacific Coast, on the contrary, the procedures were exhausted, a ballot on a "last offer" was rejected by failure of any of the men concerned to vote, and a three-month strike occurred, during which employers refused to negotiate until union officers filed non-Communist affidavits. Negotiations were, however, finally resumed in November, 1948, and resulted in settlement, again leaving the hiring-hall issue to be litigated. In the Atlantic Coast longshore dispute all the procedures were used without avoiding a strike. As the Federal Mediation Service summarized it:

This case furnishes another instance of a national emergency dispute in which (1) a strike was, in fact, forestalled by the injunction; (2) there

59. For a valuable summary and analysis of this experience see Federal Mediation and Conciliation Service, *First Annual Report*, pp. 40–57. Summaries are available also in current reports in the *Monthly Labor Review* on "Labor-Management Disputes" and "Chronology of Labor Events."

was no substantial progress made toward settlement during the injunction period; (3) all of the procedures of the act (including the ballot on the last offer of the employers) were resorted to without success; (4) a strike occurred after the discharge of the injunction; and (5) the dispute was settled at long last after many meetings between the parties, aided by mediators, but not before great injury was caused to the public and the nation.[60]

The Federal Mediation and Conciliation Service, which was in better position than any other group or individual to appraise this experience, reached conclusions which on the whole square with our analysis of the problem. It is clear from its discussion that the Service felt itself embarrassed and the most effective performance of its functions interfered with by the use of the national emergency provisions. The Service points out that appointment at an early date of a board of inquiry and the scheduling of hearings "has the effect of interfering with the collective bargaining of the parties, particularly in relationships where it is traditional not to reach a settlement until the eleventh hour." The short time allowed such boards to investigate and report exposed them to criticisms and "afforded them insufficient time to operate at maximum efficiency and effectiveness." Moreover, relatively little publicity was given to their reports, and in the absence of a recommendation there is little to mobilize public opinion behind a settlement. The issuance of an injunction in some of the cases "did much to forestall a national crisis and to assist in achieving a peaceful settlement." But the same could not be said of some others. Indeed, in some the injunction period was regarded as a "warming-up" instead of a "cooling-off" period. The Service concludes that "provision for an 80-day period of continued operations, under injunctive order of a court, tends to delay rather than facilitate settlement of a dispute." The last-offer ballots, experience demonstrated, "do nothing to promote settlement of a dispute. To the contrary, they are a disrupting influence in collective bargaining and mediation." The Service concludes: "National emergency disputes vary widely in their facts and circumstances, and it is unlikely that any machinery can be devised that will guarantee satisfactory handling in all situations."[61]

Altogether the experience of this first year and a half indicated that while the provisions for handling "national emergency" disputes served their immediate purposes in some instances, though not all, of preventing strikes, they needed reconsideration in the light of other needs which are in the long run equally important. Taft-Hartley

60. *First Annual Report*, pp. 53–54.   61. *Ibid.*, pp. 55–57.

failed to find the fair and democratic as well as efficient and workable solution needed for this very difficult problem.

STATE LAWS AND STATE LABOR RELATIONS BOARDS

Problems in the relations between federal and state powers were increased by the expansion of regulation in the field of labor relations by both the states and the federal government. Some of the resulting industrial relations and administrative problems need discussion here.[62]

In the field of conciliation of disputes, Taft-Hartley indicated an intent to encourage local and state handling of these matters.[63] In the field of union-security arrangements, also, where strict regulations were imposed, it was clearly not intended to deprive the states of power to go further and make all forms of "compulsory unionism" illegal. Section 14(b) therefore was inserted by the Conference Committee "to make it perfectly clear that nothing in the act is to be construed as authorizing compulsory union membership agreements, in states where the execution or enforcement of such agreements would be contrary to state law."[64] Senator Morse argued that, since the bill laid down a full and complete national policy as to closed- and union-shop agreements, states should not be permitted to impose a more restrictive policy, but his view did not prevail.[65] Senator Taft[66] pointed out correctly that the Wagner Act proviso as to the closed shop had not been intended to override any state prohibition of closed shops, and the amendment simply kept the law as it was, permitting states to impose greater restrictions.[67]

Except for this special case, however, Congress apparently desired

---

62. For a discussion of the complex legal issues see "State Labor Laws in the National Field," *Harvard Law Review*, 61 (1948), 840–50. Cf. also two important and interesting papers in *Proceedings of New York University First Annual Conference on Labor* (Albany: Matthew Bender & Co., 1948): Nathan P. Feinsinger, "Federal-State Relations under the Taft-Hartley Act," pp. 463–96, and E. Merrick Dodd, "Trends in State Legislation Relating to Unions," esp. pp. 530–39.

63. Cf. *supra*, p. 570.

64. *Daily Cong. Rec.*, 93:6602. The section is quoted *supra*, ch. 12, p. 435. Cf. discussion in *Taft Report*, pp. 6–7; *Hartley Report*, pp. 34, 44.

65. *Daily Cong. Rec.*, 93:6613–14.

66. *Ibid.*, p. 6679.

67. *Supra*, ch. 6, p. 203. More restrictive state laws were upheld by the Supreme Court as valid as long as they did not "run afoul of some specific Federal Constitutional prohibition, or of some valid Federal law" in Lincoln Federal Labor Union v. Northwestern Iron and Metal Co., 335 U.S. 525 (1949) and Algoma Plywood and Veneer Co. v. Wisconsin Employment Relations Board, 336 U.S. 301 (March 7, 1949).

to establish a unified national policy in regard to the prevention of unfair labor practices for industries affecting commerce. Accordingly Section 10(a), dealing with the Board's power to prevent such practices, provided:

That the Board is empowered by agreement with any agency of any State or Territory to cede to such agency jurisdiction over any cases in any industry (other than mining, manufacturing, communications, and transportation except where predominantly local in character) even though such cases may involve labor disputes affecting commerce, unless the provision of the State or Territorial statute applicable to the determination of such cases by such agency is inconsistent with the corresponding provision of this Act or has received a construction inconsistent therewith.

It had been felt necessary to clarify relationships between the national Board and the state agencies. Under the Wagner Act the Board had declined to take jurisdiction in some cases, largely local in character, and left them to the states or to the no-man's land of no control. It had worked out an agreement with the New York State Labor Relations Board, the most active of the state agencies, whereby the State Board handled cases rising in retail stores, service trades, and other specified border-line fields. There was more or less co-operation also with the boards of other states.[68] But problems sometimes arose, especially if there was a difference of policy between the state and national boards, as on the controversial issue of foremen's units for collective bargaining. In a key case the Supreme Court held that the state did not have power to apply its policy of certifying foremen's units, when the NLRB had declined to find a foremen's unit appropriate for collective bargaining, and when the national Board had made no delegation of power to deal with this subject.[69] Taft-Hartley specifically provided that jurisdiction could be ceded to such state agencies in cases predominantly local in character, but only if the law or the administrative rulings were consistent with those of Taft-Hartley.

An immediate effect was to nullify the existing agreement with the New York Board. Negotiations were entered upon between the General Counsel and the Board and the agencies of several states, in the hope, as Chairman Herzog said, that

68. For discussion of the experience of state boards and their relations with the NLRB see Charles C. Killingsworth, *State Labor Relations Acts* (Chicago: University of Chicago Press, 1948), ch. 12, "Jurisdictional Problems."

69. Bethlehem Steel Co. *et al.* v. New York State Labor Relations Board, 330 U.S. 767 (1947). Section 14(a) now specified that no employers subject to this Act might be compelled by any law, national or local, to recognize foremen as employees for purposes of collective bargaining.

some practical means can be devised whereby the paramount Federal power may be maintained, without depriving the States of the right to continue to handle essentially local controversies as they have done in the past. Moreover, it is my personal hope that this can be accomplished without imposing Federal policy too rigidly, lest we discourage experimentation in the separate compartments afforded by the several states.[70]

By the end of the first year, however, it had been impossible to conclude any agreements, because in too many respects state and federal statutes were inconsistent. Accordingly, in a year when the NLRB was inundated with new types of cases, and there was pressure to expand its jurisdiction because of the new types of unfair labor practices prohibited, it could not leave to state agencies many of the sorts of cases which they were in the habit of handling. These also were added to the Board's load and contributed to the mounting backlog of pending cases and to the inevitable delays in determining issues and eliminating causes of conflict. State boards continued to function, but at a somewhat lower level of case activity, and always with the possibility of conflict with the national Board if they attempted to act in the border-line types of cases where the NLRB might assert jurisdiction. As a result, the Board suggested to the Joint Congressional Committee that the Committee might wish to reconsider Section 10(a) under which cession to state agencies was impossible unless the state statute was substantially similar to the federal law. As the Board said:

> Because no States have chosen to enact such legislation during the current year, we have found it impossible to cede cases to State tribunals that have been accustomed to handle them in the past. There is considerable danger of creating a no-man's land, especially if the National Labor Relations Board decides to refrain from exercising its own jurisdiction to the hilt.[71]

A number of special problems came to the Board in connection with state laws. One had to do with the more restrictive anti-closed-shop laws. The majority of the Board decided not to hold union-shop elections in states where union-shop agreements were outlawed, although the Chairman and Mr. Houston dissented.[72] Such an election,

70. Address of Chairman Herzog, December 6, 1947.

71. *Ball Committee Hearings*, June 11, 1948, Pt. 2, p. 1125. Cf. also *supra*, ch. 11, pp. 400–402, on policies as to jurisdiction.

72. Giant Food Shopping Center, 77 NLRB 791 (May, 1948). Since the case involved an interstate unit, the Board held that the unit for the union-shop election might be smaller than the established unit for collective bargaining, although the Chairman thought that permitting a different unit for the union-shop election would create more problems than it would solve.

Further complexities were introduced when a multi-state agreement covered

the Board held, would "lead only to the circumvention and frustration of state law" which Congress clearly did not intend. The Chairman in his dissent thought this policy not required by the Act or its legislative history. The result, he pointed out, was to make a state offense into a federal offense, by rendering it impossible for the employer and the union to comply with federal law. He objected to thus permitting the state to set a federal standard. Another question was whether there should be both a state and a federal election where state laws required an election to authorize a union-security agreement, and whether the state or federal standard should rule when the state required more than a majority to win. Two elections were being held in a number of states, at unnecessary cost and disturbance of production;[73] but agreement was reached with the Wisconsin Board in September, 1948, that one election, conducted by the NLRB, would be accepted by both agencies.[74] It was the policy of the General Counsel, also, that regional offices should certify authorization for a union shop only when an election met the state requirements, if more than a majority was required by state law.[75] But the Board decided, in November, 1948, that in states where there was only *regulation*, not *prohibition*, of union-security agreements, the federal law should prevail.[76]

---

employees in states permitting union-security agreements, others prohibiting them, and others regulating them. The Board decided to exclude from the unit for the union-shop election employees in states forbidding such agreements; but that in states with only regulatory legislation the national law prevailed, and employees in such states were included in the unit. Chairman Herzog considered himself bound by the policy established in the Giant Food Shopping Center case and concurred here on the ground that "the formula provides the best possible solution of an almost insoluble legal and practical problem." Northland Greyhound Lines, 80 NLRB 288 (November, 1948).

73. Cf. *Ball Committee Hearings*, Pt. 2, pp. 798–99.

74. *Daily Labor Report*, No. 173:A-10 (September 3, 1948).

75. Address of Associate General Counsel Charles M. Brooks, May 12, 1948.

76. Northland Greyhound Lines, 80 NLRB 288 (November, 1948); n. 72, *supra*. Accordingly, in Safeway Stores, 81 NLRB No. 66 (January, 1949), the Board certified that the majority of the employees eligible had voted to authorize a union-security agreement, overruling the Regional Director's determination that no certificate of authority could be issued when the Colorado requirement of a three-fourths majority had not been met. The Supreme Court in the Algoma decision (*supra*, n. 67) upheld a Wisconsin Board decision requiring a company to disregard a union-shop agreement entered into after certification by the NLRB unless the state requirement of a two-thirds majority was met. But thereafter in Western Electric Co., 84 NLRB No. 111 (June, 1949), the NLRB reaffirmed its Northland policy. It held that there was no necessary conflict between the Algoma holding and the view adopted here that "the States and the Federal Govern-

The major difficulty in these situations arose from the fact that when the Board had refused to hold a qualifying union-shop election, in a state which prohibited such agreements, if the Board later found an employer or a union guilty of discrimination under a union-shop agreement a federal sanction would then be used to enforce a state law. The propriety of thus permitting states to set the standard on the basis of which a federal law is administered seems highly questionable, especially in view of the widespread reports that many states were not successfully enforcing their own more restrictive laws. This is quite different from merely permitting states to establish and enforce certain regulations for themselves.[77] Considerable difficulty in collective bargaining was of course introduced also by the variation in state laws and the complex federal policy giving "faith and credit" to these laws, at least to some degree, when collective agreements were company-wide or covered other units which crossed state lines.[78]

Another problem arose in connection with efforts of unions to demonstrate their majority status and obtain recognition when they could not use the NLRB because they had not met the filing requirements of Taft-Hartley. In a Utah case the state board held an election of Kaiser-Frazer blast-furnace workers, which the CIO Steelworkers won. Meantime, the Machinists had petitioned the NLRB for an election in the same unit. The General Counsel, on the theory that the Act gave the NLRB exclusive jurisdiction in this field, obtained a temporary injunction against the state board to prevent its certification of the Steelworkers.[79] The NLRB then ordered an election, with only the Machinists on the ballot. To do otherwise, it held, would amount to ceding its jurisdiction to the Utah State Board,

---

ment have concurrent jurisdiction to *regulate* the union shop, each being supreme in its own sphere. It follows from this view that any certification . . . is to be construed as certifying only that *federal* requirements have been met. . . . The question of compliance . . . with State laws regulating the union shop is a question of State law to be determined by State authorities in a State proceeding."

77. Feinsinger, *op. cit.*, pp. 489–91. But see also the contrary argument in *Ball Committee Report*, Pt. 1, March 15, 1948, pp. 31–32. It should be noted that the committee's comments were published before the Giant Food Shopping Center decision of the majority of the Board, which adopted the position of the committee. It is said, however, that the decision had been made before the committee's position was made known. See also *Ball Committee Report*, Pt. 3, December 31, 1948, pp. 73–74; *Thirteenth Annual Report*, pp. 40–44.

78. *Ball Committee Hearings*, Pt. 2, pp. 758, 776.

79. NLRB v. Industrial Commission of the State of Utah, District Court for State of Utah, July 9, 1948, 22 *LRRM* 2294. Cf. also Feinsinger, *op. cit.*, pp. 495–96.

which it was unable to do, since the Utah law did not impose requirements comparable to the filing requirements of the federal law.[80]
Probably it was essential thus to protect the Board's jurisdiction over
a basic industry. But the practical effect was to prolong a dispute
over recognition, even when the majority status of one union had
been demonstrated.

If these provisions of Taft-Hartley were maintained, what effects
were to be expected? It was undoubtedly desired that many states
should adopt laws patterned on Taft-Hartley, and it might be expected that to some extent this would be done, should these national
policies continue. The federal Act not only set a pattern but also
exerted pressure in that direction, at least for those states which
wished to handle some of their labor problems through state labor
relations acts. In addition, the policies of the federal Act, especially
through the loosely defined and indefinite unfair labor practices applied to union activities, might be expected to affect decisions in state
courts. A number of early decisions were reported by state courts
against nonfiling unions, indicating that they were without standing
and could be enjoined from striking or picketing.[81] A considerable
increase in the number of injunctions issued by state courts in labor
disputes was reported by many union representatives. Some of these
were based in part on alleged violations of the Taft-Hartley Act, thus
apparently assuming a concurrent jurisdiction with the NLRB to enforce federal law.[82] Undoubtedly any trend in statutory or court-
made law in the states toward the new pattern of federal labor policy
would be approved by the proponents of the latter. It is in accord
with past developments, too, that a federal policy once well established gives leadership to the states and encourages state action along
similar lines. This is sound and to be desired when federal policy is
well based and constructive.

Some of the state laws and decisions of state courts, on the other
hand, were more restrictive of union activities than Taft-Hartley. If
Congress meant to establish a uniform national policy for the prevention of unfair labor practices, what was the duty of the NLRB on
such matters? Was it not the duty of the Board to protect federal
jurisdiction by intervening in appropriate cases, not only against

80. Kaiser-Frazer Parts Corp., 80 NLRB 1050 (December, 1948).
81. See cases cited by Arthur J. Goldberg, CIO General Counsel, in testimony
before the Ball Committee, June 4, 1948, *Ball Committee Hearings*, Pt. 2, pp.
701–3.
82. A. Norman Somers, "The National Labor Relations Board from Wagner to
Taft-Hartley," *Federal Bar Journal*, 9 (1948), esp. 333–34, 357–58.

action of a state board, but also against action by other state agencies, including the courts, in order to maintain the paramount federal policy of protecting the right of self-organization and preventing unfair labor practices as defined in the federal law?[83] The desired uniformity in national labor policy would seem to require that either less liberal or more liberal standards in labor relations law as enforced by state boards or courts should give way to the paramount federal policy.

Questions must be raised finally as to how much centralization of policy and control is desirable in this area. What should be the balance between uniformity of national policy on basic rights and duties in labor relations, and the traditional freedom of the states to carry on social experiments? And how far should the federal government go in detailed regulation, and how much should rather be left to the states, if not to the parties themselves, to work out by collective bargaining processes? A case for national uniformity of policy in the law of labor relations rests upon the national character of the larger part of business enterprise, through control by corporations operating nation wide, and through competition in industry-wide markets. The accident of state borders gives no sufficient reason in such industries for important differences in the protection of rights either of workers or of employers, or in limitations upon what is permissible in the way of union activities, strikes, picketing, union-security agreements, or other matters.

On the other hand, there are practical problems which argue against uniformity and extreme centralization. One is the sheer number of the businesses, labor organizations, and collective bargaining units to be regulated once detailed regulation is decided upon. Another is the distance and variety of conditions which make uniformity difficult to achieve and centralization of control almost, if not entirely, impossible from the standpoint of administration. Decentralization is essential if the controls are to work, and the only question is whether enough decentralization of administration is possible under a federal agency, or whether substantial areas had not better be left to state control, or to none. In budgetary terms, also, it is most unlikely that a federal agency would ever be given sufficient funds and staff to handle with the needed expedition the tremendous volume of work which would come to it under a completely federal system of control. And, finally, since no sure answers have yet been given to the question of the types of control needed in this complex

83. Cf. Dodd, *op. cit.*, pp. 532–39.

and changing field of labor relations, there is still a case for an area left to experiment by the states, perhaps subject to certain standards laid down by federal law or agencies.

The Taft-Hartley Act failed to give a clear and thoroughly considered answer to these problems. Its sponsors spoke of the desirability of uniform national policy, and the Act greatly extended control over labor relations and union and employer actions. At the same time it permitted state autonomy at one crucial point, and it is not clear to what extent it intended the federal policy to override more restrictive state policies on other points. It must be noted, too, that the centralization apparently intended by the Eightieth Congress in this field is contrary to policy in other areas, such as that of the employment services which were turned back to the states, and of unemployment insurance where a wide field for experiment and variation is permitted to the states. Is more centralization really essential in labor relations? And how far did Congress intend the centralization to go? The Act was far from clear on these points.

This whole problem needs reconsideration and clear decision as to the proper areas of federal and state control in labor relations and the extent to which federal standards must rule. Perhaps wise policy would be in the direction of leaving to the states control over local and essentially local enterprises even though they "affect commerce," and permitting cession to state agencies of border-line fields, subject only to certain broad standards, without insistence upon uniformity of state and federal laws in all important details. In industries substantially affecting commerce the federal standards should rule, and more restrictive state laws should not be permitted to affect the rights and duties of the parties. With discretion in the Board to work out practicable administrative decentralization and methods of co-operation with state agencies, and with fair and reasonable standards in the federal law, a workable compromise between federal and state powers in this complex field could be achieved. Taft-Hartley, with its extension of control, posed the problem but did not solve it.

RESTRICTION ON POLITICAL CONTRIBUTIONS AND EXPENDITURES

Another restriction put upon labor organizations had only remote if any relationship to the stated purposes of the amended Act. Section 304 limited the political activity of unions by an amendment to Section 313 of the Federal Corrupt Practices Act. That Act, in effect since 1925, had proscribed the making of contributions by any corporation in connection with any election at which presidential electors, senators, or representatives are selected. The War Labor Disputes Act of 1943, which had applied these prohibitions to labor organizations also, was to expire at the end of June, 1947. Taft-Hartley amended the 1925 Act to cover labor organizations and extended the prohibition to *expenditures* as well as contributions. It made the limitation more extensive by applying it also to primary elections or political conventions or caucuses in connection with national elections. Violations were made subject to penalties of fine or imprisonment.[84] The prohibition is on its face sweeping and unrestricted.

There had been no such section in the Senate bill. The Hartley bill had included it, with the explanation that this was meant to make permanent the Smith-Connally War Labor Disputes Act restriction upon unions, with the additional limitation upon *expenditures* of both unions and corporations. It was explained to the House as meant to protect the rights of the individual union member to support any candidate he chooses and "to decide for himself whether or not his money will be spent for political purposes."[85] The only other discussion in the House was a careful and detailed statement in opposition, by Congressman Miller of California, who was never answered.[86] After the Conference Committee accepted the House clause with some additions, Senator Taft explained that the word "expenditure" had been added to "plug a loophole," since it had been thought that "contribution" was not broad enough to cover "expenditure." Under Smith-Connally unions had in some cases published political pamphlets or advertisements. The intent was stated broadly: "Labor unions are supposed to keep out of politics in the same way that corporations are supposed to keep out of politics."[87]

In the Senate the major "debate" took the form of questions and answers by which senators elicited from the committee chairman his interpretation of what the section would mean.[88] Senator Taft indicated, however, in support of the restriction, that it was unfair for a union, presumably including members of different political opinions, to be able to spend its funds for political purposes in support of particular candidates whom some of the members might oppose.[89]

84. *Supra,* ch. 13, p. 483.

85. *Daily Cong. Rec.,* 93:3535, 7507; *Hartley Report,* p. 46.

86. *Daily Cong. Rec.,* 93:3580–81. The Minority of the House Committee also had argued that the proposal was one-sided and a dangerous precedent. *Hartley Report,* p. 111.

87. *Daily Cong. Rec.,* 93:6593–94, 6597.

88. *Ibid.,* pp. 6593–98, 6604–5.   89. *Ibid.,* pp. 6594, 6598.

Moreover, it was assumed that unions and corporations were comparable for this purpose and that it was as proper to limit political activity by the former as by the latter. There was considerable uncertainty, however, as to just what a union could or could not do under this limitation. Senator Taft indicated that unions could organize separate associations, as the CIO had done in its Political Action Committee, supported by voluntary contributions. But a union could not use its funds from dues for political purposes. It could not publish a newspaper from union funds collected from dues, and use the paper for support of certain candidates, nor use its funds to publish pamphlets or for radio time in connection with an election campaign. Even the publication by a union of voting records, unless it "was not colored in any way,"[90] would apparently be unlawful. But a distinction was attempted according to the source of funds—a distinction not explicit in the language of the section. The Senator said that a union newspaper would be free of the restriction if the union charged the members for subscriptions.

> The union can separate the payment of dues from the payment for a newspaper if its members are willing to do so, that is, if the members are willing to subscribe to that kind of a newspaper. I presume the members would be willing to do so. A union can publish such a newspaper. . . . But the prohibition is against labor unions using their members' dues for political purposes, which is exactly the same as the prohibition against a corporation using its stockholders' money for political purposes, and perhaps in violation of the wishes of many of its stockholders.[91]

The opponents, notably Senators Morse, Pepper, Kilgore, and Magnuson,[92] made several points which were never directly met by the supporters of the provision. They emphasized not the issue of any dissenting minorities but rather that of the right of workers to an effective means of political action, which would be restricted by this provision. They pointed out also distinctions between a corporation and a union, "an unincorporated association of citizens," and raised the question of constitutional rights. As Senator Pepper said:

> This prohibition, therefore, is denying to citizens of this Nation the right of free press, the right of free speech, the right of disseminating information of public value. It is a chain upon the citizens' activity, and we well know that these labor organizations are composed of working people. They do not have people who are their members who can contribute hundreds of thousands or millions of dollars to political campaigns. They have to do it collectively. So they are denied the privilege of collective expression in po-

90. *Ibid.*, pp. 6604–5.   91. *Ibid.*, p. 6598.
92. *Ibid.*, pp. 6604–6, 6681–83, 6689, 6692.

litical campaigns because they are being discriminated against in favor of the corporations of the country.[93]

And Senator Morse said:

> Such attempts to weaken the political strength of labor will only serve to make the workers of this country more convinced than ever that they must take a very active part in politics if they are to protect their rights and freedoms.[94]

As Senator Morse expected, the immediate effect of the Act and this provision was to stimulate political activity on the part of the unions, partly through separate organizations set up and supported by voluntary contributions, and partly by the unions directly. It was hoped to obtain an early test of the provisions on expenditures, which labor considered clearly a restriction of constitutional rights. The AFL for the first time set up a Labor's League for Political Education and appealed to its membership for contributions of at least one dollar each for its support. The CIO continued its Political Action Committee. The International Association of Machinists organized a Machinists Non-Partisan Political League.[95] Widespread activity in different internationals and locals was directed to encouraging interest in voting and in registering in preparation for the 1948 campaign. In addition, a number of unions directly challenged the law by publishing political advertisements or supporting congressional candidates in their newspapers.[96] Unions were hampered, nevertheless, by the restrictions, the uncertainty as to what unions might lawfully do, and the increased difficulty of financing political activities if the union could not use its funds directly.

The first major test of this provision came when Philip Murray and the CIO were indicted for using the *CIO News* to promote a candidacy for Congress in a Maryland special congressional election in July, 1947. On March 15, 1948, Judge Ben Moore handed down the

93. *Ibid.*, p. 6606.
94. *Ibid.*
95. *New York Times*, December 6, 1947, August 11, 1947; International Association of Machinists, *The Truth about the Taft-Hartley Law and Its Consequences to the Labor Movement* (Washington, D.C., 1948), p. 22; *American Federationist*, 55 (January, 1948), 8–9.
96. Cf. *infra*, ch. 16, p. 653. The CIO published the voting records of members of Congress in 1947 and again in 1948. *CIO News*, July 19, 1948. A Hartford, Conn., local of the Painters, AFL, and its president were indicted and convicted for spending union funds for a political advertisement in a local newspaper and buying radio time for a political broadcast. The convictions were reversed by the Second Circuit Court, on the authority of the CIO case decision, *infra*, n. 98. 79 F. Supp. 516 (D.C., D. Conn., July 28, 1948); 23 *LRRM* 2331.

opinion of the Federal District Court for the District of Columbia, holding that the questioned portion of Section 304 "is an unconstitutional abridgment of freedom of speech, freedom of the press and freedom of assembly," and dismissed the indictment. On appeal to the Supreme Court the order of dismissal was affirmed unanimously; but the ground for so doing was a narrow one on the part of the majority, and the issue of constitutionality was not decided. Justice Reed for the majority, in spite of the plain statements of Senator Taft, construed the section as not to prohibit such newspaper publication as had occurred in this case.

It is unduly stretching language to say that the members or stockholders are unwilling participants in such normal organizational activities, including the advocacy thereby of governmental policies affecting their interests, and the support thereby of candidates thought to be favorable to their interests. . . .

. . . .

We are unwilling to say that Congress by its prohibition against corporations or labor organizations making an "expenditure in connection with any election" of candidates for federal office intended to outlaw such a publication.[97]

Justice Rutledge, with whom Justices Black, Douglas, and Murphy joined, concurred in the result, but wrote a strong dissent from the majority opinion. He considered that the majority by its interpretation had set aside "the one clearly intended feature of the statute apart from its general objectives," and in so doing had "emasculated the statute"; it should instead have faced the issue of constitutionality. In a long decision, which should be read by all concerned for civil and political liberties in the United States, he held that the amendment was clearly unconstitutional. We will quote three paragraphs, which state the central issue.

There is . . . an effect in restricting expenditures for the publicizing of political views not inherently present in restricting other types of expenditure, namely, that it necessarily deprives the electorate, the persons entitled to hear, as well as the author of the utterance, whether an individual or a group, of the advantage of free and full discussion and of the right of free assembly for that purpose.

The most complete exercise of those rights is essential to the full, fair, and untrammelled operation of the electoral process. To the extent they are curtailed the electorate is deprived of information, knowledge and opinion vital to its function. To say that labor unions as such have nothing

97. U.S. v. CIO, 335 U.S. 106, 123 (June 21, 1948), affirming 77 F. Supp. 35 (D.C. D.C.).

of value to contribute to that process and no vital or legitimate interest in it is to ignore the obvious facts of political and economic life and of their increasing interrelationship in modern society. . . .

. . . .

A statute which, in the claimed interest of free and honest elections, curtails the very freedoms that make possible exercise of the franchise by an informed and thinking electorate, and does this by indiscriminate blanketing of every expenditure in connection with an election, serving as a prior restraint upon expression not in fact forbidden as well as upon what is, cannot be squared with the First Amendment.[98]

This is not the place for a discussion of the issues involved, or of whether in fact there should be restrictions of any sort upon political expenditures of voluntary associations, since these important matters are not directly related to our major interest of industrial relations and national labor policy. The problems are complex and must be considered in relation with other efforts to insure honest and free elections. But should not the question be asked whether these matters have any proper place in a law having to do with industrial relations and labor policy, unless the provision is simply an indication of an effort to weaken unions and their influence in public life?[99] And does not experience indicate, in any event, that full publicity, rather than prohibition, is the better way to deal with whatever problems are found in this field?

THE JOINT CONGRESSIONAL COMMITTEE

Title IV set up a Joint Congressional Committee "to study and report on basic problems affecting friendly labor relations and productivity." President Truman in vetoing the Case Bill had asked for a commission to study and make recommendations for long-term

98. U.S. v. CIO, 335 U.S. 106, 144, 155.

99. A bitter statement to that effect occurs in the CIO brief to the Supreme Court in the U.S. v. CIO case. It spoke of "unconstitutional discrimination" against unions, in a law which "itself is regarded as so oppressive by labor organizations as to challenge their very existence and to create a greater need than ever for effective political action in order to secure its repeal." It charged that Congress "passed a law directed at a particular group in our society and attached to that law a device permanently to shield it from the political consequences of having passed it." *Daily Labor Report*, No. 80:A-5 (April 23, 1948). The Ball Committee in its first report indicated that it had "given some thought to the advisability of . . . an amendment . . . which would define and except particular activities of regularly circulated newspapers and periodicals," also that it would continue to study the effects of these restrictions "with a view to making recommendations for amendment if experience demonstrates that they prohibit political activity which may be desirable." *Ball Committee Report*, Pt. 1, March 15, 1948, pp. 39–40; cf. also its *Report*, Pt. 3, December 31, 1948, pp. 63–65.

legislation on labor relations, and in his January, 1947, State of the Union Message he went further and proposed a temporary joint commission to make a broad study preparatory to legislation.[100] It should include representatives of the public and of management and labor, in addition to members of both parties in the Senate and House, he said, since "the President, the Congress, and management and labor have a continuing responsibility to cooperate in seeking and finding the solution of these problems." The commission should study the problem of nation-wide strikes in vital industries, the best methods and procedures for collective bargaining, and the underlying causes of labor-management disputes, and make its first report with recommendations for legislation not later than March 15, 1947. But Congress chose to rely upon its own committee hearings and reports, and the bill which became law included provision for later study by a Joint Congressional Committee.

This committee was composed of seven members each of the Senate and House Labor Committees. An appropriation of $150,000 was authorized, and the committee was given the usual powers to hold hearings, subpoena witnesses and the production of records, and employ staff and consultants. The final report with recommendations was due not later than January 2, 1949.[101] The duties of the committee were stated as follows:

The committee, acting as a whole or by subcommittee, shall conduct a thorough study and investigation of the entire field of labor-management relations, including but not limited to—

(1) the means by which permanent friendly cooperation between employers and employees and stability of labor relations may be secured throughout the United States;

(2) the means by which the individual employee may achieve a greater productivity and higher wages, including plans for guaranteed annual wages, incentive profit-sharing and bonus systems;

(3) the internal organization and administration of labor unions, with special attention to the impact on individuals of collective agreements requiring membership in unions as a condition of employment;

(4) the labor relations policies and practices of employers and associations of employers;

(5) the desirability of welfare funds for the benefit of employees and their relation to the social-security system;

(6) the methods and procedures for best carrying out the collective-bargaining processes, with special attention to the effects of industry-wide or regional bargaining upon the national economy;

100. *Cong. Rec.* (bound), 92:6674–78; 93:137.
101. Extended to March 1, 1949, by congressional action on August 5, 1948.

(7) the administration and operation of existing Federal laws relating to labor relations; and

(8) such other problems and subjects in the field of labor-management relations as the committee deems appropriate.

There was general agreement with the objectives of this provision, although the minority of the Senate Committee argued that thorough investigation should be made before, rather than after, legislation was enacted. It also raised the question whether the committee was so constituted

as to give assurance that its studies would be productive of sound results or that its recommendations would be of a character to command the whole-hearted respect by all of the interests concerned which legislation in this field urgently requires. The problems which underlie labor unrest are deep-rooted, and involve basic and conflicting interests. These interests of management, of labor, and of the public should all be directly represented on the investigatory body, and should all participate in its deliberations and in the formulation of its recommendations.[102]

This important issue must be considered in evaluating the work of the committee.

Senator Taft, in explaining the provision to the Senate, said that Congress had not had time to study "a good many fundamental questions relating to labor relations" and that there should be "a more fundamental study leading to better relations between employer and employee."[103] Later speakers emphasized another function, that of watching the operation and administration of the new law. Senator Ives, particularly, said that the committee had two major areas of responsibility in the first instance:

First, it must see that there is no sabotage in the administration of the law . . . to see that the administration is as we intend it to be, that there is fairness and justice under the law. . . .

The second main function . . . this year will be the job of ascertaining those parts of the bill which may not be perfect, which may not work satisfactorily . . . to prepare appropriate amendments, and to see that [they] are offered and properly supported at the next session. . . .

. . . The joint committee should act in part to help formulate administrative policy and procedure as well as to perform its functions as a strictly legislative agency at the inception of the new law.[104]

When the committee was appointed, it included, naturally enough, Senators Taft and Ball and Representatives Hartley and Hoffman, all

---

102. *Taft Report*, Pt. 2, *Minority Views*, p. 40.
103. *Daily Cong. Rec.*, 93:3955.
104. *Ibid.*, p. 7684; cf. also *ibid.*, pp. 4410, 7686.

of whom had been strong supporters of this, if not a stronger, Act. Others also were counted as advocates of "strong legislation." Senators Ives, Ellender, and Smith (N.J.) had all expressed some reservations about the strengthening amendments, and Senator Ives especially was on record as willing to moderate the Act if the need were shown. Senators Murray and Pepper and Representatives Lesinski and Kelley were the minority in opposition to Taft-Hartley.[105] Senator Ball was elected chairman and announced the committee's plans, which included studies of labor relations in a series of plants, study of industry-wide bargaining, of welfare funds, of union government, and of employer associations and their part in labor relations, and "study, in cooperation with NLRB and other affected agencies, of the operation of the new law with a view to recommending promptly any changes found to be necessary or desirable."[106] For this ambitious program it assembled a small staff, of ten according to the first report, headed by Thomas E. Shroyer, chief counsel, who had been counsel for the Senate committee during the writing of the bill. It expected the co-operation of the Departments of Commerce and Labor on some of the studies and to hold hearings later in the year.

Two major questions come to mind at once. One is whether the Joint Committee was so set up as to be able to make the long-range studies needed as a basis for agreement on sound and constructive legislation or other action on important labor relations problems. The other had to do with its function as "the watchdog committee," which it was called, and the relation of this to the administration of the law. On the latter the issues were suggested by some early history.

Two days after the Joint Committee, generally called the Ball Committee, had organized, six of its seven Senate members were present at the hearing[107] of the Senate Committee on Labor and Public Welfare on the confirmation of the new appointees to the NLRB and of General Counsel Robert N. Denham. The questioning of Mr. Denham in regard to consultation with the committee was exceedingly interesting. Upon a question from Senator Ball, Mr. Denham agreed that the committee would be a source of information as to the intent in case of any questions that might not be clear in the Act.[108]

105. *New York Times,* July 18, 1948.   106. *Ibid.,* July 26, 1948.

107. U.S. Senate, Committee on Labor and Public Welfare, *Hearings, Nominations to National Labor Relations Board,* 80th Cong., 1st Sess., July 23, 1947, cited as *Senate Confirmation Hearings, 1947.*

108. *Ibid.,* pp. 2–3. There followed a colloquy in which the Senator made clear that he expected Mr. Denham to consolidate the position of the Administrative

There was agreement, however, on the necessity for co-operation between the General Counsel and the Board. Democratic senators raised question as to the relation between an administrator and Congress. Was the law to be construed as written, and as determined by the courts finally, or was it perhaps to be amended by Mr. Denham on the advice of the committee? It was agreed that if he found parts which were not working satisfactorily, he would report to the committee, but that the law was to be strictly enforced. The final word on the subject, however, was Senator Ball's question, answered in the affirmative by Mr. Denham:

> When you are confronted with possible conflicting interpretations, before you make your final decision you would merely consult with this joint commission which, as I say, contains all the members of the conference committee and men who are probably in the best position to know what the intent of Congress was, whether it is clearly expressed in the legislative history or not, before you made your decision?[109]

All this gave some basis for the fear that the Ball Committee might interfere in administration, to the detriment of the independence of the agency in performing its functions under the new Act. The fear was accentuated by the fact that the Senate adjourned without acting on the appointments. Final confirmation of all the appointees was not given until December 16, 1947.[110] Rumor had it that, while the Board and the General Counsel were working out their plans for the necessary reorganization of administration, the Ball Committee interjected itself and sought to discuss many of the details, despite objection by some members of the Board. In any event, it was reported[111] that the President summoned the Board and the General Counsel and instructed them that, while they should co-operate with the Joint Committee, they should not forget that they were an independent agency in the executive branch of the government and responsible to the President, not to the congressional committee.

The line was undoubtedly difficult to draw properly between

Director of the Field Division, held by Oscar S. Smith, with that of the General Counsel (cf. *supra*, ch. 2, pp. 53–54, and *infra*, ch. 16, pp. 619–20), also that the General Counsel should have a major voice in the selection of field personnel, and that, if any question were raised involving any present employees, they should be checked again with the FBI, and, if the report were adverse, they should be dismissed.

109. *Senate Confirmation Hearings, 1947*, p. 17. For a pertinent comment by Professor Cox on interpretation of the law cf. *supra*, ch. 11, p. 417.

110. *New York Times*, August 1, 1947; December 17, 1947.

111. *Ibid.*, August 12, 1947.

reasonable consultation and domination or interference. Rumors were abroad, though they cannot be checked, that the General Counsel consulted the committee on appointments and on policy and that in some instances members of the committee approached the General Counsel in regard to the handling of particular cases.[112] However far such attempts at interference in the day-to-day operations under the Act went, anything of the sort was clearly improper and a danger to the integrity of the administrative process. In addition, at least two points in the first report of the committee suggest pressure upon the Board as to decisions in particular cases. One was several pages of discussion of the ITU cases then pending. The other was a discussion of whether union-shop elections should be held in states which restricted or forbade union-security agreements, ending with the statement that if the Board held such elections, the committee might find it advisable to recommend amendment to the Act.[113] The committee let its displeasure with certain decisions be known to the Board. It is significant that the Board in its statement to the Joint Committee on June 11, 1948, after mentioning the difficulty in deciding the congressional intent on some matters such as "discharge for cause," and the possibility that Congress might wish to clarify or correct their interpretations by amending the Act, said very properly:

We believe, however, that we would be both shifting and abdicating our responsibilities as judicial officers if we sought the Committee's advice before we had considered and decided this or any similar difficult issue to the best of our own ability. It will be time enough to ascertain whether the Courts and the Congress share our view of the law after we have exercised our independent judgment.[114]

Little public information is available on the investigations carried on by the Joint Committee until the publication of its first report on March 15, 1948. Senator Ball in December had issued an invitation to employers, employees, and the general public to report specific examples of inequities arising under the law, although the committee stated that it would not inject itself into disputes in progress.[115] When the report was published, a controversy between the majority and the minority threw some light on the operations of the committee. The minority promptly criticized the majority report as "political

112. See *infra*, ch. 16, pp. 627–28, for a report of intervention by Senator Taft to urge filing of the contempt petition in the ITU case.
113. *Ball Committee Report*, Pt. 1, March 15, 1948, pp. 25–27, 31–32. Cf. *supra*, n. 77.
114. *Ball Committee Hearings*, Pt. 2, pp. 1125–26.
115. *New York Times*, December 18, 1947.

in its approach and misleading in its findings."[116] They said that they had not received their copies of the report until the day before the committee was called on to approve or disapprove its contents, and that the limited time had not permitted preparation of a detailed analysis. A minority report was submitted on April 1, 1948,[117] with acknowledgment to the Public Affairs Institute for aid on the factual data. Senator Ball then stated that the minority members had abstained almost entirely from participating in Joint Committee meetings and that the Public Affairs Institute, which made the study for the minority report, was a "straight propaganda organization," the head of its sponsoring committee being A. F. Whitney, president of the Brotherhood of Railroad Trainmen.[118] All this suggests that the facilities of the committee were not equally available to the minority and majority members and that the committee functioned not with an objective, nonpartisan, fact-finding and analytical approach but in a partisan spirit along the lines of the preconceptions of the two groups.

The majority report consisted of under fifty pages of analysis, followed by some one hundred and fifty pages of reports on plant studies made by the staff on seven different companies. The summary of findings reported tentatively that, "in over-all application, and basically controlling aspects, this law is working well, without undue hardship upon employer or employee, and promoting the adjustment of labor problems equitably and in more friendly and cooperative relationships."[119] The report went on to make a number of claims, such as that secondary boycotts, jurisdictional disputes, and strikes were decreasing, wages had increased, settlement of disputes had been facilitated, rights of individual workers had in no wise suffered, Communists were being eliminated from unions, and the administrative reorganization had operated to increase public confidence in the Board. About its own work the committee said:

The committee has not sought to interfere with the independence or judgment of any agency or Department charged with its enforcement or interpretation. Rather, we have conceived our function to be one of keeping in daily contact with administrative developments in order to be in a position to call to the attention of the Congress any defects which might develop in the law itself or in its administration, requiring remedial action.[120]

116. *Daily Labor Report,* No. 51:AA-11-14 (March 15, 1948).
117. *Ball Committee Report,* Pt. 2, April 1, 1948.
118. *Daily Cong. Rec.,* 94:4153–54 (April 2, 1948).
119. *Ball Committee Report,* Pt. 1, March 15, 1948, p. 2.
120. *Ibid.,* p. 4.

It stated also the unanimous agreement of the committee that every attempt should be made to obtain the co-operation of both management and labor in any studies; that all investigation was to be conducted "on an objective and impartial basis with no preconceived notions of what the facts are before they are found"; and that only in the most exceptional cases would the committee inject itself into a current dispute.[121]

The most valuable parts of the report were its rather detailed and factual account of the reorganization and operations of the Board and of the development of policies in certain types of cases. There was some inconclusive discussion of the relationship to state laws, of damage suits and other suits by private parties, of the restrictions on political expenditures, of welfare funds, and of industry-wide bargaining. Studies were said to be continuing on these questions, and recommendation for legislation might later be made. The committee concluded that "both the announced policies, and the actions taken, demonstrate that the act is being well administered."[122] They felt that "the law has adequately provided a remedy for the abuse which Congress sought to correct," and reported that no information had been received indicating a need for amendment.[123]

Senators Murray and Pepper and Representatives Lesinski and Kelley, as the minority, were highly critical of the majority report, both in their preliminary statement on March 15 and in the report published on April 1. They held that many of the claims made by the majority were unjustified and unsupported by evidence and that the majority had "failed to present many of the problems arising from the operation of the act which should be brought to public attention."[124] Among the matters on which there were serious difficulties under the Act, in their view, were the union-security provisions which caused an administrative burden on unions, employers, and the Board, and led to many "bootleg agreements," the secondary boycott and coercion provisions which were considered to be working out unfairly, the increasing use of injunctions, and the discriminatory restriction on political expenditures. They also claimed that the majority had interfered in current disputes by comments on the ITU cases and by the suggestion that they were closely watching Board decisions on certain points; and they pointed to a danger of "an unwarranted and unconstitutional intrusion in the fields preserved by our Constitution for the executive and judicial power." They criticized the plant-study reports also as uneven in quality and at some

121. *Ibid.*, p. 5.
122. *Ibid.*, p. 33.
123. *Ibid.*, p. 34.
124. *Ibid.*, Pt. 2, April 1, 1948, p. 2.

points intruding unwisely on existing bargaining relations in a number of plants. They concluded that the Act had not reduced strikes; that rather it had been the cause of work stoppages and, by encouraging antiunion employers and engendering resentment and suspicion among workers, had laid the basis for industrial unrest. Accordingly they recommended the repeal of the Act.

Looking at both reports, it is clear that each presented material important for appraisal of the operations under the Act. The minority report filled in some extremely serious gaps in the analysis of the majority, although the minority failed to give weight to fields in which certain constructive results were indicated. The work of the committee to this point would have given more ground for confidence that really constructive recommendations would be forthcoming, if the reports had been based on a more complete, objective, factual analysis; the differences in interpretation and in purposes could have been made clear by majority and minority reports, after a real effort of the whole committee in a nonpartisan spirit to examine the complex problems which they were charged to study.[125]

The long-promised public hearings were held in May and June, 1948. Senator Ball had invited testimony on specific suggestions for the improvement of the Act, but indicated that his interest was in strengthening it. He proposed especially five points as needing study: the problem of administrative delays; whether the closed-shop ban should be extended to other forms of union security, and whether the union-shop elections should be kept; should the provisions as to national emergency strikes be strengthened; what is a sound permanent solution for the problem of welfare funds; and should strikes aimed at forcing employers to agree to contracts violating or evading the law be made illegal?[126]

In three weeks of hearings the committee heard the members of the Board and the General Counsel at some length on their experience in

125. Reference may be made to the different approach of the Ives Committee, which operated in New York State under the chairmanship of Mr. Ives for eight years. The 1946 report said: "Basic to its approach has been unity of action and a bi-partisan endeavor to eliminate political considerations from its deliberations and recommendations. No minority report has been necessary at any time. . . . In preserving this non-partisan approach, the Committee's proposals have had a more universally favorable reception than might have been the case where dissension or partisan differences existed among the members on the issues involved." New York State Joint Legislative Committee on Industrial and Labor Conditions, *Report for the Year 1946*, Legislative Document (1947) No. 35 (Albany: Williams Press, Inc., 1947), p. 17.

126. *New York Times*, April 16, 1948; May 5, 1948.

administering the Act, and heard testimony from a rather wide sample of union representatives and from a number of employers, possibly less widely representative than the union spokesmen. Several strong supporters[127] of Taft-Hartley received much publicity for their testimony in favor of strengthening the Act. The range of testimony gave considerable evidence as to sore points where friction and difficulties were present under the Act, as well as to the desires of different interest groups for legislative changes. Employer representatives were much concerned over the growing demand of unions for bargaining on pensions and welfare funds, and unions over what they considered unreasonable restrictions on the right of collective action. While the Board and the General Counsel as well as others favored the elimination of the union-shop election procedure, and Senator Ives and Representative Landis introduced bills which would have modified or eliminated this requirement, the Joint Committee voted against proposing any amendment to the Act for the current session.[128]

After the national election of November, 1948, which assured a Democratic majority in both houses of Congress, and with the defeat of Senator Ball for re-election[129] and the coming retirement of Congressman Hartley, the plans of the Joint Committee underwent necessary change. Its final report was submitted on December 31, 1948. This report summarized in one hundred pages some of the experience in the development of policies and administration and in court cases. It concluded that in spite of the handicap of the campaigns against the Act, and the fact that the Board had not yet interpreted many of the provisions, the law was "working well, without undue hardship upon labor organizations, employers, or employees." It went on: "Given another year to gain the general acceptance, knowledge, and understanding of its provisions, the committee is convinced that the act will have proven beyond all doubt its effectiveness in promoting the adjustment and disposition of labor problems equitably, and in creating more friendly and cooperative relationships."[130]

The committee made a few recommendations for amendment of the Act. These included the elimination of the requirement of an

127. Among them Gerard D. Reilly, former member of the NLRB and consultant for the Senate Committee during the writing of the bill, Raymond S. Smethurst of the NAM, and Theodore R. Iserman, New York attorney.

128. *New York Times*, June 2, 1948.

129. Two other members of the committee also were defeated, Representatives Landis of Indiana and McCowen of Ohio.

130. *Ball Committee Report*, Pt. 3, December 31, 1948, p. 99.

election as a condition precedent to the right to enter into legal union-shop contracts; strengthening the non-Communist affidavit requirement and applying it also to management representatives; exclusion of local businesses from the jurisdiction of the NLRB; clarification of the sixty-day notice requirement; in national emergency cases the elimination of the "last-offer" vote, and provision that boards of inquiry should not be appointed until after the granting of the injunction; strengthening of the provisions against coercive picketing by permitting the NLRB to order a union to reimburse employees kept from their jobs by such picketing; making any strikes to compel an employer to violate the Act unfair labor practices subject to the same restrictions as boycotts, or in the alternative excluding unions and employees engaging in such strikes from any protection under the Act; other amendments where the committee thought the intent of Congress had not been followed, as in the Board's interpretation of the free-speech section as not applying in pre-election campaigns, and the interpretation of the welfare fund provisions; and further statutory delineation of the respective powers of the NLRB and the General Counsel.[131] A minority statement of Senators Murray and Pepper and Representatives Lesinski and Kelley criticized the report as "a futile attempt to sustain legislation which has already been discredited."[132] The Joint Committee then went out of existence, and the work of deciding upon the national labor policy which should replace the bitterly controversial Taft-Hartley Act went back to the standing committees and to the members of the Eighty-first Congress.

Returning to the two major questions on the Joint Committee which we posed earlier, we consider first the committee as "watch-dog." Great values are possible in a system for continuing study by a Joint Committee of the operations of a law and its administration by the agency concerned, if this could be so carried on as to result in increased understanding by Congress of the problems, co-operation with the agency by making available adequate funds so that it can do its job, and reasonably early recommendation for amendments of the law when any need becomes apparent. On the other hand, unless there is clear understanding of the different functions of a congressional committee and of the administrators of the law, there is real danger, of which there were indications in this experience, of interference by the committee with the independence of the administrative process. However disinterested such interference might be, it

131. *Ibid.*, pp. 6–7.   132. *New York Times*, December 31, 1948.

would always open the way for political and partisan pressure, direct or indirect, in the handling of certain problems or even of individual cases. Such pressure on particular cases was something of a problem under the Wagner Act, and efforts should be made to minimize its possibility, not to open the way and regularize it. The original approach of this committee was highly questionable, although its later official statements as to its functions were proper.

On the second major question, also, there are doubts as to whether such a committee was the appropriate agency to carry on the full investigation of problems and to make recommendations which could receive the needed measure of acceptance by the parties concerned and the public. We have noted the partisanship which characterized its early work. But the problems before it were of extreme complexity and great public importance, involving economic and political issues and the human relations of employees and their representatives and employers working together from day to day in countless enterprises throughout the country. Solution for these problems is not likely to be found through partisan investigations. Rather the need is for thorough study, with all the aid possible from representatives of the parties directly concerned and from people expert in various phases of the many-sided problems involved. We doubt whether such study is possible by a Joint Congressional Committee of fourteen members and its staff. Instead we believe that the importance of these problems calls for a working conference, or conferences, on presidential call, with the co-operation of Congress and carefully chosen representatives of labor and management and the public, and with the best technical aid obtainable on various aspects of the problems. A democratic society must not assume that it is impossible to find acceptable solutions for difficult problems. We think rather that such conferences could go on from the substantial accomplishments of the 1945 Labor-Management Conference to find at least the next steps toward solution of the basic problems in the relationships between employers and employees, which must be met democratically if a democratic society is to survive.

CHAPTER 16

EXPERIENCE UNDER TAFT-HARTLEY

ON AUGUST 22, 1947, the Taft-Hartley Act became fully effective. On November 2, 1948, in an election in which this law was a major issue and the Democratic party program had pledged the repeal of the Act, the voters returned a Democratic Congress. There had been only little more than a year of actual experience with the Act. This experience has been referred to in earlier chapters in connection with our analysis of the law. Here we attempt a summary and evaluation of the experience, with the differing opinions and attitudes which had become clear, before final appraisal of the 1947 Act.[1]

In many respects the first year and a half could not be conclusive as to the possible impact of the Act on unions, management, and collective bargaining. Existing contracts continued and in some cases extended even beyond the first year. It took time for unions and employers to decide upon their policies under the revised legislation. Employers, too, were advised by their associations and attorneys "to go slow" in using the Act. A time of full employment and profitable operations also gave no full test of the uses to which the Act might be put. Even by the end of 1948 relatively few of the major difficult points under the law had been interpreted by Board or court decisions, and uncertainty continued as to the meaning of the law and even of the constitutionality of certain points.

CASES HANDLED BY THE NLRB

The cases handled by the reorganized National Labor Relations Board and its General Counsel with his staff do not encompass all

1. A useful report on the development of NLRB and court policies under the Act, and effects of the Act on union contracts is available in Bureau of National Affairs, *The Taft-Hartley Act after One Year* (Washington, 1948); see also NLRB, *Thirteenth Annual Report*, and U.S. Senate, Joint Committee on Labor-Management Relations, *Labor-Management Relations*, Report No. 986, 80th Cong., 2d Sess., Pt. 1, March 15, 1948, Pt. 2, *Minority Views*, April 1, 1948, and Pt. 3, December 31, 1948, cited as *Ball Committee Reports*. Further evidence is available in the 1949 hearings and reports of the House and Senate labor committees.

aspects of the Labor Management Relations Act of 1947. Yet they are significant of major developments. Activity under the new Act began slowly, as the processing of cases was interrupted by the necessity to rebuild the administrative structure and to work out rules and procedures for handling new types of cases. An abortive "boycott" of the Board by the unions was broken except for some outstanding large unions and several smaller left-wing organizations only after the Board decided in late October, 1947, that it was not necessary for the national federations, AFL and CIO, to file the prescribed documents, including the non-Communist affidavits of their officers, before the affiliated international unions and their locals could qualify for use of the Board.[2] From November on the incoming case load rose rapidly to a peak in April, 1948, with 6,960 new cases filed.[3]

For the fiscal year from June 30, 1947, through June 30, 1948, although it was not until August 22, 1947, that the Act became fully effective, a total of 36,735 cases was filed, compared to about 15,000 in the previous fiscal year. Union-shop elections accounted for almost three-fourths of them, more than 26,000. These were filed from November, 1947, on in rapidly increasing numbers—to a peak of 5,729 in April, followed by a rapid decline to under 4,000 in June— and a continuing decline to less than 1,000 monthly by November and December, 1948. Representation cases of all sorts totaled only 7,038, compared to 10,677 in 1946–47. After a slow start, toward the end of the fiscal year petitions were filed by unions for representation elections at a rate again approaching the monthly average of the previous year. Petitions filed by employers amounted to only 471 for the year. Petitions for decertification of unions were filed in about the same numbers, only 458, far less than had been expected.

Unfair labor practice cases of all sorts also were considerably fewer than had been expected, only 3,598 cases filed for the year, compared to 4,232 in 1946–47. The great majority, 2,849, were charges against employers, although the number had fallen off because of the refusal, or in some cases inability, of particular unions to use the resources of the Board. Charges were filed against unions in only 749 cases. Union abuses expected to be remedied were apparently somewhat less widespread than had been thought.

2. *Supra,* ch. 14, pp. 546–48.
3. Unless otherwise noted the statistics which follow are from the *Thirteenth Annual Report,* and from monthly and quarterly statistical reports of the National Labor Relations Board.

By expanding its staff, especially by using large numbers of temporary and part-time employees, and streamlining its procedures as far as possible, the agency avoided being completely swamped by the flood of cases, especially of union-shop elections. It succeeded in closing 18,691 of those election cases, of the 26,099 filed. On June 30, 1948, the Board had a backlog of 7,408 union-shop election cases pending, 2,836 representation petitions of all sorts, and 2,398 unfair labor practice cases. For the latter two classes the backlog was approximately the same as a year earlier, in spite of the Board's increased appropriations and staff[4] and the decreased number of cases filed during this year. This was in spite of the fact also that the proportion of cases dismissed administratively before any formal action was about double that of the previous year; these dismissals were 13 per cent of all representation cases closed and 32 per cent of the unfair labor practices cases. Included of course were the old cases dismissed because unions involved had not qualified to use the Board's processes. By the end of December, 1948, since the union-shop petitions had greatly declined, the Board had been able to catch up on these and the representation cases, and the backlog had decreased to 1,413 union-shop petitions and 1,950 representation cases; but pending unfair labor practice cases had risen to 2,682.

Fortunately as in the past it continued to be possible to handle the great bulk of cases administratively in the regional offices. Especially was this important for the union-shop elections, of which 96 per cent were conducted by consent. But new problems in the new types of cases and in old cases which might be affected by the amendments meant that more frequently than before cases had to go to Washington either for advice or for formal action by the Board. By June 30,

4. The Board had an appropriation of $6,000,000 for the fiscal year 1947–48, subject to supplement should it be needed, and for 1948–49 received an appropriation of $9,400,000, with authority to spend it in nine months, subject to approval of the Budget Bureau. The staff had been increased from about 700 in July, 1947, to over 1,100 by April, 1948, and was expected to reach about 2,200. U.S. Senate, Subcommittee of the Committee on Appropriations, *Hearings, Labor–Federal Security Appropriation Bill for 1949*, 80th Cong., 2d Sess., March 24, 1948, pp. 197, 204; NLRB *Daily Labor News*, June 10, 1948. On February 2, 1949, the Chairman reported that "for the first time in many years the Board has had an adequate staff," with approximately 1,500–1,600 people. U.S. Senate, Committee on Labor and Public Welfare, *Hearings on S. 249, Labor Relations*, 81st Cong., 1st Sess., Pt. 1, p. 171, cited as Senate Committee on Labor and Public Welfare, *1949 Hearings*. Preliminary data for 1948–49 showed a total of 25,874 cases filed, 4,154 complaints against employers, 1,160 complaints against unions, 8,370 representation cases, and 12,190 union-shop election petitions. The backlog on June 30, 1949, was 5,723 cases, of which 3,050 were unfair labor practice cases.

1948, no complaint cases filed under the new Act had been closed after Board order, and only 168 such representation cases. Delay in handling cases, even the consent elections, continued to be the subject of much complaint and contributed to the feeling of many unions and of some employers that they could not get protection from the Board against unfair labor practices.

Some of the results of Board cases appear in the statistics. Union-shop elections, first, resulted to the surprise even of the unions themselves in victory for the unions in about 98 per cent of the cases. Of the 1.8 million eligible, 88 per cent voted, and 94 per cent of the votes were for the union shop. In only 357 elections out of 17,958 was the result adverse. In an occasional case the election was lost because of the small number voting, since a majority of all employees in the unit was required to authorize the union shop.[5] The great majority of the elections were in small units, 65 per cent involving units of less than forty employees. But they ranged up to huge elections in industrial units. The Ford Motor Company election, which came just after the close of the fiscal year, was the largest to that time. It resulted in a vote of 88,943 to 1,214, out of 98,989 eligible, in favor of the union shop. In general there was no significant difference in the proportion of votes for union-shop authorization in the larger and the small units, according to a report on results for a three-month period.[6] Most of these elections were in units where there had already been union-security agreements, if elections held in May, 1948, were typical; but of 176 cases in that month where there had not been such contracts, only 6 per cent of the elections were lost.[7] While there was of course a selection of cases among those which came to the Board for these elections, all the evidence indicates that those who thought employees would generally vote against union-security agreements, after they had accepted union representation for collective bargaining, misinterpreted the temper of American workers.[8]

5. Cf. report on elections lost up to April 30, 1948. U.S. Congress, Joint Committee on Labor-Management Relations, *Hearings, Operation of Labor-Management Relations Act, 1947*, 80th Cong., 2d Sess., Pt. 2, pp. 1176–79, cited as *Ball Committee Hearings*. Of the 158 lost elections here reported, 62 were Teamster cases and 65 other AFL cases.

6. *Ibid.*, Pt. 1, p. 54.

7. *Ibid.*, p. 63.

8. Through the months of 1948–49, as the number of union-shop elections declined to under 500 a month, unions continued to win in nearly the same proportions, with well over 90 per cent of the votes favorable and of the elections won. No union-shop "deauthorization" elections had been held by the end of October, 1948. Six such petitions had been filed, but one was dismissed and the other five withdrawn.

In decertification elections, which were relatively rare, only 97 in the first fiscal year, the petitioners succeeded in ousting the union in 62 cases. Most of these votes were in small units. The total vote was only 7,847, almost equally divided between union and no-union. Though in an occasional case the union was voted out by an overwhelming or even unanimous vote, in only three months was the total adverse vote as high as 60 per cent, and in four it ranged between 35 and 45 per cent. The unions decertified were in 38 cases AFL affiliates, in 20 CIO, and in 4 unaffiliated. The cases were widely scattered geographically, although there were relatively more in the South. Only in three states, Texas, Virginia, and New Jersey, was there a suggestion of a marked pattern of use of this device.[9]

Representation elections were conducted in 3,222 cases, in 72.5 per cent of which unions won. The vote against representation was 23 per cent, about the same as the two previous years, and relatively high in the Board's history. In the following six months, from July through December, 1948, the nonunion vote was still higher, averaging 29 per cent. Greatest difficulty in winning elections continued to be met in the South. More than one-third of these elections conducted in 1947–48 were lost, in Alabama, the District of Columbia, Florida, Maryland, New Mexico, South Carolina, Texas, and Virginia, and also in Wyoming.

Unfair labor practice charges filed against employers were much the same in type as in previous years, though in smaller numbers. Charges of interference alone and of refusal to bargain dropped a little, possibly reflecting greater difficulty in proving violations under the restrictions of the amended law. Conversely the proportion of cases involving charges of discrimination rose to over 73 per cent, the highest proportion since 1937. Fewer than usual of these cases were closed, about 3,200 as against over 4,000 the year before. But 37 company unions were disestablished, compared to 36 the year before. The number of notices posted as a part of the compliance was little more than half that of the previous year. Bargaining began following charges of refusal to bargain in only 173 cases, as against 273 in 1946–47. And, significantly, a total of only 1,150 workers were reinstated,

9. In Texas twenty-nine decertification petitions were filed, over 12 per cent of all the representation petitions in that state; in Virginia 10 per cent were decertification petitions; and in New Jersey—home of Mr. Hartley—11 per cent. It is perhaps significant that in the nine decertification elections held in Texas by the end of December, 1948, only two had resulted in displacing a union; in New Jersey five of the nine such elections by that date resulted in decertification, as did the two elections held in Virginia.

compared to over 5,000 during the year previous. The figures give credence to the charges made by the unions that they received less effective protection under Taft-Hartley than before.

Unfair labor practice charges against unions under the new Section 8(b) of the Act were filed in only 749 cases in 1947–48, but they gave some indication of the character of the "equalizing" provisions of the amended Act. They were filed in 42 instances by other unions, in 271 by individuals, and in 436 by employers. Only "restraint and coercion," Section 8(b)(1), was involved in 412 of these; 332 involved discrimination; 122 refusal to bargain; 311 illegal boycotts or jurisdictional disputes under Section 8(b)(4); 21 charges of excessive fees; and 43 charges of featherbedding. Of the important 8(b)(4) cases, 224 involved subsection (A), the broad boycott provision against forcing an employer to "cease using" certain materials or products or to "cease doing business with any other person"; 74 involved (B), organizing boycotts; only 20 involved (C), boycotts against certified unions; and 71 were jurisdictional dispute cases.

None of these cases against unions which had to go through the stages of formal action by the Board and perhaps the courts had been completed by the end of the fiscal year. But the evidence on the others is significant. Of the 749 cases, 430 had been closed. More than 53 per cent of these were withdrawn, and nearly 28 per cent were dismissed administratively. Complaints had been issued by the end of the year in only 62 cases. The figures do not tell how many of these charges were filed without justification, simply as a weapon of delay or offense, or how many of them were withdrawn when a union involved gave up illegal action. Unions also, of course, have used the filing of charges as a tactical weapon. But the unusually large proportion of the charges against unions which were withdrawn or dismissed administratively suggests misunderstanding of the Act or attempts to misuse it in a considerable number of instances.

Adjustments were achieved before hearing in only 16.5 per cent of these cases against unions, an exceptionally small proportion. The remedies obtained in the 71 cases closed after adjustment were these: individual workers received protection in one case where union membership was granted, and 20 workers were reinstated after discriminatory discharge, with back pay of $3,480; work jurisdiction was settled in 6 cases; "featherbedding" was stopped in 2; strikes were settled in 21; picketing or boycott came to an end in 4; employers were removed from union black lists in 2; collective bargaining began in 23; and notices were posted in 12 cases. It is evident that the most

615

difficult issues in the interpretation of the clauses limiting concerted activities had not yet been determined. In a few cases adjusted, however, and probably also in some of those withdrawn, one may assume that a constructive result was achieved.

Injunctions in advance of the Board's hearing and decision, the powerful weapon added to the government arsenal by Taft-Hartley, were sought in relatively few cases before June 30, 1948, only 20 of the 749 cases against unions, and twice against employers.[10] It was of course mandatory in the boycott and sympathetic strike cases to give priority to the investigation and, if it appeared that the charge was true and a complaint should issue, to petition the district court for an injunction. In other cases against unions, and in cases against employers, such injunctions might as a matter of discretion be sought when a complaint was issued.

The General Counsel took the position that the discretionary injunction was a "sacred trust," to be used only in exceptional cases, since it was not the intent to abandon the Board as the forum for the litigation of unfair labor practice cases and to resort to "the always distasteful process of regulation by injunction."[11] By the end of the first fiscal year he had sought discretionary injunctions in only five such cases, three against unions and two against employers. Injunctions were obtained against the Typographical Union, and against the United Mine Workers when it was charged with refusal to bargain with the southern operators;[12] and a third case involving closed-shop issues was withdrawn. In the first case against an employer an injunction was obtained restraining General Motors from putting into effect a unilaterally decided insurance system; and in the second, against the Boeing Airplane Company, the injunction was denied when the court upheld the company in its claim that it was under no obligation to bargain, as the union had failed to meet its obligations under the sixty-day notice provision. In the latter case the Board decided otherwise.[13] A year or more later the Board issued orders against General Motors and against the union involved in the closed-

10. *Thirteenth Annual Report,* ch. 5. esp. pp. 84 and 172. By February, 1949, there had been 42 injunction proceedings, 2 against employers and 40 against unions, 36 of the latter being mandatory under Sec. 10(l). Petitions had been granted in 1 case against an employer, in 2 discretionary proceedings against unions, and in 19 mandatory cases; they had been denied once against an employer and 6 times in union cases. The remainder were pending or otherwise disposed of. Senate Committee on Labor and Public Welfare, *1949 Hearings,* Pt. 4, pp. 1713–14.

11. Address of General Counsel, July 1, 1948.

12. *Supra,* ch. 15, p. 584.   13. *Infra,* n. 67.

616

shop case above.[14] In the Typographical Union case of course the same issues were at stake as those which were being litigated before the Board, and in which four Intermediate Reports had been issued before the end of the fiscal year. The union already, before any Board decision on the issues, had been held in contempt for failure to obey the court's order, in this complex and much-litigated controversy.[15]

In the field of mandatory injunctions it is notable how few petitions were filed, although there were 243 charges of boycotts and illegal strikes. As we have seen, the great majority of these were disposed of administratively, most of them withdrawn or dismissed, and a few adjusted, while some were still under investigation. Only 17 by the end of the first fiscal year had resulted in the issuance of complaints and in the filing of petitions for injunctions. In these cases, none of which had been decided by the Board before June 30, 1948, injunctions were granted in 11 instances, and denied in 4; and in 2 there had been no action by the court.[16] About half involved building trades strikes or boycotts against the use of nonunion subcontractors, and several of the others involved "struck work" in one or another form.

These cases were all important to the unions and involved crucial issues as to rights and obligations under the Act; but they were first litigated before district courts. Question rises therefore whether final action by the Board would be the same, or whether the Board would sometimes come to a contrary result. In those cases in which Intermediate Reports had been issued at the time of writing, Trial Examiners three times had disagreed with the court and recommended dismissal of the charges though injunctions had been issued against unions, and twice found violations although the courts had refused to grant injunctions. The Board, by the time of writing, had disagreed with the court in one case where an injunction had been denied[17] and twice had issued orders against unions which had been enjoined from boycotts.[18] In the state of a highly controversial and uncertain law

14. *Supra*, ch. 15, p. 568. Amalgamated Meat Cutters, AFL, and Great Atlantic and Pacific Tea Co., 81 NLRB No. 164 (March, 1949).

15. *Infra*, pp. 627–28.

16. *Thirteenth Annual Report*, pp. 84, 172.

17. Watson's Specialty Store, 80 NLRB 533 (November, 1948); *supra*, ch. 12, pp. 466–67.

18. Schenley Distillers Corp., 78 NLRB 504 (July, 1948); Wadsworth Building Co., 81 NLRB No. 127 (February, 1949). For two later cases in which the Board dismissed charges although injunctions had been obtained against the unions, see Supreme Rice Mill, 84 NLRB No. 47 (June, 1949); Ryan Construction Corp., 85 NLRB No. 76 (July, 1949).

the dangers were obvious when preliminary action, which might and sometimes did determine the outcome, necessarily was taken by the General Counsel and then by district courts, rather than on the authority and under the control of the Board itself.[19] As in all the work of the Board, too, the effects necessarily reached far beyond the particular conflicts involved in these cases.

The year's record under Taft-Hartley, so far as it appears in the statistics of cases, shows that some unions still obtained protection against unfair labor practices by employers, though in fewer cases, and fewer individual workers were reinstated than in previous years; that unions continued to win representation elections, though apparently with more difficulty, and with larger losses than in most of the years under the Wagner Act; but that the established unions which entered union-shop elections won in overwhelming proportions. At the same time a rather small number of employers and individuals obtained specific relief from unfair labor practices of unions in cases adjusted, and probably a somewhat larger number in cases where unions withdrew from untenable positions upon the filing of a charge. And in a very small number of cases the drastic measure of an injunction stopped action which was considered illegal under the Act. Undoubtedly in many more the threat of injunction prevented such action.

On some other important matters, such as the number of damage suits filed by unions or employers under the authority of the Act, or the number of injunctions in state courts which reflected in part the effect of the new federal proscription of certain types of action by unions, evidence is incomplete. But these also are part of the total picture and must not be forgotten.[20]

ADMINISTRATION UNDER TAFT-HARTLEY

An extraordinary amount of time and energy in the first months after Taft-Hartley became law was spent in working out the details of the division of functions and responsibility between the Board and the General Counsel and reorganizing the administrative structure.[21]

19. Legal issues in these cases need not be discussed here, since final action had not been taken. For citations and discussion cf. BNA, *The Taft-Hartley Act after One Year*, pp. 171–79; *Thirteenth Annual Report*, ch. 5, and p. 172.

20. *Supra*, ch. 13, pp. 512–13; *infra*, pp. 640–41. A. Norman Somers, "The National Labor Relations Board from Wagner to Taft-Hartley," *Federal Bar Journal*, 9 (1948), 333–34, 357–58.

21. *Supra*, ch. 11, pp. 402–6. For a news report on the struggle within the NLRB over the extent to which the Board should give the General Counsel more

The powers delegated by the Board to the General Counsel over all personnel other than the staff directly attached to the Board itself and the Trial Examiners, and over all the work in the regional offices, went far beyond what was required by the Act. Whatever the administrative advantages in this drastic separation of functions, it was arguable that the Board in going so far abdicated its responsibility to insure the best possible staff and administration, to the extent within its power, and turned over to the General Counsel more responsibility and authority than any one man could or should be expected to carry and more than was necessary under the Act.

The immediate effect upon the staff and its morale was catastrophic. The impression was widespread that all employees must be personally satisfactory to the General Counsel and that experienced administrators under the old Act were no longer desired.[22] It was thought also that attorneys would have preference over nonlegal Regional Directors and administrators. The Field Division was abolished, as had been expected, and its able and experienced top administrators left the service of the Board. The former General Counsel and one of the Associate General Counsels resigned. Several other top men, among them Regional Directors and Regional Attorneys, resigned at once or during the course of the year. Reasons for these resignations differed; some were induced by administrative changes which eliminated old positions, some by the expectation that the General Counsel would seek to eliminate certain officers, or by unwillingness to work under the General Counsel, some by unwillingness to administer a law which was considered unfair, some for other personal reasons. The net result, however, was an incalculable injury to the Board and the government service, in the loss of a dozen or more of the most able, experienced, and efficient administrators in key positions under the old Act. In addition, there was considerable turnover among field examiners and attorneys. To some extent the harm was repaired later, when it came to be believed that the General Counsel was recognizing the need for experienced men. With the expansion of the staff and the hiring of many inexperienced field examiners and attorneys, appointments to key positions in regional offices included men who had the respect of those with whom they

authority than was required by the terms of the Act, see *New York Times,* October 3, 1947.

22. The impression gained support from statements of General Counsel Denham at the confirmation hearings. Cf. *supra,* ch. 15, pp. 601–2, esp. n. 108. Cf. also reports of a meeting between the General Counsel and the NLRB union, *supra,* ch. 11, p. 408, n. 35.

had worked through the years under the Wagner Act. Many of the former Regional Directors continued to hold their posts.

Although the 1947 Act expanded the functions of the Board and added new duties, the methods of operation inevitably were much the same as in the past. The same problems as before needed solution. The General Counsel set up a new structure to supervise the regional offices and to handle cases in Washington. An Operations Division was put in charge of field operations; a Division of Policies and Appeals analyzed cases, determined whether complaints should issue in unfair labor practice cases, reviewed complaint case appeals, and recommended policy; and a Law Division was responsible for handling all litigation. The former two performed functions which had been under the Field Division, working at certain points in co-ordination with the Legal Division. It was said that the new structure would provide for more unity of command and better co-ordination.[23] Unfortunately it appeared that much of what had been learned by long experience[24] in the relations between Washington and the regional offices was disregarded, since to a large extent men inexperienced in just these problems were at the helm. Complaints of bottlenecks in the Washington office, reminiscent of older days, probably could not have been avoided when it was necessary for a time under the new law to centralize the control over handling of cases. But they might have been minimized had the General Counsel at first done more to utilize the skills and experience available from the Wagner Act days.[25]

It was of course inevitable under the amended Act that for a time the autonomy of Regional Directors should be reduced and that all types of cases should require authorization from Washington before the Regional Director could proceed. In representation cases, however, it was not long before the Regional Directors were allowed the same freedom as in the past to obtain consent election agreements or withdrawals or to dismiss cases, where there were no new problems of policy. Advice could be asked of Washington where needed. But since the Board itself could not be asked for advice, in case of doubt the tendency was to send a case to hearing in order to bring the issues

23. Abolition of the position of Regional Attorney, thus making the Regional Director the single head of a Regional Office, was expected to help in this.

24. Cf. *supra,* ch. 2, esp. pp. 53–56.

25. The appointment in the fall of 1948 of one of the experienced Regional Directors to head the Operations Division in Washington was welcomed by the staff.

before the Board for decision.[26] The result was that some cases went to the Board for formal decision when they might otherwise have been disposed of informally, with saving of time for all concerned.

In the unfair labor practice cases against employers, after some months the Regional Directors were again given authority to proceed as before and to dismiss cases or issue complaints without prior authorization, except where there were new issues. Cases against unions, on the other hand, all involved new problems; but even in these, by summer of 1948, regional offices in simple cases were going ahead on their own responsibility. In the difficult boycott cases and others where policy was still to be determined it continued to be necessary to check on every case with Washington. Here it was significant that the preliminary decisions on policy were required by the law to be made by the General Counsel, even though his theory on crucial points might turn out to be quite different from that of the Board. Under the law, no appeals could be made to the Board from decisions of the General Counsel or the Regional Directors on these cases. Appeals from the latter were handled and decided in the General Counsel's office.

The problem of the case load and how its handling could be expedited was in the foreground as administrative policies were developed.[27] Here again the original authority of the General Counsel to decide whether jurisdiction should be taken over a wider field than in the past caused delay in settling matters of policy which would finally be decided by the Board, subject to court appeal at some points.[28] But attempts were made to streamline the handling of cases both in the field and in the decision-making process in Washington, so far as this could be done without sacrifice of the requirements of

26. The Board had reserved to itself the authority to decide appeals from Regional Directors' actions in representation cases, but this did not serve exactly the same purpose as advice on policy at an earlier stage. An Appeals Committee was set up, of the five chief legal assistants to the Board members, aided by the Executive Secretary and the Solicitor, to make recommendations to the Board on the disposition of appeals. *Thirteenth Annual Report*, p. 7.

27. These matters were discussed by the Board and the General Counsel in *Ball Committee Hearings*, Pt. 2, pp. 1119–80, June 11, 1948; see also *Ball Committee Report*, Pt. I, March 15, 1948, pp. 8–9; Pt. 3, December 31, 1948, pp. 9–11.

28. Cf. *supra*, ch. 11, pp. 400–402. For evidence on a controversy between the Board and the General Counsel over his instructions to the regional offices on jurisdiction matters, see Senate Committee on Labor and Public Welfare, *1949 Hearings*, Pt. 1, pp. 138–41, 175–77. In May, 1949, the Board, in dismissing a complaint against a union, held unanimously that it had discretion to determine whether or not to assert jurisdiction in unfair labor practice cases, although the General Counsel had issued a complaint and held a hearing. A-1 Photo Service, 83 NLRB No. 86 (1949).

due process. Unfortunately the law no longer permitted prehearing elections in representation cases, though the device had formerly been effective in expediting large numbers of cases. In the union-shop election cases, however, most were handled by consent elections and others by prehearing elections. These were for the most part simple, fairly routine processes, of which the result was usually known in advance, and inexperienced and part-time employees could do much of the work. Nevertheless, because of the tremendous volume of these elections, which required attention of experienced people at least to some degree, and a large amount of clerical work, it was difficult to get on with the more important unfair labor practice cases and other representation elections. The charges against unions, involving new issues and problems, needed to be handled by people experienced in investigation and prosecution. Since some of these cases had to be given priority of handling, too, the most experienced members of the staff were obliged to stop work on other cases, however important, in order to handle the priority cases. Here was another reason for delay and the frequent complaints of unions that they were getting little protection against unfair labor practices of employers. A wasteful amount of time and energy also went into handling the paper work relating to the non-Communist affidavits and other union documents required as prerequisites for use of the Board; and the rigid requirements of the law made it impossible to achieve the most workable system.

The Trial Examiners' Division had received increased independence and responsibility. The complete independence of its staff of experienced men from control by either the Board or the General Counsel had certain advantages at a time when new issues were to be faced in applying the important new provisions case by case. Intermediate Reports on the first cases against unions explored the issues and the law. They sometimes accepted, sometimes disagreed with, the interpretations and theories of the General Counsel. These documents, expressing the independent judgment of experienced men on difficult new issues, were presumably of value to the Board as it came to decide the cases and write its own interpretation of the law. Weekly conferences of the Trial Examiners were still possible, under the Act, to discuss general policies and consider Board decisions. Of course the facts or issues in particular cases then being handled could not be discussed. There was a problem, however, in the absolute prohibition of any review of Trial Examiners' Reports before issuance; even assistants to check on the accuracy of details were apparently precluded by the terms of the Act. There was some feeling among legal assistants to the Board members that the Inter-mediate Reports as a result were less trustworthy than before and needed more thorough checking against the record. The Board in its statement to the Ball Committee in June, 1948, recommended that the employment of legal assistants to the Trial Examiners be per-mitted; such assistance would expedite the work of the Trial Examin-ers and therefore that of the Board itself in getting out its decisions.[29]

In the interest of saving time the Board decided to refuse to hear oral argument except in cases involving new issues or where for other reasons such argument was considered helpful, as had long been done in representation cases. Under the amended Act new types of cases would inevitably require oral argument, but the Board decided in others to refuse this further hearing when in its discretion it found the facts and issues adequately set forth by the record and the briefs and exceptions. Accordingly in the cases decided during the year, oral argument seems to have been denied about as many times as it was granted.[30] There was a possible disadvantage in that the Board thus isolated itself from contact with the parties and might have less "feel" for the facts in the cases decided. But used with careful dis-cretion the saving of time was justified.

Drastic changes required by Taft-Hartley in the administrative setup for review of cases and the making of decisions have been de-scribed and discussed earlier.[31] No change in structure of course could eliminate the essential steps, of consideration of the Intermedi-ate Report or the Hearing Officer's Report along with briefs and ex-ceptions of the parties, checking all against the record made at the hearing to whatever extent necessary, a process by which the five Board members themselves or a three-man panel reached agreement as to the decision, and drafting, checking, and final signing of the decision. Whatever difficulties were introduced by the rigid require-ments of the law, and whatever advantages and disadvantages in-hered in the enlargement of the Board and the resulting use of ro-tating panels, it was necessary and possible to make the new system work.[32]

29. *Ball Committee Hearings,* Pt. 2, pp. 1124–25.
30. This was indicated by a check of the decisions mimeographed for distri-bution.
31. *Supra,* ch. 11, pp. 411–16.
32. For discussion of the operation of the system see the Board's statement in *Ball Committee Hearings,* Pt. 2, pp. 1123–24; also *Ball Committee Report,* Pt. 1, March 15, 1948, pp. 6–9; *Thirteenth Annual Report,* pp. 3–9.

Review of cases was done by the legal assistants assigned directly to each Board member. Cases were assigned in rotation by the Board's Executive Secretary to Board members, each of whom acted as chairman of one of the panels. The case was analyzed by one of the fifteen or more legal assistants in that Board member's group, under the supervision of the member and his chief legal assistant. An advantage was that each member presumably had chosen a group of assistants in whom he had confidence. Good working relationships between members of the different groups provided informal means for co-ordination. Nevertheless, differences in policy on technical matters sometimes developed between different panels, so that the parties could not be sure that they knew what to expect on basic policies. There was an impression among clients of the Board that decisions were affected by the chance of which panel acted on a case, due to differences in the character of the review of the facts and of attitudes in application of the law. Apparently the problem had not been solved of insuring as careful supervision and uniform adherence to established policy as under the former centralized system with its carefully chosen specialist supervisors.

In the actual decision-making process, following the review by the legal assistants, the Board of necessity sought to devise methods for fast and efficient handling of the increased volume of cases. The Board reported in June, 1948, that the panel system was working well and handling 85 per cent of the cases decided.[33] But broad questions of policy in the new types of cases coming to the Board, or new problems in old types of cases, inevitably required decision by the full five-man Board. In simple cases it was found possible, as had been true for some time in representation cases, to make decisions without full discussion in Board meetings, on the basis of draft decisions accompanied by the Intermediate Reports or Hearing Officers' Reports, any briefs or exceptions from the parties, and where necessary memoranda from the Board member on whose responsibility the draft was circulated. In simple representation cases a system of short, printed-form decisions was adopted, with the decision and its reasons indicated briefly by a few typed-in words or footnote references to authority. These were circulated on the authority of the Board member responsible for the case, and, if no questions were raised by other members, the decisions were signed without discussion in Board meeting. Simple unfair labor practice cases were handled in something the same way, with draft decisions circulated

33. *Ball Committee Hearings,* Pt. 2, p. 1123.

with the necessary accompanying documents. When the Board member responsible thought it necessary, or another member requested it, a case was put on the agenda for discussion. Moreover, any cases involving important issues of policy supposedly went to the full Board.[34] It was thought that matters of judging evidence were appropriately handled by panels, even when there were dissents, but, if matters of policy were at stake, the full Board should take the responsibility.

Short-cut methods were necessary and desirable, in order to reduce the huge backlog of cases; and since presumably careful check was made in each member's office before decisions were signed, the chance of error was not very great. Nevertheless, there cannot have been any increase in the amount of careful consideration given by Board members to the decision of cases. The reverse would seem almost inevitable, and it would be surprising if there were not some sacrifice of quality to quantity. In addition, short decisions, which give a less full analysis of the facts and the basis for the decision, do less than fuller opinions to educate industry and labor on the policies and requirements under the Act. The necessity to streamline procedures in order to handle the increased case load, and the limits upon the delegation of functions by the Board, created a dilemma, as the Chairman pointed out in his statement to the Congressional Committee: "There is a limit to what five men can do, because they are precluded, by conscience as well as by statute, from delegating their judicial functions beyond a certain point. Short-cuts are desirable; so is careful Board consideration of the contentions of the parties to every case. The need for both creates the dilemma that faces us."[35]

The first year's experience gave added weight to the basic questions raised as to the separation of functions and division of responsibility between the Board and the General Counsel.[36] The increased

34. But the important Babcock and Wilcox case, involving "free-speech" policy, was decided by a three-man panel. *Supra*, ch. 12, p. 424.

35. *Ball Committee Hearings*, Pt. 2, p. 1124. In the last three months of 1947–48, when the panel system was in full operation, the Board turned out more than three hundred decisions each month. The output of unfair labor practice decisions was still below that of most former years; but the combined total of all representation and union-shop election decisions was about two and a half times that of the monthly average of representation decisions in any previous year. Cf. *Twelfth Annual Report*, p. 85. At the end of the second year, June 30, 1949, the Board reported that its decisions had increased to 3,051 for the year, compared to 2,099 in 1947–48. About 150 a month were contested cases requiring Board opinions. NLRB press release, August 1, 1949.

36. *Supra*, ch. 11, pp. 406–9, 415–16.

number of Board members with the use of the panel system and the saving of time on administrative details probably on the whole facilitated the handling of the work by the Board. And there was some gain in the public relations aspect from the separation of functions, in so far as employers thought the new arrangement more conducive to fair administration. Actually we find no evidence that there was need for such a separation to insure proper handling of cases, nor any reason to believe that there was any gain in the judicial quality of the Board's work. Moreover, unions complained of unfair administration under the General Counsel's direction of the earlier stages of the work. And the problem of delay in handling cases continued to be very serious. The basic problems of unity of policy and efficiency remained.

It was too soon to know whether it would be possible under the bifurcated agency in the long run to maintain the emphasis on informal disposition of cases, the essence of the administrative process, in contrast to formal action by the Board and the courts. Inevitably at first a larger proportion of cases had to come to the Board for decision, as they involved new problems. But the fact that the Board could not give advice on policy at early stages on new issues brought an unnecessarily large number of doubtful cases to the Board for its decision. This would seem to be inevitable even in the longer run.

Most important was the difficulty in achieving unity of policy and avoiding long delays and reversals of decisions. Weekly conferences between the Board and the General Counsel provided opportunity for consultation and working out methods of co-operation. But there was apparently some doubt, at least in the mind of the General Counsel, as to whether he should consult or inform the Board on developments within his jurisdiction.[37] Even important matters of policy which would affect the rights of labor and management and the entire work of the agency were not always discussed in advance of action. In addition, while the regional staffs in handling cases administered policies which were or would be determined by the Board, subject to check by the courts, once issues were settled, their instructions came from the General Counsel. The resulting division of loyalties and responsibilities carried seeds of friction and uncertainty, if not worse.

Even without the breakdown which would be possible under such an "administrative monstrosity," problems arose from delay in making final determination of policies. The General Counsel's ruling, that the

37. *Ball Committee Hearings*, Pt. 2, p. 1174.

officers of federations such as the AFL and the CIO must sign the non-Communist affidavits before affiliated unions could file charges or petitions, two months later was overruled by the Board.[38] The differences in policy between the General Counsel and the Board as to taking jurisdiction over essentially local industries was a matter of public record.[39] The General Counsel's policy against certifying authorization for a union shop unless the state standard had been met, where the state required more than a mere majority vote in the election, was finally overruled by the Board in January, 1949.[40] In unfair labor practice cases against unions, also, several Intermediate Reports indicated that the General Counsel was proceeding on rather extreme interpretations of some clauses of the Act, as in regard to the meaning of "restraint and coercion." Decisions on these matters would be made by the Board, and finally by the Supreme Court, after a long period. But unions complained bitterly that the General Counsel went beyond the requirements of the Act and that the effects upon unions involved were extensive and depressing. On the other hand, there were complaints from both unions and employers against dismissal of unfair labor practice charges by the General Counsel without hearing, subject to no appeal beyond his own office.[41] Uncertainty, conflicts of policy, and delay in establishing the Board's policies were almost inevitable. If the Board later reversed the General Counsel in any case, the complaint, hearing, and possibly injunction would already have had their effects; and when a charge had been dismissed, there would have been no recourse at all. There were serious disadvantages, from the interest both of efficiency and of due process, in having the preliminary judgments as to policy on such crucial matters made by the General Counsel rather than by the Board itself.

Illustrations of some of the difficulties in a bifurcated administration of a complex and controversial law were given in the series of cases against the Typographical Union, charging refusal to bargain and other violations in its attempts to obtain acceptable arrangements in lieu of its long-established closed shop. An injunction was obtained by the General Counsel in the national newspaper case in

---

38. *Supra,* ch. 14, pp. 546–48.
39. *Supra,* n. 28.
40. *Supra,* ch. 15, p. 589.
41. Cf. discussion by the attorney for the Children's Museum of Washington of the dismissal of a charge of featherbedding for "lack of sufficient evidence." He argued that the question of law should have been decided by the Board, not by the General Counsel. *Ball Committee Hearings,* Pt. 1, pp. 551–57.

627

March, 1948.[42] And on August 26, 1948, while the Chicago strike was still on, the General Counsel filed a petition for contempt action. It is not known whether the Board had been consulted or was in agreement with this drastic action while there still had been no decision by the Board on the complex legal issues raised in the series of cases, in which four Intermediate Reports had been issued, with some disagreement among them in interpretation of the law and the facts. It was reported that Senator Taft had summoned members of the General Counsel's staff to his office, and in the presence of representatives of the Chicago newspaper publishers and the counsel of the Joint Congressional Committee stated that the ITU and its officers should be cited for contempt for violation of the injunction, a question which was then under investigation by the General Counsel. The Senator and the counsel for the committee were reported to have suggested that to permit injunctions on suit of private parties might be the solution. The ITU protested and called for an investigation of "unwarranted interference" by Senator Taft. The General Counsel later discounted that charge and called the incident a "routine inquiry." Petition for an injunction was filed two days later.[43] The trial necessarily went into the merits of certain aspects of the case as a basis for deciding whether the union in demanding certain "competency clauses"[44] was attempting to obtain continuance of closed-shop conditions in the newspaper industry. The union was found in contempt, on October 14, 1948.[45] The strike, however, was still unsettled in the spring of 1949, and there had still been no Board decision on the merits.

Even in representation cases the Board sometimes found itself restricted in its power to make the basic decisions on policy, because of its lack of control over the General Counsel's actions at earlier stages. The problem was made clear in the Times Square Stores Corporation case late in August, 1948.[46] Charges of unfair labor

42. Evans v. Typographical Union, 76 F. Supp. 881 (S.D. Ind.). The court held it proper for the authority to seek injunctive relief to be exercised by the General Counsel. See *Thirteenth Annual Report,* p. 90.

43. *New York Times,* August 14, 19, 24, 26, 1948. A little later President Truman released an exchange of letters with the General Counsel's office, in which he held it "entirely improper for any Senator . . . to attempt to put the heat on one of the Executive Departments." For these letters and Senator Taft's answer see *ibid.,* September 15 and 16, 1948.

44. *Infra,* pp. 636–37, 641–42.

45. Evans v. Typographical Union, October 14, 1948, 22 *LRRM* 2576. For the settlement of the strike in September, 1949, and the first decisions by the Board in ITU cases, in October, 1949, see *infra,* n. 74.

46. 79 NLRB 361; see also *supra,* ch. 14, pp. 518–19.

practices against the employer had been dismissed in the regional office on the ground that the individuals who filed the charge were acting as agents for a noncomplying union. Although evidence was noted of company assistance to the AFL in its organization drive before the strike, the Board held that under the Act it was bound by the General Counsel's action in dismissing the charge. Accordingly it had to find that this strike was not caused by unfair labor practices; since the strike was therefore an economic strike, strikers who had been replaced were not entitled to reinstatement, therefore they were not entitled to vote. The Board under these circumstances found itself precluded by the terms of the Act from considering the set of facts which were crucial in the outcome of the case. The fallacy is clear in such a division of functions that the quasi-judicial body is not free to consider and decide the central issue involved in a case.

The first year's experience highlighted the difficulties and disadvantages of concentrating so much administrative responsibility in the hands of one man, subject to no appeal, or only to reversal after a long period. In fact the job of the General Counsel proved to be a back-breaking one. Pressure of work was such that sometimes snap judgments or less than thoroughly considered decisions were inevitable unless subordinates were relied on largely. Moreover, insecurity in the staff, at least in the early months, sharp criticisms on the part of the unions of what they considered unfair and unreasonable interpretations of the law, and rumors current that members of Congress and parties to cases not infrequently approached the General Counsel about the handling of individual cases,[47] all suggested danger to good administration when power and authority were so concentrated.

Gains from the separation of functions were chiefly psychological, meeting the widespread, though we think unfounded, feeling that the old administration was unfair because of the combination of other functions with the judicial. Nevertheless, the other losses, in efficiency and unity of policy, were a high price to pay for this concession to a poorly informed public opinion. Distrust of the Board had led to a far more dangerous concentration of power—as well as to a structure under which good administration was made difficult even when every effort was exerted to make it work.

POLICIES DECIDED BY THE BOARD

Interpretations of the changes made in the Wagner Act and of the new provisions added by Taft-Hartley had been made only partially

47. *Supra,* ch. 15, pp. 602–3.

by the Board even toward the end of its second year under the amended Act. On the most important new provisions, especially the new unfair labor practices proscribed to unions and their agents, the "pipe line" to the Board filled slowly, and only at the end of the summer of 1948 had the first decisions begun to be issued. Some early decisions, important in showing the meaning of various provisions, have been noted in the chapters which analyze the Act. A few of the major points which had been decided may be briefly stated.

Much of the body of doctrine built up during the twelve years of the Wagner Act was left untouched by the amendments. In representation cases the basic policies as to when a petition was timely, under what conditions existing contracts would bar a new election, what showing of representation was required before an election would be held, and others, were continued. In so far as applicable the same principles were applied also in the new types of petitions, those by employers and those by employees for decertification of an incumbent union. Policies as to collective bargaining units also were relatively little affected, except for the fact that extent of organization could not be a major factor in determining the appropriateness of a unit.[48] Even on the craft-unit issue the Board held that it was free to decide whether or not a craft unit could sever itself from an established broader unit, although it could not make its determination solely on the basis of a prior Board determination. As the problem of raiding and the opposition of many employers to the prospect of fragmentized collective bargaining became more clear, the Board worked out its tests as to the conditions under which true crafts would be permitted a choice of separate representation, and attempted a reasonable and clear balance between the opposing interests.[49]

Policies as to noncomplying unions were rather fully worked out in decisions from November, 1947, on. The Board applied the congressional intent rigidly, so that unions which did not file the required documents could not appear on ballots, except in decertification proceedings. They could intervene only when they had a current contract. They could not file charges, although their members could individually file charges of discrimination. They were rather effectively shut out for the most part from any protection from the Act. But they could be and were in a number of cases subject to charges of unfair

48. The specific limitations in the Act on units of foremen, guards, and professional employees were of course exceptions.
49. *Supra*, ch. 14, pp. 522–25.

labor practices, even when their charges of unfair labor practices by employers could not be entertained by the Board.

In deciding unfair labor practice cases against employers, the greatest change was made by the free-speech amendment. It was too soon to know how much difficulty was made by the limitation on the use of speech as evidence. Sometimes such evidence was merely supplementary and not essential for proof of the violations; but in other cases there was more serious difficulty. Proof of unfair labor practices had been made somewhat more difficult, and to that extent antiunion employers were encouraged to continue their policies. Such employers also were left more free than before to engage in campaigns against the unions. It did not appear, however, that the tightening of the rules as to evidence in general made much if any difference in the trial and decision of cases. The restriction as to "discharge for cause" also did not in the ordinary case appear to have required much if any difference in policy from that long established by Board decisions. But it was not yet clear to what extent employers might be free to discharge strikers on the ground that certain activities were not protected by the Act.

One of the most troublesome problems was created by the provisions restricting the right of economic strikers to vote in a Board election, if they had been replaced.[50] Administratively this posed questions of great difficulty; and frequently it seemed to those who had to administer it, as well as to unions and to many others, to be giving an undue aid to an employer in breaking a strike. The justice of the provision as well as the matter of its workability was in serious question.

In the unfair labor practice cases against unions even by the spring of 1949, although decisions had begun to appear, the major matters had still to be clarified by the Board and the courts. Among these were the meaning of "restraint and coercion" and union responsibility for the acts in question, the question of union "unfair lists," the meaning of the boycott provisions, the relation of the free-speech amendment to picketing in support of illegal boycotts, the effect of the featherbedding provision, and the effects in a variety of conflicts over union-security matters of the bans on union refusal to bargain and on attempts to cause an employer to discriminate.[51]

50. *Ibid.*, pp. 518–19.
51. Before August 22, 1948, when the Act had been fully effective for one year, the Board had issued only three decisions in unfair labor practice cases against unions. The first, Schenley Distillers Corp., 78 NLRB 504 (July, 1948), found an AFL union guilty of a secondary boycott against a wholesale distribu-

631

SOME EFFECTS OF TAFT-HARTLEY, 1947–49

By the fall of 1948 Taft-Hartley was acclaimed by spokesmen for employers as a success and denounced by union spokesmen as having shown all the evils which had been predicted a year earlier. The different pictures drawn obviously reflected emphasis on different parts of a complex and varied experience. There were differences in the experience in large companies and small, in different industries, in North and South, differences between mass production and small enterprises, between industrial and craft unions, and between old unions with well-established collective bargaining relationships and those which were struggling to organize unorganized areas. Various combinations of factors affected the experience of particular unions, groups of workers, and companies. It is not possible here to analyze cases in detail, although special studies of cases and industries are needed for an understanding of the full effects of the complex and far-reaching 1947 Act. Yet a bird's-eye view of the industrial relations scene after a year of Taft-Hartley disclosed several types of situations, in which different effects of the Act were to be seen. First of these were where established bargaining relationships continued; second, some types of conflict situations in which in varying degrees

---

tor of Schenley products. The Board held that "the language of the Act does not vest the Board with discretion to allow a union to engage in secondary activity, otherwise unlawful, because of an asserted alliance which rests solely on the fact that the so-called ally is an independent sales outlet for the products of the primary employer." Cf. *supra*, ch. 12, pp. 460–66.

In the second, R. H. Parr and Son, issued in August, 1948, the Board approved a stipulated settlement in which the union reimbursed the employer for payment of any money exacted for four men for services which were not performed.

In the third, National Maritime Union and the Texas Co., 78 NLRB 971 (August, 1948), the Board found the union guilty of refusal to bargain and attempting to cause the employer to discriminate by its insistence upon retention of the hiring hall, with the practices of discrimination against nonmembers which had been in use. As to the argument of the economic need for the hiring hall the Board said: "The Congress determined that the public interest required that hiring halls involving discrimination against employees who are not union members be outlawed. This determination is binding upon us. It is our duty to administer the law as written, not to pass upon the wisdom of its provisions."

In October and November, 1948, also, the Board issued two important decisions involving coercion in strikes and union responsibility: Sunset Line and Twine Co., 79 NLRB 1487, and Perry Norvell Co., 80 NLRB 225; and a secondary boycott decision, Watson's Specialty Store, 80 NLRB 533; cf. *supra*, ch. 12, pp. 444–47, 467. Analysis of the differing opinions among Trial Examiners and courts in injunction cases on many of these matters is available in BNA, *The Taft-Hartley Act after One Year*, pp. 89–113, 171–79; *Thirteenth Annual Report*, ch. 5. For later decisions see the forthcoming *Fourteenth Annual Report*.

collective bargaining was disrupted; and, third, fields where unions were trying to organize.

Union membership and the coverage of collective bargaining contracts continued, in a year of full employment, at very high levels, although the rate of growth of membership declined from that of recent years.[52] The great majority of established relationships continued, perhaps with no great effect from the changed law. In fact, in a survey by *Business Week*[53] of a sample of over five hundred management men, nearly three-fourths of them found no change in their plant relations during the year. Not infrequently employers spoke of "a new atmosphere in collective bargaining these past six months—an intangible change that is hard to define but which has manifested itself in a new bargaining approach on the part of unions and in a greater willingness to cooperate."[54] But such employers spoke also of irritations resulting from the Act. Unions recognized that many employers made every effort to co-operate with them and avoid upsetting old established relationships. It was common knowledge, too, that employers were being advised to "go slow," not to abuse their "new rights," and not to use the Act against unions unless they were very sure that they had a strong case. But union after union testified that the "new atmosphere," even when relationships continued much as in the past, was one of mutual suspicion and irritation, uncertainty, and a feeling of frustration at the bargaining table.[55] As a representative of the CIO Textile Workers said:

52. *Monthly Labor Review,* 68 (1949), 147.

53. "What 528 Management Men Think of Taft-Hartley Law," *Business Week,* August 21, 1948, pp. 19–20. The poll covered a cross-section of manufacturing industries in fifteen cities and thirteen industrial states, distributed geographically and by industry in accordance with the census distribution. Half of the plants represented had under 250 employees. It omitted nonmanufacturing enterprise, where some of the sore points arose. An NICB poll of 100 executives found a little more than half believing that the Act had improved relations with their employees, a little less than half finding no change. About three-fourths suggested changes in the Act, however, and the very interesting comments quoted show a considerable number of problems under the Act from the management point of view. National Industrial Conference Board, *Management Record,* 10 (September, 1948), 433–40.

54. E. H. Van Delden, "Management Experience under the LMRA," American Management Association, *Personnel Series,* No. 115 (1948), p. 14.

55. For important and detailed testimony on union experience under the Act see *Ball Committee Hearings,* Pt. 2, June 4 and 9, 1948. See especially statements of William Green, AFL, Arthur J. Goldberg, CIO, Isadore Katz, Textile Workers Union of America, and others. Testimony by employer spokesmen was

Not only has the Act evoked obstructions to organizing the unorganized but it has extended its baleful influence to the conference table. Here the lawyers have taken over. Union negotiators and management representatives both fear the operation of several provisions of the Act and have come to believe that they are incompetent to resolve their differences by an agreement couched in simple language comprehensible to the workers involved, as well as to themselves. . . . But the lawyers are just as confused as their clients. The result is that the parties sit helplessly by while lawyers engage in exhaustive and exhausting debates upon conflicting interpretations of the law.[56]

A somewhat more hopeful picture, though supporting the union point in some respects, was given by an employer who pointed out that efforts to resolve difficulties at the bargaining table had continued and had been successful in thousands of cases:

For after the loftily perched attorneys, representing both sides, stalk majestically from the collective bargaining room, the fog of legal terminology and procedures begins to lift and through the mists the faces of the local union officials and management's labor representatives begin to reappear. They are left alone once again to negotiate a contract or process a grievance in more or less the same old way, with all hands avoiding a work stoppage. . . . And during this first year under the Act, thousands and thousands of contracts have been peacefully negotiated . . . indicating that compromises have been effected without depriving either party of their rights at law, whether State or Federal.[57]

It is probably true that the Act's statements of union duties as well as rights brought some union representatives to the bargaining table with a rather more reasonable attitude and a desire to avoid violating the law—perhaps with more willingness to give and take. Moreover, hazards under the law made unions more anxious to avoid a breakdown and a strike; and the necessity of working out a solution for some of the problems under the law tended to make them less militant on demands for gains in wages and other conditions. All of this adds up to an increased willingness to "co-operate," as some employers reported.

---

more largely devoted to discussion of particular problems, such as union pressure for clauses which were considered evasions of the law, closed- and union-shop issues, required bargaining on pensions and welfare funds, industry-wide bargaining and industry-wide strikes, rather than to an over-all view of the effects of the Act on industrial relations. They did not therefore comment on the charges typically made against the Act by union spokesmen.

56. *Ibid.*, Pt. 2, p. 799. Cf. also AFL statement, *ibid*, p. 1045.

57. Address of John W. McCaffrey, President, New York Chapter of the Society for the Advancement of Management, at Rutgers University Labor Institute, June 16, 1948 (mimeographed).

But what were the problems set by Taft-Hartley, when neither the employer nor the union desired to challenge the other or to upset established relationships? Abolition of the closed shop and provision for a limited union shop under certain conditions[58] was the most troublesome in perhaps a majority of industries, certainly a great many. Especially was this a problem in fields where craft unions had long-established closed-shop systems, although it was postponed when existing contracts continued for most of the year. Many contracts were extended shortly before the Act became effective, and it is widely reported that many actually negotiated later were pre-dated. Sometimes the problem was solved for the time at least by assuming that the industry, such as retail trade or building, was not covered by the Act. Sometimes a clause was added, "to the extent permitted by law," or "unless and until such clause is found to be unlawful." Some clauses were continued "sub rosa"; or they were simply omitted, and presumably the status quo or something very similar continued, though perhaps with special care to see that no problem was raised by illegal discrimination under the clause.[59] As time went on and the unions began to petition for union-shop elections, many employers co-operated. While closed-shop clauses decreased in number, union-shop provisions greatly increased, especially by a shift from maintenance-of-membership systems to the broader union-security system. There were also numerous "maintenance of dues" clauses, with check-off of union dues on individual authorizations, which many unions found an acceptable substitute for other union-security arrangements.[60] But there was often fric-

58. *Supra,* ch. 12, pp. 430–40.
59. Richard T. Gray, President, Building and Construction Trades Council, AFL, stated that in the great majority of cases the building craftsmen were "still working closed shop." *Ball Committee Hearings,* Pt. 1, pp. 114, 120, May 25, 1948. Later it was reported that as agreements expired, in the absence of union-shop elections it was impossible to provide for any type of union security. "This has resulted in the almost complete stoppage of building and construction activity in a number of localities." American Federation of Labor, *Report of Executive Council to the 69th Convention,* November, 1948, p. 174. When a case involving the traditional hiring practices in this industry reached the Board, it necessarily held them illegal under the Act. Daniel Hamm Drayage Co., 84 NLRB No. 56 (June, 1949).
60. An NICB analysis of 313 contracts signed after Taft-Hartley became effective found nearly a third of them with no mention of union security, but significantly no open-shop clauses; union-shop clauses appeared in 27.5 per cent; maintenance of membership in 11.8; maintenance of dues in 23.7; and six were possibly illegal, with provision for the closed shop, preferential hiring, or a union hiring hall. Check-off arrangements were included in 70 per cent. National Industrial Conference Board, *Union Contracts since the Taft-Hartley Act,* Studies in

tion, since the law was unclear as to whether check-off of initiation fees and assessments was permitted. And sometimes resentment was aroused in the process of obtaining individual authorizations.[61]

In industries where employers had long obtained their employees from the union, and where there was no desire to challenge that system, either because it met a real need in the industry or because a powerful union insisted upon retaining such arrangements as a means to union security, various ingenious clauses were devised.[62] The legality of many of them was uncertain, and some were clearly evasive of the intent of the law. Among these were such clauses as those of the Pacific Shipowners' contract which continued the union hiring hall, with preference to men with previous experience on ships of the member companies, or if such men were not available, to graduates of the Andrew Faruseth Training School. Other hiring-hall clauses continued, subject to adjudication of their legality. Some specified that there should be no discrimination against nonmembers. Industry-wide seniority systems of preference, also, which occurred in a variety of forms in connection with hiring halls, provided substantial security in employment to union members in an industry which had been operating on a closed-shop basis. Another device, originated in the New York City wholesale and retail trades, was a "reciprocal discharge" clause, permitting the union to request discharge of an employee who interfered with harmonious relations or efficient operations, subject to arbitration should the employer refuse the request.

Where there was a high degree of craft skill, as in the printing industry, a variety of "competency" clauses were written to protect the standards of skill in the craft, with joint examining boards set up to test the competency of applicants for employment as journeymen. Preference was given in a number of industries to graduates of jointly supported schools. There were also "harmony" clauses, such as: "The Association and its members will not undertake any activity which will in any sense undermine or jeopardize the Union's strength or security or the well-being of its members." Under these clauses em-

---

Personnel Policy, No. 94, August, 1948, pp. 2–11. For the Department of Labor figures for 1946 see *supra*, ch. 12, p. 430.

61. *Supra*, ch. 15, pp. 563–64.

62. For details and discussion of some of these clauses cf. Burton A. Zorn, "New Union Responsibilities," *Proceedings of New York University First Annual Conference on Labor* (Albany: Matthew Bender & Co., 1948), pp. 304–9; statement of Robert Abelow, *Ball Committee Hearings*, June, 1948, Pt. 1, pp. 429–34; BNA, *The Taft-Hartley Act after One Year*, pp. 235–50.

ployees were in some cases hired from the open market and later admitted to the union. Or they were hired and worked beside union men when the union refused to admit them to membership. The fact that the union scale had to be paid to such employees gave protection against any attempt of employers to undercut the union, had they desired to do so.

All these types of provisions were open to the possibility that they would be used to discriminate against nonmembers, in violation of the Act, though perhaps this was not inevitable. To what extent if at all they might prove to be legal under Taft-Hartley no one knew, pending determination by the Board and the courts. Employers sometimes willingly agreed, sometimes yielded to pressure by strong unions in order to avoid interruptions of production. These were attempts to meet the need of particular situations, sometimes involving noncomplying unions. Perhaps in some cases unions wished to maintain union security without submitting to the test of an election which might have gone against the union. But even in the many industries where no one could question the fact that the great majority of employees were union members and wished to continue so, employers and unions spent time and energy seeking a way out which would continue to serve the felt needs in spite of the new law. There could be little doubt that many of the resulting agreements were evasive of the law. But bootlegging was introduced into collective bargaining by this attempt by law to change old-established habits and police collective bargaining.

Another area of co-operation between unions and employers was in working out acceptable "limited liability" agreements. The provisions for suits for violation of contracts, and for damages arising from certain outlawed activities of unions or their agents, seemed to the unions a very serious threat, opening the way for harassment by antiunion employers and to danger to union funds and the very existence of the union.[63] A solution was found first in the International Harvester and Ford agreements,[64] and later various types of clauses for a similar purpose came widely into use. Some of these provided that the union would not be held liable for any unauthor-

---

63. Cf. *supra*, ch. 13, pp. 510–12.
64. *New York Times*, August 6 and 18, 1948. The NICB report, *Union Contracts since the Taft-Hartley Act*, pp. 24–32, on 313 contracts signed after the Act became effective, found that in 25.9 per cent there was no clause prohibiting strikes, and 25.9 per cent prohibited or restricted strikes, but exempted unions from liability for unauthorized strikes. The last were almost entirely "Taft-Hartley clauses." Cf. also BNA, *The Taft-Hartley Act after One Year*, pp. 227–34.

ized stoppage, if it took specified measures to prevent or end any such interruptions of work; some specified that only the international could authorize a strike; some defined in detail the union agents for whose action the union was responsible; some relieved the union from financial responsibility but reserved the right to discipline employees involved; some provided that any issues arising over work stoppages should be handled through grievance and arbitration procedures and that the company would not in any case file suits or charges before the NLRB against the union; some set a limited sum which could be assessed by an arbitrator as damages. While there was controversy over such clauses in the early months, especially in the case of small companies which were suspicious of the motives of the union, as it worked out there are indications that often a healthy relationship was promoted by this joint effort to define responsibilities.[65] As one representative of management said, "Whether the clauses be called forgiveness, evasion, or union liability does not matter if the result is to curb strikes and to restore discipline. The value of such clauses has already been proved in a number of situations."[66] There is little doubt that as a result some unions took their responsibility to prevent violations of the contract more seriously than they had done before.

Other problems, too, required special negotiations in light of Taft-Hartley. The sixty-day provision for termination or modification of a contract was different from the terms in many contracts and required adjustments and great care to avoid violations, since the penalties for a strike in disregard of the required period were severe. Here again technicalities and uncertainty as to the requirements created difficulties.[67] There was also trouble over whether the sections barring payments to representatives of employees, with specified exceptions, or the "featherbedding" section, interfered with well-established contract clauses such as for "call-in time," rest periods, even

65. Cf. Zorn, *op. cit.*, pp. 315–19.   66. Van Delden, *op. cit.*, p. 18.

67. *Supra*, ch. 12, pp. 452–53. For an extreme case see discussion in Boeing Airplane Co., 80 NLRB 447 (November, 1948), Intermediate Report, n. 7. The company had argued that at the time of its refusal to bargain the strikers had lost their status as employees because of failure to comply with Section 8(d). A petition by the General Counsel for an injunction against the company was denied on the ground that the union had failed to give the required notice, but the judge had pointed out that the opinion of the court was not binding on the Board. The Board held that since the contract had been opened for negotiations leading to termination or modification long before the effective date of the Act, the union was not obligated to comply with the notice requirements of 8(d). The circuit court finally reversed the Board and held the strike in violation of contract and of the law. *New York Times,* June 1, 1949.

vacation pay, or, more seriously, payment for time spent in handling grievances. Such technicalities sometimes presented a real stumbling block in negotiations involving smaller employers who were fearful of violating the law, or employers who sought to use such matters as a bargaining weapon or for delay. But where employers and unions wished to settle their own affairs by collective bargaining and to continue and improve their relationships, they were able to work out the problems, by new clauses devised to meet the issues raised by the Act, or else by ignoring or evading the law. Where there was some increase in responsibility shown by union representatives, this was a gain. Against this was inevitable suspicion of motives and irritation at the upset to old habits.

One clear gain was the reduction in jurisdictional strikes, as unions, under pressure of possible action by the NLRB and threat of injunctions, found ways to settle most of these disputes themselves. The law was effective too in reducing or eliminating cases of improper pressure by boycott or other economic means by some unions against properly established representation by unions chosen by the employees.

Another development was the increase in employers' use of "free speech," under encouragement of the amendment to the Act. Many companies began programs of "employee communications," both during negotiation periods and others. This was acclaimed as making a contribution to better understanding between employees and employers, but even the proponents pointed out dangers that it might arouse resentment and create difficulties.[68]

Altogether, the verdict on the part of most employers seemed to be that the Act had improved their relationships, although in some respects it was a nuisance. The verdict on the part of unions was less favorable. At least it was clear that when employers and unions still wanted to solve their problems by collective bargaining, for most of them this was possible, although sometimes a kind of "bootlegging" was involved. It is probable that the kinds of working relationships which we have summarized were more typical in the first year than the situations of more serious conflict.

CONFLICTS ARISING UNDER TAFT-HARTLEY

It is frequently said as evidence of the success of Taft-Hartley that strikes decreased. It is true that the number of strikes decreased

68. Cf. address by Carroll E. French, Director, Industrial Relations Department, National Association of Manufacturers, *Daily Labor Report*, No. 66:E-1 (April 5, 1948).

steadily during the second half of 1947, but an equally steady increase followed during the first half of 1948. From January to June, 1948, the number of man-days lost by strikes, nearly 22 million, was only a million less than in those months of 1947. For the whole of 1948 there were about 8 per cent fewer work stoppages than in 1947, but the man-days idle, more than 34 million, were only 500,000 under 1947, and accounted for nearly the same percentage, 0.4, of the available working time. The figures suggest that many of the strikes were of long duration, as we know to have been true in important instances. The average time lost per worker involved, 17 days, was the highest since 1936, except for the great postwar strike year, 1946. Twenty large strikes, involving more than 10,000 workers each, accounted for more than half of the time lost in stoppages. There was a decline in the always small proportion of time lost which was due to jurisdictional strikes, but a noticeable increase in that due to other strikes involving union rivalry. Loss of time in strikes involving closed- or union-shop issues increased substantially, to more than 4 million man-days lost, nearly 12 per cent of the total man-days lost in work stoppages.[69]

The first year of Taft-Hartley of course was not a great strike year like 1945–46, but there were many reasons for this in addition to the change in the law. Most employers and unions wanted to avoid stoppages, because of profitable operations, or because of relatively high earnings even though the cost of living pressed hard on the pay envelope. Both sides, too, were uncertain as to the effects of the new law and hesitant to test it out. Moreover, unions and workers' families were inclined to hoard their resources for dangers possibly ahead. When strikes did occur, they tended to be bitter and long. More often than in recent years, encouraged by the Act employers opened their plants and attempted to operate. The aids available in the Act for the employer who sought to break a strike were used, and a number of important strikes were lost. In the bitterness engendered by these struggles picket-line violence and use of troops and police violence against strikers appeared again in the headlines and the pictures on newspaper front pages, as they had not to the same extent for many years.[70] Injunctions were increasingly used against unions in state

69. U.S. Bureau of Labor Statistics, *Work Stoppages in 1948—Final Data*, April 13, 1949, and preliminary report released January 13, 1949. Time lost in jurisdictional disputes in the first three quarters was reported as 0.1 per cent of the total for all stoppages; that in rival union strikes as 1.7 per cent; and that in strikes over closed- or union-shop issues as 11.8 per cent.

70. Numerous examples of such conflicts were given in union testimony in *Ball Committee Hearings*, Pt. 2, pp. 684–86, 694–98, 788–95 and elsewhere, June, 1948.

courts, some of them based in part on alleged violations of the federal Act.[71] Even the "national emergency" provisions failed to prevent several stoppages of far-reaching impact on the economy in 1948.[72] The claim that strikes were prevented by the 1947 Act needs serious qualification. Undoubtedly, however, the risks of striking were increased and unions were slower to engage in strikes. To this extent the Act accomplished one of its purposes.[73]

Serious conflicts arose in a number of situations, where the conflict stemmed directly from the restrictions imposed by Taft-Hartley. Some of these involved issues which were still in litigation before the Board or the courts at the end of the first year. Some of the most serious ones had to do with the abolition of the closed shop. In some industries, in contrast to those where accommodations were made in order to maintain more or less of the status quo, and especially where unions were not prepared to utilize the NLRB's processes, there was long conflict before adjustments were made. The Typographical Union and the maritime conflicts were the most well known of these.

The Typographical Union cases illustrate the difficulties under Taft-Hartley of a skilled craft union, with a long experience of strict apprenticeship, a closed shop, a strong bargaining position which had established high standards of wages, hours, and other conditions, and a tradition of union-imposed control over many matters which reflected its long history of organization. It is true that other unions in the printing industry accepted the necessities of the new legal framework, won union-shop elections, and worked out contracts without any head-on collision with the law or the employers. Perhaps the ITU could have done the same. A case can be made, in the experience of this industry, for a requirement that unions should not refuse to bargain collectively—that is, here, that they should not adopt unilateral rules and attempt to impose them upon employers without bargaining. Possibly also there has been something of a problem in restriction of job opportunity through restrictions upon the labor supply by a strong closed-shop union. But the sweeping restrictions in Taft-Hartley appeared to this union, rightly or wrongly, such a threat that it undertook to fight against the publishers and commercial printers who stood firm against what seemed to them

71. *Supra*, ch. 15, p. 591.
72. *Ibid.*, pp. 584–85.
73. For example, President Tobin of the Teamsters was reported to have sent a "confidential" letter to local unions urging them to take great care and to avoid strikes when possible, because of the dangers in the current situation. *New York Times,* June 4, 1948.

evasions of the Act. The NLRB had still not decided any of the ITU cases when the Chicago newspaper strike went into its second year, in November, 1948. In most areas, nevertheless, agreements or under-standings had been reached and work had gone on, in some cases after shorter strikes. The bitter strikes, costly to the union and to the industry, and the long litigation before the NLRB and the courts, were a high price to pay for changes in well-established relationships. It is to be doubted whether many, if any in the industry, had bene-fited from the costly struggle resulting from this attempt at detailed regulation of collective bargaining by the government.[74]

In the maritime and longshore industries, the hiring hall was the crucial issue. Here the problem of the unions was to prevent the re-turn of the old casual-labor, low-standard, highly competitive system of labor recruitment and to maintain the strength of the union which had brought about the changed conditions. Possibly the requirements of the law could be met by sufficient ingenuity in revising hiring-hall systems for this purpose and preventing any abuses which had occurred through control of opportunities under union hiring halls. But the drastic remedy of complete abolition of the closed shop appeared to be and could be used as a weapon to weaken the unions. The conflicts were in part at least created by Taft-Hartley.[75]

Somewhat comparable in their effects were the restrictions upon payments to unions and upon welfare funds. Extortion or the pay-ment for men clearly not needed was appropriately forbidden, and occasionally as a result a union withdrew an untenable demand. But the prohibition of such payments as the royalty on phonograph records agreed upon through collective bargaining made trouble.

74. On some of the issues cf. *supra,* pp. 627–28, 636–37; ch. 12, pp. 433, 437, 469, 477. Cf. also testimony of Woodruff Randolph, President of ITU, in *Ball Committee Hearings,* Pt. 1, pp. 285–394, May 28, 1948; *Typographical Journal,* 114 (1949), 68–75. The Chicago strike was settled on September 18, 1949, with an agreement which was believed to contain no provisions contrary to law. Union membership was not to be required for hiring or tenure of employ-ment; the definition of "journeyman" included any persons with a minimum of six years at the trade, and a method was provided for joint determination of the competency of journeymen and apprentices; the offices agreed not to require employees to process "struck work"; reproduction or "bogus" work was curtailed. *New York Times,* September 16 and 19, 1949; *ITU News,* October, 1949.

On October 28, 1949, the NLRB issued its first ITU decisions, in the Chicago and the American Newspaper Publishers Association cases. It held that the union had violated the law by its bargaining strategy, which was found a negation of the duty to bargain and to have been designed to cause discrimination against nonunion men. Chicago Newspaper Publishers Association, 86 NLRB No. 116; American Newspaper Publishers Association, 86 NLRB No. 115.

75. Cf. *supra,* n. 51; ch. 12, pp. 436–37; ch. 15, pp. 584–85.

When an agreement was finally worked out for a royalty fund to be administered by a neutral trustee appointed by the companies, it was fairly evident that the intent of the Act had been evaded, but the making of records was resumed.[76] In coal-mining the conflicts of 1947 and 1948 were sharpened by the detailed regulation of welfare funds. In their context these regulations, interfering with freedom to solve problems by mutual agreement, caused resentment and confusion in many industries, although agreements, some of them "bootleg," were finally worked out. Meanwhile, demand for extension of such welfare provisions was widespread, primarily because of the failure of Congress to meet the demand for extension of the federal social security system, and perhaps stimulated too by the publicity given to the problem by Taft-Hartley controversies. The coverage of such plans more than doubled from 1947 to mid-1948, although a considerable number of employers urged that bargaining on such matters be excluded by law from the area of required bargaining.[77]

Restrictions upon bargaining units of guards when they were included in or affiliated with unions of rank-and-file workers also upset established systems and in some cases caused trouble.[78] The elimination of foremen from the protection of the Act, apparently approved by most employers, drastically changed the relationships in some companies, although there were cases where collective bargaining continued, and others where the foremen's organization kept at least a foothold. The issue of whether foremen needed collective action in order to have satisfactory conditions was not ended by the Act.

Another important area of conflict brought on by the Act involved unions which did not file the non-Communist affidavits and other documents required for use of the NLRB.[79] Many employers continued to deal with these unions. But where employers refused to recognize or continue bargaining until the union was certified, there was serious difficulty. Sometimes it was solved by recognition after a strike, or by another union's winning an election. But in others there were long strikes and bitterness. Although the Act did not except such noncomplying unions from the right to recognition if they represented a majority of the employees, or the right to strike for recognition, they could not obtain protection from the Board or from the

76. *Supra,* ch. 15, pp. 566, 567–68.
77. *Ibid.,* pp. 565, 568.
78. For examples, see *Ball Committee Hearings,* Pt. 1, pp. 173, 256; Pt. 2, pp. 764–65; *supra,* ch. 14, pp. 521–22.
79. *Supra,* ch. 14, esp. pp. 554–57; ch. 12, n. 90.

courts. Accordingly they were thrown upon the use of their own strength, if the employer chose to go further than Congress did and to refuse to recognize a noncomplying union. There were cases where refusal to recognize and the use of other weapons provided in the Act[80] were enough to be disastrous to the union. Equally important, or sometimes even more so, was the fact that rival unions moved in to the attack. Some of the left-wing unions suffered severely, and only to a less extent some other unions which as a matter of principle refused to comply. In some instances a shift to a different affiliation, or house-cleaning by the incumbent union, brought about what appeared to be a more healthy and democratic organization and a sounder basis for collective bargaining. In others the conflicts left labor organization seriously weakened and an antiunion employer free from much of the union restraint to which he had previously been subject. In some cases employees through trial by combat became more militant and union-minded, and in the long run their unions might prove stronger than ever, if they managed to survive. Opinions differ as to whether on the whole the conflicts were worth their cost from a long-range point of view, even from that of national security. That conflicts had been promoted by the Act could not be denied. Possibly, too, as was suggested by several management representatives, this provision and employers' use of it gave basis for Communist propaganda which might more than offset any gain.[81] Nevertheless, it was clear that the process already begun before Taft-Hartley, by which the labor movement itself sought to reduce the influence of Communist leaders, had considerable success from 1947 to 1949.[82]

In a number of respects Taft-Hartley encouraged rival union competition and instability in collective bargaining. The craft-unit amendment encouraged craft unions to think they had won their argument and therefore stimulated attempts to sever craft or alleged craft groups from established plant-wide units.[83] Many employers were concerned that a less efficient and more time-consuming system of

80. Cf. *infra*, pp. 646–47. In addition in private injunction cases lower courts sometimes penalized noncomplying unions by applying, in effect, the "clean hands" doctrine against them. Several such cases in state courts are cited by Somers, *op. cit.*, pp. 357–58.

81. "Taft-Hartley Act—One Year After," *Management Record*, 10 (1948), 435–38.

82. For some details on shifts of affiliation and other aspects of the "anti-Communist movement" see *Monthly Labor Review*, 68 (1949), 148–49. See also *supra*, ch. 14, n. 100.

83. *Supra*, ch. 14, pp. 522–25.

bargaining with many unions might replace their plant-wide units. As a result there was sometimes increased attention to the problems of skilled workers in the bargaining of industrial unions and the employers.[84] The Board limited craft severance somewhat, but still unions and employers could not be sure to what extent crafts would be permitted to carve out small units, and attempts to do so were numerous. Other provisions also made raids by rival unions easier. Noncomplying unions were under extensive attack, since they could not appear on representation ballots except in the case of decertification petitions. Noncomplying unions, on the other hand, in some cases stimulated petitions for decertification against a rival and then sought by their own economic pressure to obtain recognition.

The main discouragement to raids was in the maintenance of existing contracts as a bar to new elections for periods of reasonable duration, and the Board continued to accept two-year contracts as reasonable.[85] In addition, the boycott method was not available to those unions which in the past had used it in an attempt to obtain recognition though another union had been certified or was recognized as the representative of the majority of the employees. But at the end of contracts rival unions could and frequently did use the processes of the Board to seek to overturn an incumbent union or to carve out small units from existing broader units. As always, competition in organizing served as a stimulus to active, honest, and democratic unionism. But it also put a premium on militancy and exaggerated claims in order to keep interest up and maintain lines intact against threats from outside. Taft-Hartley's concern for the protection of dissenting minorities promoted instability, at the expense of stable collective bargaining which some employers as well as unions desired. In spite of the incentive for common action in face of seen dangers, divisions within the labor movement and the resulting organizational rivalry were accentuated. Raiding was widespread between right- and left-wing unions even within the CIO, between complying and noncomplying unions, between craft and industrial unions, and between the AFL, the CIO, and the large unaffiliated unions such as District 50 and the Machinists.

Another source of conflict generally was the invitation to litigation given by the amended Act. Because of the many restrictions placed upon activities of labor organizations and upon collective bargaining in addition to the continuing restraints upon employers, and because

84. Cf. the 1948 contract of the UAW-CIO and General Motors.
85. *Thirteenth Annual Report*, pp. 29–31.

the Act was complex and technical and frequently ambiguous, an employer who wished to harass a union, or a union which wished to harass an employer, had at hand many weapons for delay and troublesome litigation. Even for the many unions and employers who were trying to work out their problems by collective bargaining, the uncertainties and technicalities brought legal issues to the fore. Lawyers had a larger role in negotiations than before, especially in case of the smaller companies. Black pictures of the results in delays and interference with frank and open discussion were drawn by several of the union representatives testifying before the Ball Committee.[86]

It was apparent that often the provisions of the Act were used as bargaining weapons, to be given up in exchange for other concessions. The possibility of filing charges with the Board, or of refusing continued recognition and insisting on new certification, or of suits for damages against the union or the employer, or of filing petitions for union-shop elections, was frequently present and used in the bargaining process, even in grievance handling. Too often attention was turned from attempts at a constructive bargaining process to seeking technical advantages from the Act. There were widespread reports of increased difficulty in settling grievances. To some union negotiators, also, Taft-Hartley appeared "a handy gadget to beat down wage demands."[87] Thus deals to perpetuate in effect closed-shop conditions, or to grant legal union-security clauses, or clauses limiting union liability to suit were made in exchange for lower wage demands.

And when strikes occurred the employer's arsenal was well stocked with weapons provided by the Act. Instances could be cited where employers refused to continue recognition, engaged in extensive campaigns by speech and letter against the union, filed employer petitions or encouraged decertification petitions, filed charges against unions for restraint and coercion or other unfair labor practices, discharged strikers for alleged violence on picket lines, obtained injunctions in state courts, and filed suits for damages for violation of contracts or for strikes allegedly illegal.[88] In answer unions filed charges

86. *Supra,* pp. 633–34.

87. A spokesman for the Textile Workers Union of America attributed to attacks upon the union and the slowing-down and obstruction to organization in the South the fact that the differential in average hourly earnings between the North and the South had increased. "The wage movement that is completed in the North has not even begun in the South." *Ball Committee Hearings,* Pt. 2, pp. 811–12, June 4, 1948.

88. Among other instances of allegations of this sort by union representatives see *Ball Committee Hearings,* Pt. 1, pp. 242, 250; Pt. 2, pp. 740–41, 794, 800, 1040–41.

against employers and suits for damages for alleged violation of contracts.[89] Possibly in some cases all these methods were justified, but in others they were merely delaying and harassing tactics, far from the needed prompt resolution of differences by a democratic process of free elections and collective bargaining. Too often, it has been said, collective bargaining was replaced by "collective litigation." The wartime tendency to run to the government unfortunately continued and was stimulated by Taft-Hartley. Many employers and unions sought to avoid such methods and solve their difficulties themselves or to go to the government only in the rare situation where there was real need, but too many found in the Act new weapons in a struggle for position and power.

EFFECTS ON NEW ORGANIZING

The immediate effect of the passage of Taft-Hartley was to slow up if not to stop entirely efforts to extend organization. Unions were worried for the security of existing organization and turned their attention to strengthening their positions against possible attack. When they began meeting the filing requirements, a heavy demand was made on the time of union officials, which left little opportunity for new organizing. Unions began to husband their resources also, and organizing activities were inevitably cut. In addition, the climate had changed, partly as a result of the antiunion propaganda in connection with the campaign for passage of the Act. In many communities antiunion sentiment had increased. Employers felt even more free than they had before to engage in very active campaigns against the unions. It was more difficult to get workers to sign up, and in the first months an unprecedented number of representation elections were lost. The antiunion vote reached the high of 38 per cent in December, 1947. In many cases where unions had obtained signed cards from an apparently safe number of workers, nevertheless at the election, and after last-minute efforts by speeches and letters from the employer, sometimes aided by community groups, the people voted strongly against the union. In addition, a considerable number of cases of violence against union organizers and sympathizers, especially in the South and small communities, were reported by union spokesmen in testifying to the Ball Committee. At the same

89. For an example of charges and countercharges cf. Seamprufe, Inc., 82 NLRB No. 106 (1949). The Trial Examiner recommended dismissal of a charge of coercion against the union, and found the company guilty of violating Sections 8(a), (1), (2), and (3). The Board on April 7, 1949, held both the employer and a union organizer in violation of the Act. For data on suits for damages see *supra,* ch. 13, pp. 512–13.

time many unions felt it useless to file charges against employers, since the regional offices were bogged down for many months with union-shop elections and necessarily also giving priority to certain cases filed against unions.[90]

Nevertheless, the sharp setback to expanding organization was only temporary. As they watched developments, unions began to find techniques to meet the hazards. In part they found that if they did a more thorough job of organizing and "selling" the union, they could still win elections. The employers' campaigns stimulated counter-attacks. Employees who had been impressed by the general anti-union feeling when the Act was passed began to think that perhaps their own welfare might be affected if unions were seriously weakened. In some instances they sought out the unions for help in organizing their plants. Unions learned too that the "crutch" which the Wagner Act had given them was no longer entirely reliable and that they must stand on their own feet. Noncomplying unions demonstrated that it was still possible to organize and win recognition, sometimes using the services of private agencies for elections or check of union cards, sometimes convincing the employer of their right to recognition by a strike. The elections held by the Board, too, began to show a substantial increase in the pro-union vote. Possibly the overwhelming votes in favor of the union shop helped to bring some change in attitude among employees. In any event organization began to move ahead again. But it was more hazardous and more costly.[91] Local unions which were organized under the stresses of the first Taft-Hartley year would long show the effects of their origin. Some of them had won recognition by battle rather than by the peaceful means which were the intent of the Wagner Act. They would be tougher, more militant, more self-reliant, perhaps also more democratic and effective, than some in the past which had won recognition with less of a fight. Whether from the employer's standpoint

90. For testimony on such matters cf. especially *Ball Committee Hearings*, Pt. 1, pp. 239–44; Pt. 2, pp. 742, 787–94, 799–802, 812, 814–15, 1041–42, 1045, May–June, 1948.

91. The AFL reported at its November, 1948, convention increases in paid-up membership of affiliated unions in 1948 over 1947 in more instances than decreases. American Federation of Labor, *Report of Executive Council to the 67th Convention*, November, 1948, pp. 12–13. President Murray reported to the CIO increases in membership for several of the internationals, and new locals chartered and new agreements signed in many others. The southern organization campaign was reported as fast approaching a gain of a half-million members. Congress of Industrial Organizations, *Report to the CIO by Philip Murray, President, Tenth Constitutional Convention*, November, 1948, pp. 25–34.

they would be easier to deal with was another question. Fighting leadership was inevitable so long as the need for it seemed to be present. And the hazards, where employers had fought the coming of the union, were still very evident to the unions.

Unions which had been in the habit of organizing from the top down, through the use of boycotts or picket lines, rather than organizing the people themselves, necessarily had to change their tactics; and this was a gain from the Act. Organization was made slower and more costly, but in these cases the interest of democratic self-organization was served by the necessity of following the methods which had always been intended by the Wagner Act. On the other hand, the blanket prohibition of boycotts removed the possibility of use of this weapon in the attempt to organize competitive plants which were a serious threat to the standards established in the organized industry.[92] Unions in the garment trades, for example, and in other industries where there had been experience with "runaway shops," were worried about possible return of extensive nonunion competition. The risk in striking in the face of strong opposition from employers and sometimes from the community also was increased, so that organizing strikes were necessarily used with caution.

Altogether it was clear that Taft-Hartley had some of its most important effects in making it more difficult to extend organization in unorganized areas and industries. But unions after the first shock began to develop methods which would work. The fact of a short labor market was important in making it possible to continue gains. Whether it would be possible to hold organization, however, should unemployment increase, was a worry for the future to many unions.

EFFECTS ON INDIVIDUALS AND THEIR RIGHTS

Protection of the rights of individual employees against abuses by unions was said to be important among the aims of the 1947 Act. Evidence as to whether the law actually gave such protection where it may have been needed is difficult to obtain, since the incidents are scattered, and no one knows to what extent there have been problems. It was assumed that many employees were unwillingly covered by closed-shop or union-shop agreements and would welcome the opportunity in secret elections to repudiate "compulsory membership." Overwhelming evidence from the thousands of union-shop elections, however, refuted any such claim, as well as indicating a broad popular support for the unions' programs. Probably in some

92. AFL, *Report of Executive Council*, November, 1948, p. 38.

cases where unions could not safely submit to the test of a vote the filing of petitions for such elections was avoided. But deauthorization elections were possible were there any strong revolt against the union; and only a handful of such petitions were filed in the first fifteen months. In a few cases employees voted against union security, and possibly in these cases the test by the secret ballot was a desirable protection. It is probable, also, that the prohibition of boycotts and coercion as organizing devices saved some employees from being brought under closed-shop contracts without having an opportunity freely to choose whether they wished to be represented by the union in question.

Decertification elections also were expected to give an opportunity for employees to free themselves from an unwanted union. Some of the petitions filed were suspect as employer-instigated, but others undoubtedly were a free expression of dissatisfaction by employees. Sometimes, in the relatively few elections held, a rather close vote indicated a real difference of opinion among the workers concerned. But occasionally a union was decertified by an overwhelming vote, such as 23 to 0 or in another case 73 to 0. In spite of the dangers seen that this device gave another tool to an antiunion employer, it probably served a useful function in some instances in making it easier for employees to rid themselves of a union which had not held their allegiance, or in stimulating the union to renewed activity in behalf of its constituents.

Whether the requirement of filing financial reports and making them available to members had much if any real effect is not known. Probably more important was the protection against loss of jobs or being shut out of jobs because of denial of union membership. In at least a few cases employees who had been excluded by unions were finally, under pressure from the filing of charges against the union, admitted to membership. It is probable that in other instances unreasonable exclusion from unions may have been prevented by the terms of the Act.

At some points, it appears, individuals did thus receive protection from the amended Act, and at these points a salutary effect was exerted upon unions to be responsible and serve their members so that they could hold their loyalty. On the other hand, in so far as Taft-Hartley made it more difficult to prove charges against employers and gave them a variety of weapons with which the bargaining position of labor organization was weakened, individual employees lost security and protection, and perhaps suffered even in their wages and conditions of work. Anyone's judgment of the net result will be affected by the weight he gives to collective activity as against individual action and interests. To many the potential or actual weakening of labor organizations seems a heavy cost to pay for whatever was gained in protection of certain individual rights—especially since these might have been protected without the weakening of collective rights.

SOME EFFECTS ON UNIONS THEMSELVES AND THEIR ACTIVITIES

Unions like other members of the American community sometimes resort to paid advertisements to take a message to the public, and on occasion these are illuminating. About a year after Taft-Hartley became effective such an ad, published in the *New York Times*[93] by a local union of the Pulp, Sulphite and Paper Mill Workers, AFL, was suggestive of some of the effects of the Act. It began:

THANKS!

Mr. Taft and Mr. Hartley
Not for what you tried to do to us and to all workers in this country, But thanks for waking us up . . . because that is precisely what your iniquitous law did.

It went on to recount its overwhelming success in a union-shop election, and then said:

We're grateful to you because your law inspired such unanimity of conviction and brought out the true strength of our Union. It enabled us to overcome the vigorous and continuous opposition of many employers in our industry to the establishment of an industry wide HEALTH and WELFARE Fund, for which our new contract provides. . . .

Many unions reported similar experiences. Their efforts to strengthen themselves against possible attacks, with increased aid from the international unions to be sure that the locals were functioning effectively, often rebuilt and strengthened the organizations. To some degree the necessity of filing the various documents prerequisite for use of the Board served educational purposes. Union-shop elections and drives to obtain individual check-off authorizations similarly proved useful. And conflict situations brought out fighting qualities which solidified ranks. Perhaps, as many were saying, the unions which survived would be stronger and better organizations.

There were certain dangers to democratic unionism, however. Because of the uncertainties and hazards to collective activity under the Act, and the increase in litigation, many international unions

93. *New York Times*, September 1, 1948.

tightened their controls over their locals. The trend toward centralized control, which had gone far in many unions—the United Mine Workers and the United Steelworkers were examples—was undoubtedly increased at the expense of local autonomy. Some unions increased their control over the negotiation of local contracts as well as control over strikes. However necessary such a trend may be, it makes it more difficult to maintain a functioning rank-and-file interest and democratic activity at the local level, and weakens the democratic base which is so vital if labor organization is to play its role in a truly democratic society. This was an unexpected and unfortunate result from a law whose sponsors wanted to strengthen the position of individuals against the great unions.

The non-Communist affidavit requirement sharpened the issue of Communist influence in the labor movement, and some such leadership was displaced. In some unions the change was more apparent than real, as former officers went on the pay roll in other capacities. By the fall of 1948, however, Communists and Communist sympathizers were losing out in a number of spots where they had had influence in the unions.

Did unions become more responsible as a result of a law which was much concerned with alleged failures of responsibility? There was a widespread impression that effort was increased to avoid violations of agreements and that undisciplined action by members and local unions was taken more seriously. The evidence is clear that unions took more responsibility to settle jurisdictional disputes themselves without interruptions of operations. Whether there was any increase in financial responsibility and democratic procedures at the points where there had been a real problem is doubtful. Whether unions that were guilty of abuses under closed-shop agreements made any very substantial changes in their methods also is to be questioned. We have noted many evasions of the Act on these points, and only more time would tell whether abuses continued. Some unions which had been irresponsible in their methods of organizing and obtaining agreements, some of them even verging on racketeering, or certainly on coercive methods, had been forced to change their methods, and at these points the Act had been useful.

In spite of the fears when the Act became law, most unions survived the tests of 1947–49. It was at the "periphery of organization" that they suffered chiefly, and some unions were having serious difficulties. Others had lost at some points but were in many respects tough and strong. Many unions increased their membership, in this time of full employment. The major tests were still to be faced, especially if depression came and the restraints upon union action were still in effect.

Finally, faced with what seemed to them a threat to their very existence by the Taft-Hartley Act and the prospect that its terms would be tightened rather than relaxed by a Republican Eighty-first Congress, and deeply dissatisfied also with the record of the Eightieth Congress on social security, housing, and the like, unions went to work in politics more actively than ever before. Many of them used their papers to promote interest and spread information about the congressional campaigns. Many if not most worked to get their members registered and paid up as to poll tax, where that was necessary, and to be sure that they voted. The labor political organizations set up and financed on the basis of voluntary contributions were active, though they never achieved their aim of getting contributions from every member. In fact, the reports to the House Clerk on expenditures in the 1948 campaign showed a total collected by six major organizations of only $696,004.[94] Labor organizations understandably took considerable credit for the results of the elections. And the AFL and CIO as well as others planned to continue their political interest and activity. An unavoidable effect of repressive, "antilabor" legislation, plus lack of action on other vital problems, was to drive labor into political action. The parallel to the development in Britain after the adoption against labor opposition of the Trades Disputes Act of 1927 was obvious. Industrial relations had been brought into the political arena, with the result which might have been expected.

SOME EFFECTS UPON ATTITUDES

Attitudes were affected in numerous ways which have been suggested in our discussion above. Employers as a whole "got a lift" from the passage of Taft-Hartley. To many of them the amendments seemed to make a much fairer law, which put responsibilities upon unions as well as employers, and gave a more equitable basis for labor relationships. They did not intend to use the law unfairly, but they were strengthened in their bargaining position, and unions found them tougher at the bargaining table. Others welcomed a law which would aid them in fighting unions and breaking strikes. Some of these were restrained by the advice and caution of others. Many

94. *Daily Labor Report,* No. 211: A-1 (October 28, 1948). The total of donations reported was as follows: CIO Political Action Committee, $306,720; AFL Labor's League for Political Education, $243,024; Railway Labor's Political League, $79,249; Labor's Committee for the Election of Truman and Barkley, $32,535; Trainmen's Political Education League, $16,435; and United Automobile Workers, CIO, $8,040.

employers were troubled at the prospect that some of their fellows would abuse their privileges under the law and recognized that there were possibilities of such abuse. And a minority of employers even during the first year were showing how the law could be used successfully to keep unions out or to get rid of an unwelcome union. These were the ones especially who gave concrete basis for much of what the unions said about the Act. And, finally, some employers were dissatisfied with the Act, partly because it proved less effective against union abuses than they had hoped, and some even more because of the great extension of government control over collective bargaining itself.

Unions, on the other hand, showed their fear and resentment and their determination to fight against a law which they considered unfair. Many admitted privately at least that some provisions of the Act were needed and that others were not so bad as painted. But the abuses and possibilities of abuse, the uncertainties, the legal pitfalls, all made unions deeply suspicious of the Act, the Board, and the General Counsel, and of employers. Increased militance, class-consciousness, and interest in political activity resulted. The fighting psychology, the atmosphere of conflict, was not conducive to the accommodations at the bargaining table that were needed in the long run for successful collective bargaining and the most productive relationships in the plants.

And in collective bargaining itself the technical requirements and limitations of the law turned the attention of the parties to legal niceties, restraints, the dangers and potentialities of litigation. The possibility of working out solutions which were acceptable and suited to the needs of particular situations was decreased. The amount of government restriction upon the bargainers was a danger to the integrity of voluntary collective bargaining. As George W. Taylor[95] has said, the most fundamental characteristic of the Taft-Hartley Act was a restriction upon the collective bargaining rights of both employees and employers. It remained to be seen whether the desire to make collective bargaining work was sufficiently strong to overcome the handicaps imposed by the law. There were encouraging signs in the number of employers and unions who succeeded in carrying on much as usual in spite of the atmosphere of conflict and of preoccupation with legal technicalities which Taft-Hartley promoted.

95. For his full discussion see George W. Taylor, *Government Regulation of Industrial Relations* (New York: Prentice-Hall, Inc., 1948), esp. pp. 10–33, and ch. 6.

CHAPTER 17

CONCLUSIONS: THE NATURE OF
THE TAFT-HARTLEY ACT

NO PHRASE or slogan is adequate for a characterization of the Labor Management Relations Act of 1947. It was not a "Slave Labor Act" nor a "Magna Carta for Employers," nor a "Bill of Rights for the Individual Workingman." Since it was complex, looked in two directions at once, and in addition was poorly drafted and unclear at many points, it meant many things to many men. Many descriptions of the Act, each with some basis in fact and experience, differ so widely that it is almost impossible to believe that they refer to the same statute. A more adequate characterization needs to break the Act down and look at a series of different sorts of things accomplished by these amendments and additions to the Wagner Act.

We find four major categories in these changes in the law. First, Taft-Hartley did a few things which were much needed, in "equalizing" the Wagner Act and imposing restraints on certain unjustifiable actions of unions—thus approaching a balanced code of labor relations. Second, it included a rather longer list of provisions, most of these also in the name of "equalizing the Act," which gave an appearance of increased fairness and met some of the attacks upon the old Act; these had a desirable psychological effect and perhaps promoted greater acceptance of the Act by employers, as well as increased acceptance of their responsibility by some unions. For most of these there was a far less strong real case for the amendment than was said by opponents of the Wagner Act. But meeting some of the adverse feeling by such concessions was at least in part constructive. Third is a series of detailed provisions which upset established practices worked out by labor and management or through the discretion of the administrators of the law, on which no adequate case was made for change, and which made unnecessary difficulty in collective bargaining and in administration. Finally, there was a still longer list of provisions which we consider unfair and discriminatory, since they reflect bias against collective bargaining and could be used unreasonably to restrict union actions which to us seem justifiable by the common interests of groups of workers. These carried the possibility of seriously undermining the position of all labor organizations, the weak as well as the strong. They are the provisions which reasonable representatives of management had in mind when they said, frequently, that they hoped the provisions of the Act would not be abused by employers. Without an exhaustive listing of provisions, some indication of major matters in each of these groups may clarify the nature of the 1947 Act. Inevitably there is some duplication, since these categories, significant as they seem to be, are not at all points mutually exclusive.

NEEDED EQUALIZING AMENDMENTS

First are the "equalizing" amendments which imposed obligations and restraints upon unions parallel to those already imposed upon employers. Some of the new prohibitions of unfair labor practices of labor organizations or their agents met the need shown by experience for restraints upon clear abuses. Among these were coercion of employers or employees or both by minority unions, contrary to the free choice of the majority of the employees; closed-shop contracts obtained by such means or by collusion between unions and employers; strikes or boycotts in the furtherance of jurisdictional disputes, or to assist employers in maintaining a monopoly of a local market; occasional cases of extortion, the extreme case of "featherbedding," in the name of collective bargaining; and occasional cases of "refusal to bargain" by unions which were inclined to put down a contract with a "take this or else" ultimatum. It was desirable, too, that the NLRB be given authority at its discretion to seek an injunction in an extreme case against a union engaging in such practices, and to order back pay from a union for victims of discrimination induced by union pressure upon employers. All this was done by the 1947 Act in its provisions on unfair labor practices and their prevention. But parts of the Act[1] went far beyond this in their restraints upon concerted activity.

EQUALIZING AMENDMENTS MEETING PSYCHOLOGICAL NEEDS

Reasonable men may disagree as to whether some of the matters in our second group do not also belong in the above group of needed amendments. These all seem to us, however, of a different sort, where the case for amendment was rather to make clear the already present

1. Esp. Sections 8(b)(1), 8(b)(4)(A), and 10(j) and (l).

intent of the law and the administration or the well-known and usually respected obligation of a union, equally with an employer, to be responsible in its behavior. These are not specific solutions for specific and well-established abuses. But the psychological effect of the apparent increase in fairness under the new specifications may have been of some significance, if only in removing openings for the use of some of the slogans, or perhaps at some points having real and sound influence on attitudes and habits. The incorporation in federal law of reasonable provisions emphasizing equality of duties and responsibilities, and fair and impartial administration of laws, may contribute to attitudes which promote responsible collective bargaining.

Important from this standpoint, for effects on feelings and therefore upon the relationships in industry, was the simple fact that unions as well as employers might be subject to restraint if they engaged in conduct contrary to the purposes of the Act. Important also was the reassurance given to employers by the free-speech amendment that their right of full and free discussion was not restricted—though this went too far in opening the door to speech that might be coercive. A number of provisions for elections also seemed to make for equity. The provisions for petitions for elections by employers or by dissatisfied employees who wished to be freed from an unwanted bargaining agent, though open to abuse, seemed on the surface fair, and on occasion they served a constructive purpose in the interest of free choice as to representation. Union-shop elections, to assure that union-security agreements rest on the decision of the majority of those covered, seemed to make for equity and perhaps actually strengthened the democratic basis of collective bargaining, as well as removing a misconception as to the prevailing attitudes of workers towards their unions. The requirement that elections, rather than a check of membership cards, be used to settle representation disputes, while hardly needed under the safeguards which had been established administratively, yet removed any doubt as to the freedom of choice of employees who selected a bargaining representative, and promoted acceptance of the results.

Canons as to fair treatment and justice in decision were given also in the provisions for equal treatment of unaffiliated and affiliated unions, and by the "discharge for cause" rule, although we have found no real basis in the evidence for the implication that these statutory rules were needed because of failure of the Board to use its discretion fairly. Perhaps the amendments as to evidence and court review were similar in their impact on feelings, though the actual change was probably more verbal than real and the effects appeared to be minor.

The sixty-day notice requirement and that as to the filing of union financial and other documents as a prerequisite for use of the NLRB also implied standards of responsibility in collective bargaining and of democratic and honest union procedures. These might affect habits at some points, as well as relieving the feelings of some employers in regard to the unions with whom they dealt.[2] And the implication that unions and employers should be equally liable for violations of contracts appeared equitable and apparently increased the attention of many unions to the necessity of seeing that contracts are observed by their members. Yet the greater ease of bringing damage suits invited litigation and on balance probably did more harm than any good accomplished by this canon of equal responsibility. On many of these points it was sound to assume that unions and employers both have responsibilities as well as rights under the law and in collective bargaining. But when the duties were made specific and enforceable, the complexities and difficulties in administration and sometimes uncertainties in the law created difficulty, turned attention to litigation, and more than counterbalanced whatever values inhered in the provisions.

The independence of the Federal Mediation and Conciliation Service, set up outside the Department of Labor, undoubtedly reassured employers as to the impartiality of the Service, and promoted the effectiveness of its work, whether or not such formal independence was necessary. The drastic separation of functions between the NLRB and the General Counsel of the Board, also, cut the ground from under one of the most widely accepted, though we think all but baseless, criticisms of the administration of the Wagner Act. Perhaps it made employers feel better about the Act; but it went so far, and introduced so many difficulties and possibilities of inefficient or unfair administration, that we are forced to consider it primarily of a quite different sort from the other changes which we find acceptable for their psychological and emotional effects.

2. The non-Communist affidavit requirement is very difficult to classify for present purposes, perhaps chiefly because it introduces an issue of an entirely different sort into a law on labor relations. To some degree it belongs in this second group, for its effects on union attitudes and employers' feelings; on the other hand, to the extent that it created interference with collective bargaining it is questionable and belongs in group three; and we consider it clearly discriminatory and open to use simply for antiunion purposes, and therefore comparable to the provisions which we place in the last group. All this is in addition to the grave questions raised as to effects upon civil liberties.

Conclusions: The Nature of the Taft-Hartley Act

Had the 1947 amendments stopped with the acceptable measures of the two groups above, and had they not been carried too far, as was done, we should have considered that on the whole the national labor policy had been strengthened, so as to provide a firmer and more equitable basis for industrial relations under the conditions which had arisen by 1947. Unfortunately, however, some of those measures were carried too far, and more than that, the amendments went farther.

In a third group are a number of extremely important provisions which interfered with well-established relationships satisfactory to the parties or worked out administratively on the basis of experience, and for which there was no sufficient evidence of any need for drastic change. Many of these promoted conflict and litigation. They led also to disregard of the law and to co-operation of employers with unions, either under pressure or by mutual agreement, to evade or ignore the restrictions of the Act. Most prominent among these was the outlawing of the closed shop, and with it apparently the hiring hall which had been established by agreement in an important group of industries where it met a real need. Any specific abuses could have been remedied without such drastic interference with acceptable programs worked out by those concerned.

Restrictions on payments to unions and on the administration of joint welfare funds also brought conflict and disturbance, rather than dealing carefully with any specific abuses found. These provisions and the sometimes related "featherbedding" clause limited the freedom of unions and management to seek through collective bargaining to work out acceptable means of dealing with their particular problems. The rigid and unclear sixty-day notice clause, with its severe penalty on strikes before the end of the period, introduced uncertainties and rigidity into collective bargaining, to the detriment of the flexibility sometimes essential for workable relationships. The encouragement of damage suits led to difficulty over no-strike clauses, though the net effect of the reconsideration at the bargaining table of the mutual responsibilities of both parties was constructive in many cases.

Concern of the Act for the protection of "the right to refrain" from collective activities, as equally important if not more important than the right to engage in such activities, led at a number of points to encouragement to dissenting groups or minorities. Permanence and stability in collective bargaining, as a means by which employers and employees work out their mutual problems, suffered as a result. The encouragement of crafts and pseudo-crafts to attempt the breaking up of many well-established plant-wide bargaining units made for instability and less effective bargaining, as many employers realized. Raiding was encouraged against unions which failed to comply with the filing requirements for access to the NLRB's processes. Decertification petitions and employer petitions at the end of contract periods similarly, though serving a sound purpose on occasion, made for instability. The rigid proscriptions as to bargaining units involving guards, professional employees, and supervisors also made for unnecessary upset in established relationships, without adequate basis. Division and competition within the labor movement, dissension over units, and attempts of minorities to upset established relationships, all were promoted by the 1947 Act. Often all of this meant conflict, and energy diverted from the more constructive matter of seeking solutions for real problems at the bargaining table.

Prominent also in this group of provisions which interrupted established procedures and interfered with efficient and satisfactory relationships were the drastic changes in the administration of the NLRA. Despite the psychological gain from this concession to the critics, we think that it was unnecessary and unsound. We find no evidence that it resulted in any higher standard of justice in administration or decision than there had been before. In fact, efficient, fair administration, with unity in policies under the Act, was made almost impossible to achieve by the bifurcation of the NLRB into the Board and the General Counsel and his staff. Division of responsibility as to *policy* in the different stages of administration resulted inevitably in delays, sometimes in reversals of prior action, and in the possibility of crucial effects upon the parties, especially labor organizations, by policy decisions in the early stages of handling cases, although the basic questions must ultimately be decided by the Board. The possibility was obvious of unfair and fatal restriction upon union activity in some cases through extreme interpretations of the Act, although if later the General Counsel were reversed by the Board, the union or the strike might be long since dead. Similar difficulty was possible in new types of cases against employers. At the same time, for the general run of cases on which there were no new issues of policy, the separation of functions made little or no difference in the actual handling of cases, except as the efficiency of the staff had been reduced by turnover, by the necessary influx of new and inexperienced employees, or by a decrease in morale resulting from some of the intangibles in the law and its administration. In addition, many of the detailed prescriptions as to the review and decision-making process and the work of Trial Examiners simply made it much more difficult to achieve efficiency in administration, without any increase in the safeguards of due process which the changes were said to intend. The increased membership of the Board, with authorization for use of a panel system, was on the whole advantageous. But the most that can be said of the detailed prescriptions as to the Board's administrative procedures is that in spite of them it was still possible to administer the Act. We find no basis for having expected any gains in the quality of the work; rather the reverse seemed inevitable. We are forced to consider these provisions as not only an unwarranted and dangerous change in a well-tested administrative process but also as a basically antiunion change in the law.

Expansion of federal power in the field of industrial relations, moreover, based on a stated desire for national uniformity of policy at least on some points, though not on all, undercut the work of the state labor relations boards and decreased the freedom of the states to experiment. There is a case for establishing a federal policy on basic matters in the relations between unions and employers. But it is significant that the Taft-Hartley Act limited the freedom of states to be less restrictive in policy than the federal law; and at the same time it was not entirely clear whether it was meant to allow them to be more restrictive. In the field of union security of course greater restrictions were permitted when states so chose. But in other aspects of labor relations and concerted activities could unions be restricted further and be deprived of basic rights stated in the federal Act? The law was uncertain on all this. At the same time excessive centralization of control over many matters brought a degree of federal intervention for which we find no sufficient basis in the evidence. The difficult problems as to the proper relationship between state and federal regulation in this field were not clarified by the 1947 law.

UNFAIR, DISCRIMINATORY, AND ANTIUNION PROVISIONS

In the fourth group is the too long list of provisions which we find unfair and discriminatory. They reflected exaggerated interest in dissenting groups, nonunion employees and individual bargaining, and distrust of collective bargaining. They unreasonably restricted concerted activities and gave weapons to an employer who wished to fight a union. They accordingly weakened potentially or actually the position of all unions. First is the free-speech amendment, going far beyond the constitutional guarantee, and permitting and encouraging employers to enter actively by the written and spoken word into election campaigns against unions seeking to represent their employees, subject only to limits upon overt acts or threats or promises of benefit. Even more serious, its limitation upon the use of speech as evidence weakened the protection of the rights of employees against interference by employers, though at some points this also modified the rigors of the proscriptions of union actions.

In marked contrast are the sweeping and poorly defined provisions as to unfair labor practices of unions and their agents. Some of them were discriminatory, not "equalizing" amendments, in their effects. The undefined prohibition of "restraint and coercion," combined with the broad definition of "agent," opened the possibility for restriction upon peaceful picketing and other activities which should be permitted if reliance is to be put upon collective bargaining rather than one-sided determination or government regulation of labor conditions. It resulted also in federal intervention into matters of policing which are, we think, better left to local authorities. The bans on payments to employee representatives, and the featherbedding clause, banning bribery, extortion, and payment "for services not rendered," were not balanced by any prohibition of "kick-backs" sometimes required by fly-by-night employers, or any effort to determine whether an employer was requiring too much service of his employees by the "stretch-out" or other device. These regulations, which opened the door to excessive federal regulation of details of labor's behavior, were essentially antiunion and unequal in effect, if not in intent. Many of these problems are better left to collective bargaining or to state laws.

The extreme case of the ban on all boycotts and sympathetic strikes, regardless of justification in direct economic interests of different groups of employees, went much further than a reasonable restraint against abuses. It interfered with activities often needed for self-protection by groups of employees affected by co-operative activities of employers, sometimes in breaking a strike. Moreover, however serious an employer's violation of the rights of his employees under the Act, no injunction against these activities was mandatory. But the fact that injunctions were mandatory in some types of cases against unions, regardless of the significance or insignificance of the case, gave powerful support occasionally to an employer at the crucial stage of his dispute with a union, even in instances where the activity restrained could easily be found reasonable when looked at in other terms than those of Taft-Hartley. In addition, the fact that in these cases priority of handling was required meant that cases against employers which might be extremely crucial for the protection of the rights of labor under the Act in the industry or area were sidetracked whenever a boycott case came in. The effectiveness of the protections against employers' unfair labor practices was considerably reduced by these changes in the law. Moreover, the clock was turned back and the use of injunctions in labor disputes was greatly increased as a direct or indirect result of the Act, in state as well as in federal courts. In addition to a decreased protection against the antiunion employer, and restrictions in the availability of union weapons at some points, unions also found themselves subject to damage suits for the same activities—and all this before the Board itself had considered whether the union was actually in violation of the law. This does not seem real equalization.

Highly effective weapons were given to an employer who sought to break a union or to break a strike. Full use of his freedom to carry on campaigns by the spoken or written word, refusal to continue recognition, filing of an employer petition or instigating a decertification petition filed by employees, with strikers not eligible to vote if it had been possible to replace them, the one-year rule protecting the employer against further efforts to obtain recognition should an election go against the union, the possibility of charges against the union and even injunctions if the union, harassed and fighting for its life, overstepped the line, or even approached it—all these added up to substantial aid and comfort to an employer who undertook to fight a union with all the help he could obtain from the law. And there was no comparable pressure upon him to seek an orderly resolution of the dispute. If a union was strong enough to hold its lines, it could survive; the union which was unable or had chosen not to use the processes of the Board was in particularly weak position,[3] but other unions too found this combination of weapons used against them. The weapons were there, available to be used by an employer at his discretion. All this invited conflict rather than reliance upon collective bargaining and peaceable means of settling disputes.[4]

3. Cf. n. 2, *supra*.
4. We would also include here the fact that foremen were barred from the protection of the Act, although we recognize the highly debatable character of this issue.

In national emergency cases, somewhat similarly, the use of the union's weapons was restricted, in the name of the public interest in uninterrupted operation, but without comparable pressure upon employers to work out an acceptable solution. No recommendation by a board of inquiry was permitted. The provision for a ballot on the employer's "last offer," also, ineffective as it proved, must have been expected to bring a repudiation of the union leaders by the rank and file. It reflected the same antiunion feeling as many others of the amendments. Recognizing all the difficulties in these problems, we are unable to find in Taft-Hartley the equitable solution needed. Finally, the ban on expenditures and contributions by unions in national elections made it more difficult for workers to be politically effective by using their own organizations to promote their interests as they see them in political campaigns.

Many of these provisions were used only in exceptional cases and had little or no direct effect on the relations of the great majority of employers and unions who preferred to work along together as in the past. Yet they increased the hazards of concerted activity, were depressive in their effect upon unions and their members, stimulated and encouraged antiunion employees, employers, and community groups, and tended to weaken labor organizations in their efforts to extend organization or to improve their bargaining position. All this had its greatest impact not upon the strong unions which were in position to abuse their power, and sometimes did, but upon unions which were weak and facing powerful employers.

THE TAFT-HARTLEY ACT AS A WHOLE

For the Act as a whole, the complexities and uncertainties and the undiscriminating limitations upon union activities, as well as the loosening of restraints upon employers, offered an inducement to resort to the Board and the courts in litigation instead of seeking to work out problems acceptably by a responsible collective-bargaining process. Although some of its provisions imposed badly needed limitations upon abuses and others might have valuable effects upon attitudes, the unprecedented extension of controls over all relations between employers and the representatives of their employees, or those who sought to become such, brought the government and its agents into the picture to an unhealthy extent; the government was present at the bargaining table; the shadow of the law and the courts was over every negotiation session, not only as a potential check upon certain abuses of power, but as a limitation upon the freedom of unions and management to work out reasonable solutions to some of their problems. Moreover, the emphasis upon protecting the interests of those who prefer individual bargaining, as against the desires of those who see concerted activity as the means to effective protection of the rights of individuals, threw the weight of the law at critical points against collective bargaining. Despite the fine words of faith in collective bargaining for the resolution of disputes, many of the new provisions inevitably had the effect of weakening unions and collective bargaining, undiscriminatingly weakening the power of organized labor as against employers rather than accepting collective bargaining as in the main to be desired as essential in a healthy society and then dealing with specific problems where they arise. They tended to create unco-operativeness and conflict, to undermine morale and spread bad behavior. In other words, Taft-Hartley tended to place industrial relations on the wrong road.

Taft-Hartley failed to meet the need of its times, to build on the Wagner Act, fill in its gaps, eliminate abuses, but at the same time strengthen the trends toward democratic and responsible self-government in industry. While some sections of the Act pointed in that direction, too much of the Act shows that it was the product of men who did not know how things work in industry or in the administration of the NLRA, and of some who wished to weaken the position of all labor organizations in the economic and political scene. On the assumption that unions and collective bargaining are essential for a free and democratic society, and that their contribution to democratic and responsible government in industry must be strengthened, not weakened by law, we conclude that the 1947 amendments to the Wagner Act failed to meet the problems posed. Taft-Hartley, with its confusion and division of purposes, its weakening of all unions rather than carefully directed restraint of specific abuses, its weakening of restraints upon employers who still seek to avoid a democratic system of labor relations, its interference with collective bargaining, its encouragement of litigation rather than of solving problems at the bargaining table, its administrative hodgepodge, was a bungling attempt to deal with difficult problems. Too largely it looked backward rather than forward. The 1947 Act needed drastic revision, based on careful and discerning analysis of the complex problems involved, before there would be a sound foundation in federal labor law on which could be built industrial peace, efficiency, and mutually responsible attitudes under representative government in industry.

Epilogue

WHAT INDUSTRIAL RELATIONS ROAD FOR THE UNITED STATES?

I N THE field of industrial relations, because of complexity and variety of experiences, researches, judgments, temperaments, and underlying philosophies and assumptions, no one can expect others to agree with him at every point.[1] Differences there will be, and some of them may be wide. All anyone can or should do is to analyze the issues in terms of what he has been caused by experience to think in this complicated and difficult field, or otherwise not set pen to paper at all. Of course anyone's judgments in the realm of industrial relations are substantially affected by the fundamentals he has come to believe in. That is true here.

One of these fundamentals is what he considers the best general road to follow in the United States—developed, politically organized, and peopled as it is. That road is not to be found in any general or extensive system of compulsory arbitration such as, in spite of its shortcomings, has found preferment in countries like New Zealand and Australia, but which could not be expected to work out as well here. One reason for this is the difference in attitude toward government control. Believing in free enterprise generally, but also in opportunity for the masses of people, we cherish and should continue to cherish "home government" in industry rather than court-made

1. This Epilogue has been made up from several notes written by Dr. Millis. It has seemed best not to expand them as he would probably have done, had he lived to complete this book. First is the statement of his basic assumptions and philosophy, which was written for this purpose early in 1947. Following are some notes on issues as to power in the relations of unions and management, written in 1945, and pertinent to the question of sound national labor policy. And finally is the credo on collective bargaining which formed part of his farewell to the NLRB staff upon his retirement in 1945 from the Chairmanship of the Board, and which seems appropriately used here as his final word. Preceding chapters have shown where in our opinions national policy was in harmony with the approach stated here, where it could be strengthened, and where it took the wrong road, if we wish to strengthen the democratic base of industrial relations as a "chief bulwark of the mode of life we cherish and are determined to maintain and to improve."—E. C. B.

standards of wages, hours, and conditions of employment which usually become the important thing in any general system of compulsory arbitration. Neither in New Zealand nor in Australia were such important end results foreseen when the initial arbitration laws were enacted.

Nor is our road to be found in a handmade, controlled unionism and industrial relations as under a Soviet state. Nor is it to be found under Fascism, which in Italy witnessed, indeed effected, the displacement of a free unionism by a Fascist organization to serve the ends of a highly centralized, authoritative state. Neither would it be found under a Nazi order where free labor organizations and collective bargaining were quickly suppressed, replaced, or narrowly controlled.

If one believes in free enterprise and representative government, what is done by government must, as a general rule, be limited to efforts to aid in the working-out of complicated problems and to limitations made to protect the public interest and to secure justice for protesting minorities. The main road, with exceptions here and there, combines free enterprise with responsible representative government in industry when representative government is elected by those immediately concerned. Otherwise, efficiency cannot be combined with free and responsible government in industry. We should seek both. Moreover, the writer believes that such government in industry, if and when obtained, is the main, continuous, and needed support of responsible, intelligent, representative government in the body politic.

In approaching the problem, emotion must be kept down. It will not do to say, "I do not like this or that—there ought to be a law against it." We have been too prone to do just that. Nor, if there is to be efficiency and freedom on the part of most people, should one fall victim to the thought that industrial relations should be, or can be, narrowly controlled by the courts. "Bureaucracy" may find a place in the conduct of war and in the period of reconversion following, but even a small amount of it is a superabundance in time of peace. On the whole our federal agencies having to do with industrial relations functioned moderately well during World War II. Some of the services rendered should have been continued, with needed improvements in administration, during the period of reconversion. Yet much that was practiced during the war needed sooner or later to be unlearned. Collective bargaining and much of the sense of responsibility so vital in it were all too frequently sacrificed during that period

670

by many in management and some of the older unions and were not really developed by most of the new. The big problem after the war was to apply our knowledge, plant by plant or industry by industry, in an effort to get a reasonably good solution of problems.

The writer is not of the belief that everything must or should be as it is, or that deep economic laws or something else are narrowly controlling, so that "not much can be done about it" without the effort necessarily begetting problems which outweigh the good effected. Rather is he of the conviction that co-operative thought and action on problems by those most directly concerned in them can accomplish much. Accordingly, he believes that the problems discussed in preceding chapters are capable of solution. Some can be solved by management and the representatives of their employees directly. In others the solution should be sought by conference and if possible agreement by representatives of management, labor, and our legislators on statutes which set reasonable standards of behavior, provide for proper checks against abuses where clearly shown, and promote the conditions in which democratic and responsible action by management, organized labor, and workers in industry can grow.

QUESTIONS OF POWER

Certain issues concerning the balance of power between unions and management are of importance in appraising the possibilities of collective bargaining and the proper role of government in industrial relations. War in industry is or should be only incidental and not inevitable. Any serious strife and conflict can usually be avoided when proper procedures and policies find place in the minds and behavior of management and unions, when they carefully sift the facts in the light of sound principles on which there is or should be general agreement.

Of course, the old-fashioned socialist and the typical present-day communist leaders have stressed power in the hands of workingmen chiefly because they think in terms of a socialist or communistic state. These minority groups among American workers—and small minority groups they have been and still are—have been tremendously interested in power in order to obtain an order visualized as quite different from the so-called capitalist state. Most American workers do not have revolutionary ideas in any such sense but are adherents of a "free enterprise" economy, with the problems of labor solved by collective bargaining, supplemented by a measure of legislation and government control.

671

From the Wagner Act to Taft-Hartley

The overwhelming evidence is that labor officials and the rank and file underneath them will dispose of such a question of power in a few words. Perhaps they would state first the truism that no union can get from management what it thinks it deserves unless it has power in numbers and leadership. Then follows the assertion that workingmen cannot get the deserved or "necessary" wages, hours, and working conditions without sufficient power to be heard effectively concerning them and, if necessary, the power and the right to stop work. Wages, hours, and working conditions, especially "job rights," are clearly the things they have in mind, and they desire sufficient power to have an effective voice in the determination of them. Following this, it will be added that, until an adequate voice can be had by labor in the determination of these matters, there will be discontent, instability, and the spread of false ideas of a different general order; and to such ideas opposition is clearly expressed, at any rate until the present order clearly fails to function moderately well—which God forbid!

Put in a word, in the general thinking of American workingmen the issue of power is not really basic but largely derivative—something to be obtained in such degree as to make the present general system work with acceptable results.

Many employers have, of course, seen in the appearance of a union a great issue of power. This has been due in large measure to the influence of custom and to fear. Management generally, depending on circumstance, temperament, and opinion, has not been habitually inclined to deal with labor in the union's "democratic way." Rather has management, once much influenced by custom, fought labor organization in ways which were declared unlawful in the National Labor Relations Act of 1935—and again in 1947.

With a widespread acceptance of the policies of the Wagner Act, however, and with the rapid expansion of the organized labor movement, custom came to have much less influence than it had before with employers, except in small industrial communities and in hard-and-fast "open shop" areas here and there. Fear of the *use of power* and of *loss of prestige with employees* are more and more decisive where unions as such are no longer denounced. It emanates largely from unresourceful management, or from union procedures—frequently none too enlightened—from specific union requests, certain union policies and practices, possibly from what has happened in particular instances, and very much from expectations of what may come next and where it may eventually end.

Thus, if this is correct, the issue of power in the minds of employers also is largely derivative, from procedures and from what unions "demand" or may later demand in wages, hours, security of tenure, and working conditions. Ordinarily when this has been present it disappears with the subsidence of fear, with the use of sound procedures, with acceptable union and management policies, with willingness to discuss and to bargain in good faith, and with recognition of the necessity of "give and take." Where instead of debate in terms of legal and natural rights there is analysis of problems and their impacts on one side and the other and the resolution of these in the light of sound principles and pertinent facts, the issue of power as such is not likely to predominate in the relationship.

The seasoned arbitrator, and seasoned management dealing with unions, realize that two fundamental things must be kept in mind. First, the union, with necessary sense of responsibility, not always found, must have sufficient power in leadership and members to maintain and strengthen its organization in such degree as to render it efficient in securing the employees' needs and appropriate aspirations. Second, management must have sufficient leeway to maintain shop discipline and to insure efficiency and quality while maintaining tolerable costs of production. Of course if there is irresponsibility, or awkwardness or exorbitance, or racketeering, there is likely to be trouble, though it must be said that in occasional cases mutual interest in racketeering smooths the way at the sacrifice of other parties. But experienced and responsible negotiators, conciliators, and arbitrators usually find that if these two fundamentals are recognized and the facts and their impacts are placed in the foreground and kept there, decisions are reached with little said about the issue of power or prerogative. Theoretically, it might be possible to draw the line between management rights and union power, but fortunately, when essential facts are kept in the foreground and carefully weighed in the light of these fundamentals, a working agreement or decision usually presents little difficulty. Certainly what to do is clarified, if not definitely disposed of.

Resolution of initial differences is made less difficult by such an attitude and approach. Yet resolution is in fact not always easy. For there are thousands of unions newly organized or attempting to organize and trying to develop sufficient power to accomplish their ends. All too frequently both leaders and management are not versed in conference procedures but are in the awkward stage. It is not sufficient to focus attention merely upon narrow-minded employers and perhaps their legal counsel. In addition, conflicting unions compete for adherence of the workers, and in an unfortunate and antisocial competitive struggle for members and prestige they make irresponsible and unrealizable promises which later plague them. Possibly there is struggle between groups or between would-be leaders in the union with like result. Not infrequently the shortcomings of policies accepted or requests presented get in the way and give rise to trouble. Certainly the problems of sound representative government within unions and as between unions have not been worked out by many of our unions, and the requisite sense of responsibility to industry developed up and down the line. The problem of maintaining rank-and-file interest and democratic participation in control in the huge unions dealing with huge corporations, or with thousands of small employers, has not been solved, and this is one reason for an adverse public opinion.

And, finally, sometimes a negative attitude on the part of employers or unions prevents recognition of the need for a balance of strength between the parties. Both "natural rights" doctrines and uneconomic policies need to be re-examined and adjusted in order to obtain the sound advantages of representative government in industry. Representative government means agreed-upon standardization with exceptions and qualifications required in the more general interest. To make it work efficiently and with justice, there must be in most industries or plants an effective Senate of Management and an effective House of Labor—also in exceptional instances agencies to end deadlocks or to protect the public against agreements adversely affecting the "general interest."

Chief concern here is the question of the desirable approach if collective bargaining is to be most successful—from the point of view of obtaining acceptable results under the present economy. Yet there is no cure-all for all the difficulties between management and organized employees over their working relations and objectives in a world changing, complicated, and presenting new opportunities, and in which cravings for a fuller life should be satisfied along what the parties most immediately involved and the general public regard as "sound lines." It would seem, nevertheless, that in a complicated and ever changing world the best possible approach to the accommodation of individual desires and the public interest is to be found in a democratic decision-making process, through responsible representative government in industry. Accordingly, public policy should be carefully framed to promote that end.

What Road for the United States?

During the period of the Wagner Act collective bargaining matured, in fact, from a hotly debated and often rejected theory to a widely used and accepted method in resolving questions in our industrial life.[2] And this was as it should be. That Act had within its operations the possibility of far-reaching by-products in this land of the free. The Wagner Act was without precedent, in scope or promise, in the history of our nation. But it was not foreign to our American way of life. On the contrary it was in close harmony with the historical traditions of our land. Even the date of its passage demonstrates its basic kinship to these traditions. In 1935 the lights of liberty were going out all over the world. Life and liberty were either being suppressed or surrendered in behalf of promised gains. But here a different choice was made, and a Magna Carta was enacted for American labor.

The Wagner Act, like all charters, was a promise, a foundation. It was a foundation on which could be built either a rude shanty or a beautiful edifice. The Act, with its full indorsement of collective bargaining and freedom of association, contemplated an edifice designed and buttressed by the best that free men can contrive. True, there were dangers of accidents of construction—self-perpetuating overseers, self-seeking leaders, those who attempted makeshift short cuts, also nonco-operative employers, as well as honest mistakes in figuring stresses and strains. However, the history of our nation shows, if it shows anything at all, that the common man, once given opportunity to construct, will usually plan and build well. That is the story of America—whether you turn to Plymouth, the Declaration of Independence, the Jacksonian era, Gettysburg, the westward trek, or TVA. The edifice built on this foundation of public policy normally houses values to our nation in economic, social, and community terms.

As an economist I am fully aware of the body of literature on the economic implications of governmental encouragement of collective bargaining, and will not add to it here. Suffice it to point out that such a national policy as that of the Wagner Act, through its remedy of unfair labor practices and determination of collective bargaining representatives, leads to collective bargaining, and collective bargaining is ordinarily concerned with better wages, shorter hours,

2. The following is freely quoted from H. A. Millis, "Credo: On Collective Bargaining," *The Wagner Act: After Ten Years,* edited by Louis G. Silverberg (Washington: Bureau of National Affairs, 1945), pp. 123–26.

protection in matters of discipline, and good working conditions in general. The collective agreement, however, means more than wages, hours, and working conditions. It means diminished turnover, increased stability, and job security. And, beyond this, industrial democracy or real-representative government in industry, when workers and employers leave off talking of rights and talk of, measure, and resolve their plant and industrial problems. Progress is made only by solving problems, with insight and in good faith.

This participation of the worker in the government of his industry is a basic fruit of collective bargaining. It is a fruit which must accompany the blossoming and continued growth of our industrial and democratic society. For, in our political life, stable and efficient representative government cannot be realized and maintained unless the great mass of the electorate become experienced in a joint solving of the many common problems. In our economic life, where lie the most immediate and continuous interests of the common man, collective bargaining through trade-unionism can contribute mightily in training and in seeking for the democratic way. In short, unless collective bargaining is developed and is successful in industry, it is unlikely that the masses of the people will receive that training in discussion, patience, tolerance, and acceptance of majority decision necessary for the development of a stable and efficient representative government.

This edifice, thus, is not concerned with economic ends alone; it is training and experience in representative government. Collective bargaining does not halt here. Once the working force is assured of economic security, as it matures in the ways of representative government, just as soon will it express itself on community problems—stability of population, strong neighborhood groups, good schools, good streets, places of worship, recreation centers, and meaningful elections to office. These are the concern of free men in a democratic society, and these are the things unreachable unless we stand and build on the foundation which exiles the labor spy from the industrial community, rejects antiunion discrimination, and encourages collective bargaining covenants openly and honestly arrived at.

And, I venture, where collective bargaining is the accepted rule, and the trade-union is an accepted institution in the community, public officials will find this to be true: Whenever they honestly try to do their duty and make war upon a labor racketeer, they will find such action popular among the mass of union people. Moreover, public officials will soon learn that trade-unions are one of the most

676

important political supports of representative government. Labor organizations have a stake in the perpetuation of a free-enterprise economy and in the perpetuation of the democratic process. A free-enterprise economy is, in fact, the only kind in which they can really bargain with employers and function as the representatives of the workers' free choosing; and a democracy is the only form of government in which they can have effective voice in securing political and social gains for themselves and their members. In a well-organized, well-led, and experienced trade-unionism and successful collective bargaining with forward-looking and able employers, I see the chief bulwark of the mode of life and the type of government we cherish and are determined to maintain and to improve.

Selected Bibliography

SELECTED BIBLIOGRAPHY

PUBLIC DOCUMENTS

ATTORNEY GENERAL'S COMMITTEE ON ADMINISTRATIVE PROCEDURE. *Final Report.* Senate Document No. 8. 77th Cong., 1st Sess., 1941.

——. *Monograph, National Labor Relations Board.* Senate Document No. 10. 77th Cong., 1st Sess., 1941.

COMMONWEALTH OF MASSACHUSETTS. *Report of the Governor's Labor-Management Committee.* House of Representatives No. 1875. March 18, 1947.

Congressional Record. Vols. 79–93.

FEDERAL MEDIATION AND CONCILIATION SERVICE. *First Annual Report, Fiscal Year Ending June 30, 1948.*

NATIONAL LABOR RELATIONS BOARD. *Annual Reports: First* (1936) *to Thirteenth* (1948).

——. *Legislative History of the Labor Management Relations Act, 1947.* 2 vols. Washington, 1948. Includes congressional committee reports and debates.

——. *Statutes and Congressional Reports Pertaining to the National Labor Relations Board.* Washington, 1943.

——. *Studies of the Results of National Labor Relations Board Activities.* Washington, 1946.

U.S. BUREAU OF LABOR STATISTICS. *Monthly Labor Review.* 1940–49.

U.S. CONGRESS, JOINT COMMITTEE ON LABOR-MANAGEMENT RELATIONS. *Hearings on Operation of Labor-Management Relations Act, 1947.* 80th Cong., 2d Sess., 1948. Cited as *Ball Committee Hearings.*

——. *Labor-Management Relations.* Senate Report No. 986. 80th Cong., 2d Sess., Pt. 1, March 15, 1948; Pt. 2, *Minority Views,* April 1, 1948; Pt. 3, December 31, 1948. Cited as *Ball Committee Reports.*

——. *Labor-Management Relations, Views of Certain Members of the Joint Committee on Labor-Management Relations.* Senate Report No. 374. 81st Cong., 1st Sess., May 13, 1949.

U.S. DEPARTMENT OF LABOR, DIVISION OF LABOR STANDARDS. *The President's National Labor-Management Conference, November 5–30, 1945.* Bulletin No. 77. Washington, 1946.

U.S. HOUSE OF REPRESENTATIVES. *Conference Report, Labor-Management Relations Act, 1947.* Report No. 510. 80th Cong., 1st Sess., June 3, 1947.

U.S. HOUSE OF REPRESENTATIVES, COMMITTEE ON EDUCATION AND LABOR. *Hearings, Amendments to the National Labor Relations Act.* 80th Cong., 1st Sess., 1947.

——. *Labor-Management Relations Act, 1947.* Report No. 245. 80th Cong., 1st Sess., April 11, 1947. Includes *Minority Report.* Cited as *Hartley Reports.*

From the Wagner Act to Taft-Hartley

U.S. HOUSE OF REPRESENTATIVES, COMMITTEE ON EDUCATION AND LABOR. *Hearings on H.R. 2032, National Labor Relations Act of 1949.* 81st Cong., 1st Sess., March, 1949.

———. *National Labor Relations Act of 1949.* Report No. 317. 81st Cong., 1st Sess., March 24, 1949; Pt. 2, *Minority Report,* March 28, 1949.

U.S. HOUSE OF REPRESENTATIVES, COMMITTEE ON EXPENDITURES IN THE EXECUTIVE DEPARTMENTS. *Twelfth Intermediate Report, Investigation To Ascertain Scope of Interpretation by General Counsel of National Labor Relations Board of the Term "Affecting Commerce" as Used in the Labor Management Relations Act, 1947.* House Report No. 2050. 80th Cong., 2d Sess., May 26, 1948.

U.S. HOUSE OF REPRESENTATIVES, COMMITTEE ON LABOR. *National Labor Relations Board.* Report No. 1147. 74th Cong., 1st Sess., June 10, 1935.

———. *Hearings, Proposed Amendments to the National Labor Relations Act.* 76th Cong., 1st Sess., 1939.

———. *Proposed Amendments to the National Labor Relations Act.* Report No. 1928. 76th Cong., 3d Sess., April 4, 1940. Includes *Minority Report,* April 12, 1940.

U.S. HOUSE OF REPRESENTATIVES, SPECIAL COMMITTEE TO INVESTIGATE THE NATIONAL LABOR RELATIONS BOARD. *Hearings, National Labor Relations Act.* 76th Cong., 2d Sess., 1939.

———. *Intermediate Report.* Report No. 1902. 76th Cong., 3d Sess., March 29, 1940; Pt. 2, *Minority Report,* April 11, 1940. Cited as *Smith Committee Reports.*

U.S. HOUSE OF REPRESENTATIVES, SUBCOMMITTEE OF THE COMMITTEE ON APPROPRIATIONS. *Hearings, Department of Labor–Federal Security Agency Appropriations Bills.* 77th to 80th Cong., 1941–47.

U.S. SENATE, COMMITTEE ON EDUCATION AND LABOR. *Hearings, To Create a National Labor Board.* 73d Cong., 2d Sess., 1934.

———. *Hearings, National Labor Relations Board.* 74th Cong., 1st Sess., 1935.

———. *National Labor Relations Board.* Report No. 573. 74th Cong., 1st Sess., May 1, 1935.

———. *Violations of Free Speech and Rights of Labor.* Reports. 75th to 78th Cong., 1937–43. Cited as *La Follette Committee Reports.*

———. *Hearings, National Labor Relations Act and Proposed Amendments.* 76th Cong., 1st Sess., 1939.

U.S. SENATE, COMMITTEE ON LABOR AND PUBLIC WELFARE. *Hearings, Labor Relations Program.* 80th Cong., 1st Sess., 1947.

———. *Federal Labor Relations Act of 1947.* Report No. 105. 80th Cong., 1st Sess., April 17, 1947; Pt. 2, *Minority Views,* April 22, 1947. Cited as *Taft Reports.*

———. *Hearings, Confirmation of Nominees for National Labor Relations Board.* 80th Cong., 1st Sess., July 23, 1947.

———. *Hearings, on S. 249, Labor Relations.* 81st Cong., 1st Sess., 1949.

———. *National Labor Relations Act of 1949.* Report No. 99. 81st Cong., 1st Sess., March 8, 1949; Pt. 2, *Minority Views,* May 4, 1949.

U.S. SENATE, SUBCOMMITTEE OF THE COMMITTEE ON APPROPRIATIONS. *Hearings, Labor–Federal Security Appropriations Bills.* 78th to 80th Cong., 1944–48.

Selected Bibliography

U.S. SENATE, SUBCOMMITTEE OF THE COMMITTEE ON THE JUDICIARY. *Hearings, Investigation of the National Labor Relations Board.* 75th Cong., 3d Sess., 1938.

BOOKS AND PAMPHLETS

AMERICAN CIVIL LIBERTIES UNION. *Democracy in Trade Unions.* New York, 1943.

BERMAN, EDWARD. *Labor and the Sherman Act.* New York: Harper & Bros., 1930.

BOWMAN, D. O. *Public Control of Labor Relations.* New York: Macmillan Co., 1942.

BUREAU OF NATIONAL AFFAIRS. *The New Labor Law.* Washington, 1947.

———. *The Taft-Hartley Act—after One Year.* Washington, 1948.

CHAMBERLAIN, JOSEPH P.; DOWLING, NOEL T.; and HAYES, PAUL R. *The Judicial Function in Federal Administrative Agencies.* New York: Commonwealth Fund, 1942.

CUSHMAN, ROBERT E. *The Independent Regulatory Commissions.* New York: Oxford University Press, 1941.

FRANKFURTER, FELIX, and GREENE, NATHAN. *The Labor Injunction.* New York: Macmillan Co., 1930.

GALENSON, WALTER. *Rival Unionism in the United States.* New York: American Council on Public Affairs, 1940.

GREGORY, CHARLES O. *Labor and the Law.* New York: W. W. Norton & Co., 1946.

HARTLEY, FRED A., JR. *Our New National Labor Policy.* New York: Funk & Wagnalls Co., 1948.

ISERMAN, THEODORE R. *Industrial Peace and the Wagner Act.* New York: McGraw-Hill Book Co., 1947.

KILLINGSWORTH, CHARLES C. *State Labor Relations Acts.* Chicago: University of Chicago Press, 1948.

LORWIN, LEWIS L., and WUBNIG, ARTHUR. *Labor Relations Boards.* Washington: Brookings Institution, 1935.

METZ, HAROLD W., and JACOBSTEIN, MEYER. *A National Labor Policy.* Washington: Brookings Institution, 1947.

MILLIS, HARRY A., and MONTGOMERY, ROYAL E. *Organized Labor.* New York: McGraw-Hill Book Co., 1945.

MORRIS, RICHARD B. *Government and Labor in Early America.* New York: Columbia University Press, 1946.

NEW YORK UNIVERSITY. *Proceedings of New York University First Annual Conference on Labor.* Albany: Matthew Bender & Co., 1948.

———. *Proceedings of New York University Second Annual Conference on Labor.* Albany: Matthew Bender & Co., 1949.

ROSENFARB, JOSEPH. *The National Labor Policy and How It Works.* New York: Harper & Bros., 1940.

SILVERBERG, LOUIS G. *The Wagner Act: After Ten Years.* Washington: Bureau of National Affairs, 1945.

TAYLOR, GEORGE W. *Government Regulation of Industrial Relations.* New York: Prentice-Hall, Inc., 1948.

From the Wagner Act to Taft-Hartley

TELLER, LUDWIG. *A Labor Policy for America.* New York: Baker, Voorhis & Co., 1945.

VAN ARKEL, GERHARD P. *An Analysis of the Labor Management Relations Act, 1947.* New York: Practising Law Institute, 1947.

WITTE, EDWIN E. *The Government in Labor Disputes.* New York: McGraw-Hill Book Co., 1932.

ZORN, BURTON A., and LICHTENSTEIN, HOWARD. *More Important Provisions of the Labor-Management Relations Act, 1947.* New York: Chamber of Commerce of the State of New York, 1947.

UNION AND MANAGEMENT PUBLICATIONS

AMERICAN FEDERATION OF LABOR. *Report of Executive Council to the Annual Convention: 57th* (1937) *to 67th* (1948).

AMERICAN MANAGEMENT ASSOCIATION. *Industrial Relations under the Taft-Hartley Law.* "Personnel Series," No. 112. New York, 1947.

———. *Problems and Experience under the Labor-Management Relations Act.* "Personnel Series," No. 115. New York, 1948.

———. *Operating under the LMRA.* "Personnel Series," No. 122. New York, 1948.

CHAMBER OF COMMERCE OF THE UNITED STATES. *Federal Regulation of Labor Relations.* Washington, May, 1937.

———. *Amendment of the National Labor Relations Act.* Washington, March, 1939.

———. *Policy Declarations, Industrial Relations in America.* Adopted May 2, 1946; May 1, 1947.

CONGRESS OF INDUSTRIAL ORGANIZATIONS. *Report of President Philip Murray to the Constitutional Convention: Seventh* (1944) *to Tenth* (1948).

INTERNATIONAL ASSOCIATION OF MACHINISTS. *The Truth about the Taft-Hartley Act and Its Consequences to the Labor Movement.* Washington, 1948.

INTERNATIONAL TYPOGRAPHICAL UNION. "Taft-Hartley and the I.T.U.," *Typographical Journal,* 114 (1949), 68–75.

NATIONAL ASSOCIATION OF MANUFACTURERS. *Why and How the Wagner Act Should Be Amended.* New York, 1939.

———. *Employer-Employee Cooperation.* New York, 1942.

———. *Collective Bargaining, a Management Guide.* New York, 1943.

———. *Collective Bargaining, Management Obligations and Rights.* New York, 1943.

———. *Government's Place in Postwar Labor-Management Relations.* New York, 1944.

———. *Labor Relations Today and Tomorrow.* New York, 1945.

———. *The Public and Industrial Peace.* New York, 1946.

———. "State Regulation of Labor Union Practices and Affairs," *NAM Law Digest,* Vol. 9 (December, 1946).

———. "Pending Labor Legislation," *NAM Law Digest,* Vol. 9 (January, 1947), Supplement No. 2.

———. *Americans Won't Stand for Monopolies.* New York, 1947.

———. "Labor-Management Relations Act, 1947," *NAM Law Digest,* Vol. 9 (June, 1947).

Selected Bibliography

——. *The Challenge and the Answer.* New York, 1947.

NATIONAL ASSOCIATION OF MANUFACTURERS, ECONOMIC PRINCIPLES COMMISSION. *The American Individual Enterprise System.* 2 vols. New York: McGraw-Hill Book Co., 1946.

NATIONAL INDUSTRIAL CONFERENCE BOARD. *Union Contracts since the Taft-Hartley Act.* "Studies in Personnel Policy," No. 94. Washington, 1948.

——. "Taft-Hartley Act—One Year After," *Personnel Management Record,* 10 (1948), 433–40.

UNITED STEELWORKERS OF AMERICA. *Legal Department Memorandum No. 3, Labor-Management Relations Act, 1947, Analysis of Provisions of the Act.* Pittsburgh, 1947.

——. *Report of Officers to the International Convention: Third* (1946) and *Fourth* (1948).

ARTICLES AND PERIODICALS

ASH, PHILIP. "The Periodical Press and the Taft-Hartley Act," *Public Opinion Quarterly,* 12 (summer, 1948), 266–71.

"Availability of NLRA Remedies to 'Unlawful' Strikers," *Harvard Law Review,* 59 (1946), 747–68.

BERNSTEIN, VICTOR H. "The Antilabor Front," *Antioch Review,* 3 (1943), 328–40.

BROWN, EMILY CLARK. "The Employer Unit for Collective Bargaining in National Labor Relations Board Decisions," *Journal of Political Economy,* 50 (1942), 321–56.

——. "Union Security," in *Proceedings of New York University Second Annual Conference on Labor,* pp. 73–110. Albany: Matthew Bender & Co., 1949.

"Change of Bargaining Representative during the Life of a Collective Agreement under the Wagner Act," *Yale Law Journal,* 51 (1942), 465–81.

CLEVELAND, ALFRED S. "NAM: Spokesman for Industry?" *Harvard Business Review,* 26 (1948), 353–71.

COX, ARCHIBALD. "Some Aspects of the Labor Management Relations Act, 1947," *Harvard Law Review,* 61 (1947–48), 1–49, 274–315.

DODD, E. MERRICK. "Some State Legislatures Go to War—on Labor Unions," *Iowa Law Review,* 29 (1944), 148–74.

FINDLING, DAVID. "NLRB Procedures: Effects of the Administrative Procedures Act," *American Bar Association Journal,* 33 (1947), 14–17, 82.

GELLHORN, WALTER, and LINFIELD, S. L. "Politics and Labor Relations—NLRB Procedure," *Columbia Law Review,* 39 (1939), 339–95.

"The G—— D—— Labor Board," *Fortune,* 18 (October, 1938), 52–57, 115–23.

HART, H. M., JR., and PRICHARD, E. F., JR. "The Fansteel Case; Employee Misconduct and the Remedial Powers of the NLRB," *Harvard Law Review,* 52 (1939), 1275–1329.

KERR, CLARK. "Employer Policies in Industrial Relations, 1945–47," in *Labor in Postwar America,* pp. 43–76. Brooklyn: Remsen Press, 1949.

KOVNER, JOSEPH. "The Legislative History of Section 6 of the Clayton Act," *Columbia Law Review,* 47 (1947), 749–65.

KOZMETSKY, GEORGE. "Unions' Financial Reporting," *Harvard Business Review*, 27 (1949), 13–23.

"The Labor Management Relations Act and the Revival of the Labor Injunction," *Columbia Law Review*, 48 (1948), 759–72.

"Labor's Economic Weapons and the Taft-Hartley Act," *University of Pennsylvania Law Review*, 96 (1947), 85–101.

LEVY, B. H. "Eligibility of Strikers To Vote under the Taft-Hartley Act," *Personnel*, 25 (1948), 60–71.

MAGRUDER, CALVERT. "A Half Century of Legal Influence upon the Development of Collective Bargaining," *Harvard Law Review*, 50 (1937), 1071–1117.

MILLIS, HARRY A., and KATZ, HAROLD A. "A Decade of State Labor Legislation: 1937–47," *University of Chicago Law Review*, 15 (1948), 282–310.

MORSE, WAYNE L. "Brookings Institution 'Fixes Up' the Facts to Anti-Union Ends," *Labor and Nation*, 3 (May–June, 1947), 14–16.

———. "Sorry, President Moulton, the Book's No Good," *ibid.*, July–August, 1947, pp. 38–40.

MOULTON, HAROLD G. "Senator Wayne L. Morse Is Wrong," *Labor and Nation*, 3 (July–August, 1947), 36–38.

NORTHRUP, HERBERT R. "A Critique of Pending Labor Legislation," *Political Science Quarterly*, 61 (1946), 205–16.

REILLY, GERARD D. "The Taft-Hartley Act," *Tennessee Law Review*, 20 (1948), 181–90.

"Renovation in N.A.M.," *Fortune*, 38 (July, 1948), 72–75, 165–69.

RICE, W. G., JR. "The Legal Significance of Labor Contracts under the NLRB," *Michigan Law Review*, 37 (1939), 693–724.

RICHBERG, DONALD R. "The Proposed Federal Industrial Relations Act," *Political Science Quarterly*, 61 (1946), 189–204.

SOMERS, A. NORMAN. "The National Labor Relations Board from Wagner to Taft-Hartley," *Federal Bar Journal*, 9 (1948), 315–59.

"State Labor Laws in the National Field," *Harvard Law Review*, 61 (1948), 840–50.

"The Taft-Hartley Act: An Administrative Chimera," *University of Pennsylvania Law Review*, 96 (1947), 67–85.

TELLER, LUDWIG. "Government Seizure in Labor Disputes," *Harvard Law Review*, 60 (1947), 1017–59.

"Union Escape Clauses and the Taft-Hartley Act," *Columbia Law Review*, 48 (1948), 105–19.

WATT, RICHARD F. "The New Deal Court, Organized Labor and the Taft-Hartley Act," *Lawyers Guild Review*, 7 (1947), 193–217, 237–51.

WEYAND, RUTH. "Majority Rule in Collective Bargaining," *Columbia Law Review*, 45 (1945), 556–97.

"What 528 Management Men Think of Taft-Hartley Law," *Business Week*, August 21, 1948, pp. 19–20.

WILLCOX, B. F. "The Tri-Boro Case, Mountain or Molehill?" *Harvard Law Review*, 56 (1943), 576–609.

WITNER, T. R. "Collective Labor Agreements in the Courts," *Yale Law Journal*, 48 (1938), 195–239.

Witte, E. E. "An Appraisal of the Taft-Hartley Act," *American Economic Review,* 38 (May, 1948), 368–82.

Daily Labor Report. Washington: Bureau of National Affairs, 1947–48.
Labor Relations Reporter. Vols. 1–23. Washington: Bureau of National Affairs, 1935–48. (Most of this material is published also semiannually in bound volumes as *Labor Relations Reference Manual,* cited as *LRRM.*)
New York Times, 1937 to 1949.

Indexes

INDEX OF MAJOR CASES CITED

Acme Air Appliance Co., 10 NLRB 1385 (1941), enforced in 117 F. 2d 417
(C.C.A. 2, 1941).. 201
Adair v. United States, 208 U.S. 161 (1908)........................11, 19
Advance Pattern Co., 80 NLRB No. 10 (1948)...................... 458
Advance Tanning Co, 60 NLRB 923 (1945)......................... 153
Algoma Plywood and Veneer Co. v. Wisconsin Employment Relations
Board, 336 U.S. 301 (1949)...................................586, 589
Allen-Bradley Co. v. Local Union No. 3, IBEW, 325 U.S. 797 (1945)..279, 459
Alliance Rubber Co., 76 NLRB 514 (1948)......................... 424
Allis-Chalmers Manufacturing Co., 4 NLRB 159 (1939)............... 141
Allison, J. H., and Co., 70 NLRB 377 (1946), enforced in 165 F. 2d 766
(C.C.A. 6, 1947), cert. denied, 335 U.S. 814 (1948)................ 117
Amazon Cotton Mill Co. v. Textile Workers Union, 167 F. 2d 183 (C.C.A.
4, 1948)..492, 555
American Can Co., 13 NLRB 1252 (1939)........................... 142
American Chain and Cable Co., 77 NLRB 850 (1948)................ 549
American Communications Association v. Douds (1948), 22 *LRRM* 2276   553
American News Co., 55 NLRB 1302 (1944)...................196, 241, 244
American Pearl Button Co., 52 NLRB 1113 (1943), modified and enforced
in 149 F. 2d 311 (C.C.A. 8, 1945)................................ 168
American Rolling Mill Co., 73 NLRB 617 (1947).................... 146
American Seating Co., 85 NLRB No. 49 (1949)...................... 548
American Smelting and Refining Co., 80 NLRB 68 (1948)............. 535
American Steel Foundries v. Tri-City Central Trades Council, 257 U.S. 184
(1921)..13, 486
American Tube Bending Co., NLRB v., 134 F. 2d 993 (C.C.A. 2, 1943),
cert. denied, 320 U.S. 768 (1943)........................166, 178, 294
American White Cross Laboratories, 66 NLRB 866 (1946), enforced in
160 F. 2d 75 (C.C.A. 2, 1947).................................... 214
Ansley Radio Corp., 18 NLRB 1028 (1939)......................... 211
A-1 Photo Service, 83 NLRB No. 86 (1949)......................... 621
Apex Hosiery Co. v. Leader, 310 U.S. 469 (1940)................... 464
Associated Shoe Industries of Southeastern Massachusetts, 81 NLRB No. 38
(1949)... 154
Atkins, E. C., and Co., NLRB v., 331 U.S. 398 (1947)............... 522
Atlantic and Pacific Tea Co. (Amalgamated Meat Cutters, AFL), 81 NLRB
No. 164 (1949)...433, 617
Augusta Chemical Corp., 83 NLRB No. 7 (1949).................... 551
Austin Co., NLRB v., 165 F. 2d 592 (C.C.A. 7, 1947)............... 417

Babcock and Wilcox Co., 77 NLRB 577 (1948)...............424, 526, 625
Bausch and Lomb Optical Co., 72 NLRB 132 (1947).................. 182
Bedford Cut Stone Co. v. Journeymen Stone Cutters' Association, 274 U.S.
37 (1927).............................12, 441, 462, 463, 465, 486, 500
Bercut-Richards Packing Co., 64 NLRB 133 (1945); 65 NLRB 1052 (1946);
68 NLRB 605 (1946); 70 NLRB 84 (1946).......164, 225, 226, 228, 229, 232
Berkshire Knitting Mills v. NLRB, 139 F. 2d 134 (C.C.A. 3, 1943)....... 71

From the Wagner Act to Taft-Hartley

Bethlehem Fairfield Shipyard, 58 NLRB 579 (1944)................... 149
Bethlehem Steel Co. *et al.* v. New York State Labor Relations Board, 330
   U.S. 767 (1947)... 587
Bibb Manufacturing Co., 82 NLRB No. 38 (1949).................... 126
Blatt, M. E., Co., NLRB v., 143 F. 2d 268 (C.C.A. 3, 1944), cert. denied,
   323 U.S. 774 (1944)... 181
Boeing Airplane Co., 80 NLRB 447 (1948).........................616, 638
Brandeis, J. L., & Sons, NLRB v., 145 F. 2d 556 (C.C.A. 8, 1944)....... 180
Budd Manufacturing Co., NLRB v., 142 F. 2d 922 (C.C.A. 3, 1944); 332
   U.S. 840 (1947)..180, 400

California Metal Trades Association, 72 NLRB 624 (1947)............. 154
Campbell Soup Co., 76 NLRB 950 (1948)........................... 551
Carleton, George F., and Co., 54 NLRB 222 (1943)................. 153
Carlisle Lumber Co., NLRB v., 94 F. 2d 138 (C.C.A. 9, 1937), cert. denied,
   304 U.S. 575 (1938)... 101
Carlson v. California, 310 U.S. 106 (1940)......................319, 330
Carpenter Steel Co., 76 NLRB 670 (1948).......................425, 427
Carson Pirie Scott and Co., 69 NLRB 935 (1946); 75 NLRB 1244 (1948) 159, 526
Case, J. I., Co. v. NLRB, 321 U.S. 332 (1944)...................... 118
Central Dispensary and Emergency Hospital, NLRB v., 145 F. 2d 852
   (C.A.D.C., 1944); cert. denied, 324 U.S. 847 (1945)............134, 399
Chicago Typographical Union and Chicago Newspaper Publishers Associ-
   ation, Case No. 13-CB-6, 86 NLRB No. 116 (1949)..........437, 469, 642
Chrysler Corp., 13 NLRB 1303 (1939); 28 NLRB 328 (1940); 31 NLRB
   400 (1941) 148, 149
Clark Bros. Co., 70 NLRB 802 (1946); 163 F. 2d 373 (C.C.A. 2, 1947) 184, 423
Cohn-Goldwater Manufacturing Co., 53 NLRB 645 (1943); 55 NLRB 1164
   (1944); 56 NLRB 749 (1944)................................. 153
Colonial Hardwood Flooring Co. (Furniture Workers), 76 NLRB 1039
   (1948); 84 NLRB No. 69 (1949)........................447, 519, 535
Colonie Fibre Co., 69 NLRB 589, 71 NLRB 354 (1946), modified and
   enforced in 163 F. 2d 65 (C.C.A. 2, 1948)...................... 214
Columbia Pictures Corp., 64 NLRB 490 (1945)...............136, 156, 199
Columbian Enameling and Stamping Corp., NLRB v., 306 U.S. 292 (1939) 72
Commonwealth v. Hunt, 4 Metcalf 111 (Mass., 1842)................ 7
Consolidated Aircraft Corp., 47 NLRB 694 (1943).................. 117
Consolidated Edison Co. v. NLRB, 305 U.S. 197 (1938)..........70, 72, 206
Container Corp., 61 NLRB 823 (1945)............................ 158
Conway's Express (Teamsters), 87 NLRB No. 130 (1949)............. 479
Coppage v. Kansas, 236 U.S. 1 (1915)............................ 11
Coronado Coal Co., United Mine Workers v., 259 U.S. 344 (1922); 268
   U.S. 295 (1925)..13, 497
Cory Corp. (Electrical Workers, CIO), 78 NLRB 923 (1948); 84 NLRB
   No. 110 (1949)...447, 519
Crompton-Highland Mills, 70 NLRB 206 (1946), enforced in 337 U.S. 217
   (1949)... 117
Cudahy Packing Co., 13 NLRB 526 (1939)......................... 133

Dadourian Export Corp., 46 NLRB 498 (1942), set aside in 138 F. 2d 891
   (C.C.A. 2, 1943).. 133
Dahlstrom Metallic Door Co., 11 NLRB 408 (1939), enforced in 112 F. 2d
   756 (C.C.A. 2, 1940)....................................... 133
Debs, *In re,* 158 U.S. 564 (1895)............................... 8

Index of Major Cases Cited

Detroit Edison Co., 74 NLRB 267 (1947)........................... 108
Di Giorgio Fruit Corp. (Farm Labor Union and Teamsters), 87 NLRB
No. 125 (1949).. 399
Diamond T. Motor Co., 64 NLRB 1225 (1945)...................... 214
Dixie Motor Coach Corp. v. Street, Electric Railway and Motor Coach Employees of America, 21 LRRM 2193 (1948)........................ 492
Donnelley, R. R., and Sons Co., 60 NLRB 635 (1945), enforced in 156 F.
2d 416 (C.C.A. 7, 1946).. 185
Donnelly Garment Co. v. NLRB, 151 F. 2d 854 (C.C.A. 8, 1945); 330
U.S. 219 (1947)... 70
Douds v. International Longshoremen's Association (Cargill, Inc.), (N.D.
N.Y.), October 2, 1947, 20 LRRM 2642.......................... 492
Douds v. Local 294, International Brotherhood of Teamsters, 75 F. Supp.
414 (D.C. N.Y.).. 492
Douds v. Metropolitan Federation of Architects, 75 F. Supp. 672 (D.C.
N.Y.).. 467
Duke Power Co., 77 NLRB 652 (1948)............................ 401
Duplex Printing Press Co. v. Deering, 254 U.S. 443 (1921)
                                        11, 441, 462, 465, 486, 500
Dyson, Joseph, & Sons, 72 NLRB 445 (1947)...................... 194

Eagle-Picher Mining and Smelting Co., 16 NLRB 727 (1939); 119 F. 2d
903 (C.C.A. 8, 1941).......................................71, 100
Easton Publishing Co., 19 NLRB 389 (1940)...................... 116
Eicor, Inc., 46 NLRB 1035 (1943).............................. 157
Electric Steel Foundry, 74 NLRB 129 (1947)..................... 182
Electric Vacuum Cleaner Co., 18 NLRB 591 (1939), enforced in 315 U.S.
685 (1942)... 206
Evans v. International Typographical Union, 76 F. Supp. 881 (S.D. Ind.,
1948); 22 LRRM 2576 (1948).............................433, 628

Fafnir Bearing Co., 73 NLRB 1008 (1947)...............183, 195, 201
Fansteel Metallurgical Corp., NLRB v., 306 U.S. 240 (1939)......103, 192, 197
Federal Shipbuilding and Drydock Co., 77 NLRB 463 (1948).......... 534
Fisher Governor Co., 71 NLRB 1291 (1946).....................182, 184
Florsheim Shoe Store Co. v. Retail Shoe Salesmen Union, 288 N.Y. 188
(1942)... 458
Ford Motor Co., 4 NLRB 621 (1937); 14 NLRB 346 (1939); and later
cases; 114 F. 2d 905 (C.C.A. 6, 1940), cert. denied, 312 U.S. 689
(1941)...70, 100, 176
Ford Motor Co. (Maywood Plant), 78 NLRB 887 (1948).............. 524
Fortenbury v. Superior Court (S.F.), 106 P. 2d 411 (1940)........... 462
Franks Brothers Co. v. NLRB, 321 U.S. 702 (1944).................. 118
Freezer, J., & Son, 75 NLRB 646 (1947)......................... 549
Fruehauf Trailer Co., 1 NLRB 68 (1935), enforced in 301 U.S. 49 (1937) 101

General Electric Co., 15 NLRB 1018 (1939); 58 NLRB 57 (1944).....137, 144
General Electric X-Ray Corp., 67 NLRB 997 (1946).................. 160
General Motors Corp., 81 NLRB No. 126 (1949)..................... 568
General Shoe Corp., 77 NLRB 124 (1948)......................424, 527
Giant Food Shopping Center, 77 NLRB 791 (1948).................. 588
Globe Machine and Stamping Co., 3 NLRB 294 (1937).............. 140
Gluek Brewing Co., 47 NLRB 1079 (1943), enforced in 144 F. 2d 847
(C.C.A. 8, 1944)... 219

From the Wagner Act to Taft-Hartley

Goldfinger v. Feintuch, 276 N.Y. 281 (1937)........................ 460
Greensboro Coca-Cola Bottling Co., 82 NLRB No. 67 (1949).......... 425
Gulf Oil Corp., 79 NLRB 1274 (1948)............................ 524

Hager, C., & Sons Hinge Manufacturing Co., 80 NLRB 163 (1948)...... 432
Hamm, Daniel, Drayage Co., 84 NLRB No. 56 (1949)................ 635
Harbison-Walker Refractories Co., 43 NLRB 936 (1942); 44 NLRB 1280
 (1942)...158, 221
Hardwicke-Etter Co., 75 NLRB 992 (1948)........................ 548
Harris Foundry and Machine Co., 76 NLRB 118 (1948).............533, 550
Hazel-Atlas Glass Co., 34 NLRB 346 (1941), modified and enforced in
 127 F. 2d 109 (C.C.A. 4, 1942)............................... 194
Hearst Publications, NLRB v., 322 U.S. 111 (1944)............140, 399, 525
Heather Handkerchief Works, 47 NLRB 800 (1943)................. 109
Heinz, H. J., Co. v. NLRB, 311 U.S. 514 (1941)...................112, 504
Hendy, Joshua, Iron Works, 53 NLRB 1411 (1943).................. 165
Hershey Metal Products Co., 76 NLRB 695 (1948)................. 427
Hill v. Florida, 325 U.S. 538 (1945).............................. 325
Hinde & Dauch Paper Co., 78 NLRB 488 (1948).................... 528
Hitchman Coal and Coke Co. v. Mitchell, 245 U.S. 229 (1917).........11, 486
Holston Manufacturing Co., 13 NLRB 783 (1939); 46 NLRB 55 (1942).. 113
Houde Engineering Corp., NLRB Case No. 12, August 30, 1934.......26, 133
Hudson Hosiery Co., 72 NLRB 1434 (1947)......................165, 183
Hughes Tool Co., 56 NLRB 981 (1944), modified and enforced in 147 F.
 2d 69 (C.C.A. 5, 1945)....................................118, 454

Illinois Bell Telephone Co., 77 NLRB 1073 (1948).................. 535
Indiana Desk Co., 56 NLRB 76 (1944); 58 NLRB 48 (1944), modified in
 149 F. 2d 987 (C.C.A. 7, 1945)..............................191, 198
Industrial Commission of Utah, NLRB v., (D.C. Utah), July 9, 1948, 22
 LRRM 2294... 590
Inland Steel Co., 77 NLRB 1 (1948), enforced in 170 F. 2d 247 (C.C.A. 7,
 1948), cert. granted in Steelworkers, CIO v. NLRB, 335 U.S. 910
 (1949), cert. denied as to welfare fund, 336 U.S. 960 (1949).......553, 568
Interlake Iron Corp., 4 NLRB 55 (1937); 2 NLRB 1036 (1937). .134, 135, 221
International Association of Machinists v. NLRB, 311 U.S. 72 (1940). .176, 206
International Harvester Co., 2 NLRB 310 (1936); 29 NLRB 456 (1941). .105, 107
International Minerals and Chemical Corp., 71 NLRB 878 (1946)....... 145
International Nickel Co., 77 NLRB 286 (1948)..................... 430
International Typographical Union and American Newspaper Publishers
 Association, Case No. 9-CB-5, 86 NLRB No. 115 (1949)
 433, 477, 494, 628, 642
International Typographical Union and Graphic Arts League, Case 5-CB-1,
 87 NLRB No. 124 (1949)..................................... 433
International Typographical Union and Union Printers Section of Printing
 Industry of America, Case No. 2-CB-30, 87 NLRB No. 164 (1949).... 469
Iron Moulders Union v. Allis-Chalmers Co., 166 Fed. 45 (C.C.A. 7, 1908) 469
Irwin Manufacturing Co., Case 15-R-1878 (1946).................. 168

Jones and Laughlin Steel Corp., 1 NLRB 503 (1936), enforced in 301
 U.S. 1 (1937); 331 U.S. 416 (1947).................40, 70, 96, 112, 522

Kaiser-Frazer Parts Corp., 80 NLRB 1050 (1948)................... 591
Kansas City Power and Light Co. v. NLRB, 111 F. 2d 340 (C.C.A. 8,
 1940); 137 F. 2d 77 (C.C.A. 8, 1943).........................71, 86

Index of Major Cases Cited

Kansas City Star Co., 76 NLRB 384 (1948)......................... 399
Kinsman Transit Co., 75 NLRB 150 (1947)......................... 549

La Fayette National Bank of Brooklyn, 77 NLRB 1210 (1948).......... 527
La Follette Shirt Co., 65 NLRB 952 (1946)........................ 164
La Salle Steel Co., 72 NLRB 411 (1947)........................... 182
Lane Wells Co., 77 NLRB 1051, 79 NLRB 252 (1948).............. 552
Lauf v. E. G. Shinner & Co., 303 U.S. 323 (1938).................... 21
Le Blond, R. K., Machine Tool Co., 22 NLRB 465 (1940).............. 135
Libbey-Owens-Ford Glass Co., 10 NLRB 1470 (1939); 31 NLRB 243
    (1941).. 148
Liddon White Truck Co., 76 NLRB 1181 (1948)..................... 401
Lincoln Federal Labor Union v. Northwestern Iron and Metal Co., 335 U.S.
    525 (1949) 436, 586
Loewe v. Lawlor, 208 U.S. 274 (1908); 235 U.S. 522 (1915)...9, 464, 497, 501
Los Angeles Building and Construction Council (Westinghouse Corp.), 83
    NLRB No. 76 (1949) 476
Lowenstein, Herman, 75 NLRB 377 (1947)......................... 550

M & M Woodworking Co., 6 NLRB 372 (1938), set aside in 101 F. 2d 938
    (C.C.A. 9, 1939)..211, 217
Mackay Radio and Telegraph Co., NLRB v., 304 U.S. 333 (1938)..71, 102, 190
Madden v. United Mine Workers, 79 F. Supp. 616 (D.C. D.C., 1948).... 443
Magnesium Casting Co., 77 NLRB 1143 (1948)..................... 550
Mallinckrodt Chemical Works, 79 NLRB 1399 (1948)............... 528
Mandel Brothers, 77 NLRB 512 (1948)............................ 526
Marshall & Bruce Co., 75 NLRB 90 (1947)......................... 550
Maryland Drydock Co., 49 NLRB 733 (1943)....................... 244
May Department Stores Co., 61 NLRB 258 (1945); 53 NLRB 1366 (1943);
    59 NLRB 976 (1944), enforced in 326 U.S. 376 (1945), 154 F. 2d 533
    (C.C.A. 8, 1946)..71, 167
Medo Photo Supply Co. v. NLRB, 321 U.S. 678 (1944).............118, 183
Midland Building Co., 78 NLRB 1243 (1948)....................... 401
Midwest Piping and Supply Co., 63 NLRB 1060 (1945).........160, 165, 199
Milk Wagon Drivers' Union v. Lake Valley Farm Products, 311 U.S. 91
    (1940).. 21
Mill B, Inc., 40 NLRB 346 (1942).............................156, 157
Monsanto Chemical Co., 78 NLRB 1249 (1948)..................... 524
Montgomery Ward and Co., 37 NLRB 100 (1941); 39 NLRB 229 (1942);
    103 F. 2d 147 (C.C.A. 8, 1939); 133 F. 2d 676 (C.C.A. 9, 1943); 157 F.
    2d 486 (C.C.A. 8, 1946).............................70, 115, 180, 184
Monumental Life Insurance Co., 69 NLRB 247 (1946), enforced in 162 F.
    2d 340 (C.C.A. 6, 1947); 75 NLRB 776 (1948)..................167, 548
Myers v. Bethlehem Shipbuilding Corp., 303 U.S. 41 (1938)........... 70
Mylan-Sparta Co., 78 NLRB 1144 (1948)......................... 424
Myrtle Desk Co., 75 NLRB 226 (1947)............................ 549

Nashville Corp., 77 NLRB 145 (1948)............................. 549
National Broadcasting Co., 61 NLRB 161 (1945), enforced in 150 F. 2d
    895 (C.C.A. 2, 1945)... 219
National Electric Products Corp., 3 NLRB 475 (1937)............... 205
National Maritime Union (The Texas Co.), 78 NLRB 971 (1948)
    433, 447, 551, 632, 642

National Maritime Union v. Herzog, 78 F. Supp. 146 (D.C. D.C., 1948);
  334 U.S. 854 (1948)..544, 557
National Silver Co., 71 NLRB 594 (1946)......................... 200
National Tube Co., 76 NLRB 1199 (1948)......................... 523
New York and Porto Rico Steamship Co., 34 NLRB 1028 (1941)....... 217
Newman, H. M., 85 NLRB No. 132 (1949)......................... 432
Newport News Shipbuilding and Dry Dock Co., NLRB v., 308 U.S. 241
  (1939)... 106
North American Aviation, 44 NLRB 604 (1942), set aside in 136 F. 2d 898
  (C.C.A. 9, 1943)... 118
North Whittier Heights Citrus Association v. NLRB, 109 F. 2d 76 (C.C.A.
  9, 1940), cert. denied, 310 U.S. 632 (1940)....................... 399
Northern Virginia Broadcasters, 75 NLRB 11 (1947)............407, 547, 627
Northland Greyhound Lines, 80 NLRB 288 (1948)................... 589
Ny-Lint Tool and Manufacturing Co., 77 NLRB 642 (1948)........... 531

Oppenheim Collins Co., 79 NLRB 435 (1948); 83 NLRB No. 47 (1949)..458, 550

Packard Motor Car Co. v. NLRB, 330 U.S. 485 (1947)............. 400
Parkinson Co. v. Building Trades Council, 154 Cal. 581 (1908).......... 461
Pennsylvania Greyhound Lines, NLRB v., 303 U.S. 261 (1938)......... 105
Perry Norvell Co., 80 NLRB 225 (1948)....................444, 495, 632
Peterson, Hal, NLRB v., 157 F. 2d 514 (C.C.A. 6, 1946), cert. denied,
  330 U.S. 838 (1947)... 181
Phelps Dodge Corp. (Morenci), 60 NLRB 1431 (1945)............... 145
Philadelphia Cordwainers–Commonwealth v. Pullis (1806)............ 4
Philip Morris & Co., 70 NLRB 274 (1946)....................... 145
Pioneer Electric Co., 75 NLRB 117 (1947)....................... 551
Pipe Machinery Co., 76 NLRB 247, 79 NLRB 1322 (1948)........... 519
Pittsburgh Plate Glass Co., 10 NLRB 1111 (1939).................147, 148
Portland Lumber Mills, 64 NLRB 159 (1945), enforced in 158 F. 2d 365
  (C.C.A. 9, 1946).. 214
Precision Castings Co., 77 NLRB 261 (1948)...................... 549
Printing Specialties and Paper Converters Union v. Le Baron, 171 F. 2d
  331 (C.C.A. 9, 1948)... 468

Queen City Warehouses, 77 NLRB 268 (1948)...................... 534

Rayonier, Inc., 52 NLRB 1269 (1943)........................... 152
R.C.A. Manufacturing Co., 2 NLRB 159 (1936)................... 134
Red Jacket Consolidated Coal & Coke Co., United Mine Workers *et al.* v.,
  18 F. 2d 839 (C.C.A. 4, 1927)................................. 13
Reed Roller Bit Co., 72 NLRB 927 (1947)....................... 159
Reliance Manufacturing Co., NLRB v., 143 F. 2d 761 (C.C.A. 7, 1944).. 181
Remington Rand, 2 NLRB 626 (1937), enforced in 94 F. 2d 862 (C.C.A. 2,
  1938), cert. denied, 304 U.S. 576 (1938); 97 F. 2d 195 (C.C.A. 2,
  1938); 130 F. 2d 919 (C.C.A. 2, 1942)...........71, 98, 99, 104, 190, 201
Republic Aviation Corp. v. NLRB, 324 U.S. 793 (1945)..............72, 73
Republic Steel Corp., NLRB v., 107 F. 2d 472 (C.C.A. 3, 1939); 310 U.S.
  655 (1940)... 191
Rite-Form Corset Co., 75 NLRB 174 (1947)...................... 548
Russell Manufacturing Co., 82 NLRB No. 136 (April, 1949)........... 126
Rutland Court Owners, 44 NLRB 587 (1942); 46 NLRB 1040 (1943)
                                                        137, 212, 431
Ryan Construction Corp., 85 NLRB No. 76 (1949).................. 617

Safeway Stores, 81 NLRB No. 66 (1949)..........................589, 627
Salant & Salant, Inc., 66 NLRB 24 (1946); 74 NLRB 1405 (1947)....124, 125
Sands Manufacturing Co., 1 NLRB 546 (1936), set aside in 306 U.S. 332
  (1939) 72, 193
Sandy Hill Iron & Brass Works, NLRB v., 165 F. 2d 660 (C.C.A. 2, 1947) 429
Sartorius, A., and Co., 10 NLRB 493 (1938)......................73, 136
Schechter Poultry Corp. v. United States, 295 U.S. 495 (1935)......... 28
Schenley Distillers Corp., 78 NLRB 504 (1948)...............467, 617, 631
Schlesinger v. Quinto, 192 N.Y.S. 564 (1921), affirmed 201 App. Div. 489
  (1922)... 503
Scullin Steel Co, 65 NLRB 1294 (1946)............................ 194
Sealright Pacific, Ltd. (Printing Specialties Union, AFL), 82 NLRB No. 64
  (1949)... 468
Seamprufe, Inc., 82 NLRB No. 106 (1949)......................... 647
Senn v. Tile Layers' Protective Union, 301 U.S. 468 (1937)............. 21
Serrick Corp., 8 NLRB 621 (1938)............................... 206
Servel, NLRB v., 149 F. 2d 542 (C.C.A. 7, 1945).................... 170
Shipowners' Association of the Pacific Coast *et al.*, 7 NLRB 1002 (1938);
  32 NLRB 668 (1941); 33 NLRB 845 (1941)..................150, 151
Singer Manufacturing Co., 24 NLRB 444 (1940); 119 F. 2d 131 (C.C.A. 7,
  1941), cert. denied, 313 U.S. 595.............................114, 120
Smith Cabinet Manufacturing Co. (Furniture Workers), 81 NLRB No. 138
  (1949)..444, 447
Solvay Process Division of Allied Chemical & Dye Corp., 78 NLRB 408
  (1948)... 533
Southern Bell Telephone and Telegraph Co., NLRB v., 319 U.S. 50 (1943) 106
Southern Steamship Co. v. NLRB, 316 U.S. 31 (1942)............... 193
Southwestern Portland Cement Co., 65 NLRB 1 (1945).............. 214
Stackpole Carbon Co., 6 NLRB 171 (1938), enforced in 105 F. 2d 167
  (C.C.A. 3, 1939), cert. denied, 308 U.S. 605 (1939).............71, 191
Standard Oil of California, 62 NLRB 1068 (1945); 63 NLRB 1174 (1945);
  and preceding cases.. 109
Star Publishing Co., 4 NLRB 498 (1937), enforced in 97 F. 2d 465
  (C.C.A. 9, 1938)... 216
Sun Tent–Luebbert Co., 37 NLRB 50 (1941), enforced in 151 F. 2d 483
  (C.C.A. 9, 1945)... 125
Sunset Line and Twine Co. (Longshoremen, CIO), 79 NLRB 1487
  (1948) 444, 495, 632
Sunset Line and Twine Co., Longshoremen v., 77 F. Supp. 119 (D.C. Cal.,
  1948)... 492
Sunshine Mining Co., 48 NLRB 301 (1943)........................ 158
Supreme Rice Mill (Teamsters, AFL), 84 NLRB No. 47 (1949)........ 617

Tabardrey Manufacturing Co., 51 NLRB 246 (1943)................. 162
Tennessee Coal, Iron and Railroad Co., 39 NLRB 617 (1942)......... 146
Texas & New Orleans Railway Co. v. Brotherhood of Railway and Steam-
  ship Clerks, 281 U.S. 548 (1930).............................19, 176
Thomas v. Collins, 323 U.S. 516 (1945)..............179, 182, 189, 325, 422
Thompson Products, Inc., 70 NLRB 13 (1946); 72 NLRB 886 (1947).... 200
Thompson Products, NLRB v., 97 F. 2d 13 (C.C.A. 6, 1938); 141 F. 2d
  794 (C.C.A. 9, 1944)..............................71, 72, 123, 170
Thornhill v. Alabama, 310 U.S. 88 (1940).......................179, 330
Times Publishing Co., 72 NLRB 676 (1947)......................116, 201
Times Square Stores Corp., 79 NLRB 361 (1948).................551, 628

From the Wagner Act to Taft-Hartley

Trojan Powder Co., 41 NLRB 1308 (1942), enforced in 135 F. 2d 337 (C.C.A. 3, 1943), cert. denied, 320 U.S. 768 (1943) 178
Truax v. Corrigan, 257 U.S. 312 (1921) 10, 13

Underwriters Salvage Co., 76 NLRB 601 (1948) 534
United Biscuit Co., 38 NLRB 778 (1942), modified in 128 F. 2d 771 (C.C.A. 7, 1942) 194
United Brotherhood of Carpenters and Joiners v. Sperry, 170 F. 2d 863 (C.C.A. 10, 1948) 468
United Elastic Corp., 84 NLRB No. 87 (1949) 196
United Mine Workers (Jones and Laughlin Steel Corp.), 83 NLRB No. 135 (1949) 434
United States v. Brotherhood of Locomotive Engineers et al., Daily Labor Report, No. 129: G-1 (July 2, 1948) 583
United States v. CIO, 335 U.S. 106 (1948), affirming 77 F. Supp. 35 (D.C. D.C.) 597
United States v. Hutcheson, 312 U.S. 219 (1941) 459
United States v. Petrillo, 332 U.S. 1 (1947) 478, 566
United States v. Railway Employees' Department, AFL, 283 Fed. 479 (D.C. Ill., 1922); 290 Fed. 978 (D.C. Ill., 1923) 486
U.S. Automatic Corp., 57 NLRB 124 (1944) 118
United States Gypsum Co., 77 NLRB 1098 (1948) 552
United Welding Co., 72 NLRB 954 (1947) 183, 202
Univis Lens Co., 82 NLRB No. 155 (1949) 550
Uxbridge Worsted Co., 60 NLRB 1395 (1945) 159

Virginia Electric and Power Co., 20 NLRB 911 (1940); 44 NLRB 404 (1942), enforced in 314 U.S. 469 (1941), 319 U.S. 533 (1943)
166, 177, 422, 424
Virginian Railway Co. v. System Federation No. 40, 300 U.S. 515 (1937)   176

Wadsworth Building Co. (Carpenters, AFL), 81 NLRB No. 127 (1949). .467, 617
Wallace Corp., 50 NLRB 138 (1943), enforced in 323 U.S. 248 (1944). .213, 431
Warshawsky and Co., 75 NLRB 1291 (1948) 552
Waterfront Employers' Association of the Pacific Coast, 71 NLRB 80 (1946); 71 NLRB 121 (1946) 154
Watson's Specialty Store (Carpenters, AFL), 80 NLRB 533 (1948)
402, 447, 467, 617, 632
Weirton Steel Co., 32 NLRB 1145 (1941); 135 F. 2d 494 (C.C.A. 3, 1943); 146 F. 2d 144 (C.C.A. 3, 1944) 71, 123, 124
Western Electric Co., 72 NLRB 738 (1947); 84 NLRB No. 111 (1949) 108, 589
Western Union Telegraph Co., 17 NLRB 34 (1939), enforced in 113 F. 2d 992 (C.C.A. 2, 1940) 106
Westinghouse Electric and Manufacturing Co., 18 NLRB 300 (1939), enforced in 112 F. 2d 657 (C.C.A. 2, 1940) 106
Whitin Machine Works, 76 NLRB 998 (1948) 533
Wholesale and Warehouse Workers Union, Local 65 v. Douds, 22 LRRM 2276, 2278 (1948) 553
Wichita Union Stockyards Co., 40 NLRB 369 (1942) 157
Wisconsin Telephone Co., 12 NLRB 375 (1939) 107
Wrought Iron Range Co., 77 NLRB 487 (1948) 424
Wurlitzer, Rudolph, Co., 32 NLRB 163 (1941) 136

Young, L. A., Spring and Wire Co. v. NLRB, 163 F. 2d 905 (C.A.D.C.), cert. denied, 333 U.S. 837 (1948) 400

GENERAL INDEX

Access to NLRB restricted, 543–44, 556–58

Administration under Taft-Hartley Act, 402–19, 493–94, 516, 539–41, 604–5, 610–13, 618–29, 660–61

Administration of Wagner Act, 30–75, 235–46, 261, 264, 266–67, 293, 334–35, 378
  1935–37, 35–40
  1937–40, 40–52
  1940–45, 52–60
  1945–47, 60–66
  regional differences in, 35, 36, 45–46, 54–56, 68, 239

Administrative discretion, limitations on, 415–16, 418–19, 494, 496, 514, 516–20, 559, 657–58

Administrative legislation; see Policies of NLRB, changes in

Administrative Procedure Act, 63–64, 66, 73, 239, 261, 335, 403, 406, 411, 415, 416, 417, 419

Administrative process
  advantage of, 136–37, 146, 173, 199, 210, 215–16, 238–40, 256, 266, 318, 493
  attitudes in Congress toward, 403, 418–19
  disadvantage of, 247
  under Taft-Hartley Act, 406–9, 415–16, 418–19, 559, 601–3, 608–9, 612–13, 626–29, 658, 660–61

Admission requirements; see Union membership, eligibility to

Affiliation, changes in, 90–91, 152, 154, 156–60, 171–72, 199, 204, 211–14, 221–22, 255, 276–77, 517

AFL; see American Federation of Labor

Agency
  under common and state law, 498–99
  under Norris–La Guardia Act, 444, 487, 502
  under Taft-Hartley Act, 398, 422, 443–44, 501, 502, 511, 637–38, 662

Agent; see Agency; Union liability

Agreements; see Contracts

Agricultural labor, 348–49, 399

Agriculture, antiunionism in, 319–20, 322, 326, 329, 399 n.

Aiken, Senator G. D., 382, 392

Amalgamated Clothing Workers, 124

Amendment of Wagner Act
  arguments for, 272, 284–85, 288–90, 293
  attempts, 1936–46, 333–62
    76th Congress, 347–54
    78th Congress, 354–56
    79th Congress, 356–62
  changes desirable, 260–62, 267
  failure of administration to propose revisions, 264, 314–15
  failure of unions to make constructive proposals, 224, 280, 295, 310, 315, 372 n.
  NLRB attitude toward, 176, 215, 264, 350, 403 n.
  proposals, 1936–46, analyzed, 333–41, 347–62
  proposed, 33–34, 50, 143, 146, 176, 183, 186, 189, 205–6, 223–24, 233, 247–49, 260–62, 271–72, 282–95, 309–11, 315, 347–49
  by Taft-Hartley Act, 395–496, 514–560, 655–65

American Can doctrine; see Appropriate unit, collective bargaining history

American Christian Association, 323

American Federation of Labor
  cases filed, 80
  charter for industrial peace, 286
  conflicts with CIO, 34, 50, 69–70, 139–46, 204–10, 221–22, 286, 347–48, 645
  and craft-unit issue, 69–70, 140–46, 524 n.
  criticisms of NLRB, 69–70, 143, 146, 152, 153 n., 204–10, 284, 347
  elections won, 89–90
  organizing efforts of, 18, 60, 645, 648 n.

American Federation of Labor—*Continued*
  policy on amendment of Wagner Act, 1947, 389
  policy on non-Communist affidavits, 546–48
  political activities of, 596, 653
  proposals for amendment of Wagner Act, 50, 143, 146, 205–6, 284, 347–49, 351–53
American Iron and Steel Institute, 287
American Liberty League, National Lawyers Committee of, 36, 282, 295
American Management Association, 291
American News doctrine, 196–200, 241
American Nurses' Association, 375
American Tube Bending statements, 178, 180–89, 294
Anti-injunction acts; *see* Injunctions
Antitrust acts
  applications to unions, 7–13, 196, 378, 386, 441 n., 455–56, 459, 462–65, 485, 497
  and Taft-Hartley Act, 490, 500
Antiunion drive, postwar, 286–87, 294–95, 297
Antiunionism, encouragement of, 280, 429, 447, 454, 481, 499–500, 515, 519, 528, 530, 533, 535, 546 n., 555–57, 559, 606, 631, 637, 640, 644, 647–48, 649–50, 653–54, 661–64
"Antiviolence" acts, 321, 323, 325, 330
Appeals Committee, 621 n.
Appeals to NLRB, under Taft-Hartley Act, 405, 407–8, 409, 494, 516, 547, 549–50, 621, 627, 629
Appeals and Review Committee, 64, 65
Appropriate time for new determination of representation, 157–58, 160, 172, 517, 520, 630
Appropriate unit, 138–55, 242, 255–56, 335
  association, 150–55, 172, 226
  antecedent legal authority of, 150–51, 154
  collective bargaining history, 142, 144–46, 148–55, 523–24, 630
  craft vs. industrial, 140–47, 149 n., 172, 241, 318 n., 320, 352, 374,

381, 522–25, 554, 630, 644–45, 660
  in decertication elections, 534–35
  difficulties in decision, 138–39, 146–47, 155
  employers' policies, 143–44, 146, 147–48, 153, 154, 310, 523–25, 630, 644–45
  factors in decisions, 139–40, 142, 144–46, 147–48, 150–55, 242, 255–56, 523–24
  free choice of small or large groups, 138–55, 241, 251–52, 522
  Globe elections, 140–42, 144–46, 151–53, 524
  multi-plant, 147–50, 172, 219
  supervisors in, 140, 521
  under Taft-Hartley Act, 381, 514, 521–26, 630
  in union-shop elections, 488 n.
  units requested and granted, 143–44
Appropriation riders, 207–10, 299, 399 n.
Appropriations, 33–34, 41, 52, 61, 74, 232, 243, 245, 254, 260
  under Taft-Hartley Act, 612
Arbitration, 309, 488, 506–8, 571, 572–73, 638, 673
  compulsory, 120, 309, 450, 473, 510, 576–77, 579, 581, 583 n., 669–70
Assessments; *see* Dues, union
Associated General Contractors of America, 474
Association unit; *see* Appropriate unit
Atomic-energy dispute, 584
Attorney-General's Committee on Administrative Procedure, 47, 50, 54, 63, 67, 73, 239, 417
Australia, 510, 578–79, 582, 669
Authorization and Appeals Committee, 54
Authorization requests, 38, 44–45, 54–55, 64, 620–21
Authorizations; *see* Check-off
Automatic renewal, 157–58, 160
Automobile Workers–CIO, United, 100, 105, 107, 149 n., 283, 653 n.
Automotive Council for War Production, 286

Baby Wagner Acts; *see* State legislation
Backlog of cases, 35, 41, 42–43, 53, 61, 588, 612, 625

Back pay, 88–89, 103, 190, 409 n., 483
  union liability for, 432 n., 483, 615,
  656
  see also Discrimination
Balance of power; see *Power*
Balkanization of market, 279, 459, 656
Ball, Senator Joseph H., 343, 345, 358,
  361, 375, 377, 379–80, 382, 403 n.,
  445–46, 491, 493, 499, 503, 511,
  564–65, 600–608
Ball-Burton-Hatch Bill, 286, 356, 358–
  60
Ball Committee; *see* Joint Congressional Committee on Labor-Management Relations
Ballot, form of, 134–35, 519–20
Ballots, marked, 126
Barden, Representative G. A., 382
Bargaining agent
  determination of, by NLRB, 129
  duty to represent all in unit, 213,
  257
  right of employer to select his representative, 442, 443
  see also Affiliation, changes in; Elections, representation; Representation cases
Bargaining in good faith, meaning,
  112–16, 119, 120–21, 448, 452–
  53; *see also* Refusal to bargain
Bargaining power; *see* Power
Barkley, Senator Alben W., 392
Basic labor law, 7–15, 271, 315, 362,
  395, 441, 450–51, 455–56, 482,
  484–86, 493, 496, 500, 505, 513,
  579, 661–65
Beer war, 218–19
Belkin, Louis S., 522 n., 537 n., 554
Bias, charges of, 32, 34, 42, 46, 50, 67–
  70, 109–10, 144, 207, 237–38, 426
Biddle, Francis, 25 n.
Bill of labor rights and duties, 280
"Bill of rights," 250, 371, 541, 655
Black, Justice Hugo L., 597
Black lists, 11, 14, 15
Blanket orders, 240
Blatnik, Representative John A., 370
Board of inquiry; *see* Fact-finding
"Bogus"; *see* "Reproduction law"
Bootleg agreements, 637, 639, 643
Boycott of NLRB by unions, 538, 544,
  546–48, 553–55, 559, 611
Boycotts, 277–79, 364, 378, 379, 383,
  455–67

under antitrust acts, 8, 11–12, 361,
  459, 462–65, 486
"common interest" as basis for dif-
  ferentiation among, 459, 460–67,
  631 n., 649, 662–63
under common law, 460–63, 466
definition of, 398, 442
and free-speech amendment, 467 n.
against nonunion contractors, 442,
  467, 615, 617
of nonunion materials and products,
  442, 452, 460–62, 464, 467, 486,
  499–500, 615
as organizing method, 171, 247, 275,
  277, 456–58, 529–30, 649, 650
in rival union disputes, 161, 211,
  216–20, 222–24, 227–29, 232–33,
  278–79, 293, 310, 442, 457–58,
  466, 473, 639, 645, 656
under state laws, 319–21, 325–31
under Taft-Hartley Act, 401, 402 n.,
  442, 455–59, 462, 466–68, 473,
  483, 489–91, 499–500, 535, 604–5,
  615–17, 621, 631 n., 645, 649, 650,
  656, 662–63
  see also Coercion; Illegality of object; Strikes
Brandeis, Justice Louis D., 12, 438,
  463–65
Budd Manufacturing Company, 23
Building and Construction Trades Department, AFL, 474
Building industry, 401, 436, 467, 468,
  473, 474–76, 536–37, 617, 635 n.
Burton, Senator H. H., 358
Business Week survey of employer
  opinion, 525 n., 556 n., 633
Byrd, Senator Harry F., 344, 380
Byrnes Anti-strikebreaking Act, 332 n.,
  445 n.

California canneries dispute, 166,
  170 n., 224–32, 458
Call-in pay, 638
Canada, 510, 575, 582
Card checks, 42, 119, 133–34, 148, 516,
  648, 657
  result posted, 134
Carmody, John M., 35
Carnegie-Illinois Steel Company, 97,
  283
Case Bill, 288, 302, 314, 332, 344 n.,
  346, 357, 360–62, 364, 370 n.,

441 n., 455, 502, 503, 562, 565, 598
Case load
1935–37, 36–37, 40
1937–40, 41–44
1940–45, 52–53
1945–47, 60–61
1947–49, 611–12
Cases filed, 76–80, 611–12, 614–15
geographical distribution, 79
industrial distribution, 79
under Taft-Hartley Act, 611–18
trend, factors in, 77–78, 95, 243, 293–94
by union groups, 80
Cease-and-desist orders; *see* Remedies
Certification, 38
increased emphasis of, 119, 241, 242, 458
and noncomplying unions, 548–50
"permanence of," 91, 120, 162–63
protection of, 200–201, 277, 327, 442, 457–59, 517, 645
and refusal to bargain, 119
required for recognition, 171
Chamber of Commerce of the United States, 24, 282, 284, 286–87, 290, 306–7, 318, 328, 348, 571
"Chamberlain squad," 48–49
Chambers of Commerce, 125, 168, 282 n., 398
Charter for industrial peace, 286, 306–7
Check-off, 330, 383, 435 n., 483, 562–64, 635–36, 651
Chief Economist, 47
Children's Museum of Washington, 627 n.
Ching, Cyrus S., 572
CIO; *see* Congress of Industrial Organizations
CIO–Political Action Committee, 595, 596, 653 n.
Citizens' Committees; *see* Community antiunion activities
Civil liberties, dangers to, 557, 559, 597–98
Civil Service status, 484, 561 n.
Clarke, Justice John H., 463
Clayton Act; *see* Antitrust acts
Clean-hands doctrine, 447, 488, 496, 507–8, 644 n.
Clifford, Clark, 389
Climate of opinion; *see* Public opinion
Closed shop
and bargaining in good faith, 113

in building industry, 436, 467, 635
case for, 431, 436–40
in clothing industry, 438
control of abuses under, 439–40
coverage, 210, 297, 430
discharges for nonmembership limited under Wagner Act, 210–16, 257, 431
effects in elections, 90–91, 137–38, 204, 532
employers' policies toward, 436, 637
and free choice, 166, 170–71, 204–16, 277–78, 431, 438, 649–50, 656
illegal when designed to effect discrimination, 213
limits under Wagner Act, 203, 431
in maritime industry, 433, 436–37, 636, 642
in printing and publishing, 433, 437, 636–37, 641–42
problems under, 166, 203–16, 277–78, 431, 439, 652, 656
prohibition of, 289–90, 297, 323 n., 329–30, 383, 428, 431–33, 452, 659
protected period under, 212–15, 257
proviso, purpose of, 430–31
under state laws, 116, 201, 203, 284, 321, 323–31, 381, 430–31, 435–36, 439, 588–90
under Taft-Hartley Act, 428, 433, 588–90, 616–17, 627–28, 635–37, 640, 641–42, 646, 652, 659
in wartime, 16, 207–10, 297
and union liability for discrimination, 214–15, 431–32
Clothing industry, 121, 438, 507, 649
Coal strikes, 285, 298, 312–14, 354, 434 n., 471 n., 567, 569, 574, 576 n., 582–83, 584, 643
Code of ethics for industry, 258
"Coercion from any source"
not included in NLRA, 27–28
proposed, 283, 285 n.
under Taft-Hartley Act, 443
Coercion by employers; *see* Company-assisted unions; Free speech; Integrity of elections
Coercion by unions
in elections, 164, 257, 446
extent in 1947, 224, 249
no defense against charge of violation of act, 216–20, 223, 257
in obtaining recognition, 163, 256–57, 277, 293, 310, 320, 442, 457–59, 529–30, 639, 645, 656

of own members, 447 n.

remedy by contempt action under Wagner Act, 218–20, 223, 458

in rival union disputes, NLRB policies to control, 222–24, 232–33, 247, 257, 276–77

in signing of cards, 133, 248, 257

under Taft-Hartley Act, 443–47, 456–59, 493–96, 529–30, 535, 563–64, 615, 627, 631, 632 n., 639, 646, 652, 662–63

to compel violation of law, 196–200, 203, 210–20, 222–24, 232–33, 247, 261, 291, 330–31, 442, 606, 608

see also Boycotts; Strikes

Collective agreements; *see* Contracts

Collective bargaining

and balance of power, 671–74

begun, after charges of refusal to bargain, 88, 614, 615

and day-to-day relationships, 505–7, 509–10, 512

defined, 441, 448, 452–53

effects of, 234, 286–87, 672, 675–77

extent of, 76–77, 172, 252–54, 272, 633

after NLRB cases, 93–94, 110–11, 122–23

NAM policy toward, 284–87, 290

national policy on, 265–68, 450–52, 569, 661, 664–65, 669–77

policies of Taft-Hartley Act toward, 271, 315, 419, 450–55, 480–81, 514–18, 558, 579–81, 661–65

principle of, 250–51

recommendations of Labor-Management Conference on, 309–10, 450, 571

regulation of, 122 n., 172, 258–59, 265–66, 271, 289, 291, 306, 311, 335–36, 661–65, 669–71

scope of, required, 117, 121, 293, 310, 448 n., 451, 568, 634 n., 643; *see also* Management prerogatives

structure of, 255–56; *see also* Appropriate unit

under Taft-Hartley Act, 632–47, 651–54, 659–65

Taft-Hartley provisions as bargaining weapons, 646–47

in wartime, 274–75, 293–94, 296–98

Collective bargaining history; *see* Appropriate unit

Collective bargaining unit; *see* Appropriate unit

Collusive contracts, 155–56, 204–10, 223, 252, 656

Combination Acts, 5–6

Combination in restraint of trade; *see* Conspiracy doctrine

"Commerce," construction of, 400–402, 499; *see also* Jurisdiction of NLRB

Committee for Constitutional Government, 367

Committee for Economic Development, 291, 367

Committee on Executive Expenditures, 401 n.

Committee To Promote Industrial Peace, 358

"Common interest" as justification in concerted activities, 459 n., 460–71, 486, 488, 493, 496, 500, 631, 649, 656, 662–63

Common law, 460–63, 482, 488, 497; *see also* Conspiracy doctrine

Communists, 169, 379, 383, 435, 545–46, 552–54, 556–57, 559, 604, 644, 652, 671; *see also* Non-Communist affidavit

Community antiunion activities, 99, 124–26, 168–69, 647, 649

Company-assisted unions, 107–11, 165–66, 204–10, 211, 213, 223, 228–30, 427

effectiveness of remedy, 207

under Taft-Hartley Act, 418, 426–28, 629

see also Independent unions

Company-dominated unions, 103–11, 123–24, 205, 207, 208–9

charges filed, 78, 104

disestablishment of, 88, 110, 426–28

in elections, 108–9

extent of collective bargaining following disestablishment, 94, 110–11

under Taft-Hartley Act, 418, 425–28, 521, 614

Company-security clauses, 195, 275, 637–38

Company unions, 14, 16–19

in 1935, 103–4

under NIRA, 22, 26, 105

outlawed by NLRA, 28, 103

Company-wide bargaining; *see* Appropriate unit

Competency clauses, 628, 636–37, 642 n.; *see also* Union security, substitutes for

Complaint cases; *see* Unfair labor practice cases

Compliance
extent of, 65, 243–44, 282
handling of, 48–49, 58–59, 64–65, 83–87
under Taft-Hartley Act, 405, 406
with Intermediate Reports, 47
meaning of, 58–59
under NIRA 7(a), 23–26, 29
with NLRB orders, 40, 42–43
under Public Resolution No. 44, 25–26
of unions with filing requirements, 546–48

Compliance unit, 58–59

Compulsory audience; *see* Free speech

Conciliation, 317, 320, 321, 340–41, 357, 361, 455, 488, 508, 569–73
not function of NLRB, 111, 234, 256

Conciliation Service, United States, 296, 297, 309, 571–72

Conciliation services, state, 570, 586

Conferences
of attorneys, 62, 264
of field staff, 53, 55, 64
see also Labor-Management Conference (1945); National Industrial Conference (1919); President's Conference of Industry and Labor (1941)

Confirmation hearings, 601–2, 619 n.

Conflicts under Taft-Hartley Act, 440, 512–13, 519, 528, 530, 533, 554–58, 581, 633–34, 638–47, 653–54, 659–60, 662–64

Congress
76th, 347–54
78th, 354–56
79th, 356–62
80th, 363–92, 653
developments in, 1936–46, 333–62
House of Representatives, attitudes in, 337, 344, 350–51, 380, 396–98, 421, 492 n., 515, 522, 532, 545, 562, 569, 572
legislative proposals, 1936–46, analyzed, 333–41, 346–62
referral of proposals to nonlabor committees, 344 n., 351 n., 360
Senate, attitudes in, 285, 337, 344, 380, 397–98, 545, 576

sponsors of legislative proposals, by region and party, 341–45
see also Legislative history of Taft-Hartley Act

Congress of Industrial Organizations (Committee for Industrial Organization)
cases filed, 80
charter for industrial peace, 286
conflicts with AFL, 34, 50, 69–70, 139–46, 204–10, 221–22, 347–48, 645
criticisms of NLRB, 146, 152, 351
elections won, 89–90
organizing efforts of, 41, 43, 60, 139, 204–5, 276, 283, 645, 648 n.
policy on amendment of Wagner Act, 351–52, 389
policy on non-Communist affidavits, 546–48
political activities of, 596–97, 653

Congressional investigations, 34, 42, 44, 49–50, 227, 262, 263, 284, 337, 346, 362

Consent elections, defined, 43 n.; *see also* Elections, representation

Conspiracy doctrine, 4–14
civil conspiracy, 8–14
and Norris–La Guardia Act, 487
prosecutions, nineteenth century, 6–7

Conspiracy of employers charged, 286, 294–95

Constitutionality
of restrictive legislation, 319, 321 n., 324–26, 330, 331, 436, 586 n.
of Taft-Hartley provisions, 436, 544, 552–53, 596–98
of Wagner Act, 27, 33, 36, 39–40, 96–97, 282, 295

Construction industry; *see* Building industry

Contempt action
against employers under Wagner Act, 59–60, 64–65, 85–87, 99–100, 115, 121, 124, 180, 181, 229, 247
against strikers, 192
against unions under Taft-Hartley Act, 314, 574 n., 617, 628
against unions under Wagner Act, 218–20, 223, 458

Context of unfair labor practices, 195, 241; *see also* Free speech

Contracting union made party to case, 206, 549; *see also* Intervening union

Contracts

as bar to election, 152, 155–60, 171–72, 241, 252, 517, 520, 529, 531, 532, 534, 549, 630, 645

changes under Taft-Hartley Act, 510–12, 563, 568, 610, 635–39, 641–42, 646

enforceability of, 211–13, 310, 453, 500–513

nature of, 155–58, 501–8

protection of, wanted by AFL, 204–13

set aside by NLRB, 104, 204–7, 210, 223

status during pre-election periods, 165–66, 223

termination or modification of, 452–53

Cooling-off periods, 361, 383, 575–76, 579–82, 584–85; *see also* Strike notices

Corporation and union compared, 595

Costs of union administration increased, 484–85, 541, 543–44, 558, 605

Countercharges, 646, 647 n.

Counterproposals, 114–15, 116, 448, 452

Court administration of labor relations laws, 320, 591–92, 670

Court review

of certifications, 322

scope of, 72–73, 416–19, 429, 657–58; *see also* Enforcement of NLRB orders

Cox, Archibald, 417, 425, 429, 451, 511, 581

Craft unions, 141, 143–44, 255–56, 438, 523–25, 630, 635–37, 641–42, 644–45, 660

Craft unit; *see* Appropriate unit

Credibility of witnesses, 47, 57, 411

Criticisms of NLRB, 236–46, 262–65

of administration, 32, 34, 49–50, 51, 66–75, 95 n.–96 n., 119, 120, 123, 237–46, 402–3, 419

appraised, 50–51, 66–75, 237–46, 260–68

on decertification issue, 162

for different treatment of affiliated and unaffiliated unions, 109–10, 207, 249, 426

on employer petition, 161, 173

for excessive interference, 241–43

for failure to enforce Act fully, 74–75, 122–24, 236, 243–46

for limitation of employers' free speech, 174–75, 176, 185–87, 248

on policy as to reinstatement, 429

relation to dislike of Act, 73, 246

for setting aside AFL contracts, 204–6, 210

on strike policy, 202–3, 236–37 n.

on unit decisions, 143, 146, 152, 153 n., 173

Criticisms of Taft-Hartley Act

administrative reorganization, 406–9, 413–16, 418–19, 480, 625–29, 660–61

broad prohibition of boycotts and sympathetic strikes, 466–70, 481, 493

changes in representation and election provisions, 514, 558–60

excessive intervention in collective bargaining, 440, 450–52, 455, 481, 512–13, 522 n., 566, 659–60, 662–65

on federal-state jurisdiction, 593

filing requirements, 544, 556–59, 658 n.

free-speech amendment, 424–25, 528, 662

individual grievance handling, 454

by Joint Congressional Committee minority, 605–6

national emergency provisions, 577–82, 585–86, 664

political expenditures provision, 595–98, 664

unfair, discriminatory, and antiunion provisions, 661–64

union-security provisions, 440, 590

weakening of protection against unfair labor practices of management, 480–81, 484–85, 613, 615, 622, 661–64

see also Conflicts under Taft-Hartley Act; Litigation; Uncertainties under Taft-Hartley Act

Criticisms of Wagner Act, 237, 246–52, 260–62

individual and minority rights, 250–52

for inequality, 246–49, 290

Cross-check; *see* Card check

Damage suits, 496–513
under antitrust acts, 9, 12–13, 497, 500
compared to injunctions, 497
effect on industrial relations, 497, 508–13, 658, 659
history of use against unions, 496–97
under Norris–La Guardia Act, 21
number filed, 512–13
under state laws, 331, 497–99, 501
under Taft-Hartley Act, 374, 378, 379, 383, 496, 499–505, 508–9, 512–13, 605, 637–38, 646–47, 663
union attitudes toward, 510–12, 637–38
used in strikes, 513, 535, 646–47
Deauthorization elections, 434, 537 n., 613 n., 650; *see also* Union-shop elections
Decertification, 162–63, 517, 528–29, 532–35, 549–50, 552 n., 558, 611, 613–14, 630, 646, 650, 657, 660, 663
Decision-making process, 36, 38, 47–48, 57–58, 65, 67, 238–39, 261, 412
compared to work of appellate courts, 414
under Taft-Hartley Act, 405, 409–16, 516–17, 621–26, 661
Decisions
effect of, 121–22, 129, 170, 185, 242, 258–59
short form, 57, 624–25
timing of, 244
tone of, 69, 238
Delay in disposition of cases, 41, 43–45, 61, 114, 119–20, 138, 163, 171, 172–73, 232, 243, 254, 275, 491
effect of prehearing election on, 62–63, 622
effect in unfair labor practice cases, 58, 61, 83, 119–20, 122–23, 243, 491, 613
by employers, 81, 114, 120, 171, 242, 295, 447, 491, 530, 533, 546 n., 559, 639, 646–47
reduced by increased efficiency, 52–53, 55, 57–59, 623, 625–26
under Taft-Hartley Act, 407, 415–16, 420, 446, 475, 540–41, 546–48,
558, 588, 606, 613, 620–22, 626–27, 647, 660–61, 663
by unions, 242, 277, 646–47
Delegation agreement, 404–5, 619
Delegation of authority, 35, 44–45, 50, 54–55, 58–59, 62, 63–65, 66–67, 236, 239, 404–5, 415, 618–19, 620–21, 625
Democracy, 669–77
effect of representation elections on, 91, 132, 171–73, 254–55
in industry, 3, 29, 129, 132, 160, 234–35, 242, 250–51, 258–60, 265–66, 268, 398, 515, 559–60, 562, 657, 664–65, 669–77
in unions, 171–72, 255, 256–57, 259, 276, 279–80, 447 n., 542–44, 559–60, 644, 645, 648–49, 651–52, 658, 674
Denham, Robert N., 404 n., 406 n., 601–2; *see also* General Counsel
Discharge
for cause, 97, 102, 195, 418, 429–30, 502, 518, 603, 631, 638, 657
of strikers, 192–202, 430, 518, 631
see also Closed shop; Discrimination; Strikers
Discipline; *see* Discharge for cause
Discipline, union; *see* Individual rights; Union membership
Discretionary powers; *see* Administrative discretion; Administrative process
Discrimination, 14, 101–3, 190–203, 207–16, 428–41
charges filed, 78, 614–15
and conflicting state and federal standards, 435, 588–90
for filing charges or testifying, 78 n., 440–41
in hiring, 432–33, 635–37, 641–42
under NIRA, 26
under railway legislation, 11, 19
under Taft-Hartley Act, 428–41, 551–52, 590, 614–15
unfair labor practice of union to cause, 432–35, 442, 443, 445, 448, 615, 631, 632 n., 650, 656
under union-security contracts, 203–4, 207–16, 223, 227, 229–30, 261, 277–78, 430–35, 438–40, 590, 635–37
under Wagner Act, 78, 88–89, 97–

99, 101–3, 120, 127, 175, 188, 190–204, 207–16, 241 n., 253
Disestablishment
   of affiliated unions, 426–28
   approved by Supreme Court, 105–6
   compared with other remedies, 207
   defined, 105
   see also Company-dominated unions
Dismissal of cases, 37–38, 40, 42–45, 48, 61, 63, 68, 243
   factors in trend, 82–83
   after hearings on charges, 83
   under Taft-Hartley Act, 407, 612, 615, 617–18, 627, 629
Disposition of cases, 80–87
   1935–36, 37–38
   1936–37, 40
   1937–38, 42–43
   1938–40, 48–49
   1940–45, 52–53
   1945–47, 63
   1947–48, 612–17
Dissents in NLRB decisions, 412
District courts, jurisdiction of
   in damage suits, 499, 500, 508
   in injunction cases, 39, 489–94, 617–18
Division of Policies and Appeals, 620
Donnell, Senator F. C., 375
Douglas, Paul H., 307 n.
Douglas, Justice William O., 597
Dual unionism, 212–15, 220, 223, 261, 277–78, 438–39
Due process, 33, 40, 45–46, 50, 67, 70–71, 83, 97, 99 n., 206, 239, 621–22, 625–26, 660–61
Dues, union, 280, 434–35, 440, 448, 538, 615; *see also* Check-off

Economic analysis, 409 n.
Economic reprisals; *see* Coercion by unions
Economic Research, Division of, 36, 51, 409 n.
Efforts of employers and unions to avoid restrictions, 455, 469, 563, 567–68, 605, 606, 634, 636–39, 642–43, 659–60
Election of 1948, 596, 607, 610, 653
Elections; *see also* Strike votes
Elections, representation
   authority of Regional Director in, 65
   for change of bargaining agent, 90–91

conducted by state or private agencies, 556, 590–91, 648
consent, 37, 42, 43 n., 46, 87, 129–31, 516
described, 129–32
effect of contracts on, 90–91, 138, 204
integrity of, 164–70, 228, 294, 424, 526–28
under NIRA, 22–23, 25
number held, 40, 76–77, 614
number of successive, 91, 171 n., 517
ordered, 38, 62, 87, 131–32
purpose of, 249, 423, 515, 526, 527
results of, 89–92, 132, 171–72, 204, 207, 254, 294, 614, 647, 648
results by industry, 90
results by union groups, 89–90
set aside, 109, 164–70, 424, 526–28
stipulated, 43 n.
under Taft-Hartley Act, 526–35, 614, 618, 647–48
votes cast, 77, 89
Elections, types under Taft-Hartley Act, 515–16; *see also* Deauthorization elections; Decertification; Employer petitions; Last-offer ballots; Union-shop elections
Electrical Workers–CIO, United, 100 n., 548, 554
Eligibility to vote, 135–36; *see also* Strikers
Ellender, Senator A. J., 374, 382, 600
Employee, defined, 190, 521
Employee communication programs, 639
Employee representation plans; *see* Company unions
Employees
   attitudes of, 98, 267, 436, 532, 536–37, 573, 580, 607, 613, 647–48, 649–50, 657, 671–72
   rights under NLRA, 31; *see also* Individual rights; Loss of employee rights
   rights under Taft-Hartley Act, 421, 514–15
Employer, definition of, 398, 422
Employer associations
   activities and influence of, 263, 281–91, 319, 322–23, 328, 349–50, 353, 367, 370, 389, 610

Employer associations—*Continued*
no filing requirements imposed on, 543, 544
unlawful to force membership in, 442, 443
Employer petitions, 51, 62, 160–63, 216, 248–49, 260, 320, 322, 352, 528–31, 535, 550, 558, 611, 630, 646, 657, 660, 663
Employer's last offer; *see* Last-offer ballots
Employers
cleared of charges, 83
difficulties in jurisdictional disputes, 216–20, 276–78, 529–30
preference for AFL, 204–5
Employers' attitudes
bases of changes in, 292–94, 672–74
in 1947, 68–69, 73–74, 95, 111, 120–21, 252–54, 293–96
toward power of unions, 672–74
under Taft-Hartley Act, 509, 512, 514, 519 n., 525, 556–57, 559, 610, 626, 632–34, 637, 639, 640, 643–44, 645–46, 653–54, 657–58, 663
Employers' policies, 14, 15, 17–18
acceptance of NLRA, 78, 121, 122, 127, 249, 252–54, 258–59, 263–64, 281, 291, 292, 296, 315, 672
under NIRA, 26
opposition to NLRA, 27–28, 30, 33, 37, 39, 41, 42, 60, 79, 95, 127, 148, 187, 191, 235, 236, 254, 259, 263, 274–75, 281–96, 322
Enforcement of NLRB orders, 39–40, 48–49, 58–59, 83–85, 97, 118, 119–21, 235, 239, 240, 243, 483, 489
compared with other agencies, 85 n.
results of litigation, 84–86
Equalization of law
demands for, 272–74, 282, 287–88, 292, 315, 317–29, 359, 377–78
under Taft-Hartley Act, 420, 444, 449–52, 455, 480–81, 496, 503–5, 528, 535, 572, 655–65
Espionage, 26, 51, 100–101, 104, 124–26, 253, 282
Evidence
adequacy of, 24, 72–73, 239, 416–19, 625, 657–58
and free-speech amendment, 422, 424–25, 631, 662

Exaction; *see* Featherbedding; Payments to employee representatives
Expenditures of NLRB, 34 n.
Expulsions; *see* Discrimination; Individual rights; Union membership
Extent of organization as factor in unit, 140, 147, 419, 525–26, 630
Extortion; *see* Featherbedding; Payments to employee representatives

Fact-finding boards, 308–9, 311–13, 327, 356–59, 361, 471 n., 489, 568 n., 570, 574–85, 608
Fahy, Charles, 51
Fair employment practices legislation, 327, 434 n.
Fair Labor Standards Act, 303
Farm Bureau, 367, 375
Farm Equipment Workers, 107, 554
Faruseth, Andrew, Training School, 636
Fascism, 670
Favoritism; *see* Company-assisted unions
Featherbedding, 387, 398, 443, 452, 476–80, 615, 627 n., 631, 632 n., 638, 656, 659, 662
applications of term, 477–79
Federal Corrupt Practices Act, 593–94
Federal employees; *see* Public employees
Federal-state relationships, 586–93, 605, 661; *see also* State legislation
Fels, Samuel S., 358
Field Division, 53–56, 238–39, 403 n., 601 n., 619
Field manual, 56
Filing requirements, 448 n., 484, 537–60
administration of, 539–41, 546–52, 558, 622
constitutionality of, 544, 552–53, 557
effects of, 553–58, 559, 590–91, 647, 651, 658
Financial reports, 280, 324–29, 484–85, 537–44, 559
effects of, 544, 559, 650, 652, 658
Fines or imprisonment under Taft-Hartley Act, 483

Food and Tobacco Workers, 226–31, 548

Ford Motor Company, 100, 175, 195, 511, 613, 637

Foreman's Association of America, 375

Foremen; *see* Supervisors

Formal cases
defined, 37 n., 80 n.
effects of, 122, 129, 170, 258–59
factors in trends, 81, 612–13, 620–21, 626
see also Disposition of cases; Informal cases

Forms, standardized, 46, 56

Forms manual, 56

Fracture doctrine, 106–8, 427

Frankfurter, Justice Felix, 459 n., 465 n.

Free choice; *see* Appropriate unit; Collusive contracts; Contract as bar to election; Elections; Integrity of elections; Majority, proof of; Stability of collective bargaining

Free collective bargaining; *see* Collective bargaining, regulation of; Government intervention

Free enterprise and industrial relations, 669–77

Free speech, 174–89, 422–25, 526–28
amendment, quoted, 422
charges dismissed by NLRB, 181–83
circuit-court decisions, 178, 180–81
and compulsory audience, 183–84, 423–24, 526
and context of unfair labor practices, 175–85, 188–89, 422, 424
effects of policies under Wagner Act, 185–89
in elections, 164, 166, 168, 178–87, 294, 526–28, 608, 631, 647, 662
and evidence of unfair labor practices, 418, 422, 424–25, 445, 631, 662
extent of employers' rights under Wagner Act, 177–83, 185–89, 201–2, 241, 293, 294, 383, 422–24
and interference with rights of employees, 101, 127, 174–89, 241, 248, 422–25, 526–28
needs of sound policy, 188–89, 248, 260, 424–25
NLRB criticized for limitation, 174–76, 185–87, 248, 422

and picketing, 179 n., 330, 447, 460, 467 n., 470, 631
policy in late years of Wagner Act, 181–85, 188–89, 423
and political expenditures, 597–98
and regulation of unions, 179, 248, 446–47, 460, 467–68, 662
and separability of speech and act, 167, 179, 182–83, 188
in strikes, 201–2, 646
Supreme Court decisions, 177–79, 422–23
under Taft-Hartley Act, 379, 387, 418, 422–25, 526–28, 639, 646–48, 657, 662–63
union attitudes toward, 186–87, 372 n., 647–48

Freedom of association; *see* Representation cases; Right to organize

Freedom of contract; *see* Collective bargaining; Government intervention

Freedom to strike, 189–203, 237 n., 246, 430 n., 468–71, 518–19, 576–77

Frey, John, 208 n., 347

Frey rider, 208–10, 252, 285 n.

Fringe groups, 242

Fur Workers, 548

Furniture Workers, 548

Garrison, Lloyd K., 25

Gellhorn, Walter, 50 n.

General Counsel, 402–9, 610, 618–21, 625–29, 658, 660–61
appointment policies of, 408, 602 n., 603, 619–20
confirmation of, 601–2
differences of opinion between Board and, 401–2, 407, 494, 546–47, 589, 617–18, 621, 626–27, 660–61
functions delegated to, 404–5, 489, 516, 618–19
in injunction cases, 616–18
instructions of, 425, 540 n., 546–47, 621 n., 622, 626–27
and Joint Congressional Committee, 602–3, 629
and NLRB union, 408 n.
powers of, 402–5, 407–8, 451, 483, 489–90, 491–92, 494, 608, 628 n.
views of, 429, 435 n., 440 n., 447 n., 468 n., 491 n., 536, 553, 555

General Motors Corporation, 283, 311–12, 507, 568, 616

Geographical distribution of cases, 79

Globe elections; *see* Appropriate unit

Goldsborough, Justice T. Alan, 434 n., 443 n., 583 n.

Government intervention, extent of, 241–43, 258–59, 265–68, 289–90, 308, 315, 331–32, 390, 592–93, 669–71, 675–77
  under Taft-Hartley Act, 395, 398, 419, 450–52, 455, 470–71, 480–81, 495, 575–86, 646–47, 653–54, 661–65

Gray, J. Copeland, 404 n., 528

Great Britain, 5–7, 486, 503, 523, 544, 579, 653

Green, William, 286, 347, 352–53

Gregory, Charles O., 460

Grievance handling, 116–17, 118 n., 195, 242, 251, 274–75, 502, 505–8, 572–73
  during election period, 165–66
  under Taft-Hartley Act, 453–54, 502, 507–8, 521, 570, 639, 646

Guards, 139 n., 521–22, 630 n., 643, 660

Harmony clauses, 636–37

Hart, Schaffner & Marx, 507

Hartley, Representative Fred A., Jr., 32, 250, 353, 365 n., 366, 369–72, 372 n., 382, 384–87, 478, 492 n., 525, 541, 566, 600, 607, 614 n.

Hartley Bill; *see* Legislative history

Hatch, Senator C. A., 358

Hearings, NLRB, 38, 46, 47, 409–10
  courts' criticisms of, 70
  courts' favorable comments on, 70–71
  on proposed changes of policy or procedure, 62, 135 n., 162, 264

Herzog, Paul M., 35 n., 60, 108, 135 n., 182, 200, 236, 367–68, 376 n., 389 n., 423, 427, 467 n., 546, 587–89, 625

Hill, Senator Lister, 374–75

Hiring halls, 432–33, 437, 452, 584, 632 n., 635 n., 636, 642, 659

Hobbs Act, 288, 314, 332 n.

Hoffman, Representative C. E., 342, 353, 382, 600

Holmes, Justice Oliver W., 463–64

Hosiery industry, 113

Hospitals, 399

"Hot-cargo" acts, 321

Houston, John M., 35 n., 52, 150, 160, 164, 181, 183, 200, 228, 232, 236, 406 n., 467 n., 550, 588

Illegality of object
  under antitrust acts, 9–13
  and charges of refusal to bargain, 433, 443 n., 449
  under conspiracy doctrine, 6–7
  under Taft-Hartley Act, 379, 442–43, 445, 455–59, 462, 466–71, 473, 476–77
  under Wagner Act, 191, 196–201, 242

Incorporation of unions, 498, 505

Independent contractor, 399

Independent unions, 34, 60, 105–10, 143–44, 207, 240–41, 283
  cases filed by, 80
  charges of unfairness to, 109–10, 207, 249, 426, 657
  in elections, 89–90, 108–10, 426–27, 521
  under Taft-Hartley Act, 418, 426–28, 657

Individual bargaining, 118 n., 201–2, 246–47, 251, 283, 285 n.
  under Taft-Hartley Act, 453–54, 515, 521, 529, 535, 661, 665

Individual filing of charges and petitions, 551–52, 630

Individual rights
  under closed shop, 210–16, 251–52, 277–78, 280, 330, 431, 438–40, 536, 636–37
  under state laws, 320–21, 323–25, 330, 331
  under Taft-Hartley Act, 396, 421, 432, 436, 443–44, 454, 471, 513, 514–15, 521, 528–35, 558–60, 573, 604, 615, 618, 649–51, 659–60, 665
  of union members, 280, 323–25, 434–35, 440, 541–43, 551–52, 563–64, 594
  under Wagner Act, 162–63, 250–51, 276–77, 454

Industrial disputes
  duty of employers and employees regarding, 570
  function of NLRB toward, 111–12
  national policy toward, 307–8, 455,

558, 569, 576–77, 599, 663–65, 671–74

settlement of, during war, 296–300, 302

see also Conciliation; Strikes

Industrial distribution of cases, 79

Industrial relations

effects of Taft-Hartley Act on, 447 n., 481, 512–13, 514, 519, 525, 528, 533, 553–60, 579–85, 632–54, 657–65

effects of Wagner Act on, 51, 252–60, 672, 675–76

Industrial unions, 141–46, 255–56, 645

Industrial unit; *see* Appropriate unit

Industry-wide bargaining, 150, 152–55, 172, 225, 248, 275, 293, 378, 379, 383, 386, 443, 449, 451, 552 n., 580, 590, 605, 634 n., 651; *see also* Appropriate unit

Industry-wide seniority, 636

Inequality of Wagner Act, 246–49

Inexperience in collective bargaining, 274–75, 293–94, 672–74

Informal cases

advantages of, 80–81, 239, 242, 258–59

defined, 37 n., 80 n.

disposition of, 81–83, 87, 612, 614–16

factors in trends, 81

importance of, 80, 122, 129, 170, 185, 406–7, 626

See also Disposition of cases; Formal cases; Settlement of cases

Ingles, William, 370 n.

Initiation fees, 431, 434–35, 440, 442–43, 445, 448, 563 n., 615, 636

Injunctions, 7–14, 485–96

in advance of hearing on unfair labor practices, 489, 616–18

anti-injunction laws, 10, 13, 20–21, 321, 458, 485–89

under antitrust laws, 9–13, 463–65, 486–87

effects of, 13–14, 493–96, 618, 662–63

against interference with certified union, 277, 458

against interference with elections, 170

limited by Norris–La Guardia Act, 20–21, 196, 279, 465, 485–89, 508 n.

mandatory, 473, 483, 489–91, 494, 616–18, 662–63

in national emergencies, 313–14, 471 n., 484, 489, 574–86, 608

in 1920's, 17–18

number of, 8, 486, 494 n., 616–17

on petition of private party, 378–80, 383, 386, 491–93, 495, 628, 644 n.

prima facie case for equitable relief, 491 n., 493–95

relation of prior actions to NLRB decisions, 494, 617–18, 628, 638 n.

in state courts, related to Taft-Hartley standards, 495, 591–92, 618, 640–41, 644 n., 646, 663

under Taft-Hartley Act, 383, 405, 480, 483–84, 489–96, 562, 568, 605, 616–18, 638 n.

to prevent hearings, 39, 282

to protect exclusive jurisdiction of NLRB, 590–91

against union unfair labor practices, 261, 378, 399 n., 433, 434 n., 443 n., 446–47, 473, 474 n., 477, 483, 489–96, 616–18, 627–28, 656, 662–63

Injustice to employers, 46, 69, 83, 238–40, 248, 277

Institute of Architects, 367

Insurance plans; *see* Welfare funds

Integrity of elections, 164–70, 228, 294, 424, 526–28, 549–50

community antiunion activities, 168–69

interference by employers, 82, 165–67, 170, 294, 526–28

interference by unions, 164

see also Free speech

Interference, general, 101, 127, 241, 246

charges filed, 79, 614

by spoken or written word, 174–89, 422–25

Intermediate Reports, 46

criticism by Attorney-General's Committee, 47, 50

increased importance of, 57, 67, 412

review of, prohibited, 622

under Taft-Hartley Act, 409–12, 617–18, 622–23

Internal affairs of unions, 256, 279–80, 323–25, 328–29, 331, 340, 383, 542–44

Internal affairs of unions—*Continued*
 under Taft-Hartley Act, 395, 434–
 35, 438–40, 443
 see also Democracy in unions; Union
 activities, regulation of
International Harvester Company, 105,
 106–7, 511, 637
International laws, union, 201, 276
International unions, relations to locals,
 552, 651–52
Interrogation of employees, 101
Intervening union, 137, 549, 630
Irresponsibility; *see* Responsibility
Iserman, T. R., 96 n., 367, 369, 370 n.,
 607 n.
Ives, Senator Irving, 345, 375, 379,
 382, 445, 491, 563, 600, 601,
 606 n., 607
Ives Committee, 606 n.

Jenner, Senator W. E., 375
Johnston, Eric, 286, 306
Joint Congressional Committee on Labor-Management Relations, 381,
 384, 396, 566, 568, 588, 590 n.,
 598–609
 amendments recommended, 607–8
 duties of, 599–600
 hearings and reports of, 601, 603–8,
 609
 as "watchdog," 600, 601–3, 604–5,
 608–9, 628
Jones and Laughlin Steel Corporation,
 96–98
Jurisdiction, union, 204, 220, 276–77,
 472
Jurisdiction of NLRB
 ceding of, to state agencies, 402,
 415, 587–88, 593
 declined by Board, 61, 242, 401,
 587, 621 n.
 exclusive or concurrent, 492–93,
 555–56, 586–93
 under Taft-Hartley Act, 400–402,
 587–93, 608, 621
Jurisdictional disputes, 199–200, 211–
 12, 216–32, 276–78, 293, 309–10,
 364, 372 n., 378–79
 methods of determination, 220–22,
 233, 471–76, 639
 NLRB awards and requirements of
 Sec. 8(a)(3), 476 n.
 NLRB policy in, 221–24, 276–78,
 476 n.

and prevention of coercion, 220–33,
 277–78, 472–73
 under state laws, 324–25, 329, 331
 under Taft-Hartley Act, 442, 456,
 471–76, 490, 495–96, 525, 604,
 615, 639, 640, 652, 656
 types of, 220–21, 472–73
Justification; *see* Common interest

Kelley, Representative A. B., 601, 605,
 608
"Kick-backs," 662
Kilgore, Senator H. M., 595
Klein, Representative A. G., 367 n.,
 369–70

Labor courts, 415, 480, 508
Labor dispute, definition of, 338, 463,
 465 n., 470
 in Norris–La Guardia Act, 21, 465,
 488–89, 504
 see also Industrial disputes
Labor-Management Conference (1945),
 117, 223–24, 287, 304, 306–11,
 312, 356, 450, 506 n., 570–71, 573,
 579, 583, 609
Labor-management conference needed,
 583–84, 609, 671
Labor Management Relations Act; *see*
 Taft-Hartley Act
Labor Relations Act, state; *see* State
 legislation, Labor Relations Acts
Labor's Committee for the Election of
 Truman and Barkley, 653 n.
Labor's League for Political Action,
 AFL, 596, 653 n.
La Follette Committee, 100–101, 283–
 85, 322, 337
Landis, Representative G. W., 382, 607
Langer, Senator William, 380, 387
Last-offer ballots, 570, 572–73 575–76,
 578, 580–81, 584–85, 608, 664
Law
 inequality of, before 1930's, 14–15
 influence of, 3, 14–15, 18
 see also Basic labor law
Lawyers
 increased use of, under Taft-Hartley
 Act, 485, 509, 517, 619, 634, 646–
 47
 influence of, 81, 121, 127, 181, 185,
 263, 295–96, 448, 610, 673–74
Lea Act, 288, 332 n., 478, 566 n.
League for Industrial Rights, 498

Legal assistants
   to Board members, 409, 411–15,
      623–24
   to Trial Examiners, 623
Legal Division, 46, 47, 54
Legislative History of the Labor Man-
   agement Relations Act, 1947,
      369 n.
Legislative history of Taft-Hartley Act,
   363–92
   Conference Committee and Report,
      365, 382–88, 492 n.
   differences in interpretation between
      House and Senate, 417, 429,
      437 n.
   Hartley Bill, 364, 369–73, 375–76,
      382–84
   charges as to writing of, 369–71
   House debates, 364–65, 371–74, 380,
      385–87, 594
   House Labor Committee, 364–73,
      562
   inadequate attention to certain major
      issues, 373–74, 380–81, 543
   legislative strategy, 369–70 n., 372–
      73, 378–79, 382–88
   Senate debate, 364–65, 379–81, 387–
      88, 391–92, 444–46, 479, 491–92,
      504–5, 541–44, 545–46, 562–63,
      575–78, 586, 594–96, 600
   Senate Labor Committee, 364–65,
      374–79
   Taft Bill, 364–65, 375–81, 382–84
   amendments, 377 n., 378, 379–80
   charges as to writing of, 376–77
   veto, 365, 382, 384–86, 388–92
Legislative proposals; *see* Congress;
   State legislation
Leiserson, Avery, 284 n.
Leiserson, William M., 44–45, 52,
   96 n., 135 n., 142, 148, 151, 156,
   212, 213, 236, 246–47
Lesinski, Representative John, 373,
   382, 386–87, 601, 605, 608
Lester, R. A., 500 n.
Levy, B. H., 519 n.
Lewis, John L., 299–300, 314, 428,
   471 n., 547, 548 n., 565, 576 n.,
   579–80
Licensing of union agents, 324–25, 331
Limited liability agreements, 501, 510–
   12, 637–38, 646; *see also* Union
   liability

Limited liability of union members,
   501–2, 505
Litigation
   promoted by Taft-Hartley Act, 406–
      7 n., 416, 419, 429, 446, 455, 496,
      508–13, 517, 641–42, 645–47,
      658–60, 663–65
   results of, 82–87; *see also* Contempt
      action; Enforcement of Board or-
      ders
Little Steel Formula, 304–5
Local business; *see* Commerce; Juris-
   diction
Local law enforcement; *see* Policing
Longshore disputes, 584
Longshoremen and Warehousemen,
   International, 548
Loss of employee rights, 453, 484, 502,
   608, 638 n., 659
Loyalty petitions, 101

McCowen, Representative E. O., 607 n.
Machinists, International Association
   of, 485 n., 547, 596, 645
Machinists   Non-Partisan   Political
   League, 596
McMahon Bill, 356, 357
Madden, J. Warren, 35, 40–41, 51, 52,
   68 n., 109, 135, 142, 175, 205–6,
   211–12, 235
Magnuson, Senator Warren G., 595
Magruder, Calvert, 3–4
Maintenance of membership, 214, 297,
   428, 430, 432, 635; *see also*
   Closed shop; Union shop
Majority
   loss of, 117–18, 120, 161–63, 204,
      530–33, 555–56
   proof of, 48, 119, 133–36, 138, 657
Majority rule, 24, 27, 118, 133–38, 171,
   204, 250–52, 454, 514–15, 519–20,
   532, 536, 657
Maladministration; *see* Administration
   of Wagner Act; Bias; Criticisms
Malone, Senator George W., 380
Management   prerogatives,   117–18,
   293, 306, 310, 473, 476 n., 568,
   643, 672–74
Maritime disputes, 584
Maritime   industry,   433,   436–37,
   632 n., 636, 642
Maritime Union, National, 433, 437,
   548, 552, 554 n.

Massachusetts, Governor's Labor-Management Committee, 327 n.

Meat-packing dispute, 584

Mediation; *see* Conciliation

Mediation and Conciliation Service, Federal, 381, 383, 395, 453, 455, 569–73, 575, 579–80, 584–85, 658

Merchants and Manufacturers Association of Los Angeles, 125

Merit increases, 117

Method of study, 95–96, 333 n.

Mid-West Piping doctrine, 165–66, 199–200, 231–32

Militant Truth, 125

Millis, H. A., 25 n., 52, 60, 74–75, 144–45, 148, 150, 151, 156, 197–98, 212 n., 236, 403 n.

assumptions of, 669–71

credo on collective bargaining, 675–77

letter to President Roosevelt, 265 n.

Mine, Mill and Smelter Workers, International Union of, 548, 554

Minority rights, 163, 203, 250–52, 454, 514–15, 520–21, 559–60, 594–95, 645, 660

Minority unions, 251–52

Mohawk Valley formula, 99

Monopoly, union, 279–80, 286–91, 439, 459, 464 n., 656

Moore, Judge Ben, 596–97

Morgan, Jerry, 370 n.

Morse, Senator Wayne, 345, 375, 376 n., 380, 382, 387, 388, 391, 446, 491, 545–46, 566, 586, 595–96

Multi-plant unit; *see* Appropriate unit

Murdock, Abe, 351 n., 352, 404 n., 467 n., 531, 550

Murphy, Justice Frank, 597

Murray, Senator James E., 380, 382, 391, 440, 479, 491, 519, 530, 542, 544, 545, 577–78, 601, 605, 608

Murray, Philip, 286, 308, 392, 596

Musicians, American Federation of, 288, 477, 479 n., 564, 566 n., 567–68, 642–43

Mutiny, 193

NLRA; *see* National Labor Relations Act

NLRB; *see* National Labor Relations Board

NLRB union, 408 n.

National Association for the Advancement of Colored People, 375

National Association of Manufacturers, 15, 23, 24, 28, 33–34, 281–91, 296, 307, 317–18, 328, 348, 352, 370, 425, 428, 571

National Defense Mediation Board, 296, 304

National emergency disputes, 381, 383, 489, 574–86, 606, 608

experience in 1947–48, 584–85, 641

National Founders Association, 15, 287 n.

National Industrial Conference (1919), 17, 311

National Industrial Conference Board, survey of management opinion, 556 n., 633 n.

National Industrial Recovery Act, 21–28

Public Resolution No. 44, 24–26

Section 7(a), 21–24

unconstitutionality of, 27–28

National Joint Board for the Settlement of Jurisdictional Disputes, 474–75

National Labor Board, 22–24, 111

National labor policy, 4, 18–29, 234, 265–68, 450–52, 558, 655–65, 669–77

uniformity issue in, 586–93, 661

National Labor Relations Act; *see* Wagner Act

National Labor Relations Board (1934), 25–26, 111, 133

National Labor Relations Board (Taft-Hartley Act)

functions of, 403–9

increase in membership of, 261 n., 403 n., 406, 623, 661

and Joint Congressional Committee, 601–3, 605, 608–9

members of, 403 n., 404 n.

staff, 612, 619–20, 629, 660–61

see also Administration; General Counsel; Jurisdiction of; Policies of NLRB; Taft-Hartley Act

National Labor Relations Board (Wagner Act)

appraisal of, 234–68

difficulties of, 33–35, 173, 266

failure to achieve public understanding, 264–65

functions of, 95, 129, 234

impartiality in policies, 69–70, 237–38, 240–41
limited time given members in 1947 House and Senate hearings, 368–69
members of, 35, 52, 60, 235–36, 266
membership, effects of changes in, 82, 235–36, 245–46
powers of, 31–32
private conferences of, 74–75, 244–45
qualifications for membership, 74–75, 237–39, 266, 413
reorganization of, by Taft-Hartley Act, 373–74, 402–16
staff
  attitudes and competency of, 41–42, 45–46, 60, 67–70, 238–39, 408, 602 n.
  in regional offices, 41, 53
  selection and training of, 35, 42, 45, 55, 67–68, 235–36, 238–39
  size of, 34–35, 41, 52–53, 61, 82–83, 123, 173, 232, 243
  see also Administration; Bias; Criticisms of; Wagner Act
National Metal Trades Association, 15, 282
National Wage Stabilization Board, 306, 313
Nazi system, labor under, 670
Negotiation while representation question unsettled, 160, 165–66, 199–200, 223, 231–32
Neutrality of employer, 166, 176–81, 423
New York State Labor Relations Board, 587–88
New Zealand, 510, 578–79, 582, 669
Newsboys, 399
Newspaper ads, 287–89, 295
Newspapers; see Press; Printing and publishing
Non-Communist affidavit requirement, 335, 379, 383, 483, 484, 537–41, 545–59, 608, 658 n.
  constitutionality of, 552–53, 557
  effects on NLRB cases, 546–52, 611
  effects on unions, 553–58, 559, 643–44, 652, 658 n.
  see also Filing requirements
Non-Communist affidavits referred to Department of Justice, 548 n.
Noncomplying unions, 548–52

cases dismissed or closed, 548–49, 552, 629
and cases filed by individuals, 551–52, 629, 630
charges against, 630–31
and conditional orders to bargain, 550–51, 553
contractual rights of, 549, 555–56, 630
in decertification elections, 532–33, 535, 549–50, 630–31, 645
and discriminatory discharges, 549 n., 551–52, 629, 630
duty to bargain, 448 n., 551 n.
in elections under state or private agencies, 556, 590–91, 648
local, and rights of international, 552
raids against, 524–25, 554–55
recognition issues, 100 n., 555–57, 584, 643–44, 648, 663
in representation cases, 524–25, 549–50, 552, 556, 630, 644–45
right as majority representative, 448 n., 492–93, 548–51, 555–57, 630
in state courts, 591, 644 n.
in unfair labor practice strikes, 447, 629
and union security, 637
Nonunion employees; see Individual rights; Minority rights
Nonunion votes, 89, 251, 614, 647–48
Normal account jobs; see Struck work
Norris–La Guardia Act
  adoption of, 20, 465
  "agency" under, 21, 444, 487
  definition of "labor dispute," 21, 465, 488–89
  effect of Taft-Hartley Act on, 489, 490, 491 n., 496, 562, 575
  effects of, 3, 21, 220, 278–79, 332, 459 n., 487–89, 497, 504, 583 n.
  policy of, 20–21, 196–97 271, 455–56, 465, 485–89, 508 n.
  proposals to repeal or modify, 288, 354–55, 360–62, 378
  Sec. 2 quoted, 20–21
  Secs. 7, 8, 13, quoted, 487–89
Norton, Representative Mary T., 351 n., 366 n.
Norton Bill, 348, 352
No-strike agreement, 194–96, 510–12, 637–38, 659

From the Wagner Act to Taft-Hartley

No-strike pledge, 162, 198, 275, 296–301, 354
Notice of dispute to Federal Mediation and Conciliation Service, 570, 572
Notice to employers of disposition of charges, 51
Notices posted in compliance, 56, 59, 88, 614, 615

Objections to elections; see Integrity of elections
O'Daniel, Senator W. L., 343, 344, 345, 380
One-union elections, 129–31
One-year rule, 118, 157, 159, 352, 418–19, 434, 517–19, 529, 531, 534, 549, 559
Open-shop movements, 15–18, 125–27, 272, 283, 294, 311, 498
Operations analysis, 60, 93–94, 118, 119–20, 122, 138, 143–44, 158–59, 161, 167, 409 n.
Operations Division, 620
Oppressive Labor Practices Act, 332 n., 336–37
Oral argument, 38, 47, 623
Organizing methods, 161, 170–71, 247, 250, 253–55, 275–79, 442, 445–46, 458, 463–64, 480–81, 529–30, 556–57, 615, 647–49, 650, 652
Organizing under Taft-Hartley Act, 634, 647–49

Packinghouse Workers, United, 554
Panel system, 403, 413, 623–26, 661
Parker, Judge John J., 493
Party influence on legislative proposals, 341–45, 364, 369–70 n., 374, 382
Payments to employee representatives, 428, 443, 477 n., 483, 492, 561–68, 632 n., 638, 642–43, 659, 662
Penalties under Taft-Hartley Act, 482–85, 545; see also Remedies; Violations unremedied
Pensions; see Welfare funds
Pepper, Senator Claude, 391, 440, 479, 491, 519, 526, 544, 545, 566, 577, 595–96, 601, 605, 608
Petrillo, James C., 428, 478 n., 566 n.
Picketing, 278–79, 330–31, 339, 383
under antitrust acts, 13–14, 486
against certified union, 277, 458 n.
under common law, 460–62

and free speech, 179 n., 330, 467 n., 470
under state laws, 317–31
under Taft-Hartley Act, 430 n., 444–47, 467–71, 495, 608, 615, 640, 646, 662
Policies of NLRB, 95–233
appraised, 240–43
changes in, 82, 145–46, 236, 240–41, 245–46, 260, 262, 264–65
under Taft-Hartley Act, 466–67, 476 n., 523–28, 531, 534–35, 546–52, 617–18, 629–32, 638 n., 642 n.
Policing of strikes, 191–93, 197–98, 202–3, 247, 446–47, 493–95, 640, 662
Political activity of unions, 450, 594–98, 653, 676–77
Political contributions or expenditures, 298, 324, 325, 328, 331, 355, 374, 381, 384, 387, 395, 450, 483, 593–98, 605, 653
Powell, Representative A. C., 370 n.
Power
attitudes of employers toward, 272–74, 292, 672–74
attitudes of labor leaders and rank and file toward, 671–72
balance of, in industrial relations, 671–74
equality of, as aim of public policy, 4, 20, 27, 234, 267, 271–74, 286, 397, 481, 671–74
meaning of, 272–74
struggles over, 234, 263, 274, 283, 290–91, 304, 312–15, 319, 582, 646–47, 653–54
of unions, 237, 263, 267, 271–74, 281, 287, 292, 317, 322, 420, 440, 510–11, 513, 560, 598, 649, 651–53, 662–65, 672
Preferential shop; see Closed shop; Hiring hall; Union security
Preferential treatment; see Company-assisted union; Company-dominated union; Neutrality of employer
Prehearing elections, 62–63, 81, 87, 169, 374, 381, 516–17, 622
Prerequisites for union use of NLRB; see Filing requirements; Financial reports; Non-Communist affidavits
President's Conference of Industry and Labor (1941), 296–97

Press
    hostility of, 262, 295, 312, 315
    treatment of Taft-Hartley issues, 295 n., 368
Pressman, Lee, 391
Pressure groups, 74–75, 303, 388–89, 607; *see also* Public opinion
Pressures on NLRB, 74–75, 123, 135 n., 146, 173, 227 232, 237–38, 243–46, 266, 407–8, 414, 602–3, 608–9, 629
Prettyman, Judge, 552, 557
Price control, 303–6, 313–14
Price Control Act, 196–97
Printing and publishing, 433, 437, 469, 627–28, 641–42
Priority of cases against unions, 420, 480, 483, 484, 489–90, 622, 648, 663
Pritchett, C. Herman, 85 n.
Private rights; *see* Jurisdiction of NLRB
Procedure, standards of, 35, 46 n., 55–56, 60, 63–64, 68, 82
Procedures
    described, 36–39, 44–49, 51, 53–59, 64–66, 409–16, 516–17, 620–26
    effects of Administrative Procedure Act on, 63–64
    see also Due process
Professional employees, 139 n., 522, 534–35, 660
Propaganda; *see* Press; Public opinion
Property rights, 486–88
"Prosecutor, judge, and jury," 238–40, 402–9
Psychological effects of amendments, 656–58
Public Affairs Institute, 604
Public attitudes
    toward Taft-Hartley Act, 558–59, 604, 626, 629, 656–58
    toward unions, 271, 311–15, 318–32, 647, 674
    toward Wagner Act, 30, 235, 236, 244–46, 252–54, 259, 262–65, 271, 366–68, 406
Public employees, strikes banned, 329, 331, 384, 395, 484, 561 n.
Public opinion
    employers' campaign to influence, 281–91, 315, 318–19, 322–28
    union campaign to influence, 294–95
Public opinion polls, 262–63
Public Resolution No. 44, 24–26, 133

Public utility strikes, 327, 329, 331, 571
Pulp, Sulphite and Paper Mill Workers, International Brotherhood of, 651
Punishment for illegal acts, 247, 446–47, 483, 485

Racial issues, 127, 132, 139 n., 168–69, 222 n., 257, 280, 327
Racketeering in unions, 171, 215, 255, 280, 319, 544, 562, 565
Raiding, 137, 160, 172, 222, 256, 276–77, 458 n., 523–25, 554–55, 559–60, 644–45
Railroad strikes, 312, 313–14, 361 n., 583 n.
Railway Labor Act, 18–19, 105, 118 n., 176 n., 359, 569
Railway Labor's Political League, 653 n.
Reciprocal discharge clauses, 636
Recognition agreements, 37, 42, 87
Recognition for reasonable period, 113, 118–19
Recognition strikes, 78, 91–92, 129, 171, 199–200, 254, 556–57, 559, 643
Reconversion, 234, 272, 293–94, 302–6, 311–15, 670
Reed, Justice Stanley F., 597
Refusal to bargain, 99, 111–22, 127, 293, 448–54
    charges filed, 79, 614
    criticisms of Taft-Hartley Act provisions on, 450–55
    criticisms of Wagner Act provisions on, 120–21, 248
    effectiveness of provision, 119–22
    penalties for, 119–20
    in strikes, 99, 190, 201–2
    under Taft-Hartley Act, 441, 442, 448–55, 550–51, 555, 614–16, 638 n.
    tests of, 111–20, 163, 448–49
    types of, 111–12
    by unions, 116, 120, 248, 258, 260, 275–76, 293, 328, 433, 442, 443 n., 448–50, 551 n., 584, 615, 627–28, 631, 632 n., 641–42, 656
Regional Directors' Committee (1939), 45
Regional influence on legislative proposals, 341–46; *see also* State legislation
Regional offices
    relations between Washington and,

36–37, 44–46, 53–56, 64, 239, 415, 619–21
responsibility of, 48, 54–55, 58–59, 64–65, 239, 612, 620–21
under Taft-Hartley Act, 404–5, 408, 619–22, 626–27
Registration of unions, 323–26, 328–29, 331, 537–44, 559; *see also* Filing requirements
Reilly, Gerard D., 52, 60, 149 n., 150, 156, 158, 167, 182 n., 183, 184, 198, 199, 200, 212 n., 236, 377, 403 n., 524 n., 550 n., 607 n.
Reinstatement, 88–89, 190, 215, 429–30, 614, 615, 618; *see also* Closed shop; Discrimination; Strikers
Religion in NLRB cases, 127, 169
Remand of cases by courts, 87
Remedies for unfair labor practices, 40, 49, 88–89, 190, 482–96
under Taft-Hartley Act, 427–28, 429, 446–47, 482–85, 495, 614–15
see also Results of NLRB cases; Violations unremedied
Remington Rand Company, 38, 98–100, 104, 112, 555
Repeal of Wagner Act, 287–88, 315, 348
Representation cases, 37–39, 47–48, 52, 55–56, 61–63, 65, 129–73, 514–35
effects of filing requirements on, 538, 546–52, 558
factors in trend, 77–78, 95
importance of, 170, 267
and jurisdictional disputes, 220–24, 309–10, 472
number filed, 76–80, 129, 611, 612 n.
results of, 129, 170–73, 254–55, 614
under Taft-Hartley Act, 404–5, 409, 412, 514–35, 548–52, 558–60, 620–21, 624, 628–29, 630, 657
see also Elections
Representation question, when exists, 136–38, 157–60, 517, 520, 529–31, 534
Representative government in industry; *see* Democracy in industry
"Reproduction law," 477, 642 n.
Responsibility of employers, 272–73, 398, 496, 505, 512–13
Responsibility of unions
conditions needed for, 438–39, 673–74

deficiency of, charged, 272–73, 275, 278, 280, 288, 293, 306, 310, 339–40, 541–42
influenced by Taft-Hartley Act, 558–60, 634, 637–39, 650, 652, 656–58
influenced by Wagner Act, 255–56
legal definition of, 496–513
see also Union liability
Rest periods, 638
Restraining orders; *see* Injunctions
Restraint or coercion; *see* Coercion
Restrictive legislation; *see* State legislation; Union activities, regulation of
Results of NLRB cases, 88–94, 103, 110–11, 119–21, 122–28, 170–73, 202–3, 207, 215, 252–62
charges against unions, 447 n., 615–18, 627, 646–47, 663
see also Industrial relations
Retail stores, New York City, 555 n.
Revenue Act of 1943, 543
Review of records under Taft-Hartley Act, 410–15, 623–24, 661
Review Section, 36, 38, 47, 57, 65, 67, 238–39, 411–12
abolition of, 411–15
Reynolds, James J., Jr., 60, 182, 200, 214–15, 236, 528, 531, 534
Richberg, Donald R., 358, 465 n.
Rifkind, Judge, 553
Right to organize
before 1930's, 7–19
under Norris–La Guardia Act and National Industrial Recovery Act, 20–28
under state laws, 317–21, 323, 329, 331–32
under Taft-Hartley Act, 396–98, 420–41, 480–81, 484–85 514–15, 546, 618, 622, 647–51
under Wagner Act, 28–29, 31, 95–128, 187, 246–47
see also Right to refrain from concerted activities; Violations unremedied
Right to refrain from concerted activities, 283, 421, 444, 514–15, 521, 525, 649–51, 659–60; *see also* Individual rights
Right to strike; *see* Freedom to strike
"Right to work," 15, 289, 317, 326–29, 432, 438–40, 641–42, 650
Rights of management and unions un-

der Taft-Hartley Act, 450–52, 480–81, 484–85
Rival unionism
and the appropriate unit, 138–55, 255–56, 522–25
and coercion, 216–20, 222–24
and collusive contracts, 203–10
and contracts in representation disputes, 157–60, 165–66, 255–56
and demand for union security, 215, 438–39
effects on industrial relations, 158–61, 235, 276–78, 524–25, 560, 644–45, 674
see also Jurisdictional disputes
Roosevelt, Franklin D., letter from H. A. Millis, 265 n.
Royalties; see Payments to employee representatives; Welfare funds
Rubber Workers, United, 100
Runaway shops, 649
Run-off elections, 62, 134–35, 519–20
Rutledge, Justice Wiley B., 597

Sabath, Representative A. J., 373
Schwellenbach, Secretary of Labor Lewis B., 389
Scoville, John W., 286–87, 367 n.
Seizure of plants by government, 298, 300, 313, 354–55, 583
Self-help by unions vs. use of NLRB, 544–47, 556–58
Self-interest; see Common interest
Separability doctrine, 167, 179, 182–83, 188
Separation of functions, 35, 48, 50, 54–58, 60, 63–67, 236, 238–39, 334–35, 383, 402–3
under Taft-Hartley Act, 402–16, 547 n., 608, 617–18, 618–29, 658, 660–61
Settlement of cases, 37–38, 40, 42–43, 46, 49, 612–13, 615
importance of informal handling, 67, 122, 239
nature of, 48–49, 69, 81–82, 103, 123, 243
policy in, 43, 48–49, 56, 58–59, 61
trends in, 81–83
written agreements in, 56, 82
Severance pay, 564
Shefferman, Nathan W., 452 n.
Sherman Act; see Antitrust acts
Shipyard cases, wartime, 207–10

Shoe Workers, United, 554
Showing of interest required, 137–38, 172, 211, 226, 520, 529–31, 534, 630
Shroyer, Thomas E., 377, 601
Sitdown strikes, 103, 192–93, 195, 278, 321, 327, 328
Sixty-day notice, 430, 453, 457 n., 470, 484, 570, 608, 616, 638–39, 658, 659
Slichter, S. H., 367, 375
Slowdown; see Strike
Smethurst, R. S., 607
Smith, Donald Wakefield, 35, 44
Smith, Edwin S., 25 n., 35, 52, 133 n., 135, 136, 141, 142, 146, 148, 151–52, 156, 211, 212 n., 217
Smith, Senator H. A. (N.J.), 375, 601
Smith, Representative Howard (Va.), 49, 342, 350, 351 n., 353, 354, 356
Smith, Oscar S., 54 n., 403 n., 602 n.
Smith Bill, 284, 332, 338, 344 n., 348, 350–53, 356, 360, 370 n.
Smith Committee; see Special Committee To Investigate the National Labor Relations Board
Smith-Connally Act; see War Labor Disputes Act
Social security, 565, 567, 643, 653
Socialists, 671
Solicitor of Department of Labor, in regard to recognition of noncomplying unions, 555–56
Southern cases, 78, 79, 121, 124–27, 187, 253–54, 614, 647
Southern organizing drive, 125–27, 293, 648 n.
Soviet industrial relations, 670
Special Committee To Investigate the National Labor Relations Board, 49–50, 161, 176, 332, 348 n., 350–52
Speed-up, 477–79, 506–7, 662
Sponsors of legislation in Congress, 341–46
Stability of collective bargaining, 91, 118, 137–38, 142–47, 149–60, 171–72, 211–13, 255–56
effects of Taft-Hartley Act on, 517–18, 523–25, 529–30, 533–35, 644–45, 659–60
Stacy, Judge Walter P., 307

State authorities, effect of Taft-Hartley Act on action by, 495
State Labor Relations Boards, ceding of NLRB jurisdiction to, 402, 415, 587–88, 590–91, 593
State legislation, 7, 10, 288, 295, 316–32, 439, 543
  campaigns for, 284–86, 288–90, 294–95, 317–19, 322–23, 328
  and federal standards, 381, 435, 446–47, 586–93, 603, 605, 661
  Labor Relations Acts, 317–22, 327, 328, 329, 587–91
  lax enforcement of restrictions, 590
  relationships to congressional developments, 285, 316, 318, 328, 332, 345–46
Statements as evidence of unfair labor practices, 188–89, 418, 422, 424–25, 428
Statements found coercive, types of, 175, 178, 181–84, 526–28
Status as employee; *see* Loss of employee rights
Statute of limitations, 420–21
Steel industry, 97–98, 110, 312, 313, 523
Steel Workers Organizing Committee, 97, 123, 283
Steelworkers of America, United, 548, 553, 652
Steelman, John, 389
Stewart, Bryce, 438
Strike, definition of, 470
Strike-breaking, 98–99, 100–101, 190, 253, 495, 499, 518–19, 535, 573, 640–41, 646–47, 662–64
Strike notices
  under state laws, 320, 321, 324
  under War Labor Disputes Act, 198, 298–99, 355
Strike votes
  results of, 299–300
  under War Labor Disputes Act, 34, 53, 60–61, 78 n., 298–300, 355, 578, 580
  see also Last-offer ballots
Strikers
  direct appeal by employer to, 183, 201–2
  effect of misconduct on rights of, 191–95, 197–98, 258, 518
  effect of purpose of strike on rights of, 191, 196–201

effect of violation of contract on rights of, 193–95, 502
eligibility to vote, 136, 190, 199–200, 419, 453, 518–19, 629, 631, 663
proposal to draft, 313–14
reinstatement of, 99, 102–3, 113, 190–200, 518
replacement of, 136, 190–203, 430, 518, 629, 663
rights under Taft-Hartley Act, 430, 453, 470–71, 484, 502, 518–19, 631, 640–41
Strikes
  causes of, 302, 578–79, 640–42
  for closed shop, 433, 628, 632 n., 640, 642
  duty to bargain during, 190, 201–2
  economic, 102, 136, 190, 518–19, 629, 631
  effect on public opinion, 263, 272, 287, 296, 304, 311–14, 322, 327–28, 339, 569
  effect of Taft-Hartley Act on, 604, 606, 639–42, 646–47, 649
  effect of Wagner Act on, 38, 92–93, 202–3, 254
  lawful, under Taft-Hartley Act, 456–57, 470, 576
  legislative restriction of, 7, 10, 285, 288, 290, 298–300, 311, 313–14, 317–31, 338–39, 354–55, 442, 470–71, 574–86
  object of; *see* Illegality of object
  postwar, 253, 272, 280, 286–87, 296, 301–2, 308–9, 311–14, 569, 578
  of public employees, 329, 374, 381, 384, 387, 561 n.
  public policy toward, 234, 256, 267, 296–300, 308–9, 455–57, 569, 575–84
  in public utilities, 327, 329
  trends in, 92, 300–302, 639–40
  unauthorized, 274–75, 471, 637–38
  unfair labor practice, 102, 136, 190, 518–19, 629
  unlawful, under Taft-Hartley Act, 442, 456–59, 465–71, 473, 483, 499
  wartime, 274–75, 280, 297–302
  see also Boycotts; Coercion by unions; Freedom to strike; Jurisdictional disputes; National emergency disputes; Sympathetic strikes

Struck work, 279, 324, 325, 447 n., 451–52, 467–70, 499–500, 617, 642 n.

Successor unions; *see* Fracture doctrine; Independent unions

Supervisors
and employee freedom of choice, 140, 164
rights under Wagner Act, 62, 139–40, 241 n., 289, 290, 293, 312, 361, 400 n.
under Taft-Hartley Act, 383, 399–400, 521, 587 n., 643, 660

Supreme Court decisions
on National Industrial Recovery Act, 27–28
before 1930, 10–13, 462–65, 486
on Taft-Hartley Act, 544, 552–53, 596–98
on Wagner Act cases, 40, 49, 59, 71–72, 84–85, 97, 105–6, 112, 118 n., 174, 176–79, 192–94, 198, 206, 213, 240, 400 n., 522, 525

Sweden, 523

Swygert, Judge Luther M., 433 n.

Sympathetic strikes, 379, 398, 467–70, 662; *see also* Struck work

Taff Vale decision, 503 n.

Taft, Senator Robert A., 251, 353 n., 361, 374–75, 379, 381, 382, 384, 386 n., 387, 391, 425, 429, 441 n., 443, 444–46, 455, 457 n., 466, 479, 503–5, 516, 517, 525, 529, 541, 545, 563, 566, 571, 575–76, 586, 594–95, 597, 600, 628

Taft Bill; *see* Legislative history

Taft-Hartley Act, 395–665
administrative reorganization under, 402–19, 618–29, 660–61
adoption of, 271, 314, 391–92
appraisal of, 419, 480–81, 558–60, 655–65
attitudes toward unions and collective bargaining, 421, 440, 450–54, 513, 514–15, 521, 558, 579, 659–60, 661, 664–65
background of
in Congress, 332–62, 363–92
employers and employer associations, 281–96
government factors in, 296–313
state legislative developments, 316–32
union factors in, 274–81

coverage of, 398–402
difficulties in enforcement of, 418–19, 650–51, 658
effects of, 632–54, 655–65
equalizing amendments, 656–58
experience under, 610–54
findings and policy quoted, 396–97
Joint Congressional Committee's appraisal of, 604–8
objections of President Truman to, 390
policy of, 396–97, 455–56, 514–15
provisions, in general, 395–98
relation to restrictive state laws, 435, 587–93, 605, 661
restriction of access to NLRB, 543–44, 556–58, 643–44
Sec. 2(13) quoted, 443–44
Sec. 7 quoted, 421
Sec. 8(a)(3), second proviso, quoted, 434
Sec. 8(b) quoted, 442–43
Sec. 8(b)(4)(D) quoted, 473
Sec. 8(b)(6) quoted, 477
Sec. 8(c) quoted, 422
Sec. 8(d) quoted, 453
Sec. 9(a) quoted, 454
Sec. 9(b) quoted, 514
Sec. 9(b)(2) quoted, 522
Sec. 9(c)(1) quoted, 529
Sec. 9(c)(2) quoted, 426, 521
Sec. 9(c)(5) quoted, 525
Sec. 9(f)(g)(h) quoted, 538–39
Sec. 10(a) quoted, 587
Sec. 10(c) quoted, 426, 429
Sec. 10(l) quoted, 489–90
Sec. 13 quoted, 430 n.
Sec. 14(b) quoted, 435
Sec. 201(a)(b) quoted, 569
Sec. 203(c) quoted, 570
Sec. 204(a) quoted, 570
Sec. 205(b) quoted, 570
Sec. 206 quoted, 574
Sec. 208(a)(ii) quoted, 575
Sec. 209(b) quoted, 575
Sec. 301(b) and (e) quoted, 500–501
Sec. 302 quoted, 561
Sec. 302(a) quoted, 428
Sec. 302(c) quoted, 564
Sec. 305 quoted, 561
Sec. 402 quoted, 599–600
Sec. 501(2) quoted, 470
title of, 395 n.

Taft-Hartley Act—*Continued*
see also Administration of; Criticisms of; Legislative history; National Labor Relations Board

Taft Report, 246, 490–91, 504–5, 564–65

Taylor, George W., 122 n., 307, 450 n., 654

Taylor, Senator Glen H., 391

Teamsters, etc., International Brotherhood of, 216, 218–19, 224–32, 247, 279, 288, 314, 399 n., 477, 479 n., 613 n., 641 n.

Technical Service Unit, 51

"Technical violation," 217–18

Teller, Ludwig, 462, 583 n.

Textile industry, 121, 646 n.

Textile Workers Union of America, 552 n.

Thomas, Senator Elbert D., 353, 376 n., 392, 440, 491, 543–44

Thompson Products, Inc., 123, 170 n.

Three-year contracts, 159, 172

Time study, 478

Timeliness; *see* Appropriate time

Trade Disputes Act of 1927, 503 n., 653

Trial Examiners, 36, 38, 46–47, 239, 410–11; *see also* Intermediate Reports

Board members as, 39

criticism and commendations of, 70–71, 623

increased importance of, 57, 67, 239

independence of, 57, 64, 65, 402, 410–11, 622

overruled by Board, 57, 412

under Taft-Hartley Act, 409–11, 617–18, 622–23, 661

Truman, President, 303, 307–8, 311, 313, 356–57, 361 n., 363–64, 388–92, 465–66, 504, 598–99, 602, 628 n.

Trumpet, The, 127

Trust funds; *see* Welfare funds

Two-year contracts, 159, 172, 645

Typographical Union, International, 201, 275–76, 433, 437, 439 n., 469, 477, 548, 603, 605, 616–17, 627–28, 641–42

UAW–CIO; *see* Automobile Workers–CIO

UE–CIO; *see* Electrical Workers–CIO

Unaffiliated unions; *see* Independent unions

Uncertainties under Taft-Hartley Act, 416, 444–47, 471 n., 479 n., 493, 502, 563 n., 596, 603, 627, 633–34, 637–39, 645–46, 658, 659, 661, 664–65

Unemployment, 303, 305, 649

Unfair labor practice cases, 36–40, 46–49, 56–60, 64–65, 95–128, 174–233

effect of filing requirements on, 550–51, 556, 558

factors in trends, 77–78, 95, 293–94, 614–15

filed as organizing or tactical device, 82, 615, 646–47

number filed, 76–80, 611, 612 n.

under Taft-Hartley Act, 404–5, 409–18, 433, 443 n., 444 n., 447, 466–68, 474 n., 476 n., 479 n., 489–96, 611–12, 614–18, 620–28, 630–31 n., 641–42, 646–47, 649–50

types of charges filed, 78–79, 614–15

Unfair labor practices

defined, 31, 421–22

of employees and unions, 233, 247, 260–61, 282, 319–31, 336–39, 350, 379

of management, under Taft-Hartley Act, 420–41, 448, 452–53, 480, 484, 614–15

in 1947, 124–27, 253–54

of unions, under Taft-Hartley Act, 383, 432–40, 441–81, 484, 557, 560, 611, 612 n., 615–18, 630–31 n., 641–42, 656, 662–63

Unfair lists, union, 467 n., 615, 631

Unfair work; *see* Struck work

Uniformity in national policy; *see* Federal-state relationships; Jurisdiction of NLRB

Union abuses, 214–15, 256–58, 263, 265, 277–81, 314–15, 371, 378–79, 397, 401, 439–40, 441, 445–46, 457–59, 467, 472–73, 477, 541–42, 563–66, 611, 656; *see also* Coercion by unions

Union activities, regulation of, 179, 265 n., 311, 669–71

indirectly by NLRB, 214–15, 255–58

not included in Wagner Act, 27–28, 256, 316

proposed, 233, 278–81, 282–91, 332–41, 349–50, 354–62, 383

by states, 285, 295, 316–32
under Taft-Hartley Act, 395, 419,
    441–81, 484–85, 543–44, 559, 563,
    593, 645–46, 661–65
Union agreements; *see* Contracts
Union attitudes under Taft-Hartley
    Act, 509, 512, 537 n., 546–48,
    579, 580, 598 n., 607, 613, 626,
    627, 629, 632–34, 639, 641–42,
    645–46, 651, 653, 654
Union elections, regulation of, 324–25,
    328, 331
Union factors in bringing Taft-Hartley,
    274–81, 314–15
Union habits, affected by NLRB cases,
    170–72, 204, 215, 255–58, 649–52
Union leadership, failure to propose
    amendments, 280, 295, 310, 315,
    372 n.
Union liability
    under antitrust laws, 9, 12–13, 497,
        501
    under common and state law, 331,
        497–99, 501–2, 504–5
    under Norris–La Guardia Act, 21,
        444, 487–88
    under Taft-Hartley Act, 443–44,
        447, 468, 470, 473, 484–85, 496–
        513, 637–38, 646, 658
    under War Labor Disputes Act, 298–
        300, 355
Union membership, 15–20, 22, 26, 76–
    77, 252–53, 271, 633, 648, 652
    eligibility to, 222 n., 257, 280, 434–
        35, 442, 443, 637
    unreasonable denial of, 330, 434–35,
        439, 545, 615, 641, 650, 652
Union security
    extent
        in 1946, 297, 430
        in 1948, 635 n.
    illegal contracts, 432 n., 433 n., 605,
        628, 637
    postwar issues on, 306
    relation of state and federal stand-
        ards, 435, 586, 588–90, 603, 661
    substitutes for, 563–64, 628, 635–37,
        641–42, 646
    Taft-Hartley policy, 428, 430–40
    wartime policy, 296–97
    see also Closed shop; Discrimination;
        Union shop
Union shop, 213–14, 296, 380, 432–35
    conditions prerequisite to, 433–34,
        452

continued pending adjudication of
    legality, 434 n., 584
defined, 432, 435
strikes for, 434
under Taft-Hartley Act, 383, 428,
    432–36, 438–40, 452, 635–36
see also Closed shop
Union-shop elections, 381, 401, 433–
    34, 436, 439–40, 536–37, 545,
    559, 588–90, 607–8, 611–13, 622,
    635, 641, 646, 648, 649–50, 657
policy in regard to state standards,
    588–90, 603, 627
results of, 536, 613, 651
Union structure, 255–56; *see also* Ap-
    propriate unit; Craft unions; In-
    dustrial unions
Unions
    and democratic system, 676–77
    effects of conflict on, 648–49, 651–
        52, 654, 665
    effects of Taft-Hartley Act on, 537 n.,
        553–60, 563–64, 618, 632–54, 656–
        65
    need for power, 671–74
Unit for collective bargaining; *see* Ap-
    propriate unit
United Mine Workers, 281, 296, 307,
    313, 314, 434 n., 443 n., 511 n.,
    547–48, 564–65, 574 n., 616, 652
United States Steel Corporation, 287
Unity of interest; *see* Common interest
Unity of policy
    under Taft-Hartley Act, 407–8, 415–
        16, 624–29, 660–61
    under Wagner Act, 65, 67, 81, 240,
        261, 266, 402, 405
Unlawful strikes; *see* Illegality of ob-
    ject
Unlawful strikes and boycotts; *see* Boy-
    cotts; Strikes; Unfair labor prac-
    tices of unions
Utah, Industrial Commission of, 590–
    91

Van Arkel, Gerhard P., 492 n., 500
Van Delden, E. H., 525, 556
Vandenberg, Senator Arthur H., 307,
    344
Violation of contract, 193–96, 321, 324,
    327, 331, 361, 374, 381, 444, 470,
    637–38, 652, 658
    extent of, 505–8
    and injunctions, 504
    solutions for, 505–8

From the Wagner Act to Taft-Hartley

Violation of contract—*Continued*
and suits for damages, 500–513, 535,
637–38, 646–47, 658
Violation of law, union attempts to induce; *see* Coercion by unions
Violations, unremedied, 49, 63, 69, 82–
83, 103, 122–24, 127, 224, 231,
240, 243–44, 252, 254, 260, 491,
613, 615, 650
Violence
by employers, 26, 99, 100, 124, 126,
176, 191–92, 253
in strikes, 14, 103, 191–93, 247, 253,
254, 258, 278, 323, 327, 330, 640,
646
under Taft-Hartley Act, 445–47, 557,
584, 640, 646, 647
by unions in elections, 164
Votes cast; *see* Elections

Wage increases, campaigning with,
182–83
Wage negotiations, 304–6, 312–14, 646
Wage-price policy, 303–8, 313–14
Wagner, Senator Robert F., 3, 22, 24,
29, 353, 391–92
Wagner Act, 28–268
accomplishments of, 252–62, 265
adoption of, 27–28
appraisal of, 234–68
attack upon, 262–64, 272, 281–91,
294–96, 333–62, 363–92
closed-shop proviso to Section 8(3)
quoted, 203
effect on extent of collective bargaining, 93–94, 122–23, 173, 252–54
effects on industrial relations, 258–
60, 675
effects on strikes, 38, 92, 253–54,
278
effects on union habits, 254–58
findings and policy quoted, 30, 396–
97
policy of, 3–4, 28–29, 30–31, 163,
190, 197–98, 200, 234, 241–42,
246, 266–68, 395
Sec. 2(3) quoted, 190
Sec. 7 quoted, 31, 190
Sec. 9(b) quoted, 515
Sec. 13 quoted, 190
see also Administration of; Amendment of; Constitutionality of; Criticisms of; National Labor Relations Board

Waivers of charges in elections, 109,
166–67, 183, 230
Walsh Bill, 347, 348
Walter-Logan Bill, 353
War, effects of, 78, 79, 81, 82, 271–72,
274–75, 285–86, 293–94, 306, 317,
322, 345, 670–71
War Labor Board
World War I, 16–17
World War II, 78, 79, 162, 196, 199,
274–75, 293, 297–98, 300–306,
354–55
War Labor Disputes Act, 34, 60–61,
198, 232, 285, 298–300, 332, 338,
344 n., 346, 354–56, 574, 578, 594
War record
of labor, 274–75, 298–302
of management, 274–75
Wartime labor policy, 196–99, 275,
296–300, 670–71
"We Don't Patronize" lists, 467 n., 615
Weirton Steel Company, 23, 24, 26 n.,
123–24
Welfare funds
bargaining on, 117, 313, 471 n., 565,
567–68, 574 n., 605, 607, 608,
616, 634, 642–43, 651
restrictions on, 361, 378, 379, 383,
386, 483, 561–62, 564–68, 584,
642–43, 659
Whiteside, Arthur N., 358
Whitney, A. F., 604
Wisconsin Employment Relations
Board, 586 n., 589
Withdrawal of cases, 122, 615
factors in, 82–83, 243, 615, 617
see also Dismissal of cases
Withdrawal of charges in elections,
109, 167
Withhold-recognition orders, 108–9,
212, 427–28; *see also* Contracts
set aside
Witte, E. E., 8, 465 n., 497
Wolman, Leo, 375
Women of the Pacific, 323 n.
Work assignment disputes; *see* Juris-
dictional disputes
Work-relief funds, 240
Written agreements required, 112, 157,
452

Yellow-dog contracts, 10, 11, 14, 18,
21, 101, 253, 486

DATE DUE

MY 9 84

GAYLORD

PRINTED IN U.S.A.